BELFAST BUILT SHIPS

H & W
H & W

ESSO
ESSO ULIDIA
LONDON

BELFAST BUILT SHIPS

JOHN LYNCH

This book is dedicated to the memory of my mother.

Gobnet (Debbie) Lynch
31 May 1927 – 18 March 2008

Worked on a hospital ward the day the NHS was introduced.

Front cover: View of the Workman Clark yard. (Courtesy of Lagan Legacy)
Back cover: Part of the riveting team at work at Harland & Wolff. (Courtesy of Lagan Legacy)

Frontispiece (top): View of Harland & Wolff yard in the early 1980s. (Courtesy of Lagan Legacy)
(Bottom): Esso Ulidia (H&W y/n 1023) outfitting in 1970. (Courtesy of Lagan Legacy)

First published 2012

The History Press
The Mill, Brimscombe Port
Stroud, Gloucestershire, GL5 2QG
www.thehistorypress.co.uk

British Library Cataloguing in Publication Data.
A catalogue record for this book is available from the British Library.

ISBN 978 0 7524 6539 5

Typesetting and origination by The History Press
Printed in Great Britain
Manufacturing managed by Jellyfish Print Solutions Ltd

CONTENTS

ACKNOWLEDGEMENTS

Many people have contributed time and knowledge to this book or have offered me encouragement and support, and I am grateful to you all. Two individuals stand out in my mind at the moment, Paul Foley of *Lloyd's List* and David Nicholas of BP, who when confronted with requests for information from a desperate author not only replied but did so promptly. People like them make research not only possible but also enjoyable. I would like to offer a special thanks to the long-suffering staff in the reference department of Belfast Central Library; hopefully you will now see that all that fetching and carrying of *Lloyd's Registers* was not wasted. I would like to thank Mark Ashby for copy-editing much of this text in a positive and supportive manner, a task which was, I know, far from easy. I would also like to thank David Henry for the work he did on illustrating this book, an amazing job done on a tight schedule. All illustrations marked DH are his work. All errors in this book are mine, but it could not have been written without the help and support of others, thank you all.

I would particularly like to thank Lee Lavis and the board of Lagan Legacy for their kind support of this project and above all for their permission to use material from their photo collection. All illustrations marked (courtesy of Lagan Legacy) remain their property.

I would also like to acknowledge a debt to the staff and students of the School of History at Queen's University Belfast, an environment that encouraged the germination of ideas such as this. I would also like to acknowledge the role of the staff and students on the part-time degree programme in the creation of this work; working with you may have been frustrating at times but was always a pleasure.

INTRODUCTION

For many years I have been fascinated by the story of Belfast shipbuilding and by developments in shipping technology; indeed some of my less kind colleagues and students have even gone so far as to describe me as a 'ship freak'. This book is not intended to be a history of Belfast's shipbuilding industry, but rather a history of ships produced there. Belfast was one of the main centres of British shipbuilding for nearly 150 years, and the story of the city's output maps the rise and fall of one of Britain's greatest industries. Others have listed the vessels produced by some of Belfast's shipyards, but I shall attempt to go further than simply cataloguing yard numbers and launch dates by providing at least a limited history of each vessel. I have not always been successful and there are gaps in my data that I hope others will fill in.

Ships are like people. Some enjoy long and uneventful lives; for others existence is short and dramatic. There are some extremely sad stories and more than a few can legitimately be described as 'tragic', including a famous White Star liner lost on her maiden voyage. There are some ships whose end is shrouded in mystery; no fewer than twenty-seven Belfast-built ships are listed as 'disappeared', although this rather dramatic-sounding fate is often rather more prosaic than it sounds. Almost one in five Belfast-built ships were lost as a consequence of war and for those launched between 1900 and 1939 the proportion is more than one in three. The ships are the 'stars' of this book and the men who owned the shipyards or worked in them are reduced to 'supporting roles'.

This study is based on a major revision of output from Belfast's shipyards and a number of generally accepted 'facts' about shipbuilding on the Lagan River have been questioned. Perhaps the most radical reinterpretation concerns the assumption that the two main yards, Harland & Wolff and Workman Clark, focused on different types of ships. My lists show that although there was considerable difference in output between these firms, this has tended to be overstated by authors in the past, including myself:

> By 1879, Harland & Wolff were one of the United Kingdom's major shipbuilders …
>
> The yard specialised increasingly in high quality passenger vessels. Workman Clark specialised increasingly in smaller and less prestigious cargo and passenger/cargo ships, supplemented, from the beginning of the twentieth century, by refrigerated and chilled vessels for the meat and fruit trades.[1]

What emerges is an industry that, in the last decades of the nineteenth century and the early twentieth century, developed a pattern of production focused on meeting the demands of a system of worldwide maritime trade that developed in the half a century before the First World War.[2] The commodities involved in international trade became increasingly diverse and

Queen Elizabeth II visited Harland & Wolff in 1954. (Courtesy of Lagan Legacy)

An aerial view of the Harland & Wolff yard in the 1980s. (Courtesy of Lagan Legacy)

Belfast's yards began to produce increasingly specialised and complex vessels to carry a wide range of cargoes.

Simple import/export statistics hide a critical aspect of European trade in these years: emigrants. These years saw a huge increase in the number of Europeans moving to other parts of the globe. Although migration statistics are notoriously inaccurate and were often collected in a very confusing manner, over 50 million Europeans migrated to other parts of the globe from the early nineteenth century to the beginning of the 1930s. This outflow increased in the decades before the First World War and peaked between 1900 and 1913.[3] The shipbuilders of Belfast responded to this: *Titanic* was designed to accommodate 1,100 third-class (emigrant) passengers compared to 750 first class and 550 second class, and when she sank there were 324 first class, 283 second and 708 third on board (of twenty-three different nationalities).[4] Belfast did not just build huge passenger vessels for the Europe–America routes; they increasingly specialised in passenger-cargo ships that carried emigrants to other destinations, which did not offer the volume of the Europe–America routes. The emigrant trade was immensely profitable, and Belfast's yards developed considerable expertise in producing ships that could carry people out and cargo back.

I will argue that the decline of Belfast's shipbuilding industry from the peak years of the 'golden era' was not simply a consequence of bad management, foreign competition or failure to innovate, but rather of fundamental changes in trading conditions. Belfast's shipyards grew and prospered in an environment of growing world trade and increasing emigration. The First World War and the economic difficulties of the interwar period, particularly the worldwide Depression created by the Wall Street Crash, ended this.[5] Of the 349 passenger and passenger-cargo ships built on the Lagan, only 85 (24.3 per cent) were built after 1920, compared to 228 (65.3 per cent) launched between 1880 and 1913. Belfast continued to build ships for 70 years, but the glory days were gone.

Perhaps the most controversial aspect of my reassessment is to question the dominance of passenger vessels in the output of Harland & Wolff, particularly before the First World War. As a result of what one reader described as a 'somewhat brutal' reassessment of the role/type of ships produced in Belfast, I have reclassified around ninety vessels normally listed as 'passenger' produced by Harland & Wolff, as well as a number of 'cargo' as 'passenger-cargo'. I looked in an equally critical manner at the more limited number of ships claimed by Workman Clark as 'passenger' and re-rated all but three of their twenty-one 'passenger' vessels as 'passenger-cargo'. Although this may appear a matter of technical definition, it raises fundamental questions about the output of yards and their relationship to each other. A couple of examples will serve to illustrate how reassessments occurred:

Six of the Royal Mail 'A'-type ships built by Harland & Wolff (H&W y/n [yard number] 367, 372, 388, 415, 434, 441) are described by Moss and Hume as 'passenger', but a seventh, *Avon* (H&W y/n 382), is described as a 'passenger-cargo' vessel. Dunn suggests that 'passengers rather than cargo were the main consideration' and states they could accommodate 305–400 first-class, 66–202 second-class and 600–760 third-class passengers. However, certain aspects of the design suggest that this apparent passenger specialism was deceptive:

> Homeward space for cargo – especially meat – was at a premium, so all the 'A' class steamers had removable accommodation for the several hundred third-class passengers. Thus on each trip, after these had been landed in Brazil, the partitions were dismantled and the space prepared to receive cargo.[6]

They were designed to carry emigrants out and meat home, a pattern that marks *Avon* as correctly defined rather than her sisters. To be consistent, I have also reclassified another 'A', Workman Clark's *Araguaya* (WC y/n 230), from 'passenger' to 'passenger-cargo'.

The next group of ships built for the Royal Mail Line were the 'D' type (H&W y/n 420, 425, 426, 427, 428), all listed as passenger ships by Moss and Hume. Strangely, two near sisters built for the Aberdeen Line (H&W y/n 412, 418) were classified as passenger-cargo ships. Again Dunn suggests that they were mixed traders:

> When new, the 'D' ships were among the world's largest meat-carriers and they could load up to 41,400 carcasses of chilled and frozen meat, with other space available for fruit and dairy produce. Besides this they had extensive passenger accommodation, for 95 first and

A view of the North Yard of Workman Clark with the South Yard and Alexandra Dock Works in the background.

HAMPTONS, SHIP DECORATORS AND FURNISHERS

THE SMOKE ROOM of the M.V. BERMUDA.

Builders:
Messrs. Workman Clark (1928), Ltd.,
Belfast, Ireland.

Architect:
A. McInnes Gardner, Esq.,
F.R.I.A.S.

The whole of the First-class Public rooms and Suites de luxe of the M.V. BERMUDA were panelled, decorated and furnished throughout by

HAMPTONS, SHIP DECORATORS AND FURNISHERS

Pall Mall East, London, S.W.1. Works: Queen's Road, Battersea, S.W.8.

Advert for Hamptons Ship Decorators and Furnishers.

> 38 second cabins as well as 860 third-class or steerage. The keynote was comfort rather than luxury; judged by contemporary standards the steerage accommodation was exceptionally good. Unlike the 'A' ships in which the cabins could be dismantled, the 'D's had permanent cabins with two, three and four berths.[7]

I have developed this argument to a greater degree elsewhere,[8] but the critical thing is that, if the employment of Belfast-built ships is examined in detail, there were far fewer 'pure' passenger ships and more passenger-cargo vessels than has previously been accepted.

The production of Harland & Wolff has been better recorded than that of other Belfast yards. A complete building list was provided by Moss and Hume in their history of the firm, which, with justification, is considered the definitive history of the company.[9] This building list was extended to the effective closure of the firm as a shipbuilder, in 2004, by Charles McConnell, who corrected a number of errors in Moss and Hume's list and added much useful information.[10] In both cases the authors listed all Harland & Wolff-built vessels and added a letter (G, M, P and D) to show those built in the company's yards on the Clyde, a rather confusing practice. I have put only minimal detail of Clyde-built ships and have numerically numbered the Belfast ones so that hopefully a clearer picture of production in Belfast is offered.

Workman Clark published an extensive building list in an advertising publication late in the firm's existence.[11] This was updated to close of production, when this booklet and another from 1903 were reprinted in 2004.[12] However, when examined in detail, this list proved to be both incomplete and inaccurate; an advertising exercise rather than an attempt to produce a serious historical record, perhaps. Specifically:

- A large number of yard numbers are left blank (82) and the only explanation offered is 'Dumb Barges and other small craft not included in this output list'. I have been able to positively identify only four of these vessels, and 32 almost certainly relate to barges built for Lloyd Brasileiro (12) or for military use during the First World War. Two others almost definitely refer to cancelled orders. However, in 44 cases it is impossible to tell if these numbers refer to barges or cancelled orders.
- The list quoted very dubious figures for engine power apparently based upon indicated horse power (ihp) but subjected to some fairly radical rounding up. Throughout my list I have used the natural horse power (nhp) as recorded by *Lloyd's* to ensure consistency with other builders.
- There are a number of errors in the list. For example, *Fort James* (y/n 34), is listed as 'Port James'. *Star of Victoria* (y/n 328) and *Star of England* (y/n 329) are listed as 'Port Melbourne' and 'Port Sydney', names they did not acquire for some years after launch. The names used by the China Mutual SS Co. caused particular confusions: *Ching Wo* (y/n 110), *Pak Ling* (y/n 120) and *Yang-Tsze* (y/n 155) being listed as 'Ching Wa', 'Pakling' and 'Yangtsze'. While trivial, such errors made tracing vessels difficult.

On balance the 1933 list gave a solid basis for research but proved inaccurate in many ways, therefore the list that appears here differs considerably from the original.

The building list of John McIlwaine and his partners, Richard Lewis (a cousin of C.S. Lewis) and later Hector McColl, proved the most difficult to reconstruct. My initial research on this yard included a building list[13] and the list published here represents the results of further research. As with Workman Clark, a considerable proportion of output consisted of barges and small harbour craft, which are almost impossible to trace, and there are 13 gaps in the list, mainly in firms' early years when they focused on barge building.[14]

As for Robert Hickson, the man who established modern shipbuilding in Belfast, his list is largely compiled from data given in the *History of Harland & Wolff* and the excellent *Miramar Ship Index*.[15]

The final result of this process of reassessment and reclassification is a fundamentally different picture of the output of the Belfast shipyards. Why was this necessary? Over the years a number of misleading 'urban myths' had grown up around Belfast's shipbuilding industry. As shipbuilding on the Lagan has finally entered the realm of history rather than industry, it is time these myths were addressed. Harland & Wolff still exists, producing wind turbines and carrying out ship-repair work, but no ship will ever again be built in Belfast. The sites of the shipyards either have or are being redeveloped for port facilities or as part of a new 'Titanic Quarter'.

Notes

1 Lynch, J.P., *An Unlikely Success Story: The Belfast Shipbuilding Industry 1880–1935* (Belfast, 2001), pp.13, 17.

2 **Average annual value of British trade by decade (£ millions)**

	Imports	Direct Exports	Re-Exports
1865–1874	316.1	208.0	52.0
1875–1884	391.3	217.9	59.7
1885–1894	399.2	230.4	61.2
1895–1904	493.3	264.3	63.9
1905–1914	660.6	421.4	95.0

Data from Mitchell, B.R., *International Historical Statistics: Europe 1750–2000* (Basingstoke, 2003), pp.575, 580.

3 **Average annual emigration from selected European countries (thousands)**

	1865–1874	1875–1884	1885–1894	1895–1904	1905–1913
Austro-Hungary	7.2	21.6	55.0	118.0	261.4
Belgium	10.5	13.6	19.8	22.6	34.4
Denmark	2.9	5.2	8.2	4.6	7.8
Germany	102.7	101.1	96.0	28.3	25.4
Italy	128.5 a	126.1	225.6	388.9	598.8
Netherlands	11.2	12.8	19.4	22.9	35.7
Norway	11.7	13.6	15.0	12.2	15.6
Portugal	9.7	14.3	23.2	25.2	50.8
Russia	12.0	10.8	28.5	37.8	94.1
Spain	—	7.3 c	17.5	5.8	110.7
Sweden	16.4	24.7	36.8	22.9	21.4
Switzerland	3 b	6.5	7.1	3.8	5.3
United Kingdom	242.1	196.8	226.7	185.8	369.4
Ireland	79.7	66.3	61.3	39.5	31.2
Total	**637.6**	**620.7**	**840.1**	**918.3**	**1,662.0**

a 1869–1874 only
b 1868–1874 only
c 1882–1884 only

Data from Mitchell, *International Historical Statistics*, pp.131–7.

4 **Third-class passengers on the *Titanic***

Nationality	Number	Survived Sinking
British	118	18
Irish	113	41
Swedish	104	23
Syrian	79	31
Finnish	55	17
Austro-Hungarian	44	7

American	43	12
Bulgarian	33	0
Norwegian	25	8
Belgian	22	5
Russian	18	6
Chinese	8	6
Turkish	8	2
Danish	7	1
Canadian	5	0
French	5	0
German	4	1
Greek	4	0
Italian	4	1
Swiss	4	0
Portuguese	3	0
Australian	1	1
South African	1	0
Total	**708**	**180 (25%)**

Comparable losses

	Number	**Survived Sinking**
First Class	324	201 (62%)
Second Class	283	120 (42%)
Third Class	708	180 (25%)
Crew & Staff	918	215 (23%)
Total	**2,233**	**716 (32%)**

Data from http://www.ithaca.edu/staff/jhenderson/titanic.html.

5 **Imports *(exports)* of selected nations, 1927–35 (millions)**

	Germany (Marks)	**France (Francs)**	**Italy (Lire)**	**UK (Pounds)**	**US (Dollars)**
1927	14,114 *(10,801)*	53,050 *(54,925)*	20,375 *(15,519)*	1,218 *(709)*	4,240 *(4,982)*
1928	13,931 *(12,055)*	53,436 *(51,375)*	21,920 *(14,444)*	1,196 *(724)*	4,159 *(5,249)*
1929	13,359 *(13,486)*	58,221 *(50,221)*	21,303 *(14,767)*	1,221 *(729)*	4,463 *(5,347)*
1930	10,349 *(12,036)*	52,511 *(42,835)*	17,347 *(12,119)*	1,044 *(571)*	3,104 *(3,929)*
1931	6,713 *(9,592)*	42,206 *(30,436)*	11,643 *(10,210)*	861 *(391)*	2,120 *(2,494)*
1932	4,653 *(5,741)*	29,808 *(19,705)*	8,268 *(6,812)*	702 *(365)*	1,343 *(1,667)*
1933	4.199 *(4,872)*	28,431 *(18,474)*	7,432 *(5,991)*	675 *(368)*	1,510 *(1,736)*
1934	4,448 *(4,178)*	23,097 *(17,850)*	7,675 *(5,224)*	731 *(396)*	1,763 *(2,238)*
1935	4,156 *(4,270)*	20,974 *(15,496)*	7,790 *(5,238)*	756 *(426)*	2,462 *(2,404)*

General view of the Harland & Wolff yard in the late 1950s. (Courtesy of Lagan Legacy)

A night-time view of the yard at around the same time. (Courtesy of Lagan Legacy)

Annual migration (thousands), 1927–35

	Finland *(Emigrants)*	**Italy** *(Emigrants)*	**Germany** *(Emigrants)*	**UK** *(Emigrants)*	**US** *(Arrivals)*
1927	6.1	218.9	59.3	153.5	335
1928	5.1	150.0	56.0	136.8	307
1929	6.4	149.8	47.8	143.7	280
1930	4.0	280.1	36.5	92.2	242
1931	0.7	165.9	13.2	34.3	97
1932	1.2	83.3	10.3	27.0	36
1933	0.7	83.1	12.9	26.3	23
1934	0.4	68.5	14.2	29.2	30
1935	0.6	57.4	12.2	29.8	35

Data from Mitchell, *International Historical Statistics*, pp.134–7; Wattenberg, B.J. *The Statistical History of the United States* (New York 1976), p. 864.

6 Dunn, L., *Famous Liners of the Past: Belfast Built* (London 1966), pp.148–52.
7 *Ibid.*, p.158.
8 Lynch, J.P., *Workman Clark: Shipbuilders of Belfast* (Manchester, forthcoming), ch.3.
9 Moss, M. & Hume, J.R., *Shipbuilders to the World: 125 years of Harland & Wolff, Belfast* (Belfast, 1986), pp.507–65.
10 McConnell, C., *The Ships of Harland & Wolff* (Carrickfergus, 2004).
11 Workman Clark (1928) Ltd, *Shipbuilding in Belfast* (Belfast, 1933), pp.58–64.
12 Lynch J.P. (ed.), *Forgotten Shipbuilders of Belfast* (Belfast, 2004).
13 Lynch J.P., 'Belfast's Third Shipyard', *Ulster Folklife*, vol.41 (1995), pp.23–4.
14 Coe, W.E., *The Engineering Industry in the North of Ireland* (Newton Abbot, 1969), p.84.
15 Moss & Hume, *Shipbuilders*, p.18.

Left: Shipwright working with an adze. (Courtesy of Lagan Legacy)

Below: General view of the Harland & Wolff foundry in the 1950s. (Courtesy of Lagan Legacy)

1

THE SHIPBUILDERS OF BELFAST

By the start of the twentieth century, Belfast had become a major British shipbuilding centre. The city's yards were producing up to 10 per cent of annual UK merchant shipping tonnage on a regular basis. This is a matter of historical fact but, as I have argued previously, it was in many ways a very unlikely success story.[1] When, in the 1830s, factory-based linen production began to transform Belfast from a prosperous but provincial commercial centre into a significant industrial town, its location offered little to induce a shipbuilder to establish business there. Unlike Cork or Dublin, Belfast had only a very limited tradition of wooden shipbuilding from which modern iron or steel construction could develop. The Lagan, upon which Belfast stands, was totally unsuited for large-scale shipbuilding until massive improvements were undertaken in the 1840s, and even after the river was dredged and straightened to form the Victoria Channel, it was far from an ideal site for the construction of large vessels. The Lagan was even more congested and restricted than the Thames, where such factors are frequently blamed for the decline of shipbuilding. Shipbuilding was dependent upon skilled labour and critical metalworking and engineering skills were available in Belfast on only a very limited scale, and would have to be recruited from other areas.

There were few local customers for potential shipbuilders in Belfast: although the city was dependent on imported raw materials and export markets for its manufactures, it was not a major ship-owning centre. Certainly, local ship owners were important to the yards in their early stages, for example supplying half of Workman Clark's early orders, but, unlike the Clyde or Mersey, they could not generate sufficient demand to keep the Lagan shipyards in business. Dependence on external customers was not unique to Belfast, but the absence of a secure local customer base was a major disadvantage compared to some regions.

How did the town, which became a city in 1888, develop into one of the world's great shipbuilding centres? The answer to this question has been presented as a matter of happy coincidences of timing, luck, nepotism or the Protestant work ethic.[2] Attractive as these reasons may be, none adequately explains the phenomenal growth of Belfast's shipbuilding industry in the 50 years before the First World War, or its success in a highly competitive market. A major cause of this 'unlikely success' was the rapid adaptation of Belfast's producers to a technological revolution within shipbuilding created by the adoption of iron, and later steel, hulls and steam propulsion.[3] Belfast was one of a number of centres with little or no tradition of shipbuilding that developed at this time on the basis of 'new technology'. Other British examples include Barrow and West Hartlepool.[4]

From its beginnings, the Belfast shipbuilding industry used state-of-the-art designs and construction methods. In part, at least, this was a strategy to allow them to compete with longer established but more conservative rivals. After Edward Harland took over Hickson's yard some of his early ships were built using the most advanced methods, as he later recalled:

> I was allowed to settle the dimensions; and the following were decided upon: length 310 feet; beam 34 feet; depth of hold 24 feet 9 inches; all of which were fully compensated for by making the upper deck entirely of iron … in this way the hull was converted into a box girder of immensely increased strength.[5]

The increased hull length and structural strength made possible by such innovations allowed a considerable increase in cargo- and passenger-carrying capacity compared to other contemporary vessels. The solid, box-like appearance of these ships earned them the nickname of 'Bibby coffins', but, despite the rather unpleasant connotation, Harland's iron 'coffin ships' proved highly popular with owners, ensuring his initial success in a highly competitive market.

The use of steel in the building of ships' hulls began in the 1860s, when it was used to construct specially built blockade runners, such as *Banshee* during the American Civil War (1861–65). In these highly specialised vessels, steel was used to reduce hull weight, thus allowing increased speed and shallow draught without sacrificing structural strength. However, steel was too expensive to compete with iron for routine shipbuilding use until widespread adoption of the Bessemer and open-hearth processes substantially lowered prices in the late 1870s. The first ocean-going steel-hulled ship *Rotomahana* was built by William Denny & Co. in 1879. This innovation was quickly adopted in Belfast: Harland & Wolff produced the steel-hulled sister ships *British Queen* (y/n 138, launched November 1880) and *British King* (y/n 139, launched January 1881). Workman Clark used steel in the construction of *Teelin Head* (y/n 14, launched February 1883), and even McIlwaine and Lewis were building colliers in steel rather than iron by the end of 1887.

Although more difficult to work than iron, a steel hull could be 15 per cent lighter than an iron one, a saving that allowed shipbuilders to increase dramatically the size of ships produced. When the first liner built by Harland & Wolff for White Star Line, iron-hulled *Oceanic*, is compared with steel *Titanic*, for the same customer, the extent of technical advance becomes clear. Both vessels were 'liners' and both, when launched, represented the very peak of marine technology.

Fig. 1: Comparative data *Oceanic* (1870) and *Titanic* (1911)[6]

	***Oceanic* (Yard No.73)**	***Titanic* (Yard No.401)**
Length (feet)	420	852.5
Gross Tonnage	3,808	46,328
Horsepower	600nhp	6,906nhp
Engines	Compound (4-cylinder)	Two 4-cylinder, triple-expansion engines with an exhaust turbine

At the same time as steel was being adopted for hull construction, the triple-expansion engines began to replace earlier compound types.[7] The first Belfast-built engine of the new type went to sea in Harland & Wolff's *Iran* (y/n 185, launched January 1886), while Workman Clark fitted *City of Dublin* (y/n 49, launched January 1888) with similar engines, built by Thompson's of Glasgow. After Workman Clark established their engine works in 1890–91 they produced almost exclusively triple-expansion power plants.

The greatest difficulty faced by Belfast's shipbuilders was recruiting and retaining the skilled and diverse labour force needed to build large ships and their propulsion machinery. Belfast had a small engineering sector, mainly concerned with the manufacture and maintenance of textile machinery, which provided limited skilled male employment. However, the emerging shipyards required a large highly skilled male labour force which the city simply could not supply, and in

Above: A marine engine seen at Harland & Wolff – note the size compared to the person in the foreground. (Courtesy of Lagan Legacy)

Left: Portable X-ray equipment, which was used to check welding. (Courtesy of Lagan Legacy)

other areas of Ireland industrial, and particularly engineering, development was too limited to meet demand. The only means whereby a shipbuilder in Belfast could obtain skilled labour was to attract workers from shipbuilding districts of Scotland and northern England.

This was not easy. Skilled workers were the element in the labour force with least reason to move, as their skills were in demand in all British industrial centres. Prejudice against Ireland and the Irish – and few differentiated between Ulster and other regions – was a feature of popular British culture. The Irish were seen as comic but intrinsically violent by inhabitants of Britain's industrial cities; angle-iron smiths from the Tyne or boilermakers from the Mersey would have seen Ireland as a foreign and very definitely hostile country. This situation was not helped by the fact that Belfast had already acquired an unenviable reputation for serious sectarian violence.[8] From the point of view of employment, a newly emerging district with only a single employer and few sources of alternative work could hardly have been an attractive proposition for skilled workers.

Why would a highly skilled and valued worker migrate from an established UK shipbuilding or engineering centre to Belfast? This question is critical; without such movement Belfast's shipyards could not have survived, let alone prosper. In historical terms, the important thing is these workers did migrate and in significant numbers. In 1870, out of 2,400 men employed at the Queen's Island yard, 200 were said to be 'mechanics from London and Liverpool engaged in fitting machinery aboard ship'.[9] When Harland & Wolff established their engine works it was nicknamed the 'English' works due to the birthplace of many of those employed there.

Fig. 2: Inhabitants of Belfast of Scottish or English birth[10]

	(A) Population of Belfast	**% of (A) English or Scottish born**	**% of all males English or Scottish born**	**% of all females English or Scottish born**
1861	121,602	5.1	n/a	n/a
1871	202,537	4.9	5.9	4.2
1881	239,280	4.9	5.4	4.5
1891	289,850	6.3	7.3	5.8
1901	349,180	6.7	7.1	6.3
1911	386,947	7.2	7.8	6.7

I have previously examined the 'quality of life' argument that such workers came to Belfast because wages were higher, housing was better, rents were lower and food costs were not too much higher than in other shipbuilding regions.[11] On balance, I argued that such advantages taken together were not sufficient to attract migrants on this scale; however, there was an additional advantage enjoyed by Belfast over her rivals. By 1901, 47 per cent of Belfast's total population was listed by the census as being employed: 63 per cent of males and 33 per cent of females. Women formed 38 per cent of the total labour force and, because of the linen industry, comprised an even higher proportion in manufacturing. This female employment was a critical difference when compared with other shipbuilding centres.

Fig. 3: Male/female employment in shipbuilding areas (1905)[12]

	Manufacturing labour force	**% male**	**% female**
Belfast	100,890	56.6	43.7
Barrow	17,787	85.9	14.1
Birkenhead	22,926	69.2	30.8

Glasgow	203,752	69.0	31.0
Greenock	19,390	78.4	21.6
Jarrow	9,159	86.7	13.3
Middlesbrough	20,376	88.4	11.6
Newcastle	49,435	77.3	22.7
South Shields	22,974	84.3	15.7
Stockton	12,039	89.9	16.1
Sunderland	31,547	80.3	19.7

The contrast between male shipyard workers and women employed in textile mills could not have been more extreme. In 1911, 31,133 people were employed in spinning, weaving or finishing linen or cotton in Belfast, with at least 13,000 others employed in making-up trades. This labour force was overwhelmingly female (79 per cent), semi-skilled and poorly paid. In 1909, a skilled shipyard worker earned 37–39*s* a week and an unskilled labourer 16–19*s*. Average female earnings in the linen industry were 10*s* 10*d* a week (girls 6*s* 5*d*) and men, who formed the skilled element in the workforce, averaged 26*s* 2*d* (boys 7*s* 8*d*).[13] In spinning rooms, the use of steam to lubricate flax resulted in working temperatures of over 27°C and high humidity levels, causing serious health problems amongst the largely female workforce. In areas in which mill workers predominated, the tuberculosis rates were 50 per cent higher than the average for the city as a whole, and the death rate was a third higher.[14]

Despite the unattractive working conditions and low pay, the fact that there was work for the wives, and more especially for the daughters, of shipyard workers – a feature almost totally absent in some other districts – was an important attraction for skilled labour moving to Belfast. For Belfast's skilled working class, income could be greatly increased by earnings of female members of the family, who would have failed to find employment in other industrial centres. Even if wives did not normally work, availability of employment for women in periods of recession in shipbuilding would have been a useful safety net for many families.

Compared to other major British shipbuilding regions, the industry in Belfast was remarkably concentrated. There were at most three producers (1880–94), much of the time only two (1894–1934) and mostly only a single producer (1854–79 and 1935–2003) on the Lagan. The Clyde, in contrast, was home to 39 shipbuilding firms in 1913, with 11 significant enough to be rated as 'important' by Pollard and Robertson.[15] This huge industry produced every type of vessel from battleships to dredgers and employed 50,000–60,000 men. The Tyne had 16 firms before the First World War, including half a dozen considered 'important'. Like the Clyde, different firms specialised in different types of ship, varying from warships (Palmers, Armstrong's) through liners (Swan Hunter, Wigham Richardson) to fishing vessels (Smith's Dock).[16] The River Wear, a major centre of shipbuilding in the days of timber construction, was home in 1900 to 13 shipyards and Sunderland boasted four yards on the 'important' list.[17] The Tees, as a district, tended to specialise in colliers and tramp steamers, and had well-established shipbuilding centres at Stockton, Middlesbrough and the Hartlepools, with eight or nine large firms, six of which appear on the 'important' list.[18]

However, despite the limited number of producers, the Lagan's share of output increased. Between 1880 and 1884 Belfast produced a modest 2.8 per cent of 4.86 million tons of shipping built in the UK. Between 1895 and 1899 production increased to just over 10 per cent of almost 5.9 million tons produced. Between 1910 and 1913, Belfast supplied 9.5 per cent of 6.6 million tons produced. When compared to other great shipbuilding regions, the status of Belfast as a 'late starter' becomes apparent.[19] Despite the constricted nature of the Lagan and absence of basic raw materials, the success of Belfast compared to well-established centres like Newcastle and Sunderland is amazing.

Robert Hickson

Robert Hickson was a Liverpool engineer who deserves the credit for establishing modern shipbuilding in Belfast. He arrived early in 1853 to take over the recently established Belfast Ironworks. In the autumn he took a lease on a shipyard that the Belfast harbour commissioners had just laid out on Queen's Island. Between September 1854 and 1859 he launched eight vessels.[20] However, it was not his shipbuilding skills that were his major contribution to the history of Belfast shipbuilding, but rather his appointment, in 1854, of a 23-year-old Yorkshire man, Edward Harland, to manage his yard. In 1855 the Belfast Ironworks was closed when the Ulster Banking Company foreclosed, but Hickson retained control of the shipyard. However, his finances did not improve and by September 1858, in the midst of an economic slump, he made his manager an offer: 'I offer you my interest and goodwill in the shipyard at the Queen's Island, Belfast together with Steam engine Boiler Plant tools, machinery and other appliances for shipbuilding as now is used by me, for the sum of five thousand pounds.'[21]

His only condition was that he be allowed to use the yard and its equipment to finish the *Bebington* for himself. Harland agreed and from 1 November 1858 the shipyard's name was changed to Edward James Harland & Company. With the completion of his ship, Hickson's interest in the yard ceased and he vanished from the story of Belfast shipbuilding.

Harland & Wolff

At times it has been suggested that the history of shipbuilding in Belfast is the history of this one firm. This is not true, but this company enjoyed the longest existence and was responsible for over 68 per cent of the ships launched in Belfast. However, Harland did not intend his stay in Belfast to be a lengthy one:

> He (Edward Harland) soon planned to set up on his own and in 1857 applied to Liverpool City Council for ground at Garstang to build a shipyard there, but he was turned down because of his 'youth and inexperience'. Further applications at Birkenhead and elsewhere on the Mersey were also rejected.[22]

Had he been successful in obtaining a yard in Liverpool, the history of Belfast shipbuilding would have been very different. However, it would be wrong to credit the success of the industry solely to Harland, despite his considerable gifts. In 1857, he engaged Gustav Wilhelm Wolff, the nephew of Gustav Christian Schwabe, an old friend of Harland's family, as his personal assistant. Wolff, a trained engineer and draughtsman, brought not only his own considerable skills but also the support of his uncle. Schwabe, amongst his other business activities, was involved in the Liverpool-based shipping firm of John Bibby & Sons: 'Harland's decision to acquire the lease of the Queen's Island Yard was almost certainly taken on Schwabe's advice and promise of financial support, for immediately John Bibby & Sons placed an order for three 1,500 gross ton iron steamers.'[23]

These ships were fairly conventional, but those ordered in a subsequent batch were built to Harland's own design, the first of the highly successful 'coffin ships'. Wolff's family ties ensured the early success of the new company: of the first 15 vessels built by Harland & Wolff, 12 were for the Bibby Line. More importantly, in terms of tonnage, out of 18,552 launched, only 1,026 (5.5 per cent) went to other customers. This family connection was vital in early days but, in reality, could only be a short-term advantage, as a single shipping line could not generate enough work to keep a yard in production.

A major factor in the long-term success of Harland & Wolff in Belfast was timing: they were fortunate enough to finish the last Bibby ship when demand for shipping was at a peak. The

The foundry department, photographed in the interwar years. (Courtesy of Lagan Legacy)

The riveting team in the early twentieth century. (Courtesy of Lagan Legacy)

American Civil War of 1861–65, whilst creating severe depression in a number of areas of the British economy, caused a boom in Belfast's linen industry, which benefited from disruption in cotton supplies and stimulated demand for shipping. Although it has been suggested that Harland built blockade runners for the Confederacy, the building list does not support this claim.[24] After completing the last Bibby vessel, the company entered a period of mixed production. Of 28 vessels delivered between October 1862 and December 1865, 16 were sailing vessels and seven were tugs or other harbour/river craft. Harland & Wolff benefited from high levels of demand within the shipbuilding industry as a whole, both for war-related activities such as blockade running and to allow British shipowners to replace American operators driven from the seas by Confederate cruisers in the lucrative 'carrying' trade. Harland & Wolff broadened their customer base, these vessels being completed for at least 19 customers, some of whom became regular clients.

Personal and family contacts were often critical in the development of business relationships in this era. According to popular legend, it was during an after-dinner game of billiards at Schwabe's Liverpool home in 1869 that Edward Harland met Thomas Ismay and obtained perhaps the most important order in his company's history. That evening, Harland was supposed to have agreed to build ships Ismay needed to allow his newly acquired White Star Line to compete in the North Atlantic emigrant trade. That game of billiards, if it took place, was to affect Belfast's shipbuilding industry profoundly.[25]

> To meet an immediate order for five 420 foot vessels at over £110,000 each, with the novel feature of financial penalty for late delivery, Harland & Wolff had to re-equip the yard completely at a cost of £30,000 ... The *Oceanic*, the first White Star ship to be launched at Queen's Island, can be regarded as the first modern liner.[26]

Following this order, Harland & Wolff established a reputation as builders of passenger vessels, and even if such vessels formed only a small proportion of total output, they were to be the best remembered. By the end of the 1870s, Harland & Wolff were recognised as one of the UK's major shipbuilders. From 1884 William Pirrie, who had trained in the yard as a premium apprentice from 1862 and became a partner in the firm in 1874 at the age of 27, effectively controlled the firm. The yard specialised increasingly in high-quality passenger and passenger-cargo vessels (see table 1). To ensure sufficient orders, Pirrie developed a system that became known as the 'commission club'. This was first adopted in dealings with White Star, but thereafter was made available to other valued customers. Under this system, the customer paid the actual cost of construction plus a proportion of the overheads, the firm's profit being fixed at 5 per cent of the final cost. The profit on such business may have been lower than might have been obtained under other conditions, but the club linked shipowners to Harland & Wolff by shared self-interest.

Table 1: Output of Harland & Wolff, 1859–1913, by type

	1859–79	**1880–99**	**1900–13**
Passenger	8	19	21
Passenger-cargo	2	52	53
Cargo	86	115	21
Military	2	3	1
Cross-Channel	3	8	5
Misc.	28	6	2
Total	**129**	**202**	**103**

There was also an increasingly complex system of mutual shareholdings and directorships between shipbuilder and customer, culminating in 1902 when Harland & Wolff became part of the International Mercantile Marine Syndicate. Under the terms of this agreement, Harland & Wolff were to receive all orders for new vessels from member companies, which they would build at preferential rates, in addition to undertaking any heavy repair work to be carried out within the UK.[27]

As a consequence of such methods, Pirrie was able to secure sufficient high-quality work of the type in which his yard specialised; although, negatively, orders tended to be dominated by a small group of companies (see table 2). Fewer than 20 vessels were built for operators who did not place a further order during these years. This 'customer loyalty' was of critical importance to the survival of both main Belfast shipyards.

Table 2: Customers of Harland & Wolff obtaining ten or more vessels, 1880–1913

Customer	Ships	Tonnage	Dates
Oceanic Steam Navigation	46	503,846	1870–1913
Union/Union-Castle SS Co.	16	129,584	1893–1911
Hamburg America Line	14	154,895	1894–1911
Pacific Steam Navigation	14	94,193	1892–1913
Royal Mail Steam Packet Co.	14	124,499	1904–1913
Leyland & Co.	13	91,436	1888–1908
Bibby Steamship Co.	12	79,291	1889–1912
T.&J. Brocklebank	12	60,539	1885–1906
African Steamship Co.	10	30,386	1881–1912
a. Total	*151*	*1,268,669*	
b. Firms' total output	*306*	*2,046,189*	
c. a. as per centage of b.	*49.3%*	*62.0%*	

The commission club and similar arrangements made it possible for the firm to insulate its labour force from fluctuations in demand to a certain degree, although periodic slumps were inevitable. Between 1880 and 1914, Harland's yard was frequently expanded and re-equipped to meet the demand for ever larger and more luxurious passenger vessels. This is best illustrated by the vast gantry erected over Nos 2 and 3 slips, which allowed the simultaneous construction of the liners *Olympic* and *Titanic*. In the years before the First World War, demand increased to the point that the Belfast yard was no longer adequate and the company was obliged to establish or acquire additional repair facilities in Liverpool and Southampton, and building yards on the Clyde.

As with many other aspects of British society, the years between 1914 and 1918 marked a turning point in the history of Harland & Wolff – the end of a golden era and the beginning of decline – although this was not recognised at the time. Harland & Wolff had never built warships in any number, although they had carried out a limited amount of work for the Admiralty.[28] As a consequence, the warship output of Harland & Wolff consisted mainly of monitors of various classes, although a couple of major warships were also constructed, notably the cruiser *Cavendish* and light battlecruiser *Glorious*.

From 1917 there was a major shift in British shipbuilding policy. The German submarine campaign was at its peak and losses in merchant shipping reached critical levels. Few merchant vessels had been laid down since 1914, so standardised merchant ships were placed at the top of construction priorities. Belfast, with its pre-war merchant shipping specialisation, inevitably played a significant role in such a programme. Furthermore, the appointment of Pirrie as controller of shipping with responsibility for the programme ensured Belfast's yards were to be major con-

The blacksmith's shop. (Courtesy of Lagan Legacy)

Pouring metal into a mould in the foundry. (Courtesy of Lagan Legacy)

tributors. The first 'Standard Merchant Ship', an 'A'-type cargo vessel named *War Shamrock*, was launched by Harland & Wolff in June 1917 and delivered in August. Another dozen were completed before the end of the war and a further 23 were at various stages of construction.

Although construction of new vessels in Belfast was considerable, the main contribution of the Lagan yards to the war effort lay in other work. Throughout the war, the north of Ireland was seen as a secure area, difficult for U-boats to reach and thus comparatively safe from German attacks. For this reason, Belfast became a major repair and refit centre for naval and merchant vessels. One of Harland & Wolff's strangest tasks in these years involved the conversion of a number of merchant ships into a dummy battle fleet to confuse German intelligence in the early days of the war.[29] A large number of ships were converted to troop or hospital ships and a huge amount of repair work was undertaken. The yard acted as the main repair and maintenance base for naval vessels of Irish Sea patrol squadrons.[30] It was this less glamorous work of repair and refit that represented Belfast's major contribution to the war at sea between 1914 and 1918.

The post-war conditions faced by Harland & Wolff were far from encouraging. After a brief boom, created by pent-up demand for replacement tonnage, the company faced a prolonged depression. It has been suggested that Belfast shipbuilders had become overspecialised and were too slow to adapt to changing conditions but this was not the case. Belfast's shipbuilders proved quick to adopt new methods; management could be poor, at times verging on the incompetent, but this was not the main reason for the yard's difficulties. The main problems faced by Belfast's shipbuilders were not created by their actions or the structure of the industry in the city, but by a massive recession in the world economy in the interwar years. This caused a reduction in levels of world trade and reduced the flow of emigrants travelling from Europe to the United States. This in turn had the effect of reducing the demand for shipping space and for the large liners and passenger-cargo vessels in which Belfast specialised.

Given the disadvantages that the region faced compared to other shipbuilding centres, adapting to changing market conditions was particularly problematic for Belfast producers. Whilst they were successful in moving into new ship types such as tankers and new technology such as motor vessels, this was not enough, as we shall see, to save Workman Clark, who faced financial difficulties of a much more serious nature than those of Harland & Wolff. However, the company faced hard times: the worst years were 1932–33, when not a single ship was launched by the Belfast yard and the Northern Irish government admitted that unemployment amongst shipbuilding and engineering workers had reached 57.1 per cent.[31]

Recovery was symbolised by the laying down of Harland & Wolff's yard no.940, HMS *Penelope*, on 30 May 1934, and certainly the yard's output began to increase and unemployment began to fall.

Table 3: Output of Harland & Wolff, 1924–38

Year	Number of hulls	Tonnage	% unemployed in shipbuilding in NI
Average 1900–13	7.4	Approx. 79,000	
1924	3	59,543	35.3
1925	5	31,536	33.3
1926	6	65,713	35.6
1927	14	62,396	27.7
1928	12	75,368	28.2
1929	10	91,256	18.2
1930	16	117,849	19.8

1931	5	61,969	45.1
1932	0	0	57.0*
1933	0	0	57.1*
1934	6	50,201	37.1*
1935	9	102,117	27.6*
1936	12	62,499	21.9*
1937	9	74,395	18.7*
1938	7	79,759	
1939	5	89,648	

* Figures cover both shipbuilding and engineering

Although output was increasing, few of the ships built in these years were the labour-intensive passenger-cargo and passenger types that had been the mainstay of the pre-war production.

During the Second World War, Harland & Wolff were swamped with work: between 1940 and 1946, 175 vessels were launched (106 military ships and 69 cargo), with a combined displacement of 848,363 tons. In addition, the firm undertook a huge amount of repair work and even established a new facility at Londonderry to support escort squadrons based there.[32] The Northern Irish government was to comment on the scale of this work: 'During the recent war Northern Ireland was called upon to undertake a considerable amount of repair and renovation work, both at Belfast and Londonderry. Between September 1939 and December 1944, more than 3,000 naval and merchant vessels were handled ...'[33] Harland & Wolff were probably never busier than during these years.

In the official history of Harland & Wolff, there is an aerial photo of the yard taken at the end of the war period[34] that shows 36 vessels (including four aircraft carriers) under construction, fitting out or being repaired. For the next decade demand for shipping, particularly tankers, remained high as the British merchant marine was reconstructed after the war. Between 1947 and 1959, the firm launched an average of just over 12 ships a year, displacing over 120,000 tons. Few of these were the passenger or passenger-cargo vessels that had been so typical of the golden era of 1900–13, but tankers and cargo vessels ensured that there was employment and the dark days of the 1930s became a distant memory. Writing in early 1957, Henry Rees saw Harland & Wolff's shipyard at its post-war peak:

> The establishment of Messrs Harland & Wolff on Queen's Island is unique. With eighteen building berths and an area of 300 acres, this is the largest shipbuilding yard, not only in the United Kingdom, but in the whole world. With 20,000 men employed here, the prosperity of this single firm is reflected in the life of the city itself. On twenty-four occasions the Belfast yard has led the world in tonnage launched ... looking to the future, we see that the Belfast yard has secured the order for a new 45,000-ton passenger liner for the P. and O. Company. She will be a ship of revolutionary design, with engines aft and twin funnels (probably side by side), and will be the largest vessel built in the United Kingdom since the *Queen Elizabeth*. She should make her first voyage to Australia in 1960, and will reduce the present four weeks for the journey to three weeks.[35]

Although fully justified at that moment, this optimism was to prove a short-lived illusion. The launch of the passenger ship mentioned above, *Canberra* (H&W y/n 1621), on 16 March 1960, can be seen as marking a moment of profound change.

As in the 1920s and 1930s, the world changed in a way that few had foreseen and the British shipbuilding industry collapsed in the face of foreign competition:

Left: One of the riveting team hard at work in the 1950s. (Courtesy of Lagan Legacy)

Below: A female member of the upholstery team. (Courtesy of Lagan Legacy)

> Finally, among declining industries, shipbuilding deserves a special mention. Again, following the short-term post-war competitive advantage because of the destruction of the shipyard capacity among other belligerents, and the inability of the rest of the world to buy tonnage launched in the dollar area, it is the relative British decline in competitiveness with the shipyards of other countries which is most striking … total merchant tonnage launched in 1950 was 1,325,000 g.t., compared with a world total of 3,489,000 g.t., and in 1966 1,094,000 g.t., out of a world total of 14,307,000. In that year Britain slipped to fourth place among the world's producing nations. In 1977, launching 1.0 m.g.t, she produced 4% of the world's output, and by 1980 had slipped to eighth place. By 1980, output had fallen dramatically once more to less than half 431,000 g.t.[36]

Harland & Wolff clearly demonstrate this process at work and output declined from the mid-1950s and all but collapsed in the following decades, although a steady increase in ship size tended to keep output in terms of tonnage up (see table 4).

Table 4: Output of Harland & Wolff, 1955–2002

	Ships	Tonnage	
1950–54	61	616,167	1950: Britain produces 38% of world shipping output
1955–59	63	607,995	1956: Britain is behind both Japan and Germany in terms of output
1960–64	32	568,140	
1965–69	20	582,947	1966: Britain slips to fourth place in terms of output (7.6% of total) 1968: H&W launch *Myrina*, first super-tanker, 95,450 tons
1970–74	15	1,215,411	1970: H&W bring building dock into use with *Esso Ulidia*, 126,538 tons
1975–79	14	1,340,780	1977: Britain produces 4% of world output of shipping 1977 & 1978: two 172,147-ton tankers produced, largest ships built by H&W
1980–84	9	339,587	1980: Britain in eighth place in terms of output
1985–89	4	161,510	1987: for the first time in 133 years, no ship launched in Belfast
1990–94	7	508,017	
1995–99	4	516,238	
2000–03	4	140,054	

After 1960, advances in air transport meant passenger vessels were effectively obsolete and Harland & Wolff increasingly focused on the production of standardised cargo vessels, with tankers and bulk carriers dominating output. The firm slowly declined as orders became scarce. In 1971 they employed 9,129 people (7,123 manual, 2,006 staff), but by 1985 this had declined to 5,163 (3,758 manual, 1,405 staff).

The end was inevitable: after a final brief flurry of tanker orders in the early 1990s and an attempt to become specialists in oil-exploration and production vessels, the firm built its last two vessels at the beginning of the twenty-first century.

The Harland & Wolff accounts office. (Courtesy of Lagan Legacy)

View of the Harland & Wolff yard in the late 1940s. (Courtesy of Lagan Legacy)

Workman Clark

Although known in Belfast as the 'wee yard', Workman Clark was a major shipbuilding firm and at its peak was amongst the top British producers in terms of tonnage. Frank Workman (b. 1856) and George Clark (b. 1861) both trained as premium apprentices at Harland & Wolff and were appointed to management positions within the firm. Their decision, in 1879–80, to establish their own yard on the opposite bank of the Lagan was probably not viewed very favourably by their former employers, not least because they took another gifted young manager from Harland & Wolff, William Campbell, to be their yard manager. Frank Workman's family had strong connections with the Belfast business community, which brought them some of their early business. George Clark's family were Scottish and his relatives included George Smith of Glasgow, who owned the City Line and not only provided 8 per cent of the initial share capital, but also gave the young men their first significant orders. As with Harland & Wolff two decades before, these family connections were of great significance in the early survival and ultimate success of the firm.

Despite important orders from Smith, the early years of the 'wee yard' gave little indication that the company would be a success. Two young, and comparatively inexperienced, men setting themselves up on a site next door to their former employer, who was less than impressed by their audacity, sounds more like a recipe for disaster. How were they going to survive in the tough competitive world of nineteenth-century British shipbuilding? The other contemporary shipbuilding business established at about the same time, McIlwaine and Lewis, in many ways comparable to Workman Clark, was eventually to collapse into bankruptcy.[37] However, unlike McIlwaine and his partners, Workman and Clark were able to reduce dependence on 'domestic' customers (although Irish owners accounted for half their orders in the early years) and establish contacts with broader 'British' markets. Initially, again probably through Clark/Smith family contacts, most of these orders came from Scotland, but over time this broadened to include other ports. Year by year, output increased and, by 1890, only a decade after they established their firm, Workman and Clark felt justified in making the investment involved in establishing a marine engineering works.

Shortly afterwards they acquired additional building slips and facilities by purchasing the yard of their bankrupt neighbours, a move that many probably saw as insane optimism. By this point, it could be argued that the 'wee yard' had come through its early difficulties and was on the brink of success as a shipbuilder. The *Belfast Trades Directory* for 1896 certainly had a very high opinion of the firm:

> [Workman Clark] have also purchased the yard and engine works belonging to the firm of MacIlwaine and McColl Ltd and thus have four separate establishments under their control. For the year 1893 they were 20th in the list of shipbuilders and for 1894 the sixth place. Thus demonstrating the great strides and growing importance of this young and enterprising firm.[38]

Although frequently presented as bitter rivals, Harland & Wolff and Workman Clark did not allow antagonisms to interfere with profit; Harland & Wolff's papers indicate that communication between yards could be amicable and even friendly. Co-operation was particularly noticeable during industrial disputes or on questions of rates of pay.[39] This co-operation was possible because the two yards had quite different customer lists, and differed significantly in output at this time.

Above: Interior of Workman Clark engine shop, early twentieth century.

Left: Hydraulic riveter employed on the centre longitudinal of a ship in Workman Clark yard, early twentieth century.

Table 5: Comparative output of specific types by Belfast shipbuilders

	Harland & Wolff		Workman Clark	
	1880–99	1900–13	1880–99	1900–13
Passenger vessels	19	21	0	1
% Total output	*9.4*	*20.2*		*0.7*
Passenger-cargo vessels	52	53	18	62
% Total output	*25.6*	*50.9*	*11.8*	*43.0*
Cargo vessels (all types)	115	21	124	79
% Total output	*56.7*	*20.2*	*81.0*	*54.9*

Whilst Workman and Clark did not develop a complex system comparable to Pirrie's commission club, they nevertheless built up a regular clientele, forming a customer base that was almost equally important in ensuring the firm's survival and success.

Table 6: Customers of Workman Clark obtaining eight or more vessels, 1880–1913

Customer	Ships	Tonnage	Dates
Alfred Holt	28	182,908	1894–1913
United Fruit	19	98,037	1904–13
J.P. Corry & Co.	12	70,067	1886–13
T.&J. Harrison	12	66,850	1891–1909
George Smith & Sons	11	49,274	1882–1901
Lampton & Holt	9	59,676	1900–13
Lloyds Brazilerio	9	25,704	1907–09
Tysor & Co.	8	60,845	1900–12
Allen Line	8	45,178	1893–1904
Houlder Bros	8	42,154	1895–1901
China Mutual SS Co.	8	41,162	1894–1902
Clark & Service	8	15,669	1883–95
a. Total	*140*	*757,524*	
b. Firms total output	*297*	*1,255,736*	
c. a. as percentage of b.	*47.1%*	*60.3%*	

As shipbuilders, Workman Clark reached maturity in the closing years of the nineteenth century and early twentieth century, when world trade and migration were expanding rapidly; hence the demand for shipping grew at an unprecedented rate. In 1904, Workman Clark completed a greater tonnage than Harland & Wolff for the first time, a feat repeated in 1912 and 1913. The nature of trade was changing, and there was a constant need to develop new types of ship capable of transporting totally new commodities to international trade, such as frozen meat, bananas and bulk oil. Workman Clark responded well to such demands and much of its success was based on a process of technical innovation. These years, with some justification, are often described as the golden age of British shipbuilding, and Workman Clark established such a reputation that they had a waiting list of customers for their vessels. The 4-acre site of 1880, employing 150 men, developed into the 50-acre, twin-site establishment, which 'usually employed' 5,000 men by 1902 and 9,000 in 1909, when they claimed the tonnage produced in the yard 'exceeded that of any other shipbuilding company in the United Kingdom'.[40]

As with Harland & Wolff, the First World War resulted in profound changes in Workman Clark's output. The company developed equipment and supplied vessels of new and highly specialist types to meet previously unimaginable developments in naval warfare, ranging from anti-submarine escorts to minesweepers. Again, as with their neighbours, perhaps the most important role played by the 'wee yard' was its contribution to the massive programme of standardised merchant tonnage construction that ultimately allowed the Allies to defeat the German U-boat blockade. They became the lead yard responsible for design of the 'G'-type standard refrigerated meat carriers, demonstrating the level of expertise they had developed in such vessels before the war. However, it was not new construction that formed the bulk of Workman Clark's work during the war years, as the firm's own history admits quite bluntly: 'during that period 1,396 vessels were handled either for building repairing or overhauling … the vessels dealt with approximated to one for every day of the war.'[41]

The management of Workman Clark, despite their clear commitment to the war effort, undoubtedly looked forward to the return of peace and the opportunity to resume building the high-quality, high-value ships in which they had specialised.

These hopes were to be disappointed: there was a brief post-war boom as wartime losses were made good, but after that the changed conditions began to adversely affect Workman Clark, and the British shipbuilding industry as a whole. The boom did, however, form the backdrop to the purchase of the 'wee yard' by the Northumberland Shipbuilding Company in 1919–20. This was, in many ways, a perfectly normal business transaction, but what was less satisfactory was the huge (even excessive) increase in share capital following purchase of the firm and the use of guaranteed dividend shares to attract investment. However, the fact that Workman Clark was able to make repeated share issues demonstrates that the firm enjoyed a good reputation and was considered a safe investment; but, unfortunately, things were not as they seemed. The burden of debt created by the financial dealings involved in the purchase of Workman Clark was eventually to drive the firm into insolvency.

How far was this the result of the somewhat cavalier management of the new board and how far was it due to the fundamental problems that beset British shipbuilding in the 1920s? Although the firm's output was significantly reduced in terms of both numbers and tonnage compared to the pre-war years, the output of the industry as a whole declined and Workman Clark managed to maintain if not slightly increase their share of the market. The problem was that the market for ships was seriously reduced and tended to fluctuate wildly, as can be seen by Workman Clark's output history.

Table 7: Output of Workman Clark, 1920–34

Year	Number of Hulls	Tonnage	
Average 1900–13	10.3	Approx. 62,000	
1920	6	34,491	
1921	9	53,600	
1922	6	51,082	
1923	5	40,704	
1924	9	45,832	
1925	5	25,554	
1926	3	26,550	
1927	6	48,366	
1928	1	360	January: Firm placed in receivership March: Reformed as Workman Clark (1928)
1929	7	52,628	

1930	10	50,488	
1931	3	33,230	
1932	1	5,739	
1933	2	14,138	
1934	4	36,896	

Between 1921 and 1927, Workman Clark launched 43 ships with a combined displacement of 291,688 tons, 59 per cent of hulls and 61 per cent of tonnage completed in the seven years before the First World War, which were perhaps the busiest in the company's history. Given the general state of the shipbuilding industry, this was still an impressive performance. Unfortunately, this simply was not sufficient to service the company's debts, and, despite a fairly full order book compared to many other yards, Workman Clark consistently made substantial losses. Just over three years after the share issues, mounting debts forced the directors of Workman Clark to suspend dividend and redemption payments, an action that created panic amongst shareholders, who eventually placed the firm in liquidation.

With hindsight, the transformation of Workman Clark into Workman Clark (1928) was a doomed venture, but this was not apparent in March 1928. The new company appeared to have a management that was not only impressively successful in obtaining orders, but also managed to resolve debt problems in a manner that freed the company from crippling responsibilities. The 'wee yard' seemed to be recovering until the Wall Street Crash of October 1929 caused a devastating reduction in world trade. The years 1928–34 saw Workman Clark launch only 28 ships (193,479 tons) – a 60 per cent drop in terms of both hulls and tonnage compared to the golden years of 1908–14. This still represented a good performance compared to many other British shipyards, but it was simply not enough to keep the yard going. These problems were compounded by the need to purchase the burned-out *Bermuda* from its owners, the company having already made a loss when building the ship in 1927.

By the beginning of 1935, the labour force was placed on a day-to-day basis and many sought more secure work in other industries or moved to other shipbuilding districts. The skilled labour that was critical to the yard's survival slowly drained away, with many employees moving to Harland & Wolff. It was increasingly recognised that Workman Clark (1928) was doomed and closure was inevitable. At the end of February 1935, most of the firm's staff were given a month's notice, leaving only a handful employed in the office, and on 13 March, in response to a question in the Northern Irish Parliament, it was suggested for the first time that National Shipbuilders Security had expressed an interest in the firm.[42] This syndicate was established in 1930 by 46 shipbuilders, including Harland & Wolff and Workman Clark, with a capital of £1 million, to purchase and dismantle redundant shipyards and so reduce capacity in the industry. On 23 March 1935, George Clark died and on 20 April the press finally announced that the yard was to be sold and closed:

> The 'Belfast Telegraph' understands that, subject to certain formalities, arrangements have been completed for the purchase of the shipbuilding yards and engineering works of Messrs Workman Clark (1928), Ltd., by National Shipbuilders Security, Ltd., the syndicate which is buying redundant shipyards and closing them down. The matter has been the subject of rumours for weeks, but has not reached the stage when an official announcement can be made. This is not likely to be available until May.[43]

Was it inevitable that Workman Clark should be the Belfast shipyard to close during the Depression of the 1930s? Harland & Wolff faced serious financial problems in these years, and, probably due to the nature of its customer base and output, the 'wee yard' enjoyed a better system of cost control and pricing. On balance, Workman Clark was probably just as viable as their neighbour, whose pre-war expansion programme left them with serious overcapacity. Both yards found it equally difficult to find new orders after 1929 and both were forced to lay off a large proportion of their skilled labour force, the vital and almost irreplaceable resource in the production of iron or steel ships and their engines. So, why did Harland & Wolff survive and Workman Clark vanish?

As early as 1923, the Northern Irish government was having doubts about the viability of Workman Clark and chose to allocate credit guarantees in a manner that favoured Harland & Wolff.[44] Was the 'wee yard' at a disadvantage because its owners were not local and did not enjoy a degree of political influence? Had the Northern Irish government recognised that rationalisation of the shipbuilding industry was inevitable in a period of falling demand and decided to support the 'big yard' at the expense of the 'wee'?

Luck was certainly a factor: the fire on the *Bermuda* could not have come at a worse moment for Workman Clark and probably drained the last financial reserves that might have allowed the yard to stay in business. Likewise, a number of the company's most important regular customers either vanished at this time or were forced to amalgamate, as the shipping industry struggled to come to terms with a changing world. If Workman Clark had been able to struggle on for a few more months, would they, like their neighbours, have begun to receive orders connected with rearmament? Could the firm have recovered and rebuilt their customer base as Harland & Wolff did in the late 1930s? We will never know, as Workman Clark simply ran out of time and vanished into history.

McIlwaine and Partners

The third Belfast shipyard offers a particularly interesting study because it was a failure. Harland & Wolff and Workman Clark were able to survive their early problems and develop into major shipbuilders; why did McIlwaine fail to do so? What can his failure tell us of the success of the other two yards?

The firm was established in the Ulster Ironworks on the newly opened Abercorn Basin in 1867. Listed as iron shipbuilders in 1868 in the *Belfast Trades Directory*, in later years McIlwaine was to claim this foundation date for his company.[45] In fact, in its early years the firm operated as ship repairers rather than builders, and it was not until 1876 that they launched their first vessel. This was the *Elizabeth Jane*, a screw tug for the Lagan Canal Company, for whom they were subsequently to build a number of iron barges prior to the yard's expansion from 1 to 4 acres in 1880.[46]

The increase in the yard's premises allowed them to extend their production. In 1880, the first vessel to merit inclusion in *Lloyd's Register*, *Parkmore*, built for Antrim Iron Ore Co. was launched. Subsequently the firm built a number of coasters and small cargo ships of between 108 and 456 tons, in addition to vessels of less than 100 tons: barges and river craft.[47] At this stage, McIlwaine and Lewis were specialising in vessels at the lower end of market, rather than ocean-going ships. Specialist yards focusing on such products survived and even prospered in other districts and the return of shipping in Belfast Harbour in the 1881 census suggests that there was local demand for small coastal and river craft:

Vessels belonging to Local Boards and Corporation	68
Vessels in Foreign Trade	29
Vessels in Home or Coasting Trade	130
Fishing Vessels	6
Vessels engaged in Inland Navigation	42
Pleasure craft	44[48]

Although the company had apparently successfully established a profitable niche market, John McIlwaine appears to have been ambitiously keen to expand into other areas of production. In 1885, the original partnership was dissolved and McIlwaine was joined by Hector McColl. The new firm, established as a limited company, acquired an extensive yard next to Harland & Wolff in 1885 or 1886.[49] Improved facilities allowed the company to compete for orders for large seagoing ships, and over the next nine years the firm completed 35 vessels. Contemporary descriptions laid great stress on the firm's capacity to construct a wide range of shipping.[50] According to the *Belfast Trades Directory* of the time, the firm 'have built very fine ships for each department of the shipbuilding trade and furnished them with all the latest and most improved machinery of the day, and are in a position to turn out vessels of the largest type'.[51]

A large proportion of their construction remained barges and small craft, and only 29 merited inclusion in *Lloyd's*. Of these, the majority were still small coasters and ferries, with only five being over 1,000 tons. Such a pattern of construction could not justify the heavy capital investment involved in the new yard and serious financial problems resulted, which came to a head in 1893–94: 'Messrs McIlwain & McColl Ltd, also built several steel steamers during 1893, but the firm has gone into liquidation, which is a source of regret to all true friends of Belfast.'[52]

The reason for McIlwaine's failure lay in the cyclic nature of the British shipbuilding industry. By the 1890s, Harland & Wolff had established the commission club and Workman Clark had created a regular clientele of customers. In both cases, these supplier/customer relationships guaranteed sufficient work in periods of slack demand. McIlwaine & Co. also had a number of regular customers, notably Cork, Passage and Blackrock Railway (four vessels), William Granger (four vessels), J. Fisher & Sons (six vessels) and Antrim Iron Ore Co. (four vessels). However, all these were relatively small-scale operators engaged in cross-Channel or coastal trades. Unlike White Star or Royal Mail, these small customers could not generate sufficient work to keep the yard active in periods of depressed demand. Another difference and a potentially critical one between McIlwaine and his neighbours is that he lacked family connections comparable to the Wolff/Schwabe or Clark/Smith relationships that proved so beneficial to the other yards. McIlwaine lacked the contacts and support to win sufficient major orders to ensure survival.

As already mentioned, McIlwaine's yard and engine works were acquired by Workman Clark and John McIlwaine returned to general engineering and ship repairing.[53] Of the legacy of this firm to the Belfast shipbuilding industry, their main contribution lies in the fact that their premises were of considerable importance to the expansion and success of Workman Clark. Nevertheless, there is one distinction that this short-lived yard can claim: it built Belfast's first *Titanic* (1,608 tons) for the Ulidian Steam Navigation Co. in 1888.

Having briefly looked at the history of the shipbuilders who operated on the Lagan, I now want to return to the ships and examine their production.

Notes

1 Lynch, J.P., *An Unlikely Success Story: The Belfast Shipbuilding Industry 1880–1935* (Belfast, 2001), ch.1.
2 Moss, M. & Hume, J.R., *Shipbuilders to the World* (Belfast, 1986), pp.11–35.
3 Lynch, J.P., 'Technology, Labour and the Growth of Belfast Shipbuilding', *Saothar* vol.24, pp.33–6.
4 Pollard, S. & Robertson, P., *The British Shipbuilding Industry 1870–1914* (Harvard, 1979), p.49.
5 Moss & Hume, *Shipbuilders*, p.19.
6 Dyos, H.J. & Aldcroft, D.H., *British Transport* (Leicester, 1971), p.244; Ulster Folk and Transport Museum *Olympic/ Titanic* publicity booklet, p.5.
7 Pounder, C.C., *Some Notable Belfast-built Engines* (Belfast, 1948), p.15.
8 Budge, I. & O'Leary, C., *Belfast Approach to Crisis* (London, 1973), p.89.
9 Pounder, *Belfast-built*, p.55.
10 BPP, census of Ireland, 1861, 1871, 1881, 1891, 1901, 1911.

11 Lynch, 'Technology, Labour and the Growth', pp.36–42; Lynch, *Unlikely Success Story*, pp.21–7.

12 BPP, Report of an enquiry by the Board of Trade into working-class housing, rents and retail prices (CD 3864), 1908.

13 BPP, Report of Board of Trade enquiry into the earnings and hours of labour of work people (CD 4545), 1909.

14 BPP, Report of the Departmental Committee on Humidity and Ventilation (CD 7433 & 7446), 1914.

15 Pollard & Robertson, *Shipbuilding*, pp.51–2, 62.

16 *Ibid.*, pp.51–2, 63.

17 *Ibid.*, pp.51–2; Smith, J.W. & Holden, T.S., *Where Ships are Born: Sunderland* (Sunderland 1953), pp.95–7. This shipbuilding district provides an interesting comparison to Belfast. In 1900 the two Belfast yards launched 16 ships with a combined tonnage of 125,109 tons (average 7,819 tons). The 13 yards on the Wear produced 70 ships, totalling 267,034 tons (average 3,815 tons).

Yard	Tonnage 1900	
Sir James Laings	40,307	One of Pollard and Robertson's 'important' yards. Specialised in tankers and liners.
Duxford & Sons	34,829	One of Pollard and Robertson's 'important' yards. Specialised in 'turret'-type cargo vessels.
J.L. Thompsons	33,649	One of Pollard and Robertson's 'important' yards.
Short Brothers	26,017	One of Pollard and Robertson's 'important' yards.
Pickergills	20,845	Specialised in cargo vessels.
Priestmans	20,362	Specialised in cargo vessels.
Bulmans	18,679	
Bartrains	18,530	
Sunderland Shipbuilders	16,358	
R. Thompsons	15,260	Specialised in medium-sized steamers.
Osborn, Grahams	9,370	
Austins	8,188	Specialised in colliers and heavily engaged in ship-repair work.
Crown	2,610	

18 Pollard & Robertson, *Shipbuilding*, pp.51–2, 63.

19 *Ibid.*, pp.252–3.

Output of major shipbuilding regions, 1880–1913

	UK output[a]	Newcastle	Sunderland	Clyde[b]	Belfast
1880–84	4,860,000	875,447 (18.0%)	734,748 (15.1%)	1,686,053 (34.7%)	136,512 (2.8%)
1885–89	3,796,820	788,416 (20.8%)	562,605 (14.8%)	1,166,498 (30.7%)	208,774 (5.5%)
1890–94	5,533,574	936,799 (16.9%)	856,036 (15.5%)	1,645,104 (29.7%)	425,503 (7.7%)
1895–99	5,847,565	1,019,396 (17.4%)	1,017,083 (17.4%)	2,078,936 (35.5%)	593,456 (10.1%)
1900–04	6,790,548	1,294,406 (19.1%)	1,161,166 (17.1%)	2,380,043 (35.0%)	654,457 (9.6%)
1905–09	6,980,136	1,345,686 (19.3%)	1,142,394 (16.4%)	2,517,383 (36.0%)	686,845 (9.8%)
1910–13	6,606,680	1,300,775 (19.7%)	971,961 (14.7%)	2,420,480 (36.6%)	630,837 (9.5%)

a This figure relates to merchant vessels of 100 tons+

b The Clyde figure includes warships so is rather too high (+2/3%)

20 Moss & Hume, *Shipbuilders*, pp.11–8.

21 *Ibid.*, p.18.
22 Bardon, J., *History of Ulster* (Belfast, 1992), p.335.
23 Moss & Hume, *Shipbuilders*, p.18.
24 Bardon, *History of Ulster*, p.335.
25 Moss & Hume, *Shipbuilders*, pp.28–9.
26 Bardon, *History of Ulster*, p.337.
27 Moss & Hume, *Shipbuilders*, pp.107–8.
28 *Ibid.*, pp.27, 40, 56, 104, 118, 123, 144.
29 *Ibid.*, *Shipbuilders*, pp.175–6.
30 *Ibid.*, p.179.
31 *Ulster Yearbook* (1938), p.176.
32 Moss & Hume, *Shipbuilders*, p.331.
33 *Ulster Yearbook* (1950), p.103.
34 Moss & Hume, *Shipbuilders*, p.356.
35 Rees, H., *British Ports and Shipping* (London, 1958), pp.256, 258.
36 Pollard, S., *The Development of the British Economy 1914–1990* (London, 1992), pp.248–9.
37 Lynch J.P., 'Belfast's Third Shipyard', *Ulster Folklife*, vol.41 (1995).
38 *Belfast Trades Directory* (1896), Introduction.
39 Harland & Wolff Papers, PRONI D2805. There are numerous examples of which the following illustrate the point:

28 March 1911: Note of a telephone conversation concerning plans to increase wages of unskilled workers.

2 December 1911: Letter from WC undertaking not to employ any striking H&W workers.

10 May 1913: Letter to WC giving details of revised apprentice pay rates agreed by H&W.

1 April 1914: Letter to WC containing list of striking boilermakers with request that they not be employed.

40 *Belfast Trades Directory* (1904 & 1914).
41 Workman Clark, *Shipbuilders of Belfast* (Belfast, 1933), p.52.
42 *Belfast Telegraph*, 13 March 1935.
43 *Ibid.*, 20 April 1935.
44 Armitage, A., 'Shipbuilding in Belfast: Workman Clark and Company, 1880–1935', in Fischer, L.R., *From Wheel House to Counting House; Essays in Maritime Business History in Honour of Professor Peter Neville Davies* (International Maritime Economic History Association, 1992), p.117. Belfast shipbuilders and their customers received £27.6 million in credit guarantees under the Trade Facilities and Loan Guarantee Acts between 1922 and 1929, compared to only £7.2 million granted to British-based yards in the same years.
45 *Belfast Trades Directory* (1868, 1884, 1887, 1890, 1892).
46 Owen, D.J., *History of Belfast* (Belfast, 1921), p.304; Moss and Hume, *Shipbuilders*, p.308.
47 Lynch, 'Third Shipyard', pp.23–4.
48 BPP, census of Ireland, 1881, City of Belfast, table E.
49 Owen, *Belfast* (Belfast, 1921), pp.304–5; Coe, W.E., *The Engineering Industry of the North of Ireland* (Newton Abbot, 1969), p.84.
50 *Industries of Ireland*, vol.2 (The North) (Belfast, 1986), p.72.
51 *Belfast Trades Directory* (1887, 1890, 1892), Introduction.
52 *Belfast Trades Directory* (1894), Introduction.
53 Coe, *Engineering*, p.84.

2

OUTPUT OF THE BELFAST SHIPYARDS

Belfast built ships for nearly 150 years. This extended time period makes the story of production complex and at times confusing. For example, *Coastal Corpus Christi* took to water (floated out of a building dock, so it would be wrong to say launched) on 18 June 1977. This ship displaced 172,147 tons and was one of the largest ever built by Harland & Wolff – she displaced slightly more than the combined tonnage of every ship launched in Belfast in the first 26 years of the industry's existence!

Modern shipbuilding began in Belfast when sailing ships dominated British output and ended in an era of super-tankers and bulk carriers. Such a complex story needs to be broken down into manageable, reasonably self-contained sections that can be examined and contrasted with each other. Many years ago I worked with an economic historian who argued that his ultimate ambition was to reduce the entire history of the world to a single table of statistics.[1] I have tried to reduce Belfast shipbuilding to a single table; all that is necessary is to explain reasons for change over time and consequences of such change for Belfast's shipyards. That is why I need a whole chapter.

Table 1: Belfast ship output by type, 1854–2003

Dates of launch	1854–79	1880–99	1900–13	1914–19	1920–39	1940–46	1947–60	1961–2003	Total
Passenger	***8*** *5.8%*	***19*** *4.7%*	***22*** *8.9%*	***5*** *3.7%*	***15*** *6.7%*	***0*** *0%*	***3*** *1.8%*	***0*** *0%*	***72*** *4.5%*
Passenger-cargo	***4*** *2.9%*	***72*** *17.9%*	***115*** *46.6%*	***19*** *14.1%*	***48*** *21.6%*	***0*** *0%*	***19*** *11.1%*	***0*** *0%*	***277*** *17.4%*
Passenger-cargo	4	67	73	11	25		14		194
Refrigerated pass-cargo		3	21	2	13		5		44
Passenger-fruiter		2	21	6	10				39
Cargo	***91*** *65.9%*	***275*** *68.6%*	***100*** *40.5*	***63*** *46.7%*	***140*** *63.0%*	***69*** *39.4%*	***116*** *67.8%*	***83*** *83.0%*	***937*** *59.0%*

General cargo	39	202	61	42	45	20	35	13	457
Sailing vessel	52	55							107
Refrigerated cargo		10	30	15	43	25	27	6	156
Fruiter			7	4	5				16
Tanker			2	2	39	22	50	37	152
Bulk carrier							2	24	26
Specialist cargo		8			8	2	2	3	23
Military vessels	***2*** *1.4%*	***4*** *1.0%*	***2*** *0.8%*	***48*** *35.5%*	***3*** *1.4%*	***106*** *60.6%*	***22*** *12.9%*	***7*** *7.0%*	***194*** *12.2%*
Cross-Channel	***3*** *2.2%*	***9*** *2.2%*	***5*** *2.0%*	***0*** *0%*	***9*** *4.0%*	***0*** *0%*	***11*** *6.4%*	***5*** *5.0%*	***42*** *2.6%*
Misc.	***30*** *21.7%*	***22*** *5.5%*	***3*** *1.2%*	***0*** *0%*	***7*** *3.1%*	***0*** *0%*	***0*** *0.0%*	***5*** *5.0%*	***67*** *4.2*
Total	**138**	**401**	**247**	**135**	**222**	**175**	**171**	**100**	**1589**

The first thing to recognise is that while cross-Channel vessels, colliers and coasters appear in the lists of Belfast's shipyards, the vast bulk of output were large ocean-going ship types. Pollard and Robertson demonstrated that this specialism meant Belfast produced vessels with the largest average tonnage in the UK.[2] There was a steady increase in average tonnage of ships produced over time, but this increase was far more marked in the case of Belfast than in most other shipbuilding districts.

Table 2: Average tonnage of major merchant shipping types produced in Belfast[3]

	Workman Clark		**Harland & Wolff**			**Merchant vessels over 100 tons**	
	Cargo	*Pass-cargo*	*Cargo*	*Pass-cargo*	*Passenger*	*UK*	*World*
1880–89	1,141	2,662	2,693	5,440	5,262	N/K	N/K
1890–99	3,421	4,338	5,050	7,212	8,700	1,706[a]	1,414[a]
1900–09	5,273	6,206	5,474	10,046	17,316	1,976	1,496
1910–19	6,779	6,365	6,357	11,596	30,642	2,653[b]	2,165[b]
1920–29	6,251	7,326	4,281	16,316	18,169	3,311	2,893
1930–35	7,299	6,384	7,351	14,956	22,606	2,729	2,282

a 1892–99 only

b Figures for 1914–18 exclude naval auxiliaries and are incomplete

Belfast primarily produced merchant shipping and while a number of naval vessels were built they were never a major element in output. Prior to the First World War, military vessels accounted for about 1 per cent of output and, if the two world wars are discounted, overall, warships accounted for 3 per cent of output. Belfast focused on big, deep-sea trading merchant ships; however, the size and type of merchant ship that was produced changed radically over time.

General view of the North Yard at Workman Clark.

1854–79

Robert Hickson produced some significant vessels, but looking at the history of this firm, and particularly the owners' somewhat unstable financial situation, the yard seemed doomed to fail. A shipbuilder operating in a resource-poor region of Britain such as Belfast hardly seemed likely to survive in the competitive world of mid-nineteenth-century shipbuilding. Hickson was probably profoundly relieved when Harland agreed to take the yard off him for £5,000 (approximately £400,000 at 2010 prices[4]).

The next decade saw Edward Harland slowly expand and develop the business. Production was more varied than in later years – he was willing or was forced to build anything he could obtain an order for. Barges and harbour craft accounted for over 20 per cent of production during this period. Cargo vessels accounted for two-thirds of output and although Harland was to make his reputation with 'coffin ships', over half of the cargo vessels launched in the first two decades were sailing vessels. This seems an anachronism. By the time Edward Harland acquired the Belfast shipyard in 1858, steamships were well established (1,926 of them on the British register compared to 25,615 sailing ships)[5] and they clearly represented the future of shipping technology. Yet for almost 40 years after this date, Belfast's yards continued to build sailing ships. Were shipbuilders on the Lagan simply old-fashioned and backward looking? Certainly there was an element of conservatism. Until the 1890s many ship owners insisted that steamers be fitted with masts and yards capable of carrying a sailing rig; for example, the first White Star liner to be completed without a sailing rig was *Teutonic* (y/n 208) in 1889. The problem was that steam engines were, initially, not terribly efficient or reliable, and a number of early disasters made shipowners cautious about adopting them unreservedly. Early ships' engines were bulky and coal consumption was high; as a consequence an often unacceptable proportion of carrying capacity had to be devoted to machinery and bunkers rather than cargo.

However, perhaps the critical point in the survival of sailing ships, in both the British merchant marine and the building lists of Belfast shipyards, is that for many purposes they were superior to steamers as cargo carriers. By the mid-nineteenth century, Britain's economy had become dependent on large-scale imports of a range of commodities that were bulky but comparatively low value (wool, jute, timber, grain, guano, metals, ores, etc.). Such cargoes did not have to be delivered quickly, but had to be transported as cheaply as possible. Conversely, one of Britain's major exports, coal (in 1850 slightly over 3¼ million tons was exported; by 1900 it was 48 million tons[6]), also fell into the category of cheap/bulky cargoes. Sailing ships were cheaper to build and operate (there were no engines and they required smaller crews) than steamers and thus were ideally suited to bulk trades and continued to be built in large numbers throughout the 1870s and 1880s. The advantages of sailing vessels were only eroded from the mid-1880s as developments in technology finally made steamships a viable option in long-distance bulk cargo transportation. Despite this, sailing ships remained efficient cargo carriers and were built in Belfast well into the 1890s. They were to be employed for decades to come.

The launch of *Oceanic* (y/n 73) in 1870 was a critical event in both the history of Harland & Wolff and in Belfast's shipbuilding industry. This ship was the first modern passenger liner and revolutionised transatlantic travel. Over the next five years Harland & Wolff supplied eight liners, of three distinctive types, to White Star.[7] Although liners comprised only 6 per cent of output in these years, their innovative design and commercial success made them the most significant ships of the era.

Harland & Wolff were interested in obtaining Admiralty work, which, it was hoped, would lead to profitable contacts from foreign customers. This proved a failure: not only did they fail to attract foreign orders,[8] but their first order, HMS *Lynx* (y/n 53), resulted in a loss of £5,000 that almost bankrupted them.[9] Their second attempt, HMS *Algerine* (y/n 131), was slightly more successful – they only lost £2,129 – but understandably this made them wary of seeking further Admiralty work on a fixed-price basis.[10] The only other significant warship order prior to the First World War was one for two gunboats, HMS *Lizard* (y/n 190) and HMS *Bramble* (y/n 191). This order was a result of the Admiralty's desire to test triple-expansion engines, which Harland & Wolff were at the forefront of introducing. In this case, the Admiralty had to agree to Harland's terms and they were built on a cost plus 5 per cent profit basis – although when the navy had finished haggling, the company made only 4 per cent profit.[11]

By the end of the 1870s, Harland & Wolff had established themselves as significant shipbuilders and the success of White Star's liners had earned them a considerable reputation. However, the Lagan was not a significant British shipbuilding district. In 1877 Belfast produced 9,072 of the 450,919 tons of merchant vessels produced in the UK (2 per cent), the Clyde produced about 35 per cent, the Tyne 19.5 per cent and Sunderland 19.4 per cent.[12]

1880–99

Harland & Wolff's success inspired imitators, and in 1879–80 two new firms began shipbuilding in Belfast; consequently these years saw an increasing number of vessels launched. The new yards, like Harland & Wolff before them, had to establish themselves and built whatever they could obtain orders for; as a result the output of the firms varied considerably.

Table 3: Output of Belfast shipyards by type, 1880–99

	Harland & Wolff	**Workman Clark**	**McIlwaine & Co.**	**Total**
Passenger	19 (9.4%)	0	0	19 (4.7%)
Passenger-Cargo	52 (25.6%)	18 (11.8%)	2 (4.4%)	72 (18.0%)
Cargo	115 (56.6%)	124 (81.0%)	36 (80.0%)	275 (68.6%)
Military	3 (1.5%)	0	1 (2.2%)	4 (1.0%)
Cross Channel	8 (3.9%)	0	1 (2.2%)	9 (2.2%)
Misc.	6 (3.0%)	11 (7.2%)	5 (11.1%)	22 (4.5%)
Total	**203**	**153**	**45**	**401**

The passenger vessel remained the prestige product of Harland & Wolff, although it comprised less than a tenth of their total output. A wide variety of different passenger configurations were adopted, depending on the customer's requirements. P&O ordered vessels for Far Eastern services that accommodated a mix of first- and second-class passengers: in *Shannon* (y/n 145) there was accommodation for 131 first-class and 94 second.[13] The Bibby Line ordered moderately sized vessels like *Cheshire* (y/n 240), which carryied about 100 passengers in single-class accommodation (first) for services to Burma, and proved highly popular with colonial officials and planters.[14] White Star continued to order huge people carriers for transatlantic routes but these developed to meet innovations by competitors. *Teutonic* (y/n 208) saw the abandonment of two-class passenger accommodation in favour of a three-class system, with accommodation being provided for 300 first-class, 190 second-class and 1,000 third-class (steerage) passengers.[15]

Although passenger vessels were the most prized products of Belfast's yards, there were relatively few routes on which such specialist ships could operate economically. What ship owners required were vessels capable of carrying fare-paying passengers (emigrants) outward and cargo on the homeward leg of the voyage. Belfast's shipbuilders were happy to supply them: such vessels comprised almost 18 per cent of output in these years. Although viewed by some as an inferior type compared to 'pure' passenger vessels, they were more complex than simple cargo carriers and were often outfitted to the highest standards for discerning owners. Ships of this type were of great importance on routes where the volume of passenger traffic was less than on transatlantic routes. Services to Africa, Latin and South America, Australia, New Zealand and the Caribbean were maintained by these useful dual-purpose vessels.

In terms of sheer numbers, the output of Belfast's yards was dominated by cargo vessels, which comprised almost 70 per cent of hulls launched. The sailing vessel slowly disappeared, with the last vessel of this type, *Lord Duffren* (WC y/n 130), being launched in 1896.[16] The majority of cargo ships launched in these years (73.5 per cent) were general cargo, albeit of considerable size. However, there were also signs of increasing specialisation in terms of function.

The UK market for meat increased dramatically in the late nineteenth century. White Star ordered specialist vessels to carry general cargo to North America and return loaded with live cattle. The first of these was *Cufic* (H&W y/n 210), which was capable of carrying 1,000 cattle, and she was followed by seven others of similar capacity. Their limitations were fairly self-evident, not least of which was the difficulty of keeping 1,000 cattle under control in heavy weather. The last of this type, *Cymric* (H&W y/n 316), was completed as an emigrant carrier with accommodation for 150 first-class passengers and 1,160 third-class (more emigrants than cattle). Technology had made livestock transporters obsolete; in 1880 the first cargo of frozen meat arrived in Britain aboard SS *Strathleven*, beginning a revolution in consumption:

> Meat which sold for 1½d. a lb. in Australia now fetched 5½d. at Smithfield, a price which put fresh meat with the reach of many for the first time. Within a few years frozen pork from the United States, beef from the Argentine and lamb from New Zealand were flooding the English market, and by 1902 had reached a value of £50 million a year, equivalent to 56lb. a year per head of population, and approximately half of total consumption.[17]

Once technical problems with refrigeration were solved this development promised huge profits for companies in the meat trade and those who built the ships they required. Harland & Wolff were rather slow to embrace this particular technology, not building their first refrigerated ship, *Norman* (y/n 280), until 1894; however, Workman Clark embraced it with vigour, launching *Celtic King* (WC y/n 73) in 1890. Refrigerated vessels became a Workman Clark specialism, with eight more refrigerated cargo and two refrigerated passenger-cargo ships launched before the turn of the century.

In 1896–97 Workman Clark introduced another new cargo-vessel type, launching a pair of vessels for Glasgow shipowners: *Belvidere* (y/n 137) and *Beverly* (y/n 138) were insulated and carefully ventilated to allow transportation of another new commodity – fruit.

Between 1880 and 1899 the Lagan developed into a major shipbuilding district, producing up to 12 per cent of British merchant shipping output in some years. The industry was about to enter its golden age.

Table 4: Belfast shipbuilding industry, 1880–99[18]

	Total UK output (Merchant vessels of 100 tons+ only)	Belfast output (Merchant vessels of 100 tons+ only)	Belfast % of UK
1880–84	4,860,000	135,920	2.8
1885–89	3,796,820	211,540	5.57
1890–94	5,533,574	429,489	7.8
1895–99	5,847,565	579,881	10.2
Total	**20,037,959**	**1,356,830**	**6.77**

1900–13

Although it is often seen as tempting fate for historians to describe any period as a golden age, it is difficult to see how the early years of twentieth century can be described as anything other than this for Belfast's shipbuilders. In these years, output was dominated by passenger and passenger-cargo vessels (55 per cent of hulls). The Belfast yards launched their most prestigious products and created fleets that dominated world shipping. Harland & Wolff built vessels that allowed White Star to become the leading shipping line on transatlantic routes while, next door, Workman Clark built the handsome passenger-fruiters that formed the 'White Fleet' of United Fruit. These were years when every building slip was occupied and potential customers had to place their names on a waiting list to have a vessel built in Belfast.

The year 1911 tends to be remembered for a single launching: Harland & Wolff's y/n 401 for Oceanic Steam Navigation (White Star). However, 19 other ships were launched that year. As a group they represent a typical example of output from the Lagan shipyards at their peak: a couple of tenders for harbour work, a cross-Channel ferry, a single general cargo ship, a refrigerated meat carrier and probably the most famous (or infamous) passenger liner in history. The other fourteen vessels launched were passenger-cargo ships of various types.

Table 5: Output of Belfast shipyards, 1911

Name	Date of launch	Yard number	Builder	Type
Aracataca	05.01.1911	300	WC	Passenger-fruiter
Anchises	12.01.1911	296	WC	Passenger-cargo
Neleus	31.01.1911	299	WC	Cargo
Demosthenes	28.01.1911	418	H&W	Passenger-cargo (Refrigerated)
Egra	14.03.1911	307	WC	Passenger-cargo
Galway Castle	12.04.1911	419	H&W	Passenger-cargo
Nomadic	25.04.1911	422	H&W	Tender
Traffic	27.04.1911	423	H&W	Tender

Carrillo	17.05.1911	305	WC	Passenger-fruiter
Titanic	31.05.1911	401	H&W	Passenger
Vandyke	01.06.1911	301	WC	Passenger-cargo
Zelandic	26.06.1911	421	H&W	Passenger-cargo
Tivives	01.08.1911	304	WC	Passenger-fruiter
Sixaola	24.08.1911	306	WC	Passenger-fruiter
Patriotic	11.09.1911	424	H&W	Cross-Channel ship
Waimana	12.09.1911	309	WC	Cargo (Refrigerated)
Ekma	21.10.1911	308	WC	Passenger-cargo
Arlanza	23.11.1911	415	H&W	Passenger-cargo
Malwa	17.12.1911	414	H&W	Passenger-cargo (Refrigerated)
Demerara	21.12.1911	425	H&W	Passenger-cargo (Refrigerated)

There was a tendency, as I have already discussed, for passenger-cargo vessels to be viewed as an inferior product, which may account for Harland & Wolff's desire to mark-up such vessels as passenger vessels in their history. However, as regular passenger/mail services were maintained using passenger-cargo vessels, the accommodation provided was frequently of a very high standard and could be comparable with that on liners on North Atlantic routes. The sister ships *Tenadores*, *Pastores* and *Calamares* (WC y/n 314–16) were for passenger-fruiter services between New York and the West Indies and had accommodation for 150 first-class passengers. One contemporary noted the design represented 'an admirable combination of artistic design and general efficiency'.[19] Workman Clark built *Patia* and *Patua* (y/n 317 and 320) for Elders & Fyffes, for passenger/mail and fruit-carrying services between Britain, the West Indies and Central America. Although slightly smaller than the American vessels, they were equally impressive in terms of accommodation:

> Accommodation is provided in each of the vessels for about sixty first-class passengers in comfortably-furnished staterooms arranged for one or two persons. These rooms are exceptionally large and bright, and no detail has been omitted that would conduce to the comfort of travellers. It is interesting to note that the Patia and Patuca are equipped with long-distance wireless telegraph installations, and that the safety of passengers is further safeguarded by the provision of sufficient lifeboat accommodation for every person on board.[20]

The closing part of this description is intended to reassure readers who had memories of the *Titanic* disaster.

Although Belfast was already a significant shipbuilding port at the end of the nineteenth century, and output increased significantly in the early twentieth century, in general, British shipbuilding was facing increasing competition. In the last seven years of the nineteenth century Britain produced over 70 per cent of world tonnage and Belfast produced 7 per cent of the world total. In the face of growing competition from German, French and American shipbuilders, in the first seven years of the twentieth century the British share, of a greatly increased total, fell to 60 per cent. In the seven years before the First World War, Britain's share of world shipping output fell to under 55 per cent. Due to the size of the vessels Belfast produced, in these years the Lagan produced less than 2 per cent of total hulls, but 5.5–6 per cent of tonnage. On 1 January 1914 the *Belfast Newsletter* carried a 'Review of Belfast trade and commerce' that must have provided reassurance to readers:

> The developments in the shipbuilding trade in Belfast promise to surpass even the wonderful achievements already to its credit, and it is now well known that the combined output in 1914 of Messrs. Harland & Wolff and Messrs. Workman, Clark & Co. will provide such an aggregate of

> big tonnage as has probably never been seen in any port in the world. The White Star line liner Britannic, which is now in course of construction at the Queen's Island will rank in size with the German leviathans Imperator and Vaterland, and with the mammoth Cunarder Aquitania …[21]

In January 1914 such optimism was well founded, but coming events would ensure the year was remembered for other reasons.

Table 6: Average annual output of merchant shipping (100 tons+), 1893–1913[22]

	Belfast			**United Kingdom**			**World**	
	Average hulls	Average tonnage	% of UK tonnage (T) and hulls (H)	Average hulls	Average tonnage	% of world tonnage (T) and hulls (H)	Average hulls	Average tonnage
1893–99	19	108,650	T = 9.8 H = 3.0	643	1,104,351	T = 73.7 H = 61.5	1,046	1,497,618
1900–06	18	134,549	T = 9.2 H = 2.5	724	1,460,294	T = 60.1 H = 45.0	1,608	2,427,530
1907–13	17.5	147,097	T = 11.2 H = 2.7	652	1,307,891	T = 53.7 H = 43.1	1,514	2,436,582

1914–19

In January 1914 nobody really believed war was possible; certainly European powers had rivalries and petty jealousies and military leaders had prepared meticulous plans for a conflict, but to most this was simply insurance. Given the horrific destructive power of modern weaponry, many argued that a major conflict in 'civilised' Europe was unthinkable and that such a war would interfere with trade and profits, which was even more unthinkable. Otto von Bismarck is reputed to have said: 'If there is ever another war in Europe, it will come out of some silly thing in the Balkans'.[23] It could be argued the 'silly thing' was Franz Ferdinand, 50-year-old heir to the Austro-Hungarian throne. On 28 June 1914 he visited the city of Sarajevo in the Balkans as part of a tour of inspection. The local authorities published exact details of the archduke's itinerary to allow loyal subjects to show their enthusiasm for the Habsburg monarchy, but also allowing Serbian nationalist terrorists to plan attacks. Under the circumstances, it should have come as no surprise that, after an unsuccessful attempt to kill him with a bomb, the archduke and his wife were killed by a student with a revolver.

The resulting crisis dragged the European powers one after another into a war none expected, but that military staffs had planned down to the last troop train. The next four years would see more than 8.5 million deaths, the end of four empires and the collapse of a way of life that had seemed fixed and stable. On 4 August 1914 when, following the invasion of Belgium, Britain declared war on Germany, the problem was that nobody, including military leaders, understood the nature of the conflict now beginning. It was assumed that it would follow the pattern of the last great continental conflict between France and Germany in 1870, and be a rapid decisive conflict lasting weeks at most. This belief in a 'short, sharp war' resulted in meticulous planning by the War Office to ensure that the British Army did not arrive too late to take part, and hundreds of trains, moving on pre-prepared timetables, carried four infantry divisions with their supporting troops and stores to embarkation ports in just five days.[24]

Another consequence of short-war thinking was that steel and other shipbuilding necessities were diverted to yards with naval construction on hand, and merchant ships were delayed or even suspended in the early stages of the war. This caused a marked drop in merchant shipping output throughout Britain (see table 7), which particularly affected centres such as Belfast as they specialised in merchant shipping. An example of the chaos produced would be three vessels under construction for the Pacific Steam Navigation Company. *Orduna* (H&W y/n 438) was launched in October 1913 and was completed and delivered in less than four months – the pre-war production pattern. Her sister ship *Orbita* (H&W y/n 440) was launched in July 1914 but, because of labour and material shortages, took over a year to complete. The third sister *Orca* (H&W y/n 442) was laid down early in 1914 and was not launched when war broke out; construction was suspended, so she was not launched until April 1917 and after that took over a year to complete. A large proportion of the merchant ships launched in Belfast between the start of 1915 and mid-1917 were vessels laid down before war and delayed by shortages of labour and materials. In 1915 the Lagan produced about 5 per cent of UK merchant tonnage, but in 1916 it produced less than half this figure.

Table 7: Merchant ship output (100 ton+ only), 1914–19[25]

	Belfast		United Kingdom	
	Hulls	**Tonnage**	**Hulls**	**Tonnage**
Average 1900–13	17.6	141,019	688	1,454,883
1914	15	224,340	656	1,683,553
1915	6	30,207	327	650,919
1916	2	14,322	306	608,235
1917	16	127,746	286	1,162,896
1918	22	139,269	301	1,348,120
1919	27	197,796	612	1,620,442
1920	19	115,308	618	2,055,624

The fate of White Star liner *Britannic* (H&W y/n 433), the source of such optimism in January 1914, shows the effects of this conflict. Launched on 26 February 1914, her fitting out (which had taken seven and ten months in the case of her sisters) was well advanced at outbreak of war, but work practically ceased. It was not until May 1915 that engine trials were completed and it was reported in such a condition that 'in an emergency' *Britannic* could be brought into use on four weeks' notice. On 13 November 1915 the liner was requisitioned and fitting out was restarted as a matter of urgency, but as a hospital ship with 3,300 beds in order to evacuate casualties from Gallipoli. On 8 December she was handed over, painted white in Red Cross livery, and four days later sailed for Alexandria from where she made five voyages evacuating casualties from the Greek port of Mudros, on the island of Limnos, to either Southampton or Marseilles. On 12 November 1916 she sailed from Southampton and, on the 21st, having refuelled at Naples, was passing to the west of the Greek island of Kea en route for Limnos when she struck a mine laid by *U-73*. Due to damage to watertight doors in the explosion and the portholes being left open to air the ship, flooding was rapid; *Britannic* sank in just under an hour. Seven members of the crew were killed in the explosion and another 21 were killed when two lifeboats were dragged into the sinking ship's propellers. *Britannic* has the dubious distinctions of being the largest Allied vessel sunk by a U-boat in the First World War and having never carried a fare-paying passenger.

The collapse in orders for merchant hulls was not compensated for by an increase in military orders. The Belfast yards lacked experience of building high-performance warships and their output was mainly minor auxiliary or support vessels rather than front-line combat ships. The major exception to this would appear to be the battlecruiser *Glorious* (H&W y/n 482, 483 and 484); this vessel was as large as many of the early Dreadnoughts but was armoured on the same scale as contemporary light cruisers. Even before *Glorious* was completed, events at Jutland demonstrated that if she were committed to the battle line she would have been a deathtrap for the 800 crew. Although a handsome ship, *Glorious* was a white elephant. In the first two years of war, Belfast's main contribution to the war effort consisted of repair and refit work, but this changed in the second half of the war.

In December 1916, in the face of increasing losses to German U-boats, the British government changed policy radically and began to order large numbers of merchantmen, built to standard designs, while increasingly assuming effective control of the shipbuilding industry. The urgency of the programme can be gauged by the fact that the Merchant Shipbuilding Advisory Committee met for first time in December 1916 and the first ship, Harland & Wolff-built *War Shamrock*, was completed in August 1917. Mitchell and Sawyer point out that this programme represented a radical departure from pre-war practice:

> Builders had, of course, special knowledge of ships that were peculiar to their yard only and were a little sensitive to their own practices being altered perhaps to the practices of another area. Nevertheless, the emergency war policy of building standard ships was accepted and if some delay in a yard building its first 'standard' occurred, the repeat ships were turned out in improved times. Designs were requested from builders with sound knowledge of the class of vessel required. The ships were to be plain cargo vessels with a maximum of cargo space and minimum use of materials, labour and expenditure.[26]

The programme demanded speed of construction rather than quality or aesthetic beauty, and both Belfast companies, with their extensive experience of merchant ship construction, were to play a major role.

In August 1918, Harland & Wolff set a record by completing a standard ship just five days after launching.[27] Workman Clark, not to be outdone, completed *War Beetle* in September, just three and three-quarter days after her launch.[28] Belfast Corporation's official history of the war noted the success of this programme:

> Some of these vessels have been turned out in very quick time. During their construction one of the firm's (Workman Clark) men established a new world's riveting record in the north yard, [John Moir drove 11,209 rivets in a normal working day on 5 June 1918] and the south yard and engine works replied by making a record in the way of finishing a standard ship, an 8,000 ton vessel being completed in 3¾ days from the time of launch.[29]

Production of standard ships continued for some time after war and Belfast eventually produced 50 such vessels.[30] This huge construction programme saw the Lagan launching over 11 per cent of total UK merchant tonnage in 1917–19. However, once slips were clear of wartime production, Belfast's shipyards found themselves facing problems.

1920–39

When I outlined the history of the Belfast shipbuilders I looked at the reasons for the slump in demand. This was not a localised problem; the same pattern of reduced demand, coupled with extreme variations year on year, affected the British shipbuilding sector as a whole (see table 8). Overall, Belfast managed to maintain its position comparative to the rest of the UK, but this average conceals a pattern of serious swings in terms of orders, which created major problems. Britain's share of world merchant shipping output, down to 55 per cent of the total immediately before the First World War, declined sharply. In 1921–28, Britain produced 46.3 per cent of world tonnage (38.7 per cent of hulls) and, in 1929–35, 44.3 per cent of tonnage (37.3 per cent of hulls). These averages conceal the fact that, once again, year-on-year output could vary dramatically.[31]

Table 8: Merchant shipping output (100 ton+ only), 1921–35[32]

	Belfast		United Kingdom	
	Hulls	**Tonnage**	**Hulls**	**Tonnage**
Average 1900–1913	17.6	141,019	688	1,454,883
1921	13	93,467	426	1,538,052
1922	9	86,869	235	1,031,081
1923	11	127,390	222	645,651
1924	12	105,375	494	1,439,885
1925	10	57,090	342	1,084,633
1926	9	92,263	197	639,568
1927	20	110,762	371	1,225,873
1928	13	75,728	420	1,445,920
1929	17	143,884	489	1,522,623
1930	26	168,337	481	1,478,563
1931	8	95,238	148	502,487
1932	1	5,939	100	187,794
1933	2	14,138	108	133,115
1934	10	87,097	173	459,877
1935	8	97,067	185	499,011
Average 1921–35	**11.3 (-36%)**	**90,710 (-36%)**	**293 (-47%)**	**922,276 (-37%)**

Compared to the golden age, the types of ship being produced were much less labour intensive. After a brief surge in demand for passenger tonnage to replace wartime losses, the market for such ships declined noticeably as the after-effects of the Wall Street Crash worked their way through the world economy. There was still a demand for passenger-cargo vessels, which accounted for 21.6 per cent of output, but overall output of labour-intensive ship types fell from 55.5 per cent of hulls to 28.3 per cent. Cargo vessels constituted 63 per cent of output, only about a third of which were general cargo ships. There was increased production of refrigerated cargo vessels and fruiters, which now accounted for nearly half of cargo and passenger-cargo hulls produced. However, a new trade created a demand for a new type of ship. Between 1904 and 1913, UK annual imports of petroleum products averaged about 1.4 million metric tons. In the post-war era, imports of oil increased dramatically until, by 1938, imports consisted of 2.3 million tons of crude oil and over 9.5 million tons of refined products.[33] Dyos and Aldcroft describe the extent of the revolution created by the adoption of oil:

> During these years the seaborne trade in fuel underwent an appreciable change. The coal trade fell from 174 million tons in 1913 to 142 in 1937 whilst world oil shipments increased from 14 million tons to 84 million tons in 1937 and by the late 1930s accounted for about one-quarter of the total tonnage of world seaborne trade. This created a demand for a specialized tanker fleet which rose from 1.5 million tons in 1914 to 10.7 in 1938.[34]

The tanker was not a new type of ship: vessels designed to carry oil in tanks, rather than in barrels or cans, dated from 1885–86, when Armstrong's launched *Glucicauf* and the *Worwarts* for German owners.[35] Such ships subsequently became a specialist product of Laing's, Sunderland, in the years before the First World War.[36] The first Belfast-built oil carriers were *Iroquois* and

Navaho (H&W y/n 385, 389), which were neither successful nor repeated. Workman Clark's involvement began with naval oiler *Appleleaf* (y/n 368), but it was the laying down of a pair of ships for British Tanker Co., *British Lantern* and *British Beacon* (WC y/n 424, 425), which marked the introduction of this type as a standard product. Between 1920 and 1935, Workman Clark built eight tankers, 10.4 per cent of output, while Harland & Wolff built 31, over a fifth of hull output. Although a welcome addition to order books of work-starved yards, these ships, which were basically only a series of tanks with an engine on the back, were far less labour intensive than passenger-cargo vessels. They kept tonnage production figures up but did not generate much employment.

1940–46

If the First World War had come as a shock to Britain, the same cannot be said of the conflict that broke out in 1939. Then most people felt it was not a case of 'will' there be another war but rather 'when' will there be another war. The British government was criticised for rearming late, but in reality they did so quickly and with remarkable efficiency. Even at the outbreak of war, Britain was producing more aircraft and tanks per month than Germany and was to mobilise more efficiently. The basic problem for the government was how to utilise resources to the maximum and allocate them in the most effective manner. The experience of the First World War had shown how this could be achieved, and lessons had not been forgotten: the government quickly assumed powers to control almost every aspect of life. The Minister of Labour was empowered to direct 'any person in the United Kingdom to perform any service required in any place', effectively giving him almost dictatorial powers. Non-essential industries were cut back, and a pool of labour was created that could be directed into any industry at any point. Conscription was introduced, with a carefully planned system of 'reserve occupations' to ensure that necessary war production was not disrupted by overenthusiastic volunteering as it had been in 1914–15.

Between 1939 and 1944, the British shipbuilding industry was to produce over 6 million tons of merchant shipping (compared to *c.* 5.4 million in 1915–19), in addition to over 1 million tons of major naval vessels.[37] The dislocation and confusion in shipyards that had been a feature of 1914–15 did not occur in 1939–40. Belfast was designated as a major centre for ship production and repair, both due to experience of previous conflict and the erroneous belief that Northern Ireland was beyond the range of German bombers.[38] Belfast's shipyards were flooded with orders: between 1940 and 1946 the Lagan launched 175 vessels and, unlike 1914–18, there were no quiet periods. Belfast continued to produce merchant vessels throughout the war years and, compared to the 1930s, output increased considerably. Of the approximately 6 million tons of merchant shipping mentioned above, Belfast contributed about 7.5 per cent.

Table 9: Belfast production of merchant shipping, 1933–46

Year	Hulls	Tonnage
1933	2	14,138
1934	9	86,950
1935	8	97,067
1936	11	62,191
1937	9	74,395
1938	6	69,586
1939	4	61,554
Average 1933–39	*7*	*66,554*

1940	8	52,000
1941	7	62,292
1942	13	103,771
1943	9	75,661
1944	12	97,799
1945	6	52,995
1946	14	123,912
Average 1940-46	*9.8*	*81,204*

* Includes passenger, passenger-cargo, cargo and cross-Channel

However, 60 per cent of hulls produced in Belfast in these years were warships (although due to the small size of many, they amounted to only just over 32 per cent of the tonnage). On 19 September 1939, just over two weeks after the declaration of war, Harland & Wolff received their first major war order: 20 Flower-class corvettes. On 8 April 1941, days after delivering the first completed corvette with four more fitted out and seven on slips, they received an order for 20 more. The design of these vessels had been prepared before the war by Smith's Dock, Middlesbrough, and was based on their 1936 whale catcher *Southern Pride* (y/n 1018). Intended as coastal escorts, 219 of these basic but effective warships were built, 145 of them in British shipyards. There was nothing complicated about these ships, as one literary description made clear:

> ... here he was, almost masquerading as Lieut.-Commander G.E. Ericson, with one of His Majesty's ships of war to commission, a crew of eighty-eight to command and a hundred things in the realm of naval routine to re-learn, quite apart from having a fighting ship to manoeuvre and to use as a weapon.
>
> A fighting ship ... He raised his eyes and looked at Compass Rose again. She was odd, definitely odd, even making allowances for her present unfinished state. She was two hundred feet long, broad, chunky, and graceless: designed purely for anti-submarine work, and not much more than a floating platform for depth-charges, she was the proto-type of a class of ship which could be produced quickly and cheaply in the future, to meet the urgent demands of convoy escort.
>
> Her mast, contrary to naval practice, was planted right in front of the bridge, and a squat funnel behind it: she had a high fo'c'stle armed with a single four-inch gun, which the senior gunnery rating was at the moment elevating and training. The depth-charge rails aft led over a whaler-type stern. Ericson knew ships, and he could guess how this one was going to behave. She would be hot in summer and cold, wet and uncomfortable at most other times. She would be a proper devil in any kind of a seaway, and in a full Atlantic gale she would be thrown about like a chip of wood. And that was really all you could say about her – except that she was his, and that, whatever her drawbacks and imperfections, he had to get her going and make her work.[39]

Belfast was eventually to deliver 34 of these ships, in most cases within five to six months of keels being laid. The Flowers formed the backbone of the British convoy escort forces in the early stages of war. Losses were heavy: 20 were sunk by U-boats and one by an Italian submarine, the very vessels they were built to hunt, while air attacks and accidents accounted for another dozen. Four of the Belfast-built Flowers became war losses.

These early orders set the pattern for much of Belfast's warship building during the war: large orders for escort vessels of standard types and increasing complexity followed one after another, with many cancelled to clear space for later types.[40] Clearly the policy was to give the yard more work than it could complete to ensure no slip was ever left empty. Belfast also produced a significant number of amphibious warfare vessels of various types from small landing craft to a large transport of over 8,000 tons. The most significant design, the LSt(1), was designed by Harland & Wolff in response to a requirement for a vessel capable of landing tanks and lorries directly onto beaches. What emerged (y/n 1143–6) were large seaworthy vessels with good speed but not suitable for mass production or capable of beaching in sufficiently shallow water: they were a failure. For most of the war, Britain employed the American-produced LSt(2) (popularly known as 'Large Slow Target') made available under lend-lease. Eventually, the Royal Navy ordered 45 LSt(3), which had frigate-type machinery to give them a more acceptable speed; eight of these were built in Belfast (y/n 1289–96).

As with the passenger vessels of earlier years, it was not the escorts and landing craft that left the greatest impression, but rather the handful of major vessels. Following *Penelope* (y/n 940), Harland & Wolff had built a number of significant warships, notably *Belfast* (y/n 1000) and more importantly *Formidable* (y/n 1007), launched shortly before the war and delivered late in 1940. During the war, Harland's major warship production consisted of aircraft carriers, seven of which were launched during hostilities; two more were on slips at the end.[41] Perhaps inevitably they will remain the best-remembered products of wartime Belfast.

1947–60

With the end of war, there was a wholesale cancellation of warship orders as the British Government, bankrupted by conflict, sought to save money to rebuild Britain and create the welfare state. The aircraft carriers already on the stocks were eventually launched, but would remain incomplete for years (y/n 1220, 1280, 1281), while another carrier (y/n 1304) and 19 frigates were cancelled. Even when peace began to be disturbed by talk of an iron curtain and a cold war there was no rush of orders: the Western Allies had a huge naval superiority due to their wartime construction programmes. Although Belfast was to contribute to the two largest post-war British military ship programmes – the type-12 frigate and the Ton-class minesweeper – warships were to form only about an eighth of Belfast's output, the yard resumed its normal focus on merchant shipping.

Unlike the post-First World War era, the late 1940s and 1950s did not see a slump in demand for merchant shipping. Rather, in terms of number of hulls launched, wartime output was maintained and, in terms of tonnage, the industry was doing better than at any point since the golden era. Towards the end of the period, annual launching figures began to slump, but compared to interwar years the yards remained busy and the ever-increasing tonnage produced seemed to provide evidence that the industry was prospering.

Table 10: Belfast production of merchant shipping, 1947–60

Year	Hulls	Tonnage
Average 1934–39	7	66,554
Average 1940–46	9.8	81,204
1947	11	122,295
1948	13	102,273
1949	12	97,766
1950	11	133,347
1951	10	118,616
1952	15	141,645
1953	10	105,446

Average 1947–53	11.7	117,341
1954	8	99,992
1955	11	121,611
1956	9	105,104
1957	13	148,377
1958	8	100,833
1959	9	121,649
1960	9	184,198
Average 1954–60	9.6	125,966

* Includes passenger, passenger-cargo, cargo and cross-Channel

The increase in tonnage launched can be explained by developments in a type of ship caused by huge expansion in the trade in one commodity in these years. Although the bulk oil trade was already well developed before the Second World War, it increased dramatically in the post-war years, partly as a consequence of increased oil consumption, but also because of a deliberate policy of expanding the British oil-processing industry.[42] Between 1926 and 1932, Belfast produced 86 merchant vessels, of which 27 had been tankers (31 per cent); however, most of these were small coastal types of 2,300–2,500 tons, with half a dozen vessels in the 8,000-ton class, which brought average tonnage up to about 4,200 tons. Of 49 merchant ships built in 1933–39, only two were tankers, although both were 8,000-ton+ ocean-going types. A third of wartime-built merchant vessels had been tankers, with 8,000-ton vessels predominating. In the post-war era the tanker again formed a third of Belfast's merchant ship output, but in 1947–53 their average size increased to over 11,000 tons, and between 1954 and 1960 to over 19,000 tons. Basically, oil was a cheap bulk cargo and the best way to transport it, particularly crude oil to feed the British refining industry, was in bulk – tankers grew steadily larger and the demand for oil increased.

Table 11: Typical Belfast tankers (Harland & Wolff), 1926–60

Name	Displacement	Length	Beam	Draft	
Ambrosio 1926	2,391	305.7	50.2	14.3	Shallow-draft coastal design for use in Venezuelan oil fields.
Empire Diamond 1941	8,236	465.6	59.5	34.0	The first of the war-built 'Ocean' type. In terms of size it was typical of late pre-war ships and remained standard after the war.
Verena 1950	18,612	619.7	80.7	45.2	This vessel marked a huge increase compared to the previous 8,000-ton standard
British Engineer 1953	21,077	640.7	85.8	46.9	The next major jump in size.
British Statesman 1958	27,586	710.9	95.4	38.8	
William Wheelwright 1960	31,320	753.6	98.5	40.7	

On 16 February 1960 Harland & Wolff launched *Canberra* (y/n 1621) for the UK–Australia service; latest in the long line of passenger ships built in the yard, what nobody knew that day was that it would be the last. Two weeks earlier a new type of ship had been launched for Norwegian owners, the bulk carrier *Tresfonn* (y/n 1599). Designed to carry unpacked bulk cargoes like grain, coal or ores, such vessels were becoming increasingly important in terms of world shipping. Belfast was keeping pace with the times. Certainly Henry Rees, writing in the late 1950s, felt considerable optimism:

> Belfast is a virile city. By nature rather poorly endowed for shipping, her people have built up a harbour which compares with our other major ports,. They are not content to rely solely on the old-fashioned exports of linen and livestock: they eagerly embrace new forms of traffic in the shape of the container and the lorry-ferry. In the manufacture of heavy electrical equipment, of ships and aircraft, the future of Belfast is assured.[43]

Yet for all this optimism, British shipbuilding was in decline. In 1956 Britain produced less than 14 per cent of world tonnage and had fallen into third place as a producer behind Japan and Germany, who had rebuilt their devastated shipyards and now aggressively competed for orders.[44] Even Rees could not ignore the decline. In 1910 Britain had produced 58 per cent of the world's merchant shipping tonnage (39 per cent of hulls), and about 120 shipbuilding firms operated in Britain.[45] The Clyde had 39 shipyards along its banks in 1911, not counting boat, yacht and barge builders, and produced 630,583 tons of shipping. By 1956 closure and amalgamation had reduced Clyde yards to a dozen, and in 1956 they produced 40 ships, displacing 391,362 tons.[46] Newcastle's 16 yards produced 412,959 tons of merchant shipping in 1911; in 1956 five survivors produced 31 ships, totalling 246,754 tons.[47] The yards of Sunderland produced 186,828 tons in 1911, and actually managed to improve to 216,784 in 1956.[48] Belfast went from 20 vessels displacing 185,280 tons in 1911 to 12 vessels displacing 106,184 in 1956. Clearly there were problems, but shipbuilding remained a major British industry and nobody foresaw what was about to happen.

1960–Closure

Britain had been slowly losing its dominance of the world shipbuilding industry since the late nineteenth century, but what was to happen during the last 40 years of the twentieth century amounted almost to a collapse, as Harland & Wolff's production shows.

Table 12: Average annual Belfast production of merchant shipping

Year	Hulls	Tonnage
Average 1934–39	7.0	66,554
Average 1940–46	9.8	81,204
Average 1947–53	11.7	117,341
Average 1954–60	9.6	125,966
Average 1961–70	4.1	117,049
Average 1971–80	2.6	231,666
Average 1981–90	1.0	43,606
Average 1991–2002	0.9	88,602

* Includes passenger, passenger-cargo, cargo and cross-Channel

The figure for average tonnage shows that the sort of ship being produced was changing: passenger and passenger-cargo ships vanished from the building list in the face of growing competition from air transport. In December 1967 *Gowanbank* (y/n 1674) marked the end of production of traditional general cargo vessels. From the late 1960s, Harland & Wolff's output was dominated by tankers and bulk carriers; this switch was a matter of policy as well as customer demand,[49] both the types in which the yard increasingly specialised.

Table 13: Typical Belfast-built (Harland & Wolff), 1961–closure

Tankers

Name	Displacement	Length	Beam	Draft	
Tindfonn 1961	31,322	753.6	98.5	40.7	A large tanker for this era
Texaco Maracaibo 1964	51,774	858.0	125.4	47.5	On completion the largest tanker built in Britain
Mrrina 1967	95,450	1,050.0	155.3	58.0	The first 'super-tanker' built in the UK
Esso Ulidia 1970	126,538	1,143.3	170.0	84.0	First tanker constructed in the building dock
Lampas 1975	161,632	1,153.0	182.0	95.0	
Coastal Corpus Christi 1977	172,147	1,204.0	182.0	95.0	One of the largest ships ever built in Belfast

Bulk Carriers

Name	Displacement	Length	Beam	Draft	
Tresfonn 1960	13,471	557.4	70.5	31.9	The first bulk carrier built in Belfast
Skaufast 1968	57,204	855.0	137.8	46.4	A fairly typical bulk carrier of the late 1960s–early 1970s
British Steel 1984	90,831	941.0	156.0	79.0	Fairly typical of vessels being produced at the end

While the average size of ship increased dramatically, keeping the yearly output figure at a respectable level in the face of Asian and Eastern European competition orders became increasingly difficult to obtain. The British government recognised this and sought to remedy the problems faced by British shipbuilders:

> As always, the basis of the British decline was the failure to invest in efficient, high productivity equipment while the market was in Britain's favour. The Geddes report of 1966 found fault with out-of-date equipment, poor sites, divided trade union allegiance leading to costly demarcation disputes and relatively high costs of labour and raw materials in British yards. The proposed remedies included rationalization, standardization and amalgamation. Government support, totalling some £68 million in credit and compensation for losses, was made available to bring about the amalgamation of the 62 yards into three or four large combines, of which two were to be in the north-east and one or two on the Clyde. The fifteen unions were similarly to amalgamate into five. In this way, the British share of the world market, which had fallen steadily to 10%, was to be raised to 12.5% ...[50]

Belfast was not affected by amalgamation proposals, but Harland & Wolff became caught up in this movement for modernisation, and in 1966–67 negotiations began with both Westminster and the Northern Irish government to obtain support for major investment. What was proposed was a whole new shipbuilding facility on the Musgrave Channel, centred on a huge building dock, which when planned was to be the largest in the world.

In the late 1960s and early 1970s, Harland & Wolff was transformed as a shipbuilder, adopting a policy of very large vessel construction and rebuilding the yard to make this possible. Unfortunately, due to problems, not all of which were within the company's or even the British government's control, orders remained difficult to obtain and even more difficult to make a profit on. The conclusion of the official history of Harland & Wolff, published in 1986, offers a blunt assessment of the problems the firm faced at this time:

> The paramount consideration was the urgent need to secure new work for the Company. With the world market demand for merchant ships at a very low ebb, competition from Japanese and Korean yards was intense. A price war between builders in the Far East, which began early in 1983, made it increasingly difficult for European yards to secure orders for bulk carriers, tankers and general cargo vessels. The severity of the depression can be gauged from the fact that Korean shipbuilding prices for these types of vessel have fallen to a level which would cover only the cost of materials for similar ships constructed in United Kingdom yards.[51]

Harland & Wolff possessed a yard adapted for construction of merchant vessels of the largest size; unfortunately they could not reduce costs to a level that would allow them to compete with Asian rivals. At the same time, the domestic market for merchant shipping declined as British shipowners left the business or re-registered their fleets abroad.[52]

As production figures demonstrate, orders became ever scarcer. In 1987, for first time since 1854, not a single ship was launched in Belfast. The Belfast shipbuilding industry was doomed. It was not murdered, as is sometimes suggested, by an uncaring or malicious government. It was not strangled by incompetent management or selfish trade unions. It was not smothered by outmoded ideas and a refusal to adapt to change. Rather, Belfast's shipbuilding industry was slowly suffocated by pressure from competitors that it could not resist. As they were driven from the market for tankers and bulk carriers, Harland & Wolff attempted to develop a capacity to produce technically advanced vessels for oil or gas exploration and exploitation. They enjoyed some success but there were never enough orders for such vessels and it proved almost impossible to make a profit on their construction. On 1 April 2003, what will almost certainly be the last Belfast-built ship was floated out of the building dock, marking the end of nearly 150 years of modern shipbuilding on the Lagan.

Notes

1 In fairness, he did admit that the explanatory footnotes would probably fill 20–30 volumes of text.

2 Pollard, S. & Robertson, P., *The British Shipbuilding Industry 1870–1914* (Harvard 1979), pp.59–60.

Average tonnage of vessels built in principal districts

District	Average 1907–13 (British flag only)	Average 1907–13 (all vessels, inc. warships)
Belfast	3,960	7,340
Wear	2,030	3,230
Tyne	1,620	3,030
Tees	1,620	2,750
Barrow	1,510	2,120

Clyde	1,260	1,590
Mersey	470	1,350
Dundee	440	1,250
Forth	290	880
Humber	160	460
Thames	70	320
Aberdeen	80	260
UK (inc. minor ports)	710	2,690

3 For UK and world output: *Lloyd's Register* vol.2, 1923–24 and 1936–37 statistical report.
4 Measuring Worth Co.
5 Mitchell, R.B., *International Historical statistics: Europe 1750–2005* (Basingstoke, 2003), p.714.
6 *Ibid.*, pp.477, 480.
7

'Type'	**Displacement (tons)**	**Launch**	**Passengers**	
			First	**Steerage**
'Oceanic' *Oceanic, Atlantic, Baltic, Republic*	3,708	1870–71	160	1,000
'Adriatic' *Adriatic, Celtic*	3,868	1871-72	166	1,000
'Britannic' *Britannic, Germanic*	5,004	1874	220	1,500

8 The only warship built in Belfast for a foreign government before the Second World War was McIlwaine and McColl's *Gorronammah* (y/n 53).
9 Moss, M. & Hume, J.R., *Shipbuilders to the World* (Belfast, 1986), p.27.
10 *Ibid.*, p.46.
11 *Ibid.*, p.56.
12 Pollard & Robinson, *Shipbuilding*, pp.250, 252.
13 http://www.theshipslist.com/ships/lines/pando.html. This company maintained regular services to India, Australia, China and Japan. Compared to transatlantic routes, fares were high. In the 1890s a voyage from London to Bombay cost £55 for first class and £35 to £37 10*s* for second class. Australia cost £60 to £70 for first class and £35 to £40 for second class. By way of comparison, skilled workers in Belfast shipyards earned 30*s* to 35*s* a week.
14 http://www.red-duster.co.uk/BIBBY3.htm. Company operated a monthly service Liverpool–Rangoon, fare £50.
15 Transatlantic fares tended to drop over time as competition increased. When *Oceanic* entered service (1871) first-class fares were £16 16*s* and steerage £6 6*s*. In 1892 fares on *Teutonic* were £10 10*s* to £12 first class, £9 to £10 second class and £5 steerage. On *Titanic* fares were £30 first class, £12 second class and £3 to £8 third class. The standard of accommodation for all classes improved considerably over this period.
16 One further sailing vessel was launched, oil barge *Navahoe* (H&W y/n 389), but it was not a traditional sailing vessel.
17 Burnett, J., *A History of the Cost of Living* (Harmondsworth, 1969), p.211.
18 *Lloyd's Register of Shipping*, 1923–24, vol.2, pp.1134–5.
19 'Review of Belfast Trade and Commerce during the year 1913', *Belfast Newsletter*, 1 January 1914, p.43.
20 *Ibid.*, p.40.
21 *Ibid.*
22 *Lloyd's Register of Shipping*, 1923–24, vol.2, pp.1134–5.
23 *Oxford Dictionary of Quotations*. Statement attributed by Herr Ballen.
24 Glover, M., *Waterloo to Mons* (London, 1980), p.244.

25 *Lloyd's Register of Shipping*, 1923–24, vol.2, pp.1134–5.

26 Mitchell, W.H. & Sawyer, L.A., *British Standard Ships of World War 1* (Liverpool, 1968), p.29.

27 *Ibid.* Launched 22nd, machinery installed 26th, steam raised 27th, trials 28th, completed 29th.

28 *Ibid.* Record held by North Eastern Marine Engineering, Wallsend, who completed a standard ship 63 hours after launch.

29 Belfast Corporation, *The Great War*, p.122.

30 **Belfast output of standard ships**

Type	Description	Harland & Wolff	Workman Clark	Years Launched
A	5,030-ton general cargo ship, single deck	6		1917–20
B	5,030-ton general cargo ship, double deck	7	7	1917–20
D	2,980-ton collier for Admiralty use	2		1918
G	8,000-ton meat carriers	3	10	1918–20
N	6,500-ton general cargo ship	15		1918–20
Total		33	17	1917–20

31 **British/world merchant shipping output (100 tons+), 1921–35**

	British output			World output	
	Hulls	**Tonnage**	**% of world total tonnage**	**Hulls**	**Tonnage**
1921	426	1,538,052	35.4	1377	4,341,679
1922	235	1,031,081	41.8	852	2,467,084
1923	222	645,651	39.3	701	1,643,181
1924	494	1,439,885	64.0	924	2,247,751
1925	342	1,084,633	49.4	855	2,193,404
1926	197	639,568	38.2	600	1,674,977
1927	371	1,225,873	53.6	802	2,285,679
1928	420	1,445,920	53.6	869	2,699,239
1921–28	***338***	***1,131,333***	***46.3***	***873***	***2,444,124***
1929	489	1,522,623	54.5	1,012	2,793,210
1930	481	1,478,563	51.2	1,084	2,889,472
1931	148	502,487	31.1	596	1,617,115
1932	100	187,794	25.8	307	726,591
1933	108	133,115	27.2	330	489,016
1934	173	459,877	47.5	536	967,419
1935	185	499,011	38.3	649	1,302,080
1929–35	***241***	***683,353***	***44.3***	***645***	***1,540,700***

32 *Lloyd's Register of Shipping*, 1923–24, vol.2, pp.1134–5.

33 Mitchell, *International Historical Statistics*, pp.489–92.

Average British oil imports/exports (thousands of metric tons)

	Crude Oil Imports	Refined Oil Imports	Exports (Re-exports)
1920–24	912	3,878	367
1925–29	2,241	5,356	710
1930–34	1,661	7,401	573
1935–39	2,143	9,012	666

34 Dyos, H.J. & Aldcroft, D.H., *British Transport* (Leicester, 1971), p.327.
35 Pollard & Robertson, *Shipbuilding*, p.22.
36 *Ibid.*, p.84.
37 Stevenson, J., *British Society 1914–45* (London, 1990), pp.444–8.
38 The capture of France and the Low Countries in 1940 brought Belfast into effective range.
30 November 1940: a German photo reconnaissance mission, unobserved at the time, identified a number of significant targets in the city.
7 April 1941: 15 German aircraft intended to attack Dumbarton in Scotland were forced by weather to divert to Belfast. Bombed harbour causing considerable damage. On return to base reported defences were 'inferior in quality, scanty and insufficient'.
15 April 1941: 180–200 German bombers from France mounted an attack on Belfast. The north of the city took the brunt of the attack and damage to housing was extensive, with over 900 lives lost and 1,500 injured in the raid.
4/5 May 1941: 200 bombers attacked the docks and shipyards causing considerable damage and killing 191.
5/6 May 1941: Two German bombers en route for Glasgow diverted to Belfast in bad weather, missed the shipyard, but killed 14 people, bringing the total for the Belfast blitz to over 1,000.
39 Monsarret, N., *The Cruel Sea*, Schools Edition (London, 1955), p.2.
40 **Escorts ordered from Harland & Wolff, 1939–45**

Type	Date of order	Number ordered	Dates laid down	Dates delivered	Notes
Flower-class corvette	19.09.1939	20	30.10.1939 to 19.07.1940	05.04.1940 to 09.01.1941	
	08.04.1940	20	19.08.1940 to 15.02.1941	03.02.1941 to 08.12.1941	Only 14 completed, others cancelled 23.01.1941
Algerine-class minesweeper/ escort	15.11.1940	16	15.03.1941 to 11.01.1943	24.03.1942 to 10.09.1943	
	30.04.1942	18	11.01.1943 to 27.11.1943	15.10.1943 to 18.01.1945	Only 11 completed, others cancelled May 1943
	24.07.1942	2	n/a	n/a	Cancelled May 1943
Castle-class corvettes	23.01.1943	4	21.06.1943	10.03.1944 to 14.07.1944	
Loch/Bay-class frigates	02.02.1943	4	28.12.1943 to 30.05.1943	15.06.1944 to 29.05.1945	
	02.05.1943	26	20.01.1944 to 24.10.1944	02.01.1945 to 19.01.1946	19 cancelled in 1945

110 escort vessels ordered, of which 76 built.

41 **Belfast-built aircraft carriers**

Ship	Class/Type	Laid Down	Launched	Completed
Formidable (y/n 1007)	Illustrious fleet carrier	17.06.1937	17.08.1939	24.11.1940
Unicorn (y/n 1031)	Light-fleet carrier	29.06.1939	20.11.1941	12.03.1943
Campania (y/n 1091)	Escort carrier	12.08.1941	17.06.1943	07.03.1944
Glory (y/n 1191)	Colossus light-fleet carrier	27.08.1942	27.11.1943	02.04.1945
Eagle (y/n 1220)	Eagle fleet carrier	24.10.1942	19.03.1946	01.10.1951
Warrior (y/n 1224)	Colossus light-fleet carrier	12.12.1942	20.05.1944	14.03.1946
Magnificent (y/n 1228)	Majestic light-fleet carrier	29.07.1943	16.11.1944	21.05.1948
Powerful/ Bonaventure (y/n 1229)	Majestic light-fleet carrier	27.11.1943	27.05.1945	17.01.1957
Centaur (y/n 1280)	Centaur light-fleet carrier	30.05.1944	22.04.1947	01.09.1953
Bulwark (y/n 1281)	Centaur light-fleet carrier	10.05.1945	22.06.1948	04.11.1954

42 Mitchell, *International Historical Statistics*, pp.489–92.

Average British oil imports/exports (thousands of metric tons)

	Crude Oil Imports	Refined Oil Imports	Exports (Re-exports)
1940–45	896	13,668	105
1946–50	4,996	11,658	626
1951–55	24,631	7,497*	6,167
1956–60	35,394	11,749	8,064

* From 1950 refinery feed stocks transferred from 'refined' to 'crude' category

43 Rees, H., *British Ports and Shipping* (London, 1958), p.259.
44 Pollard, S., *The Development of the British Economy 1914–1990* (London, 1992), p.249.
45 *Lloyd's Register of Shipping*, 1923–24, vol.2, pp.1134–5; Pollard & Robertson, *Shipbuilding*, pp.51–2.
46 Pollard & Robertson, *Shipbuilding*, pp.62, 253; Rees, *British Ports*, p.221.
47 Pollard & Robertson, *Shipbuilding*, pp.63, 253; Rees, *British Ports*, p.162.
48 Pollard & Robertson, *Shipbuilding*, pp.63, 253; Rees, *British Ports*, p.162.
49 Moss & Hume, *Shipbuilders*, p.435.
50 Pollard, *Development of the British Economy*, p.249.
51 Moss & Hume, *Shipbuilders*, p.488.
52 Mitchell, *International Historical Statistics*, p.728.

The British merchant fleet (over 500 tons), 1970–95

	Ships	Tonnage *(000s gross tons)*
1970	1,977	24,061
1975	1,682	31,489
1980	1,275	25,769
1985	693	12,208
1990	427	5,512
1995	329	4,413

3

URBAN MYTHS AND FORGOTTEN HISTORIES

Inevitably this book will be linked to the anniversary of the loss of *Titanic* in April 1912; this was not my intention, and if the entry for Harland & Wolff's y/n 401 is consulted it will be noted that it is rather brief – what more is there to say? There is considerable literature about this vessel[1] and it will grow massively in coming months.[2] Harland & Wolff built over 1,000 ships in Belfast, including some 60 for White Star; if products of other yards are added the total approaches 1,700. As such, why is *Titanic* the only Belfast-built ship that seems to be remembered? When suggestions are made to commemorate Belfast's maritime history they invariably involve *Titanic*-shaped hotels, *Titanic* light sculptures or even rebuilding the vessel. Perhaps those who run/market Belfast should remember the shipyard's reply to anyone who wanted to talk about this ship: 'She was all right when she left here.'

I hope by now that readers will realise that Belfast built more than one ship and that, in my view, *Titanic*'s importance in Belfast's shipbuilding history has been a little exaggerated. I am not, of course, suggesting that the loss of this vessel with over 1,500 passengers and crew was not a tragic disaster, I merely make the point that it was not the only such disaster in Belfast's history. If you include 27 Belfast-built vessels that vanished without trace (and hence suffered 100 per cent losses) then 48 vessels equalled or surpassed *Titanic* in terms of proportion of their passengers and crew lost when sunk (see Appendix 1). Admittedly, actual loss of life in most cases was far lower than *Titanic*, but these still represent tragedies, I would argue. What proportion of those aboard a vessel must lose their lives before the event merits 'disaster' status? If you take a figure of 20 per cent of those aboard any ship, at least another 23 vessels can be added to the list (losing between 21 and 67 per cent of those aboard).[3] Belfast suffered at least 72 maritime disasters of which only one seems to be remembered.

The greatest loss of life in a disaster involving a Belfast ship was not, as is sometimes claimed, *Titanic*, although admittedly the vessel involved suffered only six fatalities. Just after dawn on 6 December 1917, the Norwegian-owned *Imo* (formerly *Runic*, H&W y/n 211), a neutral vessel on charter to Commission for Relief in Belgium, left its anchorage in Halifax, Nova Scotia, heading for New York to load food supplies. It had to pass through the 'narrows', a restricted passage connecting an inner harbour to outer harbours and leading to the open sea. Anti-submarine nets had just been opened, and the channel was busy; *Imo* changed course to pass an incoming American freighter, a manoeuvre that left her in the port side of the channel rather than on the accepted starboard side. At about 8.15 a.m. *Imo* encountered another vessel, the French merchantman *Mont-Blanc*, and after some confusion, made worse by both captains initially refusing to alter course, a collision occurred at about 8.45 a.m. This collision and subsequent separation created a shower of sparks that started a fire aboard *Mont-Blanc* whose crew quickly took to lifeboats and rowed towards shore yelling warnings in French that nobody appeared to understand.

The panic of the French crew was fully justified; they knew what their vessel was carrying: 35 tons of benzol, 10 tons of gun cotton, 2,300 tons of picric acid (in wet and dry forms) and almost 180 tons of TNT. The ship was a floating bomb but was not, a court of inquiry later established, flying a red flag to warn others of its hazardous cargo. As the French crew reached shore and fled inland, other vessels attempted to bring the fire under control; attempts to scuttle *Mont-Blanc* were frustrated by the ship's sea cocks being corroded shut. A large crowd gathered on shore to watch the excitement as the blazing ship slowly drifted towards Halifax. At 9.04 a.m. *Mont-Blanc* exploded with a force roughly equivalent to 3 kilotons of TNT (the Hiroshima atom bomb was estimated at 21 kilotons), creating a fireball and mushroom cloud that rose 1.9km into the air. *Mont-Blanc* completely disintegrated, debris weighing up to half a ton being scattered over a 3-mile radius (the only member of *Mont-Blanc*'s crew to be killed as a consequence of these events was hit by debris). The blast shattered windows over 10 miles away and the shock wave was felt in Cape Breton, 220 miles away; it is sometimes described as 'the largest man-made explosion before the nuclear age'. The explosion created a tsunami that rose to 60ft above the high-water mark on the Halifax side of the narrows.

The entire north end of Halifax, about 325 acres, was destroyed by the blast and subsequent fires; more than 1,600 were killed instantly and the final death toll reached almost 2,000. Another 9,000 were injured, including 200 who were watching the burning ship through windows and were blinded by glass splinters. What of *Imo*? The explosion occurred before it made open sea and the captain and five crew members were killed by the blast. The shock wave tore away her funnel and most deck fittings, and the tsunami physically lifted the 4,600-ton ship and threw it ashore opposite Halifax, from where surviving crew members were rescued by the Royal Navy. Subsequently salvaged and repaired, *Imo* re-entered service as *Guvernoren*, and was finally lost when wrecked in the Falkland Islands four years after events at Halifax.

A strange mythology has grown up about *Titanic* that at times threatens to obscure the reality of this tragic vessel's history, despite the huge amount published. Harland & Wolff's y/n 401 is not unique in this; other vessels have or do suffer from a similar process of 'myth' creation. Perhaps the most striking *Titanic*-related project has been the purchase and ongoing restoration of *Nomadic* (H&W y/n 422). An attempt to save the last surviving White Star vessel (and second-oldest surviving Belfast-built ship) is, of course, totally commendable; what is more worrying is the often deliberate creation of 'myths' about vessels. Many involved in this project insist on referring to *Nomadic* as '*Titanic*'s little sister'; not only is this wrong, it is misleading. *Nomadic* was a purpose-built replacement for the paddle steamer *Gallic*, previously employed by White Star as tender at Cherbourg. Although intended to meet an anticipated increase in passenger traffic as a result of the introduction of Olympic-type liners, it would be wrong to directly link her with any particular one of these ships. She and *Traffic* (H&W y/n 423) were intended to serve all White Star ships, and any other vessel willing to pay for their services. However, such simple utilitarian explanations are not sufficient for many; they crave romance! Last year my daughter visited me in Belfast and we decided to go round the city on one of the tourist buses; during this trip we were informed that *Nomadic* was a tender to *Titanic* designed to follow her around the coast going into ports to bring out passengers! How many hundreds or thousands of unsuspecting tourists have been told this? Is this an example of how myths are born?

However, what has happened to *Nomadic* is nothing compared to *Titanic*, where the incrustation of myths has long threatened to obscure reality. Many myths date back a long time and have proved remarkably enduring. For example:

- 'The *Titanic* had the yard number No.909E.'

Titanic was 401! Yard number 909 belonged to *Conch* (1936), but did not have the letter E at the end of the yard number. No Harland & Wolff-built ship carried the letter E – there were Gs, Ms, Ps and Ds signifying vessels built in subsidiary yards on the Clyde, but no E!

- 'It was not *Titanic* that sank on the North Atlantic in April 1912 but her sister ship *Olympic*.'

This originates with Robin Gardiner's book which put forward the theory that *Olympic* was seriously damaged in a collision at Southampton and in a complex fraud her identity was switched with *Titanic*.[4] As conspiracy theories go it has the right ingredients, but there is one critical flaw. Belfast was and is a town where everyone knows everyone else's business. How was it possible, in only weeks, to change a vast number of components from y/n 400 to y/n 401 without using a large number of people? If they had, how did they keep the secret? Such activity would have been the talk of the town within hours! After the sinking, with over 1,500 dead, I find it hard to believe that everybody concerned would have ignored their conscience and kept quiet. I find it impossible to believe that White Star/Harland & Wolff were able to keep such an 'identity transfer' secret for 100 years given Belfast's love of gossip.

- 'Harland & Wolff used inferior materials in construction of *Titanic* that seriously weakened the hull.'

This is one of the most-discussed recent myths about *Titanic*, concerning its construction. The origins of this claim can be found in an article published in *Journal of Metals* in January 1998,[5] which suggested that steel plating used in *Titanic* was more brittle than material produced to modern standards. Subsequently this has been developed further and it is now suggested that a large number of iron rather than steel rivets were employed in the ship's construction.[6] This was blamed on shortages of materials and skilled labour in British shipyards at this time and a desire by J.P. Morgan, who through International Mercantile Marine controlled White Star, to save money. In reality most observers, including the authors of the original article, note that the steel used was the best quality available at the time and that comparison to modern products is potentially misleading. The question of deliberate cost cutting is more worrying; but why, despite Morgan's considerable influence, should Harland & Wolff risk their reputation as shipbuilders in such a manner? White Star may have been important, but they were not the only customer; could Harland & Wolff have afforded to compromise standards on such a prestigious vessel? In addition, there was no logical reason for Harland & Wolff to cut costs: *Titanic* was built on the 'cost-plus' system: all materials and labour expended on the job were separately accounted for and the yard charged 5 per cent of the final figure as their profit. Not only would the shipyard have saved nothing by using inferior material (White Star paid for it in full), but by doing so they would actually have cut their profit on the vessel.

If quality of construction in Belfast's shipyards was adversely affected by labour and material shortages at this time would this not be evident amongst other contemporary ships? Of 19 other ships launched that year, four were sunk during the First World War, five in the Second World War (aged 30 to 32 years), nine were broken up between 1933 and 1956 (aged 22 to 45 years) and one, *Nomadic*, is still in existence (aged 100 on 25 May 2011). I would suggest such longevity does not support the suggestion that shoddy workmanship was a feature of Belfast shipyards in 1911.

The loss of *Titanic* was a major disaster, but it was not, as is sometimes claimed, the worst peacetime tragedy in history.[7] The story of that maiden voyage has exercised a fascination over generations of historians, writers and filmmakers, and as a consequence the fates of other vessels have been ignored. What happened to the other 1,588 other ships built in Belfast? Was *Titanic* truly unique in Belfast's shipbuilding history? Once again, to try to make sense of a long and complex history, I have reduced it to a single table:

Table 1: Fate of Belfast Built Ships 1859–May 2011

	1854–79	1880–99	1900–19	1920–39	1940–59	1960–79	1980–2003	Total	%
Ships Built	***138***	***401***	***382***	***222***	***337***	***81***	***28***	***1,589***	
Accident of Sea	**51** *36.9%*	**144** *35.9%*	**44** *11.5%*	**17** *7.7%*	**27** *8.0%*	**6** *7.4%*	**0** 0%	**289**	*18.2%*
Disappeared	4	21	1	1	0	0	0	27	
Wrecked	31	74	26	10	9	2	0	152	
Foundered	5	23	7	1	6	1	0	43	
Collision	7	18	8	3	3	0	0	39	
Fire	3	5	1	2	9	3	0	23	
Other	1	3	1	0	0	0	0	5	
Act of War	**1** *0.7%*	**73** *18.2%*	**130** *34.0%*	**77** *34.7%*	**15** *4.5%*	**1** *1.2%*	**0** *0%*	**297**	*18.7%*
Torpedo	0	50	75	46	7	0	0	178	
Mine	0	3	18	7	3	0	0	31	
Gunfire	1	8	8	2	0	0	0	19	
Air Attack	0	2	17	17	5	1	0	42	
Scuttled/ Expended	0	10	12	5	0	0	0	27	
Hulked/ Scrapped	**41** *29.7%*	**163** *40.6%*	**184** *48.2%*	**126** *56.7%*	**290** *86.0%*	**68** *84.0%*	**5** *17.9%*	**877**	*55.2%*
Fate Unknown	**44** *31.9%*	**19** *4.7%*	**22** *5.7%*	**0** *0%*	**2** *0.6%*	**3** *3.7%*	**0** *0%*	**90**	*5.6%*
Extant	**1** *0.7%*	**2** *0.5%*	**2** *0.5%*	**2** *0.9%*	**3** *0.9%*	**3** *3.7%*	**23** *82.1%*	**36**	*2.3%*

I have been unable to find the ultimate fate of 90 vessels, although I suspect the majority ended up scrapped. As a result, there are 1,462 ships (plus *Titanic*) whose final fate I can state with reasonable confidence. What I would like to do with the rest of this chapter is examine them in greater detail.

Accident of Sea

Of the 1,589 ships launched in Belfast between 1854 and 2003, 289 were to be lost due to natural hazards connected with the sea (18.2 per cent of those whose ultimate fate is known). However, what is apparent from table 1 is that these losses were not consistent over time: of the 476 ships launched between 1854 and 1899, whose fates are known, 195 (41 per cent) were lost due to an accident of sea. In contrast, of 441 launched after 1940, only 33 (7.5 per cent) were lost to similar causes. Why did losses fall so dramatically during the course of the twentieth century?

- A major factor was tighter regulation of shipping, notably the Merchant Shipping Act of 1876, which made load lines compulsory on British ships, although the position of such lines was not fixed by law until 1894. From 1906 foreign-owned vessels trading with British ports also had to comply with this legislation. There has been a marked decline in the number of old ships operating over time. This is partly a consequence of improved inspection and regulation and partly a process driven by economic factors; old ships became simply unviable.

• There was a fundamental change in the composition of the merchant fleet in the late nineteenth and early twentieth centuries, which saw the sailing vessel being slowly replaced by steamers.[8] Sailing vessels had a far higher accident rate than steamers. Of 107 sail-cargo vessels built in Belfast, 62 met accidents of the sea (60 per cent); comparative figures for steam-powered cargo vessels built at the same period would be about 42 per cent lost to accident of the sea. Sailing cargo carriers accounted for just less than 20 per cent of Belfast's output in these years, but almost 32 per cent of the total Belfast-built vessels lost to the sea.
• The First World War may have been a horrendously costly experience for the British merchant marine but did bring some long-term benefits. Losses to German U-boats and raiders fell disproportionately amongst older vessels. Between 1914 and 1918 sailing ships on the UK register fell by 16.5 per cent and steamers by 12 per cent. Of the Belfast-built vessels sunk in the conflict, 46 per cent were over 20 years old at time of sinking, compared to 22 per cent under ten years (including wartime construction). By the time the British wartime merchant-shipping programme was completed the British fleet was largely composed of large seaworthy modern vessels. In addition, the downturn in trade following the war meant that much older worn-out tonnage was quickly scrapped.
• During the war, radio had become a standard fixture aboard merchant ships and this was the first of a number of developments that greatly improved the navigational efficiency and thus the safety of merchant vessels.

Over half the Belfast-built ships lost to the sea were wrecked, not surprisingly. The most dangerous stages of any voyage are the start and end, when vessels are in close proximity to land and shallow waters. Sailing vessels were particularly vulnerable, but severe weather conditions or navigational error ensured that a large proportion of steamers also met this fate. Perhaps the most famous wreck of a Belfast ship also took place near Halifax in the early hours of 1 April 1873.[9] The White Star liner *Atlantic* (H&W y/n 74) left Liverpool on 20 March on her nineteenth transatlantic voyage, but encountered rough weather and was considerably delayed. On the 31st it was decided to divert to Halifax, Nova Scotia, to refuel before making for New York. As the ship approached Halifax the weather remained poor and visibility was limited but, desperate not to lose more time on the voyage, the captain maintained almost full speed.

A critical error in navigation was made, largely, it was established, through underestimating the speed at which the ship was actually moving. The captain thought his vessel was heading for the entrance to Halifax Harbour, but in fact it was about 12 miles off course to the west. The captain left the bridge at midnight and those left in charge, despite visibility deteriorating still further, did not recall him, reduce speed, post a masthead lookout or take adequate soundings. They also failed to observe lighthouses along the shore, notably Sambro light, which warned of rocky shoals to the west of Halifax and was, investigators later found, fully visible at 9½ miles' distance just before the ship struck. The government inquiry was to be deeply critical of such behaviour:

> I feel compelled to state my belief that the conduct of Captain Williams in the management of his ship during the 12 or 14 hours preceding the disaster, was so gravely at variance with what ought to have been the conduct of a man placed in his responsible position, as to call for severe censure, and to justify me in saying that his certificate as Extra Master and Master might be cancelled; but in consideration of the praiseworthy and energetic efforts made by him to save life after the ship struck, the mitigated penalty of suspension of certificate for two years shall be imposed.

At 3.15 a.m., with most of the 957 persons on board asleep, *Atlantic* struck an underwater rock called Marr's Head about 50m from Meagher's Island, Nova Scotia. The government report into the accident records what happened next with painful clarity:

> In a few minutes after the vessel struck, several hundreds of the passengers and crew reached the deck, but the vessel having swung round and heeled over with her deck perpendicular and facing to seaward, many of the poor helpless passengers were washed off by the fearful seas which swept over her, and as she soon filled with water, those under deck were drowned, without a chance to struggle for life. From the position of the vessel it was found impossible to lower the boats and render them available for saving life, and no assistance reached the vessel from the shore till some time after the accident had happened.

Survivors were forced to swim ashore or drag themselves to a nearby rock using ropes; in the prevailing weather conditions only the fittest made it. There is some debate about exactly how many were aboard the ship and how many lives were lost, but the accident report stated 545 were lost out of 957 persons on board (57 per cent compared to 68 per cent on *Titanic*). Of a crew of 141, only ten lost their lives (7 per cent); conversely all 156 women on board died, as did all but one of 189 children (including two born on voyage); the casualty rate amongst male passengers was about 40 per cent. This was the worst civilian disaster in the North Atlantic for over 30 years (until *Norge* was lost in 1904 with a loss of 635 out of 795 on board) but has tended to be overshadowed by the loss of *Titanic* and has only recently begun to receive the attention it deserves.

Ships sinking in open sea (foundering) is a less common occurrence but still constituted a major risk. Adverse weather tends to be a major factor in such incidents, but a sharp reduction following introduction of effective load lines would indicate that overloading was also a factor. However, such accidents still occurred, as a late example demonstrates. *Vestris* (WC y/n 303) was a modern, well-maintained passenger-cargo vessel owned by Lamport & Holt and employed on the New York–River Plate route.[10] The ship was 16 years old when, on 10 November 1928, she sailed from New York with 128 passengers and 197 crew. The following day *Vestris* was hit by a severe storm and began to develop a list to starboard. A passenger later gave evidence to the federal investigation into the disaster:

> I've travelled a great deal, have been across the ocean many times, and up and down the American itself a great many times, and I know when a ship stands on one side and never turns over to the other side, something is wrong. I met a steward and told him something was decidedly wrong. The Steward said to me: 'You don't know anything about it. The cargo has shifted. The crew is working on it now. Everything will be straightened out in an hour.'[11]

The following day the list increased as the cargo and coal supply shifted still further; *Vestris* began to take water through multiple leaks. At 9.56 a.m. an SOS was sent but this gave a position that was incorrect by almost 40 miles. By midday *Vestris* was about 200 miles off Hampton Roads, Virginia, when the order was given to abandon ship.

Subsequently there were accusations that the crew were ill trained or worse:

> Suddenly, though we heard no orders and thought no officers were in sight, the crew began to take down the lifeboats. You could see that none of them had ever tried to lower a lifeboat before. There was as absolute lack of seamanship. They ran from one boat to another taking things from one and putting them into another. I didn't realize what this meant, but later I discovered ... They were fixing a few with proper equipment, planning to ride in them themselves, and they winked, to their friends to join them.[12]

At about 2 p.m. *Vestris* finally capsized and sank and despite having over two hours to abandon ship, loss of life was heavy. None of the 13 children on board survived and only eight of 33 women; overall losses amongst the passengers was 53 per cent (68 of 128). The death rate amongst the crew was just over 22 per cent (44 of 197). Later inquiries concluded that *Vestris* was overloaded, and the conduct of the captain (who went down with his ship) and some of the crew was open to criticism. There was also a view that SOS had not been sent early enough and gave an incorrect location, and finally that the evacuation of the ship had been poorly conducted and controlled.

Considering how congested major shipping routes were during the late nineteenth and early twentieth centuries, collisions were fairly uncommon amongst Belfast ships. In many cases, of course, ships survived collisions, but damage and loss of life could often be heavy. Although occurring in exceptional circumstances, the loss of *Otranto* (WC y/n 278) shows how serious such accidents could be. Launched in 1909 for Australian service of the Orient Steam Navigation Company, on the outbreak of war she was taken up by the navy and commissioned as an armed merchant cruiser, serving in the South Atlantic, Pacific and finally the North Atlantic. By late 1918 *Otranto* was employed on trooping duties bringing American troops to France. On 24 September she sailed from New York as part of convoy HX50 consisting of 13 ships and carrying 20,000 American troops. The convoy sailed in six columns each only about 600 yards apart; *Otranto* led column 3 and P&O liner *Kashmir* led column 4. As they approached Scotland the weather worsened and by the time they approached the North Channel the convoy was fixing its position by dead reckoning. On the morning of 6 October, the captains of both *Otranto* and *Kashmir* saw land ahead, and what happened next is a classic example of how collisions occur.

The officers of *Kashmir* rightly identified the land, just 2 miles off their port bow, as the Isle of Islay and turned hard to starboard to avoid impending danger. The *Otranto*'s crew wrongly assumed that the breakers a little over a mile off their bow was Inishtrahull and turned hard to port. As a consequence two large ships in close proximity were heading straight towards each other and despite desperate attempts by both vessels to avoid collision, *Kashmir* struck *Otranto* amidships at almost right angles. The collision caused huge damage to *Otranto*, her boiler rooms flooded and she lost use of her engines almost immediately. The two ships drifted apart and quickly lost contact in poor visibility; *Kashmir*, still with operating engines, followed the convoy and headed for Glasgow. In contrast, *Otranto*, now wallowing without power, was pushed, by wind and tide, towards the rocky shore of Islay despite desperate efforts to stop the ship using anchors.

At this point the destroyer *Mounsey* arrived on the scene. Captain Davidson of *Otranto* ordered her to stand clear as he felt weather conditions would make any rescue attempt suicidal. The destroyer commander, Lt Francis Worthington Craven, replied, 'Well, it must be suicide then, for we are coming over', and proceeded to bring his vessel alongside the stricken liner. An account of Worthington Craven's actions was given when he was gazetted for the DSO:

> Lieutenant Craven displayed magnificent courage and seamanship in placing H.M.S. 'Mounsey' alongside H.M.S. 'Otranto' in spite of the fact that the conditions of wind, weather and sea were exceptionally severe. After going alongside and embarking a certain number of men, it was reported that the 'Mounsey' had sustained considerable damage, and that there was a large quantity of water in the engine room. Lieutenant Craven, therefore, left the 'Otranto', but on finding the damage was not as serious as had been reported, he again went alongside, though he had previously experienced great difficulty in getting away. His action resulted in the saving of over 600 lives, which would otherwise have almost certainly have been lost. His performance was a remarkable one, and in personal courage, coolness and seamanship ranks in the very highest order.[13]

The destroyer lay alongside the stricken troopship and men jumped from one vessel to the other; a number were lost when they missed, fell into the sea and were crushed between the vessels. By the time Worthington finally left for Belfast, his damaged 1,000-ton destroyer was almost sinking under the weight of 596 rescued men. However, but for his courage and seamanship, the disaster that was about to happen would have been considerably worse.[14]

By the time the destroyer left it was clear to everyone that *Otranto* was doomed; however, there were 400 men still aboard, including almost half of the American troops, many of whom had refused to jump, preferring to take their chances aboard the stricken larger ship. The wind and tide continued to push the ship towards Islay and finally she ran aground about half a mile from shore. As he felt there was an imminent danger that the ship would break up in the heavy seas, Captain Davidson ordered survivors to abandon ship and swim ashore. Only 16 survived and the final death toll, including those killed trying to jump to the destroyer, was 431, more than three-quarters of whom were US servicemen.

One group of ships is of particular interest: 27 vanished without trace (1.7 per cent of total output). When I showed these figures to a friend the response was: 'That's it! Proof that there are sea monsters'. I cannot say he was wrong, after all, these ships disappeared without survivors, but I suspect that there are more mundane reasons for these losses. In the early years covered by this survey some ships were sent to sea in a seriously overloaded condition prior to the introduction of compulsory load lines. Even after this, heavily loaded ships could be in danger if weather conditions became extreme. Certain cargoes (coal, metal ores) were particularly hazardous if a ship hit bad weather, as they can shift suddenly, seriously affecting a ship's stability. As the loss of the *Vestris* demonstrates, such a movement of cargo or coal supplies in heavy weather could sink even a large and well-maintained vessel surprisingly quickly. Finally, a cargo vessel is designed as a load carrier and if sailing empty from one port to another it has to be carefully ballasted to ensure stability; if this is not done or is done to an insufficient degree the ship would be in grave danger if weather deteriorated. Such explanations may not be as exciting as sea monsters (alien abductions, the Bermuda triangle, piracy etc.), but probably have more to do with what really happened.

The popular image of one of these 'disappeared' vessels is probably an elderly, poorly maintained, overloaded vessel sailing out into adverse weather. However, when this sample is examined (see Appendix 2) it becomes clear that this stereotype is simply not supportable. Certainly the 39-year-old *Bensei Maru No.2* (formerly *Shahzada*, H&W y/n 123) sailing from Moji on the northern shore of Kyushu, Japan, on 20 October 1918 bound for Hong Kong at end of the typhoon season, appears to be almost a classic example of a 'coffin ship'. Likewise, the 38-year-old *Stream Fisher* sailing from Antwerp into the North Sea on Christmas Day 1928, heading for Newcastle upon Tyne, appears to have been a tragedy waiting to happen. However, the same can hardly be said of the *Naronic* (H&W y/n 251), a large modern ship that had been in her owner's hands for exactly seven months when sailed from Liverpool, on 11 February 1892, bound for New York on her seventh transatlantic voyage. Or the *Lord Dufferin* (WC y/n 130), which had been in her owner's hands for even less time when, having delivered a cargo of Welsh coal, sailed from Montevideo for New York and was never seen again. One hundred and one lives were lost when these two ships, both less than a year old, vanished. What happened? The *Lord Dufferin* was making a voyage from Rio de la Plata to New York in ballast, while the *Naronic* had only about half its cargo capacity on board when it left Liverpool and so was sailing lightly loaded; both were potentially unstable.

There is a tendency for disappearances to occur at times when the weather is at its worst in any specific area, but this is by no means a universal rule; for example, of nine ships lost in the North Atlantic, seven were lost between October and February, one was lost in May and another in August. Likewise, the majority of losses occur in open sea, but again this is by no means universal; several were lost in coastal waters, including three in the Irish Sea. *Eveleen* (WC y/n 76) was a fairly elderly vessel – she had just seen her twenty-seventh birthday – when she left the Scottish port of Ayr with a cargo of coal bound for Belfast on 6 May 1918. It was a voyage of rather less than 80 miles and one she had made probably hundreds of time before, the only difference was that she and the 12 men on board were never seen again. The obvious explanation, given the date, would be a U-boat attack and one was in the Irish Sea at this time

– *UB-65* – on 4–5 May, it attacked shipping in the area of Caernarfon Bay and on the 8th it attacked shipping at the entrance to Bristol Channel.[15] Did the boat make a brief move north and sink *Eveleen*? We will never know because on 14 July *UB-65* was lost with all hands when mined off Cornwall. Alternatively, did the cargo of coal in *Eveleen*'s holds shift suddenly?

The last ship to 'disappear' offers further evidence of how confusing such events can be. *Manaqui* (WC y/n 456) was a fairly old vessel, approaching her twenty-first birthday, but was a modern design equipped with radio. On 19 February 1942 she sailed from South Wales with general cargo for Jamaica and joined convoy OS20 assembling at Belfast, which sailed on the 23rd. She was never to arrive and according to *Miramar Ship Index* was sunk by a submarine torpedo '17.15N/61.00 W 16.3.1942'.[16] Some sources credit this sinking to *U-504*, which was certainly operating in area, but recent research suggests this boat did not sink *Manaqui*.[17] A number of sources credit the sinking to Italian submarine *Morosini*, which was also operating in the area at the time, but on 16 March she sank *Orcilla* at 19.15N/60.25W, some 250 miles away from *Manaqui*'s supposed final position. *The U-boat Net* suggests that the attack occurred on 12 March, but on that day *Morosini* claimed to have sunk *Strangarth* at 22.00N/65.00W ('kill' also claimed by *U-504*) over 400 miles away.[18] Neither of the submarines claimed *Manaqui* as a victim, and there were no survivors from *Strangarth* to say if the ship was hit once or twice. Sunk and a victim of the fog of war or foundered?

Act of War

Having brought warfare into my story, I would like to examine the effects of conflict on Belfast-built ships. It says a great deal about the nature of the late nineteenth-century world that Belfast built ships for 50 years before one was lost in conflict. When the Japanese besieged the Russian garrison of Port Arthur in 1904 a large number of merchant ships were in the town's port: two of these were Belfast-built *Kharbin* (formerly *British King*, H&W y/n 139) and *Noveic* (formerly *Corsican*, WC y/n 46). *Kharbin* appears to have been expended as a block ship in March 1904 while *Novic* was sunk late in the siege by Japanese artillery fire. The twentieth century had begun.

However, it was to be the two great wars of 1914–18 and 1939–45 that were to have profound effects on Britain, and this can be seen in the fates of Belfast-built ships: out of 297 of these vessels lost in war, 98 per cent of them were to be lost in the two world wars. Of these, 72 per cent were lost under the British flag; the other 81 ships were spread amongst 19 different countries at the time of their loss. The sheer intensity of the naval conflict waged in these years can be gauged by the fact that in just 13 years Belfast's yards produced over 19 per cent of their ships, including almost 80 per cent of their warships. If my list of Belfast 'disasters' is examined, the significance of warfare in the story of Belfast's shipping becomes apparent.

The largest war-related loss of life resulted from the sinking of HMS *Glorious* off Norway on 8 June 1940.[19] *Glorious* had been built during the First World War as a light battlecruiser but was obsolete before she was completed. The navy, not wishing to waste a large modern hull, converted the ship into an aircraft carrier in 1924–30 and she was again rebuilt in 1935–36 (her unofficial nickname in the navy was HMS *Laborious*). By early June 1940 the Allied position in Norway was becoming increasingly perilous and, with the situation worsening in France, it was decided to evacuate British forces. Two convoys of troopships sailed for Norway on the 5th; the first was fully loaded and sailed for Britain on the 7th and the second was ready to sail on the 8th. *Glorious*, which had taken on board a number of RAF aircraft and personnel for evacuation, was to form part of the escort of the second convoy, but early on the morning of departure her captain requested, and was granted, permission to proceed independently, with destroyer escort, to Scapa Flow, and parted company with the convoy at about 2.53 a.m. Later that day the carrier reduced speed to 17 knots and began zigzagging to confuse potential submarine attackers. However, it would appear that no attack was expected: no aircraft were armed and on deck, no standing air patrols were maintained and not even a masthead lookout was posted.

At 4 p.m. two strange vessels were sighted on the western horizon; a destroyer was sent to investigate and belatedly orders were given to bring five Swordfish torpedo bombers on deck. At 4.20 p.m. the ship was ordered to action stations. The approaching vessels were the German battlecruisers *Gneisenau* and *Scharnhorst*, which had seen the carrier's smoke a quarter of an hour before they were spotted themselves, allowing them to reach a speed of 29–30 knots when they began to attack. At 4.27 p.m. the leading German ship opened fire at a range of 16,000 yards (9 miles) and at 4.38 p.m. *Glorious* was hit for the first time by a 283mm shell, which damaged the flight deck and started a fire in the hangar, disrupting efforts to get aircraft off. At 4.56 p.m. another hit was scored that killed the captain and most of the bridge personnel. Shortly after this, the Germans ceased fire due to a smokescreen laid by *Glorious*' escorts, but recommenced at about 5.20 p.m. when the target again became visible. Almost immediately a hit was scored on the main engine room and the carrier began to lose speed, develop a starboard list and commence a slow circle to port. The Germans ceased fire at 5.40 p.m. and *Glorious* sank at about 6.10 p.m. Both escorting destroyers had been sunk in action and the German vessels, concerned that British reinforcements might be on their way (*Scharnhorst* had been badly damaged by a torpedo), left the scene without attempting to pick up survivors. As a consequence, only 38 of 1,245 navy and RAF personnel on board *Glorious* survived.

In terms of loss of life, the worst civilian sinking was the troopship *Ceramic* (H&W y/n 432).[20] In November 1942, *Ceramic* left Liverpool with 264 crew members, 14 gunners, 244 military and naval passengers (mostly nurses of Queen Alexandra's Imperial Military Nursing Service) and 134 fare-paying passengers, including 12 children. Although initially sailing in convoy, on 5 December she separated and sailed independently for South Africa. Shortly after midnight on 6/7 December, the ship was hit by a torpedo from *U-515* west of Azores and shortly afterwards two more torpedoes struck. The engines stopped and the vessel, clearly sinking, was plunged into darkness. There was little panic and lifeboats were successfully launched, allowing most of the passengers and crew to get off safely, despite rough seas and poor visibility. *Ceramic* stayed afloat until, three hours later, *U-515* again torpedoed the ship, which sank immediately. By this time, weather conditions were deteriorating and lifeboats were in danger of being swamped by heavy seas. The German captain reported the sinking and was ordered to return to the scene to collect intelligence information. At about midday, *U-515* reached the site and found that the weather had worsened to storm force 10 – conditions that threatened to swamp the surfaced submarine. Rather than searching for *Ceramic*'s captain as he had been ordered, the U-boat commander ordered his men to pick up the first survivor they could reach. As a consequence, Sapper Eric Munday, Royal Engineers, was dragged aboard *U-515* and the submarine left the area. A distress signal had been sent by *Ceramic* but weather conditions were so bad that rescue vessels did not reach the site of the sinking until 9 December; no survivors were found. Sapper Munday was landed at Lorient on 6 January and spent the rest of war in a German prison camp.

Troopships and transports have always been prime targets in naval warfare and some of the worst losses of life in maritime history have been connected with their sinking.[21] In the First World War *Aragon* (H&W y/n 367) was taken up for service and in December 1917 made a voyage from Marseille to Alexandria with 2,350 military personnel, 160 nurses and a crew of 190; she was delayed by weather but finally arrived at her destination on 30 December (also carrying 2,500 bags of Christmas mail). Due to congestion, when *Aragon* attempted to enter port she was turned back and ordered to wait offshore; while stationary and awaiting instructions she was torpedoed by *UC-34* and sank quickly with the loss of 610 lives (including eight nurses).[22] The largest loss of life on a Belfast-built troopship was aboard *Verona*

(WC y/n 271), which was sunk in the Straits of Messina on 11 May 1918, with a loss of 880 lives. Unfortunately, as I have been unable to establish how many were on board when she sank, I cannot tell if she belongs in the 'disaster' category, although I am sure she does.

The Italian merchant ship *Capo Noli* (*Munardan* WC y/n 354) had the somewhat old-fashioned experience of being taken as a prize by Canadian naval vessel *Bras d'Or* on 10 June 1940.[23] Subsequently she was taken over by the Canadian government, renamed *Bic Island* and employed as a general cargo vessel on North Atlantic routes. In October 1942 she was part of the inbound convoy HX212 carrying foodstuffs and government stores. On the 27th she began to fall behind the convoy when she stopped to pick up survivors from the whale factory ship *Sourabaya* (formerly *Carmarthenshire*, WC y/n 336), which had sunk inbound with 7,800 tons of fuel oil. The next day, she again stopped to pick up survivors from American tanker *Gurney E. Newlin*, inbound with 92,000 barrels of petrol and kerosene. As a result, when *Bic Island* was torpedoed shortly after midnight on 28/29 October there were 165 men on board (44 crew and 121 rescued): no survivors.

Sometimes ships could be the victims of their own weapons. HMS *Algerine* (H&W y/n 1,132) was taking part in the Allied invasion of North Africa (Operation Torch) and on 15 November 1942 had just completed clearing Bougie Roads of Axis mines. At about 3.45 a.m., while at anchor, she was torpedoed by Italian submarine *Ascianghi*. Two torpedoes were fired, both of which hit: one forward of the bridge and the other between the bridge and funnel. *Algerine* sank quickly with heavy loss of life; 32 survivors were subsequently picked up and landed at Bougie, but 24 of them died from internal injuries caused by the detonation of the minesweeper's own depth charges as she sank. The only survivors were eight men who had clambered on to a carley float and were thus protected from the explosions.

Warfare took a huge toll on the products of the Belfast shipyards. From *Kharbin* (formerly *British King*, H&W y/n 139) scuttled at Port Arthur in March 1904 to *Medusa* (formerly *Coastal Corpus Christi*, H&W y/n 1,705) damaged beyond repair by an Iraqi air-launched missile near Kharg Island in June 1986, warfare has claimed nearly 300 Belfast ships and the lives of thousands of their crews.

Scrapped and Hulked

I began this book by suggesting that ships are like people, and while it is true that some people die accidental or violent deaths, most die of age or infirmity – so too with ships. The majority of Belfast-built vessels have ended up in a scrapyard; a tendency that has become more pronounced over time: of vessels built since 1940 over 80 per cent have ended their lives in a breaker's yard. How old were these vessels when they were scrapped or reduced to hulks? Again this varied considerably over time, with a definite tendency for ships to be scrapped earlier.

Table 2: Age of Belfast-built Ships when Scrapped or Hulked (rounded to one decimal place)

	Total	1854–70	1880–99	1900–19	1920–39	1940–59	1960–79	1980+
Under 20 years	19.5%	4.8%	4.3%	12.1%	10.8%	36.1%	27.9%	60.0%
21 to 30 years	42.1%	40.5%	29.6%	40.9%	29.5%	51.4%	61.8%	40.0%
31 to 40 years	28.6%	26.2%	48.1%	35.4%	48.0%	10.8%	8.8%	
41 to 50 years	6.3%	14.3%	11.7%	7.7%	8.5%	1.4%	1.5%	
Over 50 years	3.3%	14.3%	6.2%	3.9%	3.1%	0.3%		

If we accept as a general rule that a well-maintained merchant ship could and should give 20–30 years' service, the number of Belfast-built vessels scrapped under that age appears surprisingly high, with almost one in five failing to reach that age. The peak amongst 1940–59 ships, which significantly distorts the pattern, can be explained by two factors, one of which was short term and the other which has become a long-term feature. The scrapping, after relatively brief lives, of large numbers of warships built during the Second World War that quickly became obsolete or surplus to requirements, explains much of this peak, a factor that also pushed up the 1900–19 figure. However, this was also influenced by a further long-term trend. As I explained in the previous chapter, in the years after the Second World War there was a dramatic increase in the size of tankers, and wartime-built vessels of the Ocean type quickly became uneconomical to operate compared to new vessels and thus were scrapped after fairly short careers. Closure of the Suez Canal following the Six Day War in June 1967 meant that oil from the Gulf had to be shipped around the Cape of Good Hope, and a new breed of super-tankers was developed; thus, the ships built in the 1950s went to the scrapyard. The reopening of the canal in June 1975 made the super-tankers obsolete and as a consequence many went to the scrapyard after comparatively brief working lives to be replaced by smaller vessels that could use the canal route. Compared to previous generations of merchant ships, modern tankers tend to be short-lived.

A merchant ship in its 20s can be considered as approaching the end of its useful working life: the engines and hull show signs of age and maintenance costs increase. It is noticeable that a large proportion of ships being scrapped can be found in this age bracket, with shipowners making a decision to replace an old ship rather than keep it running. Over the period as a whole, 61.6 per cent of Belfast ships were scrapped before their 31st birthday. This would probably be even more pronounced except for two significant dips among vessels built in 1880–99 and 1920–39. These can be explained by the two world wars, circumstances meaning that elderly shipping, which would normally have been scrapped, was retained in service for often quite considerable periods. It is noticeable that the scrapping of ships aged 31–40 years peaks on both of these occasions.

Any ship over 30 years old can legitimately be described as 'old' and it is the reduction in vessels reaching this venerable age that is one of the most marked features of the above table. Of vessels launched in 1854–70, whose life stories would not have been affected by the events of the two world wars, over half were over 31 when scrapped and more than one in seven were over 50 years of age. In contrast, of the ships of 1940–59, again not excessively affected by the war but which could have reached extreme old age, only one in eight survived over 31 years and less than one in 60 survived beyond 40. This change has been driven by two quite distinctive pressures. Firstly, governments and insurance bodies from the British Merchant Shipping Act of 1876 onwards have sought to improve maritime safety and a major target has always been the identification and policing of unseaworthy ships. An old ship need not be an unsafe ship, if it is properly maintained, but the temptation to economise on upkeep of an elderly vessel with a limited life expectancy was always there: more frequent and effective inspection meant that the 'coffin ship' disappeared. Secondly, the revolution in sea transport during the twentieth century meant ships became obsolete as they hadn't in the previous century; outdated vessels were worth more as scrap than as cargo carriers.

There are some spectacular examples of elderly shipping to be found in the lists of Belfast's shipbuilders, with *Germanic* (H&W y/n 85) standing out for being over 75 when finally sent to the breakers in 1950. Such an age is exceptional: only 1.1 per cent of Belfast-built ships were over 60 years old when broken up. However, some groups of vessels do seem to enjoy longevity in the same way as modern tankers tend to be short-lived. The classic example of this would be sailing vessels: as they lacked engines to wear out and were engaged in carrying trades where speed was not a necessity, they often lived to ripe old ages.[24]

Certain owners worked their ships for as long as possible: the nine ships built for Lloyd Brasileiro in the early twentieth century had an average life of almost 40 years and three were in their mid-50s before they were finally broken up. Alaska Packers made a practice of buying up old sailing ships and employing them as floating canning factories or support vessels in the fishing industry. *Ziminidar* (H&W y/n 182) was already 24 years old when they acquired her. By the time she was reduced to a non-seagoing hulk she was 52, and when broken up in 1950 she was 65. Ships sold off the UK register often seemed to survive far longer than comparable British vessels. For example, *La Nevera* (H&W y/n 160) was sold to Argentinian owners and continued in service until 1941 when she was broken up at the age of 58. The *Anselm* (WC y/n 214) also went to Argentinian owners and survived to the age of 56. Other ships survived because they were adapted to new roles: a considerable number of aged cargo and passenger-cargo vessels were converted into whaling ships in the 1920s. The passenger-cargo ship *Athenic* (H&W y/n 341) was converted into a whaling ship in 1927 at the age of 25; she served in this role, with a short break for service as a U-boat depot ship during the war, until broken up in 1962 in her 61 year.

Some specific types of ships tend to be long-lived; for example, ferries tend to survive in service far longer than average. *Caloric* (H&W y/n 187) served for nearly 30 years on the Liverpool–Belfast route before being sold to Greek owners in 1914. This ship was to pass through the hands of six further owners and, having been known by no fewer than eight different names, she was broken up in 1952 at age the of 67. *Magic* (H&W y/n 271) served over 30 years on the Belfast–Liverpool route before being sold and was 58 when wrecked in the Aegean. *Munster* (H&W y/n 1349), also in Greek ownership, was broken up in 2000 at the age of 52. *Royal Scotsman* (H&W y/n 964) served on the Belfast–Clyde route for over 30 years until bought by the Scientology Church and moved to the Mediterranean as a floating college, and was finally broken up at the age of 48. Her sister ship *Royal Ulsterman* (H&W y/n 963) also moved to the Mediterranean, where she was employed as a cruise ship; her life was cut short by a limpet mine in Beirut Harbour, at age 37. *Heroic* (H&W y/n 378) remained on Irish Sea routes until broken up in 1953 at the age of 47; her sister ship *Graphic* (H&W y/n 379) was 45 when she sank on the way to the breakers. *Leinster* (H&W y/n 995) survived to the age of 42 and *Duke of York* (H&W y/n 951) to 40.

Another group of ships that seem to have discovered the secret of longevity are those that have found employment as cruise liners. *Dunnottar Castle* (H&W y/n 959) spent over 20 years on the UK–South Africa route before being rebuilt as a cruise ship, in which role she served for over 45 years before going to the breakers at the age of 68. *Southern Cross* (H&W y/n 1,498) was designed as a round-the-world cruise liner and spent her entire life in that trade, being 48 when she went to the breakers in 2003. *Canberra* (H&W y/n 1,621), as her name would suggest, was designed for the UK–Australia route but air travel and the closure of the Suez Canal made this impractical so she was refitted as a cruise liner; she was 36 when she went to the breakers. *Port Melbourne* (H&W y/n 1,483) served for 17 years as a frozen meat carrier before being converted into a cruise ship in the 1970s. This 56-year-old vessel is four months older than the author and still, renamed the *Princess Danae*, in service.

Of the 1,589 identified vessels built in Belfast at the time of writing, only 36 are still in existence. One, *Canterbury Star* (H&W y/n 1,724), has just been renamed *Canterbury* for her last voyage to the breakers at Alang in India.[25] Another vessel that recently escaped this fate, *St Anselm* (H&W y/n 1715) built for British Rail, was sold to Spanish owners, becoming *Isla de Botafoc* in 1999. Sold to Indian breakers in March 2010, a month later she was bought by Panamanian owners and returned to service under the Cypriot flag as *Bari*. The oldest surviving Belfast-built 'vessel' is a dock caisson (H&W y/n 50); this 144-year-old hull now sits in the Hamilton Dock, for which it was built, next to *Nomadic*.[26] The oldest surviving Belfast 'ship' is *Polly Woodside* (WC y/n 38) of 1885, which has recently been fully renovated and is now on display in Melbourne.[27] The oldest working Belfast vessel is *Idalia* (H&W y/n 930), currently named *Balmoral.* This 77-year-old has been extensively rebuilt and is available for hire.[28] The oldest working 'ship' is one I have mentioned, *Port Melbourne* (H&W y/n 1,483), a refrigerated meat carrier turned cruise liner. The *Bulk Eagle* (H&W y/n 1,679) still soldiers on as the *Da Shun* despite being over 40 years old, and 11 other survivors are 20–32 years old, but will inevitably go to scrap soon. Within a decade most of these survivors will be gone.

Notes

1 In 2001 Eugene L. Rasor published *The Titanic: Historiography and Annotated Bibliography* which included 674 items. The National Maritime Museum offers an online bibliography of material in their collection (http://www.nmm.ac.uk/researchers/libraryresearch-guides/rms-titanic) which, amongst other material, lists 36 books about the sinking alone.

2 David Torrans who runs No Alibies Bookshop on Botanic Avenue, Belfast, was kind enough to search the Amazon website for me and found that in the first three months of 2012 there are over 30 books due to be published or republished relating to the building of the *Titanic* or the ship's ill-fated voyage.

3 This figure is too low as in a number of cases I have been unable, as yet, to find out how many survived. For example, the *Verona* (WC y/n 271) should almost certainly be on the list.

4 Gardiner, R., *Titanic: The ship that never sank* (London, 1998).

5 Felkins, K., Leighly, H.P. (Jr) & Jankovic, A., 'The Royal Mail Ship Titanic: Did a Metallurgical Failure Cause a Night to Remember?' in *Journal of Metals*, vol.50 (1), 1998, pp.12–8.

6 McCarty, J. & Foecke, T., *What really sank the Titanic* (New York, 2008).

7 This somewhat dubious honour belongs to *Dona Paz*, a Philippine passenger ferry that sank following a collision with the tanker *Vector* on 20 December 1987, with the loss of 4,341 lives.

8 Mitchell, R.B., *International Historical statistics: Europe 1750–2000* (Basingstoke, 2003), p.714.

Composition of British Merchant Marine, 1850–1900

	Steamers Number	Steamers Tonnage (000s)	Sailing Ships Number	Sailing Ships Tonnage (000s)
1850	1,187 (4.6%)	168 (4.7%)	24,797 (95.4%)	3,397 (95.3%)
1860	2,000 (7.2%)	454 (9.7%)	25,663 (92.3%)	4,204 (90.3%)
1870	3,178 (12.1%)	1,113 (19.6%)	23,189 (87.9%)	4,578 (80.4%)
1880	5,247 (20.8%)	2,724 (41.4%)	19,938 (79.2%)	3,851 (58.6%)
1890	7,410 (34.3%)	5,043 (65.7%)	14,181 (63.2%)	2,936 (36.8%)
1900	9,029 (44.7%)	6,917 (75.5%)	11,167 (55.3%)	2,247 (24.5%)

9 This account is largely based on the Canadian government report of the event reproduced by *The Ships List* (http://www.theshiplist.com/ships/wrecks/wreckatlantic 1873.html).

10 This account is largely based on http://www.bluestarline.org/lamports/vestris_diaster_i.html.

11 Evidence of Fred W. Puppe, quoted on http://cruiselinehistory.com/?p=4561.

12 *Ibid.*

13 http://cairogang.com/sdric-killed/craven/craven.html.

14 *Ibid.* By the end of the war Worthington Craven was in serious financial difficulties and was declared bankrupt in 1920. He left the navy on account of this and in December 1920 enlisted in the Royal Irish Constabulary as a third-class district inspector. He was killed on 3 February 1921 in an IrA ambush while serving in County Longford.

15 http:// www.uboat.net/wwi/boats/index.html?boat=UB+65.

16 http://www.miramarshipindex.org.nz, single ship report '1144255'.
17 http:// www.uboat.net/allies/merchants/removed.
18 The *Strangarth* (W. Pickersgill & Sons, Sunderland y/n 250) was on her maiden voyage, having left New York on 11 March 1942 outbound for Bombay via Cape Town.
19 The account is mainly based on http://www.warship.org/no11994.htm.
20 This account is largely based on http://www.red-duster.co.uk/WStAR.htm.
21 **Major disasters involving troopships or transports**

Vessel	Date	Nationality	Lives Lost	
Wilhelm Gustloff	Jan 1945	German	6,000–7,000	Involved in evacuation of troops and civilians in Baltic. Torpedoed by Russian submarine *S-13*.
Goya	April 1945	German	6,200	Involved in evacuation of troops from Baltic ports. Torpedoed by Russian submarine *L-3*.
Junyo Maru	Sept 1944	Japanese	5,620	Torpedoed by British submarine (HMS *Tradewind*) off Sumatra. Carrying 2,300 Allied POWs and 4,200 Japanese slave labourers.
Toyama Maru	June 1944	Japanese	5,400	Troopship torpedoed by American submarine USS *Sturgeon*.
Cap Arcona	May 1945	German	5,000–7,000	Sunk by British aircraft in the Baltic. Those on board included 2,300 concentration camp inmates.
Lancastria	June 1940	British	3,000–4,500	Troopship sunk by German aircraft off St Nazaire. Exact number on board and killed possibly higher but official report will not be released until 2040.
Orica	Jan 1944	German	4,145	Troopship transporting 4,200 Italian POWs; wrecked near Patrpoklos and broke up.
Yoshida Maru No. 1	April 1944	Japanese	3,000+	Troopship sunk by American submarine USS *Jack*.
Thielbek	May 1945	German	2,800	Involved in evacuation of Baltic ports. Sunk by British aircraft in Lubeck Bay. Passengers included inmates of Neuengamme concentration camp. No survivors.
General von Steuben	Feb 1945	German	2,700	Involved in evacuation of troops and civilians in Baltic. Torpedoed by Russian submarine *S-13*.
Petrella	Feb 1944	German	2,670	Sunk by British Submarine HMS *Sportsman* off Crete. Bulk of casualties Italian POWs.
Neptunia	Sept 1944	Italian	2,500	Italian troopship sunk by British submarine HMS *Upholder* off Tripoli.
Oceania	Sept 1944	Italian	2,500	Sunk in same attack as *Neptunia*.

22 This account is based on material from http://www.merchantnavyofficer.com/rm and *U-boat Net*.
23 This account is largely based on that given in *U-boat Net*.

24 **Age of Belfast-built Sailing Vessels at End of Career (where known)**

	Broken up or hulked	**Lost to accident of sea**	**Lost to act of war**	**% Total**
< 20 years	1	32★		36.7%
21–30	1	17	3	23.3%
31–40	10†	11★	4	27.8%
41–50	3†	2	1†	6.7%
51–60	4		1	4.5%

★ Includes one steamer converted to a sailing vessel

† Includes one sailing vessel later equipped with engines

25 I would like to acknowledge and thank Paul Foley of *Lloyd's List* for his kind and prompt help in identifying the last surviving Belfast ship (July 2007).

26 Another early Belfast product (WC y/n 47 or 48) is still in use at the Alexander Graving Dock but this is a mere 123 years old. A caisson is effectively the gate of a dry dock. A vessel is placed in the dock and then the caisson is floated across the entrance and allowed to fill with water so it sinks, effectively sealing the dock and allowing it to be drained. When the vessel in the dock is ready to leave, the dock is flooded and the caisson pumped out, allowing it to float free of the dock entrance.

27 There are two other preserved 'museum ships', *M33* (WC y/n 376) at Portsmouth and *Belfast* (H&W y/n 1,000) in London. The *Nomadic* (H&W y/n 422) is currently under renovation in Belfast.

28 http://www.charterworld.com/index.html?sub=yacht-charter&charter=Balmoral-3374 (May 2011).

Aerial view of the Harland & Wolff dry dock, with a large tanker present. (Courtesy of Lagan Legacy)

CONCLUSION

I have spent a great deal of this book trying to debunk myths surrounding Belfast's shipbuilding industry and its products. I would like to end with one final attack on a perceived 'fact'. According to tradition, it is bad luck to change a ship's name, yet looking at the building lists, one of the most commonly used words is 'renamed'. Even discounting those vessels that changed name before being completed, almost half of Belfast-built ships (49.1 per cent) changed name during their working lives. Almost one in ten (9.5 per cent) changed name three times or more and, contrary to popular belief, these did not seem any more lucky or unlucky than those that did not change identity. As a practice, name changing has become more common over time. Of ships launched between 1854 and 1899, 55.7 per cent did not change name; amongst those launched between 1960 and 2002 only 28.1 per cent retained their original name throughout their existence. However, ships have always been re-christened: significantly, the ships built as yard number 1 by both Harland & Wolff and Workman Clark changed name during their career.

In a handful of cases this practice reached ridiculous levels: about 0.5 per cent of Belfast-built ships changed name on six or more occasions. The record, eight name changes, is held by *Ulster Prince* (H&W y/n 1,667), which during its 37-year life became *Lady M.*, *Tangpakorn*, *Long Hu*, *Macmosa*, *Neptunia*, *Panther*, *Vatan* and finally *Manar.* In joint-second place with seven name changes are *Caloric* (H&W y/n 187), which in its 67-year existence became *Adriaticos*, *Syros*, *Atlantic*, *Emilie*, *Shikmona*, *Bissada* and *Castas A.*; and *Aino* (H&W y/n 1,672), which took a modest 28 years to become *Mega Star*, *Patman*, *Batman*, *Anadolu 3*, *Ziya S.*, *Zea* and *Zea I* for her last voyage to the breakers. As all ended up going to the breakers, changing name cannot be said to have brought them the expected ill luck.

I have not written a history of Belfast's shipbuilding industry; that was never my intention and I would argue a more focused and detailed history of shipbuilding on the Lagan is needed. However, looking at the output of the city's yards over nearly 150 years it is impossible not to be struck by the success of the Lagan as a shipbuilding district, albeit a singularly unlikely success story. Belfast lacked the basic necessities to create a successful iron or steel shipbuilding industry and yet became one of the leading producers of shipping in Britain. There has been something of a tendency to look at Belfast in isolation rather than as an element in a heavily interconnected national industry. To a degree this has meant that the city's success has been understated. Belfast carved a niche for itself in a highly competitive and demanding industry by specialising in large ocean-going merchant vessels and employing the latest ship technology and building techniques. Belfast's output was distinctive but it was also in other ways typical of the industry as a whole; the shipyards of the Lagan were fully integrated into the British industry and tended to follow broader trends.

Belfast can sometimes be very parochial in outlook: there is a marked tendency to look for local explanations for events rather than taking a broader view and accepting that factors beyond local control often had a profound influence on the city. This might explain why in the case of *Titanic* rumours of unlucky yard numbers or shoddy workmanship can and do retain apparent credibility. In reality, the ship was in the wrong place at the wrong time, a tragic combination of factors resulting in a maritime disaster, but 'she was all right when she left here'! The same narrow vision can be found when reasons are offered for the decline of Belfast shipbuilding: bad management, failure to innovate and the Troubles are all blamed and admittedly all might have been contributory factors. However, the critical point, so often overlooked, is the process of industrial decline that was not unique to Belfast. During the years when shipyards on the Lagan found it increasingly difficult to obtain orders and their labour force slowly declined, similar problems affected shipyards throughout Britain. There is a need for a detailed history of the industry to fully explore this process but clearly events far beyond the confines of Belfast contributed to the decline of shipbuilding.

Some may feel I have been rather harsh in my criticism of *Titanic* and the monodical cult that has grown up around her loss. I consider Harland & Wolff's yard number 401 to have been a magnificent example of Belfast shipbuilding and one of the greatest ships of her kind produced in Belfast, or indeed anywhere. I can fully understand the pride her new owners felt in this vessel:

> The 'Olympic' and 'Titanic' are not only the largest vessels in the world; they represent the highest attainments in Naval Architecture and Marine Engineering; they stand for the pre-eminence of the Anglo-Saxon race on the Ocean; for the 'Command of the Seas' is fast changing from a Naval to a Mercantile idea, and the strength of a maritime race is represented more by its instruments of commerce and less by its weapons of destruction than was formally supposed …[1]

What is forgotten is this vessel was not unique. In 1911, when White Star advertised their new addition, they talked of '*Olympic* and *Titanic*'. The third vessel of the type was ordered not, as is sometimes suggested, as a replacement for *Titanic* but rather because White Star was so happy with the performance of *Olympic*.[2] *Titanic* was not an exceptional ship, she was one of three Olympic-type liners that can be seen as a development of the preceding Celtic type (Big Four). *Titanic* was the end products of an evolving process of liner design and development on the Lagan that had been going on for over four decades before her launch; she was not a one-off. Arguably nothing like her was built again, not because *Titanic* was unlucky or because nobody felt she could be improved upon, but because the nature of world trade changed and such ships were no longer required.

Shipbuilding did much to shape Belfast's development in the late nineteenth and early twentieth centuries, stimulating immigration and creating a highly skilled, well-paid and regularly employed labour force that formed an elite within the city. The collapse of the industry during the Depression of the 1930s ensured that Belfast suffered one of the highest unemployment rates in Britain. Generations of Belfast men worked in the shipyards and even today, if the subject comes up, a surprising number of people will respond with: 'I had a father/grandfather who worked there'. The memory of the industry is deeply ingrained in Belfast's psyche; for good or ill, shipbuilding has left a legacy. On my wall I have a painting by a local artist of the launch of the last Belfast-built ship *Anvil Point*, which she did from a sketch she made after watching a news report. In the background the vessel is being floated out of the building dock but in the foreground stand three flat-capped figures watching the event. The painting, officially christened *Launch of the Anvil Point*, has always been called 'The Wee Men' – in some ways it sums up the end of an era.

What does the future hold? A decade ago I published a postscript to a brief history of the Belfast shipbuilding industry, which on re-reading seems sadly prophetic:

> CAN BELFAST'S SHIPYARD SURVIVE? The newspapers are full of stories, which are in turn optimistic and depressing, but on balance I feel the 'unlikely success story' is about to end. What went wrong? The world has changed since the 1870s and the patterns of trade and travel that once generated orders for Belfast's shipyards have long vanished. There may be a return to liner building to meet the needs of a growing cruise market but after years of 'economies' Belfast no longer has the labour force or facilities to build such vessels. It is sad to witness the passing of a great tradition but economics are brutal and accountants heartless – the end is nigh.[3]

Like so much of British industry, shipbuilding in the city on the Lagan is now a matter of history. Some insist on calling Belfast '*Titanic* Town', but that ship, as I hope I have explained, is just a very small part of the story.

Notes

1 Advertising leaflet for *Olympic* and *Titanic*, produced by White Star, May 1911, reprinted by the Ulster Folk and Transport Museum (Belfast, 1987), p.71.
2 Moss M. & Hume J.R., *Shipbuilders to the World* (Belfast, 1986), p.157.
3 Lynch, *Unlikely Success*, p.71.

General view of the yard at Harland & Wolff in the late 1950s or early 1960s. (Courtesy of Lagan Legacy)

BELFAST-BUILT SHIPS

Launchings in Belfast 1859–2003

Year	Hulls Launched	Tonnage Launched	Notes
1854	1	1,289	
1855	1	1,273	
1856	1	1,387	
1857	2	939	
1858	2	1,001	Tonnage is for 1 hull, other unknown
1859	3	3,941	Harland & Wolff – 2 hulls, 3,000 tons Robert Hickson – 1 hull, 941 tons
1860	4	2,519	
1861	4	7,688	
1862	6	5,105	
1863	8	6,691	
1864	6	5,520	
1865	12	5,490	Tonnage is for only 9 hulls, others unknown
1866	2	2,836	
1867	6	9,079	Tonnage is for only 5 hulls, other unknown
1868	6	3,845	Tonnage is for only 5 hulls, other unknown
1869	11	6,708	
1854–69	**75**	**65,311**	
1870	7	15,840	Tonnage is for 6 hulls, other unknown
1871	3	11,284	
1872	4	7,864	
1873	1	2,651	
1874	5	15,820	
1875	13	9,007	Tonnage is for 9 hulls, others unknown
1876	9	4,638	Tonnage is for 7 hulls, others unknown McIlwaine & Co. – 1 hull, tonnage unknown
1877	6	9,072	Harland & Wolff – 6 hulls, 9,072 tons
1878	8	15,416	
1879	7	10,881	
1870–79	**63**	**102,473**	
1880	14	19,668	Harland & Wolff – 9 hulls, 18,199 tons (tonnage for 8 hulls, other unknown) Workman Clark – 4 hulls, 1,208 tons McIlwaine & Co. – 1 hull, 261 tons
1881	11	19,003	Harland & Wolff – 6 hulls, 16,975 tons Workman Clark – 3 hulls, 1,479 tons McIlwaine & Co. – 2 hulls, 549 tons
1882	16	26,296	Harland & Wolff – 7 hulls, 19,940 tons Workman Clark – 5 hulls, 5,705 tons McIlwaine & Co. – 4 hulls, 951 tons
1883	25	41,467	Harland & Wolff – 13 hulls, 31,151 tons Workman Clark – 8 hulls, 8,956 tons McIlwaine & Co. – 4 hulls, 1,360 tons
1884	22	30,216	Harland & Wolff – 7 hulls, 19,407 tons Workman Clark – 12 hulls, 9,798 tons (tonnage for 11 hulls, other unknown) McIlwaine & Co. – 3 hulls, 1,011 tons

Year	Hulls Launched	Tonnage Launched	Notes
1885	19	34,050	Harland & Wolff – 14 hulls, 26,803 tons Workman Clark – 4 hulls, 6,976 tons McIlwaine & Co. – 1 hull, 271 tons
1886	16	26,361	Harland & Wolff – 10 hulls, 20,912 tons Workman Clark – 5 hulls, 4,989 tons McIlwaine & Co. – 1 hull, 460 tons
1887	17	38,487	Harland & Wolff – 8 hulls, 31,234 tons Workman Clark – 6 hulls, 6,378 tons McIlwaine & Co. – 3 hulls, 875 tons
1888	18	34,108	Harland & Wolff – 6 hulls, 21,069 tons Workman Clark – 9 hulls, 10,607 tons (tonnage for 7 hulls, others unknown) McIlwaine & Co. – 3 hulls, 2,432 tons
1889	23	80,410	Harland & Wolff – 12 hulls, 56,612 tons Workman Clark – 7 hulls, 18,091 tons McIlwaine & Co. – 4 hulls, 5,707 tons
1880–89	**181**	**350,066**	
1890	28	66,758	Harland & Wolff – 13 hulls, 48,641 tons Workman Clark – 10 hulls, 15,736 tons McIlwaine & Co. – 5 hulls, 2,381 tons
1891	30	92,872	Harland & Wolff – 13 hulls, 65963 tons Workman Clark – 12 hulls, 24,894 tons McIlwaine & Co. – 5 hulls, 2,015 tons
1892	27	93,209	Harland & Wolff – 14 hulls, 68,883 tons Workman Clark – 7 hulls, 19,204 tons McIlwaine & Co. – 6 hulls, 5,122 tons
1893	26	86,496	Harland & Wolff – 15 hulls, 65,705 tons Workman Clark – 9 hulls, 16,665 tons McIlwaine & Co. – 2 hulls, 4,126 tons
1894	21	90,486	Harland & Wolff – 13 hulls, 64,823 tons Workman Clark – 7 hulls, 25,122 tons McIlwaine & Co. – 1 hull, 541 tons *McIlwaine & Co. closes this year*
1895	19	102,995	Harland & Wolff – 7 hulls, 57,754 tons Workman Clark – 12 hulls, 45,241 tons
1896	22	123,317	Harland & Wolff – 12 hulls, 79350 tons Workman Clark – 10 hulls, 43,967 tons
1897	17	110,666	Harland & Wolff – 10 hulls, 82,832 tons Workman Clark – 7 hulls, 24,150 tons
1898	16	120,635	Harland & Wolff – 7 hulls, 67,307 tons Workman Clark – 9 hulls, 53,328 tons
1899	14	125,952	Harland & Wolff – 7 hulls, 81,698 tons Workman Clark – 7 hulls, 44,254 tons
1890–99	**220**	**1,013,386**	
1900	16	125,109	Harland & Wolff – 6 hulls, 68,998 tons Workman Clark – 10 hulls, 56,111 tons
1901	15	143,686	Harland & Wolff – 7 hulls, 91,664 tons Workman Clark – 8 hulls, 52,022 tons
1902	18	156,866	Harland & Wolff – 6 hulls, 81,450 tons Workman Clark – 12 hulls, 75,418 tons
1903	15	153,872	Harland & Wolff – 8 hulls, 109,423 tons Workman Clark – 7 hulls, 44,449 tons
1904	17	74,922	Harland & Wolff – 6 hulls, 31,843 tons Workman Clark – 11 hulls, 43,079 tons
1905	21	142,526	Harland & Wolff – 9 hulls, 84,948 tons Workman Clark – 12 hulls, 57,578 tons
1906	22	147,607	Harland & Wolff – 11 hulls, 82,710 tons Workman Clark – 11 hulls, 64,897 tons
1907	20	124,199	Harland & Wolff – 8 hulls, 64,697 tons Workman Clark – 12 hulls, 59,502 tons
1908	16	154,068	Harland & Wolff – 8 hulls, 104,433 tons Workman Clark – 8 hulls, 49,635 tons
1909	22	120,346	Harland & Wolff – 6 hulls, 30,006 tons Workman Clark – 16 hulls, 90,340 tons
1900–09	**182**	**1,343,201**	
1910	16	164,043	Harland & Wolff – 8 hulls, 114,517 tons Workman Clark – 8 hulls, 49,526 tons

Year	Hulls Launched	Tonnage Launched	Notes
1911	20	185,280	Harland & Wolff – 10 hulls, 118,586 tons Workman Clark – 10 hulls, 66,694 tons
1912	17	165,307	Harland & Wolff – 7 hulls, 77,117 tons Workman Clark – 10 hulls, 88,190 tons
1913	12	116,435	Harland & Wolff – 3 hulls, 40,543 tons Workman Clark – 9 hulls, 75,892 tons
1914	15	245,340	Harland & Wolff – 6 hulls, 151,198 tons Workman Clark – 9 hulls, 73,142 tons
1915	18	68,660	Harland & Wolff – 9 hulls, 37,120 tons Workman Clark – 9 hulls, 31,540 tons
1916	10	48,424	Harland & Wolff – 3 hulls, 38,798 tons Workman Clark – 7 hulls, 9,626 tons (tonnage for 5, others unknown)
1917	33	130,262	Harland & Wolff – 8 hulls, 67,617 tons Workman Clark – 25 hulls, 62,645 tons (tonnage for 11, others unknown)
1918	32	149,634	Harland & Wolff – 13 hulls, 84,876 tons Workman Clark – 19 hulls, 64,758 tons (tonnage for 13, others unknown)
1919	27	197,796	Harland & Wolff – 14 hulls, 109,762 tons Workman Clark – 13 hulls, 88,034 tons
1910–19	**200**	**1,426,034**	
1920	19	115,308	Harland & Wolff – 13 hulls, 80,817 tons Workman Clark – 6 hulls, 34,491 tons
1921	13	93,467	Harland & Wolff – 4 hulls, 39,867 tons Workman Clark – 9 hulls, 53,600 tons
1922	9	86,069	Harland & Wolff – 3 hulls, 35,791 tons Workman Clark – 6 hulls, 51,078 tons
1923	11	127,390	Harland & Wolff – 6 hulls, 86,686 tons Workman Clark – 5 hulls, 40,704 tons
1924	12	105,375	Harland & Wolff – 3 hulls, 59,543 tons Workman Clark – 9 hulls, 45,832 tons
1925	10	57,090	Harland & Wolff – 5 hulls, 31,536 tons Workman Clark – 5 hulls, 25,554 tons
1926	9	92,263	Harland & Wolff – 6 hulls, 65,713 tons Workman Clark – 3 hulls, 26,550 tons
1927	20	110,762	Harland & Wolff – 14 hulls, 62,396 tons Workman Clark – 6 hulls, 48,366 tons
1928	13	75,728	Harland & Wolff – 12 hulls, 75,368 tons Workman Clark – 1 hull, 360 tons
1929	17	143,884	Harland & Wolff – 10 hulls, 91,256 tons Workman Clark – 7 hulls, 52,628 tons
1920–29	**133**	**1,008,136**	
1930	26	168,337	Harland & Wolff – 16 hulls, 117,849 tons Workman Clark – 10 hulls, 50,488 tons
1931	8	95,238	Harland & Wolff – 5 hulls, 61,969 tons Workman Clark – 3 hulls, 33,270 tons
1932	1	5,939	Harland & Wolff – no launches Workman Clark – 1 hull, 5,939 tons
1933	2	14,138	Harland & Wolff – no launches Workman Clark – 2 hulls, 14,138 tons
1934	10	87,097	Harland & Wolff – 6 hulls, 50,201 tons Workman Clark – 4 hulls, 36,896 tons *Workman Clark closes this year*
1935	9	102,117	
1936	12	62,499	
1937	9	74,395	
1938	7	79,759	
1939	5	89,648	
1930–39	**89**	**779,256**	
1940	33	90,984	
1941	28	103,064	
1942	26	130,726	
1943	25	137,451	
1944	34	139,443	
1945	14	80,295	
1946	15	160,712	
1947	12	140,605	

Year	Hulls Launched	Tonnage Launched	Notes
1948	14	120,592	
1949	12	97,767	
1940–49	**213**	**1,201,639**	
1950	11	133,347	
1951	10	118,622	
1952	15	141,645	
1953	11	105,806	
1954	14	116,747	
1955	14	122,691	
1956	12	106,184	
1957	16	151,249	
1958	11	103,703	
1959	10	124,168	
1950–59	**124**	**1,224,162**	
1960	9	184,198	
1961	9	104,089	
1962	4	88,296	
1963	6	105,342	
1964	4	86,215	
1965	5	132,106	
1966	5	75,496	
1967	6	217,348	
1968	3	100,793	
1969	1	57,204	
1960–69	**52**	**1,151,087**	
1970	5	254,011	
1971	3	241,035	
1972	2	185,476	
1973	2	193,692	
1974	3	341,197	
1975	2	225,141	
1976	3	484,890	
1977	2	236,787	
1978	3	276,414	
1979	4	117,548	
1970-79	**29**	**2,556,564**	
1980	2	14,105	
1981	1	42,069	
1982	2	105,966	
1983	1	66,034	
1984	3	111,413	
1985	2	20,582	
1986	1	90,000	
1987	0		
1988	1	50,928	
1989	0		
1980–89	**13**	**501,097**	
1990	1	31,500	
1991	1	78,710	
1992	2	157,420	
1993	3	240,387	
1994	0	0	
1995	1	82,830	
1996	2	280,778	
1997	1	152,630	
1998	0		
1999	0		
2000	2	94,158	
2001	0		
2002	2	45,896	
1990–2002	**15**	**1,164,309**	
Total 1854–2002	**1,589**	**13,886,873**	

Harland & Wolff: 1,079 hulls (11,742,761 tons+)

Workman Clark: 456 hulls (2,109,220 tons+)

McIlwaine & Co.: 46 hulls (28,062 tons+)

Robert Hickson: 8 hulls (6,830 tons+)

Alphabetical Listing

Ship	Builder	Yard Number	Year of Launch	Tonnage
A.J. Balfour	McII & Co.	47	1892	3,467
Abangarez	WC	280	1909	4,960
Abelia (HMS)	H&W	1,095	1940	1,170
Abercrombie (HMS)	H&W	472	1915	6,180
Abosso	H&W	430	1912	7,782
Aburi	H&W	383	1906	3,730
Acavus	WC	536	1934	8,010
Accra	H&W	616	1926	9,337
Acute (HMS)	H&W	1,135	1942	980
Adamant (HMS)	H&W	1,023	1940	12,500
Adjutant	Hickson	7	1858	?
Adriatic	H&W	77	1871	3,868
Adriatic	H&W	358	1906	24,540
Adula	McII & Co.	34	1889	772
Aedandhue	WC	102	1893	2,091
Aeneas	WC	294	1910	10,050
Afric	H&W	322	1898	11,948
Agamemnon	WC	503	1929	7,593
Agberi	WC	220	1905	3,465
Aglaia	H&W	90	1875	821
Aino	H&W	1,672	1969	57,204
Akassa	H&W	144	1881	1,389
Alarm (HMS)	H&W	1,133	1942	980
Albacore (HMS)	H&W	1,134	1942	980
Albert	McII & Co.	13	1082	108
Albionstar	WC	439	1919	7,900
Alcantara	H&W	586	1926	22,181
Alert	WC	29	1884	?
Alexander Elder	H&W	223	1890	4,173
Alexandra	H&W	19	1863	1,352
Algerine (HMS)	H&W	131	1880	835
Algerine (HMS)	H&W	1,132	1941	980
Alice M. Craig	WC	26	1884	387
Alisma (HMS)	H&W	1,096	1940	1,170
Almanzora	H&W	441	1914	16,034
Almirante	WC	284	1909	5,010
Amazon	H&W	372	1906	10,036
Amazon	H&W	1,594	1959	20,348
Ambrosio	H&W	746	1926	2,391
Ameer	H&W	218	1889	4,014
American	H&W	294	1895	8,196
Amerika	H&W	357	1905	22,724
Anchises	WC	296	1911	10,050
Anchusa (HMS)	H&W	1,097	1941	1,170
Ancona	WC	270	1907	8,210
Andes	H&W	434	1913	15,620
Andes	H&W	1,005	1939	25,688
Anglesey	H&W	203	1887	887
Annie Sharp	H&W	41	1865	584
Anselm	WC	214	1905	5,440
Antenor	WC	129	1896	5,531
Antilochus	H&W	1,372	1948	8,238
Antinous	WC	475	1924	4,563
Antisana	H&W	260	1892	3,684
Antrim	McII & Co.	30	1888	492
Anvil Point	H&W	1,742	2003	22,996
Apapa	H&W	695	1926	9,350
Appam	H&W	431	1912	7,781
Appleby	H&W	1,708	1978	64,641
Appleleaf	WC	368	1916	5,900
Arabia	H&W	307	1896	5,550
Arabian	H&W	12	1862	1,994
Arabic	H&W	141	1881	4,368
Arabic	H&W	340	1902	15,801
Arabis (HMS)	H&W	1,058	1940	1,170
Aracataca	WC	300	1911	4,154
Aragon	H&W	367	1905	9,441
Aragon	H&W	1,595	1959	20,362
Araguaya	WC	230	1906	10,537

Chip	Builder	Yard Number	Year of Launch	Tonnage
Arankola	WC	298	1910	4,026
Araybank	H&W	1,034	1940	7,258
Arcadia	H&W	202	1887	6,362
Arcadia	H&W	308	1896	5,551
Archdale	WC	81	1891	1,557
Ardandearg	WC	121	1895	3,218
Ardandhu	WC	102	1893	2,091
Ardanmhor	WC	80	1891	2,081
Ardanrose	WC	104	1893	2,123
Ards	McI I & Co.	15	1882	133
Arlanza	H&W	415	1911	15,043
Arlanza	H&W	1,596	1960	20,362
Arlington Court	WC	469	1924	4,915
Armenian	H&W	292	1895	8,765
Armeria (HMS)	H&W	1,098	1941	1,170
Arnprior (HMCS)	H&W	1,240	1944	1,060
Arundel Castle	H&W	455	1919	19,500
Ascanius	WC	295	1910	10,050
Ascanius	H&W	1,416	1950	7,692
Ashbank	H&W	1,592	1959	8,694
Assaye	H&W	239	1891	4,296
Assiout	H&W	1,386	1949	3,422
Aster (HMS)	H&W	1,099	1941	1,170
Asturias	H&W	388	1907	12,001
Asturias	H&W	507	1925	22,048
Atenas	WC	282	1909	4,960
Athenic	H&W	341	1901	12,234
Athenic	H&W	1,326	1946	15,187
Athlone Castle	H&W	942	1935	25,567
Atlantic	H&W	74	1870	3,708
Atlantida	WC	472	1924	4,191
Auckland Star	H&W	1,017	1939	12,382
Auckland Star	H&W	1,723	1985	10,291
Auric	WC	34	1884	423
Australia Star	H&W	939	1935	11,122
Avon	H&W	382	1907	11,072
Avonbabk	H&W	1,637	1960	8,694
Bahia	WC	263	1909	3,401
Balaena	H&W	1,327	1946	15,715
Balantia	H&W	406	1909	2,379
Ballygally Head	WC	442	1919	5,180
Ballymurtagh	H&W	10	1860	41
Balniel	McI I & Co.	26	1886	460
Baltic	H&W	75	1871	3,708
Baltic	H&W	352	1903	23,875
Barabool	H&W	584	1921	13,143
Baradine	H&W	583	1920	13,143
Barbro	H&W	1,689	1971	56,915
Bardic	H&W	542	1918	8,010
Baroda	H&W	27	1864	1,364
Barrington Court	WC	470	1924	4,915
Bavarian	H&W	68	1869	3,111
Bay Fisher	McI I & Co.	22	1884	369
Bay of Panama	H&W	164	1883	2,365
Bay State	H&W	321	1898	6,824
Bayern	H&W	416	1910	7,986
BD 31 (HMS)	WC	428	1918	?
BD 32 (HMS)	WC	429	1918	?
BD 33 (HMS)	WC	430	1918	?
BD 34 (HMS)	WC	431	1918	?
BD 35 (HMS)	WC	432	1918	?
BD 36 (HMS)	WC	433	1918	?
Beacon Grange	WC	146	1898	4,018
Beaverbank	H&W	1,456	1952	5,690
Bebington	Hickson	8	1859	941
Belfast	H&W	87	1874	1,957
Belfast (HMS)	H&W	1,000	1938	10,173
Belgic	H&W	81	1873	2,651
Belgic	H&W	171	1885	4,212
Belgic	H&W	391	1914	24,147
Belgravia	WC	231	1906	6,650
Belinda	H&W	1,690	1972	56,915

Ship	Builder	Yard Number	Year of Launch	Tonnage
Bellerophon	WC	227	1905	8,920
Belvidere	WC	137	1896	1,516
Benin	H&W	169	1884	2,215
Berbice	H&W	405	1909	2,379
Bergamot (HMS)	H&W	1,100	1941	1,170
Bermuda	WC	490	1927	19,086
Berta	H&W	798	1927	2,611
Berwick (HMS)	H&W	1,590	1959	2,519
Berwindmoor	WC	467	1923	6,078
Bessfield	WC	41	1886	1,332
Beverly	WC	138	1897	1,516
Bingera	WC	225	1905	2,092
Black Diamond	H&W	51	1867	105
Black Head	H&W	136	1881	1,191
Black Prince (HMS)	H&W	1,049	1942	5,950
Blackpool (HMS)	H&W	1,473	1957	2,150
Blackwater	WC	21	1883	538
Blairmore	H&W	287	1894	2,286
Blomfontein Castle	H&W	1,421	1949	18,400
Bocaine	WC	268	1909	1,696
Bohemian	H&W	71	1870	3,113
Bolette	H&W	1,406	1950	16,394
Bologna	H&W	368	1905	4,603
Bompata	H&W	560	1920	5,570
Bonaventure (HMCS)	H&W	1,229	1945	14,000
Bonheur	H&W	547	1920	5,326
Borgny	H&W	1,380	1948	8,255
Bostonian	H&W	207	1888	4,472
Boswell	H&W	550	1920	5,327
Bovic	H&W	252	1892	6,583
Boxer (HMS)	H&W	1,155	1942	5,596
Boyne	H&W	40	1865	617
Braemar Castle	H&W	1,459	1952	17,029
Bramble (HMS)	H&W	191	1886	715
Brasilia	H&W	318	1897	10,961
Brecknockshire	H&W	453	1916	8,422
Brigida	H&W	799	1927	2,609
Brisgravia	WC	152	1899	6,575
Britannic	H&W	83	1874	5,004
Britannic	H&W	433	1914	48,158
Britannic	H&W	807	1929	26,943
British Bombardier	H&W	1,158	1942	8,202
British Centaur	H&W	1,602	1965	37,985
British Cormorant	H&W	1,604	1961	11,132
British Corporal	H&W	1,465	1953	10,071
British Crown	H&W	127	1879	3,487
British Crown	H&W	235	1890	3,204
British Cygnet	H&W	1,607	1962	11,131
British Empire	H&W	118	1878	3,361
British Empire	H&W	214	1889	3,020
British Engineer	WC	466	1922	6,993
British Engineer	H&W	1,464	1953	21,077
British Explorer	H&W	1,400	1950	8,644
British Honour	H&W	1,531	1957	21,031
British King	H&W	139	1880	3,559
British Lancer	H&W	1,600	1962	32,547
British Lantern	WC	424	1918	6,897
British Mallard	H&W	1,588	1959	11,174
British Merchant	H&W	137	1880	1,742
British Peer	H&W	32	1865	1,478
British Power	H&W	1,573	1959	27,586
British Prince	H&W	147	1882	3,973
British Princess	H&W	154	1882	3,994
British Prospector	H&W	1,401	1950	8,655
British Queen	H&W	136	1880	3,558
British Security	H&W	1,364	1948	8,583
British Skill	H&W	1,425	1952	18,550
British Skill	H&W	1,718	1982	66,034
British Statesman	H&W	1,572	1958	27,586
British Steel	H&W	1,720	1984	90,831
British Strength	H&W	1,365	1948	8,580
British Success	H&W	1,719	1983	66,034

Ship	Builder	Yard Number	Year of Launch	Tonnage
British Supremacy	H&W	1,284	1945	8,242
British Surveyor	H&W	1,402	1950	8,655
British Vine	H&W	1,601	1964	13,408
British Workman	WC	465	1922	6,993
Britmex No.2	H&W	617	1920	474
Britmex No.3	H&W	618	1920	474
Britmex No.4	H&W	619	1920	474
Britmex No.5	H&W	620	1920	475
Briton	H&W	313	1897	10,248
Broughshane	WC	43	1886	325
Broughton	H&W	44	1868	602
Bruiser (HMS)	H&W	1,154	1942	5,596
Bryony (HMS)	H&W	1,102	1941	1,170
Buchanness	WC	473	1924	4,573
Bulgarian	H&W	70	1870	3,112
Bulk Eagle	H&W	1,679	1970	17,180
Bulwark (HMS)	H&W	1,281	1948	23,300
Buttercup (HMS)	H&W	1,103	1941	1,170
BV 1 (HMS)	WC	414	1917	?
BV 2 (HMS)	WC	415	1917	?
BV 3 (HMS)	WC	416	1917	?
BV 4 (HMS)	WC	417	1917	?
BV 5 (HMS)	WC	418	1917	?
BV 6 (HMS)	WC	419	1917	?
BV 7 (HMS)	WC	420	1917	?
BV 8 (HMS)	WC	421	1917	?
BV 9 (HMS)	WC	422	1917	?
BV 10 (HMS)	WC	423	1917	?
Cadmus (HMS)	H&W	1,136	1942	980
Cairndale	H&W	1,014	1938	8,129
Calabar	H&W	954	1935	1,932
Calamares	WC	316	1913	7,782
Calchas	WC	357	1921	10,304
Calchas	H&W	1,310	1946	8,298
Calderon	WC	167	1900	4,074
Calendula (HMS)	H&W	1,061	1940	1,170
California	H&W	225	1890	3,099
Callao	H&W	175	1885	1,016
Caloric	H&W	187	1885	942
Cambria	H&W	1,368	1948	4,972
Camel	H&W	78	1870	269
Camellia (HMS)	H&W	1,064	1940	1,170
Camoens	WC	168	1900	4,074
Campania (HMS)	H&W	1,091	1943	12,450
Canada	H&W	300	1896	8,800
Canadian Bridge	H&W	1,692	1974	65,135
Canberra	H&W	1,621	1960	45,270
Candahar	H&W	45	1866	1,418
Canonesa	WC	449	1920	8,286
Canterbury Star	H&W	1,724	1985	10,291
Capetown Castle	H&W	986	1937	27,002
Cardiganshire	WC	324	1913	9,426
Carmarthanshire	WC	336	1914	7,832
Carnarvon Castle	H&W	595	1926	20,063
Carnarvonshire	WC	325	1913	9,426
Carnmoney	WC	31	1884	1,299
Carrigan Head	WC	176	1901	4,201
Carrigan Head	H&W	1,576	1958	8,271
Carrillo	WC	305	1911	5,017
Carronbank	H&W	1,550	1957	6,461
Cartago	WC	272	1908	4,940
Castilian	H&W	14	1862	607
Castilian	WC	150	1898	7,440
Castilla	WC	492	1927	4,083
Catalonian	H&W	15	1862	607
Cave Hill	WC	88	1892	2,245
Cavina	WC	338	1915	6,539
Ceara	WC	241	1907	3,324
Cedarbank	H&W	1,481	1954	5,671
Cedric	H&W	337	1902	21,073
Cedric	H&W	1,445	1952	11,232
Cefalu	WC	514	1930	5,222

Ship	Builder	Yard Number	Year of Launch	Tonnage
Celtic	H&W	79	1872	3,867
Celtic	H&W	335	1901	20,904
Celtic King	WC	73	1890	3,737
Centaur	WC	126	1895	1,900
Centaur (HMS)	H&W	1,280	1947	22,000
Ceramic	H&W	432	1912	18,481
Cerebus	WC	118	1894	1,754
Cerinthus	H&W	1,470	1954	12,194
Cestrian	H&W	296	1895	8,761
Cevic	H&W	270	1893	8,301
Chameleon (HMS)	H&W	1,207	1944	980
Champavati	H&W	1,387	1949	1,288
Charon	WC	127	1895	1,920
Charybis (HMS)	H&W	1,675	1968	2,450
Cheerful (HMS)	H&W	1,208	1944	980
Chesapeake	WC	494	1927	8,955
Cheshire	H&W	240	1891	5,656
Chichester	WC	68	1890	2,082
China	H&W	299	1896	7,899
Ching Wo	WC	110	1894	3,883
Chirripo	WC	232	1906	4,041
Chirripo	WC	365	1919	5,360
Chyebassa	WC	240	1907	6,250
Circassian	Hickson	3	1856	1,387
Circe (HMS)	H&W	1,137	1942	980
City of Agra	WC	203	1903	4,808
City of Athens	WC	171	1900	5,160
City of Benares	WC	178	1901	6,732
City of Bombay	WC	30	1885	4,491
City of Calcutta	WC	197	1903	7,380
City of Cambridge	WC	7	1882	2,576
City of Cambridge	WC	355	1920	7,055
City of Corinth	WC	147	1898	5,443
City of Dublin	WC	49	1888	3,267
City of Dundee	WC	67	1890	3,427
City of Exeter	WC	330	1914	9,373
City of Glasgow	WC	226	1906	6,444
City of Karachi	WC	216	1905	5,547
City of London	WC	236	1906	8,875
City of Madrid	WC	180	1901	4,900
City of Nagpur	WC	331	1914	8,331
City of Nagpur	WC	464	1922	10,140
City of Perth	WC	71	1890	3,427
City of Sparta	WC	133	1896	5,179
City of Sydney	WC	504	1929	6,986
City of Venice	WC	468	1924	8,308
City of Vienna	WC	59	1889	4,672
City of Vienna	WC	332	1914	6,111
City of York	WC	204	1903	7,705
Clandeboye	WC	50	1887	300
Clanrye	WC	23	1884	239
Clarkia (HMS)	H&W	1,060	1940	1,170
Cliona	H&W	908	1931	8,375
Cloverbank	H&W	1,548	1956	6,459
Clydefield	H&W	1,436	1952	11,163
Coastal Corpus Christi	H&W	1,704	1977	172,147
Coastal Hercules	H&W	1,705	1978	172,147
Colonial	WC	198	1902	4,955
Columbian	H&W	229	1890	5,088
Columbus	H&W	345	1903	15,378
Comic	H&W	306	1896	903
Commandant Drogou	H&W	1,104	1941	1,170
Commonwealth	H&W	330	1900	12,096
Conch	H&W	909	1931	8,376
Connaught Ranger	H&W	92	1875	1,200
Conus	WC	518	1931	8,132
Coppename	WC	265	1907	3,192
Coptic	H&W	142	1881	4,448
Corabank	WC	516	1930	8,898
Coranegetto	H&W	52	1867	183
Corbis	WC	519	1931	8,132
Corinthian	WC	160	1900	6,240

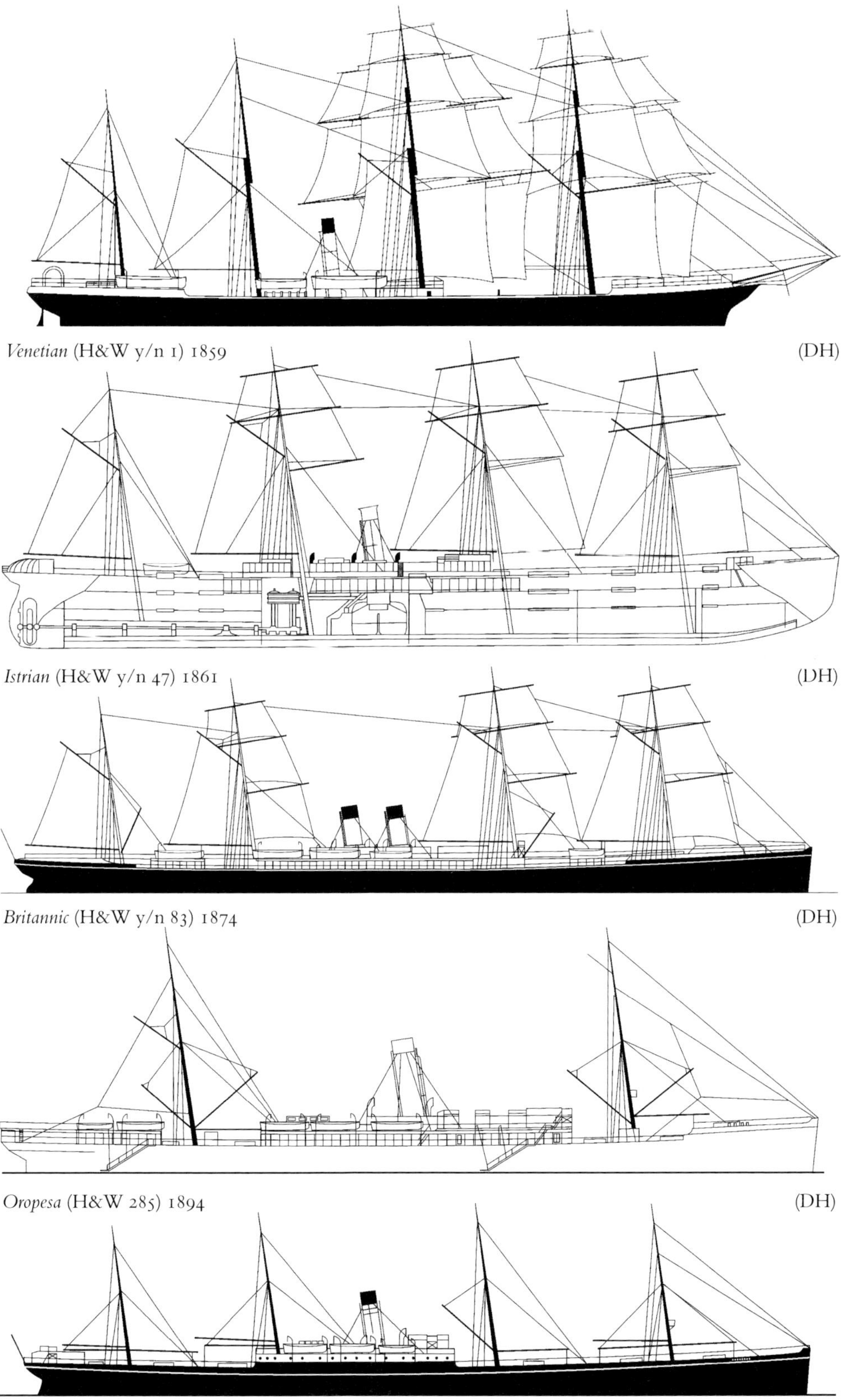

Venetian (H&W y/n 1) 1859 (DH)

Istrian (H&W y/n 47) 1861 (DH)

Britannic (H&W y/n 83) 1874 (DH)

Oropesa (H&W 285) 1894 (DH)

Scotsman (H&W 289) 1894 (DH)

Ship	Builder	Yard Number	Year of Launch	Tonnage
Corinthic	H&W	343	1902	12,231
Coronado	WC	339	1915	6,539
Corra Linn	WC	24	1884	833
Corsican	WC	46	1887	338
Costa Rican	H&W	180	1885	3,251
Councillor	WC	199	1903	4,955
Countess of Bantry	WC	28	1884	90
County Down	WC	66	1889	2,210
Cowslip (HMS)	H&W	1,105	1941	1,170
Crestbank	H&W	1,549	1957	6,459
Crown of Germany	WC	90	1892	2,241
Cufic	H&W	210	1888	4,639
Cymric	H&W	316	1897	12,551
Cymric	H&W	1,453	1952	11,182
Cypria	WC	142	1897	2,936
Dalfonn	H&W	1,407	1951	16,440
Dalmation	H&W	11	1861	1,989
Damson Hill	H&W	258	1892	2,087
Dardanus	WC	460	1923	7,857
Darro	H&W	427	1912	11,484
Darro	H&W	1,148	1942	9,733
Dartbank	H&W	1,551	1957	6,461
Dawpool	H&W	130	1880	1,697
Debrett	H&W	1,029	1940	8,104
Deebank	WC	506	1929	5,060
Defoe	H&W	1,030	1940	8,102
Defoe	H&W	1,182	1945	8,462
Delane	H&W	1,001	1937	6,054
Delius	H&W	980	1937	6,065
Delphic	H&W	309	1897	8,273
Delta	WC	218	1905	8,053
Demerara	H&W	425	1911	11,484
Demodocus	WC	311	1912	6,700
Demosthenes	H&W	418	1911	11,223
Denton Grange	WC	125	1896	5,807
Derby Park	WC	51	1887	1,333
Derbyshire	H&W	314	1897	6,635
Derwentdale	H&W	1,052	1941	8,398
Deseado	H&W	420	1911	11,471
Deseado	H&W	1,082	1942	9,641
Desna	H&W	426	1912	11,483
Devis	H&W	1,002	1937	6,054
Devis	H&W	1,181	1944	8,187
Devonian	H&W	331	1900	10,417
Dewa Gunghadur	Hickson	4	1857	594
Dharwar	H&W	30	1864	1,456
Dinsdale	H&W	1,078	1941	8,214
Diogenes	H&W	576	1922	12,341
Diomed	WC	392	1922	10,340
Divis	WC	502	1928	360
Dolius	H&W	1,497	1955	7,964
Donax	H&W	1,663	1966	42,068
Doric	H&W	153	1883	4,744
Doric	H&W	573	1922	16,484
Dorset	WC	534	1934	10,624
Dorsetshire	H&W	578	1920	7,445
Douro	H&W	31	1864	528
Drayton Grange	WC	181	1901	6,592
Drina	H&W	428	1912	11,483
Drina	H&W	1,176	1943	9,789
Duchess of Abercorn	H&W	967	1936	308
Duddon	H&W	42	1865	106
Duke of Argyll	H&W	1,541	1956	4,797
Duke of Lancaster	H&W	1,540	1955	4,797
Duke of York	H&W	951	1935	3,759
Dunaff Head	WC	326	1918	5,258
Dundela	H&W	158	1883	876
Dundonald	WC	85	1891	2,205
Dungonnell	McIl & Co.	17	1883	273
Dunluce	H&W	159	1883	877
Dunluce Castle	H&W	361	1904	8,113
Dunmore Head	WC	63	1889	2,229

Ship	Builder	Yard Number	Year of Launch	Tonnage
Dunnottar Castle	H&W	959	1930	15,007
Dunvegan Castle	H&W	960	1936	15,007
Durango	H&W	1,177	1944	9,806
Durban Castle	H&W	987	1938	17,388
Durham	WC	533	1934	10,893
Dynamic	H&W	162	1883	879
E.J. Harland	H&W	106	1876	1,333
Eagle (HMS)	H&W	1,220	1946	36,800
Earl of Peterborough (HMS)	H&W	480	1915	5,920
East Croft	H&W	91	1875	1,367
Eastern Star	H&W	1,438	1951	6,523
Ebano	H&W	899	1930	2,627
Eblana	H&W	177	1885	347
Ebro	WC	333	1914	8,463
Eden	H&W	1,544	1955	7,791
Edenfield	H&W	1,659	1965	35,805
Edinburgh Castle	H&W	410	1910	13,326
Edinburgh Castle	H&W	1,333	1947	28,705
Edward Stevinson	H&W	1,575	1960	31,317
Eglantine (HMS)	H&W	1,106	1941	1,170
Egra	WC	307	1911	5,108
Egyptian	H&W	9	1861	1,986
Ekma	WC	308	1911	5,108
Elaine	H&W	59	1869	544
Elgiva	WC	40	1886	667
Elin Knudsen	H&W	1,511	1955	20,492
Elizabeth Jane	McIl & Co.	1-9	1876	?
Elmbank	H&W	1,636	1959	8,691
Elmina	H&W	179	1885	1,764
Elpenor	H&W	1,477	1953	7,757
Elstree Grange	H&W	1,710	1979	39,626
Embiricos	McIl & Co.	36	1889	1,946
Empire Abercorn	H&W	1,230	1944	8,563
Empire Benefit	H&W	1,164	1942	8,202
Empire Bombardier	H&W	1,158	1942	8,202
Empire Castle	H&W	1,125	1942	7,356
Empire Chapman	H&W	1,080	1942	8,194
Empire Clarendon	H&W	1,231	1945	8,577
Empire Diamond	H&W	1,053	1941	8,236
Empire Falkland	H&W	1,276	1944	7,006
Empire Fletcher	H&W	1,081	1942	8,194
Empire Grace	H&W	1,051	1941	13,478
Empire Grange	H&W	1,165	1942	6,981
Empire Hope	H&W	1,050	1941	12,688
Empire Industry	H&W	1,159	1943	8,203
Empire Outpost	H&W	1,219	1943	6,978
Empire Rangoon	H&W	1,234	1944	6,988
Empire Saturn	H&W	1,242	1944	8,224
Empire Sidney	H&W	1,118	1941	6,942
Empire Spencer	H&W	1,079	1942	8,194
Empire Splendour	H&W	1,119	1941	7,335
Empire Star	H&W	957	1935	11,093
Empire Star	H&W	1,303	1946	11,860
Empire Strength	H&W	1,120	1942	7,355
Empire Traveller	H&W	1,189	1943	8,201
Enchantress (HMS)	H&W	360	1903	2,514
English Star	H&W	1,721	1984	10,291
Erica (HMS)	H&W	1,067	1940	1,170
Erin	WC	524	1932	5,739
Ernebank	H&W	984	1936	5,388
Ernesto	H&W	234	1890	2,573
Eros	H&W	966	1936	5,888
Erradale	H&W	1,733	1993	82,701
Errington Court	WC	476	1925	4,915
Esparta	WC	211	1904	3,300
Espiegle (HMS)	H&W	1,138	1942	980
Essequibo	WC	334	1914	8,463
Essi Camilla	H&W	1,699	1975	63,509
Essi Kristine	H&W	1,669	1967	41,089
Esso Caledonia	H&W	1,677	1971	126,535
Esso Glasgow	H&W	1,569	1957	10,720
Esso Ulidia	H&W	1,676	1970	126,538

Ship	Builder	Yard Number	Year of Launch	Tonnage
Ethel	WC	1	1880	265
Ethelbald	WC	42	1886	657
Ethelbert	WC	3	1881	513
Ethelwold	WC	72	1890	955
Ethelwolf	WC	8	1881	516
Etolia	H&W	196	1887	3,211
Eumaeus	WC	321	1913	6,700
Euripides	H&W	439	1914	14,947
European	H&W	303	1896	8,194
Eveleen	WC	76	1890	489
Explorador	H&W	1,382	1949	6,478
Fair Head	H&W	126	1879	1,175
Fairy Queen	H&W	38	1865	149
Fanad Head	WC	353	1917	5,200
Fanad Head	H&W	1,036	1940	5,038
Fantome (HMS)	H&W	1,139	1942	980
Faugh-a-Ballagh	H&W	119	1878	500
Fearless (HMS)	H&W	1,651	1963	11,060
Federiko Galavic	WC	481	1925	5,269
Ferric	McI I & Co.	20	1883	336
Ferry No.1	H&W	9	1872	84
Ferry No.3	WC	61	1888	15
Ferry No.4	WC	77	1890	15
Ferry No.6	WC	208	1904	25
Fiji	H&W	95	1875	1,436
Fingal	H&W	156	1883	2,570
Fjordaas	H&W	1,668	1967	41,079
Fleetbank	H&W	1,458	1953	5,690
Floridan	H&W	168	1884	3,257
Formidable (HMS)	H&W	1,007	1939	28,094
Fort George	WC	22	1884	1,756
Fort James	WC	35	1885	1,755
Fort Victoria	H&W	1,727	1990	31,500
Fort William	WC	55	1888	1,807
Forthbank	WC	508	1929	5,060
Foylebank	H&W	878	1930	5,582
Foylebank	H&W	1,514	1955	5,671
France Stove	H&W	1,411	1951	16,468
Freesia (HMS)	H&W	1,074	1940	1,170
Fritillary (HMS)	H&W	1,107	1941	1,170
Fulani	H&W	386	1907	3,730
G.W. Wolff	H&W	120	1878	1,663
Gaekwar	H&W	219	1889	4,202
Gaelic	H&W	80	1872	2,651
Gaelic	H&W	172	1885	4,205
Gaika	H&W	305	1896	6,287
Galeka	H&W	347	1899	6,767
Galgorm Castle	H&W	128	1879	192
Galgorm Castle	WC	87	1891	1,569
Galician	H&W	350	1900	6,756
Galloway Princess	H&W	1,713	1979	6,268
Galway Castle	H&W	419	1911	7,987
Gando	WC	239	1906	3,810
Garfield	H&W	146	1882	2,317
Garrybank	H&W	1,552	1957	8,693
Gascon	H&W	304	1896	6,288
Gatun	WC	485	1925	3,362
Gaul	H&W	261	1893	4,745
General Crauford (HMS)	H&W	479	1915	5,920
Genista (HMS)	H&W	1,108	1941	1,170
Gentain (HMS)	H&W	1,070	1940	1,170
George Peacock	H&W	1,626	1961	18,863
Georgian	H&W	230	1890	5,088
Georgic	H&W	293	1895	10,077
Georgic	H&W	896	1931	27,267
German	H&W	334	1898	6,763
Germanic	H&W	85	1874	5,008
Gladys	H&W	109	1876	52
Glanariff	McI I & Co.	51	1892	660
Glenarm	McI I & Co.	41	1890	524
Glenarm Head	WC	131	1897	3,910
Glenshiel	H&W	594	1924	9,415

Ship	Builder	Yard Number	Year of Launch	Tonnage
Glomar C.R. Luigs	H&W	1,739	2000	47,079
Glomar Jack Ryan	H&W	1,740	2000	47,079
Glorious (HMS)	H&W	482–4	1916	22,354
Glory (HMS)	H&W	1,191	1943	13,190
Gloucestershire	H&W	411	1910	8,324
Gloxinia (HMS)	H&W	1,068	1940	1,170
Gogra	WC	443	1919	5,181
Goodrich	WC	93	1892	2,241
Goorkha	H&W	311	1897	6,286
Gorala	WC	444	1919	5,181
Gorronammah	McIl & Co.	53	1892	150
Goth	H&W	263	1893	4,738
Gothic	H&W	267	1893	7,669
Gowanbank	H&W	1,674	1967	10,365
Graphic	H&W	379	1906	2,016
Grecian	H&W	7	1861	1,854
Greek	H&W	268	1893	4,744
Gregory Apcar	WC	192	1902	4,562
Guarani	H&W	43	1865	320
Guelph	H&W	284	1894	4,917
Guido	H&W	163	1883	3,313
Gypsy Queen	H&W	39	1865	149
Hare (HMS)	H&W	1,209	1944	980
Harold	WC	44	1887	832
Harpa	H&W	1,468	1953	12,202
Harpula	H&W	1,485	1955	12,258
Hartland Point	H&W	1,741	2002	22,900
Harvella	H&W	1,469	1956	12,224
Havelock (HMS)	H&W	473	1915	6,180
Hawks Bay	WC	313	1912	8,491
Hazelbank	H&W	1,654	1964	10,507
Heartsease (HMS)	H&W	1,063	1940	1,170
Heather (HMS)	H&W	1,073	1940	1,170
Heathmore	WC	153	1898	3,147
Hebe	H&W	54	1868	157
Hecla (HMS)	H&W	117	1878	3,360
Hector	WC	116	1894	4,660
Hector	H&W	1,377	1949	10,125
Helen Craig	WC	74	1890	417
Helenus	H&W	1,376	1949	10,125
Hercules	H&W	199	1886	818
Heredia	WC	274	1908	4,940
Herefordshire	H&W	371	1905	7,183
Heroic	H&W	378	1906	2,016
Hibernia	H&W	1,367	1948	4,972
Hibiscus (HMS)	H&W	1,062	1940	1,170
Hidalgo	WC	139	1896	1,126
Highland Brigade	H&W	812	1928	14,131
Highland Chieftain	H&W	806	1928	14,130
Highland Monarch	H&W	751	1928	14,137
Highland Patriot	H&W	916	1931	14,156
Highland Princess	H&W	814	1929	14,128
Hippomenes	WC	62	1889	2,694
Historian	H&W	69	1870	1,830
Historian	H&W	295	1895	6,857
Holkar	H&W	205	1888	3,072
Holmhurst	H&W	132	1879	495
Hooiberg	H&W	834	1928	2,395
Horn Head	H&W	165	1884	2,496
Hornby Grange	H&W	1,709	1978	39,626
Howth	WC	89	1891	2,244
Howth Head	WC	237	1906	4,440
Hyacinth (HMS)	H&W	1,071	1940	1,170
Hyson	WC	123	1895	4,445
Iberia	H&W	1,476	1954	29,614
Iberian	H&W	48	1867	2,930
Icenic	H&W	1,633	1960	11,239
Icotea	H&W	793	1927	2,402
Idalia	H&W	930	1934	147
Idar	H&W	206	1888	4,049
Idomeneus	WC	487	1926	7,882
Ikbal	H&W	279	1894	5,404

Ship	Builder	Yard Number	Year of Launch	Tonnage
Illyrian	H&W	49	1867	2,931
Imani	H&W	(a)	1897	4,582
Imaum	H&W	226	1890	4,129
Imperial Star	H&W	933	1934	10,733
Inca	H&W	275	1893	3,593
Inchanga	WC	531	1933	7,069
Incomati	WC	532	1934	7,369
Indian	WC	170	1900	9,121
Indore	WC	145	1898	7,300
Inishowen Head	H&W	189	1886	3,050
Innisfallen	H&W	870	1930	3,019
Inveravon	H&W	591	1923	6,906
Invercaibo	H&W	701	1925	2,372
Invergarry	H&W	609	1923	6,907
Invergoil	H&W	641	1922	6,966
Inverlago	H&W	699	1925	2,372
Inverleith	H&W	589	1920	6,957
Invermore	WC	86	1891	1,600
Inverrosa	H&W	700	1925	2,372
Inverruba	H&W	702	1925	2,372
Inverurie	H&W	590	1921	6,907
Ionian	H&W	242	1891	6,335
Ionian	WC	177	1901	8,265
Ionic	H&W	152	1883	4,753
Ionic	H&W	346	1902	12,232
Iowa	H&W	349	1902	8,369
Irada	WC	166	1900	8,120
Irak	WC	193	1902	8,112
Iran	H&W	185	1886	3,530
Iran	H&W	297	1896	6,250
Iredale	WC	64	1889	1,573
Irene	H&W	181	1885	897
Irex	H&W	1,460	1953	8,280
Iriona	WC	493	1927	4,083
Irisbank	WC	510	1930	5,627
Irisbank	H&W	1,655	1964	10,526
Irish Coast	H&W	1,461	1952	3,824
Iron Somersby	H&W	1,688	1971	57,250
Ironbridge	H&W	1,725	1986	90,000
Iroquois	H&W	385	1907	9,201
Isipingo	WC	530	1933	7,069
Islam	H&W	257	1892	5,402
Isocardia	H&W	1,712	1982	39,932
Isomeria	H&W	1,711	1981	42,069
Istrar	H&W	301	1896	4,582
Istrian	H&W	47	1867	2,930
Italian	H&W	8	1861	1,859
Ixion	H&W	1,417	1950	10,125
Jalta	H&W	1,373	1948	8,247
Jane Clark	WC	18	1883	838
Jane Porter	H&W	5	1860	952
Janita	H&W	1,443	1952	12,757
Janova	H&W	1,452	1952	12,765
Japan	WC	234	1906	6,013
Jaranda	H&W	1,478	1953	12,776
Jarena	H&W	1,471	1953	12,706
Jason	WC	185	1902	7,450
Jeanie Woodside	WC	100	1893	962
Jevington Court	WC	484	1925	4,544
Jewel (HMS)	H&W	1,210	1944	980
Juan Peron	H&W	1,384	1950	24,569
Juliet	H&W	58	1869	1,301
Justicia	H&W	436	1914	32,234
Kamakura Maru	WC	134	1896	6,123
Kanimbla	H&W	955	1935	10,984
Kansas	WC	293	1910	6,074
Kantara	H&W	1,359	1947	3,213
Karnak	H&W	1,360	1947	3,198
Karoola	H&W	404	1909	7,390
Kathleen	WC	45	1887	336
Katie	H&W	94	1875	107
Katoomba	H&W	437	1913	9,424

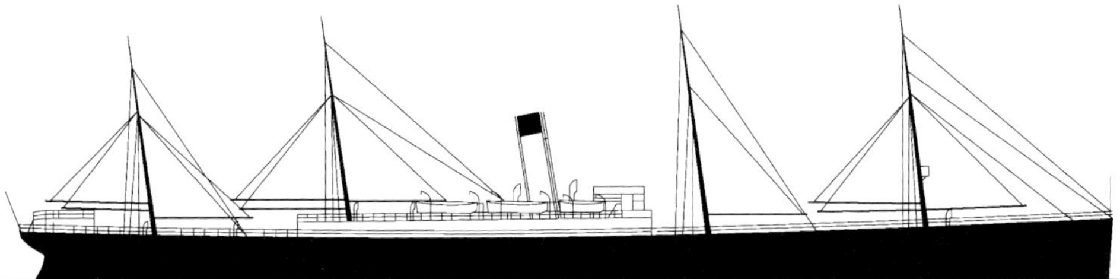

Victorian (H&W y/n 291) 1895 (DH)

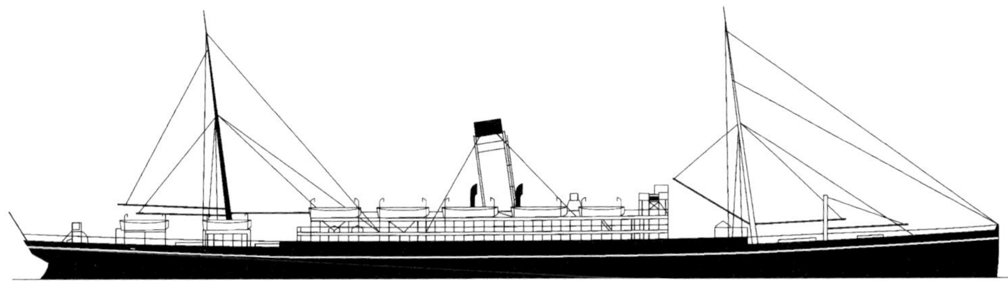

Canada (H&W y/n 300) 1896 (DH)

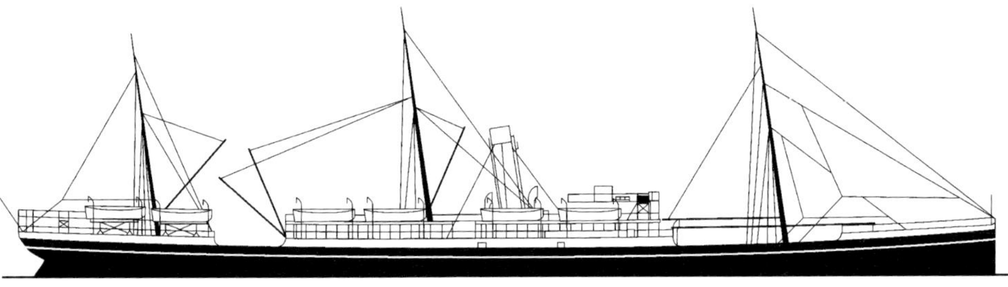

Gascon (H&W y/n 304) 1896 (DH)

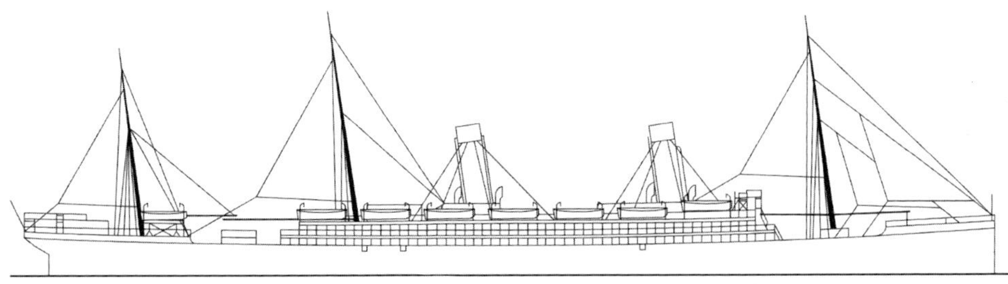

Briton (H&W y/n 313) 1897 (DH)

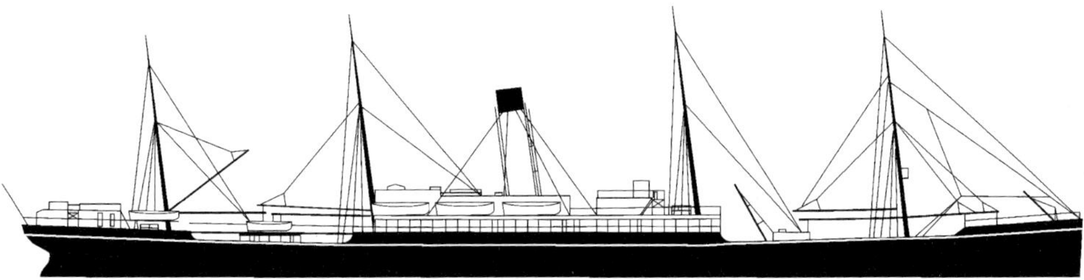

Derbyshire (H&W y/n 314) 1897 (DH)

Ship	Builder	Yard Number	Year of Launch	Tonnage
Keemun	WC	191	1902	7,642
Kemerton (HMS)	H&W	1,517	1953	360
Kenbane Head	WC	445	1919	5,180
Kenilworth Castle	H&W	356	1903	12,975
Kent (HMS)	H&W	1,632	1961	5,200
Kentucky	WC	323	1912	6,590
Kenya Castle	H&W	1,432	1951	17,041
Khersonese	Hickson	2	1855	1,273
Kia Ora	WC	255	1907	6,560
Kildarton (HMS)	H&W	1,523	1955	360
King Alexander	H&W	1,451	1952	5,883
King Arthur	H&W	763	1928	5,224
King Arthur	H&W	1,462	1952	5,883
King Charles	H&W	1,556	1957	5,993
King Edgar	H&W	757	1927	4,536
King Edwin	H&W	758	1927	4,536
King Egbert	H&W	759	1928	4,535
King George	H&W	1,557	1957	5,989
King Henry	H&W	1,587	1958	6,133
King John	H&W	760	1927	5,228
King Lud	H&W	761	1927	5,224
King Malcolm	H&W	1,450	1951	5,883
King Neptune	H&W	762	1928	5,224
King Stephen	H&W	764	1928	5,274
King William	H&W	765	1928	5,274
Kingcup (HMS)	H&W	1,076	1940	1,170
Kintuck	WC	122	1895	4,447
Kirklands	WC	56	1888	1,807
Kirkliston (HMS)	H&W	1,518	1954	360
Kitty of Coleraine	H&W	25	1863	24
Knock Adoon	H&W	1,730	1992	78,710
Knock Allan	H&W	1,728	1992	78,710
Knock An	H&W	1,735	1996	134,510
Knock Clune	H&W	1,731	1993	78,843
Knock Dun	H&W	1,732	1994	78,843
Knock Muir	H&W	1,736	1996	146,268
Knock Stocks	H&W	1,729	1992	78,710
Kohinur	H&W	174	1884	2,967
Kosmos	WC	505	1929	17,800
Kosmos II	WC	522	1931	16,966
Krossfonn	H&W	1,619	1960	13,481
Kurdistan	H&W	1,408	1949	8,322
La Estancia	H&W	1,660	1965	28,007
La Nevera	H&W	160	1883	359
La Pampa	H&W	1,678	1970	17,180
La Salina	H&W	794	1927	2,402
La Sierra	H&W	1,661	1965	28,004
Labrador	H&W	238	1891	4,737
Lackenby	H&W	1,701	1977	64,640
Lady Arthur Hill	McIl & Co.	24	1885	271
Lady Cairns	H&W	60	1869	1,311
Lady Martin	WC	60	1888	1,245
Lagan	H&W	112	1876	55
Laganbank	H&W	879	1930	5,582
Laganbank	H&W	1,515	1955	5,671
Laganfield	H&W	1,418	1950	8,196
Lagunilla	H&W	792	1927	2,402
Lairdsbank	H&W	978	1936	789
Lairdscreast	H&W	977	1936	789
Lairdswood	H&W	976	1936	789
Laleston (HMS)	H&W	1,519	1954	360
Lampas	H&W	1,695	1975	161,632
Lancashire	H&W	216	1889	3,870
Lancashire	H&W	459	1917	9,445
Lancastrian	H&W	243	1891	5,120
Langton Grange	WC	124	1896	5,850
Lanton (HMS)	H&W	1,520	1954	360
Laomedon	WC	312	1912	6,700
Lapland	H&W	393	1908	18,565
Laurentic	H&W	394	1908	14,892
Laurentic	H&W	470	1927	18,724
Lauriston	WC	97	1892	2,301

Ship	Builder	Yard Number	Year of Launch	Tonnage
LCT 11 (HMS)	H&W	1,121	1940	372
LCT 12 (HMS)	H&W	1,122	1940	372
LCT 25 (HMS)	H&W	1,126	1941	372
LCT 26 (HMS)	H&W	1,127	1941	372
LCT 100 (HMS)	H&W	1,128	1941	460
LCT 101 (HMS)	H&W	1,129	1941	460
LCT 102 (HMS)	H&W	1,130	1941	460
LCT 103 (HMS)	H&W	1,131	1941	460
Leander (HMS)	H&W	1,591	1961	2,450
Leicestershire	H&W	403	1909	8,339
Leinster	H&W	995	1937	4,302
Leinster	H&W	1,352	1947	4,115
Lenore	WC	13	1882	102
Leonia	H&W	1,697	1976	161,626
Leopoldville	H&W	402	1908	5,350
Lepeta	H&W	1,696	1976	161,632
Lepton	H&W	1,346	1946	6,446
Letterston (HMS)	H&W	1,521	1954	360
Levernbank	H&W	1,638	1961	8,694
Leverton (HMS)	H&W	1,522	1955	360
Liberty (HMS)	H&W	1,211	1944	980
Lima	H&W	1,698	1976	161,632
Limon	WC	210	1904	3,300
Lindenbank	WC	509	1929	5,060
Linga	H&W	1,309	1946	6,452
Lingula	H&W	1,347	1946	6,445
Lizard (HMS)	H&W	190	1886	715
Llandaff Castle	WC	488	1926	10,786
Loch Avon	H&W	1,329	1946	8,617
Loch Craggie (HMS)	H&W	1,246	1944	1,435
Loch Garth	H&W	1,328	1946	8,617
Loch Gorm (HMS)	H&W	1,247	1944	1,435
Loch Gowan	H&W	1,480	1954	9,718
Loch Killisport (HMS)	H&W	1,248	1944	1,435
Loch Loyal	H&W	1,562	1957	11,035
Lochmonar	H&W	517	1923	9,463
Logican	WC	109	1894	4,878
Lord Antrim	WC	186	1902	4,270
Lord Cairns	H&W	103	1877	1,372
Lord Clive (HMS)	H&W	478	1915	5,920
Lord Downshire	H&W	148	1882	2,322
Lord Downshire	WC	159	1899	4,808
Lord Dufferin	H&W	129	1879	1,697
Lord Dufferin	WC	130	1896	2,270
Lord Erne	H&W	250	1892	5,828
Lord Lansdown	H&W	170	1884	2,752
Lord Londonderry	H&W	213	1888	2,409
Lord O'Neill	H&W	166	1884	2,753
Lord Templemore	H&W	262	1892	3,045
Lord Templeton	H&W	192	1886	2,151
Lord Wolseley	H&W	157	1883	2,576
Lorton	WC	57	1888	1,419
Lossiebank	WC	511	1930	5,627
Lossiebank	H&W	1,652	1963	8,678
Lotorium	H&W	1,370	1947	6,490
Lotorium	H&W	1,694	1974	138,037
Lough Fisher	McIl & Co.	27	1887	418
Lough Fisher	McIl & Co.	38	1890	289
Lough Neagh	WC	84	1891	973
Lowlands Trassey	H&W	1,734	1995	82,830
LSt 3006 (HMS)	H&W	1,289	1944	2,300
LSt 3007 (HMS)	H&W	1,290	1944	2,300
LSt 3008 (HMS)	H&W	1,291	1944	2,300
LSt 3009 (HMS)	H&W	1,292	1944	2,300
LSt 3010 (HMS)	H&W	1,293	1944	2,300
LSt 3011 (HMS)	H&W	1,294	1945	2,300
LSt 3012 (HMS)	H&W	1,295	1945	2,300
LSt 3013 (HMS)	H&W	1,296	1945	2,300
Lullington (HMS)	H&W	1,524	1955	360
Lycia	H&W	198	1887	3,223
Lynx (HMS)	H&W	53	1868	603
Lyria	H&W	1,308	1946	6,452

Ship	Builder	Yard Number	Year of Launch	Tonnage
M.J. Hedley	WC	83	1891	442
M29 (HMS)	H&W	485	1915	360
M30 (HMS)	H&W	486	1915	360
M31 (HMS)	H&W	487	1915	360
M32 (HMS)	WC	375	1915	360
M33 (HMS)	WC	376	1915	360
Macabi	WC	455	1921	2,802
Macedonia	H&W	355	1903	10,511
Macgregor	WC	52	1888	1,047
Maddiston (HMS)	H&W	1,525	1956	360
Magdalena	H&W	1,354	1948	17,547
Magellan	H&W	273	1893	3,590
Magic	H&W	271	1893	1,630
Magician	WC	132	1896	5,065
Magnetic	H&W	269	1891	619
Magnificent (HMS)	H&W	1,228	1944	13,350
Mahana	WC	349	1917	11,800
Maharaja	H&W	124	1879	1,666
Maharani	H&W	125	1879	1,667
Mahia	WC	350	1917	7,914
Mahratta	H&W	246	1891	5,680
Mahronda	H&W	369	1905	7,630
Maine	H&W	565	1919	6,600
Majectic	H&W	209	1889	9,681
Majestic	H&W	89	1875	1,974
Makarini	WC	310	1912	8,491
Malakand	H&W	373	1905	7,653
Mallina	H&W	407	1909	3,213
Mallow (HMS)	H&W	1,065	1940	1,170
Maloja	H&W	414	1910	12,430
Maloja	H&W	588	1923	20,837
Mamari	H&W	365	1904	6,689
Manaqui	WC	456	1921	2,802
Manchester	McIl & Co.	42	1891	506
Manchester Miller	H&W	1,582	1958	9,297
Mandingo	H&W	149	1882	1,700
Manhatten	H&W	(c)	1898	8,074
Manipur	H&W	374	1905	7,654
Manitoba	H&W	248	1892	5,591
Mantiqueira	WC	267	1907	1,696
Maplebank	H&W	1,673	1967	10,365
Maracay	H&W	915	1931	3,795
Maravi	WC	457	1921	2,802
Marere	WC	194	1902	6,443
Maria	McIl & Co.	56	1893	2,642
Maria A. Hind	WC	20	1883	821
Marian Woodside	WC	79	1891	1,549
Marino	H&W	290	1894	3,819
Marlay	WC	70	1890	798
Marmora	H&W	350	1903	10,522
Marowijne	WC	266	1908	3,192
Martha C. Craig	WC	33	1884	466
Marudu	WC	471	1924	1,926
Mary E. Wadham	McIl& Co.	16	1882	602
Massachusetts	H&W	247	1891	5,590
Matatua	WC	205	1904	6,500
Matheran	H&W	375	1906	7,653
Mavis	WC	520	1930	935
Maxton (HMS)	H&W	1,526	1956	360
Mayari	WC	454	1921	2,802
Mayola	Hickson	5	1857	345
Mechanican	WC	169	1900	9,044
Median	H&W	395	1907	6,296
Medic	H&W	323	1898	11,985
Megantic	H&W	399	1908	14,877
Melmore Head	WC	327	1918	5,320
Meltonian	H&W	408	1909	6,306
Memphian	H&W	396	1908	6,305
Memphis	H&W	233	1890	3,190
Meraggio	WC	16	1883	1,126
Mercian	H&W	398	1908	6,304
Metapan	WC	286	1909	5,010

Ship	Builder	Yard Number	Year of Launch	Tonnage
Methane Progress	H&W	1,653	1903	21,875
Michigan	H&W	200	1887	4,979
Michigan	H&W	227	1890	3,722
Michigan	H&W	327	1899	9,494
Millie	H&W	93	1875	107
Mimiro	WC	162	1900	6,224
Minas Geraea	WC	264	1909	3,401
Minchbank	H&W	1,553	1958	8,693
Minneapolis	H&W	328	1899	13,401
Minnehaha	H&W	329	1900	14,714
Minnekahda	H&W	446	1917	17,220
Minnesota	H&W	197	1887	3,143
Minnetonka	H&W	339	1901	13,397
Minnetonka	H&W	614	1924	21,998
Minnewaska	H&W	397	1908	14,160
Minnewaska	H&W	613	1923	21,716
Minnie Hind	McIl & Co.	39	1890	540
Minnie Hind	McIl & Co.	45	1891	409
Miranda	H&W	6	1860	34
Mississippi	H&W	231	1890	3,731
Missouri	H&W	1,542	1956	18,751
Mobile	H&W	253	1892	5,779
Mohawk	H&W	249	1892	5,575
Monarch	McIl & Co.	23	1884	310
Monkstown	McIl & Co.	14	1882	108
Monmouth	H&W	(b)	1897	8,162
Mooltan	H&W	587	1923	20,847
Mosselbaai (SAS)	H&W	1,584	1958	360
Mount Hebron	McIl & Co.	35	1889	2,560
Mount Newman	H&W	1,691	1973	65,131
Mount Sirion	WC	111	1895	3,280
Mourne	WC	114	1895	3,223
Mousmie	H&W	105	1876	85
Moya	WC	101	1893	184
Munardan	WC	354	1917	3,813
Muneric	WC	441	1919	5,146
Munster	H&W	996	1937	4,302
Munster	H&W	1,349	1947	4,088
Muritai	WC	291	1910	7,280
Musa	WC	515	1930	5,833
Mutine (HMS)	H&W	1,140	1942	980
Myrina	H&W	1,666	1967	95,450
Mystic	H&W	266	1893	726
Nadir	H&W	221	1889	3,142
Nairnbank	H&W	1,665	1966	10,541
Nairung	H&W	255	1892	4,425
Narenta	WC	446	1919	8,266
Narica	H&W	1,173	1943	8,213
Narkunda	H&W	471	1918	16,118
Naronic	H&W	251	1892	6,594
Nasmyth	H&W	546	1919	6,509
Nassarius	H&W	1,195	1943	8,246
Navahoe	H&W	389	1907	7,718
Nawab	H&W	220	1889	3,142
Nebraska	WC	448	1919	8,266
Neleus	WC	299	1911	6,686
Neothyris	H&W	1,285	1945	8,243
Nerehana	WC	248	1907	6,600
Nessbank	H&W	1,457	1952	5,690
Nestor	WC	318	1912	14,500
New Brighton	H&W	577	1919	6,538
New Brooklyn	H&W	566	1919	6,545
New Brunswick	H&W	555	1919	6,529
New Columbia	H&W	567	1920	6,573
New England	H&W	315	1898	11,394
New Georgia	H&W	556	1919	6,566
New Mexico	H&W	1,543	1958	18,751
New Texas	H&W	559	1919	6,568
New Toronto	H&W	558	1919	6,568
New Zealand Star	H&W	934	1934	10,740
Newcombia	H&W	1,199	1944	8,292
Newhaven	WC	11	1882	906

Ship	Builder	Yard Number	Year of Launch	Tonnage
Newington	WC	17	1883	1,125
Newton	H&W	554	1919	6,509
Nictheroy	WC	450	1920	8,266
Nieuw Amsterdam	H&W	366	1905	16,913
Niger	H&W	161	1883	2,006
Niso	H&W	1,198	1944	8,273
Niwaru	WC	183	1901	6,450
Nizam	H&W	222	1889	3,142
Nomadic	H&W	236	1891	5,749
Nomadic	H&W	422	1911	1,260
Noordam	H&W	338	1901	12,316
Norah Graeme	Hickson	6	1858	1,001
Norman	H&W	280	1894	7,394
Norrisia	H&W	1,194	1943	8,246
Nowshera	WC	437	1919	7,920
Nubia	H&W	121	1878	1,958
Nuestra Senora del Carmen	WC	69	1890	389
Number 4	WC	5	1880	594
Nurani	H&W	254	1892	4,432
Nurjahan	H&W	173	1884	2,967
Nurton (HMS)	H&W	1,527	1956	360
Obuasi	H&W	1,449	1952	5,883
Oceana	H&W	201	1887	6,362
Oceanic	H&W	73	1870	3,808
Oceanic	H&W	317	1899	17,274
Olano	H&W	23	1863	445
Olivebank	H&W	1,640	1961	8,694
Olympic	H&W	400	1910	45,324
Olympic Banner	H&W	1,685	1972	128,561
Olympic Brilliance	H&W	1,686	1973	128,561
Ondo	H&W	1,554	1956	5,435
Onitsha	H&W	1,448	1952	5,802
Ontario (HMCS)	H&W	1,171	1943	8,800
Onyx (HMS)	H&W	1,141	1942	980
Oopack	WC	112	1895	3,883
Optic	H&W	188	1885	880
Orania	WC	379	1921	9,771
Oranjestad	H&W	809	1927	2,396
Orator	WC	224	1905	3,563
Oravia	H&W	310	1896	5,320
Orbita	H&W	440	1914	15,678
Orca	H&W	442	1917	15,120
Orcana	H&W	264	1893	4,821
Orchis (HMS)	H&W	1,075	1940	1,170
Orcoma	H&W	1,662	1966	10,509
Orduna	H&W	438	1913	15,499
Orellana	H&W	259	1892	4,822
Orestes	WC	486	1926	7,882
Orissa	H&W	286	1894	5,317
Orita	H&W	351	1902	9,320
Orkdal	H&W	1,412	1951	8,221
Ormidale	WC	98	1893	3,560
Ormiston	H&W	193	1886	3,158
Ormiston	WC	105	1893	3,561
Oronsa	H&W	377	1906	7,907
Oropesa	H&W	285	1894	5,317
Oroya	H&W	506	1920	12,257
Ortega	H&W	376	1906	7,970
Orvieto	WC	279	1909	12,124
Oswestry Grange	WC	182	1902	6,592
Oti	H&W	1,546	1955	5,485
Otira	H&W	541	1919	7,995
Otranto	WC	278	1909	12,124
Owerri	H&W	1,479	1954	6,240
Oxford Castle (HMS)	H&W	1,238	1943	1,060
Oxfordshire	H&W	429	1912	8,623
P15 (HMS)	WC	361	1916	613
P16 (HMS)	WC	362	1916	613
P17 (HMS)	WC	363	1915	613
P60 (HMS)	WC	380	1917	682
P61 (HMS)	WC	381	1917	682
Pacuare	WC	221	1905	3,891

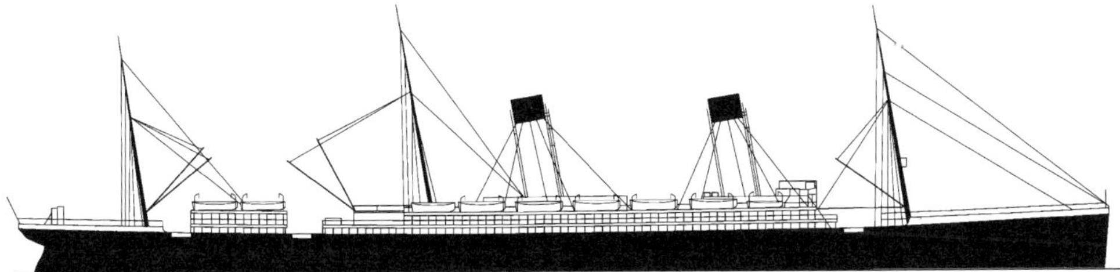

Oceanic (H&W y/n 317) 1899 (DH)

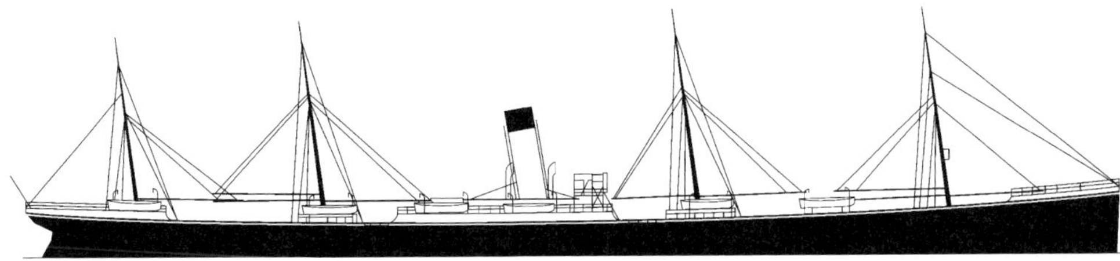

Medic (H&W y/n 323) 1898 (DH)

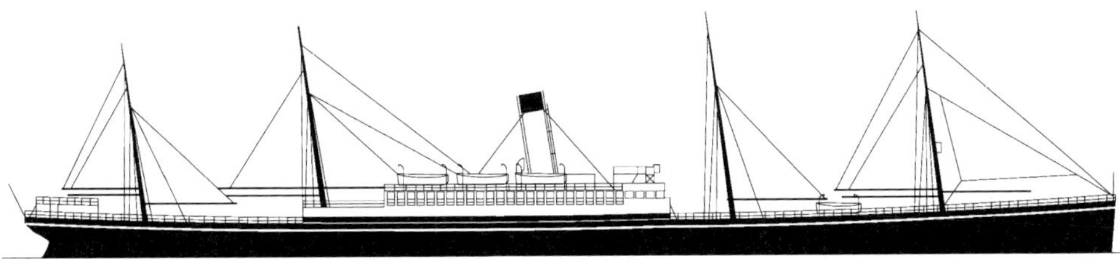

Winifredian (H&W y/n 324) 1899 (DH)

Minneapolis (H&W y/n 328) 1899 (DH)

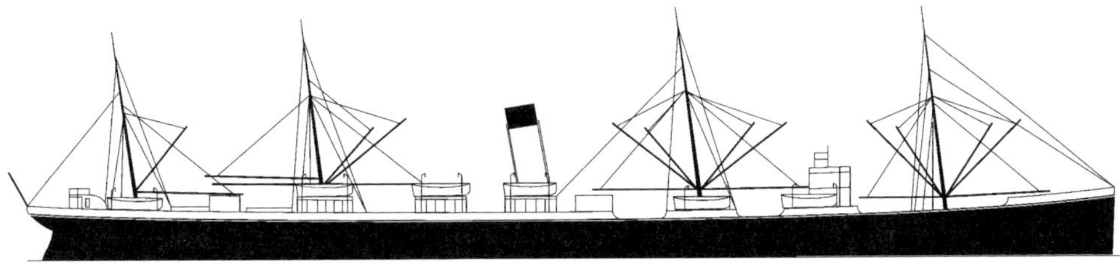

Runic (H&W y/n 332) 1900 (DH)

Ship	Builder	Yard Number	Year of Launch	Tonnage
Pak Ling	WC	120	1895	4,447
Pakeha	H&W	409	1910	7,910
Paknam	WC	174	1900	2,027
Palestine	H&W	22	1863	623
Palma	WC	202	1903	7,635
Palma	H&W	1,028	1941	5,419
Palmas	H&W	212	1888	2,428
Pampas	H&W	1,027	1940	5,415
Para	WC	242	1907	3,324
Paraguay	H&W	1,152	1944	5,560
Paramatta	H&W	1,149	1943	8,244
Parana	WC	207	1904	3,900
Pardo	H&W	363	1904	4,365
Pardo	H&W	1,025	1940	5,400
Parismina	WC	273	1908	4,940
Parkmore	McIl & Co.	10	1880	261
Parthia	H&W	1,331	1947	13,362
Pastores	WC	314	1912	7,782
Patani	WC	219	1905	3,465
Patella	H&W	1,316	1946	8,277
Patia	WC	317	1913	6,103
Patriotic	H&W	424	1911	2,254
Patroclus	WC	128	1896	5,509
Patuca	WC	320	1913	6,130
Pavia	WC	140	1897	2,936
PC69 (HMS)	WC	400	1918	682
PC70 (HMS)	WC	401	1918	682
Peleus	WC	172	1901	7,441
Pembrockshire	WC	337	1914	7,823
Pendennis Castle	H&W	1,558	1957	28,582
Penelope (HMS)	H&W	940	1935	5,050
Pennsylvania	H&W	302	1896	13,726
Pentstemon (HMS)	WC	366	1916	1,250
Peony (HMS)	H&W	1,066	1940	1,170
Pera	WC	201	1903	7,635
Pericles	H&W	392	1907	10,924
Periwinkle (HMS)	H&W	1,059	1940	1,170
Perseus	WC	275	1908	6,728
Persia	H&W	282	1894	5,857
Persian	H&W	13	1863	2,137
Persic	H&W	325	1899	11,973
Peshwa	H&W	133	1880	2,159
Petrolia (HMCS)	H&W	1,241	1944	1,060
Petunia (HMS)	WC	367	1916	1,250
Pevensey Castle (HMS)	H&W	1,239	1944	1,060
Phemius	WC	322	1913	6,700
Philadelphian	H&W	244	1891	5,120
Philadelphian	H&W	557	1919	6,566
Philadelphian	H&W	574	1919	6,585
Picardy	H&W	1,560	1957	7,306
Pickle (HMS)	H&W	1,201	1943	980
Picotee (HMS)	H&W	1,069	1940	1,170
Pilot	H&W	37	1865	34
Pimpernel (HMS)	H&W	1,077	1940	1,170
Pincher (HMS)	H&W	1,202	1943	980
Pindari	H&W	245	1891	5,674
Pinebank	H&W	1,635	1959	8,694
Ping Suey	WC	156	1899	6,457
Pioneer	McIl & Co.	29	1887	79
Pioneer	McIl & Co.	48	1891	557
Pittsburgh	H&W	457	1920	16,322
Pizarro	H&W	96	1875	1,439
Planet Mercury	WC	108	1894	3,222
Plassey	H&W	228	1890	3,176
Plucky (HMS)	H&W	1,203	1943	980
Polly Woodside	WC	38	1885	678
Poltalloch	WC	106	1893	2,254
Pontia	H&W	1,494	1954	8,904
Pontic	H&W	283	1894	395
Port Alfred	H&W	1,630	1960	9,044
Port Auckland	WC	382	1922	8,308
Port Bowen	WC	356	1918	8,267

Ship	Builder	Yard Number	Year of Launch	Tonnage
Port Brisbane	WC	462	1923	8,315
Port Campbell	WC	383	1922	8,308
Port Caroline	WC	358	1919	8,267
Port Curtis	WC	447	1919	8,287
Port Darwin	WC	351	1917	8,179
Port Denison	WC	352	1917	8,179
Port Dunedin	WC	477	1925	7,463
Port Elizabeth (SAS)	H&W	1,583	1957	360
Port Freemantle	WC	489	1927	8,072
Port Hobart	H&W	1,188	1945	11,149
Port Invercargill	H&W	1,565	1957	8,847
Port Launceston	H&W	1,534	1956	8,957
Port Melbourne	H&W	1,483	1955	10,470
Port Nelson	H&W	1,437	1951	8,375
Port Nicholson	H&W	1,646	1962	13,847
Port St Lawrence	H&W	1,631	1961	9,040
Port Wellington	WC	463	1924	7,868
Potaro	H&W	364	1904	4,378
Potaro	H&W	1,026	1940	5,409
Prahsu	H&W	387	1907	3,755
President Grant	H&W	354	1903	18,089
President Lincoln	H&W	353	1903	18,073
Pretoria Castle	H&W	1,006	1938	17,382
Pretoria Castle	H&W	1,332	1947	28,705
Princess Beatrice	H&W	100	1875	556
Professor	WC	288	1909	3,580
Prussia	H&W	281	1894	5,840
Punta Benitez	H&W	832	1928	2,394
Punta Gorda	H&W	835	1928	2,395
Pyrineus	WC	269	1909	1,696
Pyrrhus	WC	335	1914	7,603
Queens Island	H&W	184	1885	2,093
Queensmore	H&W	215	1889	4,195
Queenstown	McIl & Co.	52	1892	85
Quernmore	WC	151	1898	7,302
Race Fisher	McIl & Co.	49	1892	493
Raeburn	H&W	1,444	1952	8,312
Ramore Head	WC	75	1891	4,444
Ramore Head	H&W	1,371	1948	6,195
Rangatira	WC	289	1909	7,465
Rathdown	WC	82	1891	2,145
Rathlin Head	WC	161	1899	6,753
Rathlin Head	H&W	1,475	1953	7,439
Rattler (HMS)	H&W	1,142	1942	980
Ravenscraig	H&W	1,714	1979	64,651
Ready (HMS)	H&W	1,143	1943	980
Recife	H&W	17	1862	465
Recruit (HMS)	H&W	1,204	1943	980
Regent	H&W	1,658	1967	19,000
Regent Liverpool	H&W	1,614	1962	30,770
Regina	WC	217	1904	1,160
Reina del Mar	H&W	1,533	1955	20,225
Reina del Pacifico	H&W	852	1930	17,707
Repton (HMS)	H&W	1,528	1957	360
Republic	H&W	76	1871	3,708
Reventazon	WC	233	1906	4,041
Reventazon	WC	369	1921	5,360
Rhodesia Castle	H&W	1,431	1951	17,041
Rhododendron (HMS)	H&W	1,072	1940	1,170
Richmond Castle	H&W	1,012	1938	7,798
Richmond Castle	H&W	1,178	1944	7,971
Riebeeck Castle	H&W	1,277	1945	8,322
Rifleman (HMS)	H&W	1,205	1943	980
Rimfonn	H&W	1,620	1963	50,677
Rinaldo (HMS)	H&W	1,144	1943	980
Ringerd	H&W	1,413	1950	8,218
Rio de Janeiro	WC	246	1907	3,583
Rippingham Grange	WC	148	1898	5,790
Rita	WC	4	1880	3
River Ettrick	WC	15	1883	1,454
River Forth	WC	10	1882	1,127
River Garry	WC	19	1883	1,339

Ship	Builder	Yard Number	Year of Launch	Tonnage
River Indus	WC	25	1884	3,452
River Lagan	H&W	116	1877	895
Rochester Castle	H&W	992	1937	7,795
Rohidas	H&W	1,388	1949	1,288
Rohilla	H&W	381	1906	7,143
Roonagh Head	H&W	1,433	1951	6,153
Rosa	WC	36	1885	52
Rosario (HMS)	H&W	1,145	1943	980
Rosebank	H&W	1,593	1958	8,693
Rosetta	H&W	134	1880	3,457
Roslin Castle	H&W	943	1934	7,016
Rostellan	McIl & Co.	44	1891	82
Rothesay Castle	H&W	944	1935	7,016
Rotterdam	H&W	312	1897	8,301
Rotterdam	H&W	390	1908	23,980
Rowallan Castle	H&W	1,013	1938	7,798
Rowallan Castle	H&W	1,150	1942	7,950
Roxburgh Castle	H&W	993	1937	7,800
Roxburgh Castle	H&W	1,187	1944	8,003
Royal Scotsman	H&W	964	1936	3,244
Royal Ulsterman	H&W	963	1936	3,290
Royalstar	WC	438	1918	7,900
Roybank	H&W	1,647	1963	8,671
Royston Grange	WC	143	1898	4,018
Rudby	H&W	1,684	1970	57,245
Runic	H&W	211	1889	4,649
Runic	H&W	332	1900	12,482
Runic	H&W	1,414	1949	13,587
Rustenburg Castle	H&W	1,278	1946	8,322
Ryndam	H&W	336	1901	12,302
Sabaneta	H&W	810	1927	2,396
Sabarmati	H&W	1,375	1948	3,750
Sachem	H&W	272	1893	5,203
Sachen	H&W	413	1910	7,986
Sado Maru	WC	144	1897	5,898
Sagamore	H&W	256	1892	5,036
Saint Fillans	H&W	186	1886	3,130
Saint Kevin	McIl & Co.	18	1883	477
Saint Pancras	H&W	224	1890	4,283
Salaga	WC	238	1906	3,810
Salamanca	H&W	380	1906	5,969
Salamanca	H&W	1,358	1947	6,669
Salaverry	H&W	1,193	1946	6,612
Salinas	H&W	1,357	1947	6,669
Samanco	H&W	1,156	1943	8,336
San Andres	WC	345	1918	3,301
San Antonio	H&W	888	1930	5,986
San Benito	WC	459	1921	3,724
San Blas	WC	347	1920	3,628
San Bruno	WC	348	1920	3,628
San Carlos	H&W	795	1927	2,395
San Diego	H&W	889	1930	5,986
San Francisco	H&W	890	1930	5,894
San Gil	WC	364	1920	3,628
San Jose	WC	209	1904	3,300
San Jose	H&W	891	1930	5,982
San Mateo	WC	342	1915	3,301
San Mateo	H&W	892	1930	5,935
San Nicolas	H&W	739	1926	2,391
San Pablo	WC	343	1915	3,301
San Paulo	WC	245	1907	3,583
San Pedro	H&W	893	1930	5,935
San Rito	WC	344	1915	3,301
San Veronico	H&W	1,090	1942	8,189
Santa Marta	WC	285	1909	5,010
Santander	H&W	1,192	1946	6,612
Santiago	H&W	176	1885	1,017
Sarasvati	H&W	1,374	1948	3,750
Sarmiento	H&W	265	1893	3,603
Sarmiento	H&W	1,157	1943	8,335
Sarpedon	WC	115	1894	4,663
Saxon	H&W	326	1899	12,385

Ship	Builder	Yard Number	Year of Launch	Tonnage
Schiedyk	H&W	1,366	1948	9,592
Schiehallion	H&W	1,737	1997	152,630
Scotsman	H&W	289	1894	6,041
Scottish Coast	H&W	1,547	1956	3,817
Scottish Star	H&W	1,722	1984	10,291
Sea Fisher	McI & Co.	19	1883	274
Sea Quest	H&W	n/a	1966	7,900
Seillean	H&W	1,726	1988	50,928
Senator	WC	95	1892	4,688
Sesostris	H&W	33	1865	2,053
Shahjehan	H&W	122	1878	1,650
Shahzada	H&W	123	1879	1,677
Shannon	H&W	145	1881	4,189
Shannon	McI & Co.	50	1892	267
Shirrabank	H&W	1,035	1940	7,274
Shropshire	H&W	241	1891	5,660
Sicilian	H&W	2	1859	1,492
Sicilian	WC	158	1899	6,010
Sierra Leone	H&W	384	1906	3,730
Silistria	Hickson	1	1854	1,289
Silvercypress	H&W	882	1930	6,770
Silversandal	H&W	885	1930	6,770
Silverteak	H&W	884	1930	6,770
Silverwalnut	H&W	883	1930	6,770
Sindia	H&W	204	1887	3,067
Sir Thomas Picton (HMS)	H&W	481	1915	5,920
Sixaola	WC	306	1911	5,017
Skaufast	H&W	1,670	1968	57,204
Skegness	WC	474	1924	4,573
Skelligs	WC	9	1881	450
Skerryvore	WC	12	1882	994
Slieve Bawn	H&W	111	1877	1,749
Slieve Bawn	H&W	370	1905	1,147
Slieve More	H&W	110	1877	1,749
Slieve Roe	H&W	115	1878	1,749
Slievemore	H&W	362	1904	1,138
Sobraon	H&W	232	1890	3,185
Soesdyke	H&W	1,363	1948	9,592
Solfonn	H&W	1,493	1956	19,810
Somers Isle	H&W	1,622	1959	5,684
Somersetshire	H&W	579	1921	7,456
Sophie Kirk	WC	99	1893	958
Sophocles	H&W	575	1921	12,361
South African	WC	96	1892	438
Southern Cross	WC	91	1892	5,050
Southern Cross	H&W	1,498	1954	20,204
Spanker (HMS)	H&W	1,146	1943	980
Springbank	H&W	1,639	1961	8,694
Squirrel (HMS)	WC	215	1904	230
Squirrel (HMS)	H&W	1,206	1944	980
St Albans	WC	292	1910	4,120
St Anselm	H&W	1,715	1979	7,003
St Austell Bay (HMS)	H&W	1,249	1944	1,600
St Brides Bay (HMS)	H&W	1,250	1945	1,600
St Christopher	H&W	1,716	1980	6,996
St David	H&W	1,717	1980	7,109
Staffordshire	H&W	278	1893	6,005
Stanmore	H&W	195	1886	1,824
Star of Albion	H&W	29	1864	999
Star of Australia	WC	157	1899	7,200
Star of Austria	WC	37	1886	1,708
Star of Bengal	H&W	86	1874	1,870
Star of Canada	WC	283	1909	7,280
Star of Denmark	H&W	20	1863	998
Star of England	WC	58	1889	3,511
Star of England	WC	329	1914	9,152
Star of Erin	H&W	16	1862	948
Star of France	H&W	114	1877	1,663
Star of Germany	H&W	82	1872	1,337
Star of Greece	H&W	57	1868	1,288
Star of India	WC	297	1910	7,316
Star of Ireland	WC	200	1903	4,331

Ship	Builder	Yard Number	Year of Launch	Tonnage
Star of Italy	H&W	113	1877	1,644
Star of Japan	WC	235	1906	6,236
Star of New Zealand	WC	94	1892	4,712
Star of Persia	H&W	55	1868	1,289
Star of Russia	H&W	88	1874	1,981
Star of Scotia	H&W	24	1864	999
Star of Scotland	WC	212	1904	6,230
Star of Victoria	WC	39	1887	3,239
Star of Victoria	WC	328	1913	9,152
Start Bay (HMS)	H&W	1,252	1945	1,600
Statendam	H&W	320	1898	10,319
Statendam	H&W	612	1924	28,130
Statesman	WC	119	1895	6,322
Steelfield	H&W	108	1876	1,315
Stentor	WC	154	1898	6,773
Stirling Castle	H&W	941	1935	25,594
Storfonn	H&W	1,538	1956	24,854
Strait Fisher	McIl & Co.	40	1890	465
Stream Fisher	McIl & Co.	46	1891	479
Suevic	H&W	333	1900	12,531
Suevic	H&W	1,415	1950	13,587
Sultan	WC	107	1894	2,062
Surinam	H&W	863	1929	3,046
Susannah Kelly	McIl & Co.	43	1890	479
Suva	WC	229	1906	2,229
Swanmore	H&W	194	1886	1,821
Swift	WC	521	1930	935
Sydney Bridge	H&W	1,680	1970	35,868
Sydney Star	H&W	958	1936	11,095
Syrian	H&W	3	1860	1,492
Syringa (HMS)	WC	402	1917	1,290
Tainui	WC	277	1908	9,957
Talookdar	H&W	183	1885	2,120
Tamare	H&W	861	1929	3,046
Tanglin	WC	175	1900	2,027
Tank King	H&W	1,410	1951	16,477
Tantallon Castle	H&W	1,499	1953	7,448
Tauric	H&W	237	1891	5,727
Taybank	WC	512	1930	5,627
Teelin Head	WC	14	1883	1,715
Tela	WC	346	1915	7,226
Tela	WC	491	1927	4,083
Telemachus	WC	184	1902	7,450
Telemon	WC	213	1904	4,510
Templemore	H&W	277	1893	6,276
Tenadores	WC	315	1912	7,782
Tenasserim	H&W	46	1866	1,418
Teneriffe	H&W	178	1885	1,799
Tenet	WC	290	1910	606
Ternoy	H&W	1,392	1949	8,218
Terror (HMS)	H&W	493	1916	8,022
Teutonic	H&W	208	1889	9,685
Texan	H&W	167	1883	3,257
Texeco Maracaibo	H&W	1,656	1964	51,774
Thara	H&W	1,671	1968	41,089
Theme	McIl & Co.	21	1884	332
Theme	McIl & Co.	31	1888	332
Themistocles	H&W	412	1910	11,231
Theory	McIl & Co.	59	1894	541
Theseus	WC	276	1908	6,728
Thesis	McIl & Co.	25	1887	378
Thorshavet	H&W	1,348	1947	17,081
Thruster (HMS)	H&W	1,153	1942	5,593
Thurland Castle	H&W	107	1876	1,301
Thursby	H&W	101	1876	497
Tia Juana	H&W	833	1928	2,395
Tide Austral	H&W	1,502	1954	13,165
Tindfonn	H&W	1,597	1961	31,322
Tintagel Castle	H&W	1,500	1954	7,447
Tintoretto	WC	188	1902	4,170
Titanic	McIl & Co.	28	1888	1,608
Titanic	H&W	401	1911	46,328

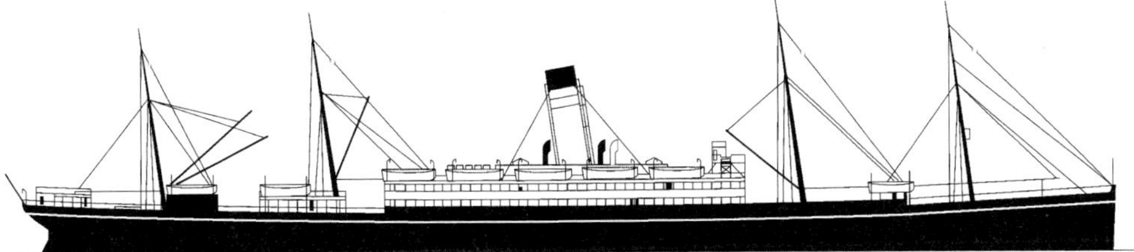

Columbus (H&W y/n 345) 1903 (DH)

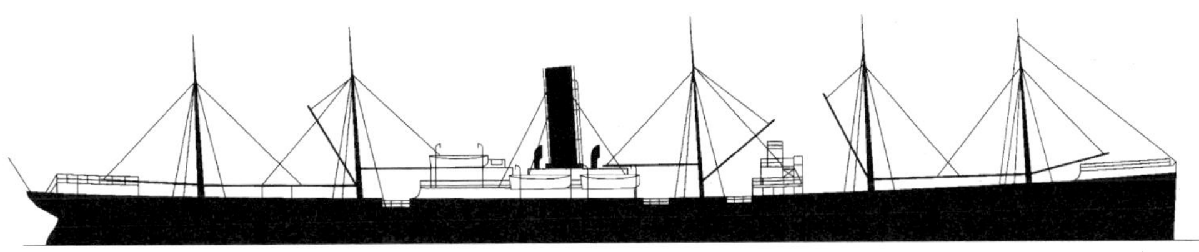

Iowa (H&W y/n 349) 1902 (DH)

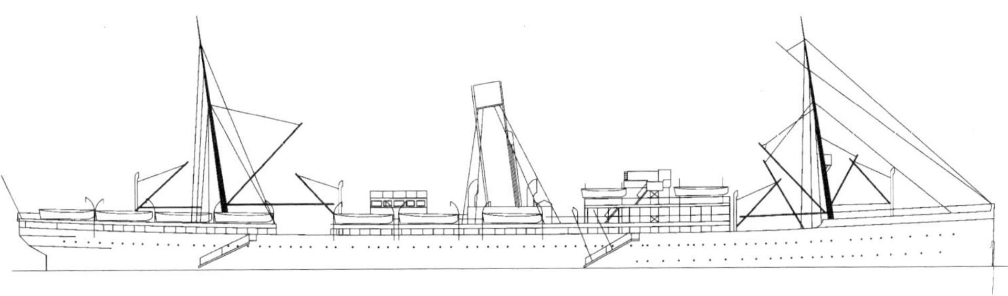

Ortega (H&W y/n 376) 1906 (DH)

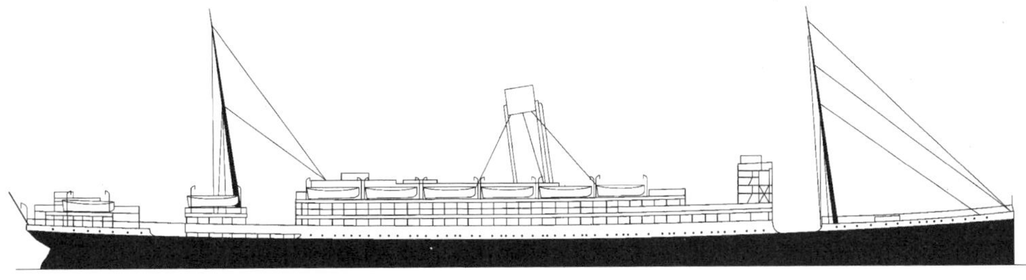

Avon (H&W y/n 382) 1907 (DH)

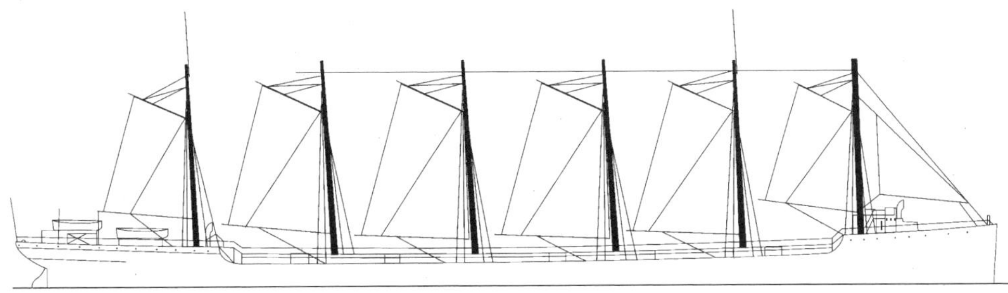

Navahoe (H&W y/n 389) 1907 (DH)

Ship	Builder	Yard Number	Year of Launch	Tonnage
Titian	WC	187	1902	4,170
Tivives	WC	304	1911	5,017
Toloa	WC	341	1917	7,452
Topic	McIl & Co.	12	1881	268
Topic	McIl & Co.	32	1889	429
Torquay (HMS)	H&W	1,472	1954	2,150
Torr Head	H&W	274	1894	5,910
Torr Head	WC	393	1923	5,221
Torr Head	H&W	994	1937	5,021
Traffic	H&W	423	1911	639
Transvaal (SAS)	H&W	1,251	1944	1,435
Tremadoc Bay (HMS)	H&W	1,253	1945	1,600
Trentbank	WC	507	1929	5,060
Tresfonn	H&W	1,599	1960	13,471
Trishul (INS)	H&W	1,555	1958	2,150
Turrialba	WC	281	1909	4,960
Tweedbank	WC	513	1930	5,627
Tydeus	WC	173	1901	7,441
Tyria	WC	141	1897	2,936
Ule	H&W	862	1929	3,046
Ulster Monarch	H&W	635	1929	3,851
Ulster Prince	H&W	697	1929	3,756
Ulster Prince	H&W	1,667	1966	4,478
Ulster Queen	H&W	696	1929	3,756
Ulster Star	H&W	1,568	1959	10,413
Ulstermore	H&W	288	1894	6,326
Ulua	WC	340	1917	7,452
Ulysses	WC	319	1913	14,500
Unicorn (HMS)	H&W	1,031	1941	14,750
Uranus	WC	65	1889	1,202
Urmston Grange	WC	113	1895	3,444
Valador	H&W	28	1864	174
Vandyke	WC	301	1911	10,328
Vandyke	WC	359	1921	13,233
Vauban	WC	302	1912	10,660
Vedamore	H&W	298	1895	6,329
Venetian	H&W	1	1859	1,508
Verdi	WC	256	1907	6,580
Verena	H&W	1,403	1950	18,612
Verona	WC	271	1908	8,210
Veronese	WC	228	1905	7,022
Vervain (HMS)	H&W	1,101	1941	1,170
Vestal (HMS)	H&W	1,147	1943	980
Vestfonn	H&W	1,578	1958	13,409
Vestfoss	H&W	1,381	1949	8,250
Vestris	WC	303	1912	10,494
Vibex	H&W	1,484	1955	20,787
Victoria Nyanza	H&W	21	1863	1,022
Victorian	H&W	291	1895	8,767
Victorian	WC	206	1904	10,630
Vikingen	H&W	1,383	1949	8,264
Vindictive (HMS)	H&W	500	1918	7,764
Vitrina	H&W	1,512	1957	20,802
Volador	H&W	28	1864	174
Volga	McIl & Co.	11	1881	281
Voltaire	WC	360	1923	13,233
Volturnus	WC	223	1904	160
W.J. Pirrie	H&W	155	1883	2,576
Waikato (HMNZS)	H&W	1,657	1965	2,305
Waimana	WC	309	1911	7,852
Waimarama	H&W	1,004	1938	11,091
Waiotira	H&W	1,019	1939	11,102
Waipara	H&W	26	1863	90
Waipawa	H&W	923	1934	10,784
Waiwera	H&W	922	1934	10,781
Waiwera	H&W	1,161	1943	12,028
Walmer Castle	H&W	342	1901	12,545
Walmer Castle	H&W	983	1936	905
Walter H. Wilson	H&W	150	1882	2,518
Walvisbaai (SAS)	H&W	1,585	1958	360
Wanderer	WC	78	1891	4,085

Ship	Builder	Yard Number	Year of Launch	Tonnage
Wanganella	H&W	849	1929	9,576
Wangaratta	WC	440	1919	7,900
War Argus	WC	436	1918	7,910
War Beetle	WC	426	1918	5,177
War Bittern	H&W	535	1918	5,178
War Buckler	H&W	536	1918	2,357
War Clover	H&W	521	1917	5,174
War Cobra	H&W	533	1917	5,155
War Dream	H&W	545	1918	6,498
War Icarus	H&W	540	1918	8,002
War Lemur	H&W	532	1918	5,185
War Leopard	WC	427	1918	5,177
War Melody	H&W	543	1918	6,533
War Music	H&W	544	1918	6,498
War Python	H&W	534	1917	5,155
War Shamrock	H&W	520	1917	5,174
War Snake	H&W	538	1918	5,222
War Tabard	H&W	537	1918	2,357
War Trefoil	H&W	522	1917	5,166
War Viper	H&W	531	1918	5,160
Warrior (HMS)	H&W	1,224	1944	13,350
Warwick Castle	H&W	840	1930	20,444
Warwickshire	H&W	344	1901	7,966
Watchman	WC	32	1884	466
Wayfarer	WC	195	1902	9,600
Wazzan	McII & Co.	57	1893	1,484
Wellington Star	H&W	1,016	1939	12,382
Weybank	H&W	1,648	1963	8,671
Whakarua	WC	247	1907	6,600
White Head	H&W	135	1880	1,192
Whitesand Bay (HMS)	H&W	1,261	1944	1,600
Widemouth Bay (HMS)	H&W	1,259	1944	1,600
Wigtown Bay (HMS)	H&W	1,260	1945	1,600
William Hind	WC	2	1880	346
William Strachan	WC	517	1930	6,157
William Wheelwright	H&W	1,574	1960	31,320
Winchester Castle	H&W	825	1929	20,108
Windflower (HMS)	WC	403	1918	1,290
Winifreda	H&W	319	1897	6,833
Winifredian	H&W	324	1899	10,404
Winnebah	H&W	143	1881	1,390
Woodhopper	H&W	140	1880	?
Woodlawn	H&W	56	1868	63
Worcestershire	H&W	359	1904	7,160
Workman	WC	27	1884	387
Workman	WC	149	1898	6,115
World Cavalier	H&W	1,693	1974	138,025
Worrell	H&W	18	1862	484
Xantippe	WC	103	1893	972
Yacatan	H&W	151	1882	2,816
Yamanota	H&W	836	1928	2,395
Yang Tsze	WC	155	1899	6,457
Yorkshire	H&W	217	1889	3,070
Yorkshire	H&W	509	1919	10,184
Zacapa	WC	287	1909	5,010
Zealandic	H&W	421	1911	10,897
Zemindar	H&W	182	1885	2,120
Zent	WC	222	1905	3,891

BUILDING LISTS

Key for Building Lists

A	B	C	D	E	F	G H	I J K	L

A. (Harland & Wolff ships only.) Sequential numbering of Belfast-built ships
B. Yard Number allocated to the ship
C. Ship's name
D. Date of launch
E. Displacement
F. Ship type
G. Ship Construction
   a. Hull material Com = Composite, Ir = Iron, St = Steel,
   b. Propulsion (not used on Sailing Vessels) Pd = Paddle Wheel, Sc = Screw (number = number of screws)
   c. Machinery (not used on sailing Vessels) St = Steam, Mv = Motor Vessel
H. Approximate Dimension (in feet) Length/Breath/Depth
I. Horsepower
   a. nhp = Natural Horse Power (simple power of engine)
   b. bhp = Brake Horse Power (effective power generated used for motor vessels)
   c. ihp = Indicated Horse Power (effective power generated used for triple/quadruple expansion ships)
   d. shp = Shaft Horse Power (effective power generated used for turbine vessels)
J. Engine Type
   a. CI = Compound Inverted (4 Cy = Double Engine)
   b. Co = Compound Oscillating
   c. COSAG = Combined Gas and Steam
   d. Cs = Compound Simple
   e. DA = Direct Acting
   f. Dies = Diesel
   g. Dies/Electric = Diesel-Electric
   h. HDAR = Horizontal, Direct-acting, Reciprocating
   i. Petrol = Petrol Engine
   j. QE = Quadruple Expansion (8 Cy = Double Engine)
   k. REC = Reciprocating
   l. SA = Single Acting
   m. TE (3 Cy) = Triple Expansion three cylinder (6 Cy = Double Engine)
   n. TE (4 Cy) = Triple Expansion four cylinder (8 Cy = Double Engine)
   o. Turb = Turbine (Exh Turb = Exhaust turbine fitted to other engine)
   p. Turb-Elect = Turbo-Electric
   q. VTE (4 Cy) = Vertical Triple Expansion (8 Cy = Double Engines)
K. Builder of Engines
L. Owner at launch

Robert Hickson

Yard No. *(Allocated not Actual)*	Name	Date Launched	Displacement Tons	Type	Construction and Dimensions	Horse Power	Owners
1	*Silistria*	??.9.1854	1,289	Sailing Vessel (Ship)	Wooden Hulled	N/A	Edward Bates Liverpool
Edward 'Bully' Bates was Conservative MP for Plymouth and notorious operator of overloaded 'coffin ships'. In one year, it was claimed, he lost six ships and made a profit by claiming on insurance. He was a public opponent of Samuel Plimsoll, whose attempt to get loading marks introduced was seen as a direct attack of Bates' business practices. Named after a Turkish fortress on the Danube besieged by Russia in May–June 1854. A fast clipper intended for India trade. Made four voyages from Scotland to New Zealand carrying emigrants.							
2	*Khersonese*	5.10.1855	1,273	Passenger-Cargo	Ir/Sc/St 240.1/38.9/23	200 nhp Randolph, Elder & Co. Glasgow	Liverpool, Newfoundland & Halifax SN Co.
When launched stuck on slip but freed without damage. The *Illustrated London News* noted on 3 November 1855: 'It is intended at present to erect a saloon for cabin-passengers aft. And house forward for the officers. Engineers &c as to leave an extensive area of main deck as a promenade clear for passengers or troops, or accommodation for the transport of horses'. In 1856 employed as Crimean War repatriation transport. In May 1897 homeward bound from Portland, Maine, lost propeller and completed voyage under sail, repaired at Birkenhead by Laird's. Shortly afterwards acquired by North Atlantic SN Co. continued on Liverpool–Canada–Portland, Maine route, carrying 400+ emigrants on each voyage. In 1857 employed as transport during Indian Mutiny. In 1863 to Robert Duncan & Co. and employed on Liverpool–New York route. In 1866 engines removed converted to sailing vessel (rigged as Barque). In 1889 to Dutch owners, S.J. Melchers. Destroyed in fire, Montevideo, July 1891.							
3	*Circassian*	18.7.1856	1,387	Passenger-Cargo	Ir/Sc/St 255.0/39.1/18.0	350 nhp Randolph, Elder & Co. Glasgow	North Atlantic Steam Navigation Co.
Provided with accommodation for cabin-class, intermediate and third-class passengers. Began maiden voyage on 17 March 1857 with 200 passengers but forced back to Liverpool a week later by weather. Made three transatlantic voyages before taken up, September 1857, as transport for Indian Mutiny. In 1858 chartered to Galway Line and made eight Galway–New York voyages, October 1858–March 1860. In May 1862 captured by USS *Somerset* on voyage Cuba–Matanzas and condemned as blockade runner. In November 1862 purchased by US Navy and commissioned as armed transport (4x9in SB, 1x100lb MLR, 1x12lb MLR) attached to Gulf Squadron. During service credited with capturing two other blockade runners. Decommissioned April 1865, sold to merchant service in June, Ruger Bros. Subsequently employed on New York–Southampton and later New York–Bremen routes. In 1874 engines removed and converted to sailing vessel. Wrecked at Bridgehampton, Long Island in 1876. No lives lost.							
4	*Dewa Gunghadur*	1857	594	Sailing Vessel (Ship)	Iron Hulled	N/A	Edward Bates Liverpool
5	*Mayola*	1857	345	Sailing Vessel (Barque)	Iron Hulled	N/A	William Porter Liverpool
Employed on Belfast–India trade.							
6	*Norah Graeme*	?.2.1858	1,001	Sailing Vessel (Barque)	Iron Hulled	N/A	Edward Bates Liverpool
7	*Adjutant*	1858		Tug	Ir/Sc/St		? Liverpool
8	*Bebington*	1859	941	Sailing Vessel (Barque)	Iron Hulled	N/A	R. Hickson & Co. Liverpool
Originally to have been called *Oceola* but completed by Hickson with this name on own account after original owner defaulted on payment. Described by contemporaries as 'a bit of an old-tub'. In 1875 sold to Shaw Savill & Co., employed on South America routes. In 1882 sold to Norwegian owners, renamed *Handel Lust*.							

Harland & Wolff

Ship	Yard No	Name	Date Launched	Displacement Tons	Type	Construction and Dimensions	Horse Power/ Engines	Owners
1	1	*Venetian*	30.7.1859	1,508	Cargo Ship	Ir/Sc/St 270.4/34.0/23.0	450 nhp CI (2Cy) **Engines** J. Rollo & Co. Liverpool	J. Bibby Sons & Co. Liverpool
Completed 14.08.1859, for Mediterranean service. Like most cargo vessels built with limited passenger accommodation in deckhouses, 28 first-class (11x double cabin and a six-berth ladies' cabin) after and ten second class in a single room amidships. In 1872 engines were modernised by Rollo & Co. In 1873 passed, with the rest of the Bibby fleet, to Leyland & Co. In 1880 to the African Steamship Co., renamed *Landana.* In 1891 to Chilean owners, E. Gerard, renamed *Tarapaca.* Wrecked on coast of Chile, July 1894.								
2	2	*Sicilian*	12.11.1859	1,492	Cargo Ship	Ir/Sc/St 270.4/34.0/23.0	450 nhp CI (2Cy) **Engines** J. Rollo & Co. Liverpool	J. Bibby Sons & Co. Liverpool
Completed 24.11.1859, sister ship of *Venetian.* To Leyland & Co. 1873. To African Steamship Co. 1880, renamed *Mayumba.* In 1882 to G.R. Gilchrist, Liverpool, following year scuttled after catching fire in Algerian port of Arzew.								
3	3	*Syrian*	26.3.1860	1,492	Cargo Ship	Ir/Sc/St 270.4/34.0/23.0	450 nhp CI (2Cy) **Engines** J. Rollo & Co. Liverpool	J. Bibby Sons & Co. Liverpool
Completed 1.4.1860, sister ship of *Venetian.* In 1869 wrecked near Cape Finisterre on voyage Corunna–Lisbon.								
	4		Cancelled					
4	5	*Jane Porter*	1.9.1860	952	Sailing Vessel (Ship)	Iron Hulled 200.5/32.0/23.0	N/A	J.P. Corry & Co. Belfast
Completed 15.9.1860, first order from Corry Line, who became significant customers of Belfast shipyards. For London–Calcutta trade via the Cape, 1889 made best time on an outward voyage of 93 days. In 1889 to William Ross & Co., Liverpool, reduced to barque. In 1896 to German owners, H. Burmester, renamed *Nanny.* Wrecked off Natal coast on voyage Bombay–East London, July 1905.								
5	6	*Miranda*	21.6.1860	34	Yacht (Schooner)	Ir/Sc/Sch 64.0/11.6/6.7	16 nhp CI (2Cy) **Engines** J.H.G. Greenhill Belfast	T. Yates
Completed June 1860. By 1890 owned by John H. Greenhill, Belfast. By 1912 no longer listed by Lloyd's.								
6	7	*Grecian*	12.1.1861	1,854	Cargo Ship	Ir/Sc/St 310/34.0/24.0	500 nhp CI (2Cy) **Engines** J. Rollo & Co. Liverpool	J. Bibby Sons & Co. Liverpool
Following success of *Venetian* 'type', the Bibby Line ordered six further vessels. In these Edward Harland introduced his 'Belfast bottom' hull form and patent iron deck to create a long, slender hull of great strength. Other state-of-the-art innovations included provision of steam winches for cargo handling and fitting of condensers to engines to reduce fuel costs and saltwater corrosion to boilers. Although initially considered unsafe, the design proved both economical and a good sea boat; rather unfairly these ships and their successors became known as 'Bibby coffins'. Completed 30.1.1861 for the North Atlantic cotton trade. On outbreak of American Civil War transferred to Mediterranean. In 1870 engines modernised by J. Rollo & Co. Disappeared at sea 1873.								
7	8	*Italian*	27.3.1861	1,859	Cargo Ship	Ir/Sc/St 313.0/34.0/24.0	500 nhp CI (2Cy) **Engines** J. Rollo & Co. Liverpool	J. Bibby Sons & Co. Liverpool
Completed 13.4.1861, sister ship of *Grecian.* Wrecked after grounding in fog, Cape Finisterre 1869.								
8	9	*Egyptian*	23.7.1861	1,986	Cargo Ship	Ir/Sc/St 335.0/34.0/24.0	500 nhp CI (2Cy) **Engines** J. Rollo & Co. Liverpool	J. Bibby Sons & Co. Liverpool
Completed 11.8.1861, lengthened half sister of *Grecian.* In 1873 to Leyland & Co.								

Ship	Yard No	Name	Date Launched	Displacement Tons	Type	Construction and Dimensions	Horse Power/ Engines	Owners
1879 refitted with compound engines by G. Forrester and rig reduced; ten years later given new boilers. In 1901 acquired by John Pierpoint Morgan when he took over Leyland in one of the early moves that led to the formation of International Mercantile Marine. *Egyptian* almost immediately passed to another Morgan-owned company, London, Liverpool & Ocean Shipping Co. (Ellerman Line) but did not serve long, being broken up 1903.								
9	10	*Ballymurtagh*	25/9/1860	41	Barge			Wicklow Mining Co.
Completed September 1860.								
10	11	*Dalmation*	19.11.1861	1,989	Cargo Ship	Ir/Sc/St 335.0/34.1/24.9	450 nhp CI (2Cy) **Engines** G. Forrester & Co. Liverpool	J. Bibby Sons & Co. Liverpool
Completed December 1861, sister ship of *Egyptian.* Wrecked Bardsey Island, North Wales, 1876.								
11	12	*Arabian*	15.4.1862	1,994	Cargo Ship	Ir/Sc/St 335.0/34.1/24.9	450 nhp CI (4Cy) **Engines** G. Forrester & Co. Liverpool	J. Bibby Sons & Co. Liverpool
Completed 2.5.1862, sister ship of *Egyptian.* As with her sister, acquired by Leyland & Co. in 1873, John Pierpoint Morgan in 1901 and passed to London, Liverpool & Ocean Shipping Co. (Ellerman Line). Broken up 1902.								
12	13	*Persian*	21.1.1863	2,137	Cargo Ship	Ir/Sc/St 361.1/34.0/24.9	450 nhp CI (4Cy) **Engines** G. Forrester & Co. Liverpool	J. Bibby Sons & Co. Liverpool
Completed February 1863, a lengthened half sister of *Egyptian.* Acquired by Leyland & Co. in 1873, engines modernised by J. Rollo & Co. in 1879 and subsequently employed on Liverpool–Boston route. Purchased by John Pierpoint Morgan in 1901 and passed to London, Liverpool & Ocean Shipping Co. (Ellerman Line). Broken up Italy (Genoa) 1902.								
13	14	*Castilian*	10.5.1862	607	Cargo Ship	Ir/Sc/St 240.0/24.0/15.5	110 nhp CI (2Cy) **Engines** J. Rollo & Co. Liverpool	J. Bibby Sons & Co. Liverpool
Completed July 1862, intended for services between Britain and Spain. Markedly smaller than previous Bibby ships and consequently nicknamed the 'baby Bibby'. Like the rest of the Bibby fleet acquired by Leyland & Co. in 1873 and John Pierpoint Morgan in 1901, being transferred to London, Liverpool & Ocean Shipping Co. (Ellerman Line). Broken up Garston (UK) 1902 (some sources suggest reduced to hulk/barge in Italy in 1915).								
14	15	*Catalonian*	15.7.1862	607	Cargo Ship	Ir/Sc/St 240.0/24.0/15.5	110 nhp CI (2Cy) **Engines** J. Rollo & Co. Liverpool	J. Bibby Sons & Co. Liverpool
Completed 2.8.1862, sister ship of *Castilian.* Wrecked 1863.								
15	16	*Star of Erin*	9.10.1862	948	Sailing Vessel (Ship)	Iron Hulled 200.0/32.0/21.9	N/A	J.P. Corry & Co. Belfast
Completed 31.10.1862, a near sister of *Jane Porter* and first Corry vessel to bear a 'Star' name, which subsequently became standard. Employed on London–Calcutta route, making best outward passage in 1873: 80 days. In 1889 to Park Bros, London. Wrecked Forveaux Straits, New Zealand, outbound for London with a cargo of wool and grain, February 1892. No lives lost.								
16	17	*Recife*	21.10.1862	465	Sailing Vessel (Barque)	Iron Hulled 150.0/26.0/17.0	N/A	James Napier Liverpool
Completed November 1862. Employed on Liverpool–South America trade. By 1875 owned by C. Morland & Co., renamed *Carolina.* Off *Lloyd's Register* by 1880.								
17	18	*Worrall*	December 1862	484	Sailing Vessel (Barque)	Iron Hulled 166.6/25.2/16.9	N/A	J. Worrall Liverpool
Completed December 1862, built to operate between European and Mediterranean ports. In 1870 to W.&J. Tyser, Liverpool, and subsequently S. Wakenham, Liverpool (1876). In 1889 to Danish owners, J. Svendsen, renamed *Else.* Sank SW off Lizard, on voyage Equador–Hamburg, January 1894. No lives lost.								
18	19	*Alexandra*	7.4.1863	1,352	Sailing Vessel (Ship)	Iron Hulled 231.5/36.5/23.9	N/A	T.&J. Brocklebank Liverpool
Completed 8.6.1893, built for India trade. In 1887 to Trinder Anderson & Co., London, employed in Australia trade. Off *Lloyd's Register* by 1900.								

<table>
<tr><th>Ship</th><th>Yard No</th><th>Name</th><th>Date Launched</th><th>Displacement Tons</th><th>Type</th><th>Construction and Dimensions</th><th>Horse Power/ Engines</th><th>Owners</th></tr>
<tr><td>19</td><td>20</td><td>Star of Denmark</td><td>19.6.1863</td><td>998</td><td>Sailing Vessel (Ship)</td><td>Iron Hulled 208.7/32.0/21.9</td><td>N/A</td><td>J.P. Corry & Co. Belfast</td></tr>
<tr><td colspan="9">Completed June 1863 for the India trade. This ship had a figurehead representing Princess Alexandria of Denmark, who married the Prince of Wales a week before launch. In 1872 sprang a leak during a cyclone but reached London unaided. In 1877 made best time London–Calcutta of 96 days. In 1881 to F.M. Tucker, London. In 1890 to Hine Bros, Workington, renamed Denton Holme; in June wrecked off Fremantle. No lives lost amongst 17-strong crew.</td></tr>
<tr><td>20</td><td>21</td><td>Victoria Nyanza</td><td>15.8.1863</td><td>1,022</td><td>Sailing Vessel (Ship)</td><td>Iron Hulled 202.2/32.5/22.5</td><td>N/A</td><td>Joshua Prouse & Co. Liverpool</td></tr>
<tr><td colspan="9">Completed August 1863. By 1875 owned by G. Fletcher; in 1880 by Lowden, Edgar & Co. Off Lloyd's Register by 1895.</td></tr>
<tr><td>21</td><td>22</td><td>Palestine</td><td>13.10.1863</td><td>623</td><td>Sailing Vessel (Barque)</td><td>Iron Hulled 184.2/27.6/17.0</td><td>N/A</td><td>W.H. Tindall Scarborough</td></tr>
<tr><td colspan="9">Completed October 1863, for Ceylon trade. Off Lloyd's Register by 1896.</td></tr>
<tr><td>22</td><td>23</td><td>Olano</td><td>29.9.1863</td><td>445</td><td>Sailing Vessel (Barque)</td><td>Iron Hulled 145.0/27.0/16.7</td><td>N/A</td><td>Larrinaga & Co. Liverpool</td></tr>
<tr><td colspan="9">Completed September 1863. Laid down as Orlando but completed with this name. Employed in Spanish trade; initially registered in Belfast but by 1881 registered in Bilbio. In 1883 to R.J. Swyny, Liverpool. Wrecked between Staten Island and New Year's Island, Patagonia, June 1884.</td></tr>
<tr><td>23</td><td>24</td><td>Star of Scotia</td><td>January 1864</td><td>999</td><td>Sailing Vessel (Ship)</td><td>Iron Hulled 207.0/32.0/22.2</td><td>N/A</td><td>J.P. Corry & Co. Belfast</td></tr>
<tr><td colspan="9">Completed January 1864, for London–Calcutta route; made best time in 1873: 90 days. In January 1885 during a voyage from Cardiff to Colombo with cargo of coal she was swept by heavy seas off Cape Cornwall which carried away the watch crew, compass and binnacle. In April 1887 she left San Francisco for London via Queenstown. Wrecked at Bull Point, Falkland Islands, 27 June. Seven lives lost.</td></tr>
<tr><td>24</td><td>25</td><td>Kitty of Coleraine</td><td>7.10.1863</td><td>24</td><td>River Boat</td><td>Ir/Sc/St 72.0/10.0/?</td><td>Cs ?</td><td>Lower Bann Steamboat Co.</td></tr>
<tr><td colspan="9">Completed 30.10.1863. Intended to provide steamer service on the Lower Bann River, but had difficulties moving upriver against the current when loaded. Left the river in January 1869 and later service and fate unknown.</td></tr>
<tr><td>25</td><td>26</td><td>Waipara</td><td>October 1863</td><td>90</td><td>Cargo Boat</td><td>Ir/Sc/St 80.5/16.0/7.0</td><td>30 nhp CI (2Cy) Engines J. Rowen & Sons Belfast</td><td>J.Ritchie Belfast</td></tr>
<tr><td colspan="9">Completed 28.11.1863; engine located aft – an uncommon feature in contemporary vessels. Although this coastal steamer was supposedly designed for this owner and was intended to carry high-value linen cargoes, its name originates in New Zealand and by 1875 the vessel was operating in New Zealand waters, owned by New Zealand Shipping Co. In c. 1880 owned by J.A. Bonar, New Zealand. Ultimate fate unknown.</td></tr>
<tr><td>26</td><td>27</td><td>Baroda</td><td>23.4.1864</td><td>1,364</td><td>Sailing Vessel (Ship)</td><td>Iron Hulled 225.0/36.5/23.9</td><td>N/A</td><td>T.&J. Brocklebank Liverpool</td></tr>
<tr><td colspan="9">Completed April 1864, for India trade. Sank following collision with SS Bucculeuch, River Mersey, 1887. No lives lost.</td></tr>
<tr><td>27</td><td>28</td><td>Volador</td><td>April 1864</td><td>174</td><td>Sailing Vessel (Barquentine)</td><td>Iron Hulled 113.2/21.0/11.8</td><td>N/A</td><td>G. Lomer Belfast</td></tr>
<tr><td colspan="9">Completed 20.7.1864, employed on Belfast–Hamburg route. Off Lloyd's Register by 1875.</td></tr>
<tr><td>28</td><td>29</td><td>Star of Albion</td><td>20.7.1864</td><td>999</td><td>Sailing Vessel (Ship)</td><td>Iron Hulled 214.0/32.1/21.5</td><td>N/A</td><td>J.P. Corry & Co. Belfast</td></tr>
<tr><td colspan="9">Completed July 1864, for India trade; best passage 1876: 83 days. In September 1886 arrived in Hooghli Delta with cargo of coal and, due to navigational error, ran aground and wrecked. No lives lost.</td></tr>
<tr><td>29</td><td>30</td><td>Dharwar</td><td>3.9.1864</td><td>1,456</td><td>Sailing Vessel (Ship)</td><td>Iron Hulled 226.2/37.2/23.3</td><td>N/A</td><td>Iron Ship Co. Ltd London</td></tr>
<tr><td colspan="9">Completed September 1864, for India trade. In 1868 to John Willis & Sons, London, fitted for passenger transport and employed in Australian emigrant trade. In 1898 to Swedish owners, Hagstrom & Lundvall. Broken up Italy (Genoa) 1909.</td></tr>
<tr><td>30</td><td>31</td><td>Douro</td><td>November 1864</td><td>528</td><td>Cargo Ship</td><td>Ir/Sc/St 198.4/27.1/15.6</td><td>168 nhp CI (2Cy) Engines J. Jack & Co. Liverepool</td><td>J. Bibby Sons & Co. Liverpool</td></tr>
<tr><td colspan="9">Completed 21.11.1864 for South African routes. In 1873 to Leyland & Co. with rest of Bibby fleet and in 1875 renamed Alcira. Subsequently to Italian owners, O. Conte, Genoa, renamed Camilla C and later Camilla. Passed to P. Milesi, Genoa, in 1894. In 1894 to Greek owners, A.A. Vagliano, Argostoli, renamed Cephalonia. By end of century owned by A.I. Diakakis, Argostoli. In 1913 to Cia de Nav. A Vapeur 'Ermopolis', Syras, renamed Nilos. In 1914 was requisitioned by Italian government for use by the railways as collier. Returned to commercial ownership after war, N.J. Eustathiadis, Piraeus; broken up Greece 1927.</td></tr>
</table>

<table>
<tr><th>Ship</th><th>Yard No</th><th>Name</th><th>Date Launched</th><th>Displacement Tons</th><th>Type</th><th>Construction and Dimensions</th><th>Horse Power/ Engines</th><th>Owners</th></tr>
<tr><td>31</td><td>32</td><td>British Peer</td><td>31.1.1865</td><td>1,478</td><td>Sailing Vessel (Ship)</td><td>Iron Hulled 218.0/36.2/22.9</td><td>N/A</td><td>British Shipowners Ltd Liverpool</td></tr>
<tr><td colspan="9">Completed February 1865, employed on Australian routes. In 1883 to Nourse Line and subsequently involved in indentured labourer trade. In December 1896 struck reef in Saldanha Bay, South Africa, and wrecked. Only four survivors from the crew of 22 (seven Britons, seven Swedes, three Norwegians, three Germans and two Finns).</td></tr>
<tr><td>32</td><td>33</td><td>Sesostris</td><td>27.5.1865</td><td>2,053</td><td>Cargo Ship</td><td>Ir/Sc/St 322.8/34.5/25.5</td><td>230 nhp CI (2Cy) Engines N.E. Marine Co. Ltd Sunderland</td><td>James Moss & Co. Liverpool</td></tr>
<tr><td colspan="9">In c. 1892 owned by T. Ward. Off Lloyd's Register by 1896.</td></tr>
<tr><td>33</td><td>34</td><td>Un-named</td><td>1865</td><td></td><td>Barge</td><td></td><td></td><td>James Moss & Co. Liverpool</td></tr>
<tr><td>34</td><td>35</td><td>Un-named</td><td>1865</td><td></td><td>Barge</td><td></td><td></td><td>James Moss & Co. Liverpool</td></tr>
<tr><td>35</td><td>36</td><td>Un-named</td><td>8.8.1865</td><td></td><td>Shearsfloat</td><td></td><td></td><td>Dublin Corporation</td></tr>
<tr><td>36</td><td>37</td><td>Pilot</td><td>1865</td><td>34</td><td>Sailing Vessel (Schooner)</td><td></td><td></td><td></td></tr>
<tr><td>37</td><td>38</td><td>Fairy Queen</td><td>1865</td><td>149</td><td>Ferry</td><td>Ir/Pd/St 135.0/20.1/7.7</td><td>70 nhp SA (2Cy) Engines Blackwood & Gordon</td><td>Rock Ferry Co. Gibraltar</td></tr>
<tr><td colspan="9">This vessel and her sister Gypsy Queen were built on same slip and launched 15 minutes apart. These small but powerful vessels were for use between Gibraltar and Tangier. Like some contemporary American Civil War gunboats, they were built on the 'double-ender' system with a rudder at each end, allowing them to sail in either direction.
By 1882 owned by T.W. Thompson and probably broken up at end of 1890s.</td></tr>
<tr><td>38</td><td>39</td><td>Gypsy Queen</td><td>1865</td><td>149</td><td>Ferry</td><td>Ir/Pd/St 135.0/20.1/7.7</td><td>70 nhp SA (2Cy) Engines Blackwood & Gordon</td><td>Rock Ferry Co. Gibraltar</td></tr>
<tr><td colspan="9">Sister ship of Fairy Queen. By 1881 owned by T.W. Thompson, broken up in mid-1880s.</td></tr>
<tr><td>39</td><td>40</td><td>Boyne</td><td>18.9.1865</td><td>617</td><td>Sailing Vessel (Barque)</td><td>Iron Hulled 185.7/28.1/16.9</td><td>N/A</td><td>W.H. Tindall Scarborough</td></tr>
<tr><td colspan="9">Completed September 1865, for the Ceylon trade. The ship appears to have had a short life, off Lloyd's Register by 1875.</td></tr>
<tr><td>40</td><td>41</td><td>Annie Sharp</td><td>November 1865</td><td>584</td><td>Sailing Vessel (Barque)</td><td>Iron Hulled 166.0/26.5/18.3</td><td>N/A</td><td>R.G. Sharp Liverpool</td></tr>
<tr><td colspan="9">For the South American trade. This ship had a short life; off Lloyd's Register by 1870.</td></tr>
<tr><td>41</td><td>42</td><td>Duddon</td><td>1865</td><td>106</td><td>Paddle Tug</td><td>Ir/Pd/St 94.4/18.1/9.3</td><td>50 nhp CO (2Cy) Engines G.K. Stothert & Co. Bristol</td><td>New Steam Navigation Co.</td></tr>
<tr><td colspan="9">By c. 1881 owned by N. Caine, Liverpool. In 1885 owned by Hodbarrow Mining Co. (W.J. Barret). By 1891 owned by G. Nelson & Sons, Whitehaven, passing back to W.J. Barret, Liverpool, c. 1898. Broken up early in the twentieth century.</td></tr>
<tr><td>42</td><td>43</td><td>Guarani</td><td>1865</td><td>320</td><td>Cargo Ship</td><td>?</td><td>?</td><td>J. Dalglish Newcastle</td></tr>
<tr><td>43</td><td>44</td><td>Broughton</td><td>25.1.1868</td><td>602</td><td>Sailing Vessel (Barque)</td><td>Iron Hulled 166.0/26.5/18.3</td><td>N/A</td><td>Ismay, Imrie & Co. Liverpool</td></tr>
<tr><td colspan="9">Completed January 1868. The original owners went bankrupt, leaving it on builders' hands, which almost bankrupted them. Wolff's uncle Gustav Schwabe introduced them to Thomas Ismay who had recently acquired the White Star Line and desperately needed new tonnage to maintain service to Australia. He brought the vessel, thus beginning a relationship that would see Harland's building some of the world's greatest ships for White Star. This ship stayed with White Star fleet for eight years before passing to William Thomas & Co., Swansea. Sank 1902 on voyage Hamburg–Glasgow.</td></tr>
<tr><td>44</td><td>45</td><td>Candahar</td><td>1.5.1866</td><td>1,418</td><td>Sailing Vessel (Ship)</td><td>Iron Hulled 239.4/36.0/23.6</td><td>N/A</td><td>T.&J. Brocklebank Liverpool</td></tr>
<tr><td colspan="9">Completed May 1866, for Indian trade. In 1890 to S. Goldberg, Swansea, and in 1897 to Norwegian owners, Akties 'Almedia'. In 1902 to Fordinand Melsom. Wrecked Novmea, New Caledonia, 1905.</td></tr>
</table>

<table>
<tr><th>Ship</th><th>Yard No</th><th>Name</th><th>Date Launched</th><th>Displacement Tons</th><th>Type</th><th>Construction and Dimensions</th><th>Horse Power/ Engines</th><th>Owners</th></tr>
<tr><td>45</td><td>46</td><td>Tenasserim</td><td>30.8.1866</td><td>1,418</td><td>Sailing Vessel (Ship)</td><td>Iron Hulled
239.4/36.0/23.6</td><td>N/A</td><td>T.&J. Brocklebank
Liverpool</td></tr>
<tr><td colspan="9">Completed September 1866, sister ship of Candahar. In 1890 to Gracie, Beazley & Co., Liverpool, and later to Australian Shipping Co., Liverpool. Ultimately to Norwegian owners. Wrecked Table Bay, South Africa, May 1902.</td></tr>
<tr><td>46</td><td>47</td><td>Istrian</td><td>9.3.1867</td><td>2,930</td><td>Cargo Ship</td><td>Ir/Sc/St
390.0/37.2/29.3</td><td>350 nhp
CI (2Cy)
Engines
J. Jack & Co.
Liverpool</td><td>J. Bibby Sons & Co.
Liverpool</td></tr>
<tr><td colspan="9">Completed 21.4.1867. In 1873 to Leyland & Co. fitted with new engines in 1877 by G. Forrester & Co., Liverpool. In 1889 to J. Glynn & Son, Liverpool. In 1894 to Furness Withy & Co. but saw little use before broken up Garston (UK) 1895.</td></tr>
<tr><td>47</td><td>48</td><td>Iberian</td><td>4.6.1867</td><td>2,930</td><td>Cargo Ship</td><td>Ir/Sc/St
390.0/37.2/29.3</td><td>350 nhp
CI (2Cy)
Engines
J. Jack & Co.
Liverpool</td><td>J. Bibby Sons & Co.
Liverpool</td></tr>
<tr><td colspan="9">Completed July 1867, sister ship of Istrian. In 1873 to Leyland & Co., fitted with new engines by Forrester in 1878. Wrecked south coast of Ireland, November 1885. No lives lost.</td></tr>
<tr><td>48</td><td>49</td><td>Illyrian</td><td>31.8.1867</td><td>2,931</td><td>Cargo Ship</td><td>Ir/Sc/St
390.0/37.2/29.3</td><td>350 nhp
CI (2Cy)
Engines
J. Jack & Co.
Liverpool</td><td>J. Bibby Sons & Co.
Liverpool</td></tr>
<tr><td colspan="9">Completed 25.9.1867, sister ship of Istrian. In 1873 to Leyland & Co., fitted with new engines by Forrester in 1878. Wrecked in fog Cape Clear, Ireland, May 1884. No lives lost.</td></tr>
<tr><td>49</td><td>50</td><td>Un-named</td><td>14.2.1867</td><td></td><td>Dock Caisson</td><td></td><td></td><td>Belfast Harbour Commissioners</td></tr>
<tr><td colspan="9">Completed 5.7.1867, for use on the Hamilton Graving Dock in Abercorn Basin. This caisson is still extant and is the oldest surviving Belfast-built vessel.</td></tr>
<tr><td>50</td><td>51</td><td>Black Diamond</td><td>?.?.1867</td><td>105</td><td>Cargo</td><td>Ir/Sc/St</td><td>?</td><td>P. Evans & Co.
Gloucester?</td></tr>
<tr><td>51</td><td>52</td><td>Corsanegetto</td><td>?.?.1867</td><td>183</td><td>Cargo</td><td>Ir/Sc/St</td><td>?</td><td>M.A. Corsanego</td></tr>
<tr><td colspan="9">Laid down as Camel.</td></tr>
<tr><td>52</td><td>53</td><td>HMS Lynx</td><td>25.4.1868</td><td>603</td><td>Gunboat</td><td>Com/Sc/St</td><td>650 ihp
HDAR</td><td>Admiralty</td></tr>
<tr><td colspan="9">Completed 12.6.1868. A Beacon-class gun vessel intended for service on overseas stations where docking and repair facilities were limited, hence a wooden hull and full sailing rig. H&W were keen to get Admiralty work as it was hoped that this would result in profitable orders from foreign governments. However, as this ship was built on a fixed-price basis the company lost £5,000 on the contract which almost bankrupted them. Armed with a 7in MLR, a 64pdr MLR and two 20 pdr BL. Discarded 1888.</td></tr>
<tr><td>53</td><td>54</td><td>Hebe</td><td>1868</td><td>157</td><td>Lighter</td><td></td><td>N/A</td><td>W.&J. Philips</td></tr>
<tr><td>54</td><td>55</td><td>Star of Persia</td><td>23.6.1868</td><td>1,289</td><td>Sailing Vessel (Ship)</td><td>Iron Hulled
227.0/35.0/22.2</td><td>N/A</td><td>J.P. Corry & Co
Belfast.</td></tr>
<tr><td colspan="9">Completed June 1868, for London–Calcutta trade; normally carried cargoes of coal outbound and jute back; best time 79 days in 1876. In 1893 to German owners, C.M. Matzen, renamed Edith; employed on Zanzibar–South America–Portland route. In 1903 sprang a leak on voyage from Puget Sound to South Australia and lost after grounded in Solomon Islands. No lives lost.</td></tr>
<tr><td>55</td><td>56</td><td>Woodlawn</td><td>1868</td><td>63</td><td>Sailing Vessel (Schooner)</td><td>Iron Hulled</td><td>N/A</td><td>S. Morland
Belfast</td></tr>
<tr><td colspan="9">Completed 1868. Short and uneventful career; hulk at Bangor Co. Down by 1875.</td></tr>
<tr><td>56</td><td>57</td><td>Star of Greece</td><td>19.9.1868</td><td>1,288</td><td>Sailing Vessel (Ship)</td><td>Iron Hulled
227.0/35.0/22.2</td><td>N/A</td><td>J.P. Corry & Co.
Belfast</td></tr>
<tr><td colspan="9">Completed September 1868, sister ship of Star of Persia. A remarkably fast ship that regularly made the voyage from London to Calcutta via the Cape in 79 days; set record for round trip to Calcutta of 5 months 27 days (80 days out, 83 days back with 10 in Calcutta). On 27 August 1883 showered with dust and debris from explosion of Krakatoa and in 1885; arrived in Calcutta with a cargo of coal smouldering in holds. In 1888 switched to Australia route and in July, homeward bound with cargo of wheat, was wrecked on reef outside Port Willunga, South Australia. Seventeen lives lost and ten saved.</td></tr>
<tr><td>57</td><td>58</td><td>Juliet</td><td>1.1.1869</td><td>1,301</td><td>Sailing Vessel (Ship)</td><td>Iron Hulled
214.0/34.0/22.5</td><td>N/A</td><td>C.T. Bowring & Co.
Liverpool</td></tr>
<tr><td colspan="9">Completed January 1869, for Australian trade. This ship had a very short life; off Lloyd's Register by 1879.</td></tr>
</table>

Ship	Yard No	Name	Date Launched	Displacement Tons	Type	Construction and Dimensions	Horse Power/ Engines	Owners
58	59	*Elaine*	16.2.1869	544	Cargo	Ir/Sc/St 196.7/24.0/15.3	80 nhp CI (2Cy) **Engines** V.&D. Coats Belfast	F. Lervick & Co. Newport
Completed 31.5.1869. In *c.* 1875 to Yeves & Co., London, renamed *Yeves.* Off *Lloyd's Register* by 1880.								
59	60	*Lady Cairns*	24.4.1869	1,311	Sailing Vessel (Ship)	Iron Hulled 214.0/34.0/22.5	N/A	Harland & Wolff Belfast
Completed April 1869. Built on speculation at cost of £17,000, when failed to find buyer H&W decided to operate ship themselves. Subsequently owned by British Shipowners, Liverpool, until 1881, then to Martin, Dublin. In March 1904 while on voyage to New Zealand was in collision with German barque *Mona* in fog and sank. All 22 crew lost their lives.								
60	61	Un-named	13.5.1869	60	Dredger			Dublin Harbour Board
61	62	Un-named	13.5.1869	60	Dredger			Dublin Harbour Board
62	63	Un-named	13.5.1869	60	Dredger			Dublin Harbour Board
63	64	Un-named	17.5.1869	60	Dredger			Dublin Harbour Board
64	65	Un-named	17.5.1869	60	Dredger			Dublin Harbour Board
65	66	Un-named	17.5.1869	60	Dredger			Dublin Harbour Board
66	67	*Carry*	31.3.1869	81	Lighter			William Gossage & Sons
67	68	*Bavarian*	7.10.1869	3,111	Cargo Ship	Ir/Sc/St 400.0/37.2/28.5	350 nhp CI (4Cy) **Engines** J. Jack & Co. Liverpool	J. Bibby Sons & Co. Liverpool
Completed 5.11.1869, improved *Istrian* for Black Sea and Levant routes. Acquired by Leyland & Co. in 1873. fitted with new engines in 1877 and then employed on Liverpool–Boston route. In 1889 to J. Glynn & Sons, Liverpool. In 1894 was acquired by Furness, Withy & Co. but saw little use before broken up, Preston (UK) 1895.								
68	69	*Historian*	5.1.1870	1,830	Cargo Ship	Ir/Sc/St 323.5/33.4/24.0	200 nhp CI (2Cy) **Engines** J. Jack & Co. Liverpool	T.&J. Harrison Liverpool
Completed 9.3.1870. To Christopher Furness in 1891, passed to Portuguese owners, Benchimol & Sobrinho, renamed *Cidade Do Porto* in 1892. By 1895 in Brazilian ownership, Cruzerio do Sul, renamed *Douro.* Foundered off Ushant December 1896.								
69	70	*Bulgarian*	17.2.1870	3,112	Cargo Ship	Ir/Sc/St 400.0/37.2/28.5	350 nhp CI (2Cy) **Engines** J. Jack & Co. Liverpool	J. Bibby Sons & Co. Liverpool
Completed 20.3.1870, sister ship of *Bavarian.* Acquired by Leyland & Co. in 1873; fitted with new engines in 1877. In 1894 to Furness, Withy & Co., but like sister saw little use, broken up, New Ferry, Mersey, 1895.								
70	71	*Bohemian*	16.4.1870	3,113	Cargo Ship	Ir/Sc/St 400.0/37.2/28.4	350 nhp CI (2Cy) **Engines** J. Jack & Co. Liverpool	J. Bibby Sons & Co. Liverpool
Completed 29.5.1870, sister ship of *Bavarian.* Acquired by Leyland & Co. in 1873 and fitted with new engines in 1877. In February 1881 wrecked near Crookhaven, Ireland. Thirty-three lives lost out of 57 on board.								
71	72	Un-named	1870		Floating Dock			Lord Erne
72	73	*Oceanic*	27.8.1870	3,808	Passenger Ship	Ir/Sc/St 420.0/40.9/23.4	600 nhp 1,990 ihp CI (4Cy) **Engines** Maudsley & Field London	Oceanic Steam Navigation Co. Liverpool
Completed 24.2.1871. Built at a cost of £120,000. Often referred to as the 'Mother of Modern Liners' being the first vessel to have promenade decks and baths with running water for passengers. This vessel and her sisters had accommodation for 160 first-class passengers and 1,000 in steerage.								

Ship	Yard No	Name	Date Launched	Displacement Tons	Type	Construction and Dimensions	Horse Power/ Engines	Owners
After a few voyages returned to builders for improvements, which included reducing masts, adding two more boilers and fitting a turtle-back to bow. In 1875 as more modern liners joined the fleet and after 33 round trips, taken off prestigious New York route and chartered to Occidental & Oriental Steamship Co., employed on San Francisco–Hong Kong–Yokohama route. Following refit in 1879 returned to this service in 1880. On 17 May 1895 arrived at H&W to be re-engined but survey revealed this was not viable. Sold, broken up Thames 1896.								
73	74	*Atlantic*	26.11.1870	3,708	Passenger Ship	Ir/Sc/St 420.0/40.9/23.4	600 nhp 1990 ihp CI (4Cy) **Engines** Maudsley & Field London	Oceanic Steam Navigation Co. Liverpool
Completed 3.6.1871, sister ship of *Oceanic*. On 20 March 1873 sailed from Liverpool on 19th, transatlantic voyage with 789 passengers and 142 crew. Ran into heavy gales on the 31st and in early hours 1 April ran aground on Marr's Rock, off Meagher's Island near Halifax; 585 of 931 persons on board drowned.								
74	75	*Baltic*	8.3.1871	3,708	Passenger Ship	Ir/Sc/St 420.0/40.0/23.4	600 nhp 1,990 ihp CI (4Cy) **Engines** Maudsley & Field London	Oceanic Steam Navigation Co. Liverpool
Completed 2.9.1871, sister ship of *Oceanic* originally to have been *Pacific* but renamed after press reports of loss of previous ship of that name. In January 1873 gained the Blue Riband for crossing the Atlantic in 7 days, 20 hours and 9 mins at an average speed of just over 15 knots. In 1883 chartered to Inman Line for 14 round voyages and again in 1885 for ten trips. By June 1888 laid up at Birkenhead before sold, for £32,000, to Dutch owners, Holland America Line, renamed *Veendam*. Fitted with new engines in 1890. Sunk February 1898 following collision with submerged wreck. No lives lost.								
75	76	*Republic*	4.7.1871	3,708	Passenger Ship	Ir/Sc/St 420.0/40.9/23.4	600 nhp 1,990 ihp CI (4Cy) **Engines** G. Forrester & Co. Liverpool	Oceanic Steam Navigation Co. Liverpool
Completed 21.1.1872, last of Oceanic-type liners. Like sisters, initially employed on Liverpool–New York route but within a year moved to South American services. From 1875 relegated to reserve ship and partially rebuilt in 1888. In 1889 sold, for £35,000, to Dutch owners, Holland America Line, renamed *Maasdam*. Fitted with new engines in 1890. In 1902 to Italian owners, 'La Veloce' Nav. Italiana, renamed *Vittoria* and later *Citta di Napoli*, employed carrying emigrants to United States. Broken up Italy (Genoa) 1909.								
76	77	*Adriatic*	17.10.1871	3,868	Passenger Ship	Ir/Sc/St 437.2/40.9/31.0	600 nhp CI (4Cy) **Engines** Maudsley & Field London	Oceanic Stream Navigation Co. Liverpool
Completed 31.3.1872, slightly enlarged near sister of *Oceanic*. Designed to carry 166 first-class passengers and 1,000 in steerage. First ship to be fitted with gas lighting. In 1874 involved in a collision with Cunard's *Parthia*. The next year ran down and sank the American schooner *Columbus* off New York in March and in December hit and sank Schooner *Harvest Queen* in Saint George's Channel. In July 1878 collided with the brigantine *G.A. Pike* causing five deaths. In 1897 laid up at Birkenhead before broken up Preston (UK) 1899.								
77	78	*Camel*	7.9.1870	269	Cargo Ship	Ir/Sc/St 175.5/21.9/12.2	70 nhp CI (2Cy) **Engines** Greenock Foundry Co.	Harland & Wolff Belfast
Completed 17.9.1870. Designed to transport iron/steel plate and ships machinery from suppliers in Scotland and Northern England. Broken up 1899.								
78	79	*Celtic*	8.6.1872	3,867	Passenger Ship	Ir/Sc/St 437.2/40.9/23.4	600 nhp CI (4Cy) **Engines** G. Forrester & Co. Liverpool	Oceanic Steam Navigation Co. Liverpool
Completed 17.10.1872, sister ship of *Adriatic*, laid down as *Artic* but completed under this name. A somewhat unlucky ship in 1874 had to be towed into Queenstown by *Gaelic* after losing two blades from propeller. In 1883 had to be towed into Liverpool by *Britannic* when propeller shaft snapped. In 1887 collided with *Britannic* in thick fog causing serious damage to both vessels. Laid up 1892 and in 1893 to Danish owners, Thingvalla Line, renamed *Amerika*, employed carrying emigrants to United States. Proved to be too large for trade and sold, broken up France (Brest) 1898.								

<table>
<tr><th>Ship</th><th>Yard No</th><th>Name</th><th>Date Launched</th><th>Displacement Tons</th><th>Type</th><th>Construction and Dimensions</th><th>Horse Power/ Engines</th><th>Owners</th></tr>
<tr><td>79</td><td>80</td><td>Gaelic</td><td>21.9.1872</td><td>2,651</td><td>Cargo Ship</td><td>Ir/Sc/St
370.0/36.3/27.9</td><td>300 nhp
CI (2Cy)
Engines
J. Jack, Rollo & Co. Liverpool</td><td>Oceanic Steam Navigation Co. Liverpool</td></tr>
<tr><td colspan="9">Completed 7.1.1873. Originally laid down for Bibby Line but acquired on stocks by White Star for South American services. Only served on these routes briefly before transferring to Liverpool–New York service. In 1875 chartered to Occidental & Oriental Steamship Co., employed on San Francisco–Japan–Hong Kong route. In 1883 sold, for £30,000, to Spanish owners, Cia de Nav 'La Flecha', renamed Hugo. In September 1896 stranded on Netherlands coast, constructive loss. The wreck refloated and broken up Holland (Amersterdam).</td></tr>
<tr><td>80</td><td>81</td><td>Belgic</td><td>17.1.1873</td><td>2,651</td><td>Cargo Ship</td><td>Ir/Sc/St
370.0/36.3/20.4</td><td>350 nhp
CI (2Cy)
Engines
J. Jack, Rollo & Co.</td><td>Oceanic Steam Navigation Co. Liverpool</td></tr>
<tr><td colspan="9">Completed 29.3.1873, near sister of Gaelic. Initially on South American service but, transferred to New York route in 1874. Subsequently chartered to O.&O. SS Co. for same service as sister. In 1883 sold, for £30,000, to Spanish owners, Cia de Nav 'La Flecha' and renamed Goefredo. In January 1884 damaged by grounding off Santiago de Cuba and sent to Liverpool for repairs. In February at beginning of voyage back to Cuba wrecked on Burbo Bank, River Mersey. No lives lost.</td></tr>
<tr><td>81</td><td>82</td><td>Star of Germany</td><td>11.3.1872</td><td>1,337</td><td>Sailing Vessel (Ship)</td><td>Iron Hulled
232.0/35.0/22.0</td><td>N/A</td><td>J.P. Corry & Co. Belfast</td></tr>
<tr><td colspan="9">Completed 20.5.1872, for Indian trade. In 1897 to Foley, Aikman & Co. in same trade. In 1904 was to Star of Germany Shipping Co., Belfast. In 1906 to Norwegian owners, Acties 'Grid', renamed Grid. In October 1906 lost masts in hurricane off Barbados and condemned, subsequently employed as harbour hulk. Survived into 1920s but by then in very poor condition.</td></tr>
<tr><td>82</td><td>83</td><td>Britannic</td><td>3.2.1874</td><td>5,004</td><td>Passenger Ship</td><td>Ir/Sc/St
455.0/45.2/33.7</td><td>760 nhp
4,900 ihp
CI (4Cy)
Engines
Maudsley Sons & Field London</td><td>Oceanic Steam Navigation Co. Liverpool</td></tr>
<tr><td colspan="9">Completed 6.6.1874. Laid down as Hellenic but completed with this name. Designed to compete with new liners being employed by other shipping lines on New York route and costing £200,000. As with earlier ships there were two classes of passenger carried: 220 first class and 1,500 steerage. On maiden voyage broke both eastward and westward records with average speed of 15.7 knots. In 1881 sank sailing ship Julia in collision off Belfast and in July was stranded in fog at Kinmore near Wexford, taken to Liverpool for repairs. In May 1887 involved in a collision with the Celtic in which three passengers were killed and two injured, had to return to New York for repairs. Speed seemed to increase with age; made fastest crossing of Atlantic in 1890: 7 days, 6 hours and 55 minutes, with an average speed of 16.1 knots. In October 1899 was requisitioned as a troopship for use in the Boer War and was temporarily renamed HM Transport No.62. As which represented Britain at the review in Sydney Harbour to mark inauguration of the Commonwealth of Australia. In October 1902 sent to Belfast to have new engines installed but survey report suggested this was not practical. In 1903 sold for £11,500, broken up Germany (Hamburg).</td></tr>
<tr><td>83</td><td>84</td><td>Ferry No.1</td><td>27.6.1872</td><td>9</td><td>River Ferry</td><td>Ir/Sc/St
44.0/13.0/?</td><td></td><td>Belfast Harbour Commissioners</td></tr>
<tr><td colspan="9">Completed 1.10.1872. Built to operate a cross-river service on the Lagan between the Custom House and Queen's Quay. This vessel was powered by two single-cylinder, directly opposed piston units fed by a single boiler and used a simple clutch system to drive one of two propellers at either end of the hull, each fitted with its own rudder. This service ceased in 1909 and this vessel and her slightly larger Napier-built companion were sold for scrap in 1912.</td></tr>
<tr><td>84</td><td>85</td><td>Germanic</td><td>15.7.1874</td><td>5,008</td><td>Passenger Ship</td><td>Ir/Sc/St
455.0/45.2/33.7</td><td>760 hp
4,900 ihp
CI (4Cy)
Engines
Maudsley Sons & Field London</td><td>Oceanic Steam Navigation Co. Liverpool</td></tr>
<tr><td colspan="9">Completed 24.4.1875, sister ship of Britannic. Triple-expansion engines and new boilers fitted in 1895. In February 1899 almost capsized while coaling in New York Harbour and it was suggested that this now elderly vessel be scrapped, but refloated and sent to Belfast for repairs that lasted four months. In September 1903 made last voyage for White Star and laid up before transferred to International Mercantile Marine Co. in 1904. Allocated initially to the American Line, but later transferred to Dominion Line for use in emigrant trade. In 1905 renamed Ottawa deployed on Canada routes before laid up at end of 1909. In 1910 to Turkish government, renamed Gul Djemal and employed as government transport. Engaged in trooping duties in Yeman in 1911 before being transferred to Black Sea in 1912. In 1915 was engaged in transporting Turkish reinforcements to Gallipoli Peninsula when torpedoed, 3 May, by British submarine E-14 in Sea of Marmara and beached. Subsequently recovered and used in November 1918 to repatriate German troops from Turkey via Dover. By 1920 was being operated by the Ottoman-America Line on emigrant service Istanbul–New York. By 1928, still government owned, known as the Gulcemal. By 1949 was a store ship (hulk) at Istanbul. After briefly being used as a floating hotel was broken up Messina (Turkey) 1950.</td></tr>
</table>

Ship	Yard No	Name	Date Launched	Displacement Tons	Type	Construction and Dimensions	Horse Power/ Engines	Owners
85	86	*Star of Bengal*	3.1.1874	1,870	Sailing Vessel (Ship)	Iron Hulled 262.8/40.2/23.5	N/A	J.P. Corry & Co. Belfast
Completed 7.3.1874. In 1898 to American owners, J.J. Smith, San Francisco. In 1903, to E.B. Smith, San Francisco, reduced to barque. Subsequently to Alaska Packers Association, San Francisco, converted into floating fish-canning factory. In September 1908 left Fort Wrangel, Alaska, under tow, with 50,000 cases of salmon, 36 crew and 110 cannery workers on board, driven ashore on Coronation Island; 110 lives lost.								
86	87	*Belfast*	15.8.1874	1,957	Sailing Vessel (Ship)	Iron Hulled 260.5/40.2/24.2	N/A	T.&J. Brocklebank Liverpool
Completed 26.10.1874. In 1900 to Shaw Savill & Albion, reduced to barque. Broken up 1925.								
87	88	*Star of Russia*	12.12.1874	1,981	Sailing Vessel (Ship)	Iron Hulled 275.5/40.6/24.2	N/A	J.P. Corry & Co. Belfast
Completed 12.2.1875, near sister of *Star of Bengal.* Considered one of smartest vessels of time; fastest time to Calcutta was 74 days (1886) and on maiden voyage reached Melbourne in 81 days. In 1898 to Shaw Savill and Albion, then to American owners J.J. More, San Francisco, briefly sailing under Hawaiian flag before island was annexed by United States. By 1901 owned by Alaska Packers Association, San Francisco. Made final voyage in 1926 then a floating warehouse in Samoa and renamed *La Perouse*; later moved to Noumea and used as a coal hulk. Finally at Port Vila Harbour, Vanuatu, again used as warehouse. Scuttled 1931.								
88	89	*Majestic*	5.5.1875	1,974	Sailing Vessel (Ship)	Iron Hulled 273.4/40.2/24.2	N/A	T.&J. Brocklebank Liverpool
Completed 24.6.1875, a lengthened half sister of *Belfast.* To Chilean government in 1899; reduced to hulk 1901.								
89	90	*Aglaia*	10.3.1875	821	Sailing Vessel (Barque)	Iron Hulled 187.8/32.0/19.7	N/A	Workman Brothers Belfast
Completed 13.4. 1875. Wrecked English Bank, River Plate, August 1889.								
90	91	*East Croft*	23.6.1875	1,367	Sailing Vessel (Ship)	Iron Hulled 228.0/35.5/22.3	N/A	J. Gambles Workington
Completed 10.8.1875. Broken up 1910.								
91	92	*Connaught Ranger*	17.8.1875	1,200	Sailing Vessel (Ship)	Iron Hulled 229.7/34.6/21.3	N/A	J.G. McCormick Dublin
Completed 23.10.1875. In 1896 to Italian owners, G.B. Schiaffiono, renamed *Stella Della Mare.* Sunk by submarine gunfire (*U-38*) NW of Majorca when inbound Baltimore–Genoa August 1916. No lives lost.								
92	93	*Millie*	July 1875	107	River Steamer Cargo	Ir/Sc/St 76.3/18.8/9.5	24 nhp CI (2Cy) (H&W)	William Gossage & Sons Widnes
Completed 27.7.1875. This company were large-scale chemical and soap manufacturers and exporters. In 1881 listed as owned by T.S. Timmis, Liverpool, but by 1886 again owned by Gossage & Sons. This small vessel spent working life on the Mersey bringing fuel and raw materials to the plant and shipping finished products to the docks; in 1889 Lloyd's noted that was for 'river use'. Broken up early twentieth century?								
93	94	*Katie*	13.8.1875	107	River Steamer Cargo	Ir/Sc/St 76.2/18.8/9.5	20 nhp CI (2Cy) (H&W)	William Gossage & Sons Widnes
Completed August 1875, sister ship of *Millie.* Like her sister, in 1881 listed as owned by T.S. Timmis, Liverpool, but the next year was owned by Prices Pattent Candle Co., London. Broken up early twentieth century?								
94	95	*Fiji*	21.9.1875	1,436	Sailing Vessel (Ship)	Iron Hulled 229.4/36.4/23.0	N/A	W.J. Myers Liverpool
Completed 29.10.1875. Wrecked near Warrnambool, Australia, September 1881.								
95	96	*Pizarro*	December 1875	1,439	Sailing Vessel (Ship)	Iron Hulled 233.0/36.3/22.8	N/A	W.J. Myers Liverpool
Completed 20.12.1875, slightly enlarged half sister of *Fiji.* Missing at sea, last seen off Gabo Island, Victoria, March 1884, on route Liverpool–Cookstown, Queensland, with cargo of railway equipment.								
96	97	Un-named	1875		Nile Barge			W. Henderson & Co.
97	98	Un-named	1875		Nile Barge			W. Henderson & Co.
98	99	Un-named	1875		Nile Barge			W. Henderson & Co.
99	100	*Princess Beatrice*	4.11.1875	556	Paddle Steamer	Ir/Pd/St 234.6/24.0/12.6	200 nhp DA (2Cy) **Engines** D. Rowan Glasgow	Larne & Stranraer Steam Packet Co.
Completed 4.2.1876. Spent career on Larne–Stranraer route. Broken up Dumbarton (UK) 1904.								

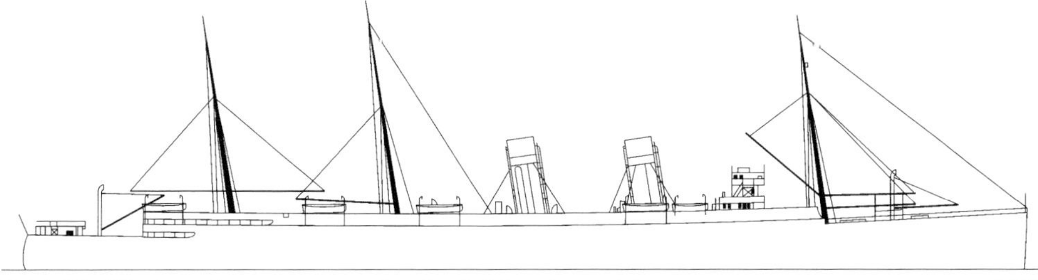

Belgic (H&W y/n 391) 1914 – as completed as freighter/troopship (DH)

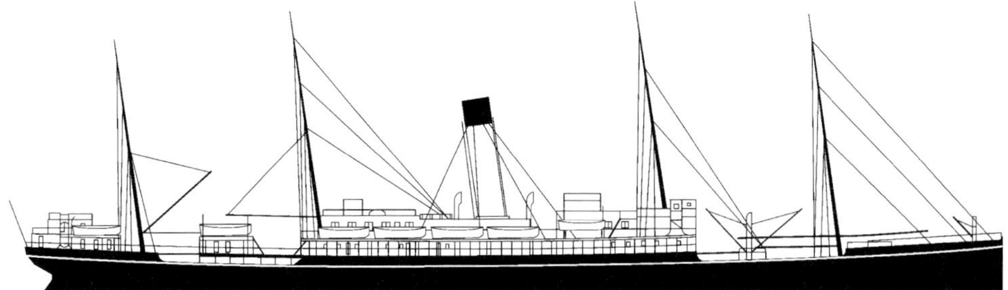

Leicestershire (H&W y/n 403) 1909 (DH)

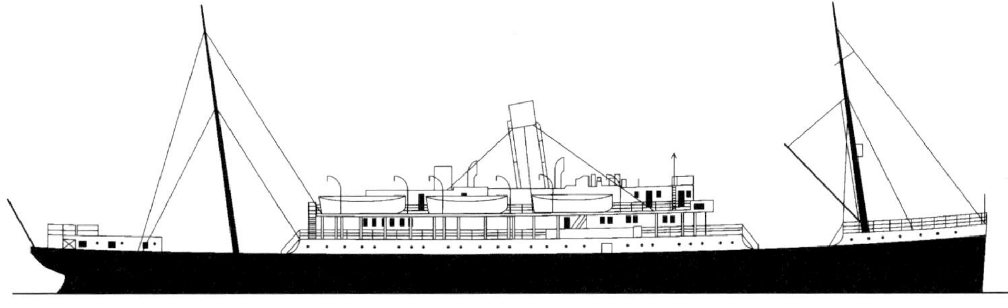

Berbice (H&W y/n 405) 1909 (DH)

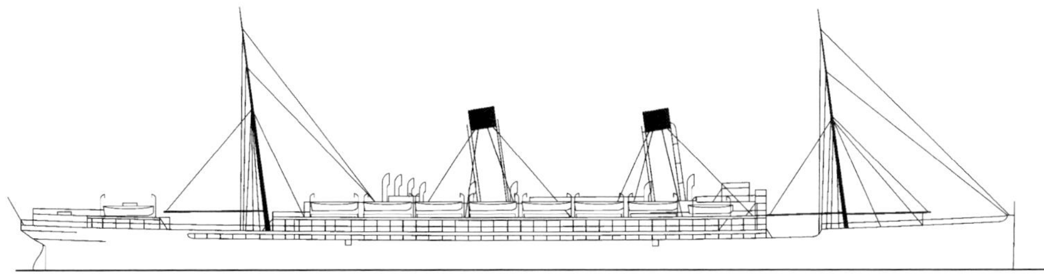

Edinburgh Castle (H&W y/n 410) 1910 (DH)

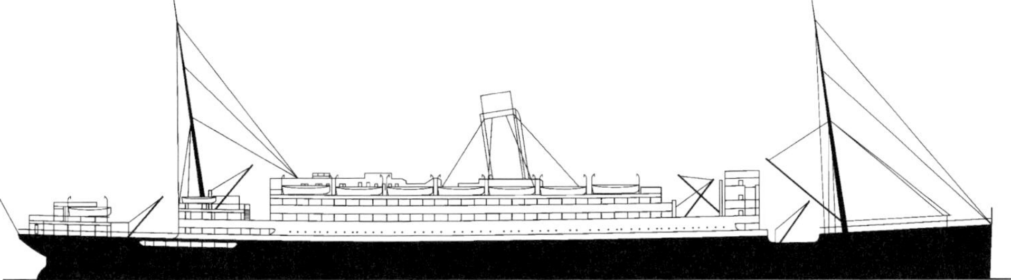

Arlanza (H&W y/n 415) 1911 (DH)

Ship	Yard No	Name	Date Launched	Displacement Tons	Type	Construction and Dimensions	Horse Power/ Engines	Owners
100	101	*Thursby*	19.2.1876	497	Cargo Ship	Ir/Sc/St 187.2/23.7/13.4	71 nhp CI (2Cy) **Engines** J. Rowan & Sons Belfast	W. Thursby Fleetwood
Completed 16.7.1876. Foundered 10 miles from Longships, August 1923.								
101	102	Un-named	4.12.1876		Hopper Barge			Cork Harbour Commissioners
Completed January 1876.								
102	103	*Lord Cairns*	12.5.1877	1,372	Sailing Vessel (Ship)	Iron Hulled 230.8/36.0/22.2	N/A	T. Dixon & Co. Belfast
In 1903 to Italian owners, L.M. Bertolotto, renamed *Spica*; fitted with a triple-expansion engine in 1920. Broken up 1923.								
103	104	Un-named	1875		Nile Barge			
104	105	*Mousmie*	1876	85	Yacht		N/A	
Off *Lloyd's Register* by 1890.								
105	106	*E.J. Harland*	20.4.1876	1,333	Sailing Vessel (Ship)	Iron Hulled 236.6/35.2/22.2	N/A	Samuel Lawther, Thomas Dixon Belfast
Completed 1.6.1876. Sunk following collision, North Atlantic, November 1879.								
106	107	*Thurland Castle*	22.7.1876	1,301	Sailing Vessel (Ship)	Iron Hulled 220.1/34.8/21.5	N/A	Lancaster Shipowners Co. Lancaster
Completed 20.9.1876. In 1895 to American owners, C.Brewer & Co., renamed *Iolani*. Sunk following collision off Astoria, Oregon, May 1900.								
107	108	*Steelfield*	2.12.1876	1,315	Sailing Vessel (Ship)	Iron Hulled 232.0/35.1/21.5	N/A	R.C. McNaughton & Co. Liverpool
Completed 1.1.1877. Missing at sea, last seen off southern Brazil, May 1889.								
108	109	*Gladys*	11.5.1876	52	Yacht (schooner)	Ir/Sc/Sch 80.6/15.7/9.1	33 nhp CI (2Cy) **Engines** Walker, Henderson & Co.	N. Mathieson
Completed May 1876.								
109	110	*Slieve More*	10.2.1877	1,749	Sailing Vessel (Ship)	Iron Hulled 257.1/38.3/23.1	N/A	W.P. Sinclair & Co. Liverpool
Completed 24.3.1877, for Indian Jute trade. Lost to fire, Indian Ocean, June 1885.								
110	111	*Slieve Bawn*	31.3.1877	1,749	Sailing Vessel (Ship)	Iron Hulled 257.1/38.2/23.1	N/A	W.P. Sinclair & Co. Liverpool
Completed 12.5.1877, sister ship of *Slieve More*. In 1894 to French owners, A.D. Bordes & Sons, renamed *Rancagua*. Wrecked off Brazil, November 1904.								
111	112	*Lagan*	12.2.1876	55	Barge	Ir/2Sc/St	6 nhp CI (2Cy) McIlwaine & Lewis, Belfast	A. Guinness & Sons Dublin
In 1873 Guinness constructed a jetty at their St James' Gate Brewery and began to acquire a fleet of steam barges, which would eventually number 13 vessels, to transport barrels of stout a mile down the river to the docks. Completed 22.2.1876, this vessel appears to have been the first to join the fleet. Served until after the Second World War when road transport replaced the barges. Subsequently to Scotts of Toomebridge and for many years hauled sand across Lough Neagh. In 1970s the hulk of this vessel was sunk to provide foundations for a new quay.								
112	113	*Star of Italy*	26.7.1877	1,644	Sailing Vessel (Ship)	Iron Hulled 257.1/38.0/22.8	N/A	J.P. Corry & Co. Belfast
Completed 18.10.1877. This vessel and sister were considered the fastest in Corry fleet; best time to Calcutta was 77 days. In 1892 carried a cargo of coal Cardiff–San Diego in 116 days. In 1898 to American owners, J.J. Moore, San Francisco, by 1903 owned by Pope and Talbot, San Francisco. The following year to Puget Sound Commercial Co., and subsequently, *c.* 1906, to Alaska Packers Association. In 1927 to Darling-Singer Shipping and Lighterage Co., San Francisco. By 1935 reduced to hulk at Buenaventura, Columbia; broken up 1938.								
113	114	*Star of France*	21.11.1877	1,663	Sailing Vessel (Ship)	Iron Hulled 258.0/38.0/22.8	N/A	J.P. Corry & Co. Belfast

Ship	Yard No	Name	Date Launched	Displacement Tons	Type	Construction and Dimensions	Horse Power/ Engines	Owners
Completed 5.1.1878, sister ship of *Star of Italy*. In 1899 to American owners, J.J. Moore, San Francisco, by 1903 was owned by Pope and Talbot, San Francisco. The following year to Puget Sound Commercial Co., and in 1905 to Alaska Packers Association.								
Used to train Sea Scouts in San Francisco in 1928 and in 1932 to Louis Rothernburg, Los Angeles. In 1933 sold to Capt. J.M. Andersen for use as fishing barge but remained moored off San Pedro breakwater until September 1940 when sank following collision with Japanese vessel.								
114	115	*Slieve Roe*	2.2.1878	1,749	Sailing Vessel (Ship)	Iron Hulled 257.1/38.3/23.1	N/A	W.P. Sinclair & Co. Liverpool
Completed 16.3.1878, sister ship of *Slieve More*. Broken up Plymouth (UK) 1910.								
115	116	*River Lagan*	30.6.1877	895	Sailing Vessel (Barque)	Iron Hulled 199.0/32.0/19.5	N/A	R. Neill & Sons Belfast
Completed 14.8.1877. Wrecked off Tierra del Fuego (New Year Islands), March 1885.								
116	117	HMS *Hecla*	7.3.1878	3,360	Torpedo Depot Ship	Ir/Sc/St 391.5/38.9/24.4	300 nhp 2,400 ihp CI (4Cy) **Engines** G. Forrester & Co. Liverpool	Admiralty
In 1870 Robert Whitehead demonstrated his 'locomotive' torpedo to the British Navy and the following year the Admiralty bought the manufacturing rights and began building experimental torpedo boats shortly afterwards. This vessel was an important element in the early development of the British Navy's torpedo force. Launched as merchantman *British Empire* but purchased by navy and completed under this name as a torpedo depot ship 24.8.1878. Capable of carrying a number of small second-class torpedo boats and acting as a 'mother ship' to larger torpedo boats, as well as meeting the torpedo and mine needs of a fleet. Initially seen as a front-line vessel and was given an armament comparable with contemporary sloops. Until replaced by the purpose-built *Vulcan* a decade later *Hecla* was largely employed with the Mediterranean fleet and many of the most important experiments in torpedo tactics were carried out under her control. As torpedo craft became larger it was no longer possible for a mother ship to carry them and *Hecla* became a more conventional depot ship, although armament was updated on a number of occasions. Rebuilt in 1912, served as destroyer depot ship until broken up Preston (UK) 1926.								
117	118	*British Empire*	18.5.1878	3,361	Passenger-Cargo	Ir/Sc/St 392.3/39.0/28.7	300 nhp CI (4Cy) **Engines** G. Forrester & Co. Liverpool	British Shipowners Ltd Liverpool
Completed 10.8.1878. In 1886 to Dutch owners, Holland-America Line, renamed *Rotterdam*; rebuilt to carry 70 first-class and 800 steerage passengers on Rotterdam–New York route. In 1895 renamed *Edam* to allow original name to be used for new liner but continued on the New York run. Broken up Italy (Genoa) 1899.								
118	119	*Faugh-a-Ballagh*	22.5.1878	500	Barge			Dublin Harbour Board
Completed 21.6.1878.								
119	120	*G.W. Wolff*	28.9.1878	1,663	Sailing Vessel (Ship)	Iron Hulled 257.1/38.3.23.1	N/A	S. Lawther Belfast
Completed 25.10.1878. Ordered as *Cyprus* and name changed to *Aerolite* on stocks but renamed again before launch. Wrecked Hummock Island, Bass Strait, August 1912. One life lost.								
120	121	*Nubia*	9.11.1878	1,958	Cargo Ship	Ir/Sc/St 321.0/34.7/22.8	188 nhp CI (2Cy) **Engines** G. Forrester & Co. Liverpool	Africa Steamship Co. London
Completed February 1879. In 1899 this company acquired by Elder Dempster, who transferred this vessel to their subsidiary the Mersey SS Co., renamed *Morocco*. Broken up Alloa (UK) 1908.								
121	122	*Shahjehan*	24.12.1878	1,650	Cargo Ship	Ir/Sc/St 305.8/31.7/22.2	190 nhp CI (2Cy) **Engines** D. Rowan Glasgow	Asiatic Steam Navigation Co. Liverpool
Completed 22.2.1879. This was a newly formed company that operated routes to Bay of Bengal. In 1907 to Li Shek Pang, renamed *Pheumpenh*. Broken up Hong Kong 1929.								
122	123	*Shahzada*	29.1.1879	1,677	Cargo Ship	Ir/Sc/St 305.8/31.7/22.2	190 nhp CI (2Cy) **Engines** D. Rowan Glasgow	Asiatic Steam Navigation Co. Liverpool

Ship	Yard No	Name	Date Launched	Displacement Tons	Type	Construction and Dimensions	Horse Power/ Engines	Owners
Completed April 1879, sister ship of *Shahjehan.* In 1907 to Hong Kong owners, Un Lai Chon (Far Eastern SS & Nav Co.), renamed *Enisey.* In 1917 to Japanese owners, K. Kusakabe, renamed *Bansei Maru No.2.* In October 1918 sailed from Moji in southern Japan for Hong Kong and never seen again.								
123	124	*Maharaja*	26.3.1879	1,666	Cargo Ship	Ir/Sc/St 305.8/31.7/22.2	190 nhp CI (2Cy) **Engines** D. Rowan Glasgow	Asiatic Steam Navigation Co. Liverpool
Completed 3.5.1879, sister ship of *Shahjehan.* In 1904 to Hong Kong owners, Un Lai Chon (Far Eastern SS & Nav Co.), not renamed as wrecked at Atiki, near Yokohama, in July that year.								
124	125	*Maharani*	26.4.1879	1,667	Cargo Ship	Ir/Sc/St 305.8/31.7/22.2	190 nhp CI (2Cy) **Engines** D. Rowan Glasgow	Asiatic Steam Navigation Co. Liverpool
Completed 5.6.1879, sister ship of *Shahjehan.* Broken up India (Bombay) 1908.								
125	126	*Fair Head*	24.5.1878	1,175	Cargo Ship	Ir/Sc/St 232.3/31.2/17.0	130nhp CI (2Cy) **Engines** D. Rowan Glasgow	Ulster Steamship Co. Belfast
Completed 3.7.1879. In 1934 to Saorstat & Continental SS Co., Dublin, renamed *City of Waterford.* Sunk following collision with a Dutch vessel in North Atlantic, September 1941. All Crew were rescued, but subsequently five killed after being transferred to rescue ship *Walmer Castle* (H&W y/n 983) when that vessel was sunk.								
126	127	*British Crown*	2.8.1879	3,487	Passenger-Cargo	Ir/Sc/St 410.8/39.0/28.9	300 nhp CI (4Cy) **Engines** G. Forrester & Co. Liverpool	British Shipowners Ltd Liverpool
(This vessel is listed by Moss & Hume as a passenger ship, re-rated) Completed 8.10.1879, slightly enlarged half sister of *British Empire.* In 1887 to Dutch owners, Holland-America Line, renamed *Amsterdam.* In 1905 to Italian owners, Cerruti Bros, renamed *Amsterda* before broken up Italy (Genoa) in that year.								
127	128	*Galgorm Castle*	June 1879	192	Cargo Ship	Ir/Sc/St 111.0/19.4/9.0	30 nhp CI (2Cy) **Engines** J. Rowan & Sons Belfast	McMullin Belfast
Completed 21.8.1879. Broken up Mersey (UK) 1926.								
128	129	*Lord Dufferin*	1.10.1879	1,697	Sailing Vessel (Ship)	Iron Hulled 262.9/38.3/23.3	N/A	T. Dixon & Sons Belfast
Completed 14.11.1879. In 1894 to French owners, J.F. Dessauer, renamed *Jupiter.* Broken up 1910.								
129	130	*Dawpool*	1.1.1880	1,697	Sailing Vessel (Ship)	Iron Hulled 262.9/38.3/23.3	N/A	North Western Shipping Co. Liverpool
Completed 24.1.1880, sister ship of *Lord Dufferin.* In 1895 to Norwegian owners, C.H.H. Winters, renamed *Willkommen.* In 1905 to A. Bech, renamed *Haakon.* In 1916 acquired by J.A. Henschien, renamed *Vestelv.* Sunk with explosive charge by submarine (*U-93*) off north of Ireland, inbound Mobil–Liverpool with cargo of timber, April 1917. No lives lost.								
130	131	HMS *Algerine*	6.11.1880	835	Gunboat	Com/Sc/St 157.0/29.5/13.5	810 ihp REC ?	Admiralty
After bad experience with *Lynx* it was not surprising that H&W did not seek further Admiralty orders. However, they agreed to build the name ship of a new class of gun vessel for £84,961, which resulted in a loss to the company of £2,129 by the time she was delivered. Completed 12.12.1880. Considerably larger than the Beacon class, armed with a 7in MLR and two 64pdr MLR. Had a fairly short service career, being sold in 1892. In civilian service survived until 1912 when crushed in ice at Ponds Inlet, Baffin Island.								
131	132	*Holmhurst*	5.11.1879	495	Cargo Ship	Ir/Sc/St 187.2/23.7/13.4	71 nhp CI (2Cy) **Engines** J. Rowan & Sons Belfast	J.H. Thursley Fleetwood
Completed 12.12.1879. Sunk following collision 7 miles south of Eddystone, February 1885. No lives lost.								

<table>
<tr><th>Ship</th><th>Yard No</th><th>Name</th><th>Date Launched</th><th>Displacement Tons</th><th>Type</th><th>Construction and Dimensions</th><th>Horse Power/ Engines</th><th>Owners</th></tr>
<tr><td>132</td><td>133</td><td>Peshwa</td><td>27.3.1880</td><td>2,159</td><td>Cargo Ship</td><td>Ir/Sc/St
333.0/34.7/23.6</td><td>188 nhp
CI (2Cy)
Engines
G. Forrester & Co. Liverpool</td><td>Asiatic S.N. Co.
Liverpool</td></tr>
<tr><td colspan="9">Completed 9.6.1880, laid down as Winnebah but completed with this name. Wrecked False Point, Calcutta, June 1890. No lives lost.</td></tr>
<tr><td>133</td><td>134</td><td>Rosetta</td><td>27.5.1880</td><td>3,457</td><td>Passenger Ship</td><td>Ir/Sc/St
390.8/40.2/26.8</td><td>700 nhp
CI (2Cy)
Engines
J. Howden & Co. Glasgow</td><td>Peninsular & Oriental Steam Navigation Co.
London</td></tr>
<tr><td colspan="9">Completed 27.8.1880. An order obtained in the face of stiff competition, ten builders bid for contract, as a consequence built at a loss in the hopes of gaining further work. Accommodation was provided for 111 passengers in first and second class. In 1900 to Japanese owners, NYK, renamed Rosetta Maru after being badly damaged; broken up Japan 1907.</td></tr>
<tr><td>134</td><td>135</td><td>White Head</td><td>5.5.1880</td><td>1,192</td><td>Cargo Ship</td><td>Ir/Sc/St
249.7/31.2/15.5</td><td>140 nhp
CI (2Cy)
Engines
J. Howden & Co. Glasgow</td><td>Ulster Steamship Co.
Belfast</td></tr>
<tr><td colspan="9">After a long and uneventful career, was taken by the British government in August 1914 for use as a stores carrier. Later chartered to the government of Montenegro. Sunk by submarine torpedo (UC-74) 14nm from Suda Bay, October 1917. Twenty-three lives lost.</td></tr>
<tr><td>135</td><td>136</td><td>Black Head</td><td>15.1.1881</td><td>1,191</td><td>Cargo Ship</td><td>Ir/Sc/St
249.7/31.2/15.5</td><td>140 nhp
CI (2Cy)
Engines
J. Howden & Co. Glasgow</td><td>Ulster Steamship Co.
Belfast</td></tr>
<tr><td colspan="9">Completed 14.3.1881, sister ship of White Head. Wrecked Bornholm Island, January 1912.</td></tr>
<tr><td>136</td><td>137</td><td>British Merchant</td><td>25.8.1880</td><td>1,742</td><td>Sailing Vessel (Ship)</td><td>Iron Hulled
262.9/38.3/23.3</td><td>N/A</td><td>British Shipowners Ltd
Liverpool</td></tr>
<tr><td colspan="9">Completed 7.10.1880. In 1895 to German owners, D. Cordes & Co., renamed Arthur Fitger. In 1908 badly damaged by fire at Seattle; purchased by local owners, J. Griffiths & Sons; converted to towed barge, renamed Quatsino. Wrecked on Lincoln Reef, near Green Island, October 1909.</td></tr>
<tr><td>137</td><td>138</td><td>British Queen</td><td>4.11.1880</td><td>3,558</td><td>Passenger-Cargo</td><td>St/Sc/St
410.4/39.6/28.8</td><td>400 nhp
CI (4Cy)
Engines
J. Jack & Co. Liverpool</td><td>British Shipowners Ltd
Liverpool</td></tr>
<tr><td colspan="9">(This vessel is listed by Moss & Hume as a passenger ship, re-rated)
Completed 15.1.1881. In 1887 to Dutch Owners, Holland-America Line, re-named Obdam. In 1898 to US Army as transport for Spanish-American War, renamed McPherson. In 1905 to Luckenbach Transportation, renamed Brooklyn and later S.V. Luckenbach. 1915 to Barber & Co., New York, renamed Onega. Sunk by submarine torpedo (UB125) English Channel on route Bordeaux–Swansea with cargo of pit-props, August 1918. Twenty-six lives lost.</td></tr>
<tr><td>138</td><td>139</td><td>British King</td><td>22.1.1880</td><td>3,559</td><td>Passenger-Cargo</td><td>St/Sc/St
410.3/39.0/28.9</td><td>400 nhp
CI (4Cy)
Engines
J. Jack & Co. Liverpool</td><td>British Shipowners Ltd
Liverpool</td></tr>
<tr><td colspan="9">(This vessel is listed by Moss & Hume as a passenger ship, re-rated)
Completed 29.3.1881, near sister of British Queen. In 1890 to Dutch owners, Holland-America Line, renamed Werkendam. In 1900 to Russian owners, Chinese Eastern Railway Co.; renamed Kharbin. Scuttled Port Arthur March 1904 during Japanese siege.</td></tr>
<tr><td>139</td><td>140</td><td>Woodhopper</td><td>18.6.1880</td><td></td><td>Barge</td><td></td><td></td><td>Oceanic Steam Navigation Co.
Liverpool</td></tr>
<tr><td>140</td><td>141</td><td>Arabic</td><td>30.4.1881</td><td>4,368</td><td>Cargo Ship</td><td>St/Sc/St
427.8/41.9/37.0</td><td>600 nhp
CI (4Cy)
Engines
J. Jack & Co. Liverpool</td><td>Oceanic Steam Navigation Co.
Liverpool</td></tr>
<tr><td colspan="9">Completed 12.8.1881, originally to have been Asiatic but completed under this name. After brief service on transatlantic routes transferred to Asiatic services. In 1887 50 second-class berths were fitted and operated on Liverpool–New York route as an intermediate ship. In 1890 to Dutch owners, Holland-America Line, for £65,000, renamed Spaarndam. Operated on Rotterdam–New York route. Broken up Preston (UK) 1901.</td></tr>
</table>

<table>
<tr><th>Ship</th><th>Yard No</th><th>Name</th><th>Date Launched</th><th>Displacement Tons</th><th>Type</th><th>Construction and Dimensions</th><th>Horse Power/ Engines</th><th>Owners</th></tr>
<tr><td>141</td><td>142</td><td>Coptic</td><td>10.8.1881</td><td>4,448</td><td>Cargo Ship</td><td>St/Sc/St
430.2/42.2/24.4</td><td>550 nhp
CI (4Cy)
Engines
J. Jack & Co.
Liverpool</td><td>Oceanic Steam Navigation Co. Liverpool</td></tr>
<tr><td colspan="9">Completed 9.11.1881, near sister of Arabic. After a couple of transatlantic journeys joined sister in Far East. In 1884 refrigeration plant installed to allow transport of meat on London–New Zealand–Cape Horn–South America–UK route. In 1894 given triple-expansion machinery by H&W. In 1906 to Pacific Mail Steamship Co., renamed Persia; given major refit 1911. In 1915 to Japanese owners, Toyo Kisen, renamed Persia Maru operated on trans-Pacific routes. Broken up Japan (Osaka) 1926.</td></tr>
<tr><td>142</td><td>143</td><td>Winnebah</td><td>16.4.1881</td><td>1,390</td><td>Cargo Ship</td><td>St/Sc/St
295.5/30.3/18.9</td><td>120 nhp
CI (2Cy)
H&W</td><td>African Steamboat Co. London</td></tr>
<tr><td colspan="9">Completed 1.7.1881, laid down as Minnehaha but completed under this name. In 1898 to W.H. Stott & Co., Liverpool, renamed Moonlight. Broken up Holland (Rotterdam) 1909.</td></tr>
<tr><td>143</td><td>144</td><td>Akassa</td><td>24.6.1881</td><td>1,389</td><td>Cargo Ship</td><td>St/Sc/St
295.5/30.3/18.9</td><td>120 nhp
CI (2Cy)
H&W</td><td>African Steamboat Co. London</td></tr>
<tr><td colspan="9">Completed 17.8.1881, sister ship of Winnebah. In 1903 to Greek owners, Simiriotti Ramsey, renamed Mina. Broken up Italy (Genoa) 1912.</td></tr>
<tr><td>144</td><td>145</td><td>Shannon</td><td>6.10.1881</td><td>4,189</td><td>Passenger Ship</td><td>St/Sc/St
400.1/42.6/32.7</td><td>750 nhp
CI (4Cy)
H&W</td><td>Peninsular and Oriental Steam Navigation Co. London</td></tr>
<tr><td colspan="9">Completed 5.1.1882. For India–Australia–China route with accommodation for 131 first-class and 94 second-class passengers. Renamed Procter before broken up India (Bombay) 1901.</td></tr>
<tr><td>145</td><td>146</td><td>Garfield</td><td>7.1.1882</td><td>2,317</td><td>Sailing Vessel (Ship)</td><td>Steel Hulled
299.8/41.2/24.8</td><td>N/A</td><td>North Western Shipping Co. Liverpool</td></tr>
<tr><td colspan="9">Completed 19.2.1882. Condemned at Coquimbo, Chile, following a fire off coast, October 1895.</td></tr>
<tr><td>146</td><td>147</td><td>British Prince</td><td>4.2.1882</td><td>3,973</td><td>Passenger-Cargo</td><td>St/Sc/St
420.1/42.2/29.0</td><td>450 nhp
CI (2Cy)
H&W</td><td>British Shipowners Ltd Liverpool</td></tr>
<tr><td colspan="9">(This vessel is listed by Moss & Hume as a passenger ship, re-rated)
Completed 4.4.1882. In 1895 to French owners, Generale TMv, renamed Les Andes. Broken up France (Marseilles) 1909.</td></tr>
<tr><td>147</td><td>148</td><td>Lord Downshire</td><td>29.4.1882</td><td>2,322</td><td>Sailing Vessel (Four-masted Barque)</td><td>Steel Hulled
299.8/41.3/24.8</td><td>N/A</td><td>T. Dixon & Sons Belfast</td></tr>
<tr><td colspan="9">Completed 31.5.1882. Disappeared at sea voyage Cuba–Hamburg, May 1895. There was speculation at the time that she was lost following a collision with the Prince Oscar in mid-July.</td></tr>
<tr><td>148</td><td>149</td><td>Mandingo</td><td>18.3.1882</td><td>1,700</td><td>Cargo Ship</td><td>St/Sc/St
305.0/34.2/20.0</td><td>160 nhp
CI (2Cy)
H&W</td><td>African Steamship Co. London</td></tr>
<tr><td colspan="9">Completed 6.5.1882. In 1905 to Greek owners, Stamatiadis Riginos, renamed Averof. In 1914 to D. Dellegrammaticas renamed Fanny. In 1916 to M. Michaeles renamed Micheal. In 1921 to Z. Oberti renamed Glauco. Broken up Italy 1904.</td></tr>
<tr><td>149</td><td>150</td><td>Walter H. Wilson</td><td>6.7.1882</td><td>2,518</td><td>Sailing Vessel (Four-masted Ship)</td><td>Iron Hulled
308.1/42.7/24.9</td><td>N/A</td><td>S. Lawther Belfast</td></tr>
<tr><td colspan="9">Completed 18.8.1882. In 1900 to J. Edgar & Co., renamed California. Wrecked St Mary's Island, Northumberland, January 1913.</td></tr>
<tr><td>150</td><td>151</td><td>Yucatan</td><td>15.6.1882</td><td>2,816</td><td>Cargo Ship</td><td>Ir/Sc/St
336.5/38.2/26.3</td><td>320 nhp
CI (4Cy)
H&W</td><td>West Indian & Pacific Steam Navigation Co. Liverpool</td></tr>
<tr><td colspan="9">Completed 19.8.1882. Broken up Preston (UK) 1912.</td></tr>
<tr><td>151</td><td>152</td><td>Ionic</td><td>11.1.1883</td><td>4,753</td><td>Passenger-Cargo</td><td>St/Sc/St
439.9/42.7/24.9</td><td>500 nhp
CI (4Cy)
H&W</td><td>Oceanic Steam Navigation Co. Liverpool</td></tr>
<tr><td colspan="9">Completed 28.3.1883, enlarged version of Arabic for UK–New Zealand routes. In 1894 returned to builders and fitted with triple-expansion engines, made last New Zealand voyage in 1899. In 1900 chartered to the Spanish government to repatriate troops from Manila following defeat by United States. Subsequently to the Aberdeen Line for £47,000, renamed Sophocles, made final voyage in 1906. Broken up Morecambe (UK) 1908.</td></tr>
</table>

<table>
<tr><th>Ship</th><th>Yard No</th><th>Name</th><th>Date Launched</th><th>Displacement Tons</th><th>Type</th><th>Construction and Dimensions</th><th>Horse Power/ Engines</th><th>Owners</th></tr>
<tr><td>152</td><td>153</td><td>Doric</td><td>10.3.1883</td><td>4,744</td><td>Passenger-Cargo</td><td>St/Sc/St
440.9/44.2/31.5</td><td>550 nhp
CI (4Cy)
H&W</td><td>Oceanic Steam Navigation Co.
Liverpool</td></tr>
<tr><td colspan="9">Completed 4.7.1883, near sister of Ionic. After use on New Zealand routes switched to San Francisco–Yokohama–Hong Kong service. In 1906 to the Pacific Mail Steamship Co., renamed Asia. In April 1911 wrecked Hea Chu Island, South China. No lives lost.</td></tr>
<tr><td>153</td><td>154</td><td>British Princess</td><td>14.12.1882</td><td>3,994</td><td>Passenger-Cargo</td><td>St/Sc/St
420.1/42.2/29.0</td><td>450 nhp
CI (2Cy)
H&W</td><td>British Shipowners Ltd
Liverpool</td></tr>
<tr><td colspan="9">(This vessel is listed by Moss & Hume as a passenger ship, re-rated)
Completed 19.4.1883, sister ship of British Prince. In 1895 to French owners, Generale TMv, renamed Les Alpes. Broken up France (Marseilles) 1910.</td></tr>
<tr><td>154</td><td>155</td><td>W.J. Pirrie</td><td>26.5.1883</td><td>2,576</td><td>Sailing Vessel (Four-masted Ship)</td><td>Iron Hulled
308.2/42.8/25.0</td><td>N/A</td><td>S. Lawther
Belfast</td></tr>
<tr><td colspan="9">Completed 29.7.1883. Condemned following fire at Tocopilla, Chile, 1904. Subsequently used as barge until 1920 when abandoned in sinking condition off Cape Flattery, Washington State.</td></tr>
<tr><td>155</td><td>156</td><td>Fingal</td><td>11.4.1883</td><td>2,570</td><td>Sailing Vessel (Four-masted Barque)</td><td>Steel Hulled
308.2/42.8/25.0</td><td>N/A</td><td>R. Martin & Co.
Dublin</td></tr>
<tr><td colspan="9">Completed 2.6.1883, sister ship of W.J. Pirrie. In 1915 twin diesel engines were installed. In 1916 to Swedish owners, A. Leffler & Sons, renamed Hugo Hamilton. Sunk by submarine gunfire (U-81) inbound Cuba–Goteburg with cargo of saltpetre off west of Ireland, February 1917. No lives lost.</td></tr>
<tr><td>156</td><td>157</td><td>Lord Wolseley</td><td>21.7.1883</td><td>2,576</td><td>Sailing Vessel (Four-masted Barque)</td><td>Iron Hulled
308.2/42.9/25.1</td><td>N/A</td><td>Irish Shipowners
(T. Dixon & Sons)
Belfast</td></tr>
<tr><td colspan="9">Completed 6.9.1883, sister ship of W.J. Pirrie. In 1896 to German owners, J. Tideman & Co., renamed Columbia. In 1906 to American owners, C.E. Peabody, renamed Everett G. Griggs, rerigged as six-masted barquentine. In 1914 to E.R. Sterling, renamed E.R. Sterling. In 1928 severely damaged in storm and subsequently broken up.</td></tr>
<tr><td>157</td><td>158</td><td>Dundela</td><td>4.8.1883</td><td>876</td><td>Cargo Ship</td><td>Ir&St/Sc/St
224.5/28.2/14.0</td><td>98 nhp
CI (2Cy)
H&W</td><td>Harland & Wolff
Belfast</td></tr>
<tr><td colspan="9">In 1883 H&W found themselves with two ships, built on speculation, that they could not sell. They were bought through the firm by the partners and their friends rather than actually owned by the company.
Completed 13.11.1883. Wrecked at Porthoe, North Wales, March 1891.</td></tr>
<tr><td>158</td><td>159</td><td>Dunluce</td><td>1.9.1883</td><td>877</td><td>Cargo Ship</td><td>Ir&St/Sc/St
224.5/28.2/14.0</td><td>98 nhp
CI (2Cy)
H&W</td><td>Harland & Wolff
Belfast</td></tr>
<tr><td colspan="9">Completed 3.11.1883, sister ship of Dundela. Wrecked Haradskar, Sweden, June 1890.</td></tr>
<tr><td>159</td><td>160</td><td>La Nevera</td><td>10.2.1883</td><td>359</td><td>Cargo Ship</td><td>Ir/Sc/St
154.9/26.2/11.0</td><td>55 nhp
CI (2Cy)
H&W</td><td>River Plate Meat Co.
Liverpool</td></tr>
<tr><td colspan="9">Completed 26.3.1883. By 1890 owned by the Argentinian firm Canals. By 1905 owned by L. Mascarello, renamed Asuncion R. In 1910 to N. Mihanovich, renamed on three occasions: Uruguay (1910), Uruguay II (1919) and Dayman (1920). Broken up 1941.</td></tr>
<tr><td>160</td><td>161</td><td>Niger</td><td>23.6.1883</td><td>2,006</td><td>Cargo Ship</td><td>St/Sc/St
320.2/35.0/21.2</td><td>180 nhp
CI (2Cy)
H&W</td><td>African Steamship Co.
London</td></tr>
<tr><td colspan="9">Completed 3.8.1883. Broken up Preston (UK) 1903.</td></tr>
<tr><td>161</td><td>162</td><td>Dynamic</td><td>19.9.1883</td><td>879</td><td>Cross-Channel Ship</td><td>Ir/Sc/St
243.3/31.9/15.3</td><td>200 nhp
CI (2Cy)
H&W</td><td>Belfast Steamship Co.
Belfast</td></tr>
<tr><td colspan="9">Completed 13.12.1883; operated Belfast–Liverpool route until replaced by new vessels. In 1900 to Union Commercial, renamed Mallorca. In 1905 to Greek owners, A. Diakaki & Co., renamed Principessa Sophia. In 1912 became Ittihad of company of that name. In 1916 in Russian naval service as Dobycha. Finally 1923 to Italian ownership, Transitaria Italiana, renamed Ambro. Broken up 1926.</td></tr>
<tr><td>162</td><td>163</td><td>Guido</td><td>17.10.1883</td><td>3,313</td><td>Cargo Ship</td><td>St/Sc/St
360.4/41.2/26.4</td><td>400 nhp
CI (2Cy)
H&W</td><td>Cia de Nav la Flecha
Bilbao</td></tr>
<tr><td colspan="9">Completed 12.1.1884. In 1898 to American owners, New York & Cuba Mail Co., renamed Matanzas. Broken up Italy (Monfalcone) 1924.</td></tr>
</table>

Ship	Yard No	Name	Date Launched	Displacement Tons	Type	Construction and Dimensions	Horse Power/ Engines	Owners
163	164	*Bay of Panama*	14.11.1883	2,365	Sailing Vessel (Four-masted Ship)	Steel Hulled 294.0/42.3/24.3	N/A	J. Bullock London
Completed 12.1.1884. Wrecked near Coverack, Cornwall, March 1891. Only 17 survived out of 40 on board.								
164	165	*Horn Head*	1.3.1884	2,496	Cargo Ship	Ir/Sc/St 321.8/37.8/25.0	275 nhp CI (2Cy) H&W	Ulster Steamship Co. Belfast
Completed 24.5.1884. Missing at sea, last seen passing Cape Henry in August 1893, heading for Dublin: 30 lives lost.								
165	166	*Lord O'Neill*	17.5.1884	2,753	Cargo Ship	Ir/Sc/St 340.5/38.3/26.0	350 nhp CI (2Cy) H&W	Irish Shipowners (T. Dixon & Sons) Belfast
Completed 12.7.1884. Wrecked on Blasket Islands, January 1898.								
166	167	*Texan*	29.12.1883	3,257	Cargo Ship	Ir/Sc/St 360.7/41.3/26.9	266 nhp CI (2Cy) H&W	West Indian & Pacific Steam Navigation Co. Liverpool
Completed 15.3.1884. Broken up Italy (Genoa) 1909.								
167	168	*Floridan*	12.4.1884	3,257	Cargo Ship	Ir/Sc/St 360.7/41.3/26.9	266 nhp CI (2Cy) H&W	West Indian & Pacific Steam Navigation Co. Liverpool
Completed 16.8.1884, sister ship of *Texan*. Broken up Preston (UK) 1908.								
168	169	*Benin*	7.6.1884	2,215	Cargo Ship	St/Sc/St 330.7/36.7/21.7	200 nhp CI (2Cy) H&W	African Steamship Co. London
Completed 24.7.1884. In 1901 chartered to Spanish owners, Cia Interinsulares Canarias, renamed *Almirante Diaz.* Transferred back 1902 and reverted to original name. In 1905 to Greek owners, S. Riginos & Co., renamed *Maraslis.* Broken up Spain (Barcelona) 1911.								
169	170	*Lord Lansdowne*	26.7.1884	2,752	Cargo Ship	Ir/Sc/St 340.5/38.3/26.0	350 nhp CI (2Cy) H&W	Irish Shipowners (T. Dixon & Sons) Belfast
Completed 15.9.1884. Sister ship of *Lord O'Neil.* Wrecked Cobbler's Reef, Barbados, May 1912.								
170	171	*Belgic*	3.1.1885	4,212	Cargo Ship	St&Ir/Sc/St 420.3/42.4/29.6	500 nhp CI (2Cy) H&W	Oceanic Steam Navigation Co. Liverpool
Completed 7.7.1885, virtual repeat of the Ionic type. Employed on Asian routes until 1898 when returned to Britain. In 1899 to Atlantic Transport Line, renamed *Mohawk* used on London–New York route. Requisitioned as transport during Boer War. Released 1902; decided not worth refurbishing; broken up Garston (UK) 1903.								
171	172	*Gaelic*	28.2.1885	4,205	Cargo Ship	St/Sc/St 420.3/42.4/29.6	500 nhp CI (2Cy) H&W	Oceanic Steam Navigation Co. Liverpool
Completed 18.7.1885, sister ship of *Belgic*; likewise on Asian routes until 1904 when returned to the United Kingdom. Overhauled by builders and passed to Pacific Steam Navigation Co., renamed *Callao.* Broken up Briton Ferry (UK) 1907.								
172	173	*Nurjahan*	23.8.1884	2,967	Cargo Ship	St/Sc/St 350.5/40.3/25.2	350 nhp CI (2Cy) H&W	Asiatic Steam Navigation Co. Liverpool
Completed 27.9.1884. Wrecked on voyage Bombay–Calcutta, November 1890.								
173	174	*Kohinur*	8.10.1884	2,967	Cargo Ship	St/Sc/St 350.5/40.3/25.2	350 nhp CI (2Cy) H&W	Asiatic Steam Navigation Co. Liverpool
Completed 16.1.1885, sister ship of *Nurjahan.* In 1905 to Japanese owners, T. Yamagata, renamed *Kohina Maru.* Sunk by submarine torpedo north of Alexandria (*UB 46*), August 1916. No lives lost.								
174	175	*Callao*	1.1.1885	1,016	Sailing Vessel (Barque)	Steel Hulled 206.7/33.1/20.0	N/A	North Western Shipping Co. Ltd Liverpool
Completed 26.1.1885. Out of use by 1925.								
175	176	*Santiago*	17.1.1885	1,017	Sailing Vessel (Barque)	Steel Hulled 206.7/33.1/20.0	N/A	North Western Shipping Co. Ltd Liverpool
Completed 4.3.1885, sister ship of *Callao.* In 1907 converted into three-masted schooner rigged oil tanker. Reduced to barge 1923. Broken up after the Second World War.								

Ship	Yard No	Name	Date Launched	Displacement Tons	Type	Construction and Dimensions	Horse Power/ Engines	Owners
176	177	*Eblana*	24.10.1885	347	Barge	Iron Hulled 116.2/30.1/12.0	N/A	Dublin Corporation
Completed 1.11.1885.								
177	178	*Teneriffe*	19.2.1885	1,799	Cargo Ship	St/Sc/St 301.0/36.0/19.8	200 nhp CI (2Cy) H&W	British & African Steam Navigation Co. Glasgow
Completed 16.4.1885. In 1920 to Spanish owners, Maritima Arenas, renamed *Zugatzarte*. Wrecked Punta Galea, northern Spain, March 1921.								
178	179	*Elmina*	23.4.1885	1,764	Cargo Ship	St/Sc/St 301.0/36.0/19.8	200 nhp CI (2Cy) H&W	British and African Steam Navigation Co. Glasgow
Completed 28.6.1885, sister ship of *Teneriffe*. Broken up Belgium (Zwijndrecht) 1907.								
179	180	*Costa Rican*	16.6.1885	3,251	Cargo Ship	St/Sc/St 360.6/41.2/26.8	266 nhp CI (2Cy) H&W	West Indian & Pacific Steam Navigation Co. Liverpool
Completed 27.8.1885. Wrecked near Plum Point, Jamaica, wreck broken up United States (Perth Amboy) 1904.								
180	181	*Irene*	10.7.1885	897	Passenger Ferry	St/2Sc/St 301.2/33.2/13.5	280 nhp CI (4Cy) H&W	London & North Western Railway Co.
Completed 29.9.1885. Built to replace *Hollyhead*. Lost in collision in 1883, on Dublin–Holyhead route. Broken up Garston (UK) 1906.								
181	182	*Zemindar*	30.6.1885	2,120	Sailing Vessel (Ship)	Steel Hulled 292.6/39.7/23.5	N/A	T.&J. Brocklebank Liverpool
Completed 14.8.1885. In 1900 to German owners, D. Cordes & Co., renamed *Otto Gildemeister*. In 1902 to Hind Rolph & Co. renamed *Homeward Bound*. In 1909 acquired by Alaska Packers, renamed *Star of Holland* in 1937; reduced to hulk/barge, broken up 1950.								
182	183	*Talookdar*	22.8.1885	2,120	Sailing Vessel (Ship)	Steel Hulled 292.6/39.7/23.5	N/A	T.&J. Brocklebank Liverpool
Completed 24.9.1885. Sank following collision with sailing ship *Libussa* near Cape of Good Hope, 1890.								
183	184	*Queen's Island*	22.9.1885	2,093	Sailing Vessel (Barque)	Steel Hulled 282.8/40.5/23.6	N/A	S. Lawther Belfast
Completed 29.9.1885. In 1890 to Aberdeen, White Star Line renamed *Strathdon*. In 1906 to French owners, A.D. Bordes & Sons, renamed *Gers*. Broken up 1924.								
184	185	*Iran*	5.1.1886	3,530	Cargo Ship	St/Sc/St 380.3/43.0/27.4	400 nhp TE (6Cy) H&W	Edward Bates & Son Liverpool
Completed 16.3.1886. Later rebuilt to carry 780 third-class passengers in transatlantic emigrant trade. In 1895 to German owners, R.M. Sloman & Co., renamed *Albano*. In 1911 to French owners, Messageries Maritimes, renamed *Breton*. Sunk by submarine torpedo (*UC-37*) north of Fratelli Rocks, Tunisia, on route Tunis–St Nazaire with cargo of grain, August 1917. No lives lost.								
185	186	*Saint Fillans*	25.2.1886	3,130	Cargo Ship	St/Sc/St 340.5/42.1/25.5	320 nhp TE (3Cy) H&W	Rankin, Gilmour & Co. Liverpool
Completed 24.9.1886. By 1890 owned by British and Foreign SS Co. In 1899 to T. Dixion & Sons, Belfast, renamed *Larne*. In 1912 to Italian owners, S. Razeto, renamed *Oriana*. Sunk by submarine gunfire (*U-35*) 3nm off Cape Huertas, Spain, outbound Genoa–Montevideo, February 1917. No lives lost.								
186	187	*Caloric*	10.10.1885	982	Cross-Channel Ship	St/Sc/St 243.9/31.9/15.3	200 nhp CI (2Cy) H&W	Belfast Steamship Co. Belfast
Completed 21.12.1885 on Belfast–Liverpool route until replaced. In 1914 to Greek owners, J. Leonidas, renamed *Adriaticos*. Following this changed ownership/name on no fewer than six further occasions: (1933) Hellenic Coast, *Syros*; (1940) S. Avgherinos, *Atlantic*; (1940) Balkans and Near East, *Emilie*; (1943) Near East Shipping Co., *Shikmona*; (1948) G. Bissada, *Bissada*; (1951) J.G. Dayanti, *Castas A*. Broken up Italy (La Spezia) 1952.								
187	188	*Optic*	12.11.1885	980	Cross-Channel Ship	St/Sc/St 243.9/31.9/15.3	200 nhp CI (2Cy) H&W	Belfast Steamship Co. Belfast
Completed 29.1.1886, sister ship of *Caloric* on same route. In 1907 to Spanish owners, SN e Industria, renamed *Delfin*. Wrecked Le Herredura, Malaga, 1937 and subsequently bombed.								
188	189	*Inishowen Head*	17.4.1886	3,050	Cargo Ship	St/Sc/St 341.6/40.2/26.4	320 nhp TE (3Cy) H&W	Ulster Steamship Co. Belfast
Completed 30.6.1886. Sunk by submarine-laid mine (*UC-65*) 1nm S of Skokholm Island, outbound Dublin–St Johns, New Brunswick, February 1917. One life lost.								

<table>
<tr><th>Ship</th><th>Yard No</th><th>Name</th><th>Date Launched</th><th>Displacement Tons</th><th>Type</th><th>Construction and Dimensions</th><th>Horse Power/ Engines</th><th>Owners</th></tr>
<tr><td>189</td><td>190</td><td>HMS Lizard</td><td>27.11.1886</td><td>715</td><td>Gunboat</td><td>Com/Sc/St
165.0/29.0/11.0</td><td>1000 ihp
TE (3Cy)
H&W</td><td>Admiralty</td></tr>
<tr><td colspan="9">Having lost money on previous Admiralty work, Harland's agreed to build these vessels on a cost plus 5 per cent basis rather than on a fixed price. The navy agreed to this because they wanted to use the firm's expertise with the new triple-expansion engine, which they had begun to build the previous year. In fact these ships and their two Elswick-built sisters can be seen as the navy experimenting with a new engine type and the results were impressive. Not only was there greater fuel efficiency, but also a 3-knot improvement in speed compared to previous classes. In addition, the Admiralty decided to fit the new light 4in QF gun in this class, making them, despite the anachronistic hull construction, some of the most technically advanced ships in the fleet.
Completed 4.2.1887. Sold out of service 1905.</td></tr>
<tr><td>190</td><td>191</td><td>HMS
Bramble</td><td>11.12.1886</td><td>715</td><td>Gunboat</td><td>Com/Sc/St
165.0/29.0/11.0</td><td>1,000 ihp
TE (3Cy)
H&W</td><td>Admiralty</td></tr>
<tr><td colspan="9">Completed 1.3.1887, sister ship of Lizard; name ship of the class. Sold out of service 1906.</td></tr>
<tr><td>191</td><td>192</td><td>Lord
Templeton</td><td>5.5.1886</td><td>2,151</td><td>Sailing Vessel
(Barque)</td><td>Steel Hulled
282.9/40.1/23.7</td><td>N/A</td><td>Irish Shipowners
(T. Dixon & Sons)
Belfast</td></tr>
<tr><td colspan="9">Completed 12.6.1886, near sister ship of Queen's Island. Reduced to hulk/barge 1933, broken up 1955.</td></tr>
<tr><td>192</td><td>193</td><td>Ormiston</td><td>31.8.1886</td><td>3,158</td><td>Cargo Ship</td><td>St/Sc/St
345.6/40.9/26.7</td><td>320 nhp
TE (3Cy)
H&W</td><td>Irish Shipowners
(T. Dixon & Sons)
Belfast</td></tr>
<tr><td colspan="9">Completed 30.10.1886. In 1888 renamed Lord Charlemont. Sunk by submarine torpedo (U-34) 22nm N of Alboran Island, Morocco, on route La Spezia–Gibraltar, April 1918. Eight lives lost.</td></tr>
<tr><td>193</td><td>194</td><td>Swanmore</td><td>22.6.1886</td><td>1,821</td><td>Sailing Vessel
(Barque)</td><td>Iron Hulled
268.6/38.2/23.3</td><td>N/A</td><td>W.J. Myers, Son & Co.
Liverpool</td></tr>
<tr><td colspan="9">Completed 10.8.1886. In 1896 to Danish owners, C.P. Holm, renamed Sixtus. Wrecked Falkland Islands, July 1905.</td></tr>
<tr><td>194</td><td>195</td><td>Stanmore</td><td>14.8.1886</td><td>1,824</td><td>Sailing Vessel
(Barque)</td><td>Iron Hulled
268.6/38.2/23.3</td><td>N/A</td><td>W.J. Myers, Son & Co.
Liverpool</td></tr>
<tr><td colspan="9">Completed 25.9.1886, sister ship of Swanmore. In 1896 to R. Thomas & Co., renamed Deudraeth Castle. Abandoned in sinking condition off Cape Horn, November 1905.</td></tr>
<tr><td>195</td><td>196</td><td>Etolia</td><td>8.1.1887</td><td>3,211</td><td>Cargo Ship</td><td>St&Ir/Sc/St
345.6/40.9/26.7</td><td>320 nhp
TE (3Cy)
H&W</td><td>City of Liverpool SN Co.
Liverpool</td></tr>
<tr><td colspan="9">Completed 9.4.1887. Wrecked Nova Scotia, June 1906.</td></tr>
<tr><td>196</td><td>197</td><td>Minnesota</td><td>2.8.1887</td><td>3,143</td><td>Cargo Ship</td><td>St/Sc/St
345.6/40.9/26.7</td><td>320 nhp
TE (3Cy)
H&W</td><td>Williams, Torrey &
Fielde
Liverpool</td></tr>
<tr><td colspan="9">Completed 22.11.1887, sister ship of Etolia. In 1917 to Atlantic Transport Co., renamed Mahopac. Broken up Holland (Rotterdam) 1923.</td></tr>
<tr><td>197</td><td>198</td><td>Lycia</td><td>5.11.1887</td><td>3,223</td><td>Cargo Ship</td><td>St/Sc/St
345.6/40.9/26.7</td><td>320 nhp
TE (3Cy)
H&W</td><td>City of Liverpool SN Co.
Liverpool</td></tr>
<tr><td colspan="9">Completed 12.5.1888, sister ship of Etolia. To Elder Dempster in 1894. In 1904 to German owners, Diederichsen Jebsen, renamed Lauschan. Hulked 1910.</td></tr>
<tr><td>198</td><td>199</td><td>Hercules</td><td>12.10.1886</td><td>818</td><td>Dredger</td><td>St&Ir/2Sc/St
200.0/37.6/14.2</td><td>200 nhp
CI (4Cy)
H&W</td><td>Londonderry Harbour
Commissioners</td></tr>
<tr><td colspan="9">Completed 8.3.1887. Broken up 1962.</td></tr>
<tr><td>199</td><td>200</td><td>Michigan</td><td>5.7.1887</td><td>4,979</td><td>Passenger-
Cargo</td><td>St /Sc/St
400.4/47.2/24.2</td><td>600 nhp
TE (3Cy)
H&W</td><td>Warren Line
Liverpool</td></tr>
<tr><td colspan="9">(This vessel is listed by Moss & Hume as a passenger ship, re-rated)
Completed 15.10.1887. In 1914 converted into dummy battleship (HMS Collingwood); employed during the Dardanelles campaign and badly damaged by Turkish gunfire. Expended as a block ship at Mudros, January 1916.</td></tr>
<tr><td>200</td><td>201</td><td>Oceana</td><td>17.9.1887</td><td>6,362</td><td>Passenger-
Cargo</td><td>St/Sc/St
468.4/52.0/26.8</td><td>1000 nhp
7000 ihp
TE (3Cy)
H&W</td><td>Peninsular and
Oriental SS Co.
London</td></tr>
<tr><td colspan="9">(This vessel is listed by Moss & Hume as a passenger ship, re-rated)</td></tr>
</table>

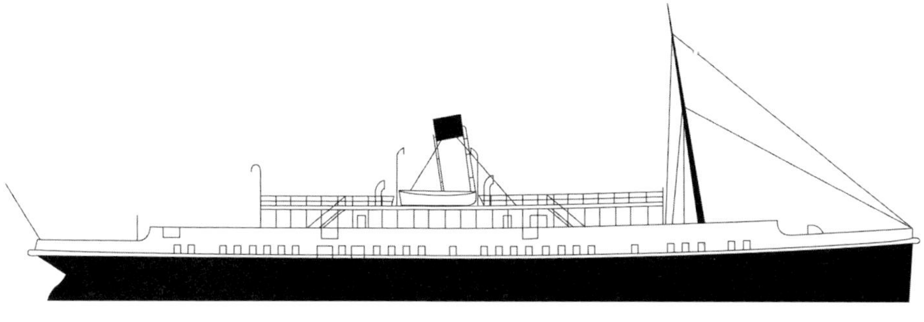

Nomadic (H&W y/n 422) 1911 (DH)

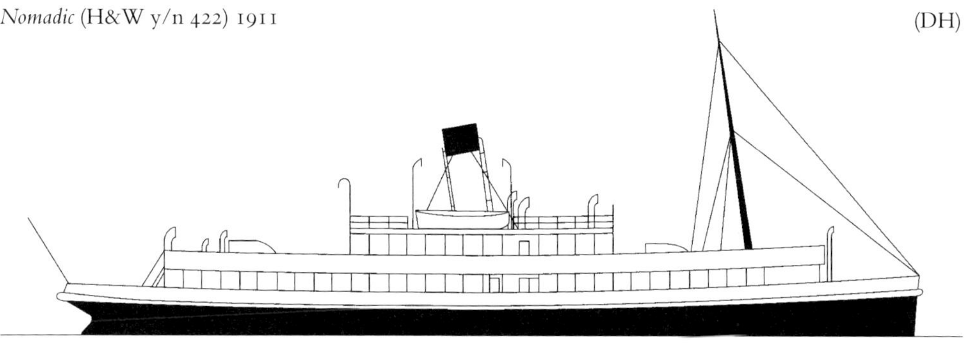

Traffic (H&W y/n 423) 1911 (DH)

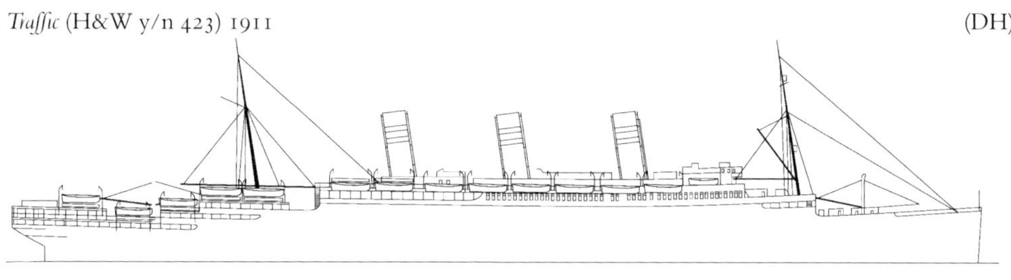

Justicia (H&W y/n 436) 1914 (DH)

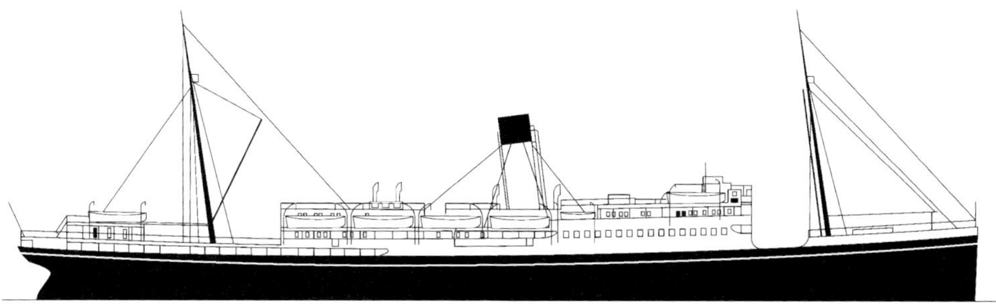

Katoomba (H&W y/n 437) 1913 (DH)

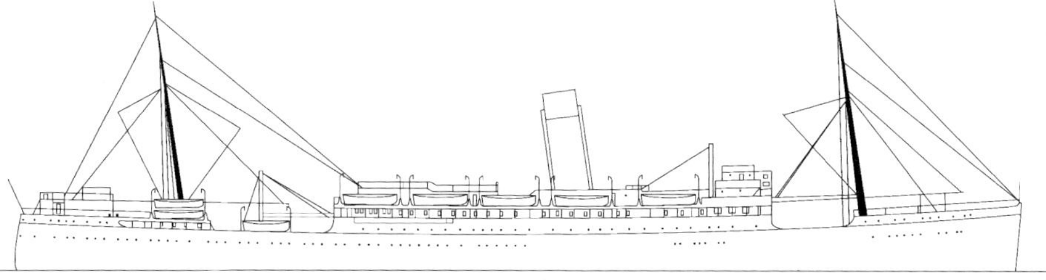

Euripides (H&W y/n 493) 1914 (DH)

<table>
<tr><th>Ship</th><th>Yard No</th><th>Name</th><th>Date Launched</th><th>Displacement Tons</th><th>Type</th><th>Construction and Dimensions</th><th>Horse Power/ Engines</th><th>Owners</th></tr>
<tr><td colspan="9">The Jubilee class was designed for Australian rather than Indian routes. They could carry just over 400 passengers and had a cargo capacity of 4,000 tons, some refrigerated. These were, by contemporary standards, fast, comfortable ships with such state-of-the-art comforts as electric lighting and mechanical ventilation. They were designed in consultation with the Admiralty to ensure they could be quickly converted into auxiliary cruisers in wartime. They cost P&O about £200,000 each, a colossal figure for the time.
Completed 26.2.1888. Lost following collision with German sailing ship Pisague in Straits of Dover, March 1912. Attempts to tow the stricken ship to port failed and it sank off Eastbourne, taking with her £700,000 in bullion that was subsequently recovered.</td></tr>
<tr><td>201</td><td>202</td><td>Arcadia</td><td>17.12.1887</td><td>6,362</td><td>Passenger-Cargo</td><td>St/Sc/St
468.4/52.1/26.8</td><td>1,000 nhp
7,000 ihp
TE (3Cy)
H&W</td><td>Peninsular and Oriental SS Co.
London</td></tr>
<tr><td colspan="9">(This vessel is listed by Moss & Hume as a passenger ship, re-rated)
Completed 12.5.1888, a sister ship of Oceana and the last of class to survive. Two Clyde-built sisters (Victoria and Britannia) went to the breakers in 1910. Engaged in trooping duties at outbreak of the First World War, sold in January 1915 and broken up Bombay.</td></tr>
<tr><td>202</td><td>203</td><td>Anglesey</td><td>20.8.1887</td><td>887</td><td>Cross-Channel Ship</td><td>St/2Sc/St
301.5/33.1/13.4</td><td>280 nhp
TE (6Cy)
H&W</td><td>London & North-Western Railway</td></tr>
<tr><td colspan="9">Completed 1.5.1888, on the Holyhead–Dublin route (passenger/cargo/cattle). Broken up 1910.</td></tr>
<tr><td>203</td><td>204</td><td>Sindia</td><td>19.11.1887</td><td>3,067</td><td>Sailing Vessel (Four-masted Ship)</td><td>Steel Hulled
329.3/45.2/26.7</td><td>N/A</td><td>T.&J. Brocklebank
Liverpool</td></tr>
<tr><td colspan="9">Completed 6.2.1888. In 1900 to Anglo-American Oil Co. Wrecked near Ocean City, New Jersey, December 1901.</td></tr>
<tr><td>204</td><td>205</td><td>Holkar</td><td>11.2.1888</td><td>3,072</td><td>Sailing Vessel (Four-masted Ship)</td><td>Steel Hulled
329.3/45.2/26.7</td><td>N/A</td><td>T.&J. Brocklebank
Liverpool</td></tr>
<tr><td colspan="9">Completed 30.4.1888, sister ship of Sindia. In 1901 to German owners, D.H. Watjen & Co., renamed Adelaide. In 1913 to Gestellschatt 1896 Co. and renamed Odessa. In 1914 captured at sea by HMS Caronir and placed under British flag as Adelaide. In 1915 to Norwegian owners, A. Meling Jr, renamed Souverain. In 1923 to E. Knudsen, renamed Hippalos. Broken up Holland 1924.</td></tr>
<tr><td>205</td><td>206</td><td>Idar</td><td>14.4.1888</td><td>4,049</td><td>Cargo Ship</td><td>St/Sc/St
400.0/45.2/28.2</td><td>450 nhp
TE (3Cy)
H&W</td><td>Edward Bates & Sons
Liverpool</td></tr>
<tr><td colspan="9">Completed 3.7.1888. In 1906 to J.H. Welsford & Co. renamed Industry. Sunk by submarine torpedo (U-45) 120nm from Fastnet outbound Barry–Newport News, April 1916. No lives lost.</td></tr>
<tr><td>206</td><td>207</td><td>Bostonian</td><td>14.3.1888</td><td>4,472</td><td>Cargo Ship</td><td>St/Sc/St
421.8/43.2/30.9</td><td>500 nhp
TE (3Cy)
H&W</td><td>Leyland & Co.
Liverpool</td></tr>
<tr><td colspan="9">Completed 11.8.1888. In 1896 to Wilson & Furness–Leyland Line on amalgamation. Broken up Falmouth (UK) 1913.</td></tr>
<tr><td>207</td><td>208</td><td>Teutonic</td><td>19.1.1889</td><td>9,685</td><td>Passenger Ship</td><td>St/2Sc/St
565.8/57.8/39.2</td><td>2,400 nhp
TE (6Cy)
H&W</td><td>Oceanic Steam Navigation Co.
Liverpool</td></tr>
<tr><td colspan="9">A new type of liner intended to overshadow competitors on New York route. The previous two-class accommodation was abandoned in this design and they could carry 300 first-class, 190 second-class and 1,000 third-class passengers. Also they were the first White Star liners to be completed without a sailing rig. They were built to a design approved by the Admiralty which allowed for rapid conversion into auxiliary cruisers.
Completed 25.7.1889, and immediately attended the Golden Jubilee Review at Spithead armed with 8x 4.7in guns. Afterwards employed on Liverpool–New York route except when employed as a transport during Boer War. From 1907 switched to Southampton–New York route. Rebuilt in 1911 and moved to Canada routes and in 1913 reconfigured to carry 550 second class and 1,000 third class. During First World War served as an armed merchant cruiser with the 10th CS and later the 2nd CS, employed in trooping duties in 1918. Broken up Germany (Emden) 1921.</td></tr>
<tr><td>208</td><td>209</td><td>Majestic</td><td>29.6.1889</td><td>9,681</td><td>Passenger Ship</td><td>St/2Sc/St
565.8/57.8/39.2</td><td>2,400 nhp
TE (6Cy)
H&W</td><td>Oceanic Steam Navigation Co.
Liverpool</td></tr>
<tr><td colspan="9">Completed 22.3.1890, sister ship of Teutonic. Served on Liverpool–New York route and as a transport during the Boer War. Rebuilt by H&W in 1902–03 and suffered serious damage in bunker fire at Liverpool in 1905. In 1907 moved to Southampton–New York service before being reduced to status of 'reserve ship' in 1911, reactivated shortly afterwards to replace the lost Titanic. Final voyage May 1914 sold for £25,000, broken up Morecambe (UK).</td></tr>
<tr><td>209</td><td>210</td><td>Cufic</td><td>10.10.1888</td><td>4,639</td><td>Livestock Carrier</td><td>St/Sc/St
430.7/45.2/36.0</td><td>520 nhp
TE (3Cy)
H&W</td><td>Oceanic Steam Navigation Co.
Liverpool</td></tr>
<tr><td colspan="9">Completed 1.12.1888, designed to carry general cargo UK–America and 1,000 head of live cattle on the return journey. In 1896 chartered to Spanish owners, Cia Trasatlantica Espanola, renamed Nuestra Senora de Guadaloupe, employed as a horse transport for Spanish Army in Cuba.</td></tr>
</table>

Ship	Yard No	Name	Date Launched	Displacement Tons	Type	Construction and Dimensions	Horse Power/ Engines	Owners
At end of charter reverted to original name. In 1901 to Mississippi and Dominion Line SS Co. renamed *Manxman*. In 1902 M&D taken over by International Mercantile Marine Co. In 1915 allocated to Elder Dempster and the following year to Canadian owners, R. Lawrence Smith, Montreal. In April 1917 taken over by the Shipping Controller. In 1919 to American owners, the Universal Transport Co., New York. In December 1919 foundered in North Atlantic on voyage Portland–Gibraltar with cargo of wheat. All 45 crew lost.								
210	211	*Runic*	1.1.1889	4,649	Livestock Carrier	St/Sc/St 430.7/45.2/36.0	520 nhp TE (3Cy) H&W	Oceanic Steam Navigation Co. Liverpool
Completed 16.2.1889, sister ship of *Cufic*. In 1895 to the West Indian & Pacific SS Co. renamed *Tampican* and in 1899 passed to Frederick Leyland & Co. with the rest of that fleet. In 1912 to H.E. Moss, Liverpool, almost immediately sold to Norwegian owners, South Pacific Whaling Co., and was converted into a whaling vessel being renamed *Imo*. On 6 December 1917 was in collision with French merchantman *Mont Blanc* in Halifax Harbour; the French vessel was loaded with explosives and blew up 15 minutes later; the blast was felt 120 miles away. The explosion destroyed Halifax suburb of Richmond, 2,000 people were killed and 9,000 injured. The *Imo* survived the blast, although six of her crew were killed and she lost her funnels, masts and deck fittings. Returned to service under the ownership of C. Christensen, renamed *Guvernoren*. Wrecked Falkland Islands, December 1921.								
211	212	*Palmas*	24.7.1888	2,428	Cargo Ship	St/Sc/St 312.0/39.2/24.7	240 nhp TE (3Cy) **Engines** McIlwaine & Lewis Belfast	Elder Dempster Liverpool
Completed 13.10.1888. Disappeared in North Atlantic, January 1903. Forty-two lives lost.								
212	213	*Lord Londonderry*	17.11.1888	2,409	Cargo Ship	St/Sc/St 312.5/39.2/24.7	240 nhp TE (3Cy) **Engines** J. Howden & Co. Glasgow	Irish Shipowners Co. (T. Dixon & Sons) Belfast
Completed 6.12.1888. Caught fire and sunk off Portuguese coast, June 1909.								
213	214	*British Empire*	28.2.1889	3,020	Passanger-Cargo	St/Sc/St 345.6/40.9/26.7	320 nhp TE (3Cy) H&W	British Shipowners Ltd Liverpool
(This vessel is listed by Moss & Hume as a cargo ship, re-rated) Completed 13.4.1889. In 1900 to Egyptian owners, Khedivial Mail, renamed *Assiout*. Seized in port by Turkey on entry to war and scuttled as block ship at entrance to Izmir (Smyma), March 1915.								
214	215	*Queensmore*	26.6.1889	4,195	Cargo Ship	St/Sc/St 400.7/46.2/29.5	560 nhp TE (3Cy) **Engines** G. Forrester & Co. Liverpool	William Johnston Liverpool
Completed 26.7.1889. Caught fire on maiden voyage, put into Dunmanus Bay, south-west Ireland and subsequently abandoned, November 1889. No lives lost.								
215	216	*Lancashire*	27.4.1889	3,870	Cargo Ship	St/Sc/St 400.5/45.2/28.1	500 nhp TE (3Cy) H&W	Bibby Steamship Co. Liverpool
The original Bibby fleet (22 vessels) was purchased by Leyland & Co. in January 1873. These two ships mark the return of the Bibby family to the shipping business. Although new firm was officially 'Bibby Brothers & Co.' they continued to be known as the Bibby Line. Completed 10.8.1889, for the Burma trade, a cargo vessel with accommodation for 12 passengers. In 1892 rebuilt to carry 70 passengers. In 1905 replaced by *Herefordshire* and passed to Danish owners, Danish East Asiatic Co., renamed *Kina*. In 1907 transferred to Russian owners, Russian East Asian Co. used on Libau–New York route, renamed *Lituaniya*. In 1913 to Japanese owners, Shosho Kisen K.K., renamed *Daiten Maru*. Sunk by submarine torpedo (*U-35*) west of Sicily inbound from Baltimore, March 1918. No lives lost.								
216	217	*Yorkshire*	27.7.1889	3,870	Cargo Ship	St/Sc/St 400.5/45.2/28.1	500 nhp TE (3Cy) H&W	Bibby Steamship Co. Liverpool
Completed 5.10.1889, sister ship of *Lancashire*. Briefly operated on Liverpool–New York route but moved to Burma trade. Modified 1891 to carry 70 passengers. In 1897 replaced by *Derbyshire* and chartered to Dominion Line. Served as a Boer War transport. In 1905 to Danish owners, East Asiatic Co., renamed *Indien*. In 1907 to Russian owners, East Asian Co., renamed *Estoniya*, employed on Libau–New York route but later transferred to Far East. In January 1913 caught fire and abandoned off Port Sudan, hulk sunk by explosive charges shortly afterwards.								
217	218	*Ameer*	24.8.1889	4,014	Cargo Ship	St/Sc/St 400.6/45.2/28.1	320 nhp TE (3Cy) H&W	T.&J. Brocklebank Liverpool
Completed 17.10.1889. In 1907 to Shire Line, renamed *Cardiganshire*. In 1911 to Japanese owners, Tatsuuma Kisen, renamed *Hakushika Maru* in 1916 to G. Katsuda, renamed *Ide Maru*. In 1920 to Hong Kong owners, Figueras SS Co., renamed *Paco Figueras*. Broken up Hong Kong 1923.								

<table>
<tr><th>Ship</th><th>Yard No</th><th>Name</th><th>Date Launched</th><th>Displacement Tons</th><th>Type</th><th>Construction and Dimensions</th><th>Horse Power/ Engines</th><th>Owners</th></tr>
<tr><td>218</td><td>219</td><td>Gaekwar</td><td>24.12.1889</td><td>4,202</td><td>Cargo Ship</td><td>St/Sc/St
400.6/45.2/28.1</td><td>320 nhp
TE (3Cy)
H&W</td><td>T.&J. Brocklebank
Liverpool</td></tr>
<tr><td colspan="9">Completed 15.3.1890, sister ship of Ameer. In 1907 to Shire Line, renamed Carnarvonshire. In 1911 to Norwegian owners, H. Fredriksen, converted into whaling supply ship, renamed Falkland. In 1914 passed to S.L. Christensen, renamed Oron 2. In 1929 to Bruun & V.D. Lippe, renamed Pontas. Broken up Norway (Tonsberg) 1934.</td></tr>
<tr><td>219</td><td>220</td><td>Nawab</td><td>28.9.1889</td><td>3,142</td><td>Cargo Ship</td><td>St/Sc/St
345.6/42.2/24.5</td><td>300 nhp
TE (3Cy)
H&W</td><td>Asiatic Steam
Navigation Co.
Liverpool</td></tr>
<tr><td colspan="9">Completed 23.11.1889. In 1914 to Indian owners, A.M. Jeevanjee, renamed Taiyabi. Foundered on approaches to English Channel, January 1918.</td></tr>
<tr><td>220</td><td>221</td><td>Nadir</td><td>26.10.1889</td><td>3,142</td><td>Cargo Ship</td><td>St/Sc/St
345.6/42.2/24.5</td><td>300 nhp
TE (3Cy)
H&W</td><td>Asiatic Steam
Navigation Co.
Liverpool</td></tr>
<tr><td colspan="9">Completed 24.12.1889, sister ship of Nawab. In 1913 to Japanese owners, Hakuyo Kisen, renamed Temmei Maru. Sunk by submarine gunfire (U-35) off south coast of France, August 1916. No lives lost.</td></tr>
<tr><td>221</td><td>222</td><td>Nizam</td><td>21.12.1889</td><td>3,142</td><td>Cargo Ship</td><td>St/Sc/St
345.6/42.2/24.5</td><td>300 nhp
TE (3Cy)
H&W</td><td>Asiatic Steam
Navigation Co.
Liverpool</td></tr>
<tr><td colspan="9">Completed 26.2.1890, sister ship of Nawab. In 1912 to Japanese owners, Y. Hachiuma, renamed Tamon Maru No.12. Broken up Japan 1935.</td></tr>
<tr><td>222</td><td>223</td><td>Alexander Elder</td><td>23.1.1890</td><td>4,173</td><td>Cargo Ship</td><td>St/Sc/St
400.6/45.2/28.2</td><td>375 nhp
TE (3Cy)
H&W</td><td>Elder Dempster
Liverpool</td></tr>
<tr><td colspan="9">Completed 19.4.1890. In 1891 chartered to Atlantic Transport Line renamed Merrimac. Subsequently returned to Elder Dempster but retained new name. Disappeared on voyage Quebec–Belfast, October 1899. Thirty-six lives lost.</td></tr>
<tr><td>223</td><td>224</td><td>Saint Pancras</td><td>8.2.1890</td><td>4,283</td><td>Cargo Ship</td><td>St/Sc/St
400.6/45.2/28.2</td><td>375 nhp
TE (3Cy)
H&W</td><td>Rankin Gilmour & Co.
Liverpool</td></tr>
<tr><td colspan="9">Completed 13.5.1890. Wrecked Labuan, Malaya, June 1895.</td></tr>
<tr><td>224</td><td>225</td><td>California</td><td>22.2.1890</td><td>3,099</td><td>Sailing Vessel (Four-masted Ship)</td><td>Steel Hulled
329.3/45.2/26.7</td><td>N/A</td><td>North Western
Shipping Co.
Liverpool</td></tr>
<tr><td colspan="9">Completed 24.4.1890. In 1896 to German owners, R.M. Sloman Jr, renamed Alster. In 1912 to F.A. Vinnen & Co., renamed Christel Vinnen. In 1926 to Italian owners, M. Aste, but does not appear to have been renamed. Wrecked off Old Providence Island, Columbia, April 1927.</td></tr>
<tr><td>225</td><td>226</td><td>Imaum</td><td>25.3.1890</td><td>4,129</td><td>Cargo Ship</td><td>St/Sc/St
400.6/45.2/28.2</td><td>450 nhp
TE (3Cy)
H&W</td><td>Edward Bates & Son
Liverpool</td></tr>
<tr><td colspan="9">Completed 31.5.1890. In 1910 to Norwegian owners, Bryde & Dahl, converted into whale factory ship, renamed Thor I. In 1931 taken out of service, broken up Germany (Hamburg) 1937.</td></tr>
<tr><td>226</td><td>227</td><td>Michigan</td><td>19.4.1890</td><td>3,722</td><td>Cargo Ship</td><td>St/Sc/St
370.8/44.2/26.0</td><td>518 nhp
TE (3Cy)
H&W</td><td>Bernard SS Co.
London</td></tr>
<tr><td colspan="9">Completed 21.6.1890. Transferred to Baltimore Storage and Lighter Co. In 1896 to National Line and in 1898 taken over by US Army as transport for Spanish-American War (40 officers, 800 men and 800 horses), renamed Kilpatrick. In 1920 to American Black Ball Line and rebuilt to carry 250 cabin-class and 600 third-class passengers, renamed Acropolis, employed on New York–Greece–Turkey route. In 1923 passed to Booras SN Co. renamed Washington but almost immediately to US & China SS Co., renamed Great Canton, not employed. Broken up Italy (Genoa) 1924.</td></tr>
<tr><td>227</td><td>228</td><td>Plassey</td><td>22.5.1890</td><td>3,176</td><td>Cargo Ship</td><td>St/Sc/St
345.6/40.9/26.7</td><td>300 nhp
TE (3Cy)
H&W</td><td>T.&J. Brocklebank
(African SS Co.)
London</td></tr>
<tr><td colspan="9">Completed 5.7.1890, laid down as Talavera for Elder Dempster name was changed when chartered to Brocklebank while on stocks. In 1893 chartered to Dominion Line, renamed Memnon. Sunk by submarine torpedo (UC-66) English Channel inbound from west coast of Africa, March 1917. Six lives lost.</td></tr>
<tr><td>228</td><td>229</td><td>Columbian</td><td>5.7.1890</td><td>5,088</td><td>Cargo Ship</td><td>St/Sc/St
442.6/45.2/31.0</td><td>500 nhp
TE (3Cy)
H&W</td><td>Leyland & Co.
Liverpool</td></tr>
<tr><td colspan="9">Completed 23.8.1890. In 1897 chartered to Wilson & Furness–Leyland Line. Caught fire and blew up in North Atlantic on voyage Antwerp–New York, May 1914. Eighteen lives lost.</td></tr>
</table>

Ship	Yard No	Name	Date Launched	Displacement Tons	Type	Construction and Dimensions	Horse Power/ Engines	Owners
229	230	*Georgian*	16.8.1890	5,088	Cargo Ship	St/Sc/St 442.6/45.2/31.0	500 nhp TE (3Cy) H&W	Leyland & Co. Liverpool
Completed 27.9.1890, sister ship of *Columbian.* In 1897 chartered to Wilson & Furness–Leyland Line later returned. Sunk by submarine torpedo (*UB-47*) near Crete, March 1917. Five lives lost.								
230	231	*Mississippi*	29.8.1890	3,731	Cargo Ship	St/Sc/St 370.8/44.2/26.6	375 nhp TE (3Cy) H&W	Atlantic Transport Co. London
Completed 18.10.1890. In 1896 to National line. Taken over by US Army in 1898 for use as transport during Spanish-American War, renamed *Burford.* Broken up Japan (Yokohama) 1929.								
231	232	*Sobraon*	17.9.1890	3,185	Cargo Ship	St/Sc/St 345.6/40.9/26.7	300 nhp TE (3Cy) H&W	African SS. Co. (Elder Dempster) London
Completed 6.11.1890, sister ship of *Plassey,* laid down as *Barrosa* completed under this name. Chartered to Brocklebank Line 1890–91. Named changed to *Mexico* 1893. Chartered to Atlantic Transport Line 1895. Wrecked near Belle Isle Light House, July 1895.								
232	233	*Memphis*	18.10.1890	3,190	Cargo Ship	St/Sc/St 345.6/40.9/26.7	300 nhp TE (3Cy) H&W	Elder Dempster Liverpool
Completed 27.11.1890, sister ship of *Plassey.* Chartered to Dominion Line from 1894. Wrecked Mizen Head, November 1896.								
233	234	*Ernesto*	1.11.1890	2,573	Cargo Ship	St/Sc/St 320.7/39.2/24.6	300 nhp TE (3Cy) H&W	Cia de Nav La Flecha Bilbao
Completed 11.12.1890. In 1918 to J.M. de Argacha, renamed *Alava.* Broken up Spain (Bilbao) 1932.								
234	235	*British Crown*	29.11.1890	3,204	Passenger-Cargo	St/Sc/St 345.6/40.9/26.6	320 nhp TE (3Cy) H&W	British Shipowners Ltd Liverpool
(This vessel is listed by Moss & Hume as a passenger ship, re-rated) Completed 17.1.1891. In 1899 to Atlantic Transport Co. renamed *Mackinaw.* Broken up Germany (Stettin) 1923.								
235	236	*Nomadic*	11.2.1891	5,749	Livestock Carrier	St/2Sc/St 460.8/49.1/31.0	600 nhp TE (6Cy) H&W	Oceanic Steam Navigation Co. Liverpool
Completed 14.4.1891, like other vessels of this type employed on Liverpool–New York route. Taken up as transport during Boer War. In 1903 to Dominion Line, renamed *Cornishman* operated on American and Canadian routes. In 1921 to Frederick Leyland & Co. Broken up Lelant (UK) 1926.								
236	237	*Tauric*	12.3.1891	5,727	Livestock Carrier	St/2Sc/St 461.0/49.1/23.2	600 nhp TE (6Cy) H&W	Oceanic Steam Navigation Co. Liverpool
Completed 16.5.1891, sister of *Nomadic.* In 1903 transferred to Dominion Line, renamed *Welshman.* To Frederick Leyland & Co. in 1921. Broken up Bo'ness (UK) 1929.								
237	238	*Labrador*	11.4.1891	4,737	Passenger-Cargo	St/Sc/St 401.0/47.2/28.3	650 nhp TE (3Cy) H&W	Mississippi & Dominion SS Co. Liverpool
(This vessel is listed by Moss & Hume as a passenger ship, re-rated) Completed 13.8.1891. Accommodation for 100 first-class, 50 second-class and 1,000 third-class passengers. Wrecked Skerryvore, inbound St Johns–Liverpool with 74 passengers and 94 crew on board in March 1899. No lives lost.								
238	239	*Assaye*	19.5.1891	4,296	Cargo Ship	St/Sc/St 401.0/45.3/28.1	375 nhp TE (3Cy) H&W	African SS Co. Elder Dempster London
Completed 4.7.1891. Wrecked off Seal Island, Bay of Fundy, when outbound Liverpool–St Johns in April 1897. No lives lost.								
239	240	*Cheshire*	6.6.1891	5,656	Passenger Ship	St/2Sc/St 445.5/49.1/29.7	630 nhp TE (6Cy) H&W	Bibby Steamship Co. Liverpool
Completed 3.9.1891, for Burma trade. Designed to carry 100 first-class passengers in considerable comfort. Requisitioned for use as a transport during Boer War. In 1911 replaced by *Gloucestershire* and passed to Burmese owners, Lim Chin, Rangoon, renamed *Seang Choon.* Requisitioned as a troopship in 1915 and after taking part in Dardanelles campaign, operated between India and UK. Sunk by submarine torpedo (*U-87*) 10 miles off Fastnet, July 1917. Seventeen lives lost.								

<table>
<tr><th>Ship</th><th>Yard No</th><th>Name</th><th>Date Launched</th><th>Displacement Tons</th><th>Type</th><th>Construction and Dimensions</th><th>Horse Power/ Engines</th><th>Owners</th></tr>
<tr><td>240</td><td>241</td><td>Shropshire</td><td>27.7.1891</td><td>5,660</td><td>Passenger Ship</td><td>St/2Sc/St
445.5/49.1/29.7</td><td>630 nhp
TE (6Cy)
H&W</td><td>Bibby Steamship Co.
Liverpool</td></tr>
<tr><td colspan="9">Completed 3.10.1891, sister ship of Cheshire replaced by Leicestershire in 1909. To Burmese owners, Lim Chin, Rangoon, renamed Seang Bee. Taken up for trooping during First World War, returned to her owners 1919. Broken up 1931.</td></tr>
<tr><td>241</td><td>242</td><td>Ionian</td><td>31.10.1891</td><td>6,335</td><td>Cargo Ship</td><td>St/2Sc/St
430.0/47.0/22.4</td><td>375 nhp
TE (6Cy)
H&W</td><td>City of Liverpool
SN Co.
Liverpool</td></tr>
<tr><td colspan="9">Completed 12.1.1892. Name almost immediately changed to Montezuma when City of Liverpool SN Co. acquired by Elder Dempster. To Union SS Co. in 1898, renamed Sandusky, employed on South Africa–North America routes. In 1899 to Mississippi & Dominion Line, renamed Englishman. Employed as transport during Boer War. In 1916 to Dominion Line. Sunk by submarine torpedo (U-43) NE of Malin Head outbound from Avonmouth, March 1916. Ten lives lost.</td></tr>
<tr><td>242</td><td>243</td><td>Lancastrian</td><td>25.7.1891</td><td>5,120</td><td>Cargo Ship</td><td>St/Sc/St
442.5/45.2/31.0</td><td>500 nhp
TE (3Cy)
H&W</td><td>Leyland & Co. Ltd
Liverpool</td></tr>
<tr><td colspan="9">Completed 17.10.1891. To Canadian owners 1921. Broken up Germany (Hamburg) 1925.</td></tr>
<tr><td>243</td><td>244</td><td>Philadelphian</td><td>20.8.1891</td><td>5,120</td><td>Cargo Ship</td><td>St/Sc/St
442.5/45.2/31.0</td><td>500 nhp
TE (3Cy)
H&W</td><td>Leyland & Co. Ltd
Liverpool</td></tr>
<tr><td colspan="9">Completed 12.11.1891, sister ship of Lancastrian. Sunk by submarine torpedo (U-82) in English Channel inbound from New York, February 1918. Four lives lost.</td></tr>
<tr><td>244</td><td>245</td><td>Pindari</td><td>17.10.1891</td><td>5,674</td><td>Cargo Ship</td><td>St/2Sc/St
446.0/49.2/30.0</td><td>375 nhp
TE (6Cy)
H&W</td><td>T.&J. Brocklebank
Liverpool</td></tr>
<tr><td colspan="9">Completed 5.12.1891. Served as Boer War transport No.93. To Shire Line 1906, renamed Breconshire. In 1912 to Japanese owners, Kishimoto Kisen, renamed Shinyo Maru. Broken up Japan 1925.</td></tr>
<tr><td>245</td><td>246</td><td>Mahratta</td><td>19.11.1891</td><td>5,680</td><td>Cargo Ship</td><td>St/Sc/St
446.0/49.2/30.0</td><td>375 nhp
TE (6Cy)
H&W</td><td>T.&J. Brocklebank
Liverpool</td></tr>
<tr><td colspan="9">Completed 28.1.1892, sister ship of Pindari. Served as Boer War transport No.94. Wrecked Goodwin Sands, April 1909.</td></tr>
<tr><td>246</td><td>247</td><td>Massachusetts</td><td>17.12.1891</td><td>5,590</td><td>Passenger-Cargo</td><td>St/2Sc/St
445.5/49.2/30.0</td><td>600 nhp
TE (6Cy)
H&W</td><td>Atlantic Transport Co.
London</td></tr>
<tr><td colspan="9">(This vessel is listed by Moss & Hume as a passenger ship, re-rated)
Completed 5.3.1892, a cargo carrier with accommodation for 80 first-class passengers. In 1896 to National line. Taken over by US Army 1898 as transport for Spanish-American War, renamed Sheridan. Ran aground Hawaiian Islands, August 1906, but salvaged and repaired. Broken up USA (San Francisco) 1923.</td></tr>
<tr><td>247</td><td>248</td><td>Manitoba</td><td>28.1.1892</td><td>5,591</td><td>Passenger-Cargo</td><td>St/2Sc/St
445.5/49.2/30.0</td><td>600 nhp
TE (6Cy)
H&W</td><td>Atlantic Transport Co.
London</td></tr>
<tr><td colspan="9">(This vessel is listed by Moss & Hume as a passenger ship, re-rated)
Completed 9.4.1892, sister ship of Massachusetts. In 1896 to National line. Taken over by US Army 1898 as transport for Spanish-American War, renamed Logan. In 1923 to E.T. Winston, renamed Candler. Broken up USA (Baltimore) 1925.</td></tr>
<tr><td>248</td><td>249</td><td>Mohawk</td><td>25.2.1892</td><td>5,575</td><td>Passenger-Cargo</td><td>St/2Sc/St
445.5/49.2/30.0</td><td>600 nhp
TE (6Cy)
H&W</td><td>African SS Co.
Elder Dempster
London</td></tr>
<tr><td colspan="9">(This vessel is listed by Moss & Hume as a passenger ship, re-rated)
Completed 7.5.1892, sister ship of Massachusetts, originally to be named Memnon. On completion chartered to Atlantic Transport Line, and sold to them in 1896. Taken up by US Army 1898 as transport for Spanish-American War and renamed Grant. In 1902 US Army engineers converted vessel into dredger, renamed Chinook. Broken up USA 1946.</td></tr>
<tr><td>249</td><td>250</td><td>Lord Erne</td><td>29.3.1892</td><td>5,828</td><td>Cargo Ship</td><td>St/2Sc/St
445.0/49.2/30.1</td><td>418 nhp
TE (6Cy)
H&W</td><td>Irish Shipowners Co.
(T. Dixon & Sons)
Belfast</td></tr>
<tr><td colspan="9">Completed 28.5.1892. In 1899 to Dominion Line, renamed Turcoman. Served as troopship during First World War. In 1921 to Leyland Line. Broken up Italy (Savona) 1926.</td></tr>
<tr><td>250</td><td>251</td><td>Naronic</td><td>26.5.1892</td><td>6,594</td><td>Livestock Carrier</td><td>St/2Sc/St
470.0/53.1/23.9</td><td>631 nhp
TE (6Cy)
H&W</td><td>Ocean Steam Navigation Co.
Liverpool</td></tr>
<tr><td colspan="9">Completed 11.7.1892. An enlarged version of previous Nomadic type with additional passenger accommodation. Left Liverpool for New York February 1893 and disappeared. Seventy-four lives lost.</td></tr>
</table>

Ship	Yard No	Name	Date Launched	Displacement Tons	Type	Construction and Dimensions	Horse Power/ Engines	Owners
251	252	*Bovic*	28.6.1892	6,583	Livestock Carrier	St/2Sc/St 470.0/53.1/23.9	631 nhp TE (6Cy) H&W	Oceanic Steam Navigation Co. Liverpool
Completed 22.8.1892, sister of *Naronic*. On Liverpool–New York route until 1914 when switched to Manchester–New York. Taken over by Shipping Controller during First World War and returned to owners 1919. In 1922 to Frederick Leyland & Co. renamed *Colonia*. Broken up Holland (Rotterdam) 1928.								
252	253	*Mobile*	17.11.1892	5,779	Passenger-Cargo	St/2Sc/St 445.5/49.2/30.0	600 nhp TE (6Cy) H&W	African SS Co. Elder Dempster London
(This vessel is listed by Moss & Hume as a cargo ship, re-rated) Completed 27.7.1893, sister ship of *Massachusetts*. On completion, chartered to Atlantic transport Line and sold to them in 1896. Taken over by US Army 1898 as transport for Spanish-American War, renamed *Sherman*. In 1923 to Los Angeles SS Co., renamed *Calawa II*. Broken up Japan (Osaka) 1933.								
253	254	*Nurani*	9.7.1892	4,432	Cargo Ship	St/2Sc/St 400.7/45.2/28.1	365 nhp TE (6Cy) H&W	Asiatic Steam Navigation Co. Liverpool
Completed 10.9.1892. In 1914 to Indian owners, Bombay & Persia SN Co. Broken up Italy (Genoa) 1922.								
254	255	*Nairung*	6.10.1892	4,425	Cargo Ship	St/2Sc/St 400.7/45.2/28.1	373 nhp TE (6Cy) H&W	Asiatic Steam Navigation Co. Liverpool
Completed 10.11.1892. Sister ship of *Nurani*. In 1914 to Indian owners, Bombay & Persia SN Co. Broken up Italy (La Spezia) 1925.								
255	256	*Sagamore*	8.9.1892	5,036	Cargo Ship	St/Sc/St 430.4/46.2/31.0	592 nhp TE (3Cy) H&W	George Warren & Co. Liverpool
(This vessel is listed by Moss & Hume as a passenger ship, re-rated) Completed 30.11.1892. Sunk by submarine torpedo (*U-49*) 150nm W of Fastnet inbound Boston–Liverpool, 3 March 1917. The crew were able to take to the boats but in bad weather two of the three were lost and the third not discovered until the 12th. Only seven of the original 17 occupants were still alive; 52 lives lost.								
256	257	*Islam*	22.10.1892	5,402	Cargo Ship	St/2Sc/St 445.0/49.2/30.1	505 nhp TE (6Cy) H&W	Edward Bates & Son Liverpool
Completed 15.12.1892. In 1894 to Japanese owners, NYK, renamed *Tosa Maru*. Broken up Japan 1925.								
257	258	*Damson Hill*	24.11.1892	2,087	Sailing Vessel (Four-masted Barque)	Steel Hulled 282.9/40.5/23.8	N/A	W.J. Myers Son & Co. Liverpool
Completed 18.1.1893. In 1896 to German owners, Gildemeister & Ries, renamed *Niobe*. Interned in Chile for duration of First World War and surrendered to British government 1920. In 1922 to German owners, Hachfeld Fischer, renamed *Harald*. Broken up 1925.								
258	259	*Orellana*	7.12.1892	4,822	Passenger-Cargo	St/Sc/St 401.0/47.6/19.9	599 nhp TE (3Cy) H&W	Pacific Steam Navigation Co. Liverpool
(This vessel is listed by Moss & Hume as a passenger ship, re-rated) Completed 23.2.1893, intended for cargo services but capable of carrying 675 emigrants from Portugal/Spain to South America during the season. In 1905 to German owners HAPAG, renamed *Allemannia*. The following year was one of a number of ships leased to the Russian East Asiatic Co., acting as colliers supplying the Russian fleet sailing from Baltic to Far East during Japo-Russian war, renamed *Kovno*. In 1907 returned to HAPAG and reverted to *Allemannia*. Interned in USA at outbreak of First World War and taken over by US Government 1917, renamed *Owasco*. Sunk by submarine torpedo (*U-64*) off southern Spain inbound for Genoa, December 1917. Two lives lost.								
259	260	*Antisana*	22.12.1892	3,684	Cargo Ship	St/Sc/St 360.8/43.2/19.5	358 nhp TE (3Cy) H&W	Pacific Steam Navigation Co. Liverpool
Completed 11.3.1893, cargo capacity of 234,000sq. ft. In 1910 to French owners, Messageries Maritimes, renamed *Basque*. Torpedoed off North African coast February 1918, beached at Malta, repaired and returned to service 1920. Broken up Italy 1924.								
260	261	*Gaul*	16.2.1893	4,745	Passenger-Cargo	St/2Sc/St 400.5/47.2/26.7	418 nhp TE (6Cy) H&W	Union SS. Co. Southampton
(This vessel is listed by Moss & Hume as a passenger ship, re-rated) Completed 6.5.1893, for use on Southampton–South Africa route. In 1900 transferred to newly formed Union-Castle Line. In 1906 to Royal Mail SP Co., renamed *Sabo* and employed on Southampton–Cuba/Mexico route. In 1909 to Shire Line, renamed *Carmarthenshire* on London–Far East routes. In 1913 to Pickford & Black, renamed *Chaleur*. Broken up Holland (Hendrik-Ido-Ambacht) 1927.								

<table>
<tr><th>Ship</th><th>Yard No</th><th>Name</th><th>Date Launched</th><th>Displacement Tons</th><th>Type</th><th>Construction and Dimensions</th><th>Horse Power/ Engines</th><th>Owners</th></tr>
<tr><td>261</td><td>262</td><td>Lord Templemore</td><td>27.2.1892</td><td>3,045</td><td>Sailing Vessel (Four-masted Barque)</td><td>Steel Hulled 329.8/45.1/26.7</td><td>N/A</td><td>Irish Shipowners Co. (T. Dixon & Son) Belfast</td></tr>
<tr><td colspan="9">Completed 19.4.1892. In 1898 to German owners, A.G. Alster, renamed Alsternixe. Disappeared on voyage Callao–Melbourne, November 1906.</td></tr>
<tr><td>262</td><td>263</td><td>Goth</td><td>16.3.1893</td><td>4,738</td><td>Passenger-Cargo</td><td>St/2Sc/St 400.5/47.2/26.8</td><td>418 nhp TE (6Cy) H&W</td><td>Union SS Co. Southampton</td></tr>
<tr><td colspan="9">(This vessel is listed by Moss & Hume as a passenger ship, re-rated)
Completed 8.6.1893, sister ship of Gaul. Served as a troopship during the Boer War. Passed to Union-Castle Line 1900. In 1913 to Royal Mail SP Co. renamed Cobequid, used on Canada–West Indies routes. Wrecked off Bay of Fundy, January 1915. No lives lost.</td></tr>
<tr><td>263</td><td>264</td><td>Orcana</td><td>7.3.1893</td><td>4,821</td><td>Passenger-Cargo</td><td>St/Sc/St 401.0/47.6/19.9</td><td>599 nhp TE (3Cy) H&W</td><td>Pacific Steam Navigation Co. Liverpool</td></tr>
<tr><td colspan="9">(This vessel is listed by Moss & Hume as a passenger ship, re-rated)
Completed 8.7.1893, sister ship of Orellana. During Boer War served as transport No.40 and later hospital ship. In 1905 to German owners, HAPAG, renamed Albingia leased to the Russian East Asiatic Co. renamed Grodno returned in 1907 and reverted to Alningia. Interned in United States at outbreak of the war and in 1916 to American owners, Jason SS Co. renamed Argonaut. Sunk by submarine torpedo (U-82) off Bishop Rock Inbound from Norfolk Viginia, June 1918. No lives lost.</td></tr>
<tr><td>264</td><td>265</td><td>Sarmiento</td><td>1.4.1893</td><td>3,603</td><td>Cargo Ship</td><td>St/Sc/St 361.0/43.2.19.5</td><td>353 nhp TE (3Cy) H&W</td><td>Pacific Steam Navigation Co. Liverpool</td></tr>
<tr><td colspan="9">(This vessel is listed by Moss & Hume as a passenger ship, re-rated)
Completed 17.6.1893, sister ship of Anaisana. In 1910 to French owners, Messageries Maritimes, renamed Normand. Broken up Italy (Genoa) 1925.</td></tr>
<tr><td>265</td><td>266</td><td>Mystic</td><td>4.2.1893</td><td>726</td><td>Cross-Channel Ship</td><td>St/2Sc/St 220.8/29.1/14.6</td><td>219 hp TE (6Cy) H&W</td><td>Belfast Steamship Co. Belfast</td></tr>
<tr><td colspan="9">Completed 1.4.1893, employed on Belfast–Liverpool route and freight services to Manchester. In 1911 to City of Dublin SP Co., renamed Carrickfergus. Subsequently operated by Sligo SN Co. In 1931 to Burns & Laird, renamed Lairdsben employed on Dublin–Heysham route. Broken up Glasgow (UK) 1937.</td></tr>
<tr><td>266</td><td>267</td><td>Gothic</td><td>28.6.1893</td><td>7,669</td><td>Passenger Ship</td><td>St/2Sc/St 490.7/53.2/33.5</td><td>846 hp TE (6Cy) H&W</td><td>Oceanic Steam Navigation Co. Liverpool</td></tr>
<tr><td colspan="9">Completed 28.11.1893, designed for North Atlantic routes but initially employed on Australian services. Seriously damaged by fire June 1906 and rebuilt to carry 104 first class and 250 third class, but first-class cabins were reduced to third shortly afterwards. In 1907 transferred to Red Star Line, and renamed Gothland operating under Belgian flag between Antwerp and North America. In 1911 returned to White Star and reverted to original name, used on Australian route carrying 1,500 steerage-class passengers. Two years later, again to Red Star and reassumed alternative name. Seriously damaged when ran aground in 1914. Final voyage for Red Star 1925. Sold for £16,000 and broken up at Bo'ness (UK) 1926.</td></tr>
<tr><td>267</td><td>268</td><td>Greek</td><td>18.5.1893</td><td>4,744</td><td>Passenger-Cargo</td><td>St/2Sc/St 400.5/47.2/26.9</td><td>418 nhp TE (6Cy) H&W</td><td>Union Steamship Co. Southampton</td></tr>
<tr><td colspan="9">(This vessel is listed by Moss & Hume as a passenger ship, re-rated)
Completed 26.8.1893, sister ship of Gaul. Troopship during Boer War. In 1906 to Royal Mail SP Co., renamed Segura. In 1909 to Shire Line, renamed Pembrokeshire. In 1913 to Royal Mail Line, renamed Chignecto. Broken up Holland (Hendrik-Ido-Ambacht) 1927.</td></tr>
<tr><td>268</td><td>269</td><td>Magnetic</td><td>28.3.1891</td><td>619</td><td>Passenger Tender</td><td>St/2Sc/St 170.5/32.0/15.0</td><td>175 nhp TE (6Cy) H&W</td><td>Oceanic Steam Navigation Co. Liverpool</td></tr>
<tr><td colspan="9">Completed 6.6.1891, for use at Liverpool, could also function as a tug or water carrier. In October 1925 seriously damaged by fire but repaired. In 1932 to the Alexandra Towing Company, renamed Ryde. Broken up Port Glasgow (UK) 1935.</td></tr>
<tr><td>269</td><td>270</td><td>Cevic</td><td>23.9.1893</td><td>8,301</td><td>Livestock Carrier</td><td>St/2Sc/St 500.0/60.0/38.0</td><td>708 nhp TE (6Cy) H&W</td><td>Oceanic Steam Navigation Co. Liverpool</td></tr>
<tr><td colspan="9">Completed 6.1.1894. On Liverpool–New York route until 1908 when transferred to Australian routes, although probably too large for that service. In 1914 converted by H&W into a dummy battleship for use on patrol duties. Decommissioned mid-1915 and restored to commercial service by H&W. In 1916 converted to oil tanker, taken up by Royal Fleet Auxiliary and renamed Boyol. In 1917 name changed to Bayleaf and used to carry fuel to naval shore establishment. In June 1920 to Anglo-Saxon Petroleum Co. (Shell) as a depot ship at New York, renamed Pyrula. Transferred to Curacao in 1925, classified as oil hulk. Broken up Italy (Genoa) 1933.</td></tr>
</table>

Ship	Yard No	Name	Date Launched	Displacement Tons	Type	Construction and Dimensions	Horse Power/ Engines	Owners
270	271	*Magic*	20.4.1893	1,630	Cross-Channel Ship	St/2Sc/St 311.3/38.3/15.1	498 nhp TE (6Cy) H&W	Belfast Steamship Co. Belfast
Completed 10.8.1893. On Belfast–Liverpool route until First World War, when became a hospital carrier. Renamed *Classic* in 1919. In 1925 to City of Cork SP Co., renamed *Killarney*. In 1947 to Bury Court Co., renamed *Attiki*. The following year to Greek owners, G. Potamianos, renamed *Adrias*. Wrecked Falconera Island, October 1951.								
271	272	*Sachem*	29.6.1893	5,203	Passenger-Cargo	St/Sc/St 445.5/46.2/31.1	591 nhp TE (3Cy) H&W	George Warren & Co. Liverpool
(This vessel is listed by Moss & Hume as a passenger ship, re-rated) Completed 28.10.1893. Broken up Morecambe (UK) 1927.								
272	273	*Magellan*	3.8.1893	3,590	Cargo Ship	St/Sc/St 360.5/43.2/27.3	353 nhp TE (3Cy) H&W	Pacific Steam Navigation Co. Liverpool
Completed 23.11.1893, sister ship of *Anaisana*. Sunk by submarine torpedo (*UB-50*) Western Mediterranean inbound Malta–UK, July 1918. One life lost.								
273	274	*Torr Head*	20.1.1894	5,910	Cargo Ship	St/2Sc/St 452.8/50.3/31.2	452 nhp TE (6Cy) H&W	Ulster Steamship Co. Belfast
Completed 7.4.1894. Sunk by submarine torpedo (*U-60*) off west of Ireland inbound St Johns–Dublin, April 1917. No lives lost.								
274	275	*Inca*	12.10.1893	3,593	Cargo Ship	St/Sc/St 360.5/43.2/27.3	353 nhp TE (3Cy) H&W	Pacific Steam Navigation Co. Liverpool
Completed 23.12.1893, sister ship of *Anaisana*. In 1923 to Argentinian owners, Braun & Blanchard, renamed *Llanquihue*. Wrecked in Magellan Strait, September 1928. Wreck subsequently broken up.								
275	276	Un-named	19.4.1893	60	Dredger			Lower Bann Navigation
Completed 11.5.1893.								
276	277	*Templemore*	9.11.1893	6,276	Cargo Ship	St/Sc/St 451.0/48.2/26.8	610 nhp TE (3Cy) H&W	William Johnston Liverpool
Completed 7.2.1894. Damaged by fire off American coast September 1913 and subsequently broken up (Boston) USA.								
277	278	*Staffordshire*	7.12.1893	6,005	Passenger-Cargo	St/2Sc/St 445.5/49.1/29.9	688 nhp TE (6Cy) H&W	Bibby Steamship Co. Liverpool
Completed 2.4.1894, employed on Liverpool–Rangoon service. Transport during Boer War. Replaced by *Oxfordshire* 1912, to French owners, Cie Sud Atlantique, renamed *Samara*. Torpedoed 1914 repaired and returned to South American routes. Broken up Italy (Genoa) 1923.								
278	279	*Ikbal*	22.2.1894	5,404	Cargo Ship	St/2Sc/St 445.2/49.1/30.2	448 nhp TE (6Cy) H&W	Edward Bates & Son Liverpool
Completed 5.5.1894. Sunk by submarine torpedo (*U-93*) approaches English Channel, inbound St John–Falmouth with cargo of ammunition, April 1917. No lives lost.								
279	280	*Norman*	19.7.1894	7,394	Passenger-Cargo (Refrigerated)	St/2Sc/St 490.8/53.2/33.5	1,090 nhp TE (6Cy) H&W	Union Steamship Co. Southampton
(This vessel is listed by Moss & Hume as a passenger ship, re-rated) Completed 13.10.1894, built to Admiralty specifications to allow rapid conversion into troopship. Employed as such in both the Boer War and First World War. Broken up Morecambe (UK) 1926.								
280	281	*Prussia*	10.4.1894	5,840	Passenger-Cargo	St/2Sc/St 445.4/50.2/29.9	594 nhp TE (6Cy) H&W	Hamburg-Amerika Line Hamburg
(This vessel is listed by Moss & Hume as a passenger ship, re-rated) Completed 31.5.1894, accommodation for 60 first-class and 1,800 third-class passengers. In 1898 to Mississippi Dominion Line, renamed *Dominion*, rebuilt to carry 200 first class, 170 second class and 750 third class on Canada routes. In 1908 to America Line and rebuilt to carry 370 second class and 750 third class on Liverpool–Philadelphia route. In First World War served as a supply ship. Returned in 1919 and converted into cargo ship. Broken up Germany (Hamburg) 1922.								
281	282	*Persia*	8.5.1894	5,857	Passenger-Cargo	St/2Sc/St 445.5/50.2/29.8	594 nhp TE (6Cy) H&W	Hamburg-Amerika Line Hamburg
(This vessel is listed by Moss & Hume as a passenger ship, re-rated)								

Ship	Yard No	Name	Date Launched	Displacement Tons	Type	Construction and Dimensions	Horse Power/ Engines	Owners
Completed 18.7.1894, sister ship of *Prussia*. In 1898 to American owners, Williams Torrey, renamed *Minnewaska*. Taken up by US Army as transport for Spanish-American War, renamed *Thomas*. Broken up USA (Oakland) 1929.								
282	283	*Pontic*	3.2.1894	395	Baggage Tender	St/Sc/St 150.5/26.1/11.1	64 nhp TE (3Cy) H&W	Oceanic Steam Navigation Co. Liverpool
Completed 13.4.1894, for use at Liverpool, could also be employed as water tender. In October 1919 to Rea Towing Co. In 1925 to John Donaldson Beardmore SS Co., used as a collier and ballast carrier. Broken up Glasgow (UK) 1930.								
283	284	*Guelph*	26.6.1894	4,917	Passenger-Cargo	St/2Sc/St 400.5/47.3/26.9	418 nhp TE (6Cy) H&W	Union Steamship Co. Southampton
(This vessel is listed by Moss & Hume as a passenger ship, re-rated) Completed 8.9.1894, slightly enlarged half sister of *Gascon*. Troopship during Boer War. In 1913 to Royal Mail SP Co., renamed *Caraquet*. Wrecked Bermuda, June 1923. No lives lost.								
284	285	*Oropesa*	29.11.1894	5,317	Passenger-Cargo	St/2Sc/St 421.0/48.3/32.0	568 nhp 3,600 ihp TE (6Cy) H&W	Pacific Steam Navigation Co. Liverpool
(This vessel is listed by Moss & Hume as a passenger ship, re-rated) Completed 9.2.1895, for South American services. At outbreak of First World War commissioned as armed merchant cruiser (6x 6in guns) and served with 10th CS. In 1915 to French Navy, renamed *Champagne*. Sunk by submarine torpedo (*U-90*) October 1917 in Irish Sea, 8nm from Calf of Man. Fifty-six lives lost out of complement of 305.								
285	286	*Orissa*	15.12.1894	5,317	Passenger-Cargo	St/2Sc/St 421.0/48.3/32.0	568 nhp 3,600 ihp TE (6Cy) H&W	Pacific Steam Navigation Co. Livorpool
(This vessel is listed by Moss & Hume as a passenger ship, re-rated) Completed 30.3.1895, sister ship of *Oropesa*. Sunk by submarine torpedo (*UB-73*) 21nm SW of Skerryvore, outbound Liverpool–Philadelphia, June 1918. Six lives lost.								
286	287	*Blairmore*	14.8.1894	2,286	Cargo Ship	St/Sc/St 313.0/38.2/22.4	245 nhp TE (3Cy) **Engines** Muir & Huston Glasgow	William Johnston Liverpool
Completed 17.10.1894. In 1912 to Monroe Rutherford, renamed *Ballater*. In 1917 to J.C. Gould & Co., Cardiff, renamed *Greleen*. Sunk by submarine torpedo (*UB-40*) near Berry Head, inbound Castro Urdialo–Tees with cargo of iron ore, September 1917. Nineteen lives lost.								
287	288	*Ulstermore*	16.10.1894	6,326	Cargo Ship	St/Sc/St 451.0/48.3/27.8	627 nhp TE (3Cy) H&W	William Johnston Liverpool
Completed 6.12.1894. Wrecked in Mersey, January 1913.								
288	289	*Scotsman*	13.12.1894	6,041	Passenger Ship	St/2Sc/St 470.7/49.2/31.9	499 nhp TE (6Cy) H&W	British & N Atlantic SN Co. (Dominion Line) Liverpool
Completed 11.4.1895, laid down as a cargo ship but altered on stocks to carry 100 first-class, 130 second-class and 800 third-class passengers. Wrecked in Straits of Belle Isle, September 1899, about a dozen lives lost. After the ship went aground the crew looted passengers' luggage, which caused considerable scandal at the time.								
289	290	*Marino*	10.11.1894	3,819	Cargo Ship	St/Sc/St 371.0/43.2/27.5	268 nhp TE (3Cy) **Engines** Muir & Huston Glasgow	Ocean Steam Transport Co. (Elder Dempster) Liverpool
Completed 2.3.1895. In 1898 to Union SS Co., renamed *Sabine*. In 1921 to Bullard King & Co., renamed *Umzinto*. Broken up Italy (Venice) 1925.								
290	291	*Victorian*	6.7.1895	8,767	Passenger-Cargo	St/Sc/St 512.5/59.2/35.0	718 nhp 4,500 ihp TE (3Cy) H&W	Leyland & Co. Ltd Liverpool
Completed 31.8.1895, for Liverpool–Boston service with accommodation for 60 saloon-class passengers. In 1903 chartered to White Star used on Liverpool–New York route. Converted to cargo vessel and renamed *Russian* in 1914, on instructions from Admiralty to avoid confusion with liner of same name. Sunk by submarine torpedo (*UB-43*) 240nm off Malta, inbound Salonica–Newport, December 1916. Twenty-eight lives lost.								

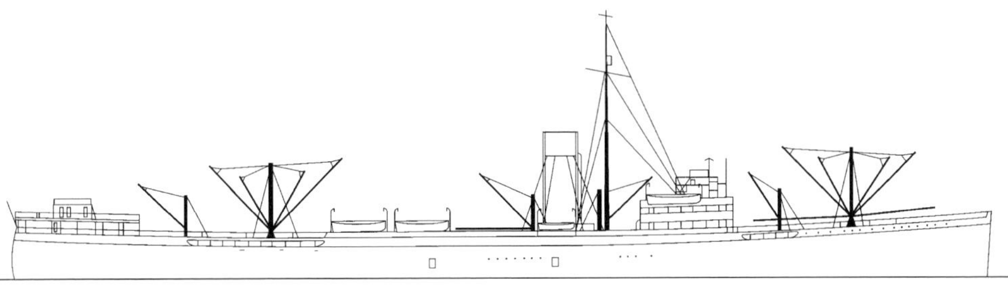

Orca (H&W y/n 442) 1917 – as originally completed (DH)

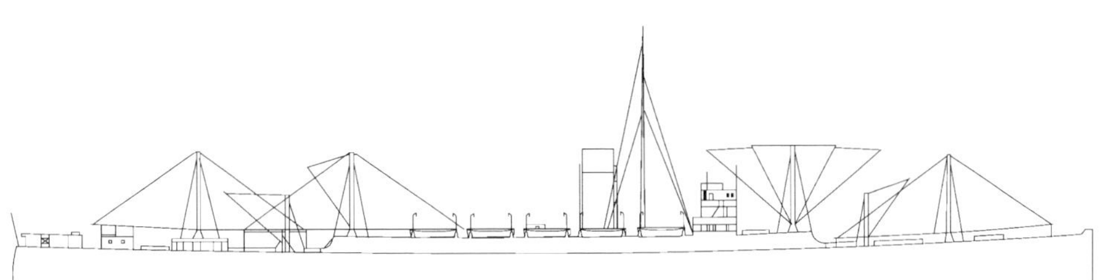

Minnekahda (H&W y/n 446) 1917 – as originally completed (DH)

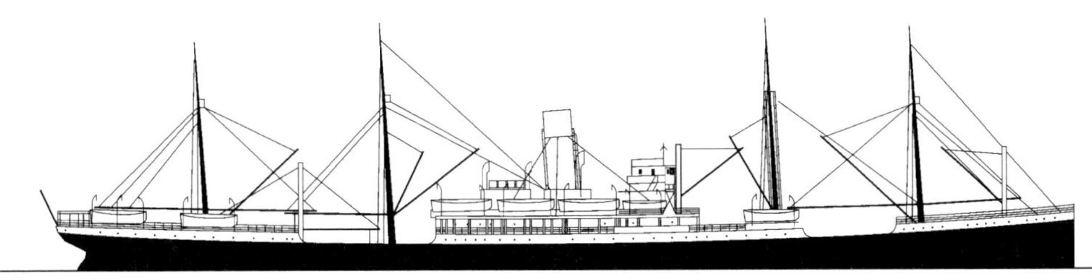

Brecknockshire (H&W y/n 453) 1916 (DH)

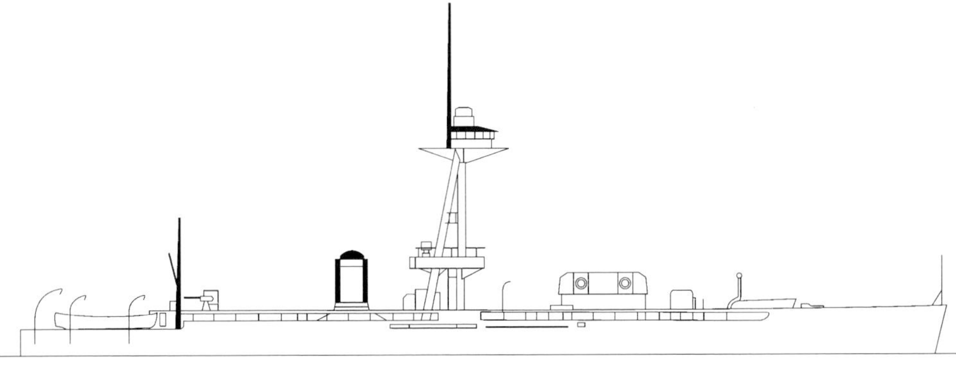

HMS *Abercrombie* (H&W y/n 472) 1915 (DH)

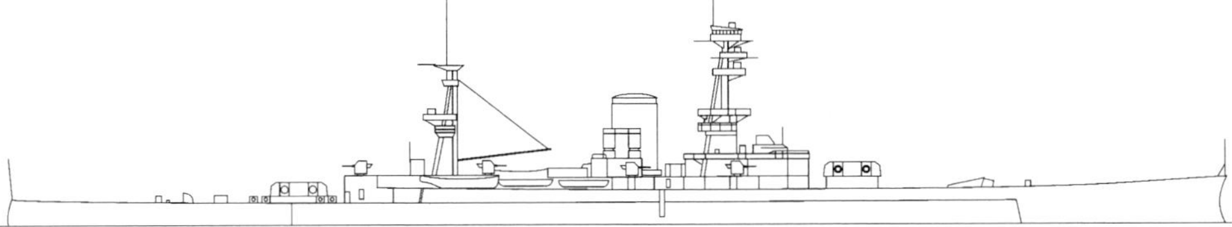

HMS *Glorious* (H&W y/n 482-4) 1916 (DH)

<table>
<tr><th>Ship</th><th>Yard No</th><th>Name</th><th>Date Launched</th><th>Displacement Tons</th><th>Type</th><th>Construction and Dimensions</th><th>Horse Power/ Engines</th><th>Owners</th></tr>
<tr><td>291</td><td>292</td><td>Armenian</td><td>25.7.1895</td><td>8,765</td><td>Passenger-
Cargo</td><td>St/Sc/St
512.5/59.2/35.0</td><td>718 nhp
4,500 ihp
TE (3Cy)
H&W</td><td>Leyland & Co. Ltd
Liverpool</td></tr>
<tr><td colspan="9">Completed 19.9.1895, laid down as Indian but completed under this name, sister ship of Victorian. In 1903 chartered to White Star employed on Liverpool–New York route. Converted to cargo vessel in 1914. Sunk by submarine torpedo (U-24) at entrance to English Channel, inbound Newport News–Avonmouth with cargo of 1,400 mules, June 1915. Twenty-nine lives lost.</td></tr>
<tr><td>292</td><td>293</td><td>Georgic</td><td>22.6.1895</td><td>10,077</td><td>Livestock
Carrier</td><td>St/2Sc/St
580.7/60.3/36.6</td><td>612 nhp
TE (6Cy)
H&W</td><td>Oceanic Steam
Navigation Co.
Liverpool</td></tr>
<tr><td colspan="9">Completed 8.8.1895, built to replace Naronic, largest of livestock carriers and last of type built. In reality too large for the trade. In December 1916 inbound Philadelphia–Brest, with a cargo that included 1,200 horses, captured and sunk by German raider Mowe.</td></tr>
<tr><td>293</td><td>294</td><td>American</td><td>8.8.1895</td><td>8,196</td><td>Cargo Ship</td><td>St/2Sc/St
475.9/55.2/35.9</td><td>375nhp
TE (6Cy)
H&W</td><td>West Indian &
Pacific Steam
Navigation Co.
Liverpool</td></tr>
<tr><td colspan="9">Completed 8.10.1895. In 1904 to Ismay Imrie & Co., Liverpool, renamed Cufic. In 1924 to Italian owners, E. Cesano, renamed Antartico. In 1927 to Bozzo & Mortola, renamed Maria Giulia. Broken up Italy (Genoa) 1932.</td></tr>
<tr><td>294</td><td>295</td><td>Historian</td><td>7.9.1895</td><td>6,857</td><td>Cargo Ship</td><td>St/Sc/St
460.7/55.2/31.5</td><td>570 nhp
TE (3Cy)
H&W</td><td>Charente SS Co.
T&J Harrison
Liverpool</td></tr>
<tr><td colspan="9">Completed 29.1.1896. In 1922 to Hong Kong owners, M.H. Nemazee, renamed Arabestan. In 1925 to Italian owners, Industrie Navali SA, renamed Delia and later Delia Terzo. Broken up Italy (Savona) 1930.</td></tr>
<tr><td>295</td><td>296</td><td>Cestrian</td><td>21.9.1895</td><td>8,761</td><td>Passenger-
Cargo</td><td>St/Sc/St
512.5/59.2/35.0</td><td>718 nhp
4,500 ihp
TE (3Cy)
H&W</td><td>Leyland & Co. Ltd
Liverpool</td></tr>
<tr><td colspan="9">(This vessel is listed by Moss & Hume as a passenger ship, re-rated)
Completed 5.3.1896, sister ship of Victorian. Sunk by submarine torpedo (UB-42) in Aegean, on route Salonica–Alexandria with cargo of horses, June 1917. Three lives lost.</td></tr>
<tr><td>296</td><td>297</td><td>Iran</td><td>29.2.1896</td><td>6,250</td><td>Cargo Ship</td><td>St/2Sc/St
452.7/52.2/31.5</td><td>478 nhp
TE (6Cy)
H&W</td><td>Edward Bates & Son
Liverpool</td></tr>
<tr><td colspan="9">Completed 30.4.1896. Sunk by submarine torpedo (U-155) 200nm of Azores, inbound Calcutta–London/Tees, August 1917. No lives lost.</td></tr>
<tr><td>297</td><td>298</td><td>Vedamore</td><td>19.10.1895</td><td>6,329</td><td>Cargo Ship
(Refrigerated)</td><td>St/Sc/St
451.1/48.3/27.3</td><td>627 nhp
TE (3Cy)
H&W</td><td>William Johnston
Liverpool</td></tr>
<tr><td colspan="9">Completed 28.3.1896. Sunk by submarine torpedo (U-85) 20nm W Fastnet, inbound Baltimore–Liverpool, February 1917. Twenty-three lives lost.</td></tr>
<tr><td>298</td><td>299</td><td>China</td><td>13.6.1896</td><td>7,899</td><td>Passenger
Ship</td><td>St/Sc/St
500.5/54.2/25.1</td><td>1,395 nhp
11,000 ihp
TE (4Cy)
H&W</td><td>Peninsular and
Oriental Steam
Navigation Co.
London</td></tr>
<tr><td colspan="9">The only one of the five 'India' type built in Belfast. Like previous ships for this customer they were designed for rapid conversion to auxiliary cruisers or troop transports able to carry 2,500 men. Accommodation was provided for 320 first-class and 160 second-class passengers and the crew numbered almost 1,000.
Completed 28.11.1896, employed on Indian and Australian routes. China was last of type to survive, sold to Japanese breakers for £24,000 in 1928.</td></tr>
<tr><td>299</td><td>300</td><td>Canada</td><td>14.5.1896</td><td>8,800</td><td>Passenger
Ship</td><td>St/2Sc/St
500.4/58.2/31.1</td><td>873 nhp
6,600 ihp
TE (6Cy)
H&W</td><td>British & N Atlantic
SN Co.
(Dominion Line)
Liverpool</td></tr>
<tr><td colspan="9">Completed 26.9.1896, designed for the Canada routes. This ship had a huge influence on medium-size liner construction, introducing enormous improvements in accommodation. Could carry 200 first-class, 200 second-class and 800 steerage passengers. Served as troopship in Boer and First World Wars. Broken up Italy (Genoa) 1926.</td></tr>
<tr><td>300</td><td>301</td><td>Istrar</td><td>14.3.1896</td><td>4,582</td><td>Cargo Ship</td><td>St/Sc/St
400.2/46.2/29.2</td><td>442 nhp
TE (3Cy)
H&W</td><td>Edward Bates & Son
Liverpool</td></tr>
<tr><td colspan="9">Completed 4.6.1896. In 1914 chartered to Brocklebank Line, bought by them in 1916. Sunk by submarine torpedo (U-39) off Alexandria, outbound for Calcutta, December 1916. One life lost.</td></tr>
</table>

<table>
<tr><th>Ship</th><th>Yard No</th><th>Name</th><th>Date Launched</th><th>Displacement Tons</th><th>Type</th><th>Construction and Dimensions</th><th>Horse Power/ Engines</th><th>Owners</th></tr>
<tr><td>301</td><td>302</td><td>Pennsylvania</td><td>10.9.1896</td><td>13,726</td><td>Passenger-Cargo</td><td>St/2Sc/St
560.0/62.0/41.0</td><td>695 nhp
6,000 ihp
QE (8Cy)
H&W</td><td>Hamburg-Amerika Line
Hamburg</td></tr>
<tr><td colspan="9">Completed 30.1.1897, prototype for a number of ships produced in German yards. As built could carry 160 first-class passengers, 180 second class and 2,000 emigrant class; later changed to 400 cabin and 2,000 steerage class. One of the 91 German ships that fell into American hands on their entry into war, operated by US Shipping Board. In January 1919 commissioned as transport, renamed Nansemond, decommissioned in September, returned to Shipping Board. Broken up USA (Baltimore) 1924.</td></tr>
<tr><td>302</td><td>303</td><td>European</td><td>9.7.1896</td><td>8,194</td><td>Cargo Ship</td><td>St/2Sc/St
475.9/55.2/35.0</td><td>375 nhp
TE (6Cy)
H&W</td><td>West Indian & Pacific Steam Navigation Co.
Liverpool</td></tr>
<tr><td colspan="9">Completed 3.12.1896, sister ship of American. In 1904 to Ismay Imrie & Co., renamed Tropic. In 1923 to Italian owners, Ligure, renamed Artico. In 1927 to L. Pittaluga, renamed Transilvania. Broken up Italy (Genoa) 1933.</td></tr>
<tr><td>303</td><td>304</td><td>Gascon</td><td>25.8.1896</td><td>6,288</td><td>Passenger-Cargo</td><td>St/2Sc/St
430.0/52.2/29.0</td><td>375 nhp
2,900 ihp
TE (6Cy)
H&W</td><td>Union Steamship Co.
Southampton</td></tr>
<tr><td colspan="9">(This vessel is listed by Moss & Hume as a passenger ship, re-rated)
Completed 13.2.1897, for South African routes. Economical vessel with good cargo capacity, carrying 80 first-class and 120 second-class passengers as well as third class. Transferred to Union-Castle in 1900. Served as hospital ship with 434 beds in First World War. Returned to regular route 1920. Broken up Inverkeithing (UK) 1928.</td></tr>
<tr><td>304</td><td>305</td><td>Gaika</td><td>22.9.1896</td><td>6,287</td><td>Passenger-Cargo</td><td>St/2Sc/St
430.0/52.2/29.0</td><td>375 nhp
2,900 ihp
TE (6Cy)
H&W</td><td>Union Steamship Co.
Southampton</td></tr>
<tr><td colspan="9">(This vessel is listed by Moss & Hume as a passenger ship, re-rated)
Completed 15.4.1897, sister ship of Gascon. Remained on South African routes during First World War. Broken up Italy (Savona) 1929.</td></tr>
<tr><td>305</td><td>306</td><td>Comic</td><td>9.6.1896</td><td>903</td><td>Cross-Channel Ship</td><td>St/2Sc/St
236.3/31.2/15.3</td><td>263 nhp
TE (6Cy)
H&W</td><td>Belfast Steamship Co.
Belfast</td></tr>
<tr><td colspan="9">Completed 25.9.1896, on Londonderry–Liverpool route until closed. In 1921 to Laird Line, renamed Cairnsmore. In 1929 to British and Irish SP Co., renamed Lady Kerry. Broken up Preston (UK) 1934.</td></tr>
<tr><td>306</td><td>307</td><td>Arabia</td><td>21.11.1896</td><td>5,550</td><td>Passenger-Cargo</td><td>St/Sc/St
398.1/49.0/31.0</td><td>330 nhp
QE (4Cy)
H&W</td><td>Hamburg-Amerika Line
Hamburg</td></tr>
<tr><td colspan="9">(This vessel is listed by Moss & Hume as a cargo ship, re-rated)
Completed 7.3.1897, accommodation for 20 first-class and up to 1,136 third-class passengers. In 1899 to R.M. Sloman & Co., renamed Barcelona. In 1916 operated by Italian government, renamed Ancona. In 1923 to E. Mazza, renamed Robinia. Broken up Italy (La Spezia) 1924.</td></tr>
<tr><td>307</td><td>308</td><td>Arcadia</td><td>8/10/1896</td><td>5,551</td><td>Passenger-Cargo</td><td>St/Sc/St
398.1/49.0/31.0</td><td>330 nhp
QE (4Cy)
H&W</td><td>Hamburg-Amerika Line
Hamburg</td></tr>
<tr><td colspan="9">(This vessel is listed by Moss & Hume as a cargo ship, re-rated)
Completed 1.4.1897, sister ship of Arabian. On maiden voyage in May 1897 ran aground in Newfoundland, and had to return to builders for repair. Interned in US on outbreak of First World War and seized 1917. In 1922 chartered to ACME Operating Co. In 1926 to California SS Co. Broken up China 1927.</td></tr>
<tr><td>308</td><td>309</td><td>Delphic</td><td>5.1.1897</td><td>8,273</td><td>Passenger-Cargo</td><td>St/2Sc/St
475.9/55.2/35.9</td><td>375 nhp
TE (6Cy)
H&W</td><td>Oceanic Steam Navigation Co.
Liverpool</td></tr>
<tr><td colspan="9">Completed 15.5.1897, briefly operated on Liverpool–New York route but designed for Asian/New Zealand services. Troopship during Boer War. In February 1917 missed by a torpedo fired by U-60 off south-west Ireland. Sunk by a submarine torpedo (UC72) 135nm of Bishops Rock, outbound Cardiff–Montevideo with cargo of coal. August 1917. Five lives lost.</td></tr>
<tr><td>309</td><td>310</td><td>Oravia</td><td>5.12.1896</td><td>5,320</td><td>Passenger-Cargo</td><td>St/2Sc/St
421.0/48.3/32.0</td><td>568 nhp
3,600 ihp
TE (6Cy)
H&W</td><td>Pacific Steam Navigation Co.
Liverpool</td></tr>
<tr><td colspan="9">(This vessel is listed by Moss & Hume as a passenger ship, re-rated)
Completed 12.6.1897, sister ship of Oropesa for use on South American routes. Wrecked Falkland Islands, November 1912.</td></tr>
</table>

<table>
<tr><th>Ship</th><th>Yard No</th><th>Name</th><th>Date Launched</th><th>Displacement Tons</th><th>Type</th><th>Construction and Dimensions</th><th>Horse Power/ Engines</th><th>Owners</th></tr>
<tr><td>310</td><td>311</td><td>Goorkha</td><td>23.1.1897</td><td>6,286</td><td>Passenger-Cargo</td><td>St/2Sc/St
430.0/52.2/29.0</td><td>375 nhp
2,900 ihp
TE (6Cy)
H&W</td><td>Union Steamship Co.
Southampton</td></tr>
<tr><td colspan="9">(This vessel is listed by Moss & Hume as a passenger ship, re-rated)
Completed 28.8.1897, sister ship of Gascon. Transferred to Union-Castle 1900. Employed on East African services from 1910. In 1914 commissioned as hospital ship, 408 beds. Damaged by submarine-laid mine (UC-25) off Malta October 1917 but repaired and returned to owners. Broken up Preston (UK) 1928.</td></tr>
<tr><td>311</td><td>312</td><td>Rotterdam</td><td>18.2.1897</td><td>8,301</td><td>Passenger Ship</td><td>St/2Sc/St
470.3/53.2/22.3</td><td>954 nhp
TE (6Cy)
H&W</td><td>Holland-America Line
Rotterdam</td></tr>
<tr><td colspan="9">Completed 29.7.1897, accommodation for 200 first-class, 150 second-class and 2,000 third-class passengers. In 1906 to Norwegian owners, Scandinavian-America Line, renamed C.F. Tietgen. In 1913 to Russian owners, East Asiatic Line, renamed Dvinsk, operating on Libau–New York route. Transferred to management of Cunard in 1917. Sunk by submarine torpedo (U-151) in North Atlantic on route Brest–New York, June 1918. Twenty-three lives lost.</td></tr>
<tr><td>312</td><td>313</td><td>Briton</td><td>5.6.1897</td><td>10,248</td><td>Passenger Ship</td><td>St/2Sc/St
530.3/60.3/36.2</td><td>632 nhp
TE (6Cy)
H&W</td><td>Union Steamship Co.
Southampton</td></tr>
<tr><td colspan="9">Completed 26.11.1897, for South Africa routes. Accommodation for 280 first-class, 200 second-class, 120 third-class and 300 steerage passengers and required crew of 237. Troopship in Boer War and First World War, returning to South Africa routes on each occasion. Broken up Italy (La Spezia) 1926.</td></tr>
<tr><td>313</td><td>314</td><td>Derbyshire</td><td>21.7.1897</td><td>6,635</td><td>Passenger-Cargo</td><td>St/2Sc/St
452.0/52.2/30.5</td><td>795 nhp
4300 ihp
TE (6Cy)
H&W</td><td>Bibby Steamship Co.
Liverpool</td></tr>
<tr><td colspan="9">(This vessel is listed by Moss & Hume as a passenger ship, re-rated)
Completed 8.10.1897, enlarged version of Staffordshire for Rangoon route. In 1899 operated on Liverpool–Boston route by the Dominion Line. In 1912 reduced to reserve steamer. From January 1915 employed as troopship initially in Asia and from 1917 carrying American troops to Europe. In 1921 became a full-time troopship when Bibby obtained the contract to transport troops to India and Middle East. Replaced in this role by Dorsetshire and reduced to cargo vessel 1927. Broken up Japan (Kobe) 1931.</td></tr>
<tr><td>314</td><td>a</td><td>Imani
(hull only)</td><td>29.6.1897</td><td>4,582</td><td>Passenger-Cargo</td><td>St/Sc/St
400.2/46.2/29.2</td><td>455 nhp
TE (3Cy)
Engines
Rowan & Sons
Glasgow</td><td>Edward Bates & Son
Liverpool</td></tr>
<tr><td colspan="9">Completed 25.11.1897. In 1914 chartered by Brocklebank Line and purchased by them 1916. Broken up Holland (Hendrik-Ido-Ambacht) 1929.</td></tr>
<tr><td>315</td><td>b</td><td>Monmouth
(hull only)</td><td>23.12.1897</td><td>8,162</td><td>Passenger Ship</td><td>St/2Sc/St
490.5/56.3/25.0</td><td>478 nhp
TE (6Cy)
Engines
Faucett, Preston & Co. Liverpool</td><td>African SS Co.
Elder Dempster
London</td></tr>
<tr><td colspan="9">Completed 20.4.1898. The 1898–99 edition of Lloyd's Register shows the owner as H&W (a stock ship?). Shortly after completion to Dominion Line, renamed Irishman. In 1903 to American ownership, National Line, renamed Michigan. In 1926 to Italian owners, E. Modiano, renamed Candido. Broken up Italy (Trieste) 1927.</td></tr>
<tr><td>316</td><td>c</td><td>Manhattan
(hull only)</td><td>13/9/1898</td><td>8,074</td><td>Passenger Ship</td><td>St/2Sc/St
490.5/56.5/25.0</td><td>478 nhp
TE (6Cy)
Engines
Faucett, Preston & Co. Liverpool</td><td>National SS. Co.
London</td></tr>
<tr><td colspan="9">Completed 31.12.1898. Chartered to the Phoenix Line 1911–14. In 1914 to Atlantic Transport Line. Broken up Italy (La Spezia) 1927.</td></tr>
<tr><td>317</td><td>315</td><td>New England</td><td>7. 4.1898</td><td>11,394</td><td>Passenger Ship</td><td>St/2Sc/St
550.3/59.3/35.9</td><td>985 nhp
TE (8Cy)
H&W</td><td>British & N Atlantic SN Co.
(Dominion Line)
Liverpool</td></tr>
<tr><td colspan="9">Completed 30.6.1898. In 1903 to White Star, renamed Romanic. In 1912 to Allan Brothers & Co., renamed Scandinavian. Troopship during First World War. Broken up Germany (Emden) 1923.</td></tr>
<tr><td>318</td><td>316</td><td>Cymric</td><td>12.10.1897</td><td>12,551</td><td>Passenger-Cargo</td><td>St/2Sc/St
585.5/64.3/37.9</td><td>838 nhp
QE (8Cy)
H&W</td><td>Oceanic Steam Navigation Co.
Liverpool</td></tr>
<tr><td colspan="9">(This vessel is listed by Moss & Hume as a passenger ship, re-rated)</td></tr>
</table>

<table>
<tr><th>Ship</th><th>Yard No</th><th>Name</th><th>Date Launched</th><th>Displacement Tons</th><th>Type</th><th>Construction and Dimensions</th><th>Horse Power/ Engines</th><th>Owners</th></tr>
<tr><td colspan="9">Completed 5.2.1898, originally an enlarged Georgic but altered on the stocks. The cattle space was converted to emigrant-class accommodation allowing her to carry 150 first-class and 1,160 third-class passengers. Employed on North Atlantic routes; although slower than contemporaries, proved economical and popular. Troopship in Boer War and afterwards employed on Liverpool–Boston route. Sunk by submarine torpedo (U-20) 140nm from Fastnet Rock inbound New York–Liverpool, May 1916. Five lives lost.</td></tr>
<tr><td>319</td><td>317</td><td>Oceanic</td><td>4.1.1899</td><td>17,274</td><td>Passenger Ship</td><td>St/2Sc/St
685.7/68.3/44.5</td><td>3,014 nhp
28,000 ihp
QE (8Cy)
H&W</td><td>Oceanic Steam Navigation Co. Liverpool</td></tr>
<tr><td colspan="9">Completed 26.8.1899, first ship to exceed Brunel's Great Eastern in length, if not tonnage. Not intended as a record breaker: very much an 'intermediate' vessel despite her size. Accommodation for 410 first-class, 300 second-class and 1,000 third-class passengers. Initially on Liverpool–New York route later switched to Southampton–New York. Commissioned as armed merchant cruiser 1914 and attached to 10th CS. In September 1914 wrecked on Hoevdi Rocks west of Foula Island as result of navigational error. No lives lost.</td></tr>
<tr><td>320</td><td>318</td><td>Brasilia</td><td>27.11.1897</td><td>10,961</td><td>Passenger Ship</td><td>St/2Sc/St
500.3/62.9/34.1</td><td>604 nhp
QE (8Cy)
H&W</td><td>Hamburg-Amerika Line Hamburg</td></tr>
<tr><td colspan="9">Completed 21.3.1898, accommodation for 300 second-class and 2,400 steerage passengers. To Dominion Line in 1900 converted to passenger-cargo ship and renamed Norseman. Troopship during the Boer War. In 1910 chartered to Aberdeen Line. Hit by submarine torpedo (U-39) off Saloniki with a cargo of munitions and mules in January 1916 and beached but declared a total loss. Wreck refloated 1920 and scrapped.</td></tr>
<tr><td>321</td><td>319</td><td>Winifreda</td><td>11.9.1897</td><td>6,833</td><td>Passenger-Cargo</td><td>St/Sc/St
482.1/52.2/31.6</td><td>772 nhp
5,000 ihp
TE (3Cy)
H&W</td><td>Leyland & Co. Ltd Liverpool</td></tr>
<tr><td colspan="9">(This vessel is listed by Moss & Hume as a passenger ship, re-rated)
Completed 17.2.1898, primarily a cargo carrier could carry 151 first-class passengers. Shortly after completion to Atlantic Transportation Co. and renamed Mesaba. Sunk by submarine torpedo (UB-118) Irish Sea, 21 miles from Tusker Rock, outbound Liverpool–Philadelphia, September 1918. Twenty lives lost.</td></tr>
<tr><td>322</td><td>320</td><td>Statendam</td><td>7.5.1898</td><td>10,319</td><td>Passenger Ship</td><td>St/2Sc/St
515.3/59.8/23.8</td><td>1,126 nhp
TE (6Cy)
H&W</td><td>Holland-America Line Rotterdam</td></tr>
<tr><td colspan="9">Completed 18.8.1898, for Rotterdam–New York route, accommodation for 200 first-class, 175 second-class and 800 third-class passengers. In 1911 to British owners, Allen Brothers, rebuilt for Canadian routes, renamed Scotian. During war operated as transport and prison ship. In the early 1920s operating in Far East, renamed Marglen in 1922. Broken up Italy (Genoa) 1927.</td></tr>
<tr><td>323</td><td>321</td><td>Bay State</td><td>4.6.1898</td><td>6,824</td><td>Cargo Ship</td><td>St/2Sc/St
490.3/52.2/32.2</td><td>755 nhp
TE (6Cy)
H&W</td><td>George Warren & Co. Liverpool</td></tr>
<tr><td colspan="9">Completed 31.8.1898. Wrecked Newfoundland, October 1899.</td></tr>
<tr><td>324</td><td>322</td><td>Afric</td><td>16.11.1898</td><td>11,948</td><td>Passenger-Cargo</td><td>St/2Sc/St
550.2/63.3/39.9</td><td>642 nhp
5,000 ihp
QE (8Cy)
H&W</td><td>Oceanic Steam Navigation Co. Liverpool</td></tr>
<tr><td colspan="9">First of 'Jubilee'-type ships for Australia routes.
Completed 2.2.1899. Troopship during Boer War. Sunk by submarine torpedo (UC-66) south of Eddystone Light outbound for Australia, February 1917. Five lives lost.</td></tr>
<tr><td>325</td><td>323</td><td>Medic</td><td>15.12.1898</td><td>11,985</td><td>Passenger-Cargo</td><td>St/2Sc/St
550.2/63.3/39.9</td><td>641 nhp
5,000 ihp
QE (8Cy)
H&W</td><td>Oceanic Steam Navigation Co. Liverpool</td></tr>
<tr><td colspan="9">Completed 6.7.1899, sister ship of Afric. In 1928 to Norwegian owners, N. Bugge, converted into whale factory ship, renamed Hektoria. Sunk by submarine torpedo (disabled by U-211 and finished off 3 hours later by U-608) North Atlantic, September 1942, while serving as oil tanker under Ministry of War. One life lost.</td></tr>
<tr><td>326</td><td>324</td><td>Winifredian</td><td>11.3.1899</td><td>10,404</td><td>Passenger-Cargo</td><td>St/Sc/St
552.5/59.3/28.9</td><td>847 hp
TE (3Cy)
H&W</td><td>Leyland & Co. Ltd Liverpool</td></tr>
<tr><td colspan="9">(This vessel is listed by Moss & Hume as a passenger ship, re-rated)
Completed 8.7.1899, for Liverpool–Boston service. A large cargo carrier with accommodation for 135 saloon-class passengers. Operated Liverpool–Boston route throughout First World War. Sold 1929 for £24,700 and broken up Italy (Genoa).</td></tr>
<tr><td>327</td><td>325</td><td>Persic</td><td>7.9.1899</td><td>11,973</td><td>Passenger-Cargo</td><td>St/2Sc/St
550.2/63.3/39.9</td><td>641 nhp
5,000 ihp
QE (8Cy)
H&W</td><td>Oceanic Steam Navigation Co. Liverpool</td></tr>
</table>

Ship	Yard No	Name	Date Launched	Displacement Tons	Type	Construction and Dimensions	Horse Power/ Engines	Owners
Completed 16.11.1899, sister ship of *Afric*. Torpedoed off Sicily (*UB-87*) in September 1918, survived. In 1926 plans to rebuild this ship were abandoned as engines found to be in poor condition. Sold for £25,000, broken up Holland (Hendrik-Ido-Ambacht) 1927.								
328	326	*Saxon*	21.12.1899	12,385	Passenger Ship	St/2Sc/St 570.5/64.4/38.6	1,396 nhp QE (8Cy) H&W	Union Steamship Co. Southampton
Completed 9.6.1900. Launched for Union SS Co. but completed for Union-Castle. Operated Southampton–South Africa routes until January 1931. Sold for £27,500, broken up Blyth (UK) 1935.								
329	327	*Michigan*	5.10.1899	9,494	Passenger-Cargo	St/2Sc/St 500.7/62.4/34.0	604 nhp QE (8Cy) H&W	Atlantic Transport Co. London
(This vessel is listed by Moss & Hume as a passenger ship, re-rated) Completed 14.12.1899, ordered by Hamburg–America line as *Belgia* but sold before launch and completed with this name and owner. In 1900 to Dominion Line, renamed *Irishman*. Broken up Holland (Rotterdam) 1924.								
330	328	*Minneapolis*	18.11.1899	13,401	Passenger-Cargo	St/2Sc/St 600.7/65.5/39.7	1,224 nhp 9,800 ihp QE (8Cy) H&W	Atlantic Transport Co. London
(This vessel is listed by Moss & Hume as a passenger ship, re-rated) First of four near sisters for London–New York service. Primarily cargo vessels but had accommodation for 250 first-class passengers. Completed 29.3.1900. Employed as troopship 1914, returned to owners, but taken up again spring 1915. Sunk by submarine torpedo (*U-35*) in central Mediterranean on route Marseille–Alexandria, March 1916. Twelve lives lost.								
331	329	*Minnehaha*	31.3.1900	14,714	Passenger-Cargo	Str/2Sc/St 600.7/65.5/39.7	1,227 nhp 9,800 ihp QE (8Cy) H&W	Atlantic Transport Co. London
(This vessel is listed by Moss & Hume as a passenger ship, re-rated) Completed 7.7.1900, near sister of *Minneapolis*. Nearly lost 1910 after grounding in Scillies. Sunk by submarine torpedo (*U-48*) off south coast of Ireland outbound London–New York, September 1917. Forty-three lives lost out of 153 on board.								
332	330	*Commonwealth*	31.5.1900	12,096	Passenger Ship	St/2Sc/St 478.3/59.3/35.8	988 nhp TE (6Cy) H&W	Dominion Line (Richard Mills & Co.) Liverpool
Completed 22.9.1900, for Liverpool–Boston route accommodation for 275 first-class, 232 second-class and 770 third-class passengers. Transferred to White Star in 1903, renamed *Canopic* and employed on New York–Boston–Genoa–Naples service. Troopship during First World War, released shortly after the Armistice. Returned to old route initially but in 1922 to Liverpool–Canada route and later that year New York–Southampton–Hamburg–Bremen. By this stage an emigrant vessel carrying 524 cabin-class and 656 third-class passengers. Broken up Briton Ferry (UK) 1925.								
333	331	*Devonian*	28.6.1900	10,417	Passenger-Cargo	St/2Sc/St 552.5/59.3/28.9	847 nhp TE (3Cy) H&W	Leyland & Co. Ltd Liverpool
(This vessel is listed by Moss & Hume as a passenger ship, re-rated) Completed 6.9.1900, sister ship of *Winifredian* for Liverpool–Boston service. Sunk by submarine torpedo (*U-53*) NE of Tory Island outbound Liverpool–Boston, August 1917. Two lives lost.								
334	332	*Runic*	25.10.1900	12,482	Passenger-Cargo	St/2Sc/St 550.2/63.3/39.9	641 nhp 5,000 ihp QE (8Cy) H&W	Oceanic Steam Navigation Co. Liverpool
(This vessel is listed by Moss & Hume as a passenger ship, re-rated) Completed 22/12/1900, an improved version of *Afric* for Australian services, accommodation for 400 emigrant class. Long and uneventful career, apart from collision with HMS *London* in 1928. In 1930 to Sevilla Whaling Co. converted into whale factory ship, renamed *New Sevilla*. Sunk by submarine torpedo (*U-138*) while outbound Liverpool–Antarctic with whaling stores 30 miles off Malin Head, September 1940. Two lives lost.								
335	333	*Suevic*	8.12.1900	12,531	Passenger-Cargo	St/2Sc/St 550.2/63.3/39.9	641 nhp 5,000 ihp QE (8Cy) H&W	Oceanic Steam Navigation Co. Liverpool
(This vessel is listed by Moss & Hume as a passenger ship, re-rated) Completed 9.3.1901, sister ship of *Runic*. In 1901 almost lost on Stag Rock near the Lizard, only recovered after blowing of bows with explosives; a new 212ft bow section was built by H&W and towed to Southampton where attached. Resumed service in 1908 on UK–Australia routes and completed her fiftieth voyage in March 1924. In October 1928 sold for £35,000 to Norwegian owners, Yngar Hvistendahl's Finnvahl A/S, converted into a whale factory ship, renamed *Skytteren*.								

<table>
<tr><th>Ship</th><th>Yard No</th><th>Name</th><th>Date Launched</th><th>Displacement Tons</th><th>Type</th><th>Construction and Dimensions</th><th>Horse Power/ Engines</th><th>Owners</th></tr>
<tr><td colspan="9">In April 1940 this vessel was amongst Norwegian ships fleeing the invading Germans that were interned in the Swedish port of Gothenburg. In April 1942 under 'Operation Performance'; 16 of these vessels attempted to break out and reach Allied-controlled waters. The Germans had been alerted and were waiting. Only two of the ships made it to safety, six were sunk and two captured inside by German forces, three returned to Gothenburg and the others, including Skytteren, were scuttled to avoid capture.</td></tr>
<tr><td>336</td><td>334</td><td>German</td><td>4.8.1898</td><td>6,763</td><td>Passenger-Cargo</td><td>St/2Sc/St
440.3/53.2/21.6</td><td>375 nhp
TE (6Cy)
H&W</td><td>Union Steamship Co.
Southampton</td></tr>
<tr><td colspan="9">(This vessel is listed by Moss & Hume as a passenger ship, re-rated)
Completed 10.11.1898, development of highly successful Gascon type for South African services. By time completed amalgamation of Union and Castle lines had occurred. In 1914, renamed Glengorm Castle in response to anti-German feeling. Served as hospital ship 1914–21 and troopship 1922–25 before return to owners. Broken up Holland (Hendrik-Ido-Ambacht) 1930.</td></tr>
<tr><td>337</td><td>335</td><td>Celtic</td><td>4.4.1901</td><td>20,904</td><td>Passenger Ship</td><td>St/2Sc/St
680.9/75.3/44.1</td><td>1,524 nhp
14,000 ihp
QE (8Cy)
H&W</td><td>Oceanic Steam Navigation Co.
Liverpool</td></tr>
<tr><td colspan="9">First of a new type of liner that became known as the 'Big Four'. Intermediate liners on Liverpool–New York route and later Southampton–New York. Accommodation for 300 first-class, 160 second-class and 2,350 third-class passengers.
Completed 11.7.1901. Commissioned as armed merchant cruiser (8x 6in guns), served with 10th CS until decommissioned in 1916 to be converted into troopship. Mined in February 1917 (U-80), but quickly repaired and back in service. In March 1918 was torpedoed in the Irish Sea (UB-77) but survived again. Returned to White Star in 1919, and after being refurbished returned to Liverpool–New York route. In 1927 rebuilt to carry 350 cabin-class, 250 tourist-class and 1,000 third-class passengers. In December 1928, driven ashore and wrecked in Cork Harbour, broken up where she lay, demolition completed 1933.</td></tr>
<tr><td>338</td><td>336</td><td>Ryndam</td><td>18.5.1901</td><td>12,302</td><td>Passenger Ship</td><td>St/2Sc/St
550.3/62.3/26.2</td><td>1,265 nhp
TE (6Cy)
H&W</td><td>Holland America Line
Rotterdam</td></tr>
<tr><td colspan="9">Completed 3.10.1901, for Rotterdam–New York service: accommodation for 286 first-class, 196 second-class and 1,800 third-class passengers. Damaged in a collision May 1915 and subsequently interned in United States. Seized by US government in March 1918 converted into troopship, 26 voyages, returned to owners October 1919. Broken up Holland (Hendrik-Ido-Ambacht) 1929.</td></tr>
<tr><td>339</td><td>337</td><td>Cedric</td><td>21.8.1902</td><td>21,073</td><td>Passenger Ship</td><td>St/2Sc/St
680.9/75.3/44.1</td><td>1,524 nhp
14,000 ihp
QE (8Cy)
H&W</td><td>Oceanic Steam Navigation Co.
Liverpool</td></tr>
<tr><td colspan="9">Completed 31.1.1903, near sister to Celtic. Commissioned as armed merchant cruiser (8x 6in guns) served with the 10th CS until decommissioned in 1916 to be converted into troopship. Returned to White Star in 1919, refurbished and returned to Liverpool–New York route. In September 1931 she made her last voyage. Sold for £22,150, broken up Inverkeithing (UK) 1932.</td></tr>
<tr><td>340</td><td>338</td><td>Noordam</td><td>28.9.1901</td><td>12,316</td><td>Passenger Ship</td><td>St/2Sc/St
550.3/62.3/26.2</td><td>1,265 nhp
TE (6Cy)
H&W</td><td>Holland America Line
Rotterdam</td></tr>
<tr><td colspan="9">Completed 29.3.1902, sister of Ryndam. In October 1914 mined; repaired and returned to transatlantic service. In August 1917 again mined and laid up for duration of the war. From March 1923 to November 1924 on charter to Swedish-America Line, renamed Kungsholm. On return assumed old name. Final voyage April 1927. Broken up Holland (Hendrik-Ido-Ambacht) 1928.</td></tr>
<tr><td>341</td><td>339</td><td>Minnetonka</td><td>12.12.1901</td><td>13,397</td><td>Passenger-Cargo</td><td>St/2Sc/St
600.7/65.5/39.7</td><td>1,227 nhp
9,800 ihp
QE (8Cy)
H&W</td><td>Atlantic Transport Co.
London</td></tr>
<tr><td colspan="9">(This vessel is listed by Moss & Hume as a passenger ship, re-rated)
Completed 7.5.1902, near sister of Minneapolis. Troopship from March 1915. Sunk by submarine torpedo (U-64) near Malta on route Port Said–Marseille with mail, January 1918. Four lives lost.</td></tr>
<tr><td>342</td><td>340</td><td>Arabic</td><td>18.12.1902</td><td>15,801</td><td>Passenger-Cargo</td><td>St/2Sc/St
650.7/65.5/47.6</td><td>1,228 nhp
9,800 ihp
QE (8Cy)
H&W</td><td>Oceanic Steam Navigation Co.
Liverpool</td></tr>
<tr><td colspan="9">(This vessel is listed by Moss & Hume as a passenger ship, re-rated)
Completed 21.6.1903, enlarged version of Minneapolis type; laid down as Minnewaska for the Atlantic Transport Co. but to White Star before launch and completed with this name. Operated Liverpool–New York/Boston routes. Sunk by submarine torpedo (U-24) outbound Liverpool–New York 50 miles off Kinsale, August 1915. Forty-four lives lost out of 184 passengers and 244 crew.</td></tr>
<tr><td>343</td><td>341</td><td>Athenic</td><td>17.8.1901</td><td>12,234</td><td>Passenger-Cargo</td><td>St/2Sc/St
500.3/63.3/45.0</td><td>641 nhp
4,800 ihp
QE (8Cy)
H&W</td><td>Oceanic Steam Navigation Co.
Liverpool</td></tr>
<tr><td colspan="9">(This vessel is listed by Moss & Hume as a passenger ship, re-rated)</td></tr>
</table>

Ship	Yard No	Name	Date Launched	Displacement Tons	Type	Construction and Dimensions	Horse Power/ Engines	Owners
First of three sister ships for New Zealand trade, combined large refrigerated hold capacity with accommodation for 121 first-class, 117 second-class and 450 third-class passengers. Completed 23.1.1902. In October 1927 sold to Norwegian owners, Bruun & V.D. Lippe, Tonsberg, for £33,000, converted into whale factory ship, renamed *Pelagos.* In January 1941 captured, along with another factory ship, a supply vessel and 11 whale catchers by German surface raider *Penguin.* Sent to Bordeaux and subsequently became a depot oiler for the 24th Submarine Flotilla; sunk at Kirkenes October 1944. Salvaged the next year and returned to service until 1962 when broken up Germany (Hamburg).								
344	342	*Walmer Castle*	6.7.1901	12,545	Passenger-Cargo	St/2Sc/St 570.5/64.4/38.6	2,040 nhp QE (8Cy) H&W	Union-Castle Steamship Co. London
(This vessel is listed by Moss & Hume as a passenger ship, re-rated) Completed 20.2.1902, laid down as the *Celt* for Union Line but renamed before launch, last of the Union ships and the first of the Union-Castle. Employed on South African routes. Troopship April 1917–19. Broken up Blyth (UK) 1932.								
345	343	*Corinthic*	10.4.1902	12,231	Passenger-Cargo	St/2Sc/St 500.3/63.3/45.0	604 nhp 4,800 ihp TE (8Cy) H&W	Oceanic Steam Navigation Co. Liverpool
(This vessel is listed by Moss & Hume as a passenger ship, re-rated) Completed 14.7.1902, sister ship of *Athenic.* Made last voyage to New Zealand 1931. Sold 1932 for £10,250, broken up Wallsend (UK).								
346	344	*Warwickshire*	28.11.1901	7,966	Passenger-Cargo	St/2Sc/St 470.3/58.2/30.9	903 nhp QE (8Cy) H&W	Bibby Steamship Co. Liverpool
(This vessel is listed by Moss & Hume as a passenger ship, re-rated) Completed 6.3.1902, for Rangoon service. Torpedoed April 1918 west of Sicily (*UB-68*) but survived and returned to service 1919. Refitted in 1920 by H&W returned to old route until replaced by *Cheshire* in 1927 then converted into a cargo vessel. Broken up Japan (Kobe) 1932.								
347	345	*Columbus*	26.2.1903	15,378	Passenger Ship	St/2Sc/St 570.0/67.8/24.0	1,180 nhp QE (8Cy) H&W	Dominion Line Richard Mills & Co. Liverpool
Completed 12.9.1903, accommodation for 280 first-class, 250 second-class and 2,830 third-class passengers. After short service with Dominion Line transferred to White Star, renamed *Republic* and employed on New York–Mediterranean routes. In January 1907, outbound from New York encountered thick fog off Nantucket and in collision with Italian liner *Florida. Republic* sank 39 hours later; fortunately the vessel was equipped with radio and assistance was quickly summoned. Three lives lost.								
348	346	*Ionic*	22.5.1902	12,232	Passenger-Cargo	St/2Sc/St 500.3/63.3/45.0	604 nhp 4,800 ihp QE (8Cy) H&W	Oceanic Steam Navigation Co. Liverpool
(This vessel is listed by Moss & Hume as a passenger ship, re-rated) Completed 15.12.1902, sister of *Athenic.* Troopship 1914–19. In September 1936 completed her seventy-ninth voyage to New Zealand. Sold January 1937 for £31,500, broken up Japan (Yokohama).								
349	347	*Galeka*	21.10.1899	6,767	Passenger-Cargo	St/2Sc/St 440.3/53.2/21.6	374 nhp TE (6Cy) H&W	Union Steamship Co. Southampton
(This vessel is listed by Moss & Hume as a passenger ship, re-rated) Completed 23.12.1899, sister ship of *German.* Damaged by a submarine-laid mine (*UC-26*) and lost after being beached near Le Havre, October 1916. Nineteen lives lost.								
350	348	*Galician*	20.9.1900	6,756	Passenger-Cargo	St/2Sc/St 440.3/53.2/21.6	374 nhp TE (6Cy) H&W	Union-Castle Steamship Co. London
(This vessel is listed by Moss & Hume as a passenger ship, re-rated) Completed 6.12.1900, sister ship of *German.* On 15 August 1914 stopped at sea by German raider *Kaiser Wilhelm der Grosse* south of Tenerife, after some hours the German captain, Max Reymann, signalled: 'I will not destroy you because of the women and children aboard, Good-bye'. Returned to Southampton, renamed *Glenart Castle* and became a hospital ship with 453 beds. Took part in Gallipoli campaign and served in the Indian Ocean and Mediterranean during 1916. In March 1917 struck a submarine-laid mine (*UC-45*) between Le Havre and Southampton, but survived and repaired. Sunk by submarine torpedo (*U-56*) 10nm W of Lundy Island, February 1918. Only 38 out of 206 crew and medical staff on board survived.								
351	349	*Iowa*	5.7.1902	8,369	Passenger-Cargo	St/2Sc/St 500.5/58.3/34.0	812 nhp TE (6Cy) H&W	George Warren & Co. Liverpool
(This vessel is listed by Moss & Hume as a passenger ship, re-rated) Completed 11.11.1902, primarily a cargo vessel for Liverpool–Boston route could carry emigrants as outwards cargo. Often carried live cattle on return journey, and pens on the shelter deck could accommodate 1,400 sheep. Later used as a cotton carrier. In 1913 to German owners, Hamburg-America Line, renamed *Bohemia.* Seized by US government on entry to war and renamed *Artemis* under US Shipping Board.								

Ship	Yard No	Name	Date Launched	Displacement Tons	Type	Construction and Dimensions	Horse Power/ Engines	Owners
Laid up in interwar years and transferred to British Ministry of Transport in 1941, renamed *Empire Brittern*. In July 1944 used as block ship to create a breakwater off landing beaches in Normandy.								
352	350	*Marmora*	9.4.1903	10,522	Passenger-Cargo	St/2Sc/St 530.4/60.4/25.5	1,799 nhp QE (8Cy) H&W	Peninsular and Oriental Steam Navigation Co. London
(This vessel is listed by Moss & Hume as a passenger ship, re-rated) Between 1903 and 1911 P&O ordered ten ships of the M type, designed to meet criticisms of previous India type and improve the standard of accommodation. Three of these ships were to be built by H&W. Designed for the Australia or India routes they carried 377 first-class passengers and 187 second class, and the considerable cargo capacity was largely refrigerated. Completed 19.11.1903. Commissioned as armed merchant cruiser in 1914. Sunk by a submarine torpedo (*UB-64*) off south coast of Ireland, July 1917. Ten lives lost.								
353	351	*Orita*	15.11.1902	9,230	Passenger-Cargo	St/2Sc/St 485.4/58.2/39.3	1,148 nhp QE (8Cy) H&W	Pacific Steam Navigation Co. Liverpool
(This vessel is listed by Moss & Hume as a passenger ship, re-rated) Completed 26.3.1903, enlarged version of previous Oropesa type for South America routes. Broken up Briton Ferry (UK) 1931.								
354	352	*Baltic*	21.11.1903	23,875	Passenger Ship	St/2Sc/St 707.2/75.6/52.6	1,524 nhp 14,000 ihp QE (8Cy) H&W	Oceanic Steam Navigation Co. Liverpool
Completed 23.6.1904, third of the 'Big Four', but not a true sister as was lengthened during construction so White Star could claim it was the largest ship in service. As the machinery remained the same as earlier vessels this change seriously reduced performance. Employed on Liverpool–New York route until 1915 when became a troopship. Returned to commercial service December 1918. She made her final voyage in 1932, broken up Japan (Osaka) 1933.								
355	353	*President Lincoln*	8.10.1903	18,073	Passenger Ship	St/2Sc/St 599.0/68.2/30.0	827 nhp 7,500 ihp QE (8Cy) H&W	Hamburg-Amerika Line Hamburg
Ordered as *Servian* for Furness-Leyland Line but laid up after launch. Finally completed for HAPAG 14.5.1907 under this name. Employed on Hamburg–New York route with accommodation for 400 first/second-class, 1,000 third-class and 2,000 steerage passengers. Interned in US at outbreak of the war taken over by US government in 1917. Sunk by submarine torpedo (*U-90*) in North Atlantic, May 1918. Twenty-six lives lost.								
356	354	*President Grant*	19.12.1903	18,089	Passenger Ship	St/2Sc/St 599.0/68.2/30.0	827 nhp 7,500 ihp QE (8Cy) H&W	Hamburg-Amerika Line Hamburg
A sister ship of *President Lincoln*, built as *Scotian* for Furness-Leyland Line but also laid up after launch. Completed for HAPAG 3.9.1907 under this name. Early history similar to sister and fell into American hands in 1917. Made 20 transatlantic voyages as a troopship and in 1920 repatriated Czech troops from Vladivostok. After war operated by US Mail Line, reconstructed and renamed *Republic*; her passenger capacity changed to 605 cabin-class and 1,396 third-class passengers. Until 1931 employed on New York–Bremerhaven service, then returned to US government and laid up. During Second World War was employed as a transport. Again laid up after hostilities. Broken up USA (San Francisco) 1951.								
357	355	*Macedonia*	9.7.1903	10,511	Passenger-Cargo	St/2Sc/St 530.4/60.4/25.5	1,799 nhp QE (8Cy) H&W	Peninsular and Oriental Steam Navigation Co. London
(This vessel is listed by Moss & Hume as a passenger ship, re-rated) Completed 28.1.1904, sister ship of *Marmora*. Commissioned as armed merchant cruiser and later converted to troopship. After war returned to Asian routes. Broken up Japan (Yokohama) 1931.								
358	356	*Kenilworth Castle*	5.12.1903	12,975	Passenger Ship	St/2Sc/St 570.2/64.7/38.7	2,174 nhp QE (8Cy) H&W	Union-Castle Steamship Co. London
Completed 14.5.1904, improved version of Saxon/Walmer Castle type, for South Africa routes. Troopship during First World War. Broken up Blyth (UK) 1937.								
359	357	*Amerika*	20.4.1905	22,724	Passenger Ship	St/2Sc/St 668.8/74.3/47.8	1,586 nhp 16,000 ihp QE (8Cy) H&W	Hamburg-Amerika Line Hamburg
Completed 21.9.1905. The poor performance of the express liner *Deutschland* (1900) caused the Hamburg-America Line to revert to slower, more comfortable intermediate-type ships of the kind favoured by White Star.								

Ship	Yard No	Name	Date Launched	Displacement Tons	Type	Construction and Dimensions	Horse Power/ Engines	Owners
In many ways this ship was a slightly faster and more luxurious version of White Star's 'Big Four' ships. The last major German liner to be ordered abroad was employed on the Hamburg–New York route with accommodation for 388 first-class, 150 second-class, 222 third-class and 1,750 steerage passengers. Took refuge in United States at outbreak of First World War and seized by US government on entry to war, renamed *America* and employed as a troopship. Sank at berth in New York in 1918 but salvaged and returned to service in six months; on one repatriation voyage carried 7,219 persons. In 1921 returned to transatlantic routes under US Mail Line and later America Line. In 1926 was severely damaged by fire at Newport News, repaired and reconstructed to carry 835 cabin-class and 516 tourist-class passengers. In 1931 returned to government and laid up for ten years. Another reconstruction transformed the ship into the military transport *Edmund B. Alexander* which transported thousands of American troops to Europe and later brought them home. Laid up 1949. Broken up USA (Baltimore) 1957.								
360	358	*Adriatic*	20.9.1906	24,540	Passenger Ship	St/2Sc/St 709.2/75.5/52.6	1,720 nhp 16,000 ihp QE (8Cy) H&W	Oceanic Steam Navigation Co. Liverpool
Completed 25.4.1907, last of the 'Big Four'. Ordered in 1903 but took four years to build, in part at least because White Star changed the design so that they could again claim the largest ship in service. Employed on Southampton–New York and later Liverpool–New York route from 1911. Following wartime service under Shipping Director refitted and returned to commercial service 1919. Later employed as a cruise ship in Mediterranean. She made last Liverpool–New York crossing in 1934 when transferred to Cunard-White Star but effectively redundant by this stage. Sold for £48,000, broken up Japan (Osaka) 1935.								
361	359	*Worcestershire*	3.3.1904	7,160	Passenger-Cargo	St/2Sc/St 452.0/54.5/22.1	819 hp QE (8Cy) H&W	Bibby Steamship Co. Liverpool
(This vessel is listed by Moss & Hume as a passenger ship, re-rated) Completed 17.9.1904, somewhat reduced near sister of *Warwickshire.* Troopship from 1914 to February 1917 when it hit a mine laid by German raider *Wolff* and sank 10 miles south of Colombo. No lives lost.								
362	360	HMS *Enchantress*	7.11.1903	2,050	Yacht	St/2Sc/St 300.0/40.0/12.0	4,500 shp Turb Parsons?	Admiralty
Completed 11.6.1904. H&W won this contract by competitive tender against three other builders (Henderson & Co., Inglis, and Ramage & Ferguson). Intended to transport and accommodate the Lords of the Admiralty when undertaking inspections or attending fleet manoeuvres, the vessel was often criticised as over luxuriant. However, as turbine powered, this ship can be seen as the test bed for this new technology, previously employed, with limited success, only in destroyers. *Enchantress* was completed and in service for over a year before the revolutionary battleship *Dreadnought* was laid down. Employed as hospital ship during First World War. After the war criticism continued until finally sold for scrap 1935.								
363	361	*Dunluce Castle*	31.3.1904	8,113	Passenger Ship	St/2Sc/St 475.5/56.9/31.7	965 nhp QE (8Cy) H&W	Union-Castle Steamship Co. London
Completed 15.9.1904, for London–South Africa routes with accommodation for 211 first-class and 264 second-class passengers. Served as troopship and later a hospital ship during First World War; returned to commercial service 1919. Listed for disposal 1939 but acquired by navy and used as an accommodation ship in Humber and Scapa Flow. Broken up Inverkeithing (UK) 1945.								
364	362	*Slievemore*	17.5.1904	1,138	Cross-Channel Ship	St/2Sc/St 299.8/37.2/15.7	239 nhp TE (8Cy) H&W	London & North Western Railway Co.
Completed 17.10.1904. Employed on Holyhead–Dublin (North Wall) cargo/passenger/cattle service. Broken up Barrow (UK) 1931.								
365	363	*Pardo*	30.6.1904	4,365	Cargo Ship (refrigerated)	St/Sc/St 375.0/48.3/25.8	378 nhp TE (3Cy) H&W	Royal Mail Steam Packet Co. London
One of three sisters for Argentine meat trade. Ordered after Owen Philips became a director of Royal Mail; two built by H&W and third by WC. Completed 1.10.1904. After long and uneventful life broken up Italy (Genoa) 1934.								
366	364	*Potaro*	10.9.1904	4,378	Cargo Ship (Refrigerated)	St/Sc/St 375.0/48.3/25.8	378 nhp TE (3Cy) H&W	Royal Mail Steam Packet Co. London
Completed 8.12.1904, sister of *Pardo.* Captured by German surface raider *Kronprinz Wilhelm* 560 nm off Pernambuco, briefly used as scout ship before being scuttled, January 1915.								
367	365	*Mamari*	24.9.1904	6,689	Passenger-Cargo (Refrigerated)	St/2Sc/St 455.4/56.4/30.6	808 nhp QE (8Cy) H&W	Shaw Savill & Albion Co. London
(This vessel is listed by Moss & Hume as a passenger ship, re-rated) Completed 3.12.1904, sister ship of WC-built *Matatua*, for UK–New Zealand trade. Accommodation for 12 first-class and 1,000 steerage passengers in temporary accommodation. In 1928 to German owners, A. Bernstein, renamed *Gerolstein.* In 1939 to Dutch owners, Westindische, renamed *Consul.* Shortly afterwards returned to German ownership, H.C. Horn, renamed *Consul Horn.* Sunk by mine off Borkum, July 1942.								

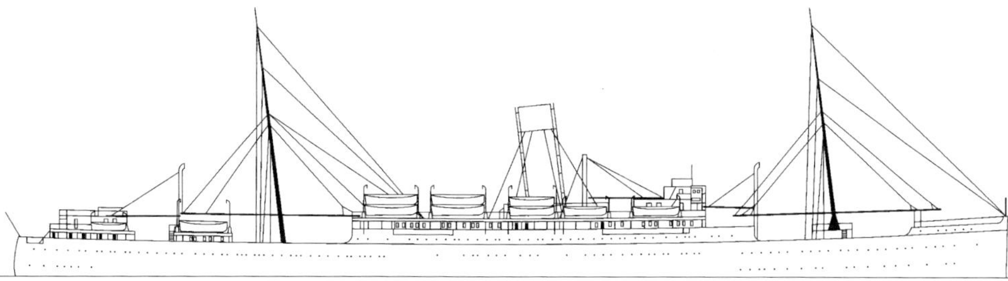

Oroya (H&W y/n 506) 1920 (DH)

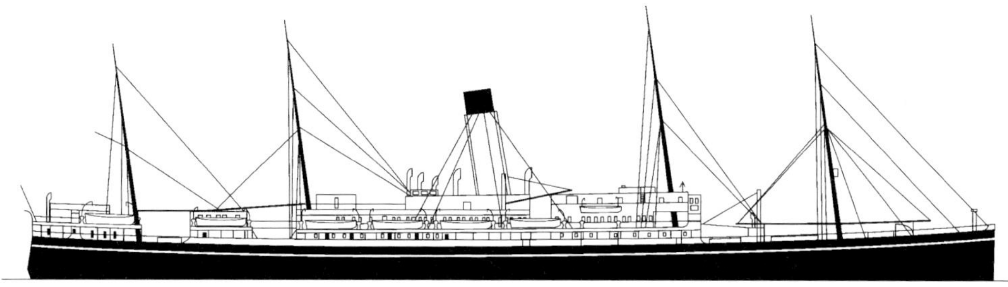

Yorkshire (H&W y/n 509) 1919 (DH)

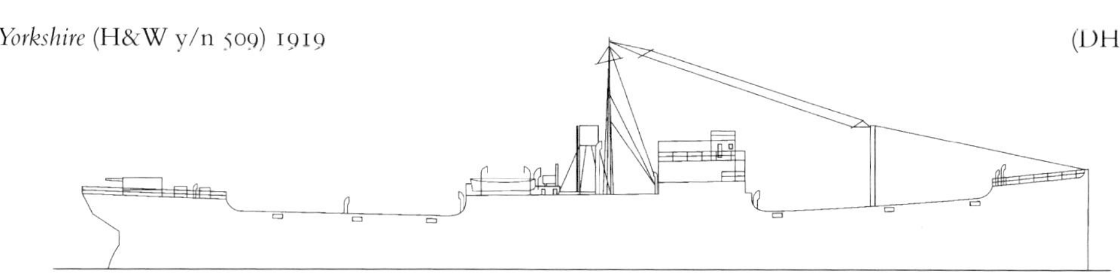

War Shamrock (H&W y/n 520) 1917. 'A' type standard merchant ship (DH)

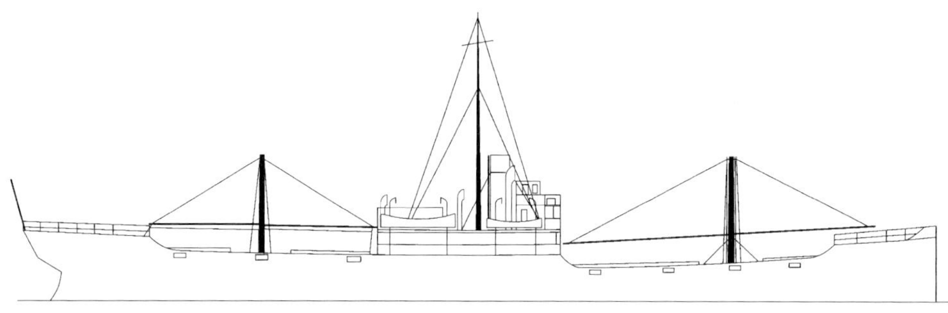

War Buckler (H&W y/n 536) 1918. 'D' type standard merchant ship (DH)

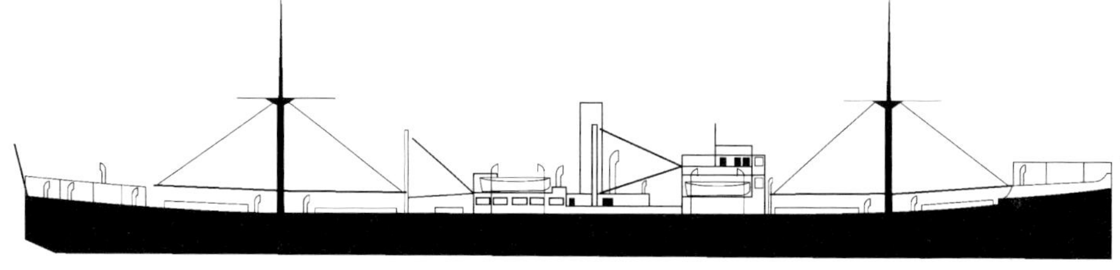

War Melody (H&W y/n 543) 1918. 'N' type standard merchant ship (DH)

<table>
<tr><th>Ship</th><th>Yard No</th><th>Name</th><th>Date Launched</th><th>Displacement Tons</th><th>Type</th><th>Construction and Dimensions</th><th>Horse Power/ Engines</th><th>Owners</th></tr>
<tr><td>368</td><td>366</td><td>Nieuw Amsterdam</td><td>28.9.1905</td><td>16,913</td><td>Passenger Ship</td><td>St/2Sc/St
600.3/68.9/35.6</td><td>1,707 nhp
QE (8Cy)
H&W</td><td>Holland-America Line
Rotterdam</td></tr>
<tr><td colspan="9">Completed 22.2.1906, represented a significant increase in size from the 12,000-tonners that previously formed Holland-America fleet. Employed on Holland–New York route with accommodation for 400 first-class, 400 second-class and 2,500 third-class passengers. Rebuilt in 1909. Maintained a service between Holland and America throughout First World War via Falmouth and north of Scotland. In 1920s rebuilt to carry 440 cabin-class and 850 tourist-class passengers. Made last transatlantic trip in 1932, shortly afterwards broken up Japan (Osaka).</td></tr>
<tr><td>369</td><td>367</td><td>Aragon</td><td>23.2.1905</td><td>9,441</td><td>Passenger-Cargo</td><td>St/2Sc/St
512.3/60.4/30.8</td><td>827 nhp
QE (8Cy)
H&W</td><td>Royal Mail Steam Packet Co.
London</td></tr>
<tr><td colspan="9">(This vessel is listed by Moss & Hume as a passenger ship, re-rated)
The first of the 'A'-class vessels for Southampton–Brazil–River Plate service which became famous for their elegance and luxury. Accommodation for 305 first-class, 66 second-class and up to 600 third-class passengers in temporary accommodation. These ships had considerable refrigerated cargo capacity for meat trade. In 1912, as part of an Admiralty plan to provide merchant ships with defensive armament, this was the first liner to be outfitted with 2x 4.7in guns.
Completed 22.6.1905. Taken up at outbreak of First World War, served as headquarters ship during Dardanelles campaign and later as a troopship. Sunk by submarine torpedo (UC-34) while off Alexandria after voyage from Marseille, December 1917. Six hundred and ten lives lost out of 2,700 on board.</td></tr>
<tr><td>370</td><td>368</td><td>Bologna</td><td>9.3.1905</td><td>4,603</td><td>Cargo Ship</td><td>St/2Sc/St
380.3/46.8/26.6</td><td>505 nhp
TE (6Cy)
H&W</td><td>Soc di Nav a Vap Italia,
Genoa</td></tr>
<tr><td colspan="9">Completed 25.5.1905. Broken up Italy (Genoa) 1928.</td></tr>
<tr><td>371</td><td>369</td><td>Mahronda</td><td>17.6.1905</td><td>7,630</td><td>Cargo Ship</td><td>St/Sc/St
470.3/58.4/31.3</td><td>658 nhp
QE (4Cy)
H&W</td><td>T.&J. Brocklebank
Liverpool</td></tr>
<tr><td colspan="9">Completed 3.8.1905. In 1923 to Norwegian owners, Rasmussen & Konow, renamed Sir James Clark Ross and converted into whale factory ship, displacement increasing to 9,755 tons. In 1930 to Danish owners, A.P. Moller, renamed Fraternitas. In 1937 to South African owners, Union Whaling Co., renamed Uniwaleco. Sunk by submarine torpedo (U-161) in Caribbean on route Curacao–Freetown with 8,800 tons of fuel oil, March 1942. Eighteen lives lost.</td></tr>
<tr><td>372</td><td>370</td><td>Slieve Bawn</td><td>6.7.1905</td><td>1,147</td><td>Cross-Channel Ship</td><td>St/2Sc/St
300.2/39.3/14.2</td><td>232 nhp
TE (6Cy)
H&W</td><td>London & North Western Railway Co.</td></tr>
<tr><td colspan="9">Completed 10.10.1905, employed on Holyhead–Dublin (North Wall) cargo/passenger/cattle service. Broken up Barrow (UK) 1935.</td></tr>
<tr><td>373</td><td>371</td><td>Herefordshire</td><td>31.8.1905</td><td>7,183</td><td>Passenger-Cargo</td><td>St/2Sc/St
452.2/54.3/34.6</td><td>833 nhp
QE (8Cy)
H&W</td><td>Bibby Steamship Co.
Liverpool</td></tr>
<tr><td colspan="9">(This vessel is listed by Moss & Hume as a passenger ship, re-rated)
Completed 29.11.1905, for Burma trade. In July 1916 taken up as hospital ship for 380 patients, served Salonika, Mesopotamia and East Africa. In January 1918 decommissioned and returned, refitted by H&W in 1920 which included conversion to oil-fired boilers. Became a cargo-only ship and laid up in 1933. Sold to Clyde ship breakers but wrecked while under tow, March 1934.</td></tr>
<tr><td>374</td><td>372</td><td>Amazon</td><td>24.2.1906</td><td>10,036</td><td>Passenger-Cargo</td><td>St/2Sc/St
512.3/60.4/30.8</td><td>827 nhp
QE (8Cy)
H&W</td><td>Royal Mail Steam Packet Co.
London</td></tr>
<tr><td colspan="9">(This vessel is listed by Moss & Hume as a passenger ship, re-rated)
Completed 5.6.1906, near sister of Aragon. In First World War remained on Liverpool–South America route. Sunk by submarine torpedo (U-110) off north coast of Ireland outbound Liverpool–Buenos Aires, March 1918. No lives lost but submarine was forced to surface by depth charges and sunk by gunfire: 39 lives lost.</td></tr>
<tr><td>375</td><td>373</td><td>Malakand</td><td>11/11/1905</td><td>7,653</td><td>Cargo Ship</td><td>St/Sc/St
470.3/58.4/31.3</td><td>685 nhp
QE (4Cy)
H&W</td><td>T.&J. Brocklebank
Liverpool</td></tr>
<tr><td colspan="9">Completed 14.12.1905, sister ship of Mahronda. Sunk by submarine torpedo North Atlantic (U-84) inbound Calcutta–Dundee with cargo of jute, April 1917. One life lost.</td></tr>
<tr><td>376</td><td>374</td><td>Manipur</td><td>14.12.1905</td><td>7,654</td><td>Cargo Ship</td><td>St/Sc/St
470.3/58.4/31.3</td><td>685 nhp
QE (4Cy)
H&W</td><td>T.&J. Brocklebank
Liverpool</td></tr>
<tr><td colspan="9">Completed 13.1.1906, sister ship of Mahronda. In 1915 converted into a dummy HMS Indomitable. In 1916 brought by Admiralty and converted by WC into repair ship, renamed Sandhurst. Served throughout interwar period and in Second World War was depot ship for Escorts at Londonderry. Broken up Dalmuir (UK) 1946.</td></tr>
<tr><td>377</td><td>375</td><td>Matheran</td><td>12.4.1906</td><td>7,653</td><td>Cargo Ship</td><td>St/Sc/St
470.3/58.4/31.3</td><td>685 nhp
QE (4Cy)
H&W</td><td>T.&J. Brocklebank
Liverpool</td></tr>
<tr><td colspan="9">Completed 12.5.1906, sister ship of Mahronda. Sunk by mine, laid by German surface raider Wolff, Cape of Good Hope, January 1917.</td></tr>
</table>

Ship	Yard No	Name	Date Launched	Displacement Tons	Type	Construction and Dimensions	Horse Power/ Engines	Owners
378	376	*Ortega*	22.3.1906	7,970	Passenger-Cargo	St/2Sc/St 465.3/56.3/35.9	1,125 nhp QE (8Cy) H&W	Pacific Steam Navigation Co. Liverpool
(This vessel is listed by Moss & Hume as a cargo ship, re-rated) Completed 28.6.1906, modified version of *Orita*, for Liverpool–west coast of South America service, accommodation for 150 first-class, 130 second-class and 800 third-class passengers. In 1914 narrowly escaped destruction by German surface raider *Dresden* by making a 100-mile voyage through uncharted waters of the Nelson Strait. Troopship during war. Broken up Briton Ferry (UK) 1927.								
379	377	*Oronsa*	24.5.1906	7,907	Passenger-Cargo	St/2Sc/St 465.3/56.3/35.9	1,125 nhp QE (8Cy) H&W	Pacific Steam Navigation Co. Liverpool
(This vessel is listed by Moss & Hume as a cargo ship, re-rated) Completed 16.8.1906, sister ship of *Ortega*. Sunk by submarine torpedo (*U-91*) inbound New York–Liverpool with general cargo, 12nm W of Bardsey Island, April 1918. Three lives lost.								
380	378	*Heroic*	13.1.1906	2,016	Cross-Channel Ship	St/2Sc/St 320.2/41.3/16.8	804 nhp QE (8Cy) H&W	Belfast Steamship Co. Belfast
Completed 23.4.1906. Employed on Belfast–Liverpool route, with break for war when commissioned as armed boarding vessel, until replaced by new vessels in 1929. To British and Irish SP Co., renamed *Lady Connaught* (1929) and *Longford* (1938) employed on Dublin–Liverpool route. Laid up during Second World War. Broken up Barrow (UK) 1953.								
381	379	*Graphic*	27.2.1906	2,016	Cross-Channel Ship	St/2Sc/St 320.2/41.3/16.8	788 nhp QE (8Cy) H&W	Belfast Steamship Co. Belfast
Completed 19.5.1906, sister ship of *Heroic*, on Belfast–Liverpool route. Sank following collision in June 1923 but salvaged and repaired. In 1929, to British and Irish SP Co., renamed *Lady Munster* (1929) and *Louth* (1938). In 1948 returned to original owners, renamed *Ulster Duke.* Sunk in tow off Cape Finisterre on way to breakers, March 1951.								
382	380	*Salamanca*	5.7.1906	5,969	Cargo Ship	St/Sc/St 392.0/50.2/28.4	360 nhp TE (3Cy) H&W	Hamburg-Amerika Line Hamburg
Completed 15.9.1906. Interned in Brazil on outbreak of war; in 1917 taken over by Brazilian government and renamed *Alegrete.* In 1923 placed under management of Lloyds Brasileiro. From 1936 training ship of Brazilian merchant marine. Sunk by submarine torpedo (*U-156*) in Caribbean on route to New Orleans, June 1942. No lives lost.								
383	381	*Rohilla*	6.9.1906	7,143	Passenger-Cargo	St/2Sc/St 460.3/56.4/30.0	1,484 nhp QE (8Cy) H&W	British India Steam Navigation Co. Glasgow
(This vessel is listed by Moss & Hume as a cargo ship, re-rated) Completed 17.11.1906. In 1914 requisitioned as hospital ship but saw no service. Wrecked 1nm S of Whitby, October 1914. Eighty-four lives lost out of 229 crew and medical staff on board.								
384	382	*Avon*	2.3.1907	11,072	Passenger-Cargo	St/2Sc/St 520.3/62.3/31.8	924 nhp 7,000 ihp QE (8Cy) H&W	Royal Mail Steam Packet Co. London
Completed 15.6.1907, slightly enlarged version of *Aragon* for Southampton–Brazil–River Plate route, also used on Australia route. Commissioned in 1916 as armed merchant cruiser, renamed HMS *Avoca*, mainly employed in Pacific. In 1919 returned to owners and reverted to original name. Sold 1930 for £31,000, broken up Briton Ferry (UK).								
385	383	*Aburi*	18.10.1906	3,730	Cargo Ship	St/Sc/St 370.6/49.3/21.8	528 nhp TE (3Cy) H&W	African SS Co. (Elder Dempster) London
Completed 2.1.1907. Sunk by submarine torpedo (*U-61*) off Ireland, outbound Liverpool–West Africa, April 1917. Twenty-five lives lost.								
386	384	*Sierra Leone*	15.11.1906	3,730	Cargo Ship	St/Sc/St 370.6/49.3/21.8	528 nhp TE (3Cy) H&W	African SS Co. (Elder Dempster) London
Completed 8.1.1907, sister ship of *Aburi.* Wrecked at Axim entrance, Ghana, July 1910.								
387	385	*Iroquois*	27.6.1907	9,201	Oil Tanker	St/2Sc/St 476.3/60.3/33.5	748 nhp QE (8Cy) H&W	Anglo-American Oil Co. New Jersey USA
Completed 19.10.1907, one of the world's largest tankers on completion, intended to operate paired to *Navahoe.* After *Navahoe* was sold in 1930 *Iroquois* was retained and used for special assignments. In 1934 towed submarine pipelines to Haifa and Tripoli; in 1946 towed a US naval floating dock from Honolulu to the South Sea Islands. Broken up Troon (UK) 1947.								

Ship	Yard No	Name	Date Launched	Displacement Tons	Type	Construction and Dimensions	Horse Power/ Engines	Owners
388	386	*Fulani*	31.1.1907	3,730	Cargo Ship	St/Sc/St 370.6/49.3/21.8	528 nhp TE (3Cy) H&W	Elder Dempster London
Completed 1.6.1907, sister ship of *Aburi.* Wrecked Carpenter Rock, Freetown, June 1914.								
389	387	*Prahsu*	28.3.1907	3,755	Cargo Ship	St/Sc/St 370.6/49.3/21.8	528 nhp TE (3Cy) H&W	Elder Dempster Liverpool
Completed 29.6.1907, sister ship of *Aburi.* Broken up Rosyth (UK) 1933.								
390	388	*Asturias*	26.9.1907	12,001	Passenger- Cargo	St/2Sc/St 520.3/62.3/31.8	924 nhp 7,000 ihp QE (8Cy) H&W	Royal Mail Steam Packet Co. London
(This vessel is listed by Moss & Hume as a passenger ship, re-rated) Completed 8.1.1908, sister ship of *Avon.* Hospital ship in First World War, March 1917, while on route Avonmouth–Southampton was torpedoed off the South Devon Coast (*UC-66*): 35 lives lost. Had to be beached, but was salvaged. Repairs required were so extensive they were deferred until after war. In 1919 brought back by Royal Mail and rebuilt as cruise ship, renamed *Arcadian*, entered service in 1923. Laid up Southampton 1930. Broken up Japan (Osaka) 1933.								
391	389	*Navahoe*	10.10.1907	7,718	Sailing Oil Carrier	St/ 6 mast/barge 450.2/58.3/31.2	N/A	Anglo-American Oil Co. New Jersey USA
Completed 18.1.1908. A towed barge paired with *Iroquois*, a combination popularly known as 'the horse and cart'. In 1930 to Creole Petroleum Corporation and became oil storage hulk in Venezuela. In 1936 scuttled off Trinidad.								
392	390	*Rotterdam*	3.3.1908	23,980	Passenger Ship	St/2Sc/St 650.5/77.4/43.5	2,451 nhp 14,500 ihp QE (8Cy) H&W	Holland-America Line Rotterdam
Completed 3.6.1908, accommodation for 520 first-class, 555 second-class and 2,500 third-class passengers on Holland–New York route. In 1916 withdrawn as dangers of wartime sailings considered too great. Returned to transatlantic service 1919 and from early 1930s employed increasingly as a cruise liner. Decommissioned 1940 after over 30 years' service; broken up Holland (Hendrik-Ido-Ambacht).								
393	391	*Belgic*	31.12.1914	24,147	Passenger Ship	St/3Sc/St 670.4/78.4/44.7	1,290 nhp 12,000 ihp TE (8Cy) + Exh Turb H&W	International Navigation Co. Liverpool
Completed 26.6.1917, for Red Star Line's Antwerp–New York service, originally named *Belgenland.* Work progressed slowly and effectively stopped at outbreak of war, eventually delivered as cargo vessel without liner superstructure and was later outfitted as troopship. After the war was operated by White Star on Liverpool–New York route. In 1922 returned to H&W and completed to original design with accommodation for 500 first-class, 600 second-class and 1,500 third-class passengers. Returned to service 1923 under original name but never served under Belgian flag. With decline in transatlantic trade increasingly used as a cruise ship. Transferred to American Atlantic Transport Co. in 1935 for use on New York–California route, renamed *Columbia.* Soon laid up and sold 1936, broken up Bo'ness (UK).								
394	392	*Pericles*	21.12.1907	10,924	Passenger- Cargo (Refrigerated)	St/2Sc/St 500.6/62.3/31.1	? QE (8Cy) H&W	George Thompson & Co. Aberdeen
(This vessel is listed by Moss & Hume as a passenger ship, re-rated) Completed 4.6.1908, for London–Australia route. Primarily a cargo carrier, but accommodation for 100 first-class and 400 third-class passengers. In March 1910, homeward bound Melbourne–London struck uncharted rock 6 miles S of Cape Leeuwin and sank in just over half an hour. There were no casualties amongst the 300 passengers and 150 crew members.								
395	393	*Lapland*	27.6.1908	18,565	Passenger Ship	St/2Sc/St 605.8/70.4/37.4	2,343 nhp 14,500 ihp QE (8Cy) H&W	Red Star Line Antwerp
Completed 27.3.1909, for Antwerp–New York route with accommodation for 450 first-class, 400 second-class and 1,500 third-class passengers. At the outbreak of war transferred to British register employed on Liverpool–New York and Southampton–New York routes. Returned to Antwerp–New York route in 1920–31. Briefly employed as a cruise ship before sold 1933 and broken up Japan (Osaka) 1934.								
396	394	*Laurentic*	10.9.1908	14,892	Passenger Ship	St/3Sc/St 550.4/67.3/27.6	11,000 ihp TE (8Cy) H&W + Exh Turb John Brown & Co., Glasgow	Oceanic Steam Navigation Co. Liverpool
Completed 15.4.1909, ordered by Dominion Line as *Alberta* and launched under this name for this owner; intended for Liverpool–Canada routes with accommodation for 230 first-class, 430 second-class and 1,000 third-class passengers.								

Ship	Yard No	Name	Date Launched	Displacement Tons	Type	Construction and Dimensions	Horse Power/ Engines	Owners
Troopship in early stages of war but commissioned as an armed merchant cruiser in 1915. In January 1917 while engaged in transporting £5 million in bullion to Canada, struck two mines laid by submarine (*U-80*) off Malin Head and sank near Lough Swilly. 354 lives lost out of the complement of 475. After the war over 90 per cent of the gold was recovered from the wreck.								
397	395	*Median*	5.12.1907	6,296	Cargo Ship	St/Sc/St 400.3/52.3/26.9	350 nhp QE (4Cy) H&W	Leyland & Co. Ltd Liverpool
Completed 25.1.1908. Broken up Briton Ferry (UK) 1933.								
398	396	*Memphian*	23.1.1908	6,305	Cargo Ship	St/Sc/St 400.3/52.3/26.9	350 nhp QE (4Cy) H&W	Leyland & Co. Ltd Liverpool
Completed 20.2.1908, a near sister of *Median*. Sunk by submarine torpedo (*U-96*) outbound Liverpool–New Orleans, near North Arklow lightship, October 1917. Thirty-two lives lost.								
399	397	*Minnewaska*	12.11.1908	14,160	Passenger-Cargo	St/2Sc/St 600.7/65.5/39.7	1,222 hp 9,800 ihp QE (8Cy) H&W	Atlantic Transport Co. London
(This vessel is listed by Moss & Hume as a passenger ship, re-rated) Completed 24.4.1909, improved version of *Minneapolis*, accommodation for 340 first-class passengers rather than 240 in earlier vessels. Ordered to create a four-ship fleet that would allow a weekly sailing schedule. Troopship during First World War. Sunk by submarine-laid mines (*UC-23*) off Mudros, on voyage Alexandria–Malta, November 1916. No lives lost.								
400	398	*Mercian*	16.4.1908	6,304	Cargo Ship	St/Sc/St 400.3/52.3/26.9	350 nhp QE (4Cy) H&W	Wilson & Furness-Leyland Line Liverpool
Completed 16.5.1908, sister ship of *Median*. Broken up Briton Ferry (UK) 1933.								
401	399	*Megantic*	10.12.1908	14,877	Passenger Ship	St/2Sc/St 550.4/67.3/41.2	1,180 nhp 11,000 ihp QE (8Cy) H&W	Oceanic Steam Navigation Co. Liverpool
Completed 3.6.1909, sister ship of *Laurentic*, ordered by Dominion Line as *Albany*, but launched under this name for this owner. Employed on the Liverpool–Canada routes, equipped quadruple-expansion engines rather than turbines to allow a comparison. Had accommodation for 230 first-class, 430 second-class and 1,000 third-class passengers. Troopship during First World War, returned in 1918 and refurbished in Belfast 1919. Employed on North Atlantic routes and as cruise ship until 1931 when, after being briefly laid up, sold. Broken up Japan (Osaka) 1933.								
402	400	*Olympic*	20.10.1910	45,324	Passenger Ship	St/3Sc/St 852.2/92.5/59.5	6,906 nhp TE = 30,000 ihp Tb = 16,000 shp TE (8Cy) + Exh Turb H&W	Oceanic Steam Navigation Co. Liverpool
The first of a new type of liner intended for Southampton–New York route and at the time of launch the biggest ship in the world. Accommodation for 1,054 first-class, 510 second-class and 1,020 third-class passengers. Completed 31.5.1911, maiden voyage began on 14 June 1911 and made the crossing in 5 days, 16 hours and 42 minutes, average speed of 21.17 knots. In September seriously damaged in collision with HMS *Hawke* in Solent and had to return to Belfast for repairs. In 1912 she was again in H&W's hands for rebuilding, following loss of *Titanic*, which lasted six months and cost £250,000. During war employed on trooping and repatriation duties, rammed and sank *U-103* off Lizard in May 1918. In August 1919 returned to Harland's to be refurbished before returning to commercial service at a cost of £500,000, including installation of oil-fired boilers. In July 1920 returned to Southampton–New York service. To Cunard-White Star in 1934, completed last transatlantic voyage in March 1935 and sold for scrap. Partly dismantled Jarrow, 1935, to relieve unemployment in town; hull broken up Inverkeithing (UK) 1937.								
403	401	*Titanic*	31.5.1911	46,328	Passenger Ship	St/3Sc/St 852.2/92.5/59.5	6,906 nhp TE = 30,000 ihp Turb = 16,000 shp TE (8Cy) + Exh Turb H&W	Oceanic Steam Navigation Co. Liverpool
Completed 2.4.1912. Sister ship of *Olympic*. Began her maiden voyage in April 1912, on 14th she hit iceberg and sank with the loss of 1,503 passengers and crew out of 2,207 on board.								
404	402	*Leopoldville*	13.8.1908	5,350	Passenger-Cargo	St/2Sc/St 400.5/53.3/31.5	816 nhp QE (8Cy) H&W	Compagne Belge Maritime du Congo Antwerp
Completed 10.11.1908, light draught, twin-screw vessel for Liverpool–West African service. At outbreak of war transferred to Elder Dempster, who had helped form CBM du C, renamed *Abinsi*. Broken up Glasgow (UK) 1933.								

<table>
<tr><th>Ship</th><th>Yard No</th><th>Name</th><th>Date Launched</th><th>Displacement Tons</th><th>Type</th><th>Construction and Dimensions</th><th>Horse Power/ Engines</th><th>Owners</th></tr>
<tr><td>405</td><td>403</td><td>Leicestershire</td><td>3.6.1909</td><td>8,339</td><td>Passenger-Cargo</td><td>St/2Sc.St
467.2/54.3/31.7</td><td>823 nhp
QE (8Cy)
H&W</td><td>Bibby Steamship Co.
Liverpool</td></tr>
<tr><td colspan="9">Completed 11.9.1909, for Rangoon trade, accommodation for 230 single-class passengers. Troopship in early months of war but returned to commercial service before taken up again in 1917. Refurbished by H&W 1919 and converted to oil burning. In 1930 to British National Exhibition Ship Co., renamed British Exhibitor, refitted at Birkenhead at cost of £100,000. Owners went bankrupt 1932 and ship laid up. In 1933 to Egyptian owners, Company for Transport and Navigation, renamed Zam Zam, employed on Egypt–Jeddah route carrying up to 600 pilgrims. In May 1934 to Societe Misr de Navigation, Alexandria. Laid up October 1939 to March 1941 then returned to service on Alexandria–Cape Town–New York route. In April 1941 captured by German surface raider Atlantis and scuttled.</td></tr>
<tr><td>406</td><td>404</td><td>Karoola</td><td>9.3.1909</td><td>7,390</td><td>Passenger-Cargo</td><td>St/2Sc/St
420.5/56.3/24.5</td><td>1,140 nhp
QE (8Cy)
H&W</td><td>McIlwraith McEachern & Co.
Melbourne</td></tr>
<tr><td colspan="9">Completed 8.7.1909. Designed for Australian coastal service. Caused a great deal of interest when entered service as far superior to any other vessel in that trade. During war employed as troopship and later as hospital ship. Broken up China (Shanghai) 1937.</td></tr>
<tr><td>407</td><td>405</td><td>Berbice</td><td>6.5.1909</td><td>2,379</td><td>Cargo Ship (Refrigerated)</td><td>St/2Sc/St
300.7/38.2/22.9</td><td>169 nhp
QE (8Cy)
H&W</td><td>Royal Mail Steam Packet Co.
London</td></tr>
<tr><td colspan="9">Completed 8.7.1909. In 1922 to South African owners, Mitchell Cotts & Co., renamed Suntemple. In 1924 to UK owners, United Baltic Corporation, renamed Baltara. Wrecked near mouth of River Vistula, January 1929.</td></tr>
<tr><td>408</td><td>406</td><td>Balantia</td><td>28.10.1909</td><td>2,379</td><td>Cargo Ship (Refrigerated)</td><td>St/2Sc/St
300.7/38.2/22.9</td><td>170 nhp
QE (8Cy)
H&W</td><td>Royal Mail Steam Packet Co.
London</td></tr>
<tr><td colspan="9">Completed 18.12.1909. Sister ship of Berbice. In 1916 taken up by Royal Navy, renamed St Margaret of Scotland; reverted to original name on return in 1919. In 1922 to Egyptian owners, Khedivial Mail SS Co., renamed Boulac. Broken up Italy 1935.</td></tr>
<tr><td>409</td><td>407</td><td>Mallina</td><td>25.3.1909</td><td>3,213</td><td>Cargo Ship</td><td>St/Sc/St
350.5/44.3/23.3</td><td>643 nhp
QE (4Cy)
H&W</td><td>Australian United Steam Navigation Co.
Brisbane</td></tr>
<tr><td colspan="9">Completed 29.4.1909. In 1929 to Japanese owners, Machida Sokai, renamed Seiko Maru. In 1935 to Kita Nippon Kisen, renamed Siberia Maru. Sunk by American aircraft in the Philippines, September 1944. One of a large number of ships sunk by US TG38 as Japanese evacuated Luzon.</td></tr>
<tr><td>410</td><td>408</td><td>Meltonian</td><td>8.7.1909</td><td>6,306</td><td>Cargo Ship</td><td>St/Sc/St
400.3/52.3/26.9</td><td>350 nhp
QE (4Cy)
H&W</td><td>Wilson & Furness-Leyland Line
Liverpool</td></tr>
<tr><td colspan="9">Completed 17.8.1909. Broken up Hayle (UK) 1933.</td></tr>
<tr><td>411</td><td>409</td><td>Pakeha</td><td>26.5.1910</td><td>7,910</td><td>Passenger-Cargo</td><td>St/2Sc/St
477.5/63.1/31.3</td><td>854 nhp
QE (8Cy)
H&W</td><td>Shaw Savill & Albion Co.
London</td></tr>
<tr><td colspan="9">Completed 20.8.1910, for UK–New Zealand routes, accommodation for 1,000 emigrant-class passengers. In 1939 purchased by Admiralty and converted into dummy Royal Sovereign-class battleship. Later rebuilt as merchant ship for Ministry of Supply, renamed Empire Pakeha. In 1946 returned to owners and reverted to original name. Broken up Briton Ferry (UK) 1950.</td></tr>
<tr><td>412</td><td>410</td><td>Edinburgh Castle</td><td>27.1.1910</td><td>13,326</td><td>Passenger Ship</td><td>St/2Sc/St
570.2/64.7/38.7</td><td>2,174 nhp
12,500 ihp
QE (8Cy)
H&W</td><td>Union-Castle Steamship Co.
London</td></tr>
<tr><td colspan="9">Completed 28.4.1910, for UK–South Africa routes, accommodation for 320 first-class, 220 second-class and 250 third-class passengers. In First World War commissioned as armed merchant cruiser and spent most of war on patrol duties on east coast of South America. After a post-war refit returned to South African run until withdrawn in December 1938, laid up at Netley. In 1939 requisitioned by Royal Navy who then bought ship outright in 1940. Employed as base ship at Freetown. In September 1945 considered surplus to requirements but unfit to be brought back to Britain; sunk off Freetown as gunnery target.</td></tr>
<tr><td>413</td><td>411</td><td>Gloucestershire</td><td>7.7.1910</td><td>8,324</td><td>Passenger-Cargo</td><td>St/2Sc/St
467.2/54.3/31.7</td><td>823 nhp
QE (8Cy)
H&W</td><td>Bibby Steamship Co.
Liverpool</td></tr>
<tr><td colspan="9">Completed 22.10.1910, sister ship of Leicestershire. Early in war troopship but later commissioned as an armed merchant cruiser and served with 10th CS. Decommissioned February 1917 and returned as troopship. On return to owners refitted and modernised before returning to original routes. Broken up Pembroke Dock (UK) 1936.</td></tr>
</table>

Ship	Yard No	Name	Date Launched	Displacement Tons	Type	Construction and Dimensions	Horse Power/ Engines	Owners
414	412	*Themistocles*	22.9.1910	11,231	Passenger-Cargo (Refrigerated)	St/2Sc/St 500.6/62.3/39.4	1,075 nhp QE (8Cy) H&W	George Thompson & Co. Aberdeen
Completed 12.1.1911, for London–Australia service, accommodation for 100 first-class and 250 third-class passengers. Troopship during war returned to the Australia route after release and subsequently passed to White Star management sailing from Liverpool rather than London. Operated on Australia route throughout Second World War. Broken up Dalmuir (UK) 1947.								
415	413	*Sachsen*	17.11.1910	7,986	Passenger-Cargo	St/Sc/St 470.0/58.0/32.4	697 nhp QE (4Cy) H&W	Hamburg-Amerika Line Hamburg
Completed 21.1.1911. Laid down as *Baron Wattenberg*, name changed before launch. Interned in America at outbreak of the war and seized by US government in 1917, renamed *Chattahoochee*. Sunk by a submarine torpedo (*UB-55*) 28nm south of Penzance on route London–St Nazaire with cargo of cement and lorries, March 1918. No lives lost.								
416	414	*Maloja*	17.12.1910	12,430	Passenger-Cargo	St/2Sc/St 550.4/62.9/34.4	1,164 nhp QE (8Cy) H&W	Peninsular and Oriental Steam Navigation Co. London
(This vessel is listed by Moss & Hume as a passenger ship, re-rated) Completed 7.9.1911, improved version of *Marmora* for Australia and India routes, with accommodation for 450 first-class and 329 second-class passengers. Sunk by a submarine-laid mine (*UC-6*) 2nm SW of Dover outbound London–Bombay, February 1916. One hundred and fifty-five lives lost out of 456 on board.								
417	415	*Arlanza*	23.11.1911	15,043	Passenger-Cargo	St/3Sc/St 570.8/65.3/33.3	? TE (8Cy) + Exh Turb H&W	Royal Mail Steam Packet Co. London
(This vessel is listed by Moss & Hume as a passenger ship, re-rated) First of final group of single-funnelled 'A'-type liners built for South American routes, accommodation for 400 first class, 230 second class and 760 third class. Completed 8.6.1912. Broken up Blyth (UK) 1938.								
418	416	*Bayern*	15.12.1910	7,986	Passenger-Cargo	St/Sc/St 470.0/58.0/32.4	697 nhp QE (4Cy) H&W	Hamburg-Amerika Line Hamburg
Completed 16.2.1911, sister ship of *Sachsen*. Taken over by Italian government 1916, renamed *Alessandria*. Sunk by submarine torpedo (*UC-74*) 100nm N of Benghazi, inbound Karachi–Naples with cargo of grain, May 1917. No lives lost.								
N/A	417	*Preussen*	Build by John Browns of Clydebank					
419	418	*Demosthenes*	28.2.1911	11,223	Passenger-Cargo (Refrigerated)	St/3Sc/St 500.6/62.3/39.4	1,240 nhp 6,000 ihp? TE (8Cy) H&W + Exh Turbine J. Brown & Co. Glasgow	George Thompson & Co. Aberdeen
Completed 5.8.1911, sister ship of *Themistocles* for London–Australia service. Troopship during First World War, returned to the Australia route on release. Passed to White Star management, sailing from Liverpool rather than London. By 1931 laid up at Rothesay and sold, broken up Blyth (UK) 1931.								
420	419	*Galway Castle*	12.4.1911	7,987	Passenger-Cargo	St/2Sc/St 452.3/56.3/30.8	722 nhp QE (8Cy) H&W	Union-Castle Steamship Co. London
(This vessel is listed by Moss & Hume as a passenger ship, re-rated) Completed 9.10.1911. Sunk by submarine torpedo (*U-82*) 160nm SW of Fastnet outbound London–Port Natal, with 400 wounded South African troops, 346 passengers and 204 crew on board, September 1918. One hundred and forty-three lives lost.								
421	420	*Deseado*	26.10.1911	11,471	Passenger-Cargo (Refrigerated)	St/2Sc/St 500.7/62.3/26.0	680 nhp QE (8Cy) H&W	Royal Mail Steam Packet Co. London
(This vessel is listed by Moss & Hume as a passenger ship, re-rated) First of five 'D'-type vessels intended to compliment the 'A's on South America routes; accommodation for 95 first-class, 38 second-class and 860 third-class/steerage passengers. Described as 'comfortable' rather than luxurious, but compared to other contemporary vessels steerage accommodation was particularly good. Unlike the 'A' ships, where third-class passenger cabins could be dismantled, these were permanent fixtures on the 'D' type. Designed primarily for carriage of frozen meat, with other space available for fruit and dairy produce, could accommodate 41,400 carcasses, making them amongst the largest vessels of this type in the world. For this reason only one of the type was briefly taken up for war service. Completed 27.6.1912. Broken up Japan (Osaka) 1934.								

<table>
<tr><th>Ship</th><th>Yard No</th><th>Name</th><th>Date Launched</th><th>Displacement Tons</th><th>Type</th><th>Construction and Dimensions</th><th>Horse Power/ Engines</th><th>Owners</th></tr>
<tr><td>422</td><td>421</td><td>Zealandic</td><td>29.6.1911</td><td>10,897</td><td>Passenger-Cargo</td><td>St/2Sc/St
477.5/63.1/31.5</td><td>596 nhp
QE (8Cy)
H&W</td><td>Oceanic Steam Navigation Co. Liverpool</td></tr>
<tr><td colspan="9">Completed 12.10.1911, for Liverpool–New Zealand routes. Chartered by Australian government as an emigrant carrier. Taken up under the Liner Requisition Scheme during the war; returned to her owners in 1919. In 1929 to Aberdeen Line, renamed Mamilius, continuing to operate on the Australian routes. In 1932 passed to Shaw Savill & Albion, renamed Mamari. To Admiralty 1939 and converted into dummy aircraft carrier (Hermes). In June 1941 while on way to be converted back into a merchant vessel was in collision with a submerged wreck and subsequently attacked by German aircraft and had to be beached at Cromer. Finished off by torpedo from an E-boat before could be salvaged.</td></tr>
<tr><td>423</td><td>422</td><td>Nomadic</td><td>25.4.1911</td><td>1,260</td><td>Passenger Tender</td><td>St/2Sc/St
220.7/37.1/12.4</td><td>54 nhp
CI (4Cy)
H&W</td><td>Oceanic Steam Navigation Co. Liverpool</td></tr>
<tr><td colspan="9">Completed 27.5.1911, capacity of 1,000 passengers, built to replace Gallic at Cherbourg 1911. During First World War served as naval tender at Brest. In 1927 IMMC decided it was no longer practical to operate vessel and sold it to Soc. Cherbourgoeise de Transbordment, retained name and employed in same activities. In 1934 to Soc. Cherbourgeoise de Remorquage et de Sauvetage, renamed Ingenieur Minard. In the Second World War operated along south coast of England, returning to Cherbourg 1945. In 1968 converted into floating restaurant. In 2006 brought back to Belfast for restoration.</td></tr>
<tr><td>424</td><td>423</td><td>Traffic</td><td>27.4.1911</td><td>639</td><td>Passenger Tender</td><td>St/2Sc/St
175.7/35.1/12.4</td><td>36 nhp
CI (4Cy)
H&W</td><td>Oceanic Steam Navigation Co. Liverpool</td></tr>
<tr><td colspan="9">Completed 27.5.1911, capacity of 500 passengers but primarily a baggage tender employed at Cherbourg 1911. During First World War served as a naval tender at Brest. In 1927 to Soc. Cherbourgoeise de Transbordment but retained name and employed in same activity. In 1934 she was acquired by Soc. Cherbourgeoise de Remorquage et de Sauvetage, renamed Ingenieur Riebell. In June 1940 scuttled at Cherbourg when town was captured by Germans. (According to some accounts subsequently raised and employed as a coastal convoy escort by German Navy, sunk in action, English Channel, January 1941.)</td></tr>
<tr><td>425</td><td>424</td><td>Patriotic</td><td>7.9.1911</td><td>2,254</td><td>Cross-Channel Ship</td><td>St/2Sc/St
325.4/41.7/16.2</td><td>840 nhp
TE (8Cy)
H&W</td><td>Belfast Steamship Co. Belfast</td></tr>
<tr><td colspan="9">Completed 28.3.1912, for Belfast–Liverpool route. During First World War served as transport. In 1930 to British and Irish SP Co., renamed Lady Leinster and later (1938) Lady Connaught. During Second World War employed on Belfast–Liverpool route, seriously damaged by mine in Mersey, December 1940; repaired and employed as troopship. In 1947 to Coast Line, renamed Lady Killarney, employed as a cruising yacht around Scottish lochs. Broken up Port Glasgow (UK) 1956.</td></tr>
<tr><td>426</td><td>425</td><td>Demerara</td><td>21.12.1911</td><td>11,484</td><td>Passenger-Cargo (Refrigerated)</td><td>St/2Sc/St
500.7/62.3/26.0</td><td>680 nhp
QE (8Cy)
H&W</td><td>Royal Mail Steam Packet Co. London</td></tr>
<tr><td colspan="9">(This vessel is listed by Moss & Hume as a passenger ship, re-rated)
Completed 8.8.1912, sister ship of Deseado for South American passenger/meat trade. During First World War had an exciting life. In 1915 drove off U-boat with gunfire near Land's End. Narrowly escaped destruction by German raider Moewe February 1916. In July 1916 was torpedoed off La Rochelle (U-84) outbound London–Buenos Aires, one life lost, and had to be beached. Subsequently repaired and returned to service. Broken up Japan (Osaka) 1933.</td></tr>
<tr><td>427</td><td>426</td><td>Desna</td><td>2.3.1912</td><td>11,483</td><td>Passenger-Cargo (Refrigerated)</td><td>St/2Sc/St
500.7/62.3/26.0</td><td>680 nhp
QE (8Cy)
H&W</td><td>Royal Mail Steam Packet Co. London</td></tr>
<tr><td colspan="9">(This vessel is listed by Moss & Hume as a passenger ship, re-rated)
Completed 3.10.1912, sister ship of Deseado. Broken up Japan (Osaka) 1933.</td></tr>
<tr><td>428</td><td>427</td><td>Darro</td><td>16.5.1912</td><td>11,484</td><td>Passenger-Cargo (Refrigerated)</td><td>St/2Sc/St
500.7/62.3/26.0</td><td>680 nhp
QE (8Cy)
H&W</td><td>Royal Mail Steam Packet Co. London</td></tr>
<tr><td colspan="9">(This vessel is listed by Moss & Hume as a passenger ship, re-rated)
Completed 31.10.1912, sister ship of Deseado. Broken up Japan (Osaka) 1933</td></tr>
<tr><td>429</td><td>428</td><td>Drina</td><td>29.6.1912</td><td>11,483</td><td>Passenger-Cargo (Refrigerated)</td><td>St/2Sc/St
500.7/62.3/26.0</td><td>680 nhp
QE (8Cy)
H&W</td><td>Royal Mail Steam Packet Co. London</td></tr>
<tr><td colspan="9">(This vessel is listed by Moss & Hume as a passenger ship, re-rated)
Completed 16.1.1913, sister ship of Deseado. During First World War served briefly as hospital ship but quickly released to trade. Sunk by submarine torpedo (UC-65) off Milford Haven inbound Buenos Aires–Liverpool, March 1917. Fifteen lives lost.</td></tr>
</table>

<table>
<tr><th>Ship</th><th>Yard No</th><th>Name</th><th>Date Launched</th><th>Displacement Tons</th><th>Type</th><th>Construction and Dimensions</th><th>Horse Power/ Engines</th><th>Owners</th></tr>
<tr><td>430</td><td>429</td><td>Oxfordshire</td><td>15.6.1912</td><td>8,623</td><td>Passenger-Cargo</td><td>St/2Sc/St
474.7/55.3/32.1</td><td>906 nhp
QE (8Cy)
H&W</td><td>Bibby Steamship Co.
Liverpool</td></tr>
<tr><td colspan="9">Completed 17.9.1912, for Rangoon service. At outbreak of war converted to hospital ship with 562 beds, served at Scapa Flow, Mudros, the Persian Gulf, German East Africa and English Channel before decommissioned March 1919. In these years made 235 voyages involving steaming 172,000 miles and had transported 50,000 sick and wounded. Refurbished by H&W and returned to commercial service. In 1939 again taken up as hospital ship serving as base hospital at Freetown before being employed in Mediterranean, Adriatic and Far East. Retained after the war on repatriation duties. Reconditioned in 1948 and subsequently operated under International Refugee Organisation, taking emigrants to Australia before reverting to trooping in 1950. In 1951 to Pakistani owners, Pan-Islamic SS Co., renamed Safina-e-Arab, employed on Jeddah pilgrimage route. Broken up Pakistan (Karachi) 1958.</td></tr>
<tr><td>431</td><td>430</td><td>Abosso</td><td>15.8.1912</td><td>7,782</td><td>Passenger-Cargo</td><td>St/2Sc/St
425.6/57.3/31.4</td><td>516 nhp
QE (8Cy)
H&W</td><td>African Steamship Co.
Elder Dempster
London</td></tr>
<tr><td colspan="9">(This vessel is listed by Moss & Hume as a cargo ship, re-rated)
Completed 19.12.1912. Sunk by submarine torpedo (U-43) 180nm NW of fastnet inbound Bathurst–Liverpool with 173 crew and 127 passengers on board, April 1917. Sixty-five lives lost.</td></tr>
<tr><td>432</td><td>431</td><td>Appam</td><td>10.10.1912</td><td>7,781</td><td>Passenger-Cargo</td><td>St/2Sc/St
425.6/57.3/31.4</td><td>516 hp
QE (8Cy)
H&W</td><td>British & African Steam Navigation Co.
Elder Dempster
Liverpool</td></tr>
<tr><td colspan="9">Completed 27.2.1913, sister ship of Abosso. In 1917 renamed Mandingo but reverted to original name 1919. Broken up Milford Haven (UK) 1936.</td></tr>
<tr><td>433</td><td>432</td><td>Ceramic</td><td>11.12.1912</td><td>18,481</td><td>Passenger-Cargo</td><td>St/3Sc/St
655.1/69.4/43.8</td><td>7,750 ihp
QE (8Cy)
+Exh Turb
H&W</td><td>Oceanic Steam Navigation Co.
Liverpool</td></tr>
<tr><td colspan="9">(This vessel is listed by Moss & Hume as a passenger ship, re-rated)
Completed 5.7.1913, for Liverpool–Australia service, the largest vessel on this route for a decade, accommodation for 600 third-class passengers and a further 220 in exceptional circumstances. In addition had 836,000cu. ft of cargo space, 321,000 of which refrigerated. Troopship early in First World War, later transferred to Shipping Controller. Returned to White Star 1919, refurbished and returned to commercial service. Transferred to Shaw Savill & Albion in 1934. In 1936 modernised by H&W at Govan, during which passenger accommodation was rebuilt as 336 cabin class. Troopship from February 1940. In November 1942 sailed Liverpool–South Africa–Australia with 378 passengers (244 military personnel, mainly nurses of Queen Alexandra's Corps, and 134 fare-paying passengers, including 12 children) and 278 crew and gunners. At midnight on 6/7th torpedoed (U-515) W of the Azores and passengers and crew took to boats. Weather conditions were appalling and soon deteriorated to Storm Force 10. As a result 655 lives were lost. Only survivor was a Royal Engineer sapper who was picked up by the U-boat to obtain intelligence data.</td></tr>
<tr><td>434</td><td>433</td><td>Britannic</td><td>26.2.1914</td><td>48,158</td><td>Passenger Ship</td><td>St/3Sc/St
852.2/94.0/59.5</td><td>6,906 nhp
TE = 30,000 ihp
Turb = 16,000 shp
TE (8Cy)
+ Exh Turb
H&W</td><td>Oceanic Steam Navigation Co.
Liverpool</td></tr>
<tr><td colspan="9">Completed 8.12.1915, near sister ship of Olympic. Originally to have been Gigantic but changed as considered too similar to ill-fated Titanic. Launch and completion were delayed awaiting outcome of court of inquiry into Titanic loss and subsequent changes in design to this ship. Converted while fitting out into hospital ship with 3,300 beds. Made five voyages, Alexandria–Mudros–Southampton or Mudros–Marseilles. Sunk by submarine-laid mines (U-73) in Aegean, November 1916. Twenty-eight lives lost.</td></tr>
<tr><td>435</td><td>434</td><td>Andes</td><td>8.5.1913</td><td>15,620</td><td>Passenger-Cargo</td><td>St/3Sc/St
570.3/67.3/33.3</td><td>?
TE (8Cy)
+ Exh Turb
H&W</td><td>Pacific Steam Navigation Co.
Liverpool</td></tr>
<tr><td colspan="9">(This vessel is listed by Moss & Hume as a passenger ship, re-rated)
Completed 12.9.1913, sister ship of Arlanza. Transferred to Royal Mail Steam Packet Co. after first voyage. Following wartime service returned to South American routes. In 1930 converted to one-class cruise vessel, renamed Atlantis. In Second World War served as transport. Afterwards chartered to New Zealand government as emigrant ship for four years. Broken up Faslane (UK) 1952.</td></tr>
<tr><td>N/A</td><td>435</td><td>Alacantara</td><td colspan="6">Govan built</td></tr>
<tr><td>436</td><td>436</td><td>Justicia</td><td>9.7.1914</td><td>32,234</td><td>Passenger Ship</td><td>St/3Sc/St
740.5/86.2/43.1</td><td>?
TE (8Cy)
+ Exh Turb
H&W</td><td>Oceanic Steam Navigation Co.
Liverpool</td></tr>
<tr><td colspan="9">Completed 7.4.1917, laid down as Statendam for Holland-American Line, launched under this name.</td></tr>
</table>

<table>
<tr><th>Ship</th><th>Yard No</th><th>Name</th><th>Date Launched</th><th>Displacement Tons</th><th>Type</th><th>Construction and Dimensions</th><th>Horse Power/ Engines</th><th>Owners</th></tr>
<tr><td colspan="9">At outbreak of war work stopped on this vessel until 1915 when requisitioned by British government. Initially to Cunard as replacement for Lusitania but that company had problems assembling a crew so assigned to White Star who had crew of the lost Britannic available. On 19 July 1918 outbound Belfast–New York hit by submarine torpedo (UB-64) 23 miles south of Skerryvore, subsequently hit by two more torpedoes from same submarine. The bulk of crew were taken off and stricken ship taken in tow, heading for Lough Swilley. At this point again hit by another submarine torpedo (UB-64) but her attacker was subsequently damaged by escorts and forced to break off action. The following morning another submarine (UB-124) finished Justicia off with two more torpedoes. Ten lives lost. Following this attack UB-124 was driven to surface by depth charges and sunk by gunfire. Sixteen lives lost.</td></tr>
<tr><td>437</td><td>437</td><td>Katoomba</td><td>10.4.1913</td><td>9,424</td><td>Passenger-Cargo</td><td>St/3Sc/St
450.4/60.3/34.2</td><td>?
TE (8Cy)
+ Exh Turb
H&W</td><td>McIlwraith McEachern & Co.
Melbourne</td></tr>
<tr><td colspan="9">(This vessel is listed by Moss & Hume as a passenger ship, re-rated)
Completed 10.7.1913, for Australian inter-state coastal trade mainly operating between Sydney and Fremantle; accommodation for 150 first class, 250 second class and 300 third class, which was described as equal to that of an ocean liner. Employed as transport late in First World War and returned to coastal routes in 1920. Again employed as transport in Second World War, released 1946. Subsequently to Italian owners, Goulandris, refitted and employed on various routes. In 1949 extensively rebuilt and converted to oil burning, renamed Columbia, for employment on Bremerhaven–Southampton–Cherbourg–Canada route from June 1950. In 1957 withdrawn from service; broken up Japan (Nagasaki) 1957.</td></tr>
<tr><td>438</td><td>438</td><td>Orduna</td><td>2.10.1913</td><td>15,499</td><td>Passenger-Cargo</td><td>St/3Sc/St
550.3/67.3/42.0</td><td>?
TE (8Cy)
+ Exh Turb
H&W</td><td>Pacific Steam Navigation Co.
Liverpool</td></tr>
<tr><td colspan="9">Completed 22.1.1914, originally named Ormeda but completed with this name, for west coast of South America service, accommodation for over 1,100 passengers which, it was noted, was of a particularly high standard. Spent the war years under charter to Cunard on Liverpool–New York route and after war transferred to Royal Mail SP Co., on North Atlantic routes. In Second World War troopship and later employed on repatriation work. When finally returned decided the ship was not worth refitting. Broken up Dalmuir (UK) 1951.</td></tr>
<tr><td>439</td><td>439</td><td>Euripides</td><td>29.1.1914</td><td>14,947</td><td>Passenger-Cargo</td><td>St/3Sc/St
550.7/67.4/44.1</td><td>1,401 nhp
7,500 ihp
TE (8Cy)
+ Exh Turb
H&W</td><td>George Thompson & Co.
Aberdeen</td></tr>
<tr><td colspan="9">Completed 6.6.1914, for the London–Australia route, accommodation for 350 first-class and 1,000 third-class passengers. Began maiden voyage to Australia in July 1914 and on arrival immediately taken up as troopship; not returned until 1919. In 1932 to Shaw Savill & Albion, modernised and renamed Akaroa. Remained on UK–Australia–New Zealand route during the Second World War, making last voyage in 1954. Sold for £130,000 and broken up Holland (Antwerp).</td></tr>
<tr><td>440</td><td>440</td><td>Orbita</td><td>7.7.1914</td><td>15,678</td><td>Passenger-Cargo</td><td>St/3Sc/St
550.3/67.3/43.0</td><td>?
TE (8Cy)
+ Exh Turb
H&W</td><td>Pacific Steam Navigation Co.
Liverpool</td></tr>
<tr><td colspan="9">Completed 31.7.1915, sister ship of Orduna. Completion delayed by outbreak of war, taken up as auxiliary cruiser and later a transport. Returned 1919 and sent to H&W to be completed to original design. Subsequent career was very similar to her sisters. Broken up Newport (UK) 1950.</td></tr>
<tr><td>441</td><td>441</td><td>Almanzora</td><td>19.11.1914</td><td>16,034</td><td>Passenger-Cargo</td><td>St/3Sc/St
570.0/67.3/33.3</td><td>?
TE (8Cy)
+ Exh Turb
H&W</td><td>Royal Mail Steam Packet Co.
London</td></tr>
<tr><td colspan="9">(This vessel is listed by Moss & Hume as a passenger ship, re-rated)
Completed 7.10.1915, a sister ship of Arlanza. Completion delayed by outbreak of war, taken up as armed merchant cruiser. Following release joined her sisters on South American routes. In Second World War served as transport. Broken up Blyth (UK) 1948.</td></tr>
<tr><td>442</td><td>442</td><td>Orca</td><td>5.4.1917</td><td>15,120</td><td>Passenger-Cargo</td><td>St/3Sc/St
550.3/67.3/43.0</td><td>28,032 ihp
QE (8Cy)
+ Exh Turb
H&W</td><td>Pacific Steam Navigation Co.
Liverpool</td></tr>
<tr><td colspan="9">Laid down in 1914, originally a sister ship of Orduna, work suspended until 1916 and vessel finally completed 25.5.1918 for Shipping Controller as cargo vessel with no passenger accommodation. In 1921 passed to H&W and rebuilt to original design, but never operated on South American Routes. In 1923 to Royal Mail Line and employed on North Atlantic routes. In 1927 to White Star, renamed Calgaric and employed on Canadian routes. In 1934 to Cunard-White Star, considered surplus to requirements, broken up Rosyth (UK) 1935–36.</td></tr>
<tr><td>N/A</td><td>443</td><td>Apapa</td><td colspan="6">Govan built</td></tr>
<tr><td>N/A</td><td>444</td><td>Egba</td><td colspan="6">Govan built</td></tr>
<tr><td>N/A</td><td>445</td><td>Egori</td><td colspan="6">Govan built</td></tr>
</table>

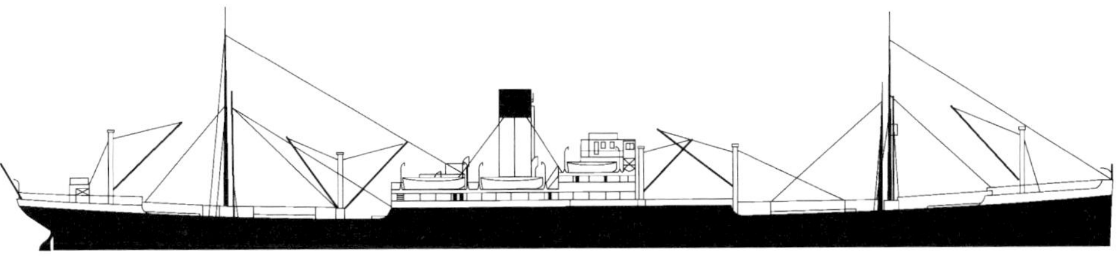

Glenshiel (H&W y/n 594) 1924 (DH)

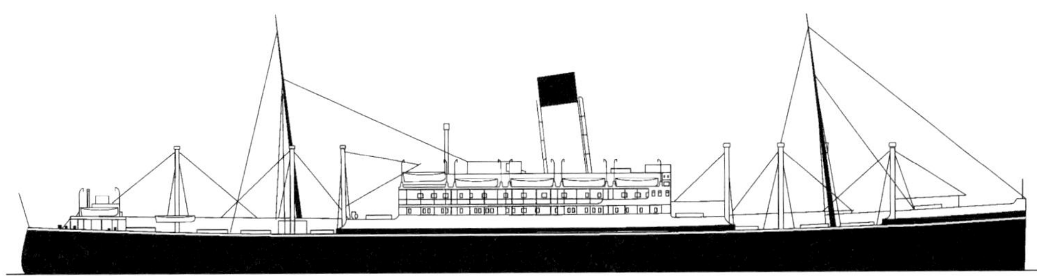

Minnewaska (H&W y/n 613) 1924 (DH)

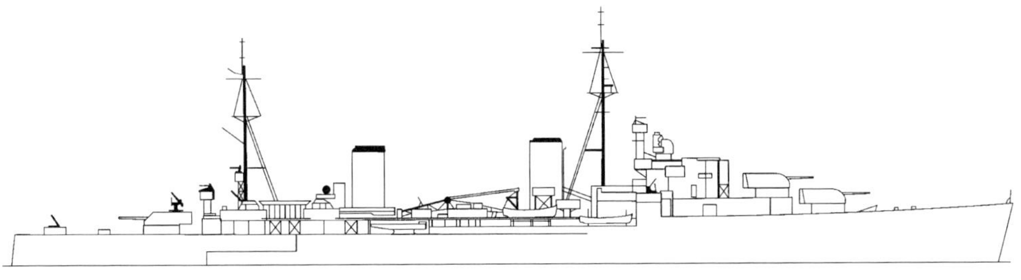

HMS *Penelope* (H&W y/n 940) 1935 (DH)

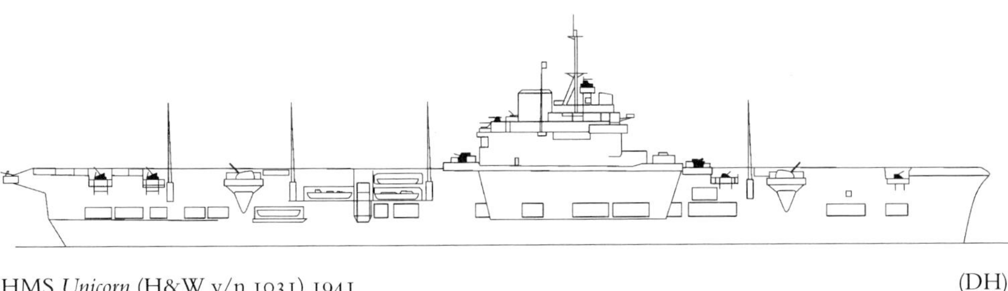

HMS *Unicorn* (H&W y/n 1031) 1941 (DH)

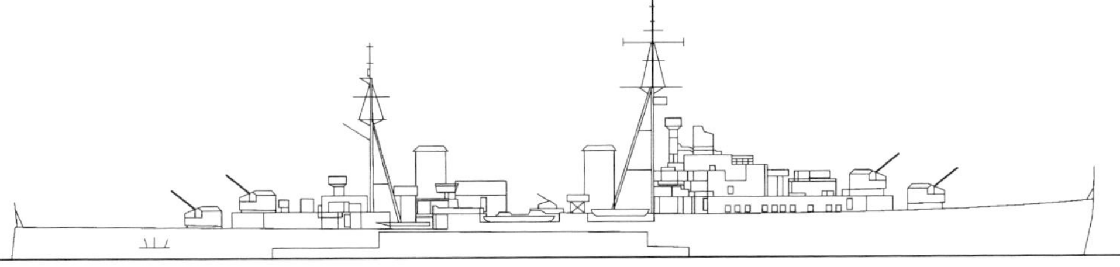

HMS *Black Prince* (H&W y/n 1049) 1942 (DH)

<table>
<tr><th>Ship</th><th>Yard No</th><th>Name</th><th>Date Launched</th><th>Displacement Tons</th><th>Type</th><th>Construction and Dimensions</th><th>Horse Power/ Engines</th><th>Owners</th></tr>
<tr><td>443</td><td>446</td><td>Minnekahda</td><td>8.3.1917</td><td>17,220</td><td>Passenger-Cargo</td><td>St/3Sc/St
620.5/66.4/47.3</td><td>?
QE (8Cy)
+ Exh Turb
H&W</td><td>Atlantic Transport Co. London</td></tr>
<tr><td colspan="9">(This vessel is listed by Moss & Hume as a passenger ship, re-rated)
Laid down before war as improved version of Minneapolis type. Construction suspended, restarted in 1916 and the vessel was finally completed 21.3.1918, as a very austere cargo carrier without superstructure or passenger accommodation. Unlike a number of other ships completed in such a manner during the war, Minnekahda was never rebuilt to original plans and as a consequence was perhaps one of the most ugly ships H&W ever built. After brief post-war service as a cargo ship on London–New York route, transferred to American registry in 1920 and rebuilt to accommodate 2,150 emigrants. After the collapse of the emigrant trade in the 1920s, was again reconstructed to accommodate 750 tourist class. However, worsening economic conditions meant the ship was increasingly unviable; laid up 1931, sold and broken up Dalmuir (UK) 1936.</td></tr>
<tr><td>N/A</td><td>447</td><td>Attendant</td><td colspan="6">Govan built</td></tr>
<tr><td>N/A</td><td>448</td><td>Maryland</td><td colspan="6">Irvine built</td></tr>
<tr><td>N/A</td><td>449</td><td>Missouri</td><td colspan="6">Irvine built</td></tr>
<tr><td>N/A</td><td>450</td><td>Mississippi</td><td colspan="6">Govan built</td></tr>
<tr><td>N/A</td><td>451</td><td>Falstria</td><td colspan="6">Irvine built</td></tr>
<tr><td>N/A</td><td>452</td><td>Lalandia</td><td colspan="6">Irvine built</td></tr>
<tr><td>444</td><td>453</td><td>Brecknockshire</td><td>12.9.1916</td><td>8,422</td><td>Cargo Ship</td><td>St/2Sc/St
470.1/60.0/?</td><td>?
QE (8Cy)
H&W</td><td>Royal Mail Steam Packet Co. London</td></tr>
<tr><td colspan="9">Laid down February 1914, considerably delayed by the outbreak of war and not completed until 11.1.1917. On maiden voyage Liverpool–Brazil suffered serious storm damage and on 2 February 1917 was intercepted by German surface raider Moewe, surrendered after being shelled and scuttled by explosive charges.</td></tr>
<tr><td>N/A</td><td>454</td><td>Pittsburgh</td><td colspan="6">Govan built</td></tr>
<tr><td>445</td><td>455</td><td>Arundel Castle</td><td>11.9.1919</td><td>19,500</td><td>Passenger Ship</td><td>St/2Sc/St
630.5/72.5/41.5</td><td>?
Turb
H&W</td><td>Union-Castle Steamship Co. London</td></tr>
<tr><td colspan="9">Originally to have been Amroth Castle. Laid down in late 1915 but not launched until late 1919 and completed 8.4.1921, clearly a very low priority. However, was not completed as an austere cargo-carrier like Orca, Belgic or Minnekahda, but emerged in 1921 as a magnificent four-funnel liner. In 1937–38 she was reconstructed by H&W, being given more powerful engines, oil-fired boilers and her appearance drastically altered by the reduction of the funnels to two. As rebuilt had accommodation for 219 first-class, 191 second-class and 194 tourist-class passengers. During Second World War served as troopship and afterwards a UK–South Africa emigrant carrier. In 1950 returned to service following a major refit with accommodation for 169 first-class and 371 tourist-class passengers. Withdrawn from service 1958; broken up Hong Kong 1959.</td></tr>
<tr><td>N/A</td><td>456</td><td>Windsor Castle</td><td colspan="6">Irvine built</td></tr>
<tr><td>446</td><td>457</td><td>Pittsburgh</td><td>11.11.1920</td><td>16,322</td><td>Passenger Ship</td><td>St/3Sc/St
574.4/67.8/41.2</td><td>TE = 8,360 ihp
Turn= 4,340 shp
TE (8Cy)
+ Exh Turb
H&W</td><td>International Navigation Co. Liverpool</td></tr>
<tr><td colspan="9">Laid down in 1913 as Regina for the American Line but completed 25.5.1922 for this owner under this name and entered service on Liverpool–Philadelphia route with accommodation for 660 cabin-class and 2,100 third-class passengers. In 1925 to Red Star, renamed Pennland, and employed on Antwerp–Southampton–New York service. In 1935 to German owner Arnold Bernstein, Hamburg, but shortly afterwards he was arrested and imprisoned by the Nazis and his ships sold off. This vessel acquired by Dutch owners, Holland-America Line, along with Antwerp–New York route on which it operated. At outbreak of Second World War became troopship, played an important role in Allied operations in Greece, engaged in evacuation when bombed and sunk by German aircraft in Gulf of Athens, April 1941. No lives lost.</td></tr>
<tr><td>N/A</td><td>458</td><td>Rimouski</td><td colspan="6">Govan built</td></tr>
<tr><td>447</td><td>459</td><td>Lancashire</td><td>11.1.1917</td><td>9,445</td><td>Passenger-Cargo</td><td>St/2Sc/St
482.4/57.3/32.1</td><td>942 hp
QE (8Cy)
H&W</td><td>Bibby Steamship Line Liverpool</td></tr>
<tr><td colspan="9">Laid down August 1914 but work suspended and not launched until January 1917, completed 9.8.1917 in very austere style. Initially in commercial service, but afterwards employed in trooping and repatriation work until released 1920. Refitted by H&W 1921. In 1930 became permanent troopship, during Second World War employed as commodore ship in trooping convoys. In 1945 converted to depot/store ship for use in Pacific but with end of conflict employed as a transport. In 1946 refurbished as troopship and served in this role for ten years before replaced by Oxfordshire. Broken up Barrow (UK) 1956.</td></tr>
<tr><td>N/A</td><td>460</td><td>Millias</td><td colspan="6">Govan built</td></tr>
<tr><td>N/A</td><td>461</td><td>Vedic</td><td colspan="6">Govan built</td></tr>
</table>

<table>
<tr><th>Ship</th><th>Yard No</th><th>Name</th><th>Date Launched</th><th>Displacement Tons</th><th>Type</th><th>Construction and Dimensions</th><th>Horse Power/ Engines</th><th>Owners</th></tr>
<tr><td>N/A</td><td>462</td><td>Marconi</td><td colspan="6">Govan built</td></tr>
<tr><td>N/A</td><td>463</td><td>Melita</td><td colspan="6">Berclay Curle built</td></tr>
<tr><td>N/A</td><td>464</td><td>Medora</td><td colspan="6">Berclay Curle built</td></tr>
<tr><td>N/A</td><td>465</td><td>Lobos</td><td colspan="6">Govan built</td></tr>
<tr><td>N/A</td><td>466</td><td>Bostonian</td><td colspan="6">Govan built</td></tr>
<tr><td>N/A</td><td>467</td><td>Montezuma</td><td colspan="6">Irvine built</td></tr>
<tr><td>N/A</td><td>468</td><td>Glenamoy</td><td colspan="6">Irvine built</td></tr>
<tr><td>N/A</td><td>469</td><td>Netherland</td><td colspan="6">Cancelled</td></tr>
<tr><td>448</td><td>470</td><td>Laurentic</td><td>16.6.1927</td><td>18,724</td><td>Passenger Ship</td><td>St/3Sc/St
578.2/75.4/40.6</td><td>?
Turb
H&W</td><td>Oceanic Steam Navigation Co. Liverpool</td></tr>
<tr><td colspan="9">Ordered before war but not laid down until slips were cleared of wartime construction. Originally to have been Germanic but changed to Homeric and again to this name under which launched. Completed 1.11.1927 with accommodation for 594 cabin-class, 406 tourist-class and 500 third-class passengers. Made maiden voyage on Liverpool–New York route November 1927, following year transferred to Canada routes. A somewhat old-fashioned ship in appearance, which resembled pre-war liners such as Laurentic (1909) rather than contemporaries. In late 1930s employed as cruise vessel and troopship before laid up in 1938. In September 1939 commissioned as armed merchant cruiser. In November 1940 was torpedoed and sunk off the Bloody Foreland by Otto Kretschmer's U-99, after going to aid of Elders & Fyffes' Casanare. When AMC Patroclus arrived to rescue both crews it was also torpedoed and sunk. Forty-nine lives lost on Laurentic out of a complement of 416, nine on Casanare and 50 on Patroclus.</td></tr>
<tr><td>449</td><td>471</td><td>Narkunda</td><td>25.4.1918</td><td>16,118</td><td>Passenger Ship</td><td>St/2Sc/St
581.4/69.4/44.5</td><td>1,428 nhp
15,300 ihp
QE (8Cy)
H&W</td><td>Peninsular and Oriental Steam Navigation Co. London</td></tr>
<tr><td colspan="9">Laid down in 1914, work suspended and this ship was not launched until 1918, for Shipping Controller. After this there were further delays caused by indecision as to how hull should be finished. Finally returned to owners still incomplete in 1919 and eventually completed 30.3.1920 to a slightly modified design, with accommodation for 426 first-class and 247 second-class passengers for UK–Australia routes. Converted to oil firing in 1930s. During the Second World War employed initially as diplomatic ship but subsequently a troopship. In this role she was sunk by aircraft bombs, November 1942, just after leaving Bougie, having participated in invasion of North Africa. Thirty-one lives lost.</td></tr>
<tr><td>450</td><td>472</td><td>HMS Abercrombie</td><td>15.4.1915</td><td>6,180</td><td>Monitor</td><td>St/2Sc/St
334.5/90.2/10.0</td><td>2,000 ihp
VTE (8Cy)
H & W</td><td>Admiralty</td></tr>
<tr><td colspan="9">In November 1914 Charles M. Schwab of Bethlehem Steel called on the First Lord, Winston Churchill, to offer him four 14in gun turrets ordered by A.G. Vulcan, Hamburg, for Greek battleship Salamis, which they then had under construction. The Americans were unable to deliver these turrets because of the British blockade of Germany and Schwab was keen to find another buyer. Churchill saw these modern weapons as an opportunity to improve the Royal Navy's capacity to support land forces in Flanders and ordered the Director of Naval Construction to prepare a design to 'armoured monitors' capable of carrying them which could be built in four months. Although the specification called for a speed of 10 knots the hull design, which included anti-torpedo bulges, was inefficient and actual speed was half this. An appalling design made worse by the determination of the Admiralty to rush these ships into service.
Laid down December 1914, originally as M1 and completed 29.5.1915, an impressive performance for a builder with limited warship experience. Before launch in February 1915 was renamed Admiral Farragut, when it was decided to give the monitors the names of American Civil War commanders to acknowledge the origins of their guns. The US authorities, already concerned about what was clearly a flagrant breach of neutrality, objected and diplomatically the ships were again renamed and this vessel became Abercrombie shortly after being commissioned. In June sailed for Dardanelles where became flagship of supporting forces, frequently in action against the Turks. After the evacuation of Cape Hellas in January 1916 moved to Imbros before refitting at Malta in May. Again stationed at Imbros in action in Aegean, on the Salonika front. Refitted at Malta in 1917 and in 1918, her worn-out American guns were replaced by British weapons of the same calibre. Returned to Britain in 1919 and paid off in May; disarmed and sold for breaking up in 1920, but retained by the navy until 1927 when resold. Broken up Inverkeithing (UK) 1927.</td></tr>
<tr><td>451</td><td>473</td><td>HMS Havelock</td><td>29.4.1915</td><td>6,180</td><td>Monitor</td><td>St/2Sc/St
334.5/90.2/10.0</td><td>2,000 ihp
VTE (8Cy)
H & W</td><td>Admiralty</td></tr>
<tr><td colspan="9">Sister ship of Abercombie, completed 29.5.1915. Originally M2 but for the same reasons as her sister renamed General Grant and Havelock shortly after commissioning. In May sailed for Dardanelles where frequently in action against Turkish forces. After evacuation returned to Britain in 1916 and employed as guard ship at Lowestoft. Paid off May 1919, disarmed and sold for breaking up 1920, again was retained by navy until 1927 when resold. Broken up Preston (UK) 1927.</td></tr>
<tr><td>N/A</td><td>474</td><td>Cargo ship</td><td colspan="6">Cancelled</td></tr>
<tr><td>N/A</td><td>475</td><td>Cargo Ship</td><td colspan="6">Cancelled</td></tr>
<tr><td>N/A</td><td>476</td><td>HMS Raglan</td><td colspan="6">Govan built</td></tr>
<tr><td>N/A</td><td>477</td><td>HMS Prince Eugene</td><td colspan="6">Govan built</td></tr>
</table>

<table>
<tr><th>Ship</th><th>Yard No</th><th>Name</th><th>Date Launched</th><th>Displacement Tons</th><th>Type</th><th>Construction and Dimensions</th><th>Horse Power/ Engines</th><th>Owners</th></tr>
<tr><td>452</td><td>478</td><td>HMS Lord Clive</td><td>10.6.1915</td><td>5,920</td><td>Monitor</td><td>St/2Sc/St
335.5/87.1/9.6</td><td>2,310 ihp
VTE (8Cy)
H&W</td><td>Admiralty</td></tr>
<tr><td colspan="9">The 'success' of the monitors encouraged the British naval authorities to order repeats before the first group was even launched and their deficiencies became apparent. No modern gun mountings were available but a large number of twin 12in turrets from obsolete pre-Dreadnought battleships were on hand. With modifications to mountings these could be given a range of 21,000 yards. As haste was seen as essential the design that emerged was virtually a repeat of 14in type.
Laid down January 1915, completed 10.7.1915. Originally M6 but subsequently renamed Lord Clive. The turret came from HMS Magnificent. Joined Dover-based monitor squadron after commissioned. At one point was fitted with an 18in gun in addition to her turret-mounted 12in. Paid off November 1918, used for gunnery tests 1920–21, laid up until sold for scrap. Broken up Bo'ness (UK) 1927.</td></tr>
<tr><td>453</td><td>479</td><td>HMS General Craufurd</td><td>8.7.1915</td><td>5,920</td><td>Monitor</td><td>St/2Sc/St
335.5/87.1/9.6</td><td>2,310 ihp
VTE (8Cy)
H&W</td><td>Admiralty</td></tr>
<tr><td colspan="9">Laid down January 1915, completed 26.8.1915, sister ship of Lord Clive. Originally M7, subsequently renamed General Crauford. The turret came from HMS Magnificent. Joined Dover-based monitor squadron after commissioning. Paid off November 1918. Briefly recommissioned as gunnery tender then sold for scrap. Broken up Holland 1921.</td></tr>
<tr><td>454</td><td>480</td><td>HMS Earl of Peterborough</td><td>26.8.1915</td><td>5,920</td><td>Monitor</td><td>St/2Sc/St
335.5/87.1/9.6</td><td>2,310 ihp
VTE (8Cy)
H&W</td><td>Admiralty</td></tr>
<tr><td colspan="9">Laid down January 1915, completed 23.9.1915, sister ship of Lord Clive. Originally M8, subsequently renamed Earl of Peterborough. The turret came from HMS Mars. Sent to Mediterranean, served in Greek and Italian waters. Paid off March 1919 and sold for scrap. Broken up Germany 1921.</td></tr>
<tr><td>455</td><td>481</td><td>HMS Sir Thomas Picton</td><td>30.9.1915</td><td>5,920</td><td>Monitor</td><td>St/2Sc/St
335.5/87.1/9.6</td><td>2,310 ihp
VTE (8Cy)
H&W</td><td>Admiralty</td></tr>
<tr><td colspan="9">Laid down January 1915, completed 4.11.1915, sister ship of Lord Clive. Originally M12, subsequently renamed Sir Thomas Picton. The turret came from HMS Mars. Sent to Mediterranean and served in Greek and Adriatic waters. Later joined Earl of Peterborough at Venice in support of Italian Army. Paid off 1919. Broken up Germany 1921.</td></tr>
<tr><td>456</td><td>482–4</td><td>HMS Glorious</td><td>20.4.1916</td><td>22,354</td><td>Light Battle Cruiser</td><td>St/4Sc/St
786.3/81.0/23.4</td><td>90,000 shp
Turb
H&W</td><td>Admiralty</td></tr>
<tr><td colspan="9">Completed 31.12.1916. Classified as a 'large light cruiser' to get around Cabinet ruling that no new capital ships should be laid down, this vessel represents one of the strangest developments of the whole misbegotten battlecruiser concept. A huge hull protected by armour more appropriate to a fleet scouting cruiser but armed with four 15in guns in massively armoured turrets, this ship had a speed of 32 knots. By the time commissioned in January 1917 events at Jutland had demonstrated that the vessel was a deathtrap and instead of joining a battle squadron was allocated to a light cruiser squadron (the 3rd) as its flagship and saw action in November 1917. In 1919 was attached to the gunnery training school at Portsmouth and later became flagship of the reserve there. In 1924–30 converted to an aircraft carrier. Off Norway in June 1940 was caught unawares by the German battlecruisers Scharnhorst and Gneisenau and destroyed by 11in shell fire in 70 minutes. Only 38 out of the 1,245 men on board survived.</td></tr>
<tr><td>457</td><td>485</td><td>HMS M29</td><td>22.5.1915</td><td>360</td><td>Monitor</td><td>St/2Sc/St
177.3/31.0/5.9</td><td>400 ihp
VTE (8Cy)
H&W</td><td>Admiralty</td></tr>
<tr><td colspan="9">Early in 1915 five battleships of the Queen Elizabeth class were ordered to land two Mk XII 6in guns each. These were powerful modern weapons with a range of 14,700 yards and a class of five small monitors were ordered to carry them. Initially all five were ordered from H&W, Belfast, but because of a shortage of slip space two (M32 and M33) were subcontracted to WC. They proved to be reliable and useful ships for coastal and river warfare.
Completed 20.6.1915. Served in Mediterranean until December 1918 when sent to support interventionist and White forces in Russian Civil War, May–September 1919. Laid up at Devonport, converted to a minelayer 1923–25, renamed Medusa. In May 1940 converted to repair ship, renamed Talbot, and by September serving as submarine depot ship. Damaged by bombs in March 1942; 1943 renamed Medway II. Broken up Dover (UK) 1946.</td></tr>
<tr><td>458</td><td>486</td><td>HMS M30</td><td>23.6.1915</td><td>360</td><td>Monitor</td><td>St/2Sc/St
177.3/31.0/5.9</td><td>400 ihp
VTE (8Cy)
H&W</td><td>Admiralty</td></tr>
<tr><td colspan="9">Completed 9.7.1915. Sister ship of M29. Served in Mediterranean from August 1915 until sunk by Turkish shore batteries in Gulf of Smyrna, May 1916.</td></tr>
<tr><td>459</td><td>487</td><td>HMS M31</td><td>24.6.1915</td><td>360</td><td>Monitor</td><td>St/2Sc/St
177.3/31.0/5.9</td><td>400 ihp
VTE (8Cy)
H&W</td><td>Admiralty</td></tr>
<tr><td colspan="9">Completed 9.7.1915. Sister ship of M29. Served in Mediterranean until March 1919 when sent to support interventionist and White forces in Russian Civil War, May–September 1919. Converted to minelayer 1921; renamed Melpomene 1925. Although listed for disposal in 1937 remained unsold in 1939, returned to naval duty as torpedo instruction vessel in 1941, renamed Menelaus. Broken up Llanelly (UK) 1948.</td></tr>
</table>

<table>
<tr><th>Ship</th><th>Yard No</th><th>Name</th><th>Date Launched</th><th>Displacement Tons</th><th>Type</th><th>Construction and Dimensions</th><th>Horse Power/ Engines</th><th>Owners</th></tr>
<tr><td>N/A</td><td>488</td><td>HMS *M32*</td><td colspan="6">Built by WC</td></tr>
<tr><td>N/A</td><td>489</td><td>HMS *M33*</td><td colspan="6">Built by WC</td></tr>
<tr><td>N/A</td><td>490</td><td>HMS *P24*</td><td colspan="6">Govan built</td></tr>
<tr><td>N/A</td><td>491</td><td>HMS *P25*</td><td colspan="6">Govan built</td></tr>
<tr><td>N/A</td><td>492</td><td>HMS *Erebus*</td><td colspan="6">Govan built</td></tr>
<tr><td>460</td><td>493</td><td>HMS *Terror*</td><td>18.5.1916</td><td>8,022</td><td>Monitor</td><td>St/2Sc/St
405.0/88.2/11.8</td><td>6,000 ihp
VTE (8Cy)
H&W</td><td>Admiralty</td></tr>
<tr><td colspan="9">After the problems with the early big-gun monitors became evident a much-improved design was prepared and two were ordered from H&W one being built at Govan and the other in Belfast. These ships were given modern 15in guns in twin mounts and in the case of *Terror* this came from the unsuccessful monitor *Marshal Ney*.
Laid down October 1915 and completed in August; exceeded design speed on trials. Joined Dover Squadron August 1916 and saw extensive action off the Belgian coast. On the night of 18/19 October 1917 hit by three torpedoes from German torpedo boats and beached, subsequently towed to Dover and repaired in ten weeks. After war used as a turret-training and experimental ship. Returned to active service during Second World War, joining the inshore squadron supporting British troops in North Africa. Was bombed and sunk off Derna, February 1941.</td></tr>
<tr><td>N/A</td><td>494</td><td>HMS *Salmon*</td><td colspan="6">Govan built</td></tr>
<tr><td>N/A</td><td>495</td><td>HMS *Sylph*</td><td colspan="6">Govan built</td></tr>
<tr><td>N/A</td><td>496</td><td>HMS *Skilful*</td><td colspan="6">Govan built</td></tr>
<tr><td>N/A</td><td>497</td><td>HMS *Springbok*</td><td colspan="6">Govan built</td></tr>
<tr><td>N/A</td><td>498</td><td>HMS *Tenacious*</td><td colspan="6">Govan built</td></tr>
<tr><td>N/A</td><td>499</td><td>HMS *Tetarch*</td><td colspan="6">Govan built</td></tr>
<tr><td>461</td><td>500</td><td>HMS *Vindictive*</td><td>17.1.1918</td><td>7,764</td><td>Seaplane Carrier</td><td>St/4Sc/St
605.0/65.0/19.3</td><td>60,000 shp
Turb
H&W</td><td>Admiralty</td></tr>
<tr><td colspan="9">Laid down June 1916 as *Cavendish*, name ship of class of 9,750-ton fleet cruisers armed with 7.5in guns. In August 1917 it was decided to convert this vessel into an aircraft carrier. Renamed *Vindictive* in June 1918 to commemorate the old cruiser used as a block ship at Zeebrugge in May. The conversion necessitated extensive alterations to the hull and as a consequence *Vindictive* wasn't launched until January 1918 and was not completed until 19.10.1918. On completion joined flying squadron of Grand Fleet, carrying six aircraft. In 1919 to Baltic where in July badly damaged when ran aground; repaired at Portsmouth August 1919–March 1920. After a period in reserve was employed as a troopship 1920–23 and then paid off and converted back into cruiser. In Second World War employed as a repair ship. Broken up 1946.</td></tr>
<tr><td>N/A</td><td>501</td><td>HMS *PC62*</td><td colspan="6">Govan built</td></tr>
<tr><td>N/A</td><td>502</td><td>*Glenogle*</td><td colspan="6">Govan built</td></tr>
<tr><td>N/A</td><td>503</td><td>*Glengarry*</td><td colspan="6">Govan built</td></tr>
<tr><td>N/A</td><td>504</td><td>*Glenfarne*</td><td colspan="6">Govan built</td></tr>
<tr><td>N/A</td><td>505</td><td>*Glenbeg*</td><td colspan="6">Govan built</td></tr>
<tr><td>462</td><td>506</td><td>*Oroya*</td><td>16.12.1920</td><td>12,257</td><td>Passenger-Cargo</td><td>St/2Sc/St
525.3/62.8/32.1</td><td>21,480 ihp
Turb
H&W</td><td>Pacific Steam Navigation Co.
Liverpool</td></tr>
<tr><td colspan="9">After launch work was stopped as owners had no use for ship; finally completed 22.3.1923. Designed for use on South America routes with accommodation for 150 first-class, 123 second-class and 450 third-class passengers. However, changes in trade patterns caused by war and opening of the Panama Canal made this vessel increasingly difficult to operate profitably. Employed on Liverpool–Panama–West Coast South America route until 1931 then laid up at Dartmouth. Broken up Italy (La Spezia) 1939.</td></tr>
<tr><td>463</td><td>507</td><td>*Asturias*</td><td>7.7.1925</td><td>22,048</td><td>Passenger-Cargo</td><td>St/2Sc/Mv
630.5/78.1/40.5</td><td>15,000 bhp
Dies
H&W</td><td>RMSP Meat Transports Ltd
London</td></tr>
<tr><td colspan="9">Completed 6.2.1926, for Southampton–River Plate service, had accommodation for 408 first-class, 200 second-class and 674 third-class passengers and a large cargo capacity. When completed was the largest and most powerful motor vessel in the world, but although technically successful the diesel engines proved too slow in service. As a consequence was re-engined with turbines (20,000 shp) and returned to service in October 1934 with a speed of 19 knots, compared to previous 16.5–17. In September 1939 commissioned as armed merchant cruiser being used on patrol and escort work in Atlantic. Refitted and rearmed in America in 1941. Torpedoed July 1943 by Italian submarine *Ammiraglio Cagni* in mid-Atlantic; towed 400 miles to Freetown where remained derelict until 1945. After war brought back to Belfast for repairs and refit prior to being employed post-war carrying emigrants to Australia and as a troopship. Broken up Faslane (UK) 1957.</td></tr>
<tr><td>N/A</td><td>508</td><td>*Lochkatrine*</td><td colspan="6">Govan built</td></tr>
<tr><td>464</td><td>509</td><td>*Yorkshire*</td><td>29.5.1919</td><td>10,184</td><td>Passenger-Cargo</td><td>St/2Sc/St
482.4/58.3/40.4</td><td>946 nhp
5,500 shp
Turb
H&W</td><td>Bibby Steamship Co.
Liverpool</td></tr>
<tr><td colspan="9">Built as replacement in quickest possible time, this vessel was something of an oddity in the Bibby fleet; last passenger ship ordered by Bibby from H&W.</td></tr>
</table>

Ship	Yard No	Name	Date Launched	Displacement Tons	Type	Construction and Dimensions	Horse Power/ Engines	Owners
Completed 2.9.1920, for UK–Ceylon/Rangoon routes, accommodation for up to 305 first-class passengers. Sunk by submarine torpedo (*U-37*) 160nm NW of Cape Finisterre inbound Burma–Liverpool with 278 passengers and crew on board, September 1939. Fifty-eight lives lost.								
N/A	510	*Coney*	Govan built					
N/A	511	*Loreta*	Govan built					
N/A	512	*Loriga*	Govan built					
N/A	513	*Salamanda*	Govan built					
N/A	514	*Glenluce*	Govan built					
N/A	515	*Dintedyk*	Govan built					
N/A	516	*Lochgoil*	Govan built					
465	517	*Lochmonar*	8.12.1923	9,463	Cargo Ship (Refrigerated)	St/2Sc/Mv 485.6/62.6/35.5	1,317 nhp Dies H&W	RMSP Meat Transports Ltd London
Completed 26.6.1924, for UK–Vancouver service. Broken up Blyth (UK) 1949								
N/A	518	Cargo Ship	Govan cancelled					
N/A	519	*Ekari*	Govan built					
466	520	*War Shamrock*	21.6.1917	5,174	Standard 'A'-type Cargo Ship	St/Sc/St 400.4/52.3/28.4	490 nhp 2,500 ihp TE (3Cy) H&W	Shipping Controller
In December 1916, faced with increasing shipping losses, the British government appointed a Shipping Controller to ensure an adequate supply of merchant tonnage to keep the country's supply routes open. The government began to order large numbers of merchantmen, built to standard designs, and increasingly assumed effective control of the shipbuilding industry. The urgency of the programme can be gauged by the fact that the Merchant Shipbuilding Advisory Committee only met for the first time in December 1916 but the first ship, this vessel, was completed by August 1917. Completed 20.8.1917, first 'standard ship' to enter service. In 1919 to Belgian ownership, Lloyd Royal Line, renamed *Belgier.* In 1927 to Africaine de Nav., renamed *Kabinda.* Wrecked E of West Goodwin buoy, December 1939, inbound from Buenos Aires with cargo of maize and general goods.								
467	521	*War Clover*	16.8.1917	5,174	Standard 'A'-type Cargo Ship	St/Sc/St 400.4/52.3/28.4	490 nhp 2,500 ihp TE (3Cy) H&W	Shipping Controller
Completed 20.9.1917. Sunk by submarine torpedo (*U-64*) 25nm NE of Pantellaria, outbound Barry–Taranto with cargo of coal, October 1917. Fourteen lives lost.								
468	522	*War Trefoil*	5.9.1917	5,166	Standard 'A'-type Cargo Ship	St/Sc/St 400.4/52.3/28.4	490 nhp 2,500 ihp TE (3Cy) H&W	Shipping Controller
Completed 16.10.1917. In 1919 to Italian owners, Ravano & Corrado, renamed *San Giuseppe.* Outbreak Second World War interned in US and seized by US government in 1941, renamed *Aneroid.* Sunk by submarine torpedo (*U-175*) E of Orinoco River, October 1942. Six lives lost.								
N/A	523	*War Legate*	Govan built					
N/A	524	*War Envoy*	Govan built					
N/A	525	*War Hostage*	Govan built					
N/A	526	*War Expert*	Govan built					
N/A	527	*War Africa*	Govan built					
N/A	528	*War Airman*	Govan built					
N/A	529	*War Cowslip*	Govan built					
N/A	530	*War Maple*	Govan built					
469	531	*War Viper*	14.2.1918	5,160	Standard 'B'-type Cargo Ship	St/Sc/St 400.4/52.3/28.4	518 nhp 2,500 ihp TE (3Cy) H&W	Shipping Controller
Completed 14.3.1918. In 1919 to Donaldson Line, renamed *Cabotia.* In 1929 to Haldin & Co., renamed *Cedrington Court.* Mined and sunk near North Goodwin light vessel, inbound Buenos Aires–Hull with cargo of wheat, January 1940.								
470	532	*War Lemur*	9.5.1918	5,185	Standard 'B'-type Cargo Ship	St/Sc/St 400.4/52.3/28.4	518 nhp 2,500 ihp TE (3Cy) H&W	Shipping Controller
Completed 28.5.1918. In 1919 to Cunard SS Co., renamed *Verentia.* In 1926 to Andrew Weir & Co., renamed *Foreric.* In 1927 to A. Holland & Co., renamed *Galvan.* In 1937 to Japanese owners, Nisshin Kaiun Shokai, renamed *Pei Tai.* In 1938 to Katagawa Sangyo, renamed *Hokutai Maru.* Sunk by US aircraft off Babelthuap, March 1944.								

<table>
<tr><th>Ship</th><th>Yard No</th><th>Name</th><th>Date Launched</th><th>Displacement Tons</th><th>Type</th><th>Construction and Dimensions</th><th>Horse Power/ Engines</th><th>Owners</th></tr>
<tr><td>471</td><td>533</td><td>War Cobra</td><td>15.11.1917</td><td>5,155</td><td>Standard
'B'-type
Cargo Ship</td><td>St/Sc/St
400.4/52.3/28.4</td><td>518 nhp
2,500 ihp
TE (3Cy)
H&W</td><td>Shipping
Controller</td></tr>
<tr><td colspan="9">Completed 20.12.1917. In 1919 to Italian owners, Veneziana, renamed Alberto Treves. In 1940 to Lloyd Triestino, renamed Romolo Gessi. Scuttled at Massawa, April 1941. Raised by British but not repaired. Broken up in situ 1951.</td></tr>
<tr><td>472</td><td>534</td><td>War Python</td><td>29.12.1917</td><td>5,155</td><td>Standard
'B'-type
Cargo Ship</td><td>St/Sc/St
400.4/52.3/28.4</td><td>518 nhp
2,500 ihp
TE (3Cy)
H&W</td><td>Shipping
Controller</td></tr>
<tr><td colspan="9">Completed 24.1.1918. In 1919 to Furness Withy, renamed Ariano. In 1929 to French owners, Chargeurs Reunis, renamed Fort Archambault. In 1951 to Italian owners, Lauro & Montella, renamed Silvano. Broken up Italy (La Spezia) 1958.</td></tr>
<tr><td>473</td><td>535</td><td>War Bittern</td><td>14.3.1918</td><td>5,178</td><td>Standard
'B'-type
Cargo Ship</td><td>St/Sc/St
400.4/52.3/28.4</td><td>518 nhp
2,500 ihp
TE (3Cy)
H&W</td><td>Shipping
Controller</td></tr>
<tr><td colspan="9">Completed 11.4.1918. In 1919 to Belgian owners, Lloyd Royal Line, renamed Patagonier. In 1932 to Greek owners, A. Andreatos, renamed Perseus. Sunk by gunfire from German surface raider Admiral Hipper NW of Madeira, February 1941. Fourteen lives lost.</td></tr>
<tr><td>474</td><td>536</td><td>War Buckler</td><td>28.3.1918</td><td>2,357</td><td>Standard
'D'-type
Cargo Ship</td><td>St/Sc/St
285.0/42.0/19.0</td><td>411 nhp
1,900 ihp
TE (3Cy)
H&W</td><td>Shipping
Controller</td></tr>
<tr><td colspan="9">Completed 30.5.1918. In 1919 to French Railway Co., renamed Portrieux. Sunk by aircraft off Gravelines, May 1940.</td></tr>
<tr><td>475</td><td>537</td><td>War Tabard</td><td>28.3.1918</td><td>2,357</td><td>Standard
'D'-type
Cargo Ship</td><td>St/Sc/St
285.0/42.0/19.0</td><td>411 nhp
1,900 ihp
TE (3Cy)
H&W</td><td>Shipping
Controller</td></tr>
<tr><td colspan="9">Completed 15.6.1918. In 1919 to French owners, S.G.A.M., renamed Jura. In 1929 to D.R. Philips, renamed Radya. Foundered Bideford Bay on voyage to Bordeaux with cargo of coal, December 1929.</td></tr>
<tr><td>476</td><td>538</td><td>War Snake</td><td>22.8.1918</td><td>5,222</td><td>Standard
'B'-type
Cargo Ship</td><td>St/Sc/St
400.4/52.3/28.4</td><td>517 nhp
2,500 ihp
TE (3Cy)
H&W</td><td>Shipping
Controller</td></tr>
<tr><td colspan="9">Completed 29.8.1918. In 1919 to Cunard SS Co., renamed Venusia. In 1923 to S.&J. Thompson, renamed River Delaware. In 1931 to Italian ownership, Corrado, renamed Rina Corrado. Sunk by British naval gunfire E of Syracuse during Duisburg Convoy battle, November 1941.</td></tr>
<tr><td>N/A</td><td>539</td><td>War Popular</td><td colspan="6">Greenock built</td></tr>
<tr><td>477</td><td>540</td><td>War Icarus</td><td>19.9.1918</td><td>8,002</td><td>Standard
'G'-type
Cargo Ship</td><td>St/2Sc/St
450.4/58.4/37.2</td><td>1,138 nhp
5,500 ihp
TE (6Cy)
H&W</td><td>Shipping
Controller</td></tr>
<tr><td colspan="9">Completed 31.10.1918. In 1919 to Atlantic Transport Co., renamed Mesaba. In 1929 to Ocean SN Co., renamed Depphic. In 1933 to Clan Line, renamed Clan Farquhar. Broken up Milford Haven (UK) 1948.</td></tr>
<tr><td>478</td><td>541</td><td>Otira</td><td>5.3.1919</td><td>7,995</td><td>Standard
'G'-type
Cargo Ship</td><td>St/2Sc/St
450.4/58.4/37.2</td><td>1,138 nhp
5,500 ihp
TE (6Cy)
H&W</td><td>Shaw Savill &
Albion Co.
London</td></tr>
<tr><td colspan="9">Completed 17.4.1919, laid down as War Paris but completed under this name. Broken up Italy (Pola) 1937.</td></tr>
<tr><td>479</td><td>542</td><td>Bardic</td><td>19.12.1918</td><td>8,010</td><td>Standard
'G'-type
Cargo Ship</td><td>St/2Sc/St
450.4/58.4/37.2</td><td>1,138 nhp
5,500 ihp
TE (6Cy)
H&W</td><td>Oceanic Steam
Navigation Co.
Liverpool</td></tr>
<tr><td colspan="9">Completed 13.3.1919, laid down as War Priam but completed under this name. In 1925 to G. Thompson & Co., renamed Horatius. In 1933 to Shaw Savill & Albion, renamed Kumara. In 1937 to Greek Owners, M. Fatsis, renamed Marathon. Captured and scuttled by German raider Scharnhorst NE of Cape Verde Islands, March 1941. No lives lost.</td></tr>
<tr><td>480</td><td>543</td><td>War Melody</td><td>19.10.1918</td><td>6,533</td><td>Standard
'N'-type
Cargo Ship</td><td>St/Sc/St
412.4/55.8/34.4</td><td>517 nhp
2,300 ihp
TE (3Cy)
H&W</td><td>Shipping
Controller</td></tr>
<tr><td colspan="9">The National of 'N'-type ship was, like later standard ships, designed with straight frames and as few curves in the hull as possible to simplify the design to the point where it could be constructed by non-shipyard engineering labour in inland yards.</td></tr>
</table>

<table>
<tr><th>Ship</th><th>Yard No</th><th>Name</th><th>Date Launched</th><th>Displacement Tons</th><th>Type</th><th>Construction and Dimensions</th><th>Horse Power/ Engines</th><th>Owners</th></tr>
<tr><td colspan="9">The design was prepared by H&W (Belfast) who subsequently built a number of these vessels, mainly launched after the war. Subsequently much of the material assembled for 'N'-type vessels was used in other ships.
Completed 7.11.1918. In 1919 to American owners, R. Dollar Co., renamed Grace Dollar. In 1924 to Japanese ownership, Tatsuuma Kisen, renamed Hakutatsu Maru. In 1937 to Ryuun Kisen, renamed Ryuun Maru. In 1942 to Nissan Kisen, renamed Nikkyu Maru. Sunk by submarine torpedo (USS Jack) in sea of Japan, July 1943.</td></tr>
<tr><td>481</td><td>544</td><td>War Music</td><td>2.11.1918</td><td>6,498</td><td>Standard
'N'-type
Cargo Ship</td><td>St/Sc/St
412.4/55.8/34.4</td><td>517 nhp
2,300 ihp
TE (3Cy)
H&W</td><td>Shipping
Controller</td></tr>
<tr><td colspan="9">Completed 5.12.1918. In 1919 to Glen Line, renamed Glenspey. In 1921 to King Line, renamed King Bleddyn. In 1937 to Dutch owners, Halcyon Line, renamed Stad Massluis. In 1950 to Italian owners, F. Pittaluga, renamed Francescu. April 1954 stranded in River Schelde, at end of voyage from Bona with cargo of ore, broke in two and wreck subsequently scrapped.</td></tr>
<tr><td>482</td><td>545</td><td>War Dream</td><td>5.12.1918</td><td>6,498</td><td>Standard
'N'-type
Cargo Ship</td><td>St/Sc/St
412.4/55.8/34.4</td><td>517 nhp
2,300 ihp
TE (3Cy)
H&W</td><td>Shipping
Controller</td></tr>
<tr><td colspan="9">Completed 9.1.1919. In 1919 to Glan Line, renamed Glenshane. In 1932 to Japanese owners. By 1934 under management of F.M. Jonas, Hong Kong, renamed Miltonia and later Sunshine. In 1935 to Chinese owners, Ding Yao Dung, renamed Chang Lung. In 1938 to Japanese owners, Shoryu Kisen, renamed Shoryu Maru. Sunk by submarine torpedo (USS Parche) in Pacific, May 1944.</td></tr>
<tr><td>483</td><td>546</td><td>Nasmyth</td><td>3.4.1919</td><td>6,509</td><td>Standard
'N'-type
Cargo Ship</td><td>St/Sc/St
412.4/55.8/34.4</td><td>517 nhp
2,300 ihp
TE (3Cy)
H&W</td><td>Liverpool
Brazil & River
Plate Steam
Navigation Co.
(Lamport & Holt)
Liverpool</td></tr>
<tr><td colspan="9">Completed 8.5.1919, laid down as War Vision but completed under this name. Severely damaged May 1938 when ran aground Tenife point, south Grand Canary, refloated and subsequently broken up Holland (Rotterdam), October 1938.</td></tr>
<tr><td>484</td><td>547</td><td>Bonheur</td><td>17.6.1920</td><td>5,326</td><td>Standard
'A'-type Cargo
Ship</td><td>St/Sc/St
400.4/52.4/28.4</td><td>590 nhp
Turb
H&W</td><td>Lamport & Holt
Ltd
Liverpool</td></tr>
<tr><td colspan="9">Completed 7.10.1920, no 'war' name appears to have been allocated. Sunk by submarine torpedo (U-138) NW of Cape Wrath outbound Liverpool–Rosario, October 1940. No lives lost.</td></tr>
<tr><td>N/A</td><td>548</td><td>War Jasmine</td><td colspan="6">Govan built</td></tr>
<tr><td>N/A</td><td>549</td><td>War Jonquil</td><td colspan="6">Govan built</td></tr>
<tr><td>485</td><td>550</td><td>Boswell</td><td>1.7.1920</td><td>5,327</td><td>Standard
'A'-type Cargo
Ship</td><td>St/Sc/St
400.4/52.4/28.4</td><td>590 hp
Turb
H&W</td><td>Lamport & Holt
Ltd
Liverpool</td></tr>
<tr><td colspan="9">Completed 19.11.1920, possibly War Bamboo? In 1934 to White Shipping Co., renamed Adderstone. In 1937 to J. Gerrard Jn, renamed Germa. In 1951 to Japanese owners, Dai-ichi Kisen, renamed Norway Maru. Broken up Japan (Sakai) 1968.</td></tr>
<tr><td>N/A</td><td>551</td><td>War Pampus</td><td colspan="6">Govan built</td></tr>
<tr><td>N/A</td><td>552</td><td>HMS St Aubin</td><td colspan="6">Govan built</td></tr>
<tr><td>N/A</td><td>553</td><td>HMS St Bees</td><td colspan="6">Govan built</td></tr>
<tr><td>486</td><td>554</td><td>Newton</td><td>30.4.1919</td><td>6,509</td><td>Standard
'N'-type
Cargo Ship</td><td>St/Sc/St
412.4/55.8/34.4</td><td>517 nhp
2,300 ihp
TE (3Cy)
H&W</td><td>Liverpool
Brazil & River
Plate Steam
Navigation Co.
(Lamport & Holt)
Liverpool</td></tr>
<tr><td colspan="9">Completed 27.5.1919, laid down as War Justice but completed under this name. In 1933 to Greek owners, Rethymnis Kulukunis (registered in London), renamed Mount Othrys. In January 1945, entering Thames with cargo of grain from St Johns, in collision off Holehaven, caught fire and beached on Mucking Flats, broke in two, total loss.</td></tr>
<tr><td>487</td><td>555</td><td>New Brunswick</td><td>15.5.1919</td><td>6,529</td><td>Standard
'N'-type
Cargo Ship</td><td>St/Sc/St
412.4/55.8/34.4</td><td>517 nhp
2,300 ihp
TE (3Cy)
H&W</td><td>Elder Dempster
Liverpool</td></tr>
<tr><td colspan="9">Completed 26.6.1919, laid down as War Liberty but completed under this name. Sunk by submarine torpedo (U-159) 140m ESE of Azores outbound UK–Lagos, May 1942. Three lives lost.</td></tr>
</table>

<table>
<tr><th>Ship</th><th>Yard No</th><th>Name</th><th>Date Launched</th><th>Displacement Tons</th><th>Type</th><th>Construction and Dimensions</th><th>Horse Power/ Engines</th><th>Owners</th></tr>
<tr><td>488</td><td>556</td><td>*New Georgia*</td><td>12.6.1919</td><td>6,566</td><td>Standard 'N'-type Cargo Ship</td><td>St/Sc/St 412.4/55.8/34.4</td><td>517 nhp 2,300 ihp TE (3Cy) H&W</td><td>Elder Dempster Liverpool</td></tr>
<tr><td colspan="9">Completed 14.8.1919, laid down as *War Triumph* but completed under this name. In 1933 to Greek owners, S. Paramythiois, renamed *Penelope* and *Penelopi* (1939). In 1956 to Hong Kong owners, C.Y. Tung, renamed *Pacific Carrier* and later *Atlantic Carrier.* Broken up Japan (Mukaishima) 1959.</td></tr>
<tr><td>489</td><td>557</td><td>*Philadelphian*</td><td>26.6.1919</td><td>6,566</td><td>Standard 'N'-type Cargo Ship</td><td>St/Sc/St 412.4/55.8/34.4</td><td>517 nhp 2,300 ihp TE (3Cy) H&W</td><td>Leyland & Co. Liverpool</td></tr>
<tr><td colspan="9">Completed 28.8.1919, no 'War' name allocated. Before completion to Elder Dempster, renamed *New Mexico.* In 1933 to Greek ownership, S.G. Razis, renamed *Andreas.* Sunk by submarine torpedo (Italian, *Leonardo da Vinci*) NE of Brazil, November 1942.</td></tr>
<tr><td>490</td><td>558</td><td>*New Toronto*</td><td>28.8.1919</td><td>6,568</td><td>Standard 'N'-type Cargo Ship</td><td>St/Sc/St 412.4/55.8/34.4</td><td>517 nhp 2,300 ihp TE (3Cy) H&W</td><td>Elder Dempster Liverpool</td></tr>
<tr><td colspan="9">Completed 9.10.1919, no 'War' name allocated. Sunk by submarine torpedo (*U-126*) off coast of Benin, West Africa, November 1942. Four lives lost.</td></tr>
<tr><td>491</td><td>559</td><td>*New Texas*</td><td>14.8.1919</td><td>6,568</td><td>Standard 'N'-type Cargo Ship</td><td>St/Sc/St 412.4/55.8/34.4</td><td>517 nhp 2,300 ihp TE (3Cy) H&W</td><td>Elder Dempster Liverpool</td></tr>
<tr><td colspan="9">Completed 18.9.1919, no 'War' name allocated. Broken up Barrow (UK) 1955.</td></tr>
<tr><td>492</td><td>560</td><td>*Bompata*</td><td>28.10.1920</td><td>5,570</td><td>Cargo Ship</td><td>St/Sc/St 410.4/54.3/27.9</td><td>590 nhp Turb H&W</td><td>Elder Dempster Liverpool</td></tr>
<tr><td colspan="9">Completed March 1921. In 1932 to Downs SS Co., renamed *Tower Dale.* In 1952 to Finnish owners, Finland-Amerika Line, renamed *Navigator.* In 1956 to Liberian owners, G.E. Panas, renamed *Kefalos.* In 1959 to J.A. Dow, renamed *Falkos.* Broken up Japan (Osaka) 1959.</td></tr>
<tr><td>N/A</td><td>561</td><td>*Boma*</td><td colspan="6">Govan built</td></tr>
<tr><td>N/A</td><td>562</td><td>*Banda*</td><td colspan="6">Govan built</td></tr>
<tr><td>N/A</td><td>563</td><td>HMS *St Mellons*</td><td colspan="6">Govan built</td></tr>
<tr><td>N/A</td><td>564</td><td>HMS *St Olaves*</td><td colspan="6">Govan built</td></tr>
<tr><td>493</td><td>565</td><td>*Maine*</td><td>27.11.1919</td><td>6,600</td><td>Standard 'N'-type Cargo Ship</td><td>St/Sc/St 412.6/55.8/34.4</td><td>517 nhp 2,300 ihp TE (3Cy) H&W</td><td>Atlantic Transport Co. London</td></tr>
<tr><td colspan="9">Completed 4.3.1920, originally *War Riddle* but completed under this name. In 1932 to Soviet government, renamed *Skala.* Deleted/broken up 1960.</td></tr>
<tr><td>494</td><td>566</td><td>*New Brooklyn*</td><td>11.12.1919</td><td>6,545</td><td>Standard 'N'-type Cargo Ship</td><td>St/S/St 412.4/55.8/34.4</td><td>517 nhp 2,300 ihp TE (3Cy) H&W</td><td>Elder Dempster Liverpool</td></tr>
<tr><td colspan="9">Completed 31.3.1920, originally *War Romance* but completed under this name. In 1954 to Greek owners, J.S. Latsis, renamed *Marianna.* Broken up Italy (La Spezia) 1959.</td></tr>
<tr><td>495</td><td>567</td><td>*New Columbia*</td><td>25.3.1920</td><td>6,573</td><td>Standard 'N'-type Cargo Ship</td><td>St/S/St 412.6/55.8/34.4</td><td>517 nhp 2,300 ihp TE (3Cy) H&W</td><td>Elder Dempster Liverpool</td></tr>
<tr><td colspan="9">Completed 30.6.1920, originally *War Pageant* but completed under this name. Sunk by submarine torpedo (*U-68*) off Ivory Coast, October 1943. No lives Lost.</td></tr>
<tr><td>N/A</td><td>568</td><td>*War Passion*</td><td colspan="6">Govan built</td></tr>
<tr><td>N/A</td><td>569</td><td>*La Paz*</td><td colspan="6">Govan built</td></tr>
<tr><td>N/A</td><td>570</td><td>*War Dahlia*</td><td colspan="6">Greenock built</td></tr>
<tr><td>N/A</td><td>571</td><td>*War Geum*</td><td colspan="6">Greenock built</td></tr>
<tr><td>N/A</td><td>572</td><td>*War Oak*</td><td colspan="6">Greenock built</td></tr>
<tr><td>496</td><td>573</td><td>*Doric*</td><td>8.8.1922</td><td>16,484</td><td>Passenger Ship</td><td>St/2Sc/St 575.5/67.9/41.2</td><td>9,000ihp? Turb H&W</td><td>Oceanic Steam Navigation Co. Liverpool</td></tr>
<tr><td colspan="9">Completed 29.5.1923, half sister of *Pittsburgh* with different machinery, employed on UK–Canada routes but surplus to requirements after formation of Cunard-White Star in 1934.</td></tr>
</table>

Ship	Yard No	Name	Date Launched	Displacement Tons	Type	Construction and Dimensions	Horse Power/ Engines	Owners
Severely damaged in collision off Cape Finisterre, September 1935; sent to Tilbury where damage was surveyed, declared a constructive loss. Sold for £35,000, broken up Newport (UK) 1935.								
497	574	*Philadelphian*	11.10.1919	6,585	Standard 'N'-type Cargo Ship	St/Sc/St 412.6/55.8/34.4	678 ihp Turb H&W	Leyland & Co. Ltd Liverpool
Completed 19.2.1920, no 'War' name allocated. Broken up Lelant (UK) 1933.								
498	575	*Sophocles*	11.9.1921	12,361	Passenger-Cargo (Refrigerated)	St/2Sc/St 500.4/63.2/39.6	1,134 nhp 5,200 shp Turb H&W	George Thompson & Co. Aberdeen
(This vessel is listed by Moss & Hume as a passenger ship, re-rated) Completed 2.2.1922, for UK–Australia passenger/frozen meat trade, accommodation for 130 first-class and 420 third-class passengers. In 1926 chartered to Shaw Savill & Albion for New Zealand trade, converted to oil fuel, renamed *Tamaroa.* In 1931 rebuilt to accommodate 130 cabin-class passengers and following year bought outright by Shaw Savill & Albion. After wartime service as transport reconditioned for New Zealand routes with passenger accommodation for 370 tourist class. Broken up Blyth (UK) 1957.								
499	576	*Diogenes*	2.3.1922	12,341	Passenger-Cargo (Refrigerated)	St/2Sc/St 500.4/63.2/39.6	1,134 nhp 5,200 shp Turb H&W	George Thompson & Co. Aberdeen
(This vessel is listed by Moss & Hume as a passenger ship, re-rated) Completed 4.7.1922, sister ship of *Sophocles.* History almost identical to sister, being renamed *Mataroa* 1926. Broken up Faslane (UK) 1957.								
500	577	*New Brighton*	6.11.1919	6,538	Standard 'N'-type Cargo Ship	St/Sc/St 412.6/55.8/34.4	679 nhp Turb H&W	Elder Dempster Liverpool
Completed 31.1.1920, no 'War' name allocated. In 1934 to Chinese owners, T.K. King, renamed *Chin Yuen.* In 1938 to Japanese owners, Kinryu Kisen, renamed *Kinryu Maru.* Broken up Japan 1952.								
501	578	*Dorsetshire*	22.4.1920	7,445	Cargo Ship	St/2Sc/St 450.3/57.3/33.7	858 nhp Dies H&W	Bibby Steamship Co. Liverpool
Completed 14.8.1920, for UK–Burma route and suitable for rapid conversion to a troopship when required. In 1927 became permanent troopship. On outbreak of war became hospital ship. Decommissioned 1948 and after refitted and employed as emigrant vessel, repatriation ship, troopship and a floating hostel before being broken up, Newport (UK) 1954.								
502	579	*Somersetshire*	24.2.1921	7,456	Cargo Ship	St/2Sc/St 450.3/57.3/33.7	858 nhp Dies H&W	Bibby Steamship Co. Liverpool
Completed 9.6.1921, sister ship of *Dorsetshire.* Life story generally similar to sister. Broken up Barrow (UK) 1954.								
N/A	580	*Lobos*	Greenock built					
N/A	581	*Losada*	Govan built					
N/A	582	*Ediba*	Govan built					
503	583	*Baradine*	27.11.1920	13,143	Passenger-Cargo (Refrigerated)	St/2Sc/St 519.9/64.4/37.8	1,322 nhp 9,500 ihp QE (8Cy) H&W	Peninsular & Oriental Steam Navigation Co. London
(This vessel is listed by Moss & Hume as a passenger ship, re-rated) First of five improved 'B'-type ships built by H&W (two in Belfast, three on Clyde) for Australian trade, had accommodation for 1,175 third-class passengers. Destined to have short lives, collapse of the emigration/trade meant they were no longer required on the route they were designed for. Fitted with new engines and converted to oil fuel to try to make them suited to conditions after 1929, but the economic situation did not improve. Completed 18.8.1921. Sold 1936, broken up Dalmuir (UK) same year.								
504	584	*Barrabool*	3.11.1921	13,143	Passenger-Cargo (Refrigerated)	St/2Sc/St 519.9/64.4/37.8	1,322 nhp 9,500 ihp QE (8Cy) H&W	Peninsular & Oriental Steam Navigation Co. London
(This vessel is listed by Moss & Hume as a passenger ship, re-rated) Completed 30.3.1922, sister ship of *Baradine.* Broken up Bo'ness (UK) 1936.								
N/A	585	*Bendigo*	Greenock built					

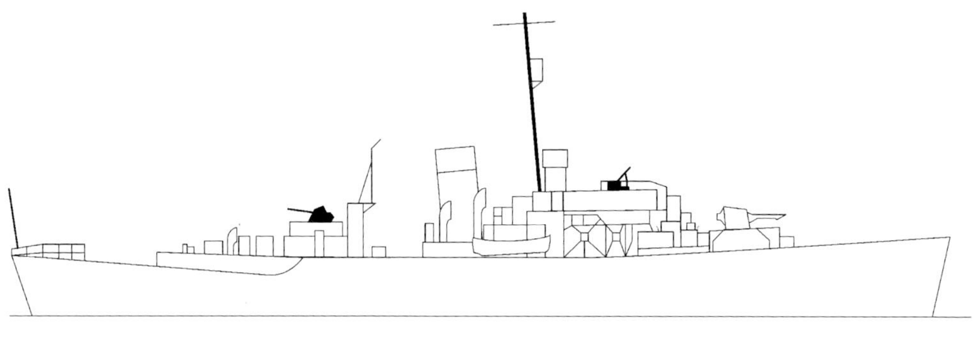

HMS *Arabis* (H&W y/n 1058) 1940 – Flower class corvette (DH)

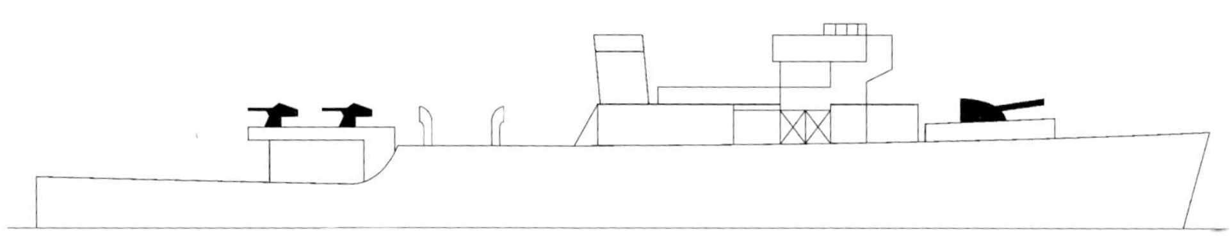

HMS *Algerine* (H&W y/n 1132) 1941 – Algerine class minesweeper (DH)

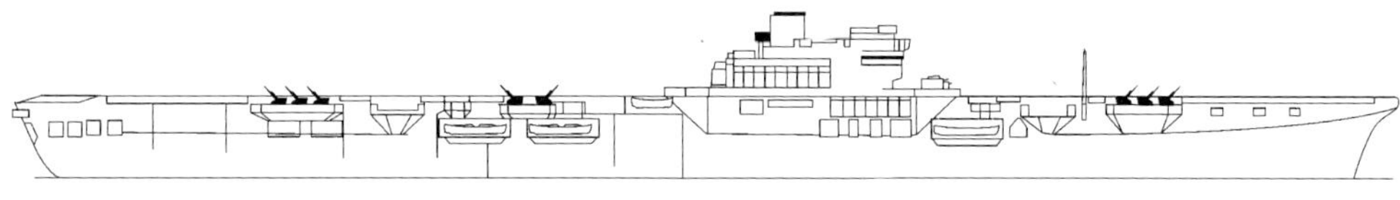

HMS *Glory* (H&W y/n 1191) 1943 – light fleet carrier (DH)

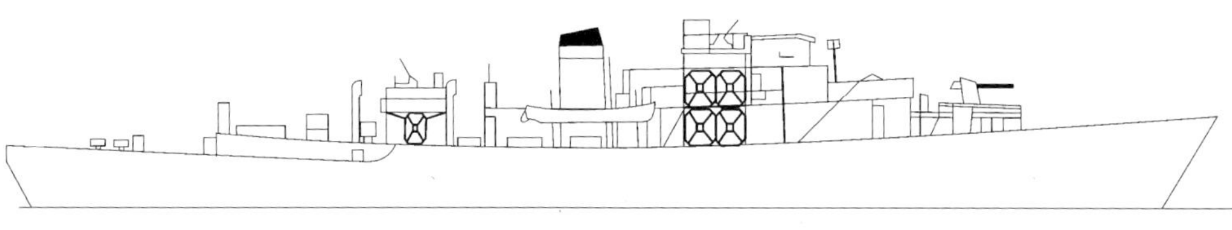

HMS *Oxford Castle* (H&W y/n 1238) 1943 – Castle class corvette (DH)

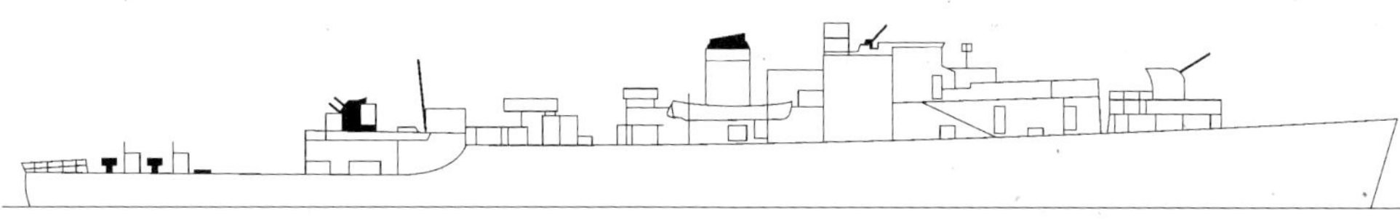

HMS *Loch Craggie* (H&W y/n 1246) 1944 – Loch class frigate (DH)

Ship	Yard No	Name	Date Launched	Displacement Tons	Type	Construction and Dimensions	Horse Power/ Engines	Owners
505	586	*Alcantara*	23.9.1926	22,181	Passenger-Cargo	St/2Sc/Mv 630.5/78.1/40.5	15,000 bhp Dies H&W	Royal Mail Steam Packet Co. London
(This vessel is listed by Moss & Hume as a passenger ship, re-rated) Completed 18.2.1927, sister ship of *Asturias*, history generally similar. In 1958 arrived at Southampton at end of 172nd round trip to South America. Sold to Japanese owners, Okadagumi, renamed *Kaisho Maru* for last voyage to breakers in Japan (Osaka).								
506	587	*Mooltan*	15.2.1923	20,847	Passenger-Cargo	St/2Sc/St 600.8/73.4/31.6	2,878 nhp 16,000 ihp QE (8Cy) H&W	Peninsular & Oriental Steam Navigation Co. London
(This vessel is listed by Moss & Hume as a passenger ship, re-rated) Completed 22.9.1923, for UK–Suez–Australia route, accommodation for 327 first-class and 329 second-class passengers in considerable comfort. During Second World War commissioned as armed merchant cruiser and later a troopship returned to owners in 1947. Refitted at Belfast to allow her to accommodate 1,030 passengers and returned to Australian service. Broken up Faslane (UK) 1954.								
507	588	*Maloja*	19.4.1923	20,837	Passenger-Cargo	St/2Sc/St 600.8/73.4/31.6	2,878 nhp 16,000 ihp QE (8Cy) H&W	Peninsular & Oriental Steam Navigation Co. London
(This vessel is listed by Moss & Hume as a passenger ship, re-rated) Completed 25.10.1923, sister ship of *Mooltan*. History is almost identical except that post-war refit was carried out in London and broken up Inverkeithing (UK) 1954.								
508	589	*Inverleith*	26.8.1920	6,957	Oil Tanker	St/Sc/St 412.6/55.8/34.4	531 nhp TE (3Cy) H&W	British Mexican Petroleum (A. Weir & Co.) Glasgow
These tankers were constructed using components prepared for 'N'-type ships which H&W purchased at the end of war. They were highly distinctive vessels with their engines mounted midships rather than at the stern and predominant expansion tanks on the main deck. Completed 3.3.1921. In 1930 management transferred to J. Hamilton. In 1937 to Italian owners, A. Vlasov, renamed *Sunstone*. In 1938 to Soc Ital Marittirii, renamed *Castelverde*. Sunk by submarine torpedo (HMS *Unruffled*) 27nm from Cape Bon, December 1942.								
509	590	*Inverurie*	6.6.1921	6,907	Oil Tanker	St/Sc/St 412.6/55.8/34.4	540 nhp TE (3Cy) H&W	British Mexican Petroleum (A. Weir & Co.) Glasgow
Completed 23.11.1922, sister ship of *Inverleith*. Broken up Rosyth (UK) 1936.								
510	591	*Inveravon*	18.1.1923	6,906	Oil Tanker	St/Sc/St 412.6/55.8/34.4	540 nhp TE (3Cy) H&W	British Mexican Petroleum (A. Weir & Co.) Glasgow
Completed 27.3.1923, sister ship of *Inverleith*. Broken up Rosyth (UK) 1936.								
N/A	592	*Somerset Coast*	Govan built					
N/A	593	*Drechytk*	Greenock built					
511	594	*Glenshiel*	24.1.1924	9,415	Cargo Ship	St/2Sc/Mv 285.7/62.2/35.5	1,317 nhp Dies H&W	Glen Line Glasgow
Completed 22.5.1924, only one of five H&W-built sisters built in the Belfast yard for UK–Far East routes and like all such ships could carry 12 first-class passengers. Sunk by a submarine torpedo (Japanese *I-7*) Indian Ocean, April 1942.								
512	595	*Carnarvon Castle*	14.1.1926	20,063	Passenger Ship	St/2Sc/Mv 630.7/73.5/41.5	3,364 nhp 13,000 bhp Dies H&W	Union-Castle Steamship Co. London
Completed 26.6.1926, for South Africa routes. In the mid-1930s re-engined and partly rebuilt to accommodate 226 first-class, 245 second-class, 48 interchangeable and 188 tourist-class passengers. Commissioned as armed merchant cruiser at outbreak of war and troopship from 1944. Served as an emigrant carrier in immediate post-war period before being refitted in late 1940s; returned to service 1950. Finished last voyage at Southampton in 1962. Broken up Japan (Mihara) 1962.								
N/A	596	*Calgary*	Clydebank built					
N/A	597	*Cochrane*	Clydebank built					
N/A	598	*Calumet*	Clydebank built					
N/A	599	*Cavally*	Clydebank built					
N/A	600	*Ayrshire Coast*	Pointhouse built					

Ship	Yard No	Name	Date Launched	Displacement Tons	Type	Construction and Dimensions	Horse Power/ Engines	Owners
N/A	601	*Scottish Coast*	Pointhouse built					
N/A	602	*Princess Caroline*	Govan built					
N/A	603	*Leighton*	Dunbarton built					
N/A	604	*Linnell*	Dunbarton built					
N/A	605	*Lassell*	Dunbarton built					
N/A	606	*Francunion*	Govan built					
N/A	607	*Lady Olive*	Pointhouse built					
N/A	608	*Ancobra*	Greenock built					
513	609	*Invergarry*	8.11.1923	6,907	Oil Tanker	St/Sc/St 412.6/55.6/34,0	540 nhp TE (3Cy) H&W	British Mexican Petroleum (A. Weir & Co.) Glasgow
Completed 17. 4.1923, sister ship of *Inverleith*. In 1937 to Greek owners, Kulukundis Sg Co., renamed *Mount Dirfys*. In 1939 to Dutch ownership, Halcyon Lijn, renamed *Stad Maastricht*. Sunk by torpedo (German MTB *S-59*) off Dutch coast, December 1940.								
N/A	610	*Gujarat*	Govan built					
N/A	611	*Kathiawar*	Govan built					
514	612	*Statendam*	11.9.1924	28,130	Passenger Ship	St/2Sc/St 674.2/81.3/49.4	4,644 nhp Turb H&W	Holland-America Line Rotterdam
Completion delayed because transatlantic passenger trade deeply depressed and changes in American emigration law, which necessitated having the third-class accommodation on the lower decks converted to cabin class. In April 1927 towed to Holland to be completed by Wilton Fijenoordand; did not make maiden voyage until April 1929. Had to supplement New York runs with cruises in Mediterranean, West Indies and South America. In 1940 laid up Rotterdam and was set on fire during fighting when Germans captured the city – after burning for five days became a total loss.								
515	613	*Minnewaska*	22.3.1923	21,716	Passenger-Cargo	St/2Sc/St 600.8/80.4/49.4	15,000 shp Turb H&W	Atlantic Transport Co. London
(This vessel is listed by Moss & Hume as a passenger ship, re-rated) Completed 25.8.1923. Following heavy war losses this company was in urgent need of new tonnage. Although having accommodation for 369 first-class passengers, this vessel was primarily a cargo carrier with a hold capacity of over a million cubic feet. With the onset of the Depression and decline in transatlantic trade such ships became increasingly difficult to run economically. The London–New York service for which it was designed closed in early 1930s and was transferred to Antwerp–New York route of Red Star Line. In late 1933 made last New York–Europe voyage and was laid up until sold for £35,000. Broken up Port Glasgow (UK) 1934.								
516	614	*Minnetonka*	10.1.1924	21,998	Passenger-Cargo	St/2Sc/St 600.8/80.4/49.4	15,000 shp Turb H&W	Atlantic Transport Co. London
(This vessel is listed by Moss & Hume as a passenger ship, re-rated) Completed 24.4.1924, sister ship of *Minnewaska*. Almost identical history to sister except broken up Bo'ness (UK) 1934.								
N/A	615	*Laurentic*	Cancelled					
N/A	615	*Oakton*	Dumbarton built					
517	616	*Accra*	18.3.1926	9,337	Passenger Ship	St/2Sc/Mv 450.8/62.3/31.3	1,651 nhp Dies H&W	Elder Dempster Liverpool
Completed 17.8.1926, for West African route, accommodation for 243 first-class and 70 second-class passengers was of very high standard. The ship set new records on route, best time Lagos–Plymouth being 11 days and 21 hours. Sunk by submarine torpedo (*U-34*) 320m W off Bloody Foreland outbound Liverpool–Freetown with 489 crew and passengers on board, July 1940. Twenty-four lives lost.								
518	617	*Britmex No.2*	15.4.1920	474	Oil Barge		N/A	British Mexican Petroleum Co. (A. Weir & Co.) Glasgow
Completed 16.6.1920, often described as 'bunkering vessel'. In 1930 passed to management of J. Hamilton. Deleted 1938.								
519	618	*Britmex No.3*	15.4.1920	474	Oil Barge		N/A	British Mexican Petroleum Co. (A. Weir & Co.) Glasgow
Completed 17.6.1920, often described as a 'bunkering vessel'. In 1930 passed to management of J. Hamilton. Deleted 1938.								

Ship	Yard No	Name	Date Launched	Displacement Tons	Type	Construction and Dimensions	Horse Power/ Engines	Owners
520	619	*Britmex No.4*	29.4.1920	474	Oil Barge		N/A	British-Mexican Petroleum Co. (A. Weir & Co.) Glasgow
Completed 4.6.1920, often described as a 'bunkering vessel'. In 1930 passed to management of J. Hamilton. Deleted 1938.								
521	620	*Britmex No.5*	29.4.1920	475	Oil Barge		N/A	British-Mexican Petroleum Co. (A. Weir & Co.) Glasgow
Completed 1.7.1920, often described as a 'bunkering vessel'. In 1930 passed to management of J. Hamilton. Deleted 1938.								
N/A	621	*Britmex No.6*	Govan built					
N/A	622	*Britmex No.7*	Govan built					
N/A	623	*Britmex No.8*	Govan built					
N/A	624	*Inveritchen*	Govan built					
N/A	625	*Inverampton*	Govan built					
N/A	626	*Princess Dagmar*	Govan built					
N/A	627	*Dorelian*	Meadowside built					
N/A	628	*Delilian*	Meadowside built					
N/A	629	*Davisian*	Meadowside built					
N/A	630	*Araby*	Dumbarton built					
N/A	631	*Cedarton*	Dumbarton built					
N/A	632	*Laguna*	Govan built					
N/A	633	*Tonbridge*	Meadowside built					
N/A	634	*Minster*	Meadowside built					
522	635	*Ulster Monarch*	24.1.1929	3,851	Cross-Channel Ship	St/2Sc/Mv 346.0/46.2/15.2	1,193 nhp 7,500 bhp Dies H&W	Belfast Steamship Co. Belfast
First of three large diesel-driven cross-Channel ships for the Belfast–Liverpool route, they replaced *Patriotic* (H&W 424, 1912), *Heroic* (H&W 378 1906) and *Graphic* (H&W 379 1906). An overnight service, the 418 first-class, but not the 86 third-class, passengers enjoyed cramped but comfortable cabin accommodation. Completed 10.6.1929. On outbreak of war taken up and converted into a landing ship [LSI(H)] capable of transporting 580 troops and carrying six landing craft to put them ashore. After war refitted and returned to old route. Broken up Belgium (Ghent) 1966.								
N/A	636	*Elmworth*	Dunbarton built					
N/A	637	*Oakworth*	Dunbarton built					
N/A	638	*Ferry No.6*	Govan built					
N/A	639	*Ferry No.7*	Govan built					
N/A	640	*Inverglass*	Dunbarton built					
523	641	*Invergoil*	21.9.1922	6,966	Oil Tanker	St/Sc/St 412.6/55.8/34.4	540 nhp TE (3Cy) H&W	British Mexican Petroleum (A. Weir & Co.) Glasgow
Completed 9.11.1922, sister ship of *Inverleith*. In 1936 to Chinese owners, Mollers, Shanghai, converted into cargo ship, renamed *Nils Moller*. In 1946 to Chinese Mar. Trust, renamed *Tien Loong*. In 1950 to Hong Kong ownership, C.Y. Tung, renamed *Atlantic Dragon*. Broken up Japan (Osaka) 1959.								
N/A	642	*Luxmi*	Govan built					
N/A	643	*Inverbank*	Govan built					
N/A	644	*Invergordan*	Clydebank built					
N/A	645	Floating Dock	Govan built					
N/A	646	*Grantleyhall*	Greenock built					
N/A	647	*Birchton*	Dunbarton built					
N/A	648	*Cable Express*	Pointhouse built					
N/A	649	*Volendam*	Govan built					
N/A	650	*Veendam*	Govan built					
N/A	651	*Britmex No.1*	Govan built					

Ship	Yard No	Name	Date Launched	Displacement Tons	Type	Construction and Dimensions	Horse Power/ Engines	Owners
N/A	652	*Britmex No.9*	Govan built					
N/A	653	*Britmex No.10*	Govan built					
N/A	654	*Britmex No.11*	Govan built					
N/A	655	*Glenbank*	Govan built					
N/A	656	*Birchbank*	Govan built					
N/A	657	*Lurcher*	Pointhouse built					
N/A	658	*Asuka Maru*	Meadowside built					
N/A	659	*Razmak*	Greenock built					
N/A	660	*Rawalpindi*	Greenock built					
N/A	661	*Rajputana*	Greenock built					
N/A	662	*Cedarbank*	Govan built					
N/A	663	*Comliebank*	Govan built					
N/A	664	*Clydebank*	Govan built					
N/A	665	Barge	Govan built					
N/A	666	Barge	Govan built					
N/A	667	Barge	Govan built					
N/A	668	Barge	Govan built					
N/A	669	Barge	Govan built					
N/A	670	Barge	Govan built					
N/A	671	Lighter	Govan built					
N/A	672	*Itu II*	Govan built					
N/A	673	Lighter	Govan built					
N/A	674	Lighter	Govan built					
N/A	675	*Thistleros*	Meadowside built					
N/A	676	*Alynbank*	Govan built					
N/A	677	*Elmwood*	Govan built					
N/A	678	*Forresbank*	Govan built					
N/A	679	*Nairnbank*	Govan built					
N/A	680	*Weirbank*	Govan built					
N/A	681	*Larchbank*	Govan built					
N/A	682	*Levernbank*	Govan built					
N/A	683	*Myrtlebank*	Govan built					
N/A	684	*Olivebank*	Govan built					
N/A	685	*Oakbank*	Govan built					
N/A	686	*Speybank*	Govan built					
N/A	687	*Springbank*	Govan built					
N/A	688	*Procris*	Pointhouse built					
N/A	689	*Fendris*	Pointhouse built					
N/A	690	*Papuan Chief*	Govan built					
N/A	691	*King James*	Meadowside built					
N/A	692	*King Malcolm*	Meadowside built					
N/A	693	*Temuco*	Govan built					
N/A	894	*Pontoon*	Govan built					
524	695	*Apapa*	26.8.1926	9,350	Passenger Ship	St/2Sc/Mv 450.8/62.3/31.3	1,651 nhp Dies H&W	Elder Dempster Liverpool
Completed 28.1.1927, sister ship of *Accra*. Sank by air attack off Ireland, November 1940. Twenty-four lives lost.								
525	696	*Ulster Queen*	28.3.1929	3,756	Cross-Channel Ship	St/2Sc/Mv 346.0/46.2/15.2	1,193 nhp 7,500 bhp Dies H&W	Belfast Steamship Co. Belfast
Completed 11.2.1930, sister ship of *Ulster Monarch*. Almost wrecked Ramsey Bay, February 1940, but refloated and taken up by Admiralty. Although sometimes stated that became an ILS(H), underwent a far more radical conversion and emerged as an auxiliary warship rated as sea-going auxiliary AA vessel.								

Ship	Yard No	Name	Date Launched	Displacement Tons	Type	Construction and Dimensions	Horse Power/ Engines	Owners
With a powerful armament of 6x 4in XVI in twin mounts and two quadruple pompoms, this ship saw extensive service as a convoy escort (out of eight ships so rated four were to become casualties). In 1943 refitted and re-rated as LSF Landing Ship (Fighter Direction) with armament changed to 4x 4in, the pompoms, 10x 20mm Oerlikon light AA guns and a depth-charge rack. However, armament was basically defensive as primary role was to act as a floating radar station and fighter control centre to ensure air superiority over landing beaches. When decommissioned, laid up at Milford Haven until 1949 when decided that alterations had been too extensive to make reconstruction for civilian use viable. Broken up Belgium (Antwerp) 1950.								
526	697	*Ulster Prince*	25.4.1929	3,756	Cross-channel Ship	St/2Sc/Mv 346.0/46.2/15.2	1,193 nhp 7,500 bhp Dies H&W	Belfast Steamship Co. Belfast
Completed 3.3.1930, sister ship of *Ulster Monarch*. Taken up as troopship and later a naval stores carrier. During evacuation of Greece ran aground near Nauplia and destroyed by German aircraft, April 1941.								
N/A	698	*Redline No.1*	Govan built					
527	699	*Inverlago*	26.2.1925	2,372	Oil Tanker	St/2Sc/St 305.7/50.2/14.3	196 nhp TE (6Cy) **Engines** A.&J. Inglis, Glasgow	Lago Shipping Co. (A. Weir & Co.) Glasgow
Completed 24.3.1925. In 1947 to Esso Transportation. In 1949 to Trinidad Shipping Co. In 1959 to Challenger Ltd of Bermuda. Broken up Spain (Santander) 1965.								
528	700	*Inverrosa*	26.3.1925	2,372	Oil Tanker	St/2Sc/St 305.7/50.2/14.3	196 nhp TE (6Cy) **Engines** A.&J. Inglis, Glasgow	Lago Shipping Co. (A. Weir & Co.) Glasgow
Completed 24.4.1925, sister ship of *Inverlago*. In 1947 to Esso Transportation. In 1949 to Trinidad Shipping Co. In 1959 to Challenger Ltd of Bermuda. In 1962 converted into ore carrier and the following year to Union Carbide Corp. Wrecked off Baca Raton, May 1968, wreck broken up Mexico (Tampico) 1973.								
529	701	*Invercaibo*	23.4.1925	2,372	Oil Tanker	St/2Sc/St 305.7/50.2/14.3	193 nhp TE (6Cy) **Engines** A.&J. Inglis, Glasgow	Lago Shipping Co. (A. Weir & Co.) Glasgow
Completed 9.6.1925, sister ship of *Inverlago*. In 1947 to Esso Transportation. In 1952 to Panama Transport Co. Broken up USA (Baltimore) 1953.								
530	702	*Inverruba*	26.5.1925	2,372	Oil Tanker	St/2Sc/St 305.7/50.2/14.3	193 nhp TE (6Cy) **Engines** A.&J. Inglis, Glasgow	Lago Shipping Co. (A. Weir & Co.) Glasgow
Completed 30.6.1925, sister ship of *Inverlago*. In 1947 to Esso Transportation. In 1950 to Trinidad Shipping Co. In 1960 to Challenger Ltd of Bermuda. Broken up Spain (Santander) 1965.								
N/A	703	*Water Carrier*	Govan built					
N/A	704	*Madrid*	Pointhouse built					
N/A	705	*Roma*	Pointhouse built					
N/A	706	*Hythe*	Meadowside built					
N/A	707	*Whitstable*	Meadowside built					
N/A	708	*Inverpool*	Govan built					
N/A	709	*Marthara*	Meadowside built					
N/A	710	Barge	Govan built					
N/A	711	Barge	Govan built					
N/A	712	Barge	Govan built					
N/A	713	Barge	Govan built					
N/A	714	Barge	Govan built					
N/A	715	Barge	Govan built					
N/A	716	*Gascony*	Dunbarton built					
N/A	717	Barge	Govan built					
N/A	718	Barge	Govan built					

Ship	Yard No	Name	Date Launched	Displacement Tons	Type	Construction and Dimensions	Horse Power/ Engines	Owners
N/A	719	*Haslemere*	Meadowside built					
N/A	720	*Fratton*	Meadowside built					
N/A	721	*Colonial*	Meadowside built					
N/A	722	*Director*	Meadowside built					
N/A	723	Lighter	Govan built					
N/A	724	Lighter	Govan built					
N/A	725	*Dolores de Urquiza*	Pointhouse built					
N/A	726	Barge	Govan built					
N/A	727	Barge	Govan built					
N/A	728	*Koolinda*	Govan built					
N/A	729	*Maidstone*	Meadowside built					
N/A	730	*Ringwood*	Meadowside built					
N/A	731	*London Mammoth*	Govan built					
N/A	732	*Begonia*	Dunbarton built					
N/A	733	*Boltonia*	Dunbarton built					
N/A	734	*George Livesey*	Govan built					
N/A	735	*Dunkwa*	Dunbarton built					
N/A	736	*Dixcove*	Dunbarton built					
N/A	737	*Daru*	Dunbarton built					
N/A	738	*Dagomba*	Dunbarton built					
531	739	*San Nicolas*	15.4.1926	2,391	Oil Tanker	St/2Sc/St 305.7/50.2/14.3	196 nhp TE (6Cy) H&W	Lago Shipping Co. (A. Weir & Co.) Glasgow
Completed 20.5.1926, sister ship of *Inverlago*. Sunk by submarine torpedo (*U-502*) 25nm SW of Punta Macolla, February 1942. Seven lives lost.								
N/A	740	*Papudo*	Govan built					
N/A	741	*Palacio*	Govan built					
N/A	742	*Pelayo*	Govan built					
N/A	743	*Pacheco*	Govan built					
N/A	744	*Pinto*	Govan built					
N/A	745	*Ponzano*	Govan built					
532	746	*Ambrosio*	3.6.1926	2,391	Oil Tanker	St/2Sc/St 305.7/50.2/14.3	196 nhp TE (6Cy) H&W	Lago Shipping Co. (A. Weir & Co.) Glasgow
Completed 7.7.1926, sister ship of *Inverlago*. In 1947 to Esso Transportation Co. In 1950 to Trinidad Shipping Co. In 1959 to Challenger Bermuda. Converted to ore carrier in 1960 and fitted with diesel engines. 1963 to Union Carbide. Hulked 1976.								
N/A	747	*Petronella*	Govan built					
N/A	748	*Paula*	Govan built					
N/A	749	*Agatha*	Govan built					
N/A	750	*Paua*	Govan built					
533	751	*Highland Monarch*	3.5.1928	14,137	Passenger-Cargo (Refrigerated)	St/2Sc/Mv 523.4/69.4/37.1	2,190 nhp 10,000 bhp Dies H&W	Royal Mail Line (W.&W. Nelson) London
First of a class of five ships for London–River Plate route, accommodation for 135 first-class, 66 intermediate and 600 emigrant-class passengers in addition to 507,000cu. ft of cargo space, most of it insulated for meat transport. Completed 2.10.1928. During war employed as a transport. Broken up Dalmuir (UK) 1960.								
N/A	752	*Sin Kheng Seng*	Govan built					
N/A	753	Floating Dock	Govan built					
N/A	754	*La Falaise*	Pointhouse built					
N/A	755	*Casson*	Govan built					

Ship	Yard No	Name	Date Launched	Displacement Tons	Type	Construction and Dimensions	Horse Power/ Engines	Owners
N/A	756	*Minmi*	Meadowside built					
534	757	*King Edgar*	15.9.1927	4,536	Cargo Ship	St/Sc/Mv 400.6/58.4/23.6	489 nhp Dies H&W	King Line Ltd London
Completed 30.11.1927. Sunk by submarine torpedo (*U-1302*) St George's Channel, inbound Halifax–London, March 1945. Four lives lost.								
535	758	*King Edwin*	29.9.1927	4,536	Cargo Ship	St/Sc/Mv 400.6/58.4/23.6	489 nhp Dies H&W	King Line Ltd London
Completed 20.12.1927, sister ship of *King Edgar.* Scuttled after caught fire while unloading in Grand Harbour, Valletta, Malta, April 1943. In 1945 wreck raised, towed out to sea and sunk.								
536	759	*King Egbert*	27.10.1927	4,535	Cargo Ship	St/Sc/Mv 400.6/58.4/23.6	489 nhp Dies H&W	King Line Ltd London
Completed 17.1.1928, sister ship of *King Edgar.* Sunk by mine 4nm SW of Haisboro light vessel, December 1939. One life lost.								
537	760	*King John*	24.11.1927	5,228	Cargo Ship	St/Sc/Mv 400.7/58.4/27.2	489 nhp Dies H&W	King Line Ltd London
Completed 16.2.1928, a slightly enlarged version of *King Edgar.* Sunk by German surface raider *Widder*, July 1940.								
538	761	*King Lud*	22.12.1927	5,224	Cargo Ship	St/Sc/Mv 400.7/58.4/27.2	489 nhp Dies H&W	King Line Ltd London
Completed 15.3.1928, sister ship of *King John.* Torpedoed and sunk by Japanese submarine (*I-10*), June 1942. Thirty-nine lives lost.								
539	762	*King Neptune*	26.1.1928	5,224	Cargo Ship	St/Sc/Mv 400.7/58.4/27.2	489 nhp Dies H&W	King Line Ltd London
Completed 17.4.1928, sister ship of *King John.* In 1957 to Singapore owners, Chip Hwa Shipping & Trading Co., renamed *Wing On.* In 1962 to Hong Kong owners, Hwa Aun, not renamed. In 1963 to Panamanian owners, Transportes Dorados SA, not renamed. Broken up Taiwan (Kaohsiung) 1968.								
540	763	*King Arthur*	22.3.1928	5,224	Cargo Ship	St/Sc/Mv 400.7/58.4/27.2	489 nhp Dies H&W	King Line Ltd London
Completed 17.5.1928, sister ship of *King John.* Sunk by submarine torpedo (*U-67*) W of Trinidad, inbound Trinidad–UK, November 1942. No lives lost.								
541	764	*King Stephen*	24.4.1928	5,274	Cargo Ship	St/Sc/Mv 400.7/58.4/27.2	489 nhp Dies H&W	King Line Ltd London
Completed 14.6.1928, sister ship of *King John.* In 1957 to Hong Kong owners, Vanguard Shipping Co., renamed *Golden Delta.* In 1962 to Corinthian Shipping Co. not renamed. Broken up Hong Kong 1965.								
542	765	*King William*	19.5.1928	5,274	Cargo Ship	St/Sc/Mv 400.7/58.4/27.2	489 nhp Dies H&W	King Line Ltd London
Completed 5.7.1928, sister ship of *King John.* Broken up Japan (Tokyo) 1959.								
N/A	766	Barge	Govan built					
N/A	767	Barge	Govan built					
N/A	768	Barge	Govan built					
N/A	769	Barge	Govan built					
N/A	770	Barge	Govan built					
N/A	771	Barge	Govan built					
N/A	772	Barge	Govan built					
N/A	773	Barge	Govan built					
N/A	774	Barge	Govan built					
N/A	775	Barge	Govan built					
N/A	776	Barge	Govan built					
N/A	777	Barge	Govan built					
N/A	778	Barge	Govan built					
N/A	779	Barge	Govan built					

Ship	Yard No	Name	Date Launched	Displacement Tons	Type	Construction and Dimensions	Horse Power/ Engines	Owners
N/A	780	Lighter	Govan built					
N/A	781	Lighter	Govan built					
N/A	782	Lighter	Govan built					
N/A	783	Lighter	Govan built					
N/A	784	Lighter	Govan built					
N/A	785	Lighter	Govan built					
N/A	786	*Portwey*	Govan built					
N/A	787	*Eddystone*	Meadowside built					
N/A	788	Barge	Govan built					
N/A	789	Barge	Govan built					
N/A	790	Barge	Govan built					
N/A	791	*Uganda*	Meadowside built					
543	792	*Lagunilla*	26.5.1927	2,402	Oil Tanker	St/2Sc/St 305.7/50.2/14.3	196 nhp TE (6Cy) H&W	Lago Shipping Co. (A. Weir & Co.) Glasgow
Completed 16.6.1927, sister ship of *Inverlago*. In 1938 to Standard Oil (Venezuela). In 1943 to Cia de Petroleo, Lago. Broken up USA (Boston) 1953.								
544	793	*Icotea*	26.5.1927	2,402	Oil Tanker	St/2Sc/St 305.7/50.2/14.3	196 nhp TE (6Cy) H&W	Lago Shipping Co. (A. Weir & Co.) Glasgow
Completed 17.6.1927, sister ship of *Inverlago*. In 1938 to Cia de Petroleo, Lago. In 1955 to Island Tug & Barge, rebuilt as rail wagon-carrying barge, renamed *Cedar Island*.								
545	794	*La Salina*	31.5.1927	2,402	Oil Tanker	St/2Sc/St 305.7/50.2/14.3	196 nhp TE (6Cy) H&W	Lago Shipping Co. (A. Weir & Co.) Glasgow
Completed 28.6.1927, sister ship of *Inverlago*. Later to Cia de Petroleo Lago. Broken up USA (Mobile) 1953.								
546	795	*San Carlos*	28.6.1927	2,395	Oil Tanker	St/2Sc/St 305.7/50.2/14.3	196 nhp TE (6Cy) H&W	Lago Shipping Co. (A. Weir & Co.) Glasgow
Completed 29.7.1927, sister ship of *Inverlago*. In 1947 to Esso Transportation Co. In 1952 to Panama Transport Co. In 1953 to Dominican government. Wrecked Rio Haina, May 1965.								
N/A	796	*Lahej*	Greenock built					
N/A	797	*Nimoda*	Greenock built					
547	798	*Berta*	30.6.1927	2,611	Oil Tanker	St/2Sc/St 305.0/50.2/15.0	238 nhp TE (6Cy) H&W	Anglo-Saxon Petroleum Co. London
Completed 14.7.1927, near sister of *Inverlago* type. In 1939 to Shell and renamed *Shell Dezoito*. Broken up Holland (Flushing) 1962.								
548	799	*Brigida*	11.8.1927	2,609	Oil Tanker	St/2Sc/St 305.0/50.2/15.0	238 nhp TE (6Cy) H&W	Anglo-Saxon Petroleum Co. London
Completed 30.8.1927, sister ship of *Berta*. Later to Dutch ownership. Broken up Belgium (Ghent) 1954.								
N/A	800	*Kheti*	Greenock built					
N/A	801	*Saugor*	Greenock built					
N/A	802	*Cabo Espichel*	Govan built					
N/A	803	*Cabo Raso*	Govan built					
N/A	804	*Cabo Sardao*	Govan built					
N/A	805	*Iguazu*	Pointhouse built					
549	806	*Highland Chieftain*	21.6.1928	14,130	Passenger-Cargo (Refrigerated)	St/2Sc/Mv 523.4/69.4/37.1	2,190 nhp 10,000 bhp Dies H&W	Royal Mail Line (W.&W. Nelson) London
Completed 26.1.1929, sister ship of *Highland Monarch*. Twice damaged at Liverpool during 1940 in air raids. In 1958 to Gibraltar owners, Calpean Shipping, for use in whaling industry, renamed *Calpean Star*. In June 1960 disabled by engine room explosion and while under tow to Montevideo ran aground and lost.								

<table>
<tr><th>Ship</th><th>Yard No</th><th>Name</th><th>Date Launched</th><th>Displacement Tons</th><th>Type</th><th>Construction and Dimensions</th><th>Horse Power/ Engines</th><th>Owners</th></tr>
<tr><td>550</td><td>807</td><td>Britannic</td><td>6.8.1929</td><td>26,943</td><td>Passenger Ship</td><td>St/2Sc/Mv
683.6/82.4/48.6</td><td>4,214 nhp
20,000 bhp
Dies
H&W</td><td>Oceanic Steam Navigation Co.
Liverpool</td></tr>
<tr><td colspan="9">Completed 21.5.1930, for Liverpool–New York route accommodation for 504 cabin-class, 551 tourist-class and 498 third-class passengers. Maiden voyage in June 1930. Following merger with Cunard in 1935 transferred to Southampton–New York route. In 1939 requisitioned as troopship carrying 3,000–5,000 men and during war carried 180,000 men and steamed 376,000 miles. After repatriation duties, returned to owners in March 1947 and refitted by H&W to accommodate 430 first-class and 570 tourist-class passengers. Returned to Liverpool–New York route in May 1948. In November 1960 she completed her 275th voyage and was sold. Broken up Inverkeithing (UK) December 1960.</td></tr>
<tr><td>N/A</td><td>808</td><td>Clydefield</td><td colspan="6">Meadowside built</td></tr>
<tr><td>551</td><td>809</td><td>Oranjestad</td><td>1.9.1927</td><td>2,396</td><td>Oil Tanker</td><td>St/2Sc/St
305.7/50.2/14.3</td><td>196 nhp
TE (6Cy)
H&W</td><td>Andrew Weir & Co.
Glasgow</td></tr>
<tr><td colspan="9">Completed 23.9.1927, a sister ship of Inverlago. In 1936 management transferred to F.J. Wolfe. Sunk by submarine torpedo (U-156) in San Nicholas Harbour, Caribbean, February 1942. Fifteen lives lost.</td></tr>
<tr><td>552</td><td>810</td><td>Sabaneta</td><td>8.9.1927</td><td>2,396</td><td>Oil Tanker</td><td>St/2Sc/St
305.7/50.2/14.3</td><td>196 nhp
TE (6Cy)
H&W</td><td>Andrew Weir & Co.
Glasgow</td></tr>
<tr><td colspan="9">Completed 30.9.1927, sister ship of Inverlago. In 1936 management transferred to F.J. Wolfe. In 1947 to Esso Transportation Co. In 1952 to Panama Transport Co. In 1954 to Esso Argentina, renamed Esso Santa Fe. In 1963 to Petromar SA de Nav. Argentina, following year reduced to a bunkering hulk. Broken up Argentina 1971.</td></tr>
<tr><td>N/A</td><td>811</td><td>Zahra</td><td colspan="6">Govan built</td></tr>
<tr><td>553</td><td>812</td><td>Highland Brigade</td><td>1.11.1928</td><td>14,131</td><td>Passenger-Cargo (Refrigerated)</td><td>St/2Sc/Mv
523.4/69.4/37.1</td><td>2,190 nhp
10,000 bhp
Dies
H&W</td><td>Royal Mail Line (W.&W. Nelson)
London</td></tr>
<tr><td colspan="9">Completed 27.4.1929, sister ship of Highland Monarch. Mined off Singapore, January 1946, survived. In 1959 to Greek owners, J.S. Latsis, renamed Henrietta and later (1960) Marianna (II). Broken up Taiwan (Kaohsiung) 1965.</td></tr>
<tr><td>N/A</td><td>813</td><td>Highland Hope</td><td colspan="6">Govan built</td></tr>
<tr><td>554</td><td>814</td><td>Highland Princess</td><td>11.4.1929</td><td>14,128</td><td>Passenger-Cargo (Refrigerated)</td><td>St/2Sc/Mv
523.4/69.4/37.1</td><td>2,190 nhp
10,000 bhp
Dies
H&W</td><td>Royal Mail Line (W.&W. Nelson)
London</td></tr>
<tr><td colspan="9">Completed 25.2.1930, sister ship of Highland Monarch. In 1959 to Greek owners, J.S. Latsis, renamed Marianna. In 1960 to Chinese government, renamed Guang Hua. Shortly afterwards to Czechoslovakian government, renamed Slapy. Broken up China 1992.</td></tr>
<tr><td>N/A</td><td>815</td><td>Delfina Mitre</td><td colspan="6">Pointhouse built</td></tr>
<tr><td>N/A</td><td>816</td><td>Dafila</td><td colspan="6">Meadowside built</td></tr>
<tr><td>N/A</td><td>817</td><td>Nyanza</td><td colspan="6">Meadowside built</td></tr>
<tr><td>N/A</td><td>818</td><td>Deal</td><td colspan="6">Meadowside built</td></tr>
<tr><td>N/A</td><td>819</td><td>JJ1</td><td colspan="6">Govan built</td></tr>
<tr><td>N/A</td><td>820</td><td>JJ2</td><td colspan="6">Govan built</td></tr>
<tr><td>N/A</td><td>821</td><td>JJ3</td><td colspan="6">Govan built</td></tr>
<tr><td>N/A</td><td>822</td><td>JJ4</td><td colspan="6">Govan built</td></tr>
<tr><td>N/A</td><td>823</td><td>Oil Barge</td><td colspan="6">Pointhouse built</td></tr>
<tr><td>N/A</td><td>824</td><td>Brittany</td><td colspan="6">D built</td></tr>
<tr><td>555</td><td>825</td><td>Winchester Castle</td><td>19.11.1929</td><td>20,108</td><td>Passenger Ship</td><td>St/2Sc/Mv
631.6/75.7/37.5</td><td>3,360 nhp
Dies
H&W</td><td>Union-Castle Steamship Co.
London</td></tr>
<tr><td colspan="9">Completed 11.10.1930, for South African routes, accommodation for 259 first-class, 243 second-class and 254 third-class passengers. Modernised in 1938. At outbreak of the war taken up as troopship but subsequently employed as HQ ship of Mountbatten's Combined Operations force. Served as HQ ship for invasion of Vichy-held Madagascar (Operation Ironclad), and afterwards involved in landings in North Africa (Operation Torch), Italy (Operation Avalanche) and southern France (Operation Dragoon). Returned to South Africa route after war. Broken up Japan (Mihara) 1960.</td></tr>
<tr><td>N/A</td><td>826</td><td>Designer</td><td colspan="6">Meadowside built</td></tr>
<tr><td>N/A</td><td>827</td><td>Sefwi</td><td colspan="6">Govan built</td></tr>
<tr><td>N/A</td><td>828</td><td>Wala</td><td colspan="6">Govan built</td></tr>
<tr><td>N/A</td><td>829</td><td>Ciudad del Salto</td><td colspan="6">Govan built</td></tr>
</table>

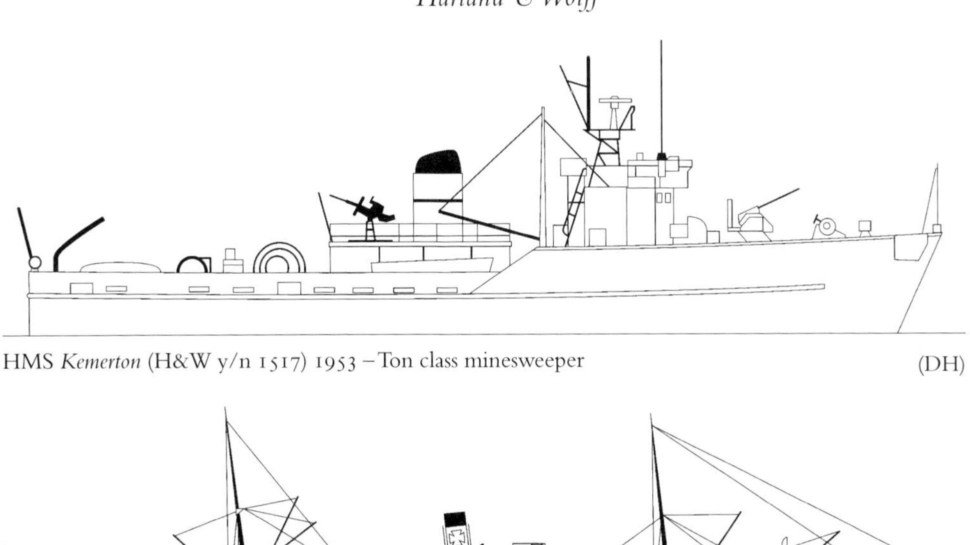

HMS *Kemerton* (H&W y/n 1517) 1953 – Ton class minesweeper (DH)

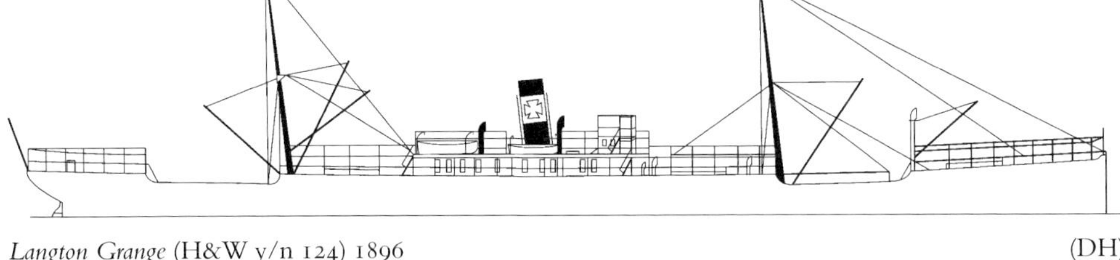

Langton Grange (H&W y/n 124) 1896 (DH)

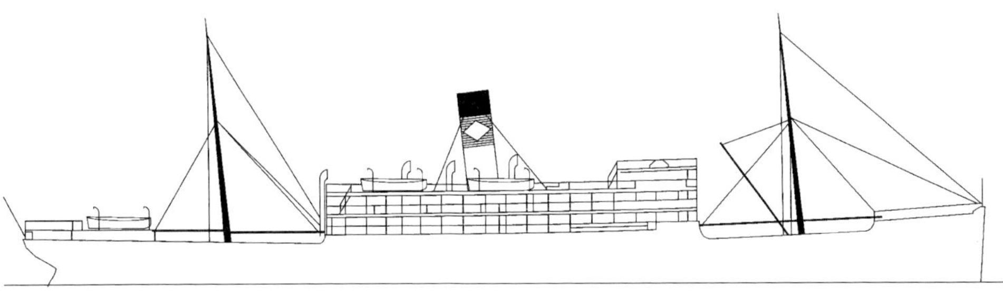

Cartago (H&W y/n 272) 1908 (DH)

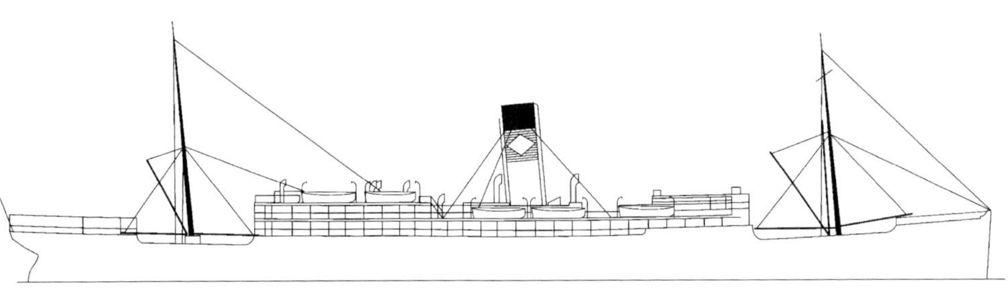

Pastores (H&W y/n 314) 1912 (DH)

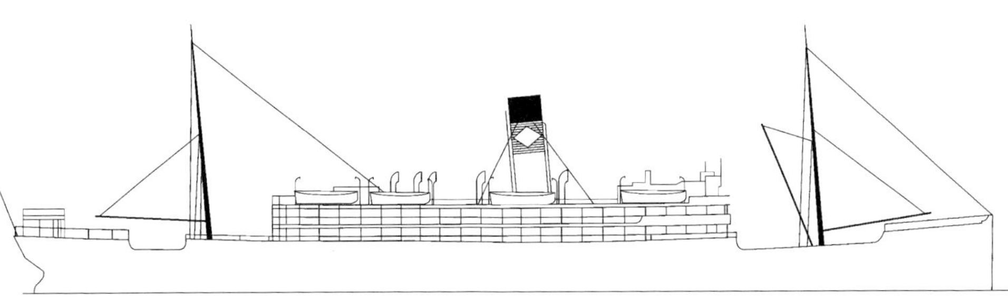

Ulua (H&W y/n 340) 1917 (DH)

Ship	Yard No	Name	Date Launched	Displacement Tons	Type	Construction and Dimensions	Horse Power/ Engines	Owners
N/A	830	*Behar*	Greenock built					
N/A	831	*Kerma*	Meadowside built					
556	832	*Punta Benitez*	21.2.1928	2,394	Oil Tanker	St/2Sc/St 305.7/50.2/14.3	196 nhp TE (6Cy) H&W	Lago Shipping Co. (A. Weir & Co.) Glasgow
Completed 16.3.1928, sister ship of *Inverlago.* In 1937 to Argentinian owners, Cia Transportadora de Petroleo SA, renamed *Criollo Fiel.* In 1938 to Esso (Argentina) and renamed *ESSO Campana.* In 1963 to Petromar SA de Nav. In 1971 returned to Esso. Broken up Argentina (Campans) 1978.								
557	833	*Tia Juana*	8.3.1928	2,395	Oil Tanker	St/2Sc/St 305.7/50.2/14.3	196 nhp TE (6Cy) H&W	Lago Shipping Co. (A. Weir & Co.) Glasgow
Completed 4.4.1928, sister ship of *Inverlago.* Sunk by submarine torpedo (*U-502*) 25nm SW of Punta Macolla, February 1942. Seventeen lives lost out of 27 on board.								
558	834	*Hooiberg*	27.3.1928	2,395	Oil Tanker	St/2Sc/St 305.7/50.2/14.3	196 nhp TE (6Cy) H&W	Lago Shipping Co. (A. Weir & Co.) Glasgow
Completed 25.4.1928, sister ship of *Inverlago.* In 1947 to Esso. In 1953 to Esso (Argentina) and renamed *ESSO Entre Rios.* In 1963 to Rio Lujan Nav., renamed *Entre Rios.* Broken up Argentina (Buenos Aires) 1981.								
559	835	*Punta Gorda*	23.4.1928	2,395	Oil Tanker	St/2Sc/St 305.7/50.2/14.3	196 nhp TE (6Cy) H&W	Lago Shipping Co. (A. Weir & Co.) Glasgow
Completed 18.5.1928, sister ship of *Inverlago.* Sank following collision 5nm off Cape San Roman, Aruba, September 1944.								
560	836	*Yamanota*	22.5.1928	2,395	Oil Tanker	St/2Sc/St 305.7/50.2/14.3	196 nhp TE (6Cy) H&W	Lago Shipping Co. (A. Weir & Co.) Glasgow
Completed 13.6.1928, sister ship of *Inverlago.* In 1948 transferred to Esso. In 1953 to ESSO (Argentina), renamed *ESSO Formosa.* In 1963 to SA de Nav. Petromar. Broken up Argentina (Buenos Aires) 1966.								
N/A	837	*Celtic Monarch*	Meadowside built					
N/A	838	*Centauta*	Pointhouse built					
N/A	839	Oil Barge	Pointhouse built					
561	840	*Warwick Castle*	29.4.1930	20,444	Passenger Ship	St/2Sc/Mv 651.2/75.5/37.4	3,360 nhp Dies H&W	Union-Castle Steamship Co. London
Completed 16.1.1931, a slightly longer half sister of *Winchester Castle.* Modernised in 1938. At outbreak of war taken up as troopship. In 1942 took part in Operation Torch but on return journey was sunk by submarine torpedo (*U-413*) 200m NW of Cape Espichel, Portugal, November 1942. Ninety-six lives lost out of 462 on board.								
N/A	841	*Llangibby Castle*	Govan built					
N/A	842	*Bhutan*	Govan built					
N/A	843	*Westralia*	Govan built					
N/A	844	*Oceanic*	Cancelled					
N/A	845	*Cardiff*	Pointhouse built					
N/A	846	*Glasgow*	Pointhouse built					
N/A	847	*Ciudad de Ascuncion*	Pointhouse built					
N/A	848	*Ciudad de Corrientes*	Pointhouse built					
562	849	*Wanganella*	17.12.1929	9,576	Passenger-Cargo	St/2Sc/Mv 461.2/63.9/29.1	1,305 nhp 8,500 bhp Dies H&W	Huddart Parker Melbourne
(This vessel is listed by Moss & Hume as a passenger ship, re-rated) Launched as *Achimota* for Elder Dempster with accommodation for 304 first-class and 104 second-class passengers. Before the vessel was completed the Kylsant business empire had collapsed and Elder Dempster could not pay for her, so repossessed by H&W and offered for sale. Although valued at £580,000 under the company's 'costs-plus' system, the best offer received was from Huddart Parker of £346,376 and sold at that price. Finally completed 29.11.1932, and from 1933 employed on Melbourne–Sydney–Auckland route. From 1962 employed as an accommodation ship. Broken up Taiwan (Kaohsiung), June 1970.								
N/A	850	*Idomo*	Pointhouse built					
N/A	851	*Dunbar Castle*	Govan built					

Ship	Yard No	Name	Date Launched	Displacement Tons	Type	Construction and Dimensions	Horse Power/ Engines	Owners
563	852	*Reina del Pacifico*	23.9.1930	17,707	Passenger-Cargo	St/4Sc/Mv 551.3/76.3/37.8	2,844 nhp Dies H&W	Pacific Steam Navigation Co. Liverpool
(This vessel is listed by Moss & Hume as a passenger ship, re-rated) Completed 24.3.1931, for Liverpool–Caribbean–South America route, accommodation for 280 first-class, 162 second-class and 446 third-class passengers. At start of war employed as troopship and later as an assault transport. After repatriation duties was returned to H&W for refit. On 11 September 1947 while undergoing sea trials there was a serious engine room explosion which killed 28 members of the crew and the company's technical staff. In July 1957 ran aground in Bermuda and refloated with great difficulty. This was the first of a number of accidents that gave the vessel the reputation of being a 'jinx' ship. Withdrawn from service March 1958 and broken up Newport (UK).								
N/A	853	*David Livingstone*	Dunbarton built					
N/A	854	*Mary Slessor*	Dunbarton built					
N/A	855	*William Wilberforce*	Meadowside built					
N/A	856	*Baron Vernon*	Meadowside built					
N/A	857	*Baron Ramsey*	Meadowside built					
N/A	858	*Kufra*	Govan built					
N/A	659	*Irwin*	Meadowside built					
N/A	660	*Goschen*	Meadowside built					
564	861	*Tamare*	23.4.1929	3,046	Oil Tanker	St/2Sc/St 325.0/55.2/15.3	228 nhp TE (6Cy) H&W	Lago Shipping Co. (A. Weir & Co.) Glasgow
Completed 7.5.1929. A new type of tanker somewhat larger than preceding Inverlago type. In 1938 to Venezuelan owners, Cia de Petrolo Lago, not renamed. In 1954 to Canadian owners, Island Tug & Barge, converted into oil hulk/barge, renamed *Island Maple*. Broken in two and lost in October 1963.								
565	862	*Ule*	30.4.1929	3,046	Oil Tanker	St/2Sc/St 325.0/55.2/15.3	228 nhp TE (6Cy) H&W	Lago Shipping Co. (A. Weir & Co.) Glasgow
Completed 20.5.1929, sister ship of *Tamare*. In 1932 to Standard Oil (Venezuela), not renamed. In 1943 to Cia de Petrolo Lago. In 1954 to Canadian owners, Island Tug & Barge, converted to oil hulk/barge, renamed *Island Balsam*. In 1969 to Goodwin Johnston, renamed *Nahat II*. Subsequently sunk in breakwater at Queen Charlotte Island, Vancouver.								
566	863	*Surinam*	9.5.1929	3,046	Oil Tanker	St/2Sc/St 325.0/55.2/15.3	228 nhp TE (6Cy) H&W	Lago Shipping Co. (A. Weir & Co.) Glasgow
Completed 29.5.1929, sister ship of *Tamare*. In 1933 to Standard Oil (Venezuela), not renamed. In 1947 to Cia de Petrolo Lago. In 1954 to Canadian owners, Island Tug & Barge, and converted into oil hulk/barge, renamed *Island Cypress*. Broke in two and sank October 1963.								
N/A	864	*Kavak*	Dunbarton built					
N/A	865	*Kana*	Dunbarton built					
N/A	866	*Carmen Avellaneda*	Pointhouse built					
N/A	867	*Edward Blyden*	Govan built					
N/A	868	*Alfred Jones*	Govan built					
N/A	869	*Macgregor Laird*	Meadowside built					
567	870	*Innisfallen*	4.3.1930	3,019	Passenger Ferry	St/2Sc/Mv 321.0/45.7/15.2	1,193 nhp Dies H&W	City of Cork Steam Packet Co. Cork
Completed 14.6.1930, for Cork–Fishguard passenger/cattle service. At outbreak of war this service was suspended and the ship operated between Cork and Liverpool. Mined off Canada Dock, Liverpool, December 1940. Four lives lost.								
N/A	871	*Ardanbhan*	Meadowside built					
N/A	872	*Lochness*	Govan built					
N/A	873	*Amberes*	Pointhouse built					
N/A	874	*Barcelona*	Govan built					
N/A	875	*Genova*	Govan built					
N/A	876	*Hamburgo*	Pointhouse built					
N/A	877	*Guayra*	Pointhouse built					

Ship	Yard No	Name	Date Launched	Displacement Tons	Type	Construction and Dimensions	Horse Power/ Engines	Owners
568	878	*Foylebank*	12.6.1930	5,582	Cargo Ship	St/2Sc/Mv 426.8/57.3/25.8	830 nhp Dies H&W	Andrew Weir & Co. Glasgow
Completed 14.11.1930. In 1939 converted into auxiliary anti-aircraft vessel, armed with 8x 4in guns and two quadruple pompoms. Sunk July 1940 at Portland during air attack. Sixteen lives lost. Wreck salvaged in two sections, forward half broken up Falmouth 1947 and stern Essex 1952.								
569	879	*Laganbank*	10.7.1930	5,582	Cargo Ship	St/2Sc/Mv 426.8/57.3/25.8	830 nhp Dies H&W	Andrew Weir & Co. Glasgow
Completed 11.12.1930, sister ship of *Foylebank*. Wrecked Maldive Islands, January 1938.								
N/A	880	*Dorothy Rose*	Meadowside built					
N/A	881	*Dudley Rose*	Meadowside built					
570	882	*Silvercypress*	18.2.1930	6,770	Cargo Ship (Refrigerated)	St/2Sc/Mv 456.3/62.0/25.6	979 nhp Dies H&W	Silver Line Ltd (S.&J. Thompson) London
Completed 18.6.1930. In 1939 to Japanese owners, Kawasaki Kisen, renamed *Yasukawa Maru*. Sunk in air attack off New Guinea, November 1942.								
571	883	*Silverwalnut*	15.4.1930	6,770	Cargo Ship (Refrigerated)	St/2Sc/Mv 456.3/62.0/25.6	979 nhp Dies H&W	Silver Line Ltd (S.&J. Thompson) London
Completed 23.7.1930, sister ship of *Silvercypress*. In 1954 to Italian owners, Gastaldi & Co., renamed *Samundar*. Broken up Japan (Izumi-Ohtsu) 1960.								
572	884	*Silverteak*	29.5.1930	6,770	Cargo Ship (Refrigerated)	St/2Sc/Mv 456.3/62.0/25.6	979 nhp Dies H&W	Silver Line Ltd (S.&J. Thompson) London
Completed 2.9.1930, sister ship of *Silvercypress*. In 1954 to Italian owners, Gastaldi & Co., renamed *Gardigan*. Broken up Japan (Izumi-Ohtsu) 1960.								
573	885	*Silversandal*	26.6.1930	6,770	Cargo Ship (Refrigerated)	St/2Sc/Mv 456.3/62.0/25.6	979 nhp Dies H&W	Silver Line Ltd (S.&J. Thompson) London
Completed 19.9.1930, sister ship of *Silvercypress*. In 1954 to Blyth DD & SB Co., renamed *Blyth Trader*. Broken up Hong Kong 1960.								
N/A	886	*Baron Napier*	Meadowside built					
N/A	887	*Baron Erskine*	Meadowside built					
574	888	*San Antonio*	1.7.1930	5,986	Cargo Ship (Refrigerated)	St/Sc/St 431.5/57.3/26.7	557 nhp TE (4Cy) H&W	Compagnie Generale Transatlantique Le Havre
Completed 24.9.1930. Seized by Germans in 1942, employed as transport. Sunk by Allied aircraft off Cape San Vito Siculo, May 1943.								
575	889	*San Diego*	14.8.1930	5,986	Cargo Ship (Refrigerated)	St/Sc/St 431.5/57.3/26.7	557 nhp TE (4Cy) H&W	Compagnie Generale Transatlantique Le Havre
Completed 11.11.1930, sister ship of *San Antonio*. Seized by Germans in 1942, employed as transport. Sunk by aircraft bombs near Bizerta, April 1944.								
576	890	*San Francisco*	11.9.1930	5,894	Cargo Ship (Refrigerated)	St/Sc/St 431.5/57.3/26.7	557nhp TE (4Cy) H&W	Compagnie Generale Transatlantique Le Havre
Completed 10.12.1930, sister ship of *San Antonio*. Seized by Germans in 1942, employed as transport. Sunk by aircraft bombs north of Cape Corse, July 1943.								
577	891	*San Jose*	23.10.1930	5,982	Cargo Ship (Refrigerated)	St/Sc/St 431.5/57.3/26.7	557 nhp TE (4Cy) H&W	Compagnie Generale Transatlantique Le Havre
Completed 23.1.1931, sister ship of *San Antonio*. In 1954 to Hong Kong owners, Wheelock Marden, renamed *San Rolando* and again in 1957 *Loraine*. Broken up Hong Kong 1958.								
578	892	*San Mateo*	20.11.1930	5,935	Cargo Ship (Refrigerated)	St/Sc/St 431.5/57.3/26.7	557nhp TE (4Cy) H&W	Compagnie Generale Transatlantique Le Havre
Completed 6.3.1931, sister ship of *San Antonio*. In 1954 to Hong Kong owners, Wheelock Marden, renamed *San Mardeno*. Wrecked in Indian waters, July 1954.								

Ship	Yard No	Name	Date Launched	Displacement Tons	Type	Construction and Dimensions	Horse Power/ Engines	Owners
579	893	*San Pedro*	20.12.1930	5,935	Cargo Ship (Refrigerated)	St/Sc/St 431.5/57.3/26.7	557 nhp TE (4Cy) H&W	Companie Generale Transatlantique Le Havre
Completed 17.4.1931, sister ship of *San Antonio.* In 1953 renamed *Uranus.* In 1954 to Hong Kong owners, Wheelock Marden, renamed *Anto.* In 1957 to Great Southern SS Co., renamed *Eastwind.* Broken up Japan (Osaka) 1959.								
N/A	894	*Ciudad de Concepcion*	Pointhouse built					
N/A	895	Lighter	Dumbarton built					
580	896	*Georgic*	12.11.1931	27,267	Passenger Ship	St/2Sc/Mv 683.6/82.4/48.6	4,214 nhp 20,000 bhp Dies H&W	Oceanic Steam Navigation Co. Liverpool
Completed 10.6.1932, sister ship of *Britannic*, accommodation for 475 cabin-class, 557 tourist-class and 506 third-class passengers. Served as troopship in Second World War until sunk in air attack at Suez, July 1941. Salvaged and temporarily repaired at Bombay before being returned to H&W for reconstruction, re-entered service as troopship in December 1944. After war employed on Australia emigrant route but later returned to North Atlantic, 1950. Broken up Faslane (UK) 1956.								
N/A	897	*Ganges*	Govan built					
N/A	898	*Somali*	Govan built					
581	899	*Ebano*	27.5.1930	2,627	Asphalt Carrier	St/Sc/St 290.2/47.2/17.7	229 nhp TE (3Cy) H&W	Ebano Oil Co. (A. Weir & Co.) London
Completed 30.10.1930. In 1933 to French owners, Auxiliaire se Transports, renamed *Petrophalt.* At the fall of France was in a British port, and was requisitioned, operated by Ministry of Supply. After the war returned to owners. In 1952 passed to Esso/Standard (France), renamed *ESSO La Mailleraye.* Broken up France (Aviles) 1953.								
N/A	900	*Prestatyn Rose*	Meadowside built					
N/A	901	*Anglesea Rose*	Meadowside built					
N/A	902	*Medoc*	Meadowside built					
N/A	903	*Pomerol*	Meadowside built					
N/A	904	*Chateau Larose*	Meadowside built					
N/A	905	*Chateau Pavie*	Meadowside built					
N/A	906	*Maurice Rose*	Meadowside built					
N/A	907	*Dennis Rose*	Meadowside built					
582	908	*Cliona*	14.5.1931	8,375	Oil Tanker	St/2Sc/Mv 456.6/62.0/34.1	877 nhp Dies H&W	Anglo-Saxon Petroleum Co. London
Completed 14.10.1931. In 1948 to M. Whitwill & Son, Bristol, renamed *Avon Venturer.* In 1955 converted to ore carrier. In 1958 to Finnish owners, A. Johansson, renamed *Avony.* Broken up Spain (Santander) 1963.								
583	909	*Conch*	2.7.1931	8,376	Oil Tanker	St/2Sc/Mv 456.6/62.0/34.1	877 nhp Dies H&W	Anglo-Saxon Petroleum Co. London
Completed 22.12.1931, sister ship of *Cliona.* Damaged by submarine torpedo (*U-47*) 370m W of Bloody Foreland and fell astern of convoy. Hit by three further torpedoes (*U-95*) and lost engines but stayed afloat and attacker driven off by escorts. Finally, almost 30 hours after first hit, sunk by a torpedo (*U-99*), December 1940. No lives lost.								
N/A	910	*Rockabill*	Meadowside built					
N/A	911	*Triona*	Govan built					
N/A	912	*Autocarrier*	Meadowside built					
N/A	913	*Orgeni*	Govan built					
N/A	914	*East Goodwin*	Pointhouse built					
584	915	*Maracay*	21.5.1931	3,795	Oil Tanker	St/2Sc/St	314 nhp TE (6Cy) H&W	Lago Shipping Co. (A. Weir & Co.) London
Completed 16.6.1931. In 1947 to Esso. In 1952 to Panamanian owners, Panama Transport Co. and later (1953) to Creole Petroleum Corp, Panama. In 1957 to Cia de Petrolo Lago, renamed *ESSO Maracay.* The following year to Dutch owners, Simons Metaalhandel, renamed *Waalhaven* for voyage to brakers. Broken up Japan (Osaka) 1959.								

<table>
<tr><th>Ship</th><th>Yard No</th><th>Name</th><th>Date Launched</th><th>Displacement Tons</th><th>Type</th><th>Construction and Dimensions</th><th>Horse Power/ Engines</th><th>Owners</th></tr>
<tr><td>585</td><td>916</td><td>Highland Patriot</td><td>10.12.1931</td><td>14,156</td><td>Passenger-Cargo (Refrigerated)</td><td>St/2Sc/Mv
523.4/69.4/37.1</td><td>2,190 nhp
10,000 bhp
Dies
H&W</td><td>Nelson Steam Navigation Co.
Liverpool</td></tr>
<tr><td colspan="9">Completed 13.5.1932, sister ship of Highland Monarch, built to replace Highland Hope (built by H&W at Govan) lost in 1930. In December 1939 was attacked by the French submarine Fresnal after being mistaken for a German blockade runner; submarine driven off by gunfire with no damage to either side. Sunk by submarine torpedo (U-38) 500m W of Bishops Rock, October 1940. Three lives lost.</td></tr>
<tr><td>N/A</td><td>917</td><td>Floating Crane</td><td colspan="6">Govan built</td></tr>
<tr><td>N/A</td><td>918</td><td>Royal Iris II</td><td colspan="6">Govan built</td></tr>
<tr><td>N/A</td><td>919</td><td>Baron Ardrossan</td><td colspan="6">Meadowside built</td></tr>
<tr><td>N/A</td><td>920</td><td>Duchess of Hamilton</td><td colspan="6">Govan built</td></tr>
<tr><td>N/A</td><td>921</td><td>North Carr</td><td colspan="6">Pointhouse built</td></tr>
<tr><td>586</td><td>922</td><td>Waiwera</td><td>1.5.1934</td><td>10,781</td><td>Cargo Ship (Refrigerated)</td><td>St/2Sc/Mv
516.2/70.4/32.4</td><td>1,631 nhp
10,000 bhp
Dies
H&W</td><td>Shaw Savill & Albion
London</td></tr>
<tr><td colspan="9">Completed 13.8.1934, designed as 'Empire Food Ship' with top speed of almost 17 knots, sometimes described as a cargo liner but had accommodation for only the usual 12 passengers. Sunk by submarine torpedo (U-574) 450m N of Azores, inbound Auckland–Liverpool, June 1942. Eight lives lost.</td></tr>
<tr><td>587</td><td>923</td><td>Waipawa</td><td>28.6.1934</td><td>10,704</td><td>Cargo Ship (Refrigerated)</td><td>St/2Sc/Mv
516.2/70.4/32.4</td><td>1,631 nhp
10,000 bhp
Dies
H&W</td><td>Shaw Savill & Albion
London</td></tr>
<tr><td colspan="9">Completed 19.10.1934, sister ship of Waiwera. In 1967 to Greek owners, Astro Protector, renamed Aramis for final voyage to breakers. Broken up Taiwan (Kaohsiung) 1968.</td></tr>
<tr><td>N/A</td><td>924</td><td>Wairangi</td><td colspan="6">Govan built</td></tr>
<tr><td>N/A</td><td>925</td><td>Bhadravati</td><td colspan="6">Govan built</td></tr>
<tr><td>N/A</td><td>926</td><td>Chandravati</td><td colspan="6">Govan built</td></tr>
<tr><td>N/A</td><td>927</td><td>Baron Dunmore</td><td colspan="6">Meadowside built</td></tr>
<tr><td>N/A</td><td>928</td><td>Baron Elgin</td><td colspan="6">Meadowside built</td></tr>
<tr><td>N/A</td><td>929</td><td>Prabhavati</td><td colspan="6">Govan built</td></tr>
<tr><td>588</td><td>930</td><td>Idalia</td><td>29.5.1934</td><td>147</td><td>Yacht (Schooner)</td><td>St/2Sc/Mv
101.7/19.2/8.8</td><td>73 nhp
Dies
H&W</td><td>Alan F. Craig
Belfast</td></tr>
<tr><td colspan="9">Completed 2.7.1934. By 1938 owned by Sir Raymond Dennis KBE. Appears to have been taken into naval service during Second World War as re-engined in 1944. In 1950 owned by George B. Butler of Belfast. In early 1950s name changed briefly to Greeba but by 1956 had returned to original name and was owned by H.A. Andreae of Belfast. By 1959 owned by Vicount Camrose and moved to Southampton. In the 1970s to Hi-Tec Corp. Name changed to Alicia Dawn. In 1984 was rebuilt and given a large aluminium superstructure and about this time renamed Endeavour. Still extant in May 2011 and named Balmoral.</td></tr>
<tr><td>N/A</td><td>931</td><td>Lough Lomand</td><td colspan="6">Meadowside built</td></tr>
<tr><td>N/A</td><td>932</td><td>Ansdara</td><td colspan="6">Govan built</td></tr>
<tr><td>589</td><td>933</td><td>Imperial Star</td><td>9.10.1934</td><td>10,733</td><td>Cargo Ship (Refrigerated)</td><td>St/2Sc/Mv
524.2/70.4/32.3</td><td>1,631 nhp
10,000 bhp
Dies
H&W</td><td>Blue Star Line
(Leyland & Co.)
Liverpool</td></tr>
<tr><td colspan="9">Completed 29.12.1934, near sister of Waiwera type, originally New Zealand Star launched under this name. Hit by air-launched torpedo western Mediterranean and subsequently scuttled, September 1941.</td></tr>
<tr><td>590</td><td>934</td><td>New Zealand Star</td><td>22.11.1934</td><td>10,740</td><td>Cargo Ship (Refrigerated)</td><td>St/2Sc/Mv
516.2/70.4/32.4</td><td>1,631 nhp
10,000 bhp
Dies
H&W</td><td>Blue Star Line
(Leyland & Co.)
Liverpool</td></tr>
<tr><td colspan="9">Completed 1.3.1935, sister ship of Imperial Star, originally Australia Star but launched under this name. Broken up Japan (Kure) 1967.</td></tr>
<tr><td>N/A</td><td>935</td><td>Sir Hastings Anderson</td><td colspan="6">Govan built</td></tr>
<tr><td>N/A</td><td>936</td><td>John Dock</td><td colspan="6">Govan built</td></tr>
</table>

Ship	Yard No	Name	Date Launched	Displacement Tons	Type	Construction and Dimensions	Horse Power/ Engines	Owners
N/A	937	*W.H. Fuller*	Govan built					
N/A	938	*San Acradio*	Govan built					
591	939	*Australia Star*	8.1.1935	11,122	Cargo Ship (Refrigerated)	St/2Sc/Mv 524.2/70.4/32.7	2,463 nhp Dies H&W	Blue Star Line (Leyland & Co.) Liverpool
Completed 17.4.1935 slightly enlarged half sister of *Imperial Star*, originally *Imperial Star* but launched under this name. Broken up Faslane (UK) 1964.								
592	940	HMS *Penelope*	15.10.1935	5,050	Cruiser	St/4Sc/St 506.0/51.0/16.6	64,000 shp Turb H&W	Admiralty
This vessel is normally seen as marking the beginning of re-armament in terms of the history of H&W. An Arethusa-class vessel which were reduced versions of the preceding Perth class and represented an attempt to build the smallest possible modern cruiser. Completed 13.11.1936. Damaged during the Norwegian campaign and after repair was sent to the Mediterranean where it spent most of the rest of its career. In February 1944 hit by a submarine torpedo (*U-410*) while steaming at 27 knots off the Anzio Beachhead; a second torpedo 16 minutes later sank the ship. Four hundred and fifteen lives lost, 206 survivors.								
593	941	*Stirling Castle*	15.8.1935	25,594	Passenger-Cargo	St/2Sc/Mv 696.0/82.5/41.4	4,650 nhp Dies H&W	Union-Castle Steamship Co. London
(This vessel is listed by Moss & Hume as a passenger ship, re-rated) Completed 29.1.1936, accommodation for over 780 passengers. On outbreak of war requisitioned as troopship, capable of carrying 6,000 men (eating and sleeping in two sessions), during the war carried 128,000 troops and sailed 500,000 miles without incident. Refitted and returned to South Africa route until sold for £360,000; broken up Japan (Mihara) 1966.								
594	942	*Athlone Castle*	28.11.1935	25,567	Passenger-Cargo	St/2Sc/Mv 696.0/82.5/41.4	4,650 nhp Dies H&W	Union-Castle Steamship Co. London
(This vessel is listed by Moss & Hume as a passenger ship, re-rated) Completed 13.5.1936, sister ship of *Stirling Castle*. Troopship during war carrying 150,000 men without incident. Refitted and returned to South African routes until 1965 when, having completed her 141st voyage, sold; broken up Taiwan (Kaohsiung) 1965.								
595	943	*Roslin Castle*	20.12.1934	7,016	Cargo Ship (Refrigerated)	St/Sc/Mv 426.5/61.3/32.0	1,643 nhp 8,750 bhp Dies H&W	Union-Castle Steamship Co. London
(This vessel is listed by Moss & Hume and a passenger-cargo ship, re-rated) Completed 4.5.1935, completely refrigerated and equipped to carry different produce in separate holds. Spent much of year laid up between the fruit seasons, but was still highly profitable. Broken up Taiwan (Kaohsiung) 1967.								
596	944	*Rothesay Castle*	21.2.1935	7,016	Cargo Ship (Refrigerated)	St/Sc/Mv 426.5/61.3/32.0	1,643 nhp 8,750 bhp Dies H&W	Union-Castle Steamship Co. London
(This vessel is listed by Moss & Hume and a passenger-cargo ship, re-rated) Completed 11.5.1935, sister ship of *Roslin Castle*. Wrecked Isle of Islay, inbound from New York, January 1940. No lives lost.								
N/A	945	*Henzada*	Meadowside built					
N/A	946	*Martaban*	Meadowside built					
N/A	947	*Baron Renfrew*	Meadowside built					
N/A	948	*Baron Cawdor*	Meadowside built					
N/A	949	*Flying Falcon*	Pointhouse built					
N/A	950	*Saganaga*	Meadowside built					
597	951	*Duke of York*	7.3.1935	3,759	Passenger Ferry	St/2Sc/St 339.2/52.2/17.9	1,494 nhp 9,000 shp Turb H&W	London Midland & Scottish Railway
Completed 4.6.1935, employed on Belfast–Heysham route. Taken up 1942 converted into Landing Ship Infantry (H), renamed *Duke of Wellington* (presumably to avoid confusion with the 36,727-ton battleship of the same name) accommodation for 420 combat-ready troops and carried six landing craft to ferry them ashore. After war returned to owners and assumed original name. In 1963 to Chandris, London, and renamed initially *York* and later *Fantasia*. Broken up Greece (Piraeus) 1975.								
N/A	952	*Mpasa*	Pointhouse built					
N/A	953	*Inventor*	Meadowside built					

<table>
<tr><th>Ship</th><th>Yard No</th><th>Name</th><th>Date Launched</th><th>Displacement Tons</th><th>Type</th><th>Construction and Dimensions</th><th>Horse Power/ Engines</th><th>Owners</th></tr>
<tr><td>598</td><td>954</td><td>Calabar</td><td>7.2.1935</td><td>1,932</td><td>Passenger-
Cargo</td><td>St/Sc/Mv
249.4/41.2/16.3</td><td>404 nhp
1,700 bhp
Dies
H&W</td><td>Elder Dempster Line
Liverpool</td></tr>
<tr><td colspan="9">Completed 19.3.1935. In 1953 to Greek owners, G. Potamianos, renamed Semiramis. Broken up Singapore 1980.</td></tr>
<tr><td>599</td><td>955</td><td>Kanimbla</td><td>12.12.1935</td><td>10,984</td><td>Passenger-
Cargo</td><td>St/2Sc/Mv
468.8/66.3/30.2</td><td>1,305 hp
8,500 bhp
Dies
H&W</td><td>McIlwraith McEachern
& Co.
Melbourne</td></tr>
<tr><td colspan="9">Completed 26.4.1936. Operated in Australian waters until 1939 when taken up by the Royal Navy and converted into an armed merchant cruiser (7x 6in guns 2x 3in AA) later converted to a Landing Ship Infantry and operated by the Royal Australian Navy. Returned to civilian owners in 1950. In 1961 to Japanese owners, Toyo Yusen, renamed Oriental Queen. Broken up Taiwan (Kaohsiung) 1973.</td></tr>
<tr><td>N/A</td><td>956</td><td>Talisman</td><td colspan="6">Pointhouse built</td></tr>
<tr><td>600</td><td>957</td><td>Empire Star</td><td>26.9.1935</td><td>11,093</td><td>Cargo Ship
(Refrigerated)</td><td>St/2Sc/Mv
524.2/70.4/32.3</td><td>2,463 nhp
Dies
H&W</td><td>Blue Star Line
(Leyland & Co.)
Liverpool</td></tr>
<tr><td colspan="9">Completed 20.12.1935, sister ship of Australia Star, originally Sydney Star but launched under this name. Sunk by submarine torpedo (U-615) N of Azores outbound Liverpool–East London, October 1942. Forty-two lives lost out of 103 on board.</td></tr>
<tr><td>601</td><td>958</td><td>Sydney Star</td><td>11.1.1936</td><td>11,095</td><td>Cargo Ship
(Refrigerated)</td><td>St/2Sc/Mv
524.2/70.4/32.3</td><td>2,463 nhp
Dies
H&W</td><td>Blue Star Line Ltd
(Leyland & Co.)
Liverpool</td></tr>
<tr><td colspan="9">Completed 19.3.1936, sister ship of Australia Star, originally Melbourne Star but launched under this name. In July 1941 torpedoed by German E-boat while on route to Malta – reached destination and subsequently repaired. In 1967 to Embajada Cia Nav, renamed Kent. Broken up Taiwan (Kaohsiung) 1967.</td></tr>
<tr><td>602</td><td>959</td><td>Dunnottar Castle</td><td>25.1.1936</td><td>15,007</td><td>Passenger-
Cargo</td><td>St/2Sc/Mv
540.0/71.9/37.8</td><td>1,931 nhp
1,4000 bhp
Dies
H&W</td><td>Union-Castle
Steamship Co.
London</td></tr>
<tr><td colspan="9">(This vessel is listed by Moss & Hume as a passenger ship, re-rated)
Completed 27.6.1936, accommodation for 285 first-class and 250 tourist-class passengers. Commissioned August 1939 as armed merchant cruiser (2x 6in guns and 2x 3in AA), served in South Atlantic. In 1942 became a troopship and carried some 250,000 men including running a shuttle service between Normandy and Southampton after D-Day. Returned to owners and refurbished by H&W before returning to South Africa routes. In 1958, having completed 94 voyages, to Liberian owners, Incres SS Co., renamed Victoria; rebuilt in Holland as a cruise liner, initially in Mediterranean but later employed between New York and the West Indies. Later to Chandris, transferred to Greek registry as The Victoria. In 1993 to Cypriot owners, Interorient Nav Co., renamed Princesa Victoria. In 2004 after 68 years in service, broken up in India (Alang).</td></tr>
<tr><td>603</td><td>960</td><td>Dunvegan Castle</td><td>26.3.1936</td><td>15,007</td><td>Passenger-
Cargo</td><td>St/2Sc/Mv
540.0/71.9/37.8</td><td>1,931 nhp
14,000 bhp
Dies
H&W</td><td>Union-Castle
Steamship Co.
London</td></tr>
<tr><td colspan="9">(This vessel is listed by Moss & Hume as a passenger ship, re-rated)
Completed 27.8.1936, sister ship of Dunnottar Castle. Commissioned August 1939 as armed merchant cruiser (2x 6in guns and 2x 12 lber AA). Sunk by submarine torpedo (U-46) off western Ireland escorting an inbound convoy from Freetown, August 1940. Twenty-seven lives lost out of 277 on board.</td></tr>
<tr><td>N/A</td><td>961</td><td>Standella</td><td colspan="6">Govan built</td></tr>
<tr><td>N/A</td><td>962</td><td>Simnia</td><td colspan="6">Govan built</td></tr>
<tr><td>604</td><td>963</td><td>Royal Ulsterman</td><td>10.3.1936</td><td>3,290</td><td>Passenger-
Cargo Ferry</td><td>St/2Sc/Mv
327.9/47.77/13.6</td><td>1,077 nhp
5,200 bhp
Dies
H&W</td><td>Burns & Laird Line
Glasgow</td></tr>
<tr><td colspan="9">Completed 13.6.1936, originally Laird of Ulster but launched under this name, employed on Belfast–Clyde route. During war served as troop-ship. In 1968 to Cammell Laird & Co., renamed Cammell Laird, used as accommodation ship. In 1970 to Greek owners, G. Karydas, renamed Sounion, employed as a cruise ship. Sunk by a limpet mine at Beirut, March 1973. Wreck raised and broken up Perama 1973.</td></tr>
<tr><td>605</td><td>964</td><td>Royal Scotsman</td><td>11.3.1936</td><td>3,244</td><td>Passenger-
Cargo Ferry</td><td>St/2Sc/Mv
327.9/47.77/13.6</td><td>1,077 nhp
5,200 bhp
Dies
H&W</td><td>Burns & Laird Line
Glasgow</td></tr>
<tr><td colspan="9">Completed 29.5.1936, sister ship of Royal Ulsterman, originally Laird of Scotia but launched under this name. History similar to sister until sold in 1968. Passed to Scientology Church, renamed Apollo, becoming floating college and home of founder of movement Ron Hubbard based in Mediterranean. In 1984 to Panamanian owners, Zanzibar Inc., renamed Artic Star. Broken up shortly afterwards USA (Brownsville).</td></tr>
</table>

Ship	Yard No	Name	Date Launched	Displacement Tons	Type	Construction and Dimensions	Horse Power/ Engines	Owners
N/A	965	*Sonavati*	Govan built					
606	966	*Eros*	9.1.1936	5,888	Fruit Carrier	St/Sc/St 415.4/54.8/30.4	1,084 nhp 6,400 ihp TE (4Cy) H&W	Erin Steamship Co. (Standard Fruit) New York
Completed 8.4.1936. In 1939 to Morant SS Co., London. At outbreak of war taken over by Ministry of Supply, managed by Elders & Fyffes. In June 1940, while inbound Montreal–Liverpool, with cargo of 300 tons of copper, 100 tons of chrome and 200 tons of small arms, was torpedoed (*U-48*) off Northern Ireland. Beached on Tory Island from where salvaged and repaired. In 1947 to Canadian register. In 1963 to Australian owners, Rigryth Ltd, renamed *Trangie.* Broken up Taiwan (Kaohsiung) 1968.								
607	967	*Duchess of Abercorn*	25.8.1936	308	Tug/Tender	St/2Sc/Mv 119.7/27.1/11.2	208 nhp Dies-Elect H&W	Belfast Harbour Commissioners
Completed 17.3.1937. In 1948 to W.E. McCaig, renamed *Wimaisia.* In 1949 to City of Liverpool, renamed *William Gregson.* In 1963 to Collins Pipe Lines, renamed *Collinstar.* Capsized and sank 100nm S of Luderitz, February 1965.								
N/A	968	*British Power*	Govan built					
N/A	969	*British Destiny*	Govan built					
N/A	970	*Adelong*	Govan built					
N/A	971	*Boardale*	Govan built					
N/A	972	*British Integrity*	Govan built					
N/A	973	*Broomdale*	Govan built					
N/A	974	*British Security*	Govan built					
N/A	975	*Charles MacIver*	Pointhouse built					
608	976	*Lairdswood*	21.7.1936	789	Cargo	St/2Sc/Mv 229.0/37.2/11.5	332 nhp 1,400 bhp Dies H&W	Burns & Laird Line Glasgow
Completed 15.8.1936. In 1959 to Belfast SS Co., renamed *Ulster Sportsman.* In 1967 to Haiti owners, Transrodopi, renamed *Transrodopi IV.* In 1968 acquired by Belgian government, renamed *Alnilam.* Broken up Spain (La Felguera) 1970.								
609	977	*Lairdscrest*	6.8.1936	789	Cargo	St/2Sc/Mv 229.0/37.2/11.5	332 nhp 1,400 bhp Dies H&W	Burns & Laird Line Glasgow
Completed 26.8.1936, sister ship of *Lairdswood.* In 1968 to Greek owners, S.C. Vazeos, renamed *San Marco* and subsequently *Kronos* (1974). Broken up Greece 1978.								
610	978	*Lairdsbank*	3.9.1936	789	Cargo	St/2Sc/Mv 229.0/37.2/11.5	332 nhp 1,400 bhp Dies H&W	Burns & Laird Line Glasgow
Completed 24.9.1936, sister ship of *Lairdswood.* In 1963 to British & Irish SP Co., renamed *Glanmire.* Broken up Dalmuir (UK) 1969.								
N/A	979	*Cameo*	Pointhouse built					
611	980	*Delius*	12.4.1937	6,065	Cargo Ship	St/Sc/Mv 438.6/62.3/25.4	898 nhp Dies H&W	Lamport & Holt Line Liverpool
Completed 6.7.1937. In 1954 to Blue Star Line, renamed *Portland Star.* In 1958 returned to Lamport & Holt, reverted to original name. In 1961 to Moroccan owners, Miniere et Metal, renamed *Kettara VII.* Broken up Japan 1962.								
N/A	981	*Sitala*	Govan built					
N/A	982	*Salacia*	Govan built					
612	983	*Walmer Castle*	17.9.1936	905	Cargo Ship	St/Sc/Mv 236.2/39.3/12.5	539 nhp Dies H&W	Union-Castle Steamship Co. London
Completed 30.11.1936, for Germany–Southampton feeder services. In 1940 requisitioned and initially employed as armed supply ship at Scapa Flow. In June 1941 converted into convoy rescue ship, in September joined OG75. On the 21st, with 54 rescued survivors from three different ships on board, attacked by a Condor bomber 700nm W of Ushant. Suffered a direct hit which killed the captain, ten crew members and two of the rescued survivors. Subsequently scuttled.								
613	984	*Ernebank*	17.11.1936	5,388	Cargo Ship	St/Sc/Mv 431.7/57.3/24.9	490 nhp Dies H&W	Andrew Weir & Co. Glasgow
Completed 18.2.1937. Broken up Hong Kong 1963.								

Ship	Yard No	Name	Date Launched	Displacement Tons	Type	Construction and Dimensions	Horse Power/ Engines	Owners
N/A	985	*Dipavati*	Govan built					
614	986	*Capetown Castle*	23.9.1937	27,002	Passenger-Cargo	St/2Sc/Mv 702.9/82.5/42.0	4,650 nhp Dies H&W	Union-Castle Steamship Co. London
(This vessel is listed by Moss & Hume as a passenger ship, re-rated) Completed 31.3.1938, enlarged half sister of *Stirling Castle.* Troopship in Second World War carrying 164,000 troops over 484,000 miles. On release refitted for commercial service by H&W with accommodation for 244 first-class and 553 cabin/tourist-class passengers; returned to South Africa route. Severely damaged by an engine room explosion in 1960; repaired by H&W and returned to service. Broken up Italy (La Spezia) 1967.								
615	987	*Durban Castle*	14.6.1938	17,388	Passenger-Cargo	St/2Sc/Mv 560.0/76.0/37.0	3,284 nhp Dies H&W	Union-Castle Steamship Co. London
(This vessel is listed by Moss & Hume as a passenger ship, re-rated) Completed 15.12.1938, for round-Africa service. Troopship from September 1939. In 1941 transported King of Greece and family into exile. In 1942 became infantry landing ship equipped with 18 landing craft, saw extensive service in Mediterranean. Returned to commercial service 1946, but not refurbished until 1947. Broken up Germany (Hamburg) 1962.								
N/A	988	*Crossgar*	Pointhouse built					
N/A	989	*Leonora*	Pointhouse built					
N/A	990	*Comara*	Govan built					
N/A	991	*May*	Pointhouse built					
616	992	*Rochester Castle*	11.2.1937	7,795	Cargo Ship (Refrigerated)	St/Sc/Mv 457.1/63.3/34.3	1,642 nhp 7,500 bhp Dies H&W	Union-Castle Steamship Co. London
Completed 29.4.1937, first of four similar ships, enlarged versions of *Roslin Castle* type for UK–South Africa fruit trade. In August 1942 formed part of convoy sent to resupply Malta under Operation Pedestal, hit by two torpedoes from an E-boat, but one of only five ships out of 15 dispatched which actually reached Valetta. Due to damage sustained remained at Malta until December when made dash to Alexandria and from there to New York via Cape Town. In 1970 to Cypriot owners, Mavroleon Bros, renamed *Glenda* for final voyage to breakers; broken up China (Whampoa).								
617	993	*Roxburgh Castle*	25.3.1937	7,800	Cargo Ship (Refrigerated)	St/Sc/Mv 457.1/63.3/34.3	1,642 nhp 7,500 bhp Dies H&W	Union-Castle Steamship Co. London
Completed 26.6.1937, sister ship of *Rochester Castle.* In December 1940 damaged at Liverpool in German air raid; this happened again in May 1941. Sunk by submarine torpedo (*U-107*) off Ferraria Point, Azores, February 1943. No lives lost.								
618	994	*Torr Head*	25.2.1937	5,021	Cargo Ship	St/Sc/St 407.3/58.9/24.8	2,400 ihp TE (3Cy) + Exh Turb H&W	Ulster Steamship Co. Belfast
Completed 10.4.1937. In 1961 to Hong Kong owners, Haven Crest, renamed *Balboa.* Broken up Taiwan (Kaohsiung) 1967.								
619	995	*Leinster*	24.6.1937	4,302	Passenger Ferry	St/2Sc/Mv 353.0/50.2/14.6	1,347 nhp 5,100 bhp Dies H&W	British & Irish Steam Packet Co. Dublin
Completed 2.11.1937, by reputation the most comfortable ship on Dublin–Liverpool route. During war employed as hospital ship. In 1946 to Belfast SS Co., renamed *Ulster Prince,* employed on Belfast–Liverpool service. In 1968 to Greek owners, Epirotiki SS Co., renamed *Adria* and subsequently *Odysseus.* Broken up Faslane (UK) 1979.								
620	996	*Munster*	3.11.1937	4,302	Passenger Ferry	St/2Sc/Mv 353.0/50.2/14.6	1,347 nhp 5,100 bhp Dies H&W	British & Irish Steam Packet Co. Dublin
Completed 22.2.1938, sister ship of *Leinster* for same service. Sunk by submarine-laid mine (*U-30*) off Mersey, February 1940. No lives lost.								
N/A	997	*Lady Sylvia*	Pointhouse built					
N/A	998	*Donaghadee*	Pointhouse built					
N/A	999	*Lochavon*	Govan built					
621	1,000	HMS *Belfast*	17.3.1938	10,173	Cruiser	St/4Sc/St 613.6/63.4/21.3	80,000 shp Turb H&W?	Admiralty
Completed 3.8.1939, one of two members of Edinburgh class. Badly damaged by a submarine-laid mine (*U-21*) in November 1939, did not return to service until October 1942. Recommissioned for Korean War but planned modernisation in 1955–56 was shelved because of lack of dockyard capacity. In 1963 paid off and became flagship of reserve fleet at Portsmouth. Preserved as museum ship 1971.								

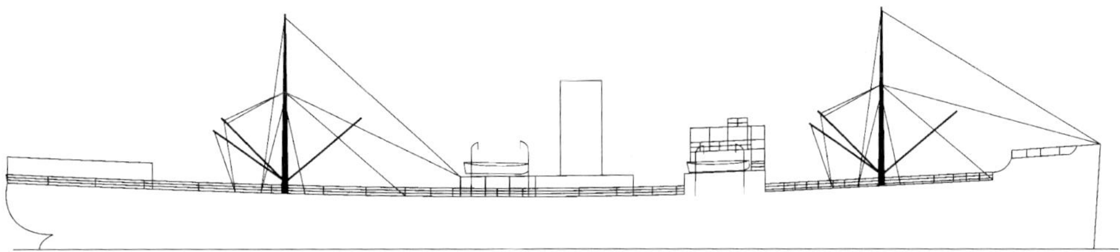

War Argus (H&W y/n 436) 1918 – 'G' type standard merchant ship (DH)

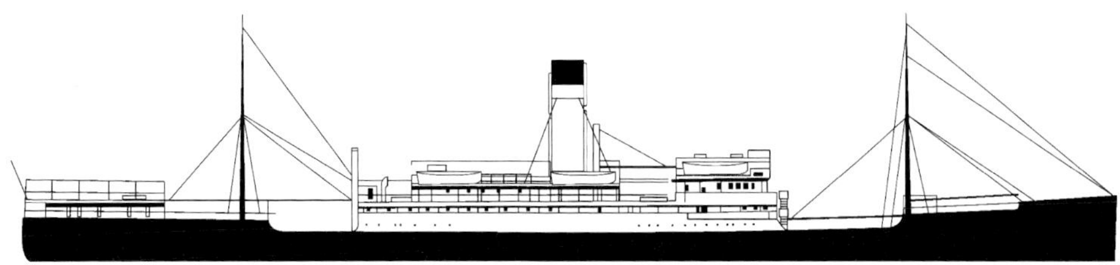

City of Venice (H&W y/n 468) 1924 (DH)

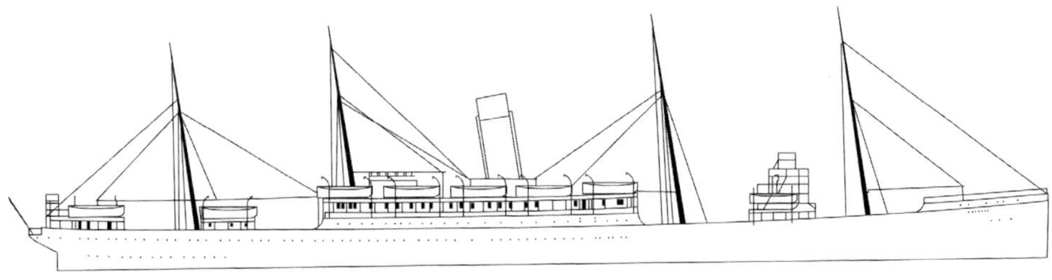

Pericles (H&W y/n 392) 1907 (DH)

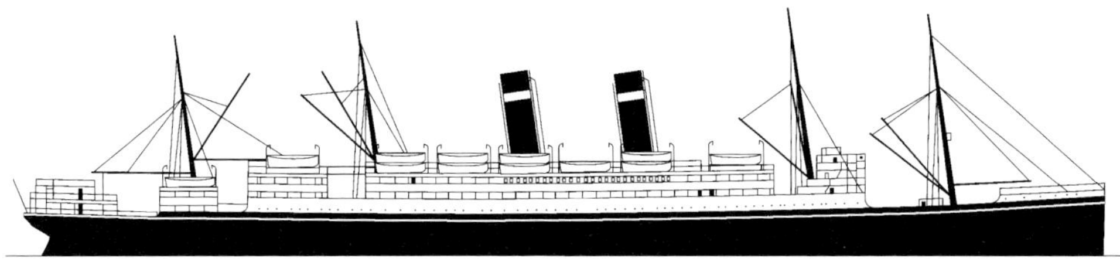

Lapland (H&W y/n 393) 1908 (DH)

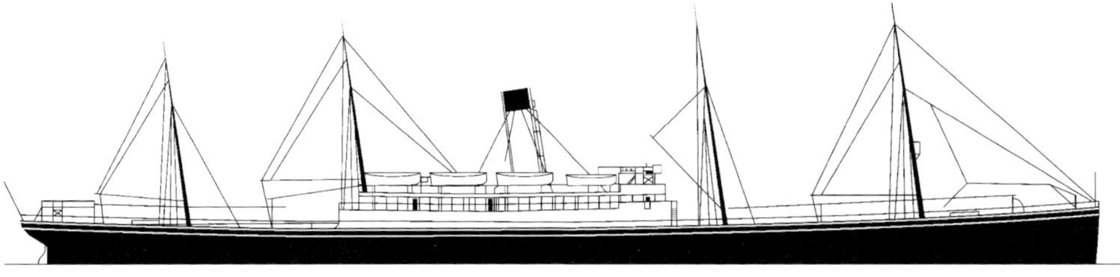

Winifreda (H&W y/n 319) 1897 (DH)

Ship	Yard No	Name	Date Launched	Displacement Tons	Type	Construction and Dimensions	Horse Power/ Engines	Owners
622	1,001	*Delane*	21.10.1937	6,054	Cargo Ship	St/Sc/Mv 438.6/62.3/25.4	898 nhp Dies H&W	Lamport & Holt Line Liverpool
Completed 17.1.1938. In 1954 to Blue Star Line, refrigeration equipment installed by H&W, renamed *Seattle Star.* In 1961 to Moroccan owners, Miniere & Metal, for £90,000, renamed *Kettara VI*, broken up Hong Kong 1961.								
623	1,002	*Devis*	21.12.1937	6,054	Cargo Ship	St/Sc/Mv 438.6/62.3/25.4	898 nhp Dies H&W	Lamport & Holt Line Liverpool
Completed 14.2.1938, sister ship of *Delane.* Sunk by submarine torpedo (*U-593*) off Algeria while transporting 289 Canadian troops for invasion of Sicily, July 1943. Fifty-two lives lost out of 343 on board.								
N/A	1,003	*Koolama*	Govan built					
624	1,004	*Waimarama*	31.5.1938	11,091	Cargo Ship (Refrigerated)	St/2Sc/Mv 515.0/70.0/43.4	2,463 nhp Dies H&W	Shaw Savill & Albion Co. London
Completed 6.10.1938. Sunk by air attack during attempt to reach Malta (Operation Pedestal), August 1942. Eighty-seven lives lost out of 107 on board.								
625	1,005	*Andes*	7.3.1939	25,688	Passenger Ship	St/2Sc/St 643.3/83.5/43.6	5,599 nhp 30,000 shp Turb H&W	Royal Mail Line London
Completed as troopship 24.9.1939. In 1947 returned to builders and rebuilt to original design with accommodation for 300 first-class and 200 second-class passengers. In 1959 became cruise ship with accommodation for 500 one-class passengers. Broken up Belgium (Ghent) 1971.								
626	1,006	*Pretoria Castle*	12.10.1938	17,382	Passenger-Cargo Ship	St/2Sc/Mv 560.0/76.0/37.0	3,281 nhp Dies H&W	Union-Castle Steamship Co. London
(This vessel is listed by Moss & Hume as a passenger ship, re-rated) Completed 18.4.1939, sister ship of *Durban Castle.* Made maiden voyage April 1939. Commissioned as armed merchant cruiser (6x 6in and 2x 12pdr AA). In 1942 bought outright by Admiralty and converted into aircraft carrier by Swan Hunter, commissioned in March 1943 for training purposes. Brought back by Union-Castle in 1946 and reconstructed to original plans, renamed *Warwick Castle.* Resumed service on South Africa routes. Broken up Spain (Barcelona) 1962.								
627	1,007	HMS *Formidable*	17.8.1939	28,094	Aircraft Carrier	St/3Sc/St 753.3/95.7/28.5	111,000 shp Turb H&W	Admiralty
Completed 24.11.1940, Illustrious-class fleet carrier, first such vessels to have fully armoured hangars, although this permitted only one hangar deck. Badly damaged by two bomb hits off Island of Scarpanto in Aegean, May 1941; out of action for six months. Later, while operating in Far East, seriously damaged by Kamikaze attack. As with most wartime carriers, increasingly obsolete post-war environment and never modernised. Broken up Inverkeithing (UK) 1953.								
N/A	1,008	*Donax*	Govan built					
N/A	1,009	*Dromus*	Govan built					
N/A	1,010	*British Fidelity*	Govan built					
N/A	1,011	*British Trust*	Govan built					
628	1,012	*Richmond Castle*	8.11.1938	7,798	Cargo Ship (Refrigerated)	St/Sc/Mv 457.4/63.3/34.3	1,643 nhp 7,500 bhp Dies H&W	Union-Castle Steamship Co. London
Completed 11.2.1939, sister ship of *Rochester Castle.* Sunk by submarine torpedo (*U-176*) SE of Cape Farewell, inbound Montevideo–Liverpool, August 1942. Fourteen lives lost out of 64 on board.								
629	1,013	*Rowallan Castle*	8.12.1938	7,798	Cargo Ship (Refrigerated)	St/Sc/Mv 457.4/63.3/34.3	1,643 nhp 7,500 bhp Dies H&W	Union-Castle Steamship Co. London
Completed 11.3.1939, sister ship of *Rochester Castle.* In February 1942 part of convoy MW9B Alexandria-Malta. Hit by German aircraft and disabled, taken in tow by destroyer it became clear was sinking and consequently scuttled.								
630	1,014	*Cairndale*	25.10.1938	8,129	Oil Tanker	St/Sc/Mv 465.6/59.5/33.9	502 nhp Dies H&W	Admiralty
Completed 26.1.1939, laid down for Anglo-Saxon/Shell Oil Co. as *Eraro.* Completed as Royal Fleet Auxiliary under this name. Sunk by submarine torpedo (Italian *Guglielmo Marconi*) 188m WSW of Gibraltar, May 1941. Four lives lost.								
N/A	1,015	*San Emiliano*	Govan built					

<table>
<tr><th>Ship</th><th>Yard No</th><th>Name</th><th>Date Launched</th><th>Displacement Tons</th><th>Type</th><th>Construction and Dimensions</th><th>Horse Power/ Engines</th><th>Owners</th></tr>
<tr><td>631</td><td>1,016</td><td>Wellington Star</td><td>20.4.1939</td><td>12,382</td><td>Cargo Ship (Refrigerated)</td><td>St/2Sc/Mv 534.4/70.3/32.3</td><td>2,463 nhp Dies H&W</td><td>Blue Star Line (Leyland & Co.) Liverpool</td></tr>
<tr><td colspan="9">Completed 24.8.1939, an enlarged version of Empire Star. Sunk by submarine torpedo (U-101) 300m W of Cape Finisterre, June 1940. No lives lost.</td></tr>
<tr><td>632</td><td>1,017</td><td>Auckland Star</td><td>20.6.1939</td><td>12,382</td><td>Cargo Ship (Refrigerated)</td><td>St/2Sc/Mv 535.1/70.3/32.3</td><td>2,463 nhp Dies H&W</td><td>Blue Star Line (Leyland & Co.) Liverpool</td></tr>
<tr><td colspan="9">Completed 4.11.1939, sister ship of Wellington Star. Sunk by submarine torpedo (U-99) 80m SW of Valentia Island, Co. Kerry, July 1940. No lives lost.</td></tr>
<tr><td>N/A</td><td>1,018</td><td>Bangalow</td><td colspan="6">Govan built</td></tr>
<tr><td>633</td><td>1,019</td><td>Waiotira</td><td>1.8.1939</td><td>11,102</td><td>Cargo Ship (Refrigerated)</td><td>St/2Sc/Mv 516.9/70.4/32.3</td><td>2,463 hp Dies H&W</td><td>Shaw Savill & Albion Co. London</td></tr>
<tr><td colspan="9">(This vessel is listed by Moss & Hume and a passenger-cargo ship, re-rated)
Completed 24.11.1939, a near sister of Waimarama. Damaged by submarine torpedo (U-95) and subsequently finished off by torpedo from another (U-38) near Rockall, inbound Sydney–UK, December 1940. One life lost.</td></tr>
<tr><td>N/A</td><td>1,020</td><td>Theodor Woker</td><td colspan="6">Pointhouse built</td></tr>
<tr><td>N/A</td><td>1,021</td><td>Watermeyer</td><td colspan="6">Pointhouse built</td></tr>
<tr><td>N/A</td><td>1,022</td><td>Degei</td><td colspan="6">Pointhouse built</td></tr>
<tr><td>634</td><td>1,023</td><td>HMS Adamant</td><td>30.11.1940</td><td>12,500</td><td>Submarine Depot Ship</td><td>St/2Sc/St 658.0/70.5/21.3</td><td>8,000 shp Turb H&W</td><td>Admiralty</td></tr>
<tr><td colspan="9">Completed 28.2.1942, an enlarged version of the previous Tyne class, well armed and designed to withstand torpedo attacks. On completion became depot ship of the 4th Submarine Flotilla in Far East and Australian until 1950. From 1954 to 1962 was base ship of 3rd Submarine Flotilla on Clyde. From 1964 attached to 2nd Submarine Flotilla at Devonport. Broken up Inverkeithing (UK) 1970.</td></tr>
<tr><td>N/A</td><td>1,024</td><td>Lincoln Castle</td><td colspan="6">Pointhouse built</td></tr>
<tr><td>635</td><td>1,025</td><td>Pardo</td><td>21.5.1940</td><td>5,400</td><td>Cargo Ship (Refrigerated)</td><td>St/Sc/Mv 433.3/61.3/22.7</td><td>1,236 nhp 6,000 bhp Dies H&W</td><td>Royal Mail Line London</td></tr>
<tr><td colspan="9">Completed 15.8.1940. In 1965 to Greek owners, M.A. Karageorgis, renamed Aristarchos. Broken up Taiwan (Kaohsiung) 1967.</td></tr>
<tr><td>636</td><td>1,026</td><td>Potaro</td><td>4.9.1940</td><td>5,409</td><td>Cargo Ship (Refrigerated)</td><td>St/Sc/Mv 433.3/61.3/22.7</td><td>1,236 nhp 6,000 bhp Dies H&W</td><td>Royal Mail Line London</td></tr>
<tr><td colspan="9">Completed 19.11.1940, sister ship of Pardo. In 1965 to Greek owners, M.A. Karageorgis, renamed Aristipos. Broken up China (Shanghai) 1970.</td></tr>
<tr><td>637</td><td>1,027</td><td>Pampas</td><td>2.11.1940</td><td>5,415</td><td>Cargo Ship (Refrigerated)</td><td>St/Sc/Mv 433.3/61.3/22.7</td><td>1,236 nhp 6,000 bhp Dies H&W</td><td>Royal Mail Line London</td></tr>
<tr><td colspan="9">Completed 23.1.1941, sister ship of Pardo. Sunk in air attack, Malta, April 1942.</td></tr>
<tr><td>638</td><td>1,028</td><td>Palma</td><td>14.1.1941</td><td>5,419</td><td>Cargo Ship (Refrigerated)</td><td>St/Sc/Mv 433.3/61.3/22.7</td><td>1,236 nhp 6,000 bhp Dies H&W</td><td>Royal Mail Line London</td></tr>
<tr><td colspan="9">Completed 2.4.1941, sister ship of Pardo, laid down as Pelotas but launched under this name. In July 1941 attacked in North Atlantic (U-95); after two torpedoes missed, U-boat surfaced and began to use its gun. After scoring three hits, this malfunctioned and Palma escaped. Sunk by submarine torpedo (U-183) off Ceylon, February 1944. Seven lives lost.</td></tr>
<tr><td>639</td><td>1,029</td><td>Debrett</td><td>23.3.1940</td><td>8,104</td><td>Cargo Ship</td><td>St/Sc/Mv 438.8/62.3/33.9</td><td>898 nhp Dies H&W</td><td>Lamport & Holt Line Liverpool</td></tr>
<tr><td colspan="9">Completed 23.5.1940. In 1955 to Blue Star Line, renamed Washington Star. In 1956 reverted to Lamport & Holt and original name. In 1964 badly damaged by an engine room fire; to Greek owners, Embajada, renamed Ambasciata, but not repaired; broken up Japan (Osaka) 1964.</td></tr>
<tr><td>640</td><td>1,030</td><td>Defoe</td><td>20.6.1940</td><td>8,102</td><td>Cargo Ship</td><td>St/Sc/Mv 438.8/62.3/33.9</td><td>898 nhp Dies H&W</td><td>Lamport & Holt Line Liverpool</td></tr>
<tr><td colspan="9">Completed 30.8.1940, sister ship of Debrett. Abandoned when cargo of liquid chlorine, aircraft lacquer and explosives caught fire and exploded off Rockall, September 1942.</td></tr>
</table>

Ship	Yard No	Name	Date Launched	Displacement Tons	Type	Construction and Dimensions	Horse Power/ Engines	Owners
641	1,031	HMS *Unicorn*	20.11.1941	14,750	Aircraft Maintenance Carrier	St/2Sc/St 646.0/90.0/24.0	40,000 shp Turb H&W	Admiralty
Completed 12.3.1943, employed as light fleet carrier operating 35 aircraft. By the end of the war obsolete as an aircraft carrier and not modernised. In 1949 commissioned to transport aircraft and stores to the Far East in support of aircraft carrier *Triumph* and saw service during Korean War. Decommissioned to reserve 1953. Broken up Dalmuir (UK) 1959.								
N/A	1,032	*Lavington Court*	Govan built					
N/A	1,033	*Novelist*	Govan built					
642	1,034	*Araybank*	6.6.1940	7,258	Cargo Ship	St/Sc/Mv 433.2/57.3/33.6	490 nhp 6,250 bhp Dies H&W	Andrew Weir & Co. Glasgow
Completed 24.10.1940. Bombed and sunk by German aircraft Suda Bay, Crete, May 1941. In 1947 salvaged and repaired. In 1948 to Italian owners, A. Lauro, renamed *Napoli*. Employed as an immigrant carrier initially to Australia and later to South America. In 1960 converted into cargo vessel. Broken up Italy (La Spezia) 1971.								
643	1,035	*Shirrabank*	20.7.1940	7,274	Cargo Ship	St/Sc/Mv 433.2/57.3/33.6	490 nhp 6,250 bhp Dies H&W	Andrew Weir & Co. Glasgow
Completed 5.12.1940, sister ship of *Araybank*. Broken up Hong Kong 1963.								
644	1,036	*Fanad Head*	3.9.1940	5,038	Cargo Ship	St/Sc/St 407.3/58.9/24.8	432 nhp TE (3Cy) + Exh Turb H&W	Ulster Steamship Co. Belfast
Completed 19.12.1940. In 1961 to Panamanian owners, Wallem & Co., renamed *Bogota*. Broken up Hong Kong 1965.								
N/A	1,037	HMS *Elm*	Pointhouse built					
N/A	1,038	HMS *Fir*	Pointhouse built					
N/A	1,039	HMS *Bangor*	Govan built					
N/A	1,040	HMS *Blackpool*	Govan built					
N/A	1,041	HMS *Coreopsis*	Pointhouse built					
N/A	1,042	HMS *Crocus*	Pointhouse built					
N/A	1,043	*Vipya*	Pointhouse built					
N/A	1,044	*Dingdale*	Govan built					
N/A	1,045	*Empire Gem*	Govan built					
N/A	1,046	HMS *Black Ranger*	Govan Built					
N/A	1,047	HMS *Blue Ranger*	Govan built					
N/A	1,048	HMS *Brown Ranger*	Govan built					
645	1,049	HMS *Black Prince*	27.8.1942	5,950	Cruiser	St/4Sc/St 485.0/50.5/17.8	62,000 shp Turb H&W	Admiralty
Completed 20.11.1943, Bellona-class light cruiser. Loaned to New Zealand Navy 1948–56. Broken up Japan 1962.								
646	1,050	*Empire Hope*	27.3.1941	12,688	Cargo Ship (Refrigerated)	St/2Sc/Mv 535.1/70.3/32.3	2,472 nhp Dies H&W	Ministry of Supply
Completed 22.10.1941, repeat of Wellington Star type. In August 1942 was part of convoy WS21, with a cargo of kerosene, coal and explosives when attacked by German aircraft and disabled by 18 near misses and two direct hits; the crew abandoned ship. That night hit by a torpedo from the Italian submarine *Bronzo* but did not sink. Eventually wreck scuttled by British naval ships off Galeta Island.								
647	1,051	*Empire Grace*	25.8.1941	13,478	Cargo Ship (Refrigerated)	St/2Sc/Mv 521.4/70.4/40.5	2,472 nhp Dies H&W	Ministry of Supply
Completed 1.4.1942, near sister of *Empire Hope*. In 1946 to Shaw Savill & Albion, renamed *Wairangi*. Ran aground near Stockholm, August 1963; refloated but not repaired. Broken up Faslane (UK).								

<table>
<tr><th>Ship</th><th>Yard No</th><th>Name</th><th>Date Launched</th><th>Displacement Tons</th><th>Type</th><th>Construction and Dimensions</th><th>Horse Power/ Engines</th><th>Owners</th></tr>
<tr><td>648</td><td>1,052</td><td>Derwentdale</td><td>12.4.1941</td><td>8,398</td><td>Landing Craft Carrier</td><td>St/Sc/Mv
465.6/59.5/34.0</td><td>670 nhp
Dies
J.G. Kincaid
& Co.
Grennock</td><td>Admiralty</td></tr>
<tr><td colspan="9">Completed 30.8.1941, an RFA tanker converted on stocks into landing ship (gantry) capable of carrying 257 combat troops and 15 LCM(1) landing craft and launching them with loads of up to 10 tons. Sold to merchant service 1960, J.D. Irving, renamed Irvingdale I. Broken up Spain (El Ferrol) 1966.</td></tr>
<tr><td>649</td><td>1,053</td><td>Empire Diamond</td><td>10.7.1941</td><td>8,236</td><td>Oil Tanker</td><td>St/Sc/Mv
465.6/59.5/34.0</td><td>502 nhp
Dies
H&W</td><td>Ministry of Supply</td></tr>
<tr><td colspan="9">A new type of tanker of fairly basic design sometimes called the Ocean type.
Completed 12.11.1941. In 1942 to Norwegian government, renamed Norsol. In 1946 to Norwegian commercial owners, Aktieselskaper Kollbiorg, renamed Kollbjorg. In 1956 to Swedish ownership, A.F. Andersson, renamed Storo. Broken up Hong Kong 1959.</td></tr>
<tr><td>N/A</td><td>1,054</td><td>HMS Rumba</td><td colspan="6">Pointhouse built</td></tr>
<tr><td>N/A</td><td>1,055</td><td>HMS Sarabande</td><td colspan="6">Pointhouse built</td></tr>
<tr><td>N/A</td><td>1,056</td><td>HMS Spirea</td><td colspan="6">Pointhouse built</td></tr>
<tr><td>N/A</td><td>1,057</td><td>HMS Starwort</td><td colspan="6">Pointhouse built</td></tr>
<tr><td>650</td><td>1,058</td><td>HMS Arabis</td><td>14.2.1940</td><td>1,170</td><td>Corvette</td><td>St/Sc/St
205.0/33.2/15.0</td><td>2,750 ihp
VTE (4Cy)
H&W</td><td>Admiralty</td></tr>
<tr><td colspan="9">The Flower-class corvettes were based on a sketch design prepared by Smith's Dock based on their pre-war whale catcher Southern Pride. Ordered in large numbers from British and Canadian yards under the 1939–40 and War Emergency building programmes. They varied considerably in terms of armament and construction but were primarily anti-submarine vessels. They formed a vital element in the British convoy system early in the war. H&W were to build no fewer than 34 of these vessels in Belfast and orders for another six were cancelled as more efficient designs became available.
Laid down 30 October 1939 and completed on 5 April 1940 (158 days); such rapid construction was typical of this class. In 1942 to US Navy, renamed Saucy. Returned to RN in 1947 and given name Snapdragon. In 1947 to commercial use, Albatros Nav. Co., renamed Katina. In 1950 to Egyptian owners, F. Awad, renamed Tewfik. Broken up Italy (Le Grazie) 1964.</td></tr>
<tr><td>651</td><td>1,059</td><td>HMS Periwinkle</td><td>24.2.1940</td><td>1,170</td><td>Corvette</td><td>St/Sc/St
205.0/33.2/15.0</td><td>2,750 ihp
VTE (4Cy)
H&W</td><td>Admiralty</td></tr>
<tr><td colspan="9">Completed 8.4.1940, sister ship of Arabis. In 1942 to US Navy, renamed Restless. In 1946 to commercial use and Hong Kong owners, Wheelock Marden, renamed Perilock. Broken up Hong Kong 1953.</td></tr>
<tr><td>652</td><td>1,060</td><td>HMS Clarkia</td><td>7.3.1940</td><td>1,170</td><td>Corvette</td><td>St/Sc/St
205.0/33.2/15.0</td><td>2,750 ihp
VTE (4Cy)
H&W</td><td>Admiralty</td></tr>
<tr><td colspan="9">Completed 22.4.1940, sister ship of Arabis. Broken up Hayle (UK) 1947.</td></tr>
<tr><td>653</td><td>1,061</td><td>HMS Calendula</td><td>21.3.1940</td><td>1,170</td><td>Corvette</td><td>St/Sc/St
205.0/33.2/15.0</td><td>2,750 ihp
VTE (4Cy)
H&W</td><td>Admiralty</td></tr>
<tr><td colspan="9">Completed 6.5.1940, sister ship of Arabis. In 1942 to US Navy, renamed Ready; returned to RN 1945, reverted to original name. In 1946 to commercial use, Spanish owners, Zubi Sg Co., renamed Villa Cisneros. In 1949 to Africana Fisheries, renamed Villa Bens. In 1965 taken over by Spanish Army; still in existence 1968, final fate is unknown.</td></tr>
<tr><td>654</td><td>1,062</td><td>HMS Hibiscus</td><td>6.4.1940</td><td>1,170</td><td>Corvette</td><td>St/Sc/St
205.0/33.2/15.0</td><td>2,750 ihp
VTE (4Cy)
H&W</td><td>Admiralty</td></tr>
<tr><td colspan="9">Completed 21.5.1940, sister ship of Arabis. In 1942 to US Navy, renamed Spry. Returned to RN 1945, reverted to original name. In 1948 to commercial use, Greek owners, J.P. Hadoulis, renamed Madonna. Broken up Hong Kong 1955.</td></tr>
<tr><td>655</td><td>1,063</td><td>HMS Heartsease</td><td>20.4.1940</td><td>1,170</td><td>Corvette</td><td>St/Sc/St
205.0/33.2/15.0</td><td>2,750 ihp
VTE (4Cy)
H&W</td><td>Admiralty</td></tr>
<tr><td colspan="9">Completed 4.6.1940, sister ship of Arabis, laid down as Pansy but completed under this name. In 1942 to US Navy, renamed Courage; returned to RN 1945, reverted to original name. In 1951 to commercial use, Norwegian owners, Giertsen & Co., renamed Roskva. In 1956 to S. Jansen, renamed Douglas. In 1958 to Carrara & Co., renamed Seabird. Sunk by government aircraft while engaged in gun running to rebel forces in Western Sumatra, December 1958.</td></tr>
</table>

Ship	Yard No	Name	Date Launched	Displacement Tons	Type	Construction and Dimensions	Horse Power/ Engines	Owners
656	1,064	HMS *Camellia*	4.5.1940	1,170	Corvette	St/Sc/St 205.0/33.2/15.0	2,750 ihp VTE (4Cy) H&W	Admiralty
Completed 18.6.1940, sister ship of *Arabis.* In 1948 to commercial use, South African owners, Vinke & Sons, renamed *Hetty W. Vinke.* Broken up South Africa (Cape Town) 1969.								
657	1,065	HMS *Mallow*	22.5.1940	1,170	Corvette	St/Sc/St 205.0/33.2/15.0	2,750 ihp VTE (4Cy) H&W	Admiralty
Completed 2.7.1940, sister ship of *Arabis.* In 1944 to Yugoslavian Navy, renamed *Nada* and later (1945*) Partizanka.* Returned to RN reverted to original name. To Egyptian Navy 1948, renamed *El Sudan.* Used as training ship from *c.* 1970, deleted 1975.								
658	1,066	HMS *Peony*	4.6.1940	1,170	Corvette	St/Sc/St 205.0/33.2/15.0	2,750 ihp VTE (4Cy) H&W	Admiralty
Completed 2.8.1940, sister ship of *Arabis.* In 1943 to Greek Navy, renamed *Sakhtouris.* Returned to RN 1951 reverted to original name. Broken up Dunston (UK) 1952.								
659	1,067	HMS *Erica*	18.6.1940	1,170	Corvette	St/Sc/St 205.0/33.2/15.0	2,750 ihp VTE (4Cy) H&W	Admiralty
Completed 9.8.1940, sister ship of *Arabis.* Sunk by submarine-laid mine (HMS *Rorqual,* laid July 1941) off Libyan coast while escorting convoy Benghazi–Alexandria, February 1943. No lives Lost.								
660	1,068	HMS *Gloxinia*	2.7.1940	1,170	Corvette	St/Sc/St 205.0/33.2/15.0	2,750 ihp VTE (4Cy) H&W	Admiralty
Completed 22.8.1940, sister ship of *Arabis.* Broken up Purfleet (UK) 1947.								
661	1,069	HMS *Picotee*	19.7.1940	1,170	Corvette	St/Sc/St 205.0/33.2/15.0	2,750 ihp VTE (4Cy) H&W	Admiralty
Completed 5.9.1940, sister ship of *Arabis.* Sunk by submarine torpedo (*U-568*) near Iceland, August 1941. Sixty-six lives lost (no survivors).								
662	1,070	HMS *Gentian*	6.8.1940	1,170	Corvette	St/Sc/St 205.0/33.2/15.0	2,750 ihp VTE (4Cy) H&W	Admiralty
Completed 20.9.1940, sister ship of *Arabis.* Broken up Purfleet (UK) 1947.								
663	1,071	HMS *Hyacinth*	19.8.1940	1,170	Corvette	St/Sc/St 205.0/33.2/15.0	2,750 ihp VTE (4Cy) H&W	Admiralty
Completed 3.10.1940, sister ship of *Arabis.* In 1943 to Greek Navy, renamed *Apostolis.* Broken up Italy 1961.								
664	1,072	HMS *Rhododendron*	2.9.1940	1,170	Corvette	St/Sc/St 205.0/33.2/15.0	2,750 ihp VTE (4Cy) H&W	Admiralty
Completed 18.10.1940, sister ship of *Arabis.* In 1950 to commercial use, South African owners, Vinke & Sons, renamed *Maj Vinke.* Broken up South Africa (Cape Town) 1968.								
665	1,073	HMS *Heather*	17.9.1940	1,170	Corvette	St/Sc/St 205.0/33.2/15.0	2,750 ihp VTE (4Cy) H&W	Admiralty
Completed 1.11.1940, sister ship of *Arabis.* Broken up Grays (UK) 1947.								
666	1,074	HMS *Freesia*	3.10.1940	1,170	Corvette	St/Sc/St 205.0/33.2/15.0	2,750 ihp VTE (4Cy) H&W	Admiralty
Completed 19.11.1940, sister ship of *Arabis.* In 1946 to commercial use, Hong Kong owners, Wheelock Marden, renamed *Freelock.* Wrecked San Jorge, April 1947, being towed London–Shanghai.								
667	1,075	HMS *Orchis*	15.10.1940	1,170	Corvette	St/Sc/St 205.0/33.2/15.0	2,750 ihp VTE (4Cy) H&W	Admiralty
Completed 29.11.1940, sister ship of *Arabis.* On 15 August 1944 sank *U-741* while escorting invasion convoy during D-Day operations, 48 crew killed and one survivor. On 21st mined off Normandy and lost after beached.								

Ship	Yard No	Name	Date Launched	Displacement Tons	Type	Construction and Dimensions	Horse Power/ Engines	Owners
668	1,076	HMS *Kingcup*	31.10.1940	1,170	Corvette	St/Sc/St 205.0/33.2/15.0	2,750 ihp VTE (4Cy) H&W	Admiralty
Completed 3.1.1941, sister ship of *Arabis.* In 1946 to commercial use, Belgian owners, J. Cockerill, renamed *Rubis.* In 1954 to Seismograph Service, renamed *Seislim.* Broken up Belgium (Utrecht) 1959.								
669	1,077	HMS *Pimpernel*	16.11.1940	1,170	Corvette	St/Sc/St 205.0/33.2/15.0	2,750 ihp VTE (4Cy) H&W	Admiralty
Completed 9.1.1941, sister ship of *Arabis.* Broken up Portaferry (UK) 1948.								
670	1,078	*Dinsdale*	21.10.1941	8,214	Oil Tanker	St/Sc/Mv 465.6/59.5/33.8	502 nhp Dies H&W	Admiralty
Completed 11.4.1942, sister ship of *Empire Diamond*, laid down as *Empire Norseman* but completed with this name as a naval auxiliary. Sunk by submarine torpedo (Italian Commandante Cappellini) in South Atlantic, May 1942. Thirteen lives lost.								
671	1,079	*Empire Spenser*	17.2.1942	8,194	Oil Tanker	St/Sc/Mv 465.6/59.5/33.8	502 nhp Dies H&W	Ministry of Supply
Completed 29.9.1942, sister ship of *Empire Diamond.* Sunk by submarine torpedo (*U-524*) on maiden voyage North Atlantic, December 1942. One life lost.								
672	1,080	*Empire Chapman*	17.1.1942	8,194	Oil Tanker	St/Sc/Mv 465.6/59.5/33.8	502 nhp Dies H&W	Ministry of Supply
Completed 25.6.1942, sister ship of *Empire Diamond.* In 1946 to British Tanker Co., renamed *British Commando.* Broken up Belgium (Bruges) 1959.								
673	1,081	*Empire Fletcher*	4.4.1942	8,194	Oil Tanker	St/Sc/Mv 465.6/59.5/33.8	502 nhp Dies H&W	Ministry of Supply
Completed 31.7.1942, sister ship of *Empire Diamond.* In 1944 to Dutch government, renamed *Backhuysen.* In 1946 to Royal Dutch/Shell, renamed *Chama.* In 1955 to Panamanian owners, Dema Compagnia Navigazione SA, renamed *Anastasia.* Broken up Italy (Savona) 1959.								
674	1,082	*Deseado*	17.3.1942	9,641	Cargo Ship (Refrigerated)	St/2Sc/Mv 453.3/65.3/35.3	1,803 nhp 9,600 bhp Dies H&W	Royal Mail Line London
Completed 28.11.1942. Broken up Germany (Hamburg) 1968.								
N/A	1,083	*Empire Onyx*	Govan built					
N/A	1,084	HMS *Romeo*	Pointhouse built					
N/A	1,085	HMS *Rosalind*	Pointhouse built					
N/A	1,086	HMS *Oxlip*	Pointhouse built					
N/A	1,087	HMS *Pennywort*	Pointhouse built					
N/A	1,088	*Empire Gat*	Pointhouse built					
N/A	1,089	*Empire Spinney*	Pointhouse built					
675	1,090	*San Veronico*	30.5.1942	8,189	Oil Tanker	St/Sc/Mv 465.6/59.5/33.8	502 nhp Dies H&W	Eagle Oil & Shipping Co. London
Completed 31.12.1942, sister ship of *Empire Diamond.* Broken up Germany (Hamburg) 1964.								
676	1,091	HMS *Campania*	17.6.1943	12,450	Aircraft Carrier	St/2Sc/Mv 540.0/70.0/22.8	10,700 bhp Dies H&W	Admiralty
Completed 7.3.1944, escort carrier based on a merchant ship taken over on stocks (refrigerated cargo vessel for Shaw Savill & Albion). Could operate 18 aircraft; obsolete by end of war and could not be modernised. In the late 1940s re-rated as a ferry carrier. In 1951 was converted into a floating exhibition for Festival of Britain. In 1952 acted as transport and accommodation ship in support of the British nuclear tests at Monte Bello Islands. Laid up 1952. Broken up Blyth (UK) 1955.								
N/A	1,092	*Empire Shoal*	Govan built					
N/A	1,093	*Empire Ballantyne*	Govan built					
N/A	1,094	*Empire Bede*	Govan built					

<table>
<tr><th>Ship</th><th>Yard No</th><th>Name</th><th>Date Launched</th><th>Displacement Tons</th><th>Type</th><th>Construction and Dimensions</th><th>Horse Power/ Engines</th><th>Owners</th></tr>
<tr><td>677</td><td>1,095</td><td>HMS Abelia</td><td>28.11.1940</td><td>1,170</td><td>Corvette</td><td>St/Sc/St
205.0/33.2/15.0</td><td>2,750 ihp
VTE (4Cy)
H&W</td><td>Admiralty</td></tr>
<tr><td colspan="9">In 1939 the French Navy ordered a large number of Flower-class corvettes. Only a few were delivered before the fall of France and the remainder were taken over by Royal Navy. Abelia was one of these.
Completed 3.2.1941, sister ship of Arabis. In 1947 to commercial use, Norwegian owners, A. van der Lippe, converted into whale catcher, renamed Kraft. In 1954 to A. Jahre, renamed Arne Skontorp. Broken up Norway (Grimstad) 1966.</td></tr>
<tr><td>678</td><td>1,096</td><td>HMS Alisma</td><td>17.12.1940</td><td>1,170</td><td>Corvette</td><td>St/Sc/St
205.0/33.2/15.0</td><td>2,750 ihp
VTE (4Cy)
H&W</td><td>Admiralty</td></tr>
<tr><td colspan="9">Completed 13.2.1941, sister ship of Arabis, ordered by French as Pertuisane but completed under this name. In 1948 to commercial use, Indian owners, Memsabe Maritime, renamed Laconia. In 1950 to Greek owners, K. Samartzopoulos, renamed Constantine S. In 1952 to D. Efthimiou, renamed Parnon. Foundered July 1954 on voyage Marseilles–Eleusis.</td></tr>
<tr><td>679</td><td>1,097</td><td>HMS Anchusa</td><td>15.1.1941</td><td>1,170</td><td>Corvette</td><td>St/Sc/St
205.0/33.2/15.0</td><td>2,750 ihp
VTE (4Cy)
H&W</td><td>Admiralty</td></tr>
<tr><td colspan="9">Completed 1.3.1941, sister ship of Arabis. Ordered by French Navy but completed for RN. In 1949 to commercial use, Indian Ocean Trading Co., renamed Silverlord. In 1954 to G. O'Brian Davis, renamed Sir Edgar. Foundered off Port Louis, January 1960. Wreck subsequently broken up in Mauritius.</td></tr>
<tr><td>680</td><td>1,098</td><td>HMS Armeria</td><td>16.1.1941</td><td>1,170</td><td>Corvette</td><td>St/Sc/St
205.0/33.2/15.0</td><td>2,750 ihp
VTE (4Cy)
H&W</td><td>Admiralty</td></tr>
<tr><td colspan="9">Completed 28.3.1941, sister ship of Arabis, ordered by French Navy but completed for RN. In 1948 to commercial use, French owners, Faralon Nav., renamed Deppie. In 1950 to Italian owners, Scotto Ambrosino P., renamed Canastel. In 1952 to Chilean owners, Salvo & Fontaine, renamed Rio Blanco. In 1955 to H. Ossa, renamed Lilian. Broken up Chile 1961.</td></tr>
<tr><td>681</td><td>1,099</td><td>HMS Aster</td><td>12.2.1941</td><td>1,170</td><td>Corvette</td><td>St/Sc/St
205.0/33.2/15.0</td><td>2,750 ihp
VTE (4Cy)
H&W</td><td>Admiralty</td></tr>
<tr><td colspan="9">Completed 11.4.1941, sister ship of Arabis. Broken up Bo'ness 1946.</td></tr>
<tr><td>682</td><td>1,100</td><td>HMS Bergamot</td><td>15.2.1941</td><td>1,170</td><td>Corvette</td><td>St/Sc/St
205.0/33.2/15.0</td><td>2,750 ihp
VTE (4Cy)
H&W</td><td>Admiralty</td></tr>
<tr><td colspan="9">Completed 9.5.1941, sister ship of Arabis, ordered by French Navy but completed for RN. To Greek government 1947, converted to merchant ship, renamed Syros. In 1951 to Greek owners, Kovounides Sg Co., renamed Delphini and Ekaterini (1955). Broken up Greece (Perama) 1974.</td></tr>
<tr><td>683</td><td>1,101</td><td>HMS Vervain</td><td>12.3.1941</td><td>1,170</td><td>Corvette</td><td>St/Sc/St
205.0/33.2/15.0</td><td>2,750 ihp
VTE (4Cy)
H&W</td><td>Admiralty</td></tr>
<tr><td colspan="9">Completed 9.6.1941, sister ship of Arabis, originally Broom, completed under this name. Sunk by submarine torpedo (U-1276) 25nm SE of Dungarvin, Ireland, February 1945. Sixty-one lives lost out of 94 on board. Shortly afterwards U-boat sunk by HMS Amethyst. Forty-nine lives lost.</td></tr>
<tr><td>684</td><td>1,102</td><td>HMS Bryony</td><td>15.3.1941</td><td>1,170</td><td>Corvette</td><td>St/Sc/St
205.0/33.2/15.0</td><td>2,750 ihp
VTE (4Cy)
H&W</td><td>Admiralty</td></tr>
<tr><td colspan="9">Completed 16.6.1942, sister ship of Arabis, completion delayed by serious damage during air raid May 1941. To Norwegian government 1947, converted to weather ship, renamed Polarfront II. Broken up 1980.</td></tr>
<tr><td>685</td><td>1,103</td><td>HMS Buttercup</td><td>10.4.1941</td><td>1,170</td><td>Corvette</td><td>St/Sc/St
205.0/33.2/15.0</td><td>2,750 ihp
VTE (4Cy)
H&W</td><td>Admiralty</td></tr>
<tr><td colspan="9">Completed 24.4.1942, sister ship of Arabis. Completion delayed by serious damage during air raid May 1941. To Norwegian Navy 1946, renamed Nordkyn. In 1958 to T. Dahl, renamed Thoris. Broken up Norway (Grimstad) 1970.</td></tr>
<tr><td>686</td><td>1,104</td><td>FNFL Commandant Drogou</td><td>11.4.1941</td><td>1,170</td><td>Corvette</td><td>St/Sc/St
205.0/33.2/15.0</td><td>2,750 ihp
VTE (4Cy)
H&W</td><td>French Navy</td></tr>
<tr><td colspan="9">Completed 26.1.1942, sister ship of Arabis, originally Chrysanthemum, completed for Free French Navy under this name. Completion delayed by serious damage during an air raid May 1941. In 1948 to United Whalers, renamed Terje X. In 1959 to Portuguese Navy, renamed Carvalho Araujo. Stricken 1975.</td></tr>
<tr><td>687</td><td>1,105</td><td>HMS Cowslip</td><td>28.5.1941</td><td>1,170</td><td>Corvette</td><td>St/Sc/St
205.0/33.2/15.0</td><td>2,750 ihp
VTE (4Cy)
H&W</td><td>Admiralty</td></tr>
<tr><td colspan="9">Completed 9.8.1941, sister ship of Arabis. Broken up Troon (UK) 1949.</td></tr>
</table>

Ship	Yard No	Name	Date Launched	Displacement Tons	Type	Construction and Dimensions	Horse Power/ Engines	Owners
688	1,106	HMS *Eglantine*	11.6.1941	1,170	Corvette	St/Sc/St 205.0/33.2/15.0	2,750 ihp VTE (4Cy) H&W	Admiralty
Completed 27.8.1941, sister ship of *Arabis*. To Norwegian Navy 1946, renamed *Soroy*. To Norwegian commercial owners, T. Dahl 1957, renamed *Thorglimt*. Broken up Norway (Grimstad) 1970.								
689	1,107	HMS *Fritillary*	22.7.1941	1,170	Corvette	St/Sc/St 205.0/33.2/15.0	2,750 ihp VTE (4Cy) H&W	Admiralty
Completed 31.10.1941, sister ship of *Arabis*. In 1947 to commercial use, Indian owners, Memsabe Maritime, renamed *Andria*. In 1949 to Air, Steamer & General, renamed *V.O. Chidambaram*. Broken up India (Bombay) 1955.								
690	1,108	HMS *Genista*	24.7.1941	1,170	Corvette	St/Sc/St 205.0/33.2/15.0	2,750 ihp VTE (4Cy) H&W	Admiralty
Completed 18.12.1941, sister ship of *Arabis*. In 1952 converted to weather ship, renamed *Weather Recorder*. Broken up Belgium (Antwerp) 1961.								
N/A	1,109	HMS *Gloriosa*	Cancelled					
N/A	1,110	HMS *Harebell*	Cancelled					
N/A	1,111	HMS *Hemlock*	Cancelled					
N/A	1,112	HMS *Ivy*	Cancelled					
N/A	1,113	HMS *Ling*	Cancelled					
N/A	1,114	HMS *Marjoram*	Cancelled					
N/A	1,115	*Empire Deep*	Govan built					
N/A	1,116	*British Vigilance*	Govan built					
N/A	1,117	*British Merit*	Govan built					
691	1,118	*Empire Sidney*	4.9.1941	6,942	Standard 'X'-type Cargo Ship	St/Sc/Mv 432.9/56.3/34.3	489 nhp 3,300 bhp Dies H&W	Ministry of Transport
Completed 7.5.1942. In 1943 to Dutch government, renamed *Van Der Helst*. In 1947 to commercial Dutch owners, Java-China-Japan Co., renamed *Tjimenteng*. In 1963 to Greek owners, A. Halcoussis & Co., renamed *Diamandis*. Broken up Spain (Cartagena) 1970.								
692	1,119	*Empire Splendour*	18.12.1941	7,335	Standard 'D'-type Cargo Ship	St/Sc/Mv 431.9/57.3/33.6	490 nhp 2,650 bhp Dies H&W	Ministry of Transport
Completed 1.9.1942. In 1946 to Holt & Co., renamed *Medon*. In 1963 to Greek owners, A. Frangistas, renamed *Tina*. Broken up China (Shanghai) 1970.								
693	1,120	*Empire Strength*	28.5.1942	7,355	Standard 'D'-type Cargo Ship	St/Sc/Mv 431.9/57.3/33.6	490 nhp 2,650 bhp Dies H&W	Ministry of Transport
Completed 22.12.1942. In 1946 to Blue Star Line, renamed *Saxon Star*. In 1961 to Welsh owners D.L. Street, renamed *Redbrook*. In 1965 to Greek owners, H. Embiricos, renamed *E. Evangelia*. Wrecked, Black Sea, October 1968.								
694	1,121	*LCT 11*	9.12.1940	372	Landing Craft	St/2Sc/Mv 152.0/29.0/4.4	840 bhp Petrol H&W?	Admiralty
Completed 16.12.1940. LCT(1)-type landing craft, first specialist landing vessels. Cellular construction so could be divided into four sections to store on transports. Could carry 3x 40t or 6x 30t tanks.								
695	1,122	*LCT 12*	9.12.1940	372	Landing Craft	St/2Sc/Mv 152.0/29.0/4.4	840 bhp Petrol H&W?	Admiralty
Completed 16.12.1940, sister ship of *LCT 11*.								
N/A	1123	HMS *Stronsay*	Pointhouse built					
N/A	1124	HMS *Switha*	Pointhouse built					
696	1125	*Empire Castle*	25.8.1942	7,356	Standard 'D'-type Cargo Ship	St/Sc/Mv 431.4/57.3/33.6	530 nhp 2,650 bhp Dies H&W	Ministry of Transport
Completed 31.1.1943. In 1946 to Blue Star Line, renamed *Gothic Star*, *Nelson Star* (1947) and *Patagonis Star* (1958). In 1961 to Greek owners, G.A. Theodorou, renamed *Eirini* and later ((1970) *Byzantium*. Broken up Spain (Puerto de Santa Maria) 1971.								

Ship	Yard No	Name	Date Launched	Displacement Tons	Type	Construction and Dimensions	Horse Power/ Engines	Owners
697	1,126	*LCT 25*	11.3.1941	372	Landing Craft	St/2Sc/Mv 152.0/29.0/4.4	840 bhp Petrol H&W?	Admiralty
Completed 25.3.1941, sister ship of *LCT 11.*								
698	1,127	*LCT 26*	11.3.1941	372	Landing Craft	St/2Sc/Mv 152.0/29.0/4.4	840 bhp Petrol H&W?	Admiralty
Completed 25.3.1941, sister ship of *LCT 11.*								
699	1,128	*LCT 100*	9.6.1941	460	Landing Craft	St/3Sc/Mv 159.9/31.0/5.3	1,050 bhp Petrol H&W?	Admiralty
Completed 29.6.1941. LCT(2) larger three-shaft versions of the original type; could carry 3x 40t or 7x 20t tanks.								
700	1,129	*LCT 101*	9.6.1941	460	Landing Craft	St/3Sc/Mv 159.9/31.0/5.3	1,050 bhp Petrol H&W?	Admiralty
Completed 11.7.1941, sister ship of *LCT 100.*								
701	1,130	*LCT 102*	17.6.1941	460	Landing Craft	St/3Sc/Mv 159.9/31.0/5.3	1,050 bhp Petrol H&W?	Admiralty
Completed 31.8.1941, sister ship of *LCT 100.*								
702	1,131	*LCT 103*	17.6.1941	460	Landing Craft	St/3Sc/Mv 159.9/31.0/5.3	1,050 bhp Petrol H&W?	Admiralty
Completed 16.9.1941, sister ship of *LCT 100.*								
703	1,132	HMS *Algerine*	22.12.1941	980	Minesweeper	St/2Sc/St 225.0/35.5/10.5	2,000 shp Turb H&W	Admiralty
By September 1940 it was recognised that a larger minesweeper with better sea-keeping qualities than the current Bangor-class vessels was needed. A design was quickly drawn up for a ship capable of sweeping moored, magnetic and acoustic mines in seas of up to force 5 and also capable of acting as an anti-submarine escort. This was the name ship of this highly successful and versatile design. The H&W ships differed from those built in most other yards in that they were fitted with turbine machinery rather than triple expansion. Completed 24.3.1942. Sunk by submarine torpedo (Italian *Ascianghi*), western Mediterranean, while taking part in Operation Torch, November 1942. One hundred and fourteen lives lost, only eight survivors.								
704	1,133	HMS *Alarm*	5.2.1942	980	Minesweeper	St/2Sc/St 225.0/35.5/10.5	2,000 shp Turb H&W	Admiralty
Completed 16.5.1942, sister ship of *Algerine.* Total loss after being beached following damaged in air attack, Bone, January 1943. Wreck broken up 1944.								
705	1,134	HMS *Albacore*	2.4.1942	980	Minesweeper	St/2Sc/St 225.0/35.5/10.5	2,000 shp Turb H&W	Admiralty
Completed 16.6.1942, sister ship of *Algerine.* Broken up Port Glasgow (UK) 1963.								
706	1,135	HMS *Acute*	14.4.1942	980	Minesweeper	St/2Sc/St 225.0/35.5/10.5	2,000 shp Turb H&W	Admiralty
Completed 30.7.1942, sister ship of *Algerine*, laid down as *Alert.* Sunk as target 1964.								
707	1,136	HMS *Cadmus*	27.5.1942	980	Minesweeper	St/2Sc/St 225.0/35.5/10.5	2,000 shp Turb H&W	Admiralty
Completed 9.9.1942, sister ship of *Algerine.* In 1950 to Belgian Navy, renamed *Georges Lecointe.* Broken up Belgium 1960.								
708	1,137	HMS *Circe*	27.6.1942	980	Minesweeper	St/2Sc/St 225.0/35.5/10.5	2,000 shp Turb H&W	Admiralty
Completed 16.10.1942, sister ship of *Algerine* Broken up Dalmuir (UK) 1966.								
709	1,138	HMS *Espiegle*	12.8.1942	980	Minesweeper	St/2Sc/St 225.0/35.5/10.5	2,000 shp Turb H&W	Admiralty
Completed 1.12.1942, sister ship of *Algerine.* Broken up Dalmuir (UK) 1967.								

The launch of *Belinda* (H&W y/n 1690) 1972. (Courtesy of Lagan Legacy)

British Success (H&W y/n 1719) 1983. (Courtesy of Lagan Legacy)

British Vine (H&W y/n 1601) 1964. (Courtesy of Lagan Legacy)

British Steel (H&W y/n 1720) 1984. (Courtesy of Lagan Legacy)

Ship	Yard No	Name	Date Launched	Displacement Tons	Type	Construction and Dimensions	Horse Power/ Engines	Owners
710	1,139	HMS *Fantome*	22.9.1942	980	Minesweeper	St/2Sc/St 225.0/35.5/10.5	2,000 shp Turb H&W	Admiralty
Completed 23.1.1943, sister ship of *Algerine* Mined off Cape Bon, May 1943, not repaired. Broken up Milford Haven 1947.								
711	1,140	HMS *Mutine*	10.10.1942	980	Minesweeper	St/2Sc/St 225.0/35.5/10.5	2,000 shp Turb H&W	Admiralty
Completed 26.2.1943, sister ship of *Algerine.* Broken up Barrow (UK) 1967.								
712	1,141	HMS *Onyx*	27.10.1942	980	Minesweeper	St/2Sc/St 225.0/35.5/10.5	2,000 shp Turb H&W	Admiralty
Completed 26.3.1943, sister ship of *Algerine.* Broken up Inverkeithing (UK) 1967.								
713	1,142	HMS *Rattler*	9.12.1942	980	Minesweeper	St/2Sc/St 225.0/35.5/10.5	2,000 shp Turb H&W	Admiralty
Completed 22.4.1943, sister ship of *Algerine.* Renamed *Loyalty.* Sunk by submarine torpedo (*U-480*), English Channel while returning to Portsmouth from Normandy, August 1944. Twenty lives lost.								
714	1,143	HMS *Ready*	11.1.1943	980	Minesweeper	St/2Sc/St 225.0/35.5/10.5	2,000 shp Turb H&W	Admiralty
Completed 21.5.1943, sister ship of *Algerine.* In 1951 to Belgian Navy, renamed *Jan Van Haverbeke.* Broken up Belgium 1961.								
715	1,144	HMS *Rinaldo*	20.3.1943	980	Minesweeper	St/2Sc/St 225.0/35.5/10.5	2,000 shp Turb H&W	Admiralty
Completed 18.6.1943, sister ship of *Algerine.* Broken up Gateshead (UK) 1961.								
716	1,145	HMS *Rosario*	3.4.1943	980	Minesweeper	St/2Sc/St 225.0/35.5/10.5	2,000 shp Turb H&W	Admiralty
Completed 9.7.1943, sister ship of *Algerine.* In 1954 to Belgian Navy, renamed *De Moor.* Broken up Belgium 1969.								
717	1,146	HMS *Spanker*	20.4.1943	980	Minesweeper	St/2Sc/St 225.0/35.5/10.5	2,000 shp Turb H&W	Admiralty
Completed 20.8.1943, sister ship of *Algerine.* In 1953 to Belgian Navy, renamed *De Brouwer.* Broken up 1963.								
718	1,147	HMS *Vestal*	19.6.1943	980	Minesweeper	St/2Sc/St 225.0/35.5/10.5	2,000 shp Turb H&W	Admiralty
Completed 10.9.1943, sister ship of *Algerine.* Scuttled following damage in kamikaze attack. Andaman Sea, July 1945.								
719	1,148	*Darro*	21.11.1942	9,733	Cargo Ship (Refrigerated)	St/2Sc/Mv 453.3/65.3/35.3	1,803 nhp 9,600 bhp Dies H&W	Royal Mail Line London
Completed 29.6.1943, sister ship of *Deseado.* In 1967 to Greek owners, Embajada Cia Nav., renamed *Surrey.* Broken up Taiwan (Kaohsiung) 1967.								
720	1,149	*Paramatta*	25.9.1943	8,244	Cargo Ship	St/Sc/Mv 433.3/61.2/23.7	1,236 nhp 6,000 bhp Dies H&W	Royal Mail Line London
Completed 1.2.1944, name changed to *Pampas.* Wartime service as infantry landing ship (large) operating 19 LCA and one LCM, accommodating up to 1,631 troops, renamed *Persimmon.* Returned to owners 1946, reverted to *Pampas.* In 1965 to, M.A. Karageorgeoris, renamed *Aristodimos.* Broken up Taiwan (Kaohsiung) 1967.								
721	1,150	*Rowallan Castle*	23.12.1942	7,950	Cargo Ship (Refrigerated)	St/Sc/Mv 457.4/63.3/34.3	1,647 nhp 9,375 bhp Dies H&W	Union-Castle Steamship Co. London
Completed 23.4.1943, sister ship of *Richmond Castle*, completion delayed by late delivery of engines. Not taken up for military use but employed on South Africa–UK route, fitted with anti-aircraft guns and mine defences. After war made a number of voyages to US. Broken up Taiwan (Kaohsiung) 1971.								
N/A	1,151	*Empire Maiden*	Pointhouse built					

Ship	Yard No	Name	Date Launched	Displacement Tons	Type	Construction and Dimensions	Horse Power/ Engines	Owners
722	1,152	*Paraguay*	8.2.1944	5,560	Cargo Ship	St/Sc/Mv 433.3/61.3/22.7	1,236 nhp 6,000 bhp Dies H&W	Royal Mail Line London
Completed 7.9.1944, sister ship of *Pampas*. In 1964 to Greek owners, M.A. Garageorgis, renamed *Elire*. Broken up China (Shanghai) 1969.								
723	1,153	HMS *Thruster*	24.9.1942	5,593	Landing Ship Tank	St/2Sc/St 390.0/49.0/18.5	7,000 shp Turb H&W	Admiralty
The first purpose-built landing ships capable of sea-going voyages. Funnels were set to starboard, giving a clear tank deck, which was loaded/landed via bow doors fitted with a 145ft-long extending ramp. Capacity to carry 13x 40t tanks or 20x 25t tanks on tank deck plus 27x 3t lorries stowed on upper deck. The design was not successful as could not beach in sufficiently shallow water when fully loaded and too complex for mass production. Completed 14.3.1943. To Dutch Navy in 1945, renamed *Pelicaan*, employed as store ship and accommodation vessel. Broken up Spain (Bilbao) 1975.								
724	1,154	HMS *Bruiser*	24.10.1942	5,596	Landing Ship Tank	St/2Sc/St 390.0/49.0/18.5	7,000 shp Turb H&W	Admiralty
Completed 2.4.1943, sister ship of *Thruster*. Sold in 1947.								
725	1,155	HMS *Boxer*	12.12.1942	5,596	Landing Ship Tank	St/2Sc/St 390.0/49.0/18.5	7,000 shp Turb H&W	Admiralty
Completed 1.5.1943, sister ship of *Thruster*. Converted into fighter direction ship (LSF) 1944, radar training ship 1947. Broken up 1958.								
726	1,156	*Samanco*	23.3.1943	8,336	Cargo Ship	St/Sc/Mv 448.2/62.8/34.8	1,643 nhp 7,500 bhp Dies H&W	Pacific Steam Navigation Co. Liverpool
Completed 9.8.1943. In 1956 to German owners, D.D.G. Hansa, and renamed *Reichenfels*. Broken up Spain (Bilbao) 1962.								
727	1,157	*Sarmiento*	17.8.1943	8,335	Cargo Ship	St/Sc/Mv 448.2/62.8/34.8	1,643 nhp 7,500 bhp Dies H&W	Pacific Steam Navigation Co. Liverpool
Completed 28.10.1943. In 1967 to Cypriot owners, Lemos Bros, and renamed *Monomachos* and *Gladiator* (1969). Broken up China (Shanghai) 1971.								
728	1,158	*Empire Bombardier*	8.8.1942	8,202	Oil Tanker	St/Sc/Mv 465.6/59.5/33.8	502 nhp Dies H&W	Minister of Transport
Completed 18.2.1943, sister ship of *Empire Diamond*, originally *Empire Fusilier* but completed under this name. In 1946 to British Tanker Co., renamed *British Bombardier*. Broken up Haiti (Tamise) 1959.								
729	1,159	*Empire Industry*	4.5.1943	8,203	Oil Tanker	St/Sc/Mv 465.6/59.5/33.8	502 nhp Dies H&W	Ministry of Transport
Completed 16.9.1943, sister ship of *Empire Diamond*. In 1946 to Anglo-Saxon/Shell, renamed *Flammulina*. Broken up Hong Kong 1960.								
N/A	1,160	*Empire Metal*	Govan built					
730	1,161	*Waiwera*	30.9.1943	12,028	Cargo Ship (Refrigerated)	St/2Sc/Mv 520.8/70.4/32.3	2,552 nhp 12,000 bhp Dies H&W	Shaw Savill & Albion Co. London
Completed 29.10.1944. In 1967 to Greek owners, Embajada Cia Nav., renamed *Julia*. Broken up Taiwan (Kaohsiung) 1968.								
N/A	1,162	HMS *Kale*	Pointhouse built					
N/A	1,163	*San Vulfranco*	Govan built					
731	1,164	*Empire Benefit*	24.11.1942	8,202	Oil Tanker	St/Sc/Mv 465.6/59.5/33.8	490 nhp Dies H&W	Ministry of Transport
Completed 20.4.1943, sister ship of *Empire Diamond*. In 1945 to Athel Line, renamed *Athelqueen*. In 1955 to Greek owners, Chandris, renamed *Mariverda*. Broken up Japan (Kure) 1961.								

Ship	Yard No	Name	Date Launched	Displacement Tons	Type	Construction and Dimensions	Horse Power/ Engines	Owners
732	1,165	*Empire Grange*	23.9.1942	6,981	Standard 'X'-type Cargo Ship	St/Sc/Mv 432.9/56.3/34.3	489 nhp 3,300 bhp Dies H&W	Ministry of Transport
Completed 17.3.1943. In 1946 to Dodd Thompson & Co., renamed *King Robert.* In 1961 to Hong Kong owners, Mullion & Co., renamed *Ardgem.* In 1967 to Gibraltar owners Kelso Shipping Co., renamed *Kelso.* Broken up Taiwan (Kaohsiung) 1969.								
N/A	1,166	*British Patience*	Govan built					
N/A	1,167	*British Wisdom*	Govan built					
N/A	1,168	*Empire Torrent*	Govan built					
N/A	1,169	*Empire Nerissa*	Govan built					
N/A	1,170	HMS *Tweed*	Pointhouse built					
733	1,171	HMCS *Ontario*	29.7.1943	8,800	Cruiser	St/4Sc/St 555.6/63.0/20.8	72,500 shp Turb H&W	Royal Canadian Navy
Completed 25. 5.1945, Swiftsure-class cruiser, originally named *Minotaur* but completed for Canadian Navy under this name. Broken up Japan (Osaka) 1960.								
N/A	1,172	HMS *Oxna*	Pointhouse built					
734	1,173	*Narica*	17.2.1943	8,213	Oil Tanker	St/Sc/Mv 465.6/59.5/33.8	520 nhp Dies H&W	Anglo-Saxon Petroleum Co. London
Completed 28.5.1943, sister ship of *Empire Diamond.* Broken up Hong Kong 1960.								
N/A	1,174	*Neritina*	Govan built					
N/A	1,175	*Empire Gypsy*	Pointhouse built					
735	1,176	*Drina*	30.12.1943	9,789	Cargo Ship (Refrigerated)	St/2Sc/Mv 453.1/65.3/33.3	1,803 nhp 9,600 bhp Dies H&W	Royal Mail Line London
Completed 25.7.1944, sister ship of *Deseado.* In 1965 to Shaw Savill & Albion, renamed *Romanic.* Broken up Taiwan (Kaohsiung) 1968.								
736	1,177	*Durango*	5.9.1944	9,806	Cargo Ship (Refrigerated)	St/2Sc/Mv 453.1/65.3/33.3	1,803 nhp 9,600 bhp Dies H&W	Royal Mail Line London
Completed 20.12.1944, sister ship of *Deseado.* In 1966 to Shaw Savill & Albion, renamed *Ruthenic.* In 1967 to Greek owners, Embajada Cia Nav., renamed *Sussex.* Broken up Taiwan (Kaohsiung) 1968.								
737	1,178	*Richmond Castle*	23.3.1944	7,971	Cargo Ship (Refrigerated)	St/Sc/Mv 457.4/63.3/34.3	1,647 nhp 9,375 bhp Dies H&W	Union-Castle Steamship Co. London
Completed 28.9.1944, sister ship of *Rochester Castle,* for South Africa–UK fruit trade. In 1971 sold for £146,000, broken up China (Shanghai).								
N/A	1,179	Un-named	Cancelled					
N/A	1,180	Un-named	Cancelled					
738	1,181	*Devis*	12.4.1944	8,187	Cargo Ship (Refrigerated)	St/Sc/Mv 439.0/62.3/33.9	1,275 nhp 6,000 bhp Dies H&W	Lamport & Holt Line Liverpool
Completed 20.8.1944. Renamed *Oakland Star* (1955) but resumed her original name the following year. Broken up Italy (La Spezia) 1962.								
739	1,182	*Defoe*	28.2.1945	8,462	Cargo Ship (Refrigerated)	St/Sc/Mv 439.0/62.3/33.9	1,275 nhp 6,000 bhp Dies H&W	Lamport & Holt Line Liverpool
Completed 31.5.1945, sister ship of *Devis.* Renamed *Geelong Star* in 1954 but later resumed original name. In 1966 to Greek owners, P.B. Metaxas, renamed *Argolis Star.* Broken up China (Shanghai) 1969.								
N/A	1,183	*San Vito*	Govan built					
N/A	1,184	*Empire Fay*	Pointhouse built					
N/A	1,185	HMS *Helmsdale*	Pointhouse built					
N/A	1,186	HMS *Meon*	Pointhouse built					

Ship	Yard No	Name	Date Launched	Displacement Tons	Type	Construction and Dimensions	Horse Power/ Engines	Owners
740	1,187	*Roxburgh Castle*	31.10.1944	8,003	Cargo Ship (Refrigerated)	St/Sc/Mv 457.4/63.3/34.3	1,647 nhp 9,375 bhp Dies H&W	Union-Castle Steamship Co. London
Completed 14.2.1945, sister ship of *Rochester Castle*, for South Africa–UK fruit trade. In 1971 sold for £146,000, broken up China (Shanghai).								
741	1,188	*Port Hobart*	5.12.1945	11,149	Standard 'Fast' Cargo Ship (Refrigerated)	St/2Sc/Mv 521.4/70.5/30.9	4,000 nhp 16,000 bhp Dies H&W	Port Line London
Completed 29.8.1946, originally *Empire Wessex* but completed under this name. Broken up China (Shanghai) 1970.								
742	1,189	*Empire Traveller*	29.6.1943	8,201	Oil Tanker	St/Sc/Mv 465.6/59.5/33.8	520 nhp 4,800 bhp Dies H&W	Ministry of Transport
Completed 28.10.1943, sister ship of *Empire Diamond*. In 1946 to French government, renamed *Pechelbronn*. In 1955 to French commercial owners, J.A. Galani, renamed *Eagle*. In 1959 to Yugoslavia, renamed *Jajce*. Broken up Spain (Valencia) 1969.								
N/A	1,190	*Empire Coppice*	Pointhouse built					
743	1,191	HMS *Glory*	27.11.1943	13,190	Aircraft Carrier	St/2Sc/St 695.0/80.0/13.3	40,000 shp Turb H&W	Admiralty
Completed 2.4.1945, light fleet carrier of Colossus class. Served in Korean War but increasingly obsolete due to developments in aircraft design which ship could not be modified to meet. After period in reserve broken up Inverkeithing (UK) 1961.								
744	1,192	*Santander*	17.1.1946	6,612	Cargo Ship	St/Sc/Mv 448.2/62.8/25.5	1,933 nhp 7,500 bhp Dies H&W	Pacific Steam Navigation Co. Liverpool
Completed 2.5.1946. In 1967 to Greek owners, G. Lemos Bros, renamed *Navmachos*. Broken up Spain (Villanueva y Geltru) 1971.								
745	1,193	*Salaverry*	2.4.1946	6,612	Cargo Ship	St/Sc/Mv 448.2/62.8/25.5	1,933 nhp 7,500 bhp Dies H&W	Pacific Steam Navigation Co. Liverpool
Completed 16.8.1946, sister ship of *Santander*, In 1967 to Greek owners, Stravelalis Bros, renamed *Pelias*. Foundered off South Africa, December 1972.								
746	1,194	*Norrisia*	14.10.1943	8,246	Oil Tanker	St/Sc/Mv 465.6/59.5/33.8	490 nhp Dies H&W	Anglo-Saxon Petroleum Co. London
Completed 3.3.1944, sister ship of *Empire Diamond*. Broken up Italy (La Spezia) 1960.								
747	1,195	*Nassarius*	14.12.1943	8,246	Oil Tanker	St/Sc/Mv 465.6/59.5/33.8	490 nhp Dies H&W	Anglo-Saxon Petroleum Co. London
Completed 30.3.1944, sister ship of *Empire Diamond*. Broken up Hong Kong 1959.								
N/A	1,196	*British Might*	Govan built					
N/A	1,197	*Empire Grenade*	Govan built					
748	1,198	*Niso*	3.8.1944	8,273	Oil Tanker	St/Sc/Mv 465.6/59.5/33.8	490 nhp Dies H&W	Anglo-Saxon Petroleum Co. London
Completed 20.12.1944, sister ship of *Empire Diamond*. Broken up Dalmuir (UK) 1961.								
749	1,199	*Newcombia*	17.11.1944	8,292	Oil Tanker	St/Sc/Mv 465.6/59.5/33.8	490 nhp Dies H&W	Anglo-Saxon Petroleum Co. London
Completed 22.3.1945, sister ship of *Empire Diamond*. Broken up Belgium (Antwerp) 1959.								
N/A	1,200	*Parina*	Govan built					
750	1,201	HMS *Pickle*	3.8.1943	980	Minesweeper	St/Sc/St 225.0/35.5/10.5	2,000 shp Turb H&W	Admiralty
Completed 15.10.1943, sister ship of *Algerine*. Transferred to Ceylonese Navy 1958, renamed *Parakrama*. Broken up Hong Kong 1964.								

Ship	Yard No	Name	Date Launched	Displacement Tons	Type	Construction and Dimensions	Horse Power/ Engines	Owners
751	1,202	HMS *Pincher*	19.8.1943	980	Minesweeper	St/Sc/St 225.0/35.5/10.5	2,000 shp Turb H&W	Admiralty
Completed 12.11.1943, sister ship of *Algerine*. Broken up Dunston (UK) 1962.								
752	1,203	HMS *Plucky*	29.9.1943	980	Minesweeper	St/Sc/St 225.0/35.5/10.5	2,000 shp Turb H&W	Admiralty
Completed 10.12.1943, sister ship of *Algerine*. Broken up Dunston (UK) 1962.								
753	1,204	HMS *Recruit*	26.10.1943	980	Minesweeper	St/Sc/St 225.0/35.5/10.5	2,000 shp Turb H&W	Admiralty
Completed 14.1.1944, sister ship of *Algerine*. Broken up Barrow (UK) 1965.								
754	1,205	HMS *Rifleman*	25.11.1943	980	Minesweeper	St/Sc/St 225.0/35.5/10.5	2,000 shp Turb H&W	Admiralty
Completed 11.2.1944, sister ship of *Algerine*. Broken up Dalmuir (UK) 1972.								
755	1,206	HMS *Squirrel*	20.4.1944	980	Minesweeper	St/Sc/St 225.0/35.5/10.5	2,000 shp Turb H&W	Admiralty
Completed 16.8.1944, sister ship of *Algerine*. Scuttled following damage by mine off Thailand, July 1945.								
756	1,207	HMS *Chameleon*	6.5.1944	980	Minesweeper	St/Sc/St 225.0/35.5/10.5	2,000 shp Turb H&W	Admiralty
Completed 14.9.1944, sister ship of *Algerine*. Broken up Silloth (UK) 1966.								
757	1,208	HMS *Cheerful*	22.5.1944	980	Minesweeper	St/Sc/St 225.0/35.5/10.5	2,000 shp Turb H&W	Admiralty
Completed 13.10.1944, sister ship of *Algerine*. Broken up Queenborough (UK) 1963.								
758	1,209	HMS *Hare*	20.6.1944	980	Minesweeper	St/Sc/St 225.0/35.5/10.5	2,000 shp Turb H&W	Admiralty
Completed 10.11.1944, sister ship of *Algerine*. Transferred to Nigerian Navy 1959, renamed *Nigeria*. Broken up Faslane (UK) 1962.								
759	1,210	HMS *Jewel*	20.7.1944	980	Minesweeper	St/Sc/St 225.0/35.5/10.5	2,000 shp Turb H&W	Admiralty
Completed 9.12.1944, sister ship of *Algerine*. Broken up Inverkeithing (UK) 1967.								
760	1,211	HMS *Liberty*	22.8.1944	980	Minesweeper	St/Sc/St 225.0/35.5/10.5	2,000 shp Turb H&W	Admiralty
Completed 18.1.1945, sister ship of *Algerine*. Transferred to Belgian Navy 1949, renamed *Adrien De Gerlache*. Broken up 1969.								
N/A	1,212	HMS *Lysander*	Cancelled					
N/A	1,213	HMS *Mariner*	Cancelled					
N/A	1,214	HMS *Marmion*	Cancelled					
N/A	1,215	HMS *Mary Rose*	Cancelled					
N/A	1,216	HMS *Moon*	Cancelled					
N/A	1,217	HMS *Provident*	Cancelled					
N/A	1,218	HMS *Regulus*	Cancelled					
761	1,219	*Empire Outpost*	31.5.1943	6,978	Standard 'X'-type Cargo Ship	St/Sc/Mv 432.9/56.3/34.3	489 nhp 3,300 bhp Dies H&W	Ministry of Transport
Completed 31.7.1943. In 1945 to French government, renamed *Pilote Garnier*. In 1960 to Greek owners, Franco Sg Co., renamed *Kyra Hariklia*. Broken up Germany (Hamburg) 1966.								
762	1,220	HMS *Eagle*	19.3.1946	36,800	Aircraft Carrier	St/4Sc/St 803.9/112.9/31.1	152,000 shp Turb H&W	Admiralty
Originally *Audacious*, improved version of preceding Implacable-class fleet carriers. Laid down in October 1942, not completed until October 1951 when emerged as the most modern carrier in Royal Navy and one of few that could operate new generation of jet aircraft.								

Ship	Yard No	Name	Date Launched	Displacement Tons	Type	Construction and Dimensions	Horse Power/ Engines	Owners
In mid-1950s refitted, emerged with angled flight deck and improved aircraft-handling facilities. Modernised 1959–64. Although the navy's most modern carrier, fell victim in 1966 to decision to axe carrier force and paid off 1972. Placed in reserve; 'cannibalised' to keep *Ark Royal* operational. Broken up Cairnryan (UK) 1978.								
N/A	1,221	HMS *Candytuft*	Pointhouse built					
N/A	1,222	*Empire Sheba*	Govan built					
N/A	1,223	*Empire Venus*	Govan built					
763	1,224	HMS *Warrior*	20.5.1944	13,350	Aircraft Carrier	St/2Sc/St 695.0/80.0/23.3	40,000 shp Turb H&W	Admiralty
Completed 14.3.1946, light fleet carrier of Colossus class, originally *Brave* but completed under this name. Loaned to Canadian Navy, returned 1948 and used as experimental ship. In 1958 to Argentina, renamed *Independencia*. In 1970 placed in reserve, following year sold for scrap.								
N/A	1,225	*Empire Harvest*	Pointhouse built					
N/A	1,226	HMS *Halladale*	Pointhouse built					
N/A	1,227	*Empire Dombey*	Pointhouse built					
764	1,228	HMS *Magnificent*	16.11.1944	14,000	Aircraft Carrier	St/2Sc/St 695.0/80.0/23.0	40,000 shp Turb H&W	Admiralty
Completed 21.5.1948, light fleet carrier of Majestic class; work suspended at end of war. Completed to modified design for Australian Navy, renamed *Melbourne*. She served as flagship of Australian Navy. Modified 1967–68 and again 1972–73. In reserve from 1982, sold 1985; broken up China (Shanghai).								
765	1,229	HMCS *Bonaventure*	27.2.1945	14,000	Aircraft Carrier	St/2Sc/St 695.0/80.0/23.0	40,000 shp Turb H&W	Admiralty
Completed 17.1.1957, light fleet carrier of Majestic class originally named *Powerful*; work suspended at end of war restarted 1952. Completed to a modified design for Canadian Navy under this name. Modified 1966–67. Paid off 1970, broken up Taiwan.								
766	1,230	*Empire Abercorn*	30.12.1944	8,563	Standard 'Fast' Cargo Ship (Refrigerated)	St/Sc/Mv 457.3/63.3/35.0	1,700 nhp 7,500 bhp Dies H&W	Ministry of Transport
Completed 30.6.1945. In 1946 to New Zealand Sg Co., renamed *Rakaia*. Broken up Hong Kong 1971.								
767	1,231	*Empire Clarendon*	14.5.1945	8,577	Standard 'Fast' Cargo Ship (Refrigerated)	St/Sc/Mv 457.3/63.3/35.0	1,700 nhp 7,500 bhp Dies H&W	Ministry of Transport
Completed 26.10.1945. In 1947 to Blue Star Line, renamed *Tuscan Star*, *Timaru Star* (1948) and *California Star* (1958). Broken up Taiwan (Kaohsiung) 1969.								
N/A	1,232	HMS *Seabear*	Cancelled					
N/A	1,233	HMS *Serene*	Cancelled					
768	1,234	*Empire Rangoon*	25.1.1944	6,988	Standard 'X'-type Cargo Ship	St/Sc/Mv 432.9/56.3/34.3	489 nhp 3,250 bhp Dies H&W	Ministry of Transport
Completed 30.5.1944. In 1947 to Reardon Smith & Sons, renamed *Homer City*. In 1960 to Hong Kong owners, Mollers, renamed *Grovenor Mariner*. In 1966 to Chinese government, renamed *Red Sea*. Wrecked Hong Kong, August 1971 and broken up.								
N/A	1,235	HMS *Northampton Castle*	Pointhouse built					
N/A	1,236	HMS *Oakham Castle*	Pointhouse built					
N/A	1,237	HMS *Dover Castle*	Pointhouse built					
769	1,238	HMS *Oxford Castle*	11.12.1943	1,060	Corvette	St/Sc/St 252.0/36.8/13.9	2,750 ihp VTE (4Cy) H&W	Admiralty
Although the Flower class had proved capable of meeting the need for a quickly produced convoy escort, the design was far from perfect. The Castle class represented an attempt to rectify the worst of the Flower's faults by increasing size and sea worthiness. Completed 10.3.1944. Broken up Briton Ferry (UK) 1960.								

Ship	Yard No	Name	Date Launched	Displacement Tons	Type	Construction and Dimensions	Horse Power/ Engines	Owners
770	1,239	HMS *Pevensey Castle*	11.1.1944	1,060	Corvette	St/Sc/St 252.0/36.8/13.9	2,750 ihp VTE (4Cy) H&W	Admiralty
Completed 10.6.1944, sister ship of *Oxford Castle.* Rebuilt as weather ship 1960–61, renamed *Weather Monitor* and *Admiral Beaufort* (1977). Broken up Troon (UK) 1982.								
771	1,240	HMCS *Arnprior*	8.2.1944	1,060	Corvette	St/Sc/St 252.0/36.8/13.9	2,750 ihp VTE (4Cy) H&W	Royal Canadian Navy
Completed 26.6.1944, sister ship of *Oxford Castle*, originally *Rising Castle* but completed for Canada under this name. In 1956 to Uruguayan Navy, renamed *Montevideo.* Used as a training ship until deleted 1975.								
772	1,241	HMCS *Petrolia*	24.2.1944	1,060	Corvette	St/Sc/St 252.0/36.8/13.9	2,750 ihp VTE (4Cy) H&W	Royal Canadian Navy
Completed 14.7.1944, sister ship of *Oxford Castle*, originally *Sherbourne Castle* but completed for Canada under this name. In 1946 to commercial use, American owners, Castle Sg, renamed *Maid of Athens.* In 1947 to Indian ownership, Bharat Line, renamed *Bharatlaxmi.* Broken up India (Bombay) 1965.								
773	1,242	*Empire Saturn*	6.5.1944	8,224	Oil Tanker	St/Sc/Mv 465.6/59.5/33.8	490 nhp Dies H&W	Ministry of Transport
Completed 20.9.1944, sister ship of *Empire Diamond.* In 1946 to Anglo-Saxon/Shell, renamed *Nayadis.* Broken up Japan (Hirao) 1961.								
N/A	1,243	*Empire Jupiter*	Govan built					
N/A	1,244	HMS *Calshot Castle*	Pointhouse cancelled					
N/A	1,245	HMS *Dudley Castle*	Pointhouse cancelled					
774	1,246	HMS *Loch Craggie*	23.5.1944	1,435	Frigate	St/2Sc/St 307.0/38.6/12.3	5,500 ihp VTE (8Cy) H&W	Admiralty
The limitations of the early corvettes were clearly understood by the British Navy; the Castle class were, at best, an intermediate measure while a larger ocean-going anti-submarine escort was designed, given designation 'frigate'. The first ships of this type were the River class (not built in Belfast); the Loch class were improved versions intended as ocean-going anti-submarine escorts. Completed 15.6.1944. Broken up Portugal (Lisbon) 1963.								
775	1,247	HMS *Loch Gorm*	8.6.1944	1,435	Frigate	St/2Sc/St 307.0/38.6/12.3	5,500 ihp VTE (8Cy) H&W	Admiralty
Completed 7.7.1944, sister ship of *Loch Craggie.* In 1961 to mercantile use, Greek owners, Kavounides, renamed *Orion.* Broken up Greece 1966.								
776	1,248	HMS *Loch Killisport*	6.7.1944	1,435	Frigate	St/2Sc/St 307.0/38.6/12.3	5,500 ihp VTE (8Cy) H&W	Admiralty
Completed 9.9.1945, sister ship of *Loch Craggie.* Broken up Blyth (UK) 1970.								
777	1,249	HMS *St Austell Bay*	8.11.1944	1,600	Frigate	St/2Sc/St 307.0/38.6/12.9	5,500 ihp VTE (8Cy) H&W	Admiralty
Bay-class frigates were anti-aircraft escort version of anti-submarine Loch class for Pacific rather than Atlantic conditions. Many began as Lochs but were altered on stocks. Completed 29.5.1945, originally *Loch Lydoch* but completed under this name. Broken up Charlestown (UK) 1959.								
778	1,250	HMS *St Brides Bay*	16.1.1945	1,600	Frigate	St/2Sc/St 307.0/38.6/12.9	5,500 ihp VTE (8Cy) H&W	Admiralty
Completed 15.6.1945, sister ship of *St Austell Bay*, originally *Loch Achilty* but completed under this name. Broken up Faslane (UK) 1962.								
779	1,251	SAS *Transvaal*	2.8.1944	1,435	Frigate	St/2Sc/St 307.0/38.6/12.9	5,500 ihp VTE (8Cy) H&W	South African Navy
Completed 2.1.1945, sister ship of *Lough Craggie*, originally *Loch Ard* completed for South Africa under this name. Scuttled to form breakwater 1976.								
780	1,252	HMS *Start Bay*	15.2.1945	1,600	Frigate	St/2Sc/St 307.0/38.6/12.9	5,500 ihp VTE (8Cy) H&W	Admiralty
Completed 6.9.1945, sister ship of *St Austell Bay.* Originally *Loch Arklet* but completed under this name. Broken up Newport (UK) 1958.								

Ship	Yard No	Name	Date Launched	Displacement Tons	Type	Construction and Dimensions	Horse Power/ Engines	Owners
781	1,253	HMS *Tremadoc Bay*	29.3.1945	1,600	Frigate	St/2Sc/St 307.0/38.6/12.9	5,500 ihp VTE (8Cy) H&W	Admiralty
Completed 11.10.1945, sister ship of *St Austell Bay*, originally *Loch Arnish* but completed under this name. Broken up Italy (Genoa) 1959.								
N/A	1,254	HMS *Loch Kirkaig*	Cancelled					
N/A	1,255	HMS *Loch Hourn*	Cancelled					
N/A	1,256	HMS *Loch Goil*	Cancelled					
N/A	1,257	HMS *Loch Awe*	Cancelled					
N/A	1,258	HMS *Loch Striven*	Cancelled					
782	1,259	HMS *Widemouth Bay*	19.10.1944	1,600	Frigate	St/2Sc/St 307.0/38.6/12.9	5,500 ihp VTE (8Cy) H&W	Admiralty
Completed 13.4.1945, sister ship of *St Austell Bay*, originally *Loch Frisa* but completed under this name. Broken up Blyth (UK) 1957.								
783	1,260	HMS *Wigtown Bay*	26.4.1945	1,600	Frigate	St/2Sc/St 307.0/38.6/12.9	5,500 ihp VTE (8Cy) H&W	Admiralty
Completed 19.1.1946, sister ship of *St Austell Bay*, originally *Loch Garasdale* but completed under this name. Broken up Faslane (UK) 1959.								
84	1,261	HMS *Whitesand Bay*	16.12.1944	1,600	Frigate	St/2Sc/St 307.0/38.6/12.9	5,500 ihp VTE (8Cy) H&W	Admiralty
Completed 30.7.1945, sister ship of *St Austell Bay*, originally to have been *Loch Lubnaig*. Broken up Charlestown (UK) 1956.								
N/A	1,262	HMS *Loch Ronald*	Cancelled					
N/A	1,263	HMS *Loch Stemster*	Cancelled					
N/A	1,264	HMS *Loch Tummell*	Cancelled					
N/A	1,265	HMS *Loch Eye*	Cancelled					
N/A	1,266	HMS *Loch Lurgain*	Cancelled					
N/A	1,267	HMS *Loch Shiel*	Cancelled					
N/A	1,268	HMS *Loch Laro*	Cancelled					
N/A	1,269	HMS *Loch Inchard*	Cancelled					
N/A	1,270	HMS *Loch Vanavie*	Cancelled					
N/A	1,271	HMS *Loch Swin*	Cancelled					
N/A	1,272	HMS *Loch Enoch*	Cancelled					
N/A	1,273	HMS *Loch Sunart*	Cancelled					
N/A	1,274	HMS *Loch Sheallag*	Cancelled					
N/A	1,275	HMS *Loch Eynort*	Cancelled					
785	1,276	*Empire Falkland*	2.9.1944	7,006	Standard 'X'-type Cargo Ship	St/Sc/Mv 432.9/56.3/34.3	489 nhp 3,300 bhp Dies H&W	Ministry of Transport
Completed 21.2.1945. To Scottish Line 1946, renamed *Stirlingshire*. In 1956 to Turnbull Martin & Co. Broken up Belgium (Bruges) 1966.								
786	1,277	*Riebeeck Castle*	23.10.1945	8,322	Cargo Ship (Refrigerated)	St/Sc/Mv 457.4/63.3/35.5	1,938 nhp 9,375 bhp Dies H&W	Union-Castle Steamship Co. London
Completed 11.3.1946, for South African fruit trade. Broken up Taiwan (Kaohsiung) 1971.								

<table>
<tr><th>Ship</th><th>Yard No</th><th>Name</th><th>Date Launched</th><th>Displacement Tons</th><th>Type</th><th>Construction and Dimensions</th><th>Horse Power/ Engines</th><th>Owners</th></tr>
<tr><td>787</td><td>1,278</td><td>*Rustenburg Castle*</td><td>5.3.1946</td><td>8,322</td><td>Cargo Ship (Refrigerated)</td><td>St/Sc/Mv
457.4/63.3/35.5</td><td>1,938 nhp
9,375 bhp
Dies
H&W</td><td>Union-Castle Steamship Co. London</td></tr>
<tr><td colspan="9">Completed 25.6.1946, sister ship of *Riebeeck Castle.* Broken up China (Shanghai) 1971.</td></tr>
<tr><td>N/A</td><td>1,279</td><td>*Pilcomayo*</td><td colspan="6">Govan built</td></tr>
<tr><td>788</td><td>1,280</td><td>HMS *Centaur*</td><td>22.4.1947</td><td>18,310</td><td>Aircraft Carrier</td><td>St/2Sc/St
737.0/90.0/24.8</td><td>76,000 shp
Turb
H&W</td><td>Admiralty</td></tr>
<tr><td colspan="9">Completed 1.9.1953, name ship of a class of intermediate fleet carriers incorporating wartime experience; however, like other wartime carriers, proved too small to operate new generation of jet aircraft coming into service in late 1950s. In early 1960s was proposed to rebuild as commando carrier (as done with sisters *Bulwark* and *Albion*) but plans shelved due to rising costs. In reserve 1966, broken up Cairnryan (UK) 1971.</td></tr>
<tr><td>789</td><td>1,281</td><td>HMS *Bulwark*</td><td>22.6.1948</td><td>18,319</td><td>Aircraft Carrier</td><td>St/2Sc/St
737.0/90.0/24.8</td><td>76,000 shp
Turb
H&W</td><td>Admiralty</td></tr>
<tr><td colspan="9">Completed 2.11.1954, sister ship of *Centaur*, by time completed obsolete as aircraft carrier. In 1959–60 converted into commando carrier which employed helicopters and landing craft to land up to 733 Royal Marines. In reserve 1976; commissioned in 1980 to release *Hermes* from amphibious warfare role to embark Sea Harriers. Fell victim to 1981 defence cuts, broken up Cairnryan (UK) 1984.</td></tr>
<tr><td>N/A</td><td>1,282</td><td>*Empire Jura*</td><td colspan="6">Pointhouse built</td></tr>
<tr><td>N/A</td><td>1,283</td><td>*Empire Gambia*</td><td colspan="6">Govan built</td></tr>
<tr><td>790</td><td>1,284</td><td>*British Supremacy*</td><td>26.7.1945</td><td>8,242</td><td>Oil Tanker</td><td>St/Sc/Mv
466.0/59.5/34.8</td><td>490 nhp
Dies
H&W</td><td>British Tanker Co. London</td></tr>
<tr><td colspan="9">Completed 21.12.1945, sister ship of *Empire Diamond.* Originally for Ministry of Transport, completed for these owners. Broken up Troon (UK) 1961.</td></tr>
<tr><td>791</td><td>1,285</td><td>*Neothyris*</td><td>24.10.1945</td><td>8,243</td><td>Oil Tanker</td><td>St/Sc/Mv
466.0/59.5/34.8</td><td>502 nhp
Dies
H&W</td><td>Anglo-Saxon Petroleum Co. London</td></tr>
<tr><td colspan="9">Completed 24.1.1946, sister ship of *Empire Diamond.* Broken up Hong Kong 1960.</td></tr>
<tr><td>N/A</td><td>1,286</td><td>*Empire Bute*</td><td colspan="6">Pointhouse built</td></tr>
<tr><td>N/A</td><td>1,287</td><td>*Empire Orkney*</td><td colspan="6">Pointhouse built</td></tr>
<tr><td>N/A</td><td>1,288</td><td>*Empire Shetland*</td><td colspan="6">Pointhouse built</td></tr>
<tr><td>792</td><td>1,289</td><td>*LSt 3006*</td><td>3.9.1944</td><td>2,300</td><td>Landing Ship</td><td>St/2Sc/St
347.5/55.3/12.5</td><td>5,500 ihp
VTE (8Cy)
H&W</td><td>Admiralty</td></tr>
<tr><td colspan="9">After the failure of LSt(1) type and experience of operating American-built LSt(2), British Navy designed the LSt(3) which used frigate-type machinery to give an increased speed, 13.5 knots compared to 9 knots (the popular nickname for American LSt was 'Large Slow Target'). Could carry 15x 40t or 20x 25t tanks and 14x 3t lorries.
Completed 15.9.1944. In 1946 given name *Tromso.* In 1956 chartered for commercial use, renamed *Empire Gannet.* Broken up Singapore 1968.</td></tr>
<tr><td>793</td><td>1,290</td><td>*LSt 3007*</td><td>16.9.1944</td><td>2,300</td><td>Landing Ship</td><td>St/2Sc/St
347.5/55.3/12.5</td><td>5,500 ihp
VTE (8Cy)
H&W</td><td>Admiralty</td></tr>
<tr><td colspan="9">Completed 28.9.1944, sister ship of *LSt 3006.* In 1947 to Greek Navy, renamed *Axios.* Returned to RN 1962. Broken up Italy (Genoa) 1962.</td></tr>
<tr><td>794</td><td>1,291</td><td>*LSt 3008*</td><td>31.10.1944</td><td>2,300</td><td>Landing Ship</td><td>St/2Sc/St
347.5/55.3/12.5</td><td>5,500 ihp
VTE (8Cy)
H&W</td><td>Admiralty</td></tr>
<tr><td colspan="9">Completed 4.5.1945, sister ship of *LSt 3006.* Broken up Australia (Sydney) 1950.</td></tr>
<tr><td>795</td><td>1,292</td><td>*LSt 3009*</td><td>30.12.1944</td><td>2,300</td><td>Landing Ship</td><td>St/2Sc/St
347.5/55.3/12.5</td><td>5,500 ihp
VTE (8Cy)
H&W</td><td>Admiralty</td></tr>
<tr><td colspan="9">Completed 11.5.1945, sister ship of *LSt 3006.* In 1946 to British Army, renamed *Reginald Kerr.* Broken up Singapore 1966.</td></tr>
<tr><td>796</td><td>1,293</td><td>*LSt 3010*</td><td>30.9.1944</td><td>2,300</td><td>Landing Ship</td><td>St/2Sc/St
347.5/55.3/12.5</td><td>5,500 ihp
VTE (8Cy)
H&W</td><td>Admiralty</td></tr>
<tr><td colspan="9">Completed 5.4.1945, sister ship of *LSt 3006.* In 1947 renamed *Attacker.* In 1954 chartered for commercial use, renamed *Empire Cymric.* Broken up Faslane (UK) 1963.</td></tr>
</table>

The fitting out of *Canberra* (H&W y/n 1621) took place in 1960–1. (Courtesy of Lagan Legacy)

Essi Kristine (H&W y/n 1669) 1967. (Courtesy of Lagan Legacy)

View of the yard at Harland & Wolff in 1952 with *Cymric* (H&W y/n 1453) seen on the stocks. (Courtesy of Lagan Legacy)

View of the deck of a bulk carrier. (Courtesy of Lagan Legacy)

Ship	Yard No	Name	Date Launched	Displacement Tons	Type	Construction and Dimensions	Horse Power/ Engines	Owners
797	1,294	*LSt 3011*	12.2.1945	2,300	Landing Ship	St/2Sc/St 347.5/55.3/12.5	5,500 ihp VTE (8Cy) H&W	Admiralty
Completed 14.8.1945, sister ship of *LSt 3006*. In 1947 given name *Avenger.* In 1951 to Indian Navy, renamed *Magar.* Broken up India 1988.								
798	1,295	*LSt 3012*	12.3.1945	2,300	Landing Ship	St/2Sc/St 347.5/55.3/12.5	5,500 ihp VTE (8Cy) H&W	Admiralty
Completed 25.9.1945, sister ship of *LSt 3006* In 1945 renumbered LSt(Q) 1, when converted to 'mother ship', providing additional accommodation and supplies for squadron of LSts. In 1947 renamed *Ben Nevis.* Broken up Faslane (UK) 1965.								
799	1,296	*LSt 3013*	24.4.1945	2,300	Landing Ship	St/2Sc/St 347.5/55.3/12.5	5,500 ihp VTE (8Cy) H&W	Admiralty
Completed 24.11.1945, sister ship of *LSt 3006.* In 1945 renumbered LSt(Q) 2. In 1947 renamed *Ben Lomond.* Broken up Grays (UK) 1960.								
N/A	1,297	*LSt 3041*	Govan built					
N/A	1,298	*LSt 3042*	Govan built					
N/A	1,299	*Empire Belgrave*	Pointhouse built					
N/A	1,300	*Empire Campden*	Pointhouse built					
N/A	1,301	*Empire Fitzroy*	Pointhouse built					
N/A	1,302	*Empire Grosvenor*	Pointhouse built					
800	1,303	*Empire Star*	4.3.1946	11,860	Standard 'Fast' Cargo Ship (Refrigerated)	St/2Sc/Mv 521.4/70.5/30.9	4,000 nhp 16,000 bhp Dies H&W	Blue Star Line (Frederick Leyland & Co.) London
Completed 18.12.1946, originally *Empire Mercia* for Ministry of Transport completed under this name. Broken up Taiwan (Kaohsiung) 1971.								
N/A	1,304	HMS *New Zealand*	Cancelled					
N/A	1,305	Un-named Tanker	Govan cancelled					
N/A	1,306	*Empire Edgehill*	Govan built					
N/A	1,307	*British Knight*	Govan built					
801	1,308	*Lyria*	6.3.1946	6,452	Oil Tanker	St/Sc/Mv 431.3/54.7/30.6	538 nhp Dies H&W	Anglo-Saxon Petroleum Co. London
Completed 20.6.1946. In 1955 to Spanish owners, M. Yllera, renamed *Yebala.* Converted to bulk carrier 1956. Broken up Spain (Aviles) 1975.								
802	1,309	*Linga*	16.4.1946	6,452	Oil Tanker	St/Sc/Mv 431.3/54.7/30.6	538 nhp Dies H&W	Anglo-Saxon Petroleum Co. London
Completed 19.9.1946, sister ship of *Lyria.* Broken up Belgium (Willebroek) 1963.								
803	1,310	*Calchas*	27.8.1946	8,298	Cargo Ship	St/Sc/Mv 466.0/59.5/34.0	1,360 nhp 6,800 bhp Dies H&W	Alfred Holt & Co. Liverpool
Completed 17.1.1947. In 1957 to Glen Line, renamed *Glenfinlas*; returned to Holt & Co., assumed original name (1962). Damaged by fire, Port Kelang, July 1973, broken up Taiwan (Kaohsiung).								
N/A	1,311	*Empire Tedship*	Pointhouse built					
N/A	1,312	*Empire Tedport*	Pointhouse built					
N/A	1,313	*Empire Tedmuir*	Pointhouse built					
N/A	1,314	*Empire Tedrita*	Pointhouse built					
N/A	1,315	*Empire Tesland*	Govan built					
804	1,316	*Patella*	28.6.1946	8,277	Bitumen Tanker	St/Sc/Mv 466.0/59.5/34.0	714 nhp Dies H&W	Anglo-Saxon Petroleum Co. London
Completed 17.12.1946. Broken up Belgium (Bruges) 1967.								
N/A	1,317	*Empire Tescombe*	Govan built					
N/A	1,318	*Empire Tesella*	Govan built					

Ship	Yard No	Name	Date Launched	Displacement Tons	Type	Construction and Dimensions	Horse Power/ Engines	Owners
N/A	1,319	*Empire Tedmont*	Pointhouse cancelled					
N/A	1,320	*Empire Tedlake*	Pointhouse cancelled					
N/A	1,321	*Empire Tedellen*	Pointhouse cancelled					
N/A	1,322	*Empire Tedrose*	Pointhouse cancelled					
N/A	1,323	*Empire Tesdown*	Govan cancelled					
N/A	1,324	*Empire Tesgrove*	Govan cancelled					
N/A	1,325	*Empire Tes***?*	Govan cancelled					
805	1,326	*Athenic*	26.11.1946	15,187	Cargo Ship (Refrigerated)	St/2Sc/St 536.3/71.3/38.3	3,720 nhp 15,400 shp Turb H&W	Shaw Savill & Albion Co. London
(This vessel is listed by Moss & Hume as a passenger-cargo ship, re-rated) Completed 16.7.1947. Scrapped Taiwan (Kaohsiung) 1969.								
806	1,327	*Balaena*	18.4.1946	15,715	Whale Factory Ship	St/2Sc/St 539.7/77.4/34.1	1,653 nhp 7,300 ihp TE (6Cy) H&W	United Whalers Ltd London
Completed 28.9.1946. In 1960 to Japanese owners, Kyokuyo Hogei, renamed *Kyokuyo Maru No.3.* Broken up Japan 1978.								
807	1,328	*Loch Garth*	24.9.1946	8,617	Cargo Ship (Refrigerated)	St/Sc/St 478.9/66.3/38.0	2,914 nhp 11,550 shp Turb H&W	Royal Mail Lines Ltd London
Completed 29.5.1947. Broken up Belgium (Tamise) 1967.								
808	1,329	*Loch Avon*	27.11.1946	8,617	Cargo Ship (Refrigerated)	St/Sc/St 478.9/66.3/38.0	2,914 nhp 11,550 shp Turb H&W	Royal Mail Lines Ltd London
Completed 3.9.1947. In 1967 to Hong Kong owners, C.Y. Tung, renamed *Hongkong Observer.* Broken up Taiwan 1973.								
N/A	1,330	*Waverley*	Pointhouse built					
809	1,331	*Parthia*	25.2.1947	13,362	Passenger-Cargo	St/2Sc/St 509.5/70.2/33.0	2,970 nhp 15,000 shp Turb H&W	Cunard-White Star Steamship Co. Liverpool
(This vessel is listed by Moss & Hume as a passenger ship, re-rated) Completed 7.4.1948. In 1962 to New Zealand Sg Co., renamed *Remuera.* In 1964 to Eastern & Australian, renamed *Aramac.* Broken up Taiwan (Kaohsiung) 1969.								
810	1,332	*Pretoria Castle*	19.8.1947	28,705	Passenger-Cargo	St/2Sc/St 717.9/84.0/43.9	7,873 nhp 35,000 shp Turb H&W	Union-Castle Steamship Co. London
(This vessel is listed by Moss & Hume as a passenger ship, re-rated) Completed 10.7.1948, replacement for *Windsor Castle,* enlarged version of *Capetown Castle.* In 1966 to South African Mariner Corporation, renamed *Oranje,* continued on old routes with Union-Castle crew. After 187 sailings and carrying 250,000 passengers, broken up Taiwan (Kaohsiung) 1975.								
811	1,333	*Edinburgh Castle*	16.10.1947	28,705	Passenger-Cargo	St/2Sc/St 717.9/84.0/43.9	7,873 nhp 35,000 shp Turb H&W	Union-Castle Steamship Co. London
(This vessel is listed by Moss & Hume as a passenger ship, re-rated) Completed 26.11.1948, sister ship of *Pretoria Castle,* replacement for *Warwick Castle.* Broken up Taiwan (Kaohsiung) 1976.								
N/A	1,334	*Linswe*	Pointhouse built					
N/A	1,335	*Linwet*	Pointhouse built					
N/A	1,336	*Linyon*	Pointhouse built					
N/A	1,337	*Linno*	Pointhouse built					
N/A	1,338	*Linda*	Pointhouse built					
N/A	1,339	*Limpya*	Pointhouse built					
N/A	1,340	Un-named Launch	Pointhouse built					

Ship	Yard No	Name	Date Launched	Displacement Tons	Type	Construction and Dimensions	Horse Power/ Engines	Owners
N/A	1,341	Un-named Launch	Pointhouse built					
N/A	1,342	Un-named Launch	Pointhouse built					
N/A	1,343	*La Hague*	Govan built					
N/A	1,344	*Franck Delmas*	Govan built					
N/A	1,345	*La Heve*	Govan built					
812	1,346	*Lepton*	26.9.1946	6,446	Oil Tanker	St/Sc/Mv 431.3/54.7/30.6	560 nhp Dies H&W	Anglo-Saxon Petroleum Co. London
Completed 6.2.1947, sister ship of *Lyria*. Broken up Rosyth (UK) 1960.								
813	1,347	*Lingula*	11.10.1946	6,445	Oil Tanker	St/Sc/Mv 431.3/54.7/30.6	538 nhp Dies H&W	Anglo-Saxon Petroleum Co. London
Completed 25.3.1947, sister ship of *Lyria*. Broken up Inverkeithing (UK) 1961.								
814	1,348	*Thorshavet*	19.6.1947	17,081	Whale Factory Ship	St/2Sc/Mv 571.1/77.3/39.9	1,392 nhp 7,000 bhp Dies H&W	A/S Thor Dahl Sandefiord Norway
Completed 9.10.1947. In 1970 converted to fish meal factory ship, renamed *Astra*. Sank following collision, April 1974.								
815	1,349	*Munster*	25.3.1947	4,088	Passenger-Cargo Ferry	St/2Sc/Mv 353.2/50.2/14.5	1,590 nhp 5,600 bhp Dies H&W	British & Irish SP Co. Dublin
Completed 17.1.1948, for Liverpool–Dublin route. Withdrawn October 1967. In 1968 to Greek owners, G. Potamianos, renamed *Theseus* and *Orpheus* (1969). Broken up India (Alang) 2000.								
N/A	1,350	*Imperial Star*	Govan built					
N/A	1,351	*Melbourne Star*	Govan built					
816	1,352	*Leinster*	20.5.1947	4,115	Passenger-Cargo Ferry	St/2Sc/Mv 353.2/50.2/14.5	1,590 nhp 5,600 bhp Dies H&W	British & Irish SP Co. Dublin
Completed 25.3.1948, sister ship of *Munster*, for Liverpool–Dublin route. In 1969 to Greek owners, Mediterranean Sun Lines, renamed *Aphrodite*. Broken up Turkey (Aliaga) 1987.								
N/A	1,353	*Soochow*	Pointhouse built					
817	1,354	*Magdalena*	11.5.1948	17,547	Passenger-Cargo Ship	St/2Sc/St 570.2/73.2/?	? Turb H&W	Royal Mail Lines London
Completed 18.2.1949 On maiden voyage wrecked S of Tijucas Island and sank off Rio de Janeiro, April 1949.								
N/A	1,355	*Pelorus*	Pointhouse built					
N/A	1,356	*Penlee*	Pointhouse built					
818	1,357	*Salinas*	7.3.1947	6,669	Cargo Ship	St/Sc/Mv 448.2/62.8/25.5	1,933 nhp 7,500 bhp Dies H&W	Pacific Steam Navigation Co. Liverpool
Completed 18.11.1947, sister ship of *Santander*. In 1968 to Greek owners, Stravelakis Bros, renamed *Polyfimos*. Broken up China (Shanghai) 1972.								
819	1,358	*Salamanca*	29.8.1947	6,669	Cargo Ship	St/Sc/Mv 448.2/62.8/25.5	1,933 nhp 7,500 bhp Dies H&W	Pacific Steam Navigation Co. Liverpool
Completed 20.3.1948, sister ship of *Santander*. In 1968 to Greek owners, Stravelakis Bros, renamed *Kronos*. Broken up China (Shanghai) 1972.								
820	1,359	*Kantara*	3.6.1947	3,213	Cargo Ship	St/Sc/Mv 352.3/52.2/16.8	536 nhp 2,500 bhp Dies H&W	Moss Hutchinson Line Liverpool
Completed 19.11.1947. In 1972 to Greek owners, A. Bousses, renamed *Constantis II*. Broken up Spain (Castellon) 1980.								

Ship	Yard No	Name	Date Launched	Displacement Tons	Type	Construction and Dimensions	Horse Power/ Engines	Owners
821	1,360	*Karnak*	2.10.1947	3,198	Cargo Ship	St/Sc/Mv 352.3/52.2/16.8	536 nhp 2,500 bhp Dies H&W	Moss Hutchinson Line Liverpool
Completed 30.1.1948, sister ship of *Kantara*. In 1971 to Greek owners, Grecomer Sg Agency, renamed *Eudocia*. Broken up India (Bombay) 1981.								
N/A	1,361	*Granuaile*	Pointhouse built					
N/A	1,362	*British Ranger*	Govan built					
822	1,363	*Soesdyke*	11.3.1948	9,592	Cargo Ship (Refrigerated)	St/Sc/St 465.5/65.9/38.0	2,912 nhp 10,400 shp Turb H&W	Holland-America Line Rotterdam
Completed 14.10.1948. In 1967 to Greek owners, Gourdomichalis, renamed *Kavo Peiratis*. In 1970 to Italian owners, D'Amico, renamed *Lorenzo D'Amico*. Damaged in collision at Terminal Island, January 1978, subsequently broken up.								
823	1,364	*British Security*	27.2.1948	8,583	Oil Tanker	St/Sc/Mv 470.6/61.8/33.8	695 nhp 3,200 bhp Dies H&W	British Tanker Co. London
Completed 7.7.1948. In 1966 to Greek Owners A. Halcoussis, renamed *Mana* and *Ypatia* (1967). Wrecked Danae Reef, Mozambique. September 1968, wreck broken up Taiwan (Kaohsiung).								
824	1,365	*British Strength*	8.6.1948	8,580	Oil Tanker	St/Sc/Mv 470.6/61.8/33.8	695 nhp 3,200 bhp Dies H&W	British Tanker Co. London
Completed 12.11.1948, sister ship of *British Security*. Broken up Spain (Santander) 1966.								
825	1,366	*Schiedijk*	10.6.1948	9,592	Cargo Ship (Refrigerated)	St/Sc/St 471.9/65.9/38.3	2,912 nhp 10,400 bhp Turb H&W	Holland-America Line Rotterdam
Completed 19.2.1949, sister ship of *Soesdyke*. In 1954 renamed *Schiedyk*. Wrecked Bligh Island, Nootka Sound, January 1968.								
826	1,367	*Hibernia*	22.7.1948	4,972	Passenger- Cargo Ferry	St/2Sc/Mv 379.5/54.2/28.0	1,883 nhp 10,700 bhp Dies H&W	London Midland & Scottish Railway London
Completed 5.4.1949, delivered to British Transport Commission (British Rail) for Holyhead–Dublin route. The first cross-Channel ship to be fitted with stabilisers. Extensively refitted 1964–65 to increase second-class passenger accommodation at expense of first class, an indication of changing pattern of travel. In 1976 to Greek owners, Agapitos Bros, renamed *Express Apollon*. Broken up India (Bombay) 1981.								
827	1,368	*Cambria*	21.9.1948	4,972	Passenger- Cargo Ferry	St/2Sc/Mv 379.5/54.2/28.0	1,883 nhp 10,700 bhp Dies H&W	London Midland & Scottish Railway London
Completed 17.5.1949, sister ship of *Hibernia* delivered to British Transport Commission (British Rail). Career similar to sisters. In 1976 to Saudi owners, Oriental Navigation Line, renamed *Al Taif*. Foundered Suez Roads, January 1981.								
N/A	1,369	*Liparus*	Govan built					
828	1,370	*Lotorium*	30.9.1947	6,490	Oil Tanker	St/Sc/Mv 431.3/54.7/30.6	560 nhp Dies H&W	Anglo-Saxon Petroleum Co. London
Completed 30.12.1947, sister ship of *Lyria*. Broken up Japan (Osaka) 1960.								
829	1,371	*Ramore Head*	25.5.1948	6,195	Cargo Ship	St/Sc/St 437.1/59.5/27.4	1,100 nhp 5,500 shp Turb H&W	Ulster Steamship Co. Belfast
Completed 26.8.1948. In 1968 to Iranian owners, Shipping & General, renamed *Xerxes II*. Broken up Spain (Valencia) 1968.								
830	1,372	*Antilochus*	2.11.1948	8,238	Cargo Ship (Refrigerated)	St/Sc/Mv 462.9/62.3/31.7	6,800 bhp Dies H&W	Alfred Holt & Co. Liverpool
Completed 3.5.1949. In 1976 to Pakistani owners, Gokal Group, renamed *Gulf Orient*. Broken up Pakistan (Gadani) 1978.								

Ship	Yard No	Name	Date Launched	Displacement Tons	Type	Construction and Dimensions	Horse Power/ Engines	Owners
831	1,373	*Jalta*	6.7.1948	8,247	Oil Tanker	St/Sc/Mv 470.2/59.5/34.8	695 nhp 3,200 bhp Dies H&W	A/S Bulls Tankrederi Sandeifiord Norway
Completed 17.9.1948. In 1961 to Greek owners, N. Konialidis, renamed *Albacara* and *Albazero* (1967). Broken up Spain (Santander) 1968.								
832	1,374	*Sarasvati*	19.10.1948	3,750	Passenger-Cargo Ferry	St/Sc/St 329.3/52.7/25.7	1,241 nhp 7,100 shp Turb H&W	Bombay Steam Navigation Co.
Completed 20.6.1949. Broken up India (Bombay) 1969.								
833	1,375	*Sabarmati*	19.10.1948	3,750	Passenger-Cargo Ferry	St/Sc/St 329.3/52.7/25.7	1,241 nhp 7,100 shp Turb H&W	Bombay Steam Navigation Co.
Completed 20.8.1949, sister ship of *Saravati*. Broken up India (Bombay) 1969.								
834	1,376	*Helenus*	13.4.1949	10,125	Passenger-Cargo (Refrigerated)	St/Sc/St 496.3/69.3/34.7	3,000 nhp 15,000 shp Turb H&W	Ocean Steamship Co. Liverpool
Completed 29.10.1949, for Australian routes. Broken up Taiwan (Kaohsiung) 1972.								
835	1,377	*Hector*	27.7.1949	10,125	Passenger-Cargo (Refrigerated)	St/Sc/St 496.3/69.3/34.7	3,000 nhp 15,000 shp Turb H&W	Ocean Steamship Co. Liverpool
Completed 31.3.1950, sister ship of *Helenus*. Broken up Taiwan (Kaohsiung) 1972.								
N/A	1,378	*British Mariner*	Govan built					
N/A	1,379	*British Workman*	Govan built					
836	1,380	*Borgny*	4.11.1948	8,255	Oil Tanker	St/Sc/Mv 470.2/59.5/34.8	695 nhp 3,200 bhp Dies H&W	Fred Olsen & Co. Oslo Norway
Completed 31.3.1949, sister ship of *Jalta*. In 1954 to Mexican owners, Petroleos Mexicanos, renamed *Miguel Hidalgo* and *PEMEX B* (1968). Broken up Mexico (Manzanillo) 1968.								
837	1,381	*Vestfoss*	17.3.1949	8,250	Oil Tanker	St/Sc/Mv 470.2/59.5/34.8	695 nhp 3,200 bhp Dies H&W	A/S Thor Thoresen Oslo Norway
Completed 27.6.1949, sister ship of *Jalta*. In 1961 to H. Tangvald-Pedersen, renamed *Vestsund*. Broken up Japan (Yokohama) 1963.								
838	1,382	*Explorador*	15.2.1949	6,478	Oil Tanker	St/Sc/Mv 431.3/54.5/30.6	536 nhp 2,800 bhp Dies H&W	Estrella Maritima S.A. Argintina
Completed 6.7.1949, a near sister of *Lyria*. Caught fire and exploded at San Lorenzo, February 1967. Wreck broken up 1968.								
839	1,383	*Vikingen*	10.6.1949	8,264	Oil Tanker	St/Sc/Mv 470.2/59.5/34.8	695 nhp 3,200 bhp Dies H&W	Tanker Corp. of Panama City
Completed 7.10.1949, sister ship of *Jalta*. In 1955 to Norwegian owners, T. Moe, renamed *Fossvik*. In 1961 to J. Stolt-Neilsen, renamed *Stolt Avenir*. In 1967 to Italian owners, R. Salvatori, renamed *Avenir* and *Avenir S* (1971). Broken up Italy (La Spezia) 1975.								
840	1,384	*Juan Peron*	4.4.1950	24,569	Whale Factory Ship	St/2Sc/Mv 648.1/80.3/59.9	1,390 nhp 3,500 bhp Dies H&W	Campania Argentina de Pesca SA
Completed 15.10.1951. In 1955 taken over by Argentine government, renamed *Cruz Del Sur*. In 1968 converted to tanker. In 1970 cut in two to form barges *Western Offshore VII* and *Western Offshore VIII*.								
N/A	1,385	*Amarna*	Govan built					

Ship	Yard No	Name	Date Launched	Displacement Tons	Type	Construction and Dimensions	Horse Power/ Engines	Owners
841	1,386	*Assiout*	31.5.1949	3,422	Cargo Ship (Refrigerated)	St/Sc/Mv 352.6/52.2/16.6	726 nhp 3,500 bhp Dies H&W	Moss Hutchinson Line Liverpool
Completed 12.10.1949, a half sister of *Kantara.* In 1973 to Greek owners, Grecomar, renamed *Chryssoula II.* Broken up Pakistan (Gadani) 1981.								
842	1,387	*Champavati*	29.3.1949	1,288	Passenger Ferry	St/2Sc/St 223.0/38.1/17.5	490 nhp 2,530 shp Turb H&W	Bombay Steam Navigation Co.
Completed 20.10.1949. Broken up India (Bombay) 1968.								
843	1,388	*Rohidas*	30.3.1949	1,288	Passenger Ferry	St/2Sc/St 223.0/38.1/17.5	490 nhp 2,530 shp Turb H&W	Indian Co-operative Navigation and Trading Co.
Completed 20.10.1949, sister ship of *Champavati.* Broken up India 1969								
N/A	1,389	*Cazador*	Govan built					
N/A	1,390	*Setter I*	Pointhouse built					
N/A	1,391	*Setter II*	Pointhouse built					
844	1,392	*Ternoy*	22.9.1949	8,218	Oil Tanker	St/Sc/Mv 470.2/59.5/34.8	695 nhp 3,200 bhp Dies H&W	Skips A/S Truma Norway
Completed 27.1.1950, sister ship of Jalta. In 1955 to A. Bech, renamed *Elise.* Broken up China (Shanghai) 1969.								
N/A	1,393	*Setter III*	Pointhouse built					
N/A	1,394	*Setter IV*	Pointhouse built					
N/A	1,395	*Setter V*	Pointhouse built					
N/A	1,396	*Setter VI*	Pointhouse built					
N/A	1,397	*British Captain*	Govan built					
N/A	1,398	*British Commander*	Govan built					
N/A	1,399	*British Consul*	Govan built					
845	1,400	*British Explorer*	21.3.1950	8,644	Oil Tanker	St/Sc/Mv 470.6/61.8/33.8	700 nhp Dies H&W	British Tanker Co. London
Completed 8.7.1950, sister ship of *British Security.* In 1958 to BP Clyde Tanker Co., renamed *Clyde Explorer.* Broken up Spain (Santander) 1964.								
846	1,401	*British Prospector*	1.6.1950	8,655	Oil Tanker	St/Sc/Mv 470.6/61.8/33.8	700 nhp Dies H&W	British Tanker Co. London
Completed 28.9.1950, sister ship of *British Security.* In 1958 to BP Clyde Tanker Co., renamed *Clyde Prospector.* Broken up Holland (Willebroek) 1964.								
847	1,402	*British Surveyor*	15.8.1950	8,655	Oil Tanker	St/Sc/Mv 470.6/61.8/33.8	700 nhp Dies H&W	British Tanker Co. London
Completed 8.12.1950, sister ship of *British Security.* In 1958 to BP Clyde Tanker Co., renamed *Clyde Surveyor.* Broken up Sweden (Ystad) 1964.								
848	1,403	*Verena*	29.6.1950	18,612	Oil Tanker	St/Sc/St 619.7/80.7/45.2	2,600 nhp 13,000 shp Turb H&W	Anglo-Saxon Petroleum Co. London
Completed 9.11.1950. Broken up Italy (Castellon) 1971.								
N/A	1,404	*Bratsberg*	Govan built					
N/A	1,405	*Binta*	Govan built					
849	1,406	*Bolette*	28.9.1950	16,394	Oil Tanker	St/Sc/Mv 595.0/78.5/42.6	1,650 nhp 8,250 bhp Dies H&W	Fred Olsen & Co. Oslo, Norway
Completed 17.1.1951. In 1964 to Greek owners, J.S. Latsis, renamed *Marianna III* and *Petrola XXXIII* (1975). Broken up Taiwan (Kaohsiung) 1984.								

<table>
<tr><th>Ship</th><th>Yard No</th><th>Name</th><th>Date Launched</th><th>Displacement Tons</th><th>Type</th><th>Construction and Dimensions</th><th>Horse Power/ Engines</th><th>Owners</th></tr>
<tr><td>850</td><td>1,407</td><td>Dalfonn</td><td>12.1.1951</td><td>16,440</td><td>Oil Tanker</td><td>St/Sc/Mv
595.0/78.5/42.6</td><td>1,650 nhp
8,200 bhp
Dies
H&W</td><td>Sigval Bergesen
Stavanger, Norway</td></tr>
<tr><td colspan="9">Completed 15.5.1951, sister ship of Bolette. In 1964 to Greek owners, J.S. Latsis, renamed Margarita II and Petrola XXXI (1975). Broken up Taiwan (Kaohsiung) 1984.</td></tr>
<tr><td>851</td><td>1408</td><td>Kurdistan</td><td>26.10.1949</td><td>8322</td><td>Oil Tanker</td><td>St/Sc/Mv
470.4/59.5/34.7</td><td>640 nhp
3,200 bhp
Dies
H&W</td><td>Common Brothers Ltd
Newcastle on Tyne</td></tr>
<tr><td colspan="9">Completed 24.2.1950. In 1961 to Bulgarian government, renamed Arda. Broken up Yugoslavia (Split) 1977.</td></tr>
<tr><td>N/A</td><td>1,409</td><td>Africana II</td><td colspan="6">Pointhouse built</td></tr>
<tr><td>852</td><td>1,410</td><td>Tank King</td><td>22.5.1951</td><td>16,477</td><td>Oil Tanker</td><td>St/Sc/Mv
595.0/78.5/42.6</td><td>1,650 nhp
7,500 bhp
Dies
H&W</td><td>Sigurd Herlofsen A/S
Norway</td></tr>
<tr><td colspan="9">Completed 31.8.1951, sister ship of Bolette. In 1964 to Greek owners, Meditermar, renamed Maurice. Broken up Spain (Villanueva y Geltru) 1975.</td></tr>
<tr><td>853</td><td>1,411</td><td>France Stove</td><td>2.7.1951</td><td>16,468</td><td>Oil Tanker</td><td>St/Sc/Mv
595.0/78.5/42.6</td><td>1,650 nhp
7,500 bhp
Dies
H&W</td><td>Lorentzen A/S
Oslo, Norway</td></tr>
<tr><td colspan="9">Completed 12.11.1951, sister ship of Bolette. In 1962 to Christen Smith, renamed Belfri. In 1968 to British owners, Arimec, renamed Philemon. In 1974 to Vental, renamed Moonlight. Broken up Taiwan (Kaohsiung) 1975.</td></tr>
<tr><td>854</td><td>1,412</td><td>Orkdal</td><td>8.2.1951</td><td>8,221</td><td>Oil Tanker</td><td>St/Sc/Mv
470.4/59.5/34.7</td><td>640 nhp
3,200 bhp
Dies
H&W</td><td>Moltzaus & Christensen
Oslo, Norway</td></tr>
<tr><td colspan="9">Completed 17.4.1951, sister ship of Kurdistan. In 1959 to, A.C. Olsen, renamed Granvik. Broken up Italy (Castellon) 1965.</td></tr>
<tr><td>855</td><td>1,413</td><td>Ringerd</td><td>12.12.1950</td><td>8,218</td><td>Oil Tanker</td><td>St/Sc/Mv
470.2/59.5/34.8</td><td>640 nhp
3,200 bhp
Dies
H&W</td><td>Olav Ringdal
Oslo, Norway</td></tr>
<tr><td colspan="9">Completed 12.3.1951, sister ship of Kurdistan. In 1961 to J. Stolt-Neilsen, renamed Stolt Victor. Broken up Spain (Valencia) 1965.</td></tr>
<tr><td>856</td><td>1,414</td><td>Runic</td><td>21.10.1949</td><td>13,587</td><td>Cargo Ship (Refrigerated)</td><td>St/2Sc/St
539.8/72.2/40.8</td><td>3,080 nhp
15,400 shp
Turb
H&W</td><td>Shaw Savill & Albion Co.
London</td></tr>
<tr><td colspan="9">Completed 24.3.1950. Wrecked 120nm N of Lord Howe Island during hurricane, February 1961. No lives lost.</td></tr>
<tr><td>857</td><td>1,415</td><td>Suevic</td><td>7.3.1950</td><td>13,587</td><td>Cargo Ship (Refrigerated)</td><td>St/2Sc/St
539.8/72.2/40.8</td><td>3,080 nhp
15,400 shp
Turb
H&W</td><td>Shaw Savill & Albion Co.
London</td></tr>
<tr><td colspan="9">Completed 5.7.1950, sister ship of Runic. Broken up Taiwan (Kaohsiung) 1974.</td></tr>
<tr><td>858</td><td>1,416</td><td>Ascanius</td><td>15.6.1950</td><td>7,692</td><td>Passenger-Cargo (Refrigerated)</td><td>St/Sc/Mv
462.9/62.3/31.7</td><td>1,520 nhp
7,600 bhp
Dies
H&W</td><td>Ocean Steamship Co. (Holt & Co.)
Liverpool</td></tr>
<tr><td colspan="9">Completed 21.11.1950. In 1972 to Elder Dempster, renamed Akosombo; following year returned to Holts and former name. In 1976 to Saudi-Europe Line, renamed Mastura. Broken up Blyth (UK) 1978.</td></tr>
<tr><td>859</td><td>1,417</td><td>Ixion</td><td>28.7.1950</td><td>10,125</td><td>Passenger-Cargo (Refrigerated)</td><td>St/Sc/St
496.3/69.3/34.7</td><td>3,000 nhp
15,000 shp
Turb
H&W</td><td>Ocean Steamship Co. (Holt & Co.)
Liverpool.</td></tr>
<tr><td colspan="9">Completed 5.1.1951, sister ship of Helenus. Broken up Spain (Villanueve y Geltru) 1972.</td></tr>
<tr><td>860</td><td>1,418</td><td>Laganfield</td><td>26.9.1950</td><td>8,196</td><td>Oil Tanker</td><td>St/Sc/Mv
469.4/59.3/34.8</td><td>640 nhp
3,500 bhp
Dies
H&W</td><td>Hunting & Son Ltd
Newcastle</td></tr>
<tr><td colspan="9">Completed 29.12.1950. In 1961 to Argentine owners, P.&M. Martini, renamed Anna Maria Martini and Netin (1974). Broken up Italy (La Spezia) 1978.</td></tr>
</table>

Ship	Yard No	Name	Date Launched	Displacement Tons	Type	Construction and Dimensions	Horse Power/ Engines	Owners
N/A	1,419	*Bollsta*	Govan built					
N/A	1,420	Un-named	Govan cancelled					
861	1,421	*Bloemfontein Castle*	25.8.1949	18,400	Passenger-Cargo	St/2Sc/Mv 570.7/76.4/39.5	4,000 nhp 20,000 bhp Dies H&W	Union-Castle Steamship Co. London
Completed 25.3.1950, emigrant carrier East Africa, unsuccessful in role, never really effective as part of Union-Castle fleet. In 1959 to Greek owners, Chandris, renamed *Patris*. Refitted, transferred to National Greek-Australia Line and employed on Sydney–Singapore route. In 1976 returned to Greece where converted to car ferry. In 1979 to M.A. Karageorgis, renamed *Mediterranean Island* and *Mediterranean Star* (1981). In 1987, renamed *Terra* for final voyage to breakers in Pakistan (Gadani).								
N/A	1,422	*Ernst Larsen*	Pointhouse built					
N/A	1,423	*Arnt Karlsen*	Pointhouse built					
N/A	1,424	Un-named	Govan cancelled					
862	1,425	*British Skill*	16.1.1952	18,550	Oil Tanker	St/Sc/St 619.5/81.3/44.7	2,750 nhp 13,750 shp Turb H&W	British Tanker Co. London
Completed 12.6.1952. Broken up Taiwan (Kaohsiung) 1972.								
N/A	1,426	Un-named Lighter	Pointhouse cancelled					
N/A	1,427	Un-named Lighter	Pointhouse cancelled					
N/A	1,428	*Carnarvon*	Pointhouse built					
N/A	1,429	*Simba*	Pointhouse built					
N/A	1,430	*Nyati*	Pointhouse built					
863	1,431	*Rhodesia Castle*	5.4.1951	17,041	Passenger-Cargo	St/2Sc/St 556.4/74.3/40.3	2,880 nhp 14,400 shp Turb H&W	Union-Castle Steamship Co. London
Completed 6.10.1951, similar to *Bloemfontein Castle* but not strictly a sister ship, for round-Africa route. By 1960 had accommodation for 442 one-class passengers. Broken up Taiwan (Kaohsiung) 1967.								
864	1,432	*Kenya Castle*	21.6.1951	17,041	Passenger-Cargo	St/2Sc/St 556.4/74.3/40.3	2,880 nhp 14,400 shp Turb H&W	Union-Castle Steamship Co. London
Completed 16.2.1952, sister ship of *Rhodesia Castle*. In 1967 to Greek owners, Chandris, renamed *Amerikanis* refitted to accommodate 920 passengers between Greece and New York. Later used as cruise ship with accommodation for 617 passengers. In 1989 when replaced by more modern ships returned to Greece and laid up. At one point suggested might be converted to floating hotel on Thames but broken up India (Alang) 2001.								
865	1,433	*Roonagh Head*	17.12.1951	6,153	Cargo Ship	St/Sc/St 438.2/59.5/27.4	1,210 nhp 6,050 shp Turb H&W	Ulster Steamship Co. Belfast
Completed 20.3.1952. Broken up Italy (Castellon) 1971.								
N/A	1,434	*Kvint*	Pointhouse built					
N/A	1,435	*La Rochelle*	Govan built					
866	1,436	*Clydefield*	16.9.1952	11,163	Oil Tanker	St/Sc/Mv 526.7/70.3/31.7	1,500 nhp Dies H&W	Hunting & Son Ltd Newcastle
Completed 21.1.1953. Badly damaged by fire Cutuco, El Salvador, November 1964. Broken up Japan (Hirao) 1965.								
867	1,437	*Port Nelson*	19.6.1951	8,375	Cargo Ship (Refrigerated)	St/Sc/Mv 472.0/64.8/29.4	1,390 nhp 7,500 bhp Dies H&W	Port Line Ltd London
Completed 31.10.1951. Broken up Italy (Castellon) 1972.								
868	1,438	*Eastern Star*	2.8.1951	6,523	Cargo Ship (Refrigerated)	St/Sc/St 443.4/60.0/26.7	1,670 nhp 7,250 shp Turb H&W	Australia China Line Ltd Hong Kong
Completed 20.12.1951. Seriously damaged by fire at Hong Kong, July 1969, broken up Taiwan (Keelung).								

Ship	Yard No	Name	Date Launched	Displacement Tons	Type	Construction and Dimensions	Horse Power/ Engines	Owners
N/A	1,439	*Setter VII*	Pointhouse built					
N/A	1,440	*Setter VIII*	Pointhouse built					
N/A	1,441	*Star XI*	Pointhouse built					
N/A	1,442	*Tuscany*	Govan built					
869	1,443	*Janita*	25.3.1952	12,757	Oil Tanker	St/Sc/Mv 546.2/73.3/39.3	1,500 nhp 7,500 bhp Dies H&W	Spermacet Whaling SA Panama
Completed 9.7.1952. In 1964 to Hong Kong owners, C.Y. Tung, renamed *Atlantic Endeavour.* Broken up Taiwan (Kaohsiung) 1976.								
870	1,444	*Raeburn*	6.8.1952	8,312	Cargo Ship	St/Sc/Mv 447.6/63.3/35.1	1,606 nhp 8,000 bhp Dies H&W	Lamport & Holt Ltd Liverpool
Completed 28.11.1952. In 1958 renamed *Colorado Star.* In 1972 to Singapore owners, Austasia Line, renamed *Mahsuri.* Returned to Lamport & Holt 1977, renamed *Roland.* Broken up Faslane (UK) 1978.								
871	1,445	*Cedric*	22.5.1952	11,232	Cargo Ship (Refrigerated)	St/2Sc/Mv 493.5/69.3/37.7	2,860 nhp 14,300 bhp Dies H&W	Shaw Savill & Albion Co. London
Completed 11.11.1952. In 1976 to Liberian owners, Fife Shipping, renamed *Sea Condor.* Broken up Taiwan (Kaohsiung) 1976.								
N/A	1,446	*J.K. Hansen*	Pointhouse built					
N/A	1,447	*Essequibo*	Govan built					
872	1,448	*Unitsha*	29.1.1952	5,802	Cargo Ship	St/Sc/Mv 428.9/62.3/20.8	750 nhp 3,750 bhp Dies H&W	Elder Dempster Lines Ltd Liverpool
Completed 5.6.1952. In 1972 to Greek owners, G. Dracopoulos, renamed *Amvourgon.* Damaged by fire Quebec, January 1975, broken up Spain (Santander).								
873	1,449	*Obuasi*	24.6.1952	5,883	Cargo Ship	St/Sc/Mv 429.0/60.3/21.5	750 nhp 3,750 bhp Dies H&W	Elder Dempster Lines Ltd Liverpool
Completed 12.11.1952, near sister of *Onitsha.* In 1972 to Hong Kong ownership, Anglo-Eastern Sg Co., renamed *Amoy.* Wrecked off Burma, August 1972.								
874	1,450	*King Malcolm*	29.11.1951	5,883	Cargo Ship	St/Sc/Mv 477.8/59.2/25.2	660 nhp 3,300 bhp Dies H&W	King Line Ltd London
Completed 29.2.1952. In 1959 to Clan Line. In 1963 to Hector Whaling. In 1972 to Cypriot ownership, V. Haji Ioannou, renamed *Kanaris.* In 1980 to Greek owners, Dimitra Sg Co., renamed *Dimitra K.* Broken up Bangladesh (Chittagong) 1981.								
875	1,451	*King Alexander*	14.2.1952	5,883	Cargo Ship	St/Sc/Mv 477.8/59.2/25.2	660 nhp 3,300 bhp Dies H&W	King Line Ltd London
Completed 6.5.1952, sister ship of *King Malcolm.* In 1972 to Cypriot ownership, V. Haji Ioannou, renamed *Elli 2.* In 1980 to Thai owners, Bangkok Marine, renamed *Bangkok 2.* Broken up Pakistan (Gadani) 1982.								
876	1,452	*Janova*	8.7.1952	12,765	Oil Tanker	St/Sc/Mv 546.2/73.3/39.3	1,500 nhp 7,500 bhp Dies H&W	Spermacet Whaling SA Panama
Completed 30.1.1953, sister ship of *Janita.* In 1965 to Bulgarian government, renamed *Hydrophane* and *Lom* (1971). Lost following collision Black Sea, January 1972.								
877	1,453	*Cymric*	5.11.1952	11,182	Cargo Ship (Refrigerated)	St/2Sc/Mv 493.5/69.3/37.7	2,860 nhp 14,300 bhp Dies H&W	Shaw Savill & Albion Co. London
Completed 15.5.1953, sister ship of *Cedric.* In 1973 to Royal Mail, renamed *Durango.* Broken up Taiwan (Kaohsiung) 1975.								
N/A	1,454	*Blandford*	Govan built					
N/A	1,455	*Anders Arvesen*	Pointhouse built					

Floating out of *Esso Ulidia* (H&W y/n 1676) 1970. (Courtesy of Lagan Legacy)

Gowanbank (H&W y/n 1674) 1967. (Courtesy of Lagan Legacy)

Iron Somersby (H&W y/n 1688) 1971. (Courtesy of Lagan Legacy)

Isomeria (H&W y/n 1711) 1981. (Courtesy of Lagan Legacy)

Ship	Yard No	Name	Date Launched	Displacement Tons	Type	Construction and Dimensions	Horse Power/ Engines	Owners
878	1,456	*Beaverbank*	3.12.1952	5,690	Cargo Ship (Refrigerated)	St/Sc/Mv 431.9/59.3/25.4	1,020 nhp 5,100 bhp Dies H&W	Andrew Weir & Co. Glasgow
Completed 26.2.1953. In 1970 to Greek owners, J. Starvropoulos, renamed *Eratini*. In 1972 to D.G. Arapis, renamed *Provimi Star*. Broken up Pakistan (Gadani) 1982.								
879	1,457	*Nessbank*	18.12.1952	5,690	Cargo Ship (Refrigerated)	St/Sc/Mv 431.9/59.3/25.4	1,020 nhp 5,100 bhp Dies H&W	Andrew Weir & Co. Glasgow
Completed 24.6.1953, sister ship of *Beaverbank*. In 1973 to Cypriot owners, S. Stravelakis, renamed *Paris* and *Tithis* (1978). Broken up Pakistan (Gadani) 1981.								
880	1,458	*Fleetbank*	29.6.1953	5,690	Cargo Ship (Refrigerated)	St/Sc/Mv 431.9/59.3/25.4	1,020 nhp 5,100 bhp Dies H&W	Andrew Weir & Co. Glasgow
Completed 14.10.1953, sister ship of *Beaverbank*. In 1970 to Greek owners, S. Lalis & Co., renamed *Lady Ute*. In 1976 to G. Kotsovilis, renamed *Osia Irini Chrysovalandou II*. Arrested Sidon April 1978 with illegally diverted cargo under name *Camelia* (does not seem to have been an official change). Broken up Tunisia (Bizerta) 1983.								
881	1,459	*Braemar Castle*	24.4.1952	17,029	Passenger-Cargo	St/2Sc/St 556.4/74.3/40.3	2,880 nhp 14,400 shp Turb H&W	Union-Castle Steamship Co. London
Completed 8.11.1952, sister ship of *Rhodesia Castle*. After less than 14 years' service, broken up Faslane (UK) 1966.								
882	1,460	*Irex*	15.4.1953	8,280	Oil Tanker	St/Sc/Mv 470.2/59.5/34.8	640 nhp 3,200 bhp Dies H&W	A/S Fjeld Fredrikstad, Norway
Completed 8.7.1953, sister ship of *Kurdistan*. In 1965 to J. Stolt-Neilsen, renamed *Stolt Atlantic*, almost immediately to A. Langvik, renamed *Stolt Bjorn*. Broken up Pakistan (Gadani) 1975.								
883	1,461	*Irish Coast*	8.5.1952	3,824	Passenger-Cargo Ferry	St/2Sc/Mv 327.7/51.6/14.6	1,300 nhp 6,500 bhp Dies H&W	Coast Lines Ltd Liverpool
Completed 17.10.1952, for Dublin–Glasgow route. In 1969 to Greek owners, Epirotiki Lines, renamed *Achilleus* and *Apollon II*. Soon afterwards to G. Potamianos, renamed *Semiramis II*. In 1981 to International, renamed *Regency*. Wrecked at Batangas in the Philippines, October 1989 and broken up (Manila).								
884	1,462	*King Arthur*	19.11.1952	5,883	Cargo Ship	St/Sc/Mv 477.8/59.2/25.2	660 nhp 3,300 bhp Dies H&W	King Line Ltd London
Completed 19.3.1953, sister ship of *King Malcolm*. In 1952 to Clan Line returned to King Line 1963. In 1972 to Cypriot owners, V. Haji loannou, renamed *Toulla* and *Despo* (1979). In 1980 to Turkish owners, Basco Enterprises, renamed *Pearl Rainbow*. In 1981 to Greenleaf Navigation, renamed *Greenleaf*. Broken up Bangladesh (Chittagong) 1983.								
N/A	1,463	*Britta*	Govan built					
885	1,464	*British Engineer*	24.11.1953	21,077	Oil Tanker	St/Sc/St 640.7/85.8/46.9	15,750 shp Turb H&W	British Tanker Co. London
Completed 30.4.1954. In 1972 to Greek owners, J.S. Latsis, renamed *Petrola V*. Broken up Italy (Castellon) 1976.								
886	1,465	*British Corporal*	9.12.1953	10,071	Oil Tanker	St/Sc/Mv 497.1/65.3/35.9	4,950 bhp Dies H&W	British Tanker Co. London
Completed 1.7.1954. In 1960 renamed *Clyde Corporal* but later resumed original name 1964. Broken up Taiwan (Kaohsiung) 1972.								
N/A	1,466	*British Gunner*	Govan built					
N/A	1,467	*British Sergeant*	Govan built					
887	1,468	*Harpa*	29.1.1953	12,202	Oil Tanker	St/Sc/Mv 537.6/69.5/30.0	8,250 shp Turb H&W	Anglo-Saxon Petroleum Co. London
Completed 11.6.1953. In 1955 to Dutch owners, La Corona/Shell, renamed *Kellia*. In 1961 to Argentine owners, Star Marine, not renamed. In 1973 to Cimba, renamed *Fabiana*. Broken up Argentina (Zarate) 1975.								

Ship	Yard No	Name	Date Launched	Displacement Tons	Type	Construction and Dimensions	Horse Power/ Engines	Owners
888	1,469	*Harvella*	26.4.1956	12,224	Oil Tanker	St/Sc/Mv 555.9/69.5/29.9	8,250 shp Turb H&W	Shell Bermuda (Overseas) Ltd London
Completed 20.9.1956, sister ship of *Harpa*. Served under Argentine flag. Broken up Argentina (Villa Constitucion) 1984.								
889	1,470	*Cerinthus*	29.6.1954	12,194	Oil Tanker	St/Sc/Mv 555.8/69.5/29.8	8,250 shp Turb H&W	Hadley Shipping Co. London
Completed 9.11.1954, sister ship of *Harpa*. Broken up Faslane (UK) 1976.								
890	1,471	*Jarena*	25.8.1953	12,706	Oil Tanker	St/Sc/Mv 553.2/73.3/39.3	7,500 bhp Dies H&W	A/S Kosmos Sandefjord, Norway
Completed 20.11.1953. In 1965 to Hong Kong owners, Y.K. Pao, renamed *World Goodwill* and *Dolphin* (1971). In 1972 to Greek owner, N. Konialidis, renamed *Albacara*. Broken up Pakistan (Gadani) 1975.								
891	1,472	HMS *Torquay*	1.7.1954	2,150	Frigate	St/2Sc/St 370.0/41.0/17.0	30,000 shp Turb H&W	Admiralty
In the mid-1950s the Royal Navy escort force, which consisted of wartime-built vessels, was beginning to show its age. At the same time there was a huge expansion of Russian submarine forces following the introduction of the Project 613 'Whiskey' class in 1951 (215 delivered 1951–58). The navy issued a requirement for a new escort capable of maintaining 27 knots in a seaway to hunt the new generation of fast submarines. The resulting Type 12 were arguably one of the finest small warship designs of the twentieth century. The initial vessels were the Whitby class and H&W were given orders for two of these vessels. Completed 10.5.1956. Employed as training vessel with Dartmouth squadron and later as a navigation and direction training ship before being converted to a trials vessel for Computer-Assisted Action Information System (CAAIS). As a result was last of class to go to breakers in 1987 almost a decade after some of sisters.								
892	1,473	HMS *Blackpool*	14.2.1957	2,150	Frigate	St/2Sc/St 370.0/41.0/17.0	30,000 shp Turb H&W	Admiralty
Completed 14.8.1958. Sister ship of *Torquay*. On loan to New Zealand Navy 1966–71. Broken up 1978.								
N/A	1,474	*Maid of the Loch*	Pointhouse built					
893	1,475	*Rathlin Head*	10.8.1953	7,439	Cargo Ship	St/Sc/St 430.4/59.0/28.0	6,050 shp Turb H&W	Ulster Steamship Co. Belfast
Completed 4.11.1953. In 1970 to Cypriot owners, Zela Sg Co., renamed *George*. Broken up Spain (Vigo) 1972.								
894	1,476	*Iberia*	21.1.1954	29,614	Passenger-Cargo	St/2Sc/St 718.8/90.1/30.5	42,500 shp Turb H&W	Peninsular & Oriental Steam Navigation Co. London
Completed 10.9.1954. In 1960 extensively refitted, including the installation of air conditioning throughout for UK–Australia route. Not considered a reliable ship and withdrawn 1972. Broken up Taiwan (Kaohsiung) 1973.								
895	1,477	*Elpenor*	11.11.1953	7,757	Cargo Ship (Refrigerated)	St/Sc/Mv 487.0/62.4/28.3	7,600 bhp Dies H&W	Ocean Steamship Co. (Andrew Holt) Liverpool
Completed 22.4.1954. In 1978 to Liberian owners, Cremorne Bay Shipping Co., renamed *United Concord*. Broken up Taiwan (Kaohsiung) 1979.								
896	1,478	*Jaranda*	23.10.1953	12,776	Oil Tanker	St/Sc/Mv 572.6/73.4/30.8	7,500 bhp Dies H&W	Anders Jahre A/S Sanderfjord, Norway
Completed 9.1.1954. In 1965 to Marfama Cia Nav., renamed *Spyridon*. In 1973 to Comninos Bros, renamed *Armonia* and *Moni* (1976). Broken up Pakistan (Gadani) 1976.								
897	1,479	*Owerri*	14.10.1954	6,240	Cargo Ship	St/Sc/Mv 450.0/62.4/23.0	3,750 bhp Dies H&W	Elder Dempster Lines Ltd Liverpool
Completed 21.1.1955. In 1972 renamed *Maldive Courage*. Broken up Pakistan (Karachi) 1983.								
898	1,480	*Loch Gowan*	19.1.1954	9,718	Cargo Ship (Refrigerated)	St/Sc/St 502.9/68.4/28.6	11,550 shp Turb H&W	Royal Mail Lines Ltd London
Completed 27.6.1954, for Pacific services. Broken up Taiwan (Kaohsiung) 1970.								
899	1,481	*Cedarbank*	29.9.1954	5,671	Cargo Ship (Refrigerated)	St/Sc/Mv 455.0/59.4/26.1	4,500 bhp Dies H&W	Andrew Weir & Co. Glasgow
Completed 5.1.1955. In 1973 to Cypriot owners, Jacaransa Shipping, renamed *Pola Monika*. Broken up Pakistan (Gadani) 1979.								

Ship	Yard No	Name	Date Launched	Displacement Tons	Type	Construction and Dimensions	Horse Power/ Engines	Owners
N/A	1,482	*Port Montreal*	Govan built					
900	1,483	*Port Melbourne*	10.3.1955	10,470	Cargo Ship (Refrigerated)	St/2Sc/Mv 532.6/70.4/28.9	13,200 bhp Dies H&W	Port Line Ltd London
Completed 7.7.1955. In 1972 to Greek owners, J.C. Carras, renamed *Therisos Express*. In 1974 to Delian Artemis Cruises, rebuilt as cruise ship, renamed *Danae.* In 1992 to Harbour Marine, renamed *Anar*, later in year to Capricorn Maritime, renamed *Starlight Princess.* In 1994 to Flax International, renamed *Baltica.* In 1996 to Arcalia Shipping/Classic International Cruises, renamed *Princess Danae.* Still extant; can carry 657 passengers, rated at 17,074 tons (May 2011).								
901	1,484	*Vibex*	5.5.1955	20,787	Oil Tanker	St/Sc/St 659.9/84.6/34.9	14,500 shp Turb H&W	Shell Bermuda (Overseas) Ltd London
Completed 20.10.1955. Broken up Holland 1972.								
902	1,485	*Harpula*	6.7.1955	12,258	Oil Tanker	St/Sc/Mv 555.8/69.5/29.8	8,250 shp Turb H&W	Shell Tankers Ltd London
Completed 21.12.1955, near sister of *Cerinthus.* Broken up Taiwan (Kaohsiung) 1975.								
N/A	1,486	*Belfast*	Govan built					
N/A	1,487	Un-named	Cancelled					
N/A	1,488	HMS *Brayford*	Pointhouse built					
N/A	1,489	HMS *Bryansford*	Pointhouse built					
N/A	1,490	Un-named	Govan cancelled					
N/A	1,491	*Maid of Argyll*	Pointhouse built					
N/A	1,492	*Maid of Skelmorlie*	Pointhouse built					
903	1,493	*Solfonn*	2.3.1956	19,810	Oil Tanker	St/Sc/St 649.7/84.4/34.9	13,750 shp Turb H&W	Sigval Bergesen Stavanger, Norway
Completed 13.6.1956. In 1967 to American owners, Burbank & Co., renamed *Wabash River.* In 1969 to Greek owners, N.J. Vardinoyannis, renamed *Vardis V.* Broken up Taiwan (Kaohsiung) 1979.								
904	1,494	*Pontia*	2.6.1954	8,904	Oil Tanker	St/Sc/Mv 498.6/61.9/27.9	3,200 bhp Dies H&W	Hvalfangerselskapet Pelagos A/S Tonsberg, Norway
Completed 15.9.1954. In 1971 to Greek Owners, A.P. Kefallonitis, renamed *Kef George* and *Poros* (1978). Broken up Taiwan (Kaohsiung) 1978.								
N/A	1,495	Unnamed Tanker	Cancelled					
N/A	1,496	*Triaster*	Govan built					
905	1,497	*Dolius*	4.8.1955	7,964	Passenger-Cargo (Refrigerated)	St/Sc/Mv 491.4/62.4/28.5	8,000 bhp Dies H&W	Ocean Steamship Co. (Alfred Holt) Liverpool
Completed 5.1.1956. To Glen Line 1970, renamed *Glenfruin*; reverted to Holts and original name 1972. In 1972 to Nan Yang Shipping Co., Macao, renamed *Hungmein.* Subsequently to Panamanian ownership operating under Somali flag. In 1977 to Chinese government, renamed *Hng Qi 119* and *Zhan Dou 51* (1984). Fate unknown; deleted by Lloyd's 1992.								
906	1,498	*Southern Cross*	17.8.1954	20,204	Passenger Ship	St/2Sc/St 603.9/78.6/25.9	20,000 shp Turb H&W	Shaw Savill & Albion Co. London
Completed 28.2.1955, a round-the-world cruise liner with accommodation for 1,100 one-class passengers. In 1973 to Ulysses Line, renamed *Calypso*, employed as cruise liner. In 1980 to Western Cruise Lines, renamed *Azure Seas.* In 1991 to Dolphin Cruise Line, renamed *Ocean Breeze.* Finally to Imperial Majesty Cruises, renamed *Imperial Majesty.* Broken up Bangladesh (Chittagong) 2003.								
907	1,499	*Tantallon Castle*	22.10.1953	7,448	Cargo Ship	St/Sc/Mv 494.7/65.9/27.8	9,850 bhp Dies H&W	Union-Castle Steamship Co. London
Completed 5.3.1954, for South Africa-UK/USA routes. In 1971 to Cypriot owners, J.N. & D.N. Pateras, renamed *Aris II* and *Aris* (1972). Broken up Japan (Aioi) 1978.								
908	1,500	*Tintagel Castle*	4.2.1954	7,447	Cargo Ship	St/Sc/Mv 494.7/65.9/27.8	9,850 bhp Dies H&W	Union-Castle Steamship Co. London
Completed 5.6.1954, sister ship of *Tantallon Castle.* In 1971 to Cypriot owners, J.N. & D.N. Pateras, renamed *Armar.* Broken up Taiwan (Kaohsiung) 1978.								
N/A	1,501	*YC327* Lighter	Pointhouse built					

Ship	Yard No	Name	Date Launched	Displacement Tons	Type	Construction and Dimensions	Horse Power/ Engines	Owners
909	1,502	RAFA *Tide Austral*	1.9.1954	13,165	Fleet Tanker	St/Sc/St 583.2/71.4/32.0	? Turb H&W	Royal Australian Navy
Completed 28.5.1955, Tide-class replenishment oiler originally for Australian Navy as HMAS *Supply*; because of manpower shortages and financial restrictions loaned to Royal Navy and operated under this name until 1962. In that year transferred to Australia and assumed her original name. Deleted 1985.								
N/A	1,503	*Busen 5*	Pointhouse built					
N/A	1,504	*Ballylumford*	Pointhouse built					
N/A	1,505	Un-named Tanker	Cancelled					
N/A	1,506	Un-named Tanker	Cancelled					
N/A	1,507	*Setter IX*	Pointhouse built					
N/A	1,508	*Western Prince*	Govan built					
N/A	1,509	*Rowanmore*	Govan built					
N/A	1,510	Cargo Ship	Cancelled					
910	1,511	*Elin Knudsen*	17.11.1955	20,492	Oil Tanker	St/Sc/St 664.9/85.9/34.9	13,750 bhp Turb H&W	Knut Knutsen OAS Haugesund, Norway
Completed 11.4.1956. In 1967 to Stephanson-Smith, renamed *Camilla*. In 1969 to Liberian owners, Whitehall International, renamed *Nepco Dauntless*. Broken up Taiwan (Kaohsiung) 1976.								
911	1,512	*Vitrina*	16.4.1957	20,802	Oil Tanker	St/Sc/St 659.9/84.6/34.9	14,500 shp Turb H&W	Shell Tankers UK London
Completed 4.7.1957, sister ship of *Vibex*. In 1974 to Singapore owners, Independent Shipping, renamed *Cherry King*. Broken up Taiwan (Kaohsiung) 1978.								
N/A	1,513	*Southern Prince*	Govan built					
912	1,514	*Foylebank*	24.3.1955	5,671	Cargo Ship (Refrigerated)	St/Sc/Mv 455.0/59.4/26.1	5,100 bhp Dies H&W	Andrew Weir & Co. Glasgow
Completed 4.8.1955, near sister of *Cederbank*. In 1972 to Cypriot owners, Patroclos Shipping Co., renamed *Patroclos*. Broken up Cuba 1989.								
913	1,515	*Laganbank*	5.7.1955	5,671	Cargo Ship (Refrigerated)	St/Sc/Mv 455.0/59.4/26.1	5,100 bhp Dies H&W	Andrew Weir & Co. Glasgow
Completed 27.10.1955, sister ship of *Foylebank*. In 1972 to Cypriot owners, Tower Shipping Co., renamed *Pola Anna*, *Golden Sea* (1973) and *Eastern Saturn* (1974). Foundered Gulf of Guinea, February 1978.								
N/A	1,516	Un-named Cargo Ship	Cancelled					
914	1,517	HMS *Kemerton*	27.11.1953	360	Minesweeper	Wd/2Sc/Mv 152.0/28.8/8.2	2,500 bhp Dies H&W	Admiralty
During Korean War was discovered that contemporary Russian magnetic mines could no longer be countered by degaussing; consequently, steel-hulled minesweepers were obsolete. A huge programme of minesweeper construction began based on an aluminium-framed wooden hull with non-magnetic fittings. The Ton class were intended for coastal work but were capable of undertaking ocean passages. One hundred and eighteen were authorised, of which H&W built 15. Completed 21.5.1954. Broken up 1971.								
915	1,518	HMS *Kirkliston*	18.2.1954	360	Minesweeper	Wd/2Sc/Mv 152.0/28.8/8.2	2,500 bhp Dies H&W	Admiralty
Completed 21.8.1954, sister ship of *Kemerton*. Served as RNVR/RNR vessel, temporarily renamed *Kilmorey*. Broken up 1991.								
916	1,519	HMS *Laleston*	18.5.1954	360	Minesweeper	Wd/2Sc/Mv 152.0/28.8/8.2	2,500 bhp Dies H&W	Admiralty
Completed 10.11.1954, sister ship of *Kemerton*. Broken up 1985.								

Ship	Yard No	Name	Date Launched	Displacement Tons	Type	Construction and Dimensions	Horse Power/ Engines	Owners
917	1,520	HMS *Lanton*	30.7.1954	360	Minesweeper	Wd/2Sc/Mv 152.0/28.8/8.2	2,500 bhp Dies H&W	Admiralty
Completed 10.3.1955, sister ship of *Kemerton*. Broken up 1970.								
918	1,521	HMS *Letterston*	26.10.1954	360	Minesweeper	Wd/2Sc/Mv 152.0/28.8/8.2	2,500 bhp Dies H&W	Admiralty
Completed 29.6.1955, sister ship of *Kemerton*. Broken up 1971.								
919	1,522	HMS *Leverton*	2.3.1955	360	Minesweeper	Wd/2Sc/Mv 152.0/28.8/8.2	2,500 bhp Dies H&W	Admiralty
Completed 25.8.1955, sister ship of *Kemerton*. Broken up 1972.								
920	1,523	HMS *Kildarton*	23.5.1955	360	Minesweeper	Wd/2Sc/Mv 152.0/28.8/8.2	2,500 bhp Dies H&W	Admiralty
Completed 25.11.1955, sister ship of *Kemerton*, originally to have been *Liston*. Broken up 1969.								
921	1,524	HMS *Lullington*	31.8.1955	360	Minesweeper	Wd/2Sc/Mv 152.0/28.8/8.2	2,500 bhp Dies H&W	Admiralty
Completed 1.6.1956, sister ship of *Kemerton*. To Malaysia 1966, renamed *Tahan*. Deleted in 1980s.								
922	1,525	HMS *Maddiston*	27.1.1956	360	Minesweeper	Wd/2Sc/Mv 152.0/28.8/8.2	2,500 bhp Dies H&W	Admiralty
Completed 8.11.1956, sister ship of *Kemerton*. Broken up 1975.								
923	1,526	HMS *Maxton*	24.5.1956	360	Minesweeper	Wd/2Sc/Mv 152.0/28.8/8.2	2,500 bhp Dies H&W	Admiralty
Completed 19.2.1957, sister ship of *Kemerton*. Broken up 1989.								
924	1,527	HMS *Nurton*	22.10.1956	360	Minesweeper	Wd/2Sc/Mv 152.0/28.8/8.2	2,500 bhp Dies H&W	Admiralty
Completed 21.8.1957, sister ship of *Kemerton*. Sold 1995.								
925	1,528	HMS *Repton*	1.5.1957	360	Minesweeper	Wd/2Sc/Mv 152.0/28.8/8.2	2,500 bhp Dies H&W	Admiralty
Completed 11.12.1957, sister ship of *Kemerton*. Sold 1982.								
N/A	1,529	HMS *Confiance*	Pointhouse built					
N/A	1,530	HMS *Confident*	Pointhouse built					
926	1,531	*British Honour*	25.9.1957	21,031	Oil Tanker	St/Sc/St 664.8/85.9/33.0	15,500 shp Turb H&W	British Tanker Co. London
Completed 31.1.1958. In 1973 to Cypriot owners, Troodos Shipping, renamed *Nedi*. Broken up Taiwan (Kaohsiung) 1976.								
N/A	1,532	Un-named Tanker	Cancelled					
927	1,533	*Reina Del Mar*	7.6.1955	20,225	Passenger Ship	St/2Sc/St 600.9/78.4/30.1	18,700 shp Turb H&W	Pacific Steam Navigation Co. Liverpool
Completed 8.4.1956, for UK–west coast of South America (via Panama Canal) route, accommodation for 207 first-class, 216 cabin-class and 343 tourist-class passengers. In 1964 withdrawn from South America services and converted to cruise liner. To Union-Castle 1973, withdrawn from service 1975, broken up Taiwan (Kaohsiung).								
928	1,534	*Port Launceston*	21.11.1956	8,957	Cargo Ship (Refrigerated)	St/Sc/Mv 490.6/66.0/28.9	7,700 bhp Dies H&W	Port Line Ltd London
Completed 12.3.1957. In 1977 to Singapore owners, Woburn Shipping Co., renamed *United Vantage*. Broken up Taiwan (Kaohsiung) 1980.								
N/A	1,535	Un-named Tanker	Cancelled					
N/A	1,536	Un-named Bulk Carrier	Cancelled					

Ship	Yard No	Name	Date Launched	Displacement Tons	Type	Construction and Dimensions	Horse Power/ Engines	Owners
N/A	1,537	*Ulster Premier*	Pointhouse built					
929	1,538	*Storfonn*	20.11.1956	24,854	Oil Tanker	St/Sc/St 660.3/86.3/37.1	13,750 shp Turb H&W	Sigval Bergesen Stravanger, Norway
Completed 31.1.1957. In 1968 to Panamanian owners, Astro-Proctor, renamed *Capetan Elias.* In 1975 to Marbrisas Armadora SA, renamed *Rockport.* Broken up Spain (Castellon) 1979.								
N/A	1,539	*Escalante*	Govan built					
930	1,540	*Duke of Lancaster*	1.12.1955	4,797	Passenger-Cargo Ferry	St/2Sc/St 376.1/57.4/14.9	10,500 shp Turb H&W	British Transport Commission
Completed 22.8.1956, one of three near sisters (third Denny-built *Duke of Rothesay*). Almost last examples of classic passenger/rail ferries. For Belfast–Heysham overnight route; had accommodation for 600 first-class and 1,200 second-class passengers. Subsequently converted to car ferry by H&W in 1970; main deck converted to car deck and stern door fitted. With closure of Heysham route in 1974 was transferred to other routes. In 1978 laid up at Barrow, subsequently to Empirewise, Liverpool, for use as an exhibition centre at Llanerch-Y-Mor, North Wales, renamed *Duke of Llanerch-Y-Mor.* Extant 2011 but derelict.								
931	1,541	*Duke of Argyll*	12.1.1956	4,797	Passenger-Cargo Ferry	St/2Sc/St 376.1/57.4/14.9	10,500 shp Turb H&W	British Transport Commission
Completed 22.9.1956, sister ship of *Duke of Lancaster*, rebuilt as a car ferry in early 1970s. In 1975 to Greek owners, Libra Marine, renamed *Neptuna.* In 1987 to Hellenic Maritime Lines, renamed *Corinthia.* In 1993 to Panamanian owners, Power Sea Transportation, renamed *Faith Power*, *Fairy Princess* (1994) and *Zenith* (1995). In 1995 severely damaged by fire at Hong Kong. Broken up China (Zhongshan) 1996.								
932	1,542	*Missouri*	7.8.1956	18,751	Oil Tanker	St/Sc/St 629.9/84.3/33.5	13,750 shp Turb H&W	General Tankers (Panama)
Completed 26.1.1957. In 1960 to Texaco, renamed *Texaco Missouri.* Broken up Taiwan (Kaohsiung) 1976.								
933	1,543	*New Mexico*	20.3.1958	18,751	Oil Tanker	St/Sc/St 629.9/84.3/33.5	13,750 shp Turb H&W	General Tankers (Panama)
Completed 13.9.1958, sister ship of *Missouri.* In 1960 to Texaco, renamed *Texaco New Mexico.* Broken up Taiwan (Kaohsiung) 1981.								
934	1,544	*Eden*	19.10.1955	7,791	Cargo Ship (Refrigerated)	St/Sc/Mv 444.7/58.8/26.9	4,500 bhp Dies H&W	Royal Mail Lines Ltd London
Completed 1.2.1956. In 1969 to Singapore owners, Neptune Orient Line, renamed *Neptune Garnet.* Broken up Taiwan (Kaohsiung) 1979.								
N/A	1,545	*Tuscany*	Govan built					
935	1,546	*Oti*	15.12.1955	5,485	Cargo Ship	St/Sc/Mv 450.0/62.3/27.0	3,750 bhp Dies H&W	Elder Dempster Lines Ltd Liverpool
Completed 26.4.1956. In 1972 to Cypriot owners, Mimimeth Shipping Ltd, renamed *Mimi Methantis.* In 1976 to Goldbeach Shipping, renamed *Goldbeach* (1976). In 1978 renamed *Nicolas K.* Broken up Taiwan (Kaohsiung) 1979.								
936	1,547	*Scottish Coast*	21.8.1956	3,817	Passenger-Cargo	St/2Sc/Mv 342.3/52.8/15.0	6,500 bhp Dies H&W	Coast Lines Ltd Liverpool
Completed 1.3.1957. In 1969 to Greek owners, Kavounides Shipping Co., renamed *Galaxias.* In 1989 to Cypriot owners, Almarco Marine Co., renamed *Princesa Amorosa.* Broken up India (Mumbai) 2002.								
937	1,548	*Cloverbank*	21.12.1956	6,459	Cargo Ship	St/Sc/Mv 483.3/62.9/26.0	6,700 bhp Dies H&W	Andrew Weir & Co. Glasgow
Completed 7.3.1957. In 1977 to Singapore owners, Pacific International line, renamed *Kota Rakyat.* Broken up Pakistan (Gadani) 1981.								
938	1,549	*Crestbank*	15.2.1957	6,459	Cargo Ship	St/Sc/Mv 483.3/62.9/26.0	6,700 bhp Dies H&W	Andrew Weir & Co. Glasgow
Completed 7.6.1957, sister ship of *Cloverbank.* In 1973 to Greek owners, Black Lion Shipping Co., renamed *Rena K.* Broken up Yugoslavia (Split) 1978.								
939	1,550	*Carronbank*	30.5.1957	6,461	Cargo Ship	St/Sc/Mv 483.3/62.9/26.0	6,700 bhp Dies H&W	Andrew Weir & Co. Glasgow
Completed 27.9.1957, sister ship of *Cloverbank.* In 1974 to Cypriot owners, Tafimar Nav. Co., renamed *Aris Carrier.* In 1976 to Lebanese owners, Eurabia Shipping, renamed *Eurabia Ocean* (1976), *Neptun* (1979) and *Maystar* (1980). Broken up India (Bombay) 1982.								

Ship	Yard No	Name	Date Launched	Displacement Tons	Type	Construction and Dimensions	Horse Power/ Engines	Owners
940	1,551	*Dartbank*	28.8.1957	6,461	Cargo Ship	St/Sc/Mv 483.3/62.9/26.0	6,700 bhp Dies H&W	Andrew Weir & Co. Glasgow
Completed 17.1.1958, sister ship of *Cloverbank*. In 1975 to Ceylon Shipping Co., renamed *Lanka Keeri*. Broken up Pakistan (Gadani) 1985.								
941	1,552	*Garrybank*	27.12.1957	8,693	Cargo Ship	St/Sc/Mv 483.3/62.9/29.3	6,700 bhp Dies H&W	Andrew Weir & Co. Glasgow
Completed 2.4.1958, near sister of Cloverbank type. In 1974 to Panamanian owners, Lee Lai Marine, renamed *Chieh Sheng* and *Chi Ho* (1976). Broken up Taiwan (Kaohsiung) 1979.								
942	1,553	*Minchbank*	19.6.1958	8,693	Cargo Ship	St/Sc/Mv 483.3/62.9/29.3	6,700 bhp Dies H&W	Andrew Weir & Co. Glasgow
Completed 25.9.1958, sister ship of *Garrybank*. In 1972 to Cypriot owners, Imperiana Transport Ltd, renamed *Aegis Grace* and *Grace* (1978). Broken up Taiwan (Kaohsiung) 1979.								
943	1,554	*Ondo*	7.6.1956	5,435	Cargo Ship	St/Sc/Mv 450.0/62.3/23.0	3,750 bhp Dies H&W	Elder Dempster Lines Ltd Liverpool
Completed 24.10.1956, sister ship of *Oti*. Wrecked near Kiel, December 1961.								
944	1,555	INS *Trishul*	18.6.1958	2,150	Frigate	St/2Sc/St 370.0/41.0/17.0	30,000 shp Turb H&W	Indian Navy
Completed 13.1.1960. A modified version of the Type 12. Deleted *c.* 1997.								
945	1,556	*King Charles*	15.3.1957	5,993	Cargo Ship	St/Sc/Mv 466.6/59.3/25.9	3,300 bhp Dies H&W	King Line Ltd London
Completed 25.6.1957. To Clan Line 1959 and Houston Line 1970. In 1973 to Cypriot owners, Aegis Shipping Co., renamed *Aegis Might*. Broken up Taiwan (Kaohsiung) 1979.								
946	1,557	*King George*	27.8.1957	5,989	Cargo Ship	St/Sc/Mv 466.6/59.3/25.9	3,300 bhp Dies H&W	King Line Ltd London
Completed 19.12.1957, sister ship of *King Charles*. To Clan Line 1959 and Houston Line 1970. In 1973 to Cypriot owners, Alassia Shipping Co., renamed *Eleni 2*. In 1980 to Hong Kong Marine, renamed *Taichung 2*. Broken up Taiwan (Kaohsiung) 1982.								
947	1,558	*Pendennis Castle*	24.12.1957	28,582	Passenger-Cargo	St/2Sc/St 763.3/83.9/32.2	46,000 shp Turb H&W	Union-Castle Steamship Co. London
Completed 14.11.1958, largest ship built for Union-Castle, for Southampton–Cape Town mail service. In 1976 to Panamanian owners, Ocean Queen Navigation Corp, renamed *Ocean Queen* and laid up Hong Kong .In 1978, still laid up, to Liberian owners, Kinvarra Bay Shipping Co., renamed *Sinbad* and *Sinbad I*. Broken up Taiwan (Kaohsiung) 1980.								
N/A	1,559	*Albany*	Govan built					
948	1,560	*Picardy*	30.4.1957	7,306	Cargo Ship (Refrigerated)	St/Sc/Mv 447.7/58.8/28.9	6,700 bhp Dies H&W	Royal Mail Lines Ltd London
Completed 22.8.1957. In 1971 to Liberian owners, Union SS Co., renamed *Europe*. In 1976 to Singapore owners, Lira Shipping Co., renamed *Lira*. Lost following explosion and fire, Indian Ocean, August 1977.								
N/A	1,561	*Thessaly*	Govan built					
949	1,562	*Loch Loyal*	9.8.1957	11,035	Cargo Ship (Refrigerated)	St/Sc/Mv 502.8/68.5/30.6	10,300 bhp Dies H&W	Royal Mail Lines Ltd London
Completed 30.12.1957, for North Pacific services. In 1971 to Greek owners, Aegis Group, renamed *Aegis Loyal*. Broken up China (Shanghai) 1974.								
N/A	1,563	*Toucan Lappe*	Pointhouse built					
N/A	1,564	*Flying Duck*	Pointhouse built					
950	1,565	*Port Invercargill*	22.11.1957	8,847	Cargo Ship (Refrigerated)	St/Sc/Mv 490.6/66.0/28.9	7,700 bhp Dies H&W	Port Line Ltd London
Completed 26.3.1958, sister ship of *Port Launceston*. Spent 1967–75 trapped in Great Bitter Lake by closure of Suez Canal and abandoned to underwriters. In 1975 to Greek owners, Deferon Corp, renamed *Kavo Kolones*. Broken up Taiwan (Kaohsiung) 1979.								
N/A	1,566	*Alaric*	Govan built					

Ship	Yard No	Name	Date Launched	Displacement Tons	Type	Construction and Dimensions	Horse Power/ Engines	Owners
N/A	1,567	*Afghanistan*	Govan built					
951	1,568	*Ulster Star*	26.2.1959	10,413	Cargo Ship (Refrigerated)	St/Sc/Mv 519.3/70.3/27.6	10,000 bhp Dies H&W	Blue Star Line Ltd London
Completed 3.7.1959. Broken up Taiwan (Kaohsiung) 1979.								
952	1,569	(Mid-ship section) *Esso Glasgow*	14.3.1957	10,720	Oil Tanker	N/A	N/A	Esso Petroleum Co. London
Delivered 17.8.1957, ordered as part of major rebuild of 1944 vintage American-built tanker. The ship, and new mid-ships, broken up Spain (Bilbao) 1971.								
N/A	1,570	*Flying Drake*	Pointhouse built					
N/A	1,571	*Eskfield*	Govan built					
953	1,572	*British Statesman*	27.11.1958	27,586	Oil Tanker	St/Sc/St 710.0/95.4/38.8	17,600 shp Turb H&W	BP Tanker Co. London
Completed 18.4.1959. Broken up Taiwan (Kaohsiung) 1975.								
954	1,573	*British Power*	22.5.1959	27,586	Oil Tanker	St/Sc/St 710.0/95.4/38.8	17,600 shp Turb H&W	BP Tanker Co. London
Completed 15.11.1959, sister ship of *British Statesman.* Broken up Taiwan (Kaohsiung) 1975.								
955	1,574	*William Wheelwright*	15.1.1960	31,320	Oil Tanker	St/Sc/St 753.6/98.5/40.7	16,000 shp Turb H&W	Pacific Steam Navigation Co. Liverpool
Completed 1.7.1960, spent most of life chartered to Shell Tankers. Ran aground December 1975 off Liberia, refloated but found damaged beyond repair. Broken up Spain (Santander) 1976.								
956	1,575	*Edward Stevinson*	24.8.1960	31,317	Oil Tanker	St/Sc/St 753.6/98.5/40.7	16,000 shp Turb H&W	Stevinson Hardy & Co. London
Completed 27.2.1961, sister ship of *William Wheelwright*, spent most of life chartered to Shell Tankers. Broken up Taiwan (Kaohsiung) 1981.								
957	1,576	*Carrigan Head*	2.7.1958	8,271	Cargo Ship	St/Sc/St 459.4/61.9/28.0	7,400 shp Turb H&W	Ulster Steamship Co. Belfast
Completed 18.11.1958. In 1972 to Cypriot owners, Chrysanthi Shipping Co., renamed *Chrysanthi.* In 1980 renamed *Rysan* and broken up Pakistan (Gadani).								
N/A	1,577	*Iron Age*	Govan built					
958	1,578	*Vestfonn*	7.3.1958	13,409	Oil Tanker	St/Sc/Mv 560.0/72.1/31.2	10,000 bhp Dies H&W	Sigval Bergesen Stravanger, Norway
Completed 11.7.1958. In 1965 to Stolt-Nielsen, converted into chemical carrier, renamed *Stolt Vestfonn.* In 1971 to Greek owners, Pyrgos De Nav, renamed *Stolt Fuji.* Renamed *Fuji* and broken up Taiwan (Kaohsiung) 1976.								
N/A	1,579	*Accord*	Pointhouse built					
N/A	1,580	*Advice*	Pointhouse built					
N/A	1,581	*Tri-Ellis*	Govan built					
959	1,582	*Manchester Miller*	12.12.1958	9,297	Cargo Ship	St/Sc/St 467.9/62.4/28.7	7,700 shp Turb H&W	Manchester Liners Ltd Manchester
Completed 19.3.1959. In 1970 converted to container ship, renamed *Manchester Quest.* Broken up Taiwan (Kaohsiung) 1976.								
960	1,583	SAS *Port Elizabeth*	8.11.1957	360	Minesweeper	Wd/2Sc/Mv 152.0/28.8/8.2	2,500 bhp Dies H&W	South African Navy
Following the Simonstown agreement of 1955 the South African Navy was expanded to defend Cape route. A number of ships were obtained from Britain. Amongst these were ten Ton-class minesweepers, three of which were built by H&W. Completed 10.7.1958, sister ship of *Kemerton*, originally *Dumbleton.* Rebuilt 1979–80 as minehunter, broken up 1987.								
961	1,584	SAS *Mosselbaai*	3.7.1958	360	Minesweeper	Wd/2Sc/Mv 152.0/28.8/8.2	2,500 bhp Dies H&W	South African Navy
Completed 11.2.1959, sister ship of *Kemerton*, originally *Oakington.* Broken up 1987.								

Ship	Yard No	Name	Date Launched	Displacement Tons	Type	Construction and Dimensions	Horse Power/ Engines	Owners
962	1,585	SAS *Walvisbaai*	10.12.1958	360	Minesweeper	Wd/2Sc/Mv 152.0/28.8/8.2	2,500 bhp Dies H&W	South African Navy
Completed 21.5.1959, sister ship of *Kemerton*, originally *Packington*. Rebuilt in 1995. In 2003 to Walt Disney Co. and became R/V *Belafonte* in film *The Life Aquatic*. Sold into private ownership and converted to yacht. Extant 2011.								
N/A	1,586	Un-named Tanker	Cancelled					
963	1,587	*King Henry*	15.8.1958	6,133	Cargo Ship	St/Sc/Mv 466.6/59.3/26.0	3,300 bhp Dies H&W	King Line Ltd London
Completed 5.12.1958, sister ship of *King Charles*. To Clan Line 1959 and Houston Line 1970. In 1972 to Greek owners, A. Marcopoulos, renamed *African Lady*. Passed to Grandmar Cia Naviera SA, renamed *African Lion*. In 1981 to Grifos Marine, renamed *Kladitis Emmanuel*. Renamed *Verbier* and broken up Pakistan (Gadani) 1983.								
964	1,588	*British Mallard*	3.11.1959	11,174	Oil Tanker	St/Sc/Mv 525.2/69.2/30.1	8,600 bhp Dies H&W	BP Tanker Co. London
Completed 6.5.1960. In 1978 to French owners, Soc Maritime d'Arm, renamed *Penhors*. In 1984 to Fal Bunkering Co., United Arab Emirates, renamed *Fal XII*. In 1987 renamed *Fame 2* and broken up Pakistan.								
N/A	1,589	*British Gull*	Govan built					
965	1,590	HMS *Berwick*	15.12.1959	2,519	Frigate	St/2Sc/St 370.0/41.0/17.0	30,000 shp Turb H&W	Admiralty
Completed 1.6.1961. A Rothesay-class Type-12 frigate. Effectively repeats of the earlier Whitby class. Sunk as a target, August 1986.								
966	1,591	HMS *Leander*	28.6.1961	2,450	Frigate	St/2Sc/St 372.0/41.0/18.0	30,000 shp Turb H&W	Admiralty
Originally sister ship of *Berwick* named *Weymouth*. In 1960 order cancelled and replaced by one for new vessel which, while still designated 'Type 12', are better known as Leander class. Completed 28.3.1963, first of 26 ships built to constantly evolving design over next decade, considered by many the most handsome warships ever built for Royal Navy. Sunk as target 1989.								
967	1,592	*Ashbank*	27.1.1959	8,694	Cargo Ship	St/Sc/Mv 483.3/62.9/29.3	6,700 bhp Dies H&W	Andrew Weir & Co. Glasgow
Completed 2.5.1959, sister ship of *Garrybank*. In 1979 to Liberian owners, Crest Shipping Ltd, renamed *Newcrest*. Broke tow and wrecked Santa Catalina Peninsula, Gijon, February 1983.								
968	1,593	*Rosebank*	30.12.1958	8,693	Cargo Ship	St/Sc/Mv 483.3/62.9/29.3	6,700 bhp Dies H&W	Andrew Weir & Co. Glasgow
Completed 3.4.1959, sister ship of *Garrybank*. In 1976 to Liberian owners, Transocean Shipping Co., renamed *Newbreeze* and *Newbeach* (1977). Broken up Bangladesh (Chittagong) 1982.								
969	1,594	*Amazon*	7.7.1959	20,348	Passenger-Cargo	St/2Sc/Mv 584.0/78.3/28.9	20,000 bhp Dies H&W	Royal Mail Lines Ltd London
Completed 31.12.1959. In 1968 to Shaw Savill & Albion, renamed *Akaroa*. In 1971 to Norwegian owners, A/S Uglands Rederi, converted to car carrier, renamed *Akarita*. In 1977 to Liberian ownership, Sagitta, renamed *Hual Akarita* and *Akarita* (1980). Broken up Taiwan (Kaohsiung) 1982.								
970	1,595	*Aragon*	20.10.1959	20,362	Passenger-Cargo	St/2Sc/Mv 584.0/78.3/28.9	20,000 bhp Dies H&W	Royal Mail Lines Ltd London
Completed 12.4.1960, sister ship of *Amazon*. In 1968 to Shaw Savill & Albion, renamed *Aranda*. In 1971 to Norwegian owners, A/S Leif Hoegh & Co., converted to car carrier, renamed *Hoegh Traveller*. In 1977 to Liberian ownership, Ace Nav. Co., renamed *Hual Traveller* and *Traveller* (1980). Broken up Taiwan (Kaohsiung) 1981.								
971	1,596	*Arlanza*	13.4.1960	20,362	Passenger-Cargo	St/2Sc/Mv 584.0/78.3/28.9	20,000 bhp Dies H&W	Royal Mail Lines Ltd London
Completed 23.9.1960, sister ship of *Amazon*. In 1968 to Shaw Savill & Albion, renamed *Arawa*. In 1971 to Norwegian owners, A/S Leif Hoegh & Co., converted to car carrier, renamed *Hoegh Transit* and *Hoegh Trotter* (1972). In 1977 to Liberian ownership, Ace Nav. Co., renamed *Hual Trotter* and *Trotter* (1980). Broken up Taiwan (Kaohsiung) 1981.								

La Pampa (H&W y/n 1678) 1970. (Courtesy of Lagan Legacy)

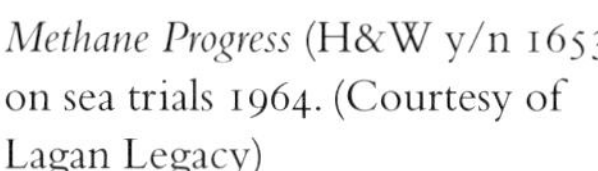

Methane Progress (H&W y/n 1653) on sea trials 1964. (Courtesy of Lagan Legacy)

Onitsha (H&W y/n 1448) 1952. (Courtesy of Lagan Legacy)

The launch of *Sea Quest* (H&W no y/n) 1966. (Courtesy of Lagan Legacy)

<table>
<tr><th>Ship</th><th>Yard No</th><th>Name</th><th>Date Launched</th><th>Displacement Tons</th><th>Type</th><th>Construction and Dimensions</th><th>Horse Power/ Engines</th><th>Owners</th></tr>
<tr><td>972</td><td>1,597</td><td>Tindfonn</td><td>31.1.1961</td><td>31,322</td><td>Oil Tanker</td><td>St/Sc/St
753.6/98.5/40.7</td><td>16,000 shp
Turb
H&W</td><td>Sigval Bergesen
Stavanger, Norway</td></tr>
<tr><td colspan="9">Completed 30.5.1961, sister ship of William Wheelwright. In 1976 to Atlas Livestock Carriers SA, converted to livestock carrier, renamed Atlas Pioneer. In 1977 to Lebanese owners, Raschid Fares Ent, renamed Danny F. Broken up Pakistan (Gadani) 1995.</td></tr>
<tr><td>N/A</td><td>1,598</td><td>Torr Head</td><td colspan="6">Cancelled</td></tr>
<tr><td>973</td><td>1,599</td><td>Tresfonn</td><td>1.3.1960</td><td>13,471</td><td>Bulk Carrier</td><td>St/2Sc/Mv
557.4/70.5/31.9</td><td>7,000 bhp
Dies
H&W</td><td>Sigval Bergesen
Stavanger, Norway</td></tr>
<tr><td colspan="9">Completed 11.6.1960. In 1973 to Panamanian owners, Noramarsa, renamed St Mary. In 1974 to Cypriot owners, Anassa Navigation, renamed Drymos. In 1976 to Argentine owners, registered in Liberia, Faramond Shipping and Trading Co., renamed Cuyo. In 1978 to Greek owners, Anemes Shipping Corp renamed Rio Bravo. Lost to flooding and fire 500 miles from Azores, March 1981.</td></tr>
<tr><td>974</td><td>1,600</td><td>British Lancer</td><td>28.9.1962</td><td>32,547</td><td>Oil Tanker</td><td>St/Sc/St
759.6/97.4/42.9</td><td>16,000 shp
Turb
H&W</td><td>BP Tanker Co.
London</td></tr>
<tr><td colspan="9">Completed 28.6.1963. In 1976 renamed Lancer and broken up Taiwan (Kaohsiung).</td></tr>
<tr><td>975</td><td>1,601</td><td>British Vine</td><td>23.9.1964</td><td>13,408</td><td>Oil Tanker</td><td>St/2Sc/Mv
559.0/73.9/30.1</td><td>7,500 bhp
Dies
H&W</td><td>BP Tanker Co.
London</td></tr>
<tr><td colspan="9">Completed 26.3.1965. In 1983 to Greek owners J.S. Latsis, renamed Petrolina VI. In 1987 to Cypriot ownership, Leficartis Bros, renamed Vine. In 1996 to Iranian owners, Iranian Marine Services (registered in Panama), renamed Saveh. Broken up India (Alang) 1997.</td></tr>
<tr><td>976</td><td>1,602</td><td>British Centaur</td><td>15.6.1965</td><td>37,985</td><td>Oil Tanker</td><td>St/2Sc/Mv
815.9/108.4/42.3</td><td>18,000 bhp
Dies
H&W</td><td>BP Tanker Co.
London</td></tr>
<tr><td colspan="9">Completed 11.1.1966. In 1983 renamed Earl of Skye; proposed to convert into livestock carrier but not undertaken. Broken up Korea (Ulsan) 1984.</td></tr>
<tr><td>N/A</td><td>1,603</td><td>Norsk Drott</td><td colspan="6">Govan built</td></tr>
<tr><td>977</td><td>1,604</td><td>British Cormorant</td><td>9.1.1961</td><td>11,132</td><td>Oil Tanker</td><td>St/2Sc/Mv
525.2/69.4/30.1</td><td>8,600 bhp
Dies
H&W</td><td>BP Tanker Co.
London</td></tr>
<tr><td colspan="9">Completed 6.7.1961. In 1977 to Liberian owners, Atlantic Tanker Transport Inc., renamed Oriental Unity. Broken up Indonesia (Djakarta) 1982.</td></tr>
<tr><td>N/A</td><td>1,605</td><td>British Osprey</td><td colspan="6">Govan built</td></tr>
<tr><td>N/A</td><td>1,606</td><td>British Merlin</td><td colspan="6">Govan built</td></tr>
<tr><td>978</td><td>1,607</td><td>British Cygnet</td><td>19.1.1962</td><td>11,131</td><td>Oil Tanker</td><td>St/2Sc/Mv
525.2/69.4/30.1</td><td>8,600 bhp
Dies
H&W</td><td>BP Tanker Co.
London</td></tr>
<tr><td colspan="9">Completed 7.6.1962, sister ship of British Cormorant. Renamed BP Endeavour (1967) and BP Explorer (1969) but resumed original name in 1970. In 1977 to Liberian owners, Transocean Marine Transport, renamed Oriental Endeavour and Oriental Banker. Broken up Indonesia (Djakarta) 1982.</td></tr>
<tr><td>N/A</td><td>1,608</td><td>Un-named Tanker</td><td colspan="6">Govan Cancelled</td></tr>
<tr><td>N/A</td><td>1,609</td><td>Bulimba</td><td colspan="6">Govan built</td></tr>
<tr><td>N/A</td><td>1,610</td><td>Bankura</td><td colspan="6">Govan built</td></tr>
<tr><td>N/A</td><td>1,611</td><td>Barpeta</td><td colspan="6">Govan built</td></tr>
<tr><td>N/A</td><td>1,612</td><td>Bamora</td><td colspan="6">Govan built</td></tr>
<tr><td>N/A</td><td>1,613</td><td>Bombala</td><td colspan="6">Govan built</td></tr>
<tr><td>979</td><td>1,614</td><td>Regent Liverpool</td><td>5.4.1962</td><td>30,770</td><td>Oil Tanker</td><td>St/Sc/St
746.3/98.4/39.7</td><td>16,500 shp
Turb
H&W</td><td>Regent Petroleum
Tankship Co.
London</td></tr>
<tr><td colspan="9">Completed 23.11.1962. In 1969 to Texaco, renamed Texaco Liverpool. Broken up Taiwan (Kaohsiung) 1982.</td></tr>
<tr><td>N/A</td><td>1,615</td><td>Flying Dipper</td><td colspan="6">Pointhouse built</td></tr>
<tr><td>N/A</td><td>1,616</td><td>Un-named Cargo Ship</td><td colspan="6">Cancelled</td></tr>
<tr><td>N/A</td><td>1,617</td><td>Un-named Cargo Ship</td><td colspan="6">Govan cancelled</td></tr>
<tr><td>N/A</td><td>1,618</td><td>Un-named Oil Tanker</td><td colspan="6">Cancelled</td></tr>
</table>

Ship	Yard No	Name	Date Launched	Displacement Tons	Type	Construction and Dimensions	Horse Power/ Engines	Owners
980	1,619	*Krossfonn*	23.11.1960	13,481	Bulk Carrier	St/2Sc/Mv 557.4/70.5/31.8	7,000 bhp Dies H&W	Sigval Bergesen Stavanger, Norway
Completed 8.4.1961. In 1971 to Panamanian owners, Elmar SA, renamed *San Francisco.* In 1974 to Argentinian owners, Solgt Til Navimar, renamed *Sarandi.* In 1982 to Greek owners, C. Tamasos, renamed *Leros Island.* Broken up China (Jiangsu) 1984.								
981	1,620	*Rimfonn*	19.8.1963	50,677	Oil Tanker	St/Sc/St 869.3/122.0/45.0	22,500 bhp Turb H&W	Sigval Bergesen Stavanger, Norway
Completed 18.12.1963. In 1975 to Dutch owners, Naess Shipping (registered Bermuda), renamed *Rama Notomas.* Broken up Taiwan (Kaohsiung) 1977.								
982	1,621	*Canberra*	16.3.1960	45,270	Passenger Ship	St/2Sc/St 818.6/102.6/32.8	42,500 shp Turb-Elect **Engines** Associated Electrical Ind.	Peninsular and Oriental Steam Navigation Co. London
Completed 19.5.1961, for London–Australia service, accommodation for 548 first-class and 1,690 tourist-class passengers and crew of 960. By early 1970s air travel and decline in emigration to Australia, combined with closure of Suez Canal, made service unprofitable. In 1973–74 refitted as cruise liner with accommodation for 1,737 passengers and 795 crew. In 1984 serviced as troopship in Falklands War, during which nicknamed 'Great White Whale'. After being used to repatriate Argentine troops from Falklands, refitted and returned to civilian service. By 1990s age and high running costs meant the vessel was increasingly uneconomic to operate. Withdrawn September 1997, broken up Pakistan (Gadani).								
983	1,622	*Somers Isle*	9.4.1959	5,684	Cargo Ship	St/Sc/Mv 396.0/54.3/26.2	4,500 bhp Dies H&W	Pacific Steam Navigation Co. Liverpool
Completed 10.7.1959, for Bermuda–Caribbean–Panama routes. In 1971 to Cypriot owners, Sealord Shipping Co., renamed *Eldina.* In 1975 to Commencement Companis Naviera, renamed *Commencement* and *Carribbean* (1981). In 1981 to Commercial Maritime Enterprises of Jersey, renamed *Melpol.* In December 1983 severely damaged by fire, English Channel, broken up Belgium (Ghent).								
N/A	1,623	*York*	Pointhouse built					
N/A	1,624	*Leeds*	Pointhouse built					
N/A	1,625	*Wakefield*	Pointhouse built					
984	1,626	*George Peacock*	17.3.1961	18,863	Oil Tanker	St/Sc/Mv 643.3/80.9/35.7	11,600 bhp Dies H&W	Pacific Steam Navigation Co. Liverpool
Completed 6.7.1961. In 1969 to Greek owners, V.J. Virdinoyannis, renamed *Georgis V.* In 1981 to Varnima Corp. Laid up in later years. Broken up Pakistan (Gadani) 1992.								
N/A	1,627	Un-named Bulk Carrier	Cancelled					
N/A	1,628	Un-named Bulk Carrier	Cancelled					
N/A	1,629	Un-named Bulk Carrier	Cancelled					
985	1,630	*Port Alfred*	8.9.1960	9,044	Cargo Ship (Refrigerated)	St/Sc/Mv 500.2/67.9/31.3	11,500 bhp Dies H&W	Port Line Ltd London
Completed 1.3.1961. In 1976 to Cunard. In 1978 to Brocklebank Line, renamed *Masirah.* In 1982 to Gibraltan owners, Orpheus Ltd, renamed *Masir.* Broken up Thailand (Siracha) 1986.								
986	1,631	*Port St Lawrence*	31.5.1961	9,040	Cargo Ship (Refrigerated)	St/Sc/Mv 500.2/67.9/31.3	11,500 bhp Dies H&W	Port Line Ltd London
Completed 20.10.1961, sister ship of *Port Alfred.* In 1976 to Cunard. In 1978 to Brocklebank Line, renamed *Matangi.* In 1982 to Maltese owners, Armier Shipping Co., renamed *Nordave.* Broken up Pakistan (Gadani) 1983.								
987	1,632	HMS *Kent*	27.9.1961	5,200	Destroyer	St/2Sc/St 521.5/54.0/20.5	60,000 shp COSAG H&W?	Admiralty
Completed 15.8.1963. A County-class guided missile destroyer. Often listed in contemporary naval publications as cruisers, a classification reinforced by use of county names, which had been used by navy for cruisers. These big handsome ships had limited service life as too expensive to operate (their crew was almost twice that of a Leander) and their main weapon system, the 'Seaslug' SAM, rapidly became obsolete. Deleted April 1980 but retained as harbour training vessel until 1997 when towed to India for breaking up.								

Ship	Yard No	Name	Date Launched	Displacement Tons	Type	Construction and Dimensions	Horse Power/ Engines	Owners
988	1,633	*Icenic*	23.6.1960	11,239	Cargo Ship (Refrigerated)	St/Sc/Mv 513.3/70.5/32.7	6,700 bhp Dies H&W	Shaw Savill & Albion Ltd London
Completed 19.12.1960. In 1978 to Greek owners, Atacos Cia, renamed *Agean Unity.* Broken up Taiwan (Kaohsiung) 1979.								
N/A	1,634	Un-named Oil Tanker	Cancelled					
989	1,635	*Pinebank*	5.6.1959	8,694	Cargo Ship	St/Sc/Mv 483.3/62.9/29.3	6,700 bhp Dies H&W	Andrew Weir & Co. Glasgow
Completed 24.9.1959, sister ship of *Garrybank.* In 1976 to Liberian owners, Ark Shipping Ltd, renamed *Newark.* Broken up Spain (Villanueva y Geltru) 1978.								
990	1,636	*Elmbank*	29.12.1959	8,694	Cargo Ship	St/Sc/Mv 483.3/62.9/29.3	6,700 bhp Dies H&W	Andrew Weir & Co. Glasgow
Completed 28.4.1960, sister ship to *Garrybank.* In 1976 to Greek owners, Maritime Corp, renamed *Blue Wave.* In 1984 renamed *Minoas* and broken up Pakistan (Karachi).								
991	1,637	*Avonbank*	6.10.1960	8,694	Cargo Ship	St/Sc/Mv 483.3/62.9/29.3	6,700 bhp Dies H&W	Andrew Weir & Co. Glasgow
Completed 13.1.1961, sister ship of *Garrybank.* In 1977 to Panamanian owners, Evolution Marine, renamed *Fortune Star.* Broken up China 1984.								
992	1,638	*Levernbank*	28/4/1961	8,694	Cargo Ship	St/Sc/Mv 483.3/62.9/29.3	6,700 bhp Dies H&W	Andrew Weir & Co. Glasgow
Completed 11.8.1961, sister ship of *Garrybank.* In July 1973 stranded in fog near Martarani, Peru, refloated but subsequently sank.								
993	1,639	*Springbank*	26/10/1961	8,694	Cargo Ship	St/Sc/Mv 483.3/62.9/29.3	6,700 bhp Dies H&W	Andrew Weir & Co. Glasgow
Completed 26.1.1962, sister ship of *Garrybank.* In 1978 to Liberian owners, Transorient Fright Transport, renamed *Global Med* and *Terrie U* (1979). Broken up Taiwan (Kaohsiung) 1984.								
994	1,640	*Olivebank*	21.12.1961	8,694	Cargo Ship	St/Sc/Mv 483.3/62.9/29.3	6,700 bhp Dies H&W	Andrew Weir & Co. Glasgow
Completed 12.4.1962, sister ship of *Garrybank.* In 1976 to Panamanian owners, Good Companion Shipping Co., renamed *Golden Lasos.* Broken up Taiwan (Kaohsiung) 1984.								
N/A	1,641	Un-named Oil tanker	Cancelled					
N/A	1,642	*Daghestan*	Govan built					
N/A	1,643	*Clyde*	Pointhouse built					
N/A	1,644	*Cressington*	Pointhouse built					
N/A	1,645	*Aigburth*	Pointhouse built					
995	1,646	*Port Nicholson*	4.5.1962	13,847	Refrigerated Cargo Ship	St/2Sc/Mv 573.6/76.2/35.1	17,000 bhp Dies H&W	Port Line Ltd London
Completed 9.11.1962. After only 17 years' service broken up Taiwan (Kaohsiung) 1979.								
996	1,647	*Roybank*	21.6.1963	6,526	Cargo Ship	St/Sc/Mv 483.4/62.9/29.2	6,700 bhp Dies H&W	Andrew Weir & Co. Glasgow
Completed 31.10.1963, sister ship of *Garrybank.* In 1979 to Cypriot owners, Cynthos Maritime Co., renamed *Castor* and *Byron I* (1983). Wrecked Kalilimenes, Crete, January 1985.								
997	1,648	*Weybank*	31.12.1963	6,527	Cargo Ship	St/Sc/Mv 483.4/62.9/29.2	6,700 bhp Dies H&W	Andrew Weir & Co. Glasgow
Completed 26.3.1964, sister ship of *Garrybank.* In 1979 to Panamanian owners, Chung Hsing Shipping Co., renamed *Golden Nigeria.* Broken up Taiwan (Kaohsiung) 1984.								
N/A	1,649	*Ring Wood*	Govan built					
N/A	1,650	*Belisland*	Govan built					

Ship	Yard No	Name	Date Launched	Displacement Tons	Type	Construction and Dimensions	Horse Power/ Engines	Owners
998	1,651	HMS *Fearless*	19.12.1963	11,060	Assault Ship	St/2Sc/St 520.0/80.0/20.5	22,000 shp Turb H&W	Admiralty
Completed 25.11.1965. Assault ship capable of accommodating 400 troops (700 for short periods), 17 tanks and 27 other vehicles. In 1976 downgraded to training squadron, but kept available for emergencies. Took part in Falklands campaign. Modernised in 1989–90. Broken up Belgium (Ghent) 2007.								
999	1,652	*Lossiebank*	25.1.1963	8,678	Cargo Ship	St/Sc/Mv 483.4/62.9/29.2	6,700 bhp Dies H&W	Andrew Weir & Co. Glasgow
Completed 3.7.1963, sister ship of *Garrybank*. In 1979 to Greek owners, Evicos Shipping Co., renamed *Evoicos Gulf.* Broken up India (Alang) 1985.								
1,000	1,653	*Methane Progress*	19.9.1963	21,875	Liquefied-gas Carrier	St/Sc/St 621.0/81.9/35.1	13,750 shp Turb H&W	Conch International Methane London
Completed 26.5.1964, this ship (and Vickers-built sister *Methane Princess*) first specifically built LNG carrier in service. Had capacity of 27,400cu. m. Operated between Algeria and Canvey Island, Thames supplying British Gas. After 467 voyages broken up Spain (Castellon) 1986.								
1,001	1,654	*Hazelbank*	27.1.1964	10,507	Cargo Ship	St/Sc/Mv 513.3/67.8/31.2	7,000 bhp Dies H&W	Andrew Weir & Co. Glasgow
Completed 20.5.1964. In 1979 to Greek owners, Alciana Bay Shipping Co., renamed *Argonaut.* In 1982 to Saudi owners, Good Harvest Marine, renamed *Mastura Zahabia.* In 1984 renamed *Golden Singapore* and broken up South Korea (Pusan) 1985.								
1,002	1,655	*Irisbank*	25.6.1964	10,526	Cargo Ship	St/Sc/Mv 513.3/67.8/31.2	7,000 bhp Dies H&W	Andrew Weir & Co. Glasgow
Completed 9.9.1964, sister ship of *Hazelbank.* In 1979 to Greek owners, Ormond Bay Shipping Co., renamed *Oceanaut.* In 1980 to North Korean government, renamed *Kang Dong.* Broken up India (Alang) 1994.								
1,003	1,656	*Texaco Maracaibo*	6.8.1964	51,774	Oil Tanker	St/Sc/St 858.0/125.4/47.5	27,500 shp Turb H&W	Texaco (Panama) Inc. Panama
Completed 14.1.1965, at time of launch largest British-built tanker. Broken up Taiwan (Kaohsiung) 1978.								
1,004	1,657	HMNZS *Waikato*	18.2.1965	2,305	Frigate	St/2Sc/St 372.0/41.0/18.0	30,000 shp Turb H&W	Royal New Zealand Navy
Completed 19.9.1966, sister ship of *Leander.* Scuttled off Tutukaka 2000.								
1,005	N/A	*Sea Quest*	7.1.1966	7,900	Oil Drilling Rig	N/A	N/A	BP Clyde Tanker Co.
Completed 5.7.1966, never allocated an order number. Launched from conventional slipways of Musgrave Yard, a feat many said was impossible. An exploration rig responsible for first major oil finds in North Sea. By 1977 search for oil in North Sea had moved into deeper waters and this rig was no longer suitable for operations. Transferred to Sedco, subsequently employed in Nigerian waters. In January 1980 badly damaged when a blow-out caught fire; wreck towed to deep water and scuttled.								
1,006	1,658	RFA *Regent*	9.3.1967	19,000	Fleet Replenishment Ship	St/Sc/St 640.0/77.3/26.1	20,000 shp Turb H&W	Admiralty
Completed 6.6.1967. Served in both Falklands and First Gulf War. Decommissioned 1992. Renamed *Shahzadelal* for last voyage to India where broken up (Alang) 1993.								
1,007	1,659	*Edenfield*	5.3.1965	35,805	Oil Tanker	St/Sc/Mv 774.6/107.9/41.5	17,000 bhp Dies H&W	Hunting (Eden) Tankers Ltd Newcastle
Completed 2.7.1967, almost immediately to Ministry of Defence, renamed *Dewdale*, employed as Royal Fleet Auxiliary east of Suez, officially classified as a mobile reserve tanker and had no RAS (Replenishment at Sea) capacity. In 1978 returned to owners before going to Liberian ownership, Liberian Athene Transport, renamed *World Field.* Broken up Taiwan (Kaohsiung) 1982.								
1,008	1,660	*La Estancia*	30.6.1965	28,007	Bulk Carrier	St/Sc/Mv 720.0/92.4/40.1	13,800 bhp Dies H&W	Buries Markes Ltd London
Completed 30.9.1965. In 1978 to Greek owners, Comninos Bros, renamed *Emmanuel Comninos.* In 1985 renamed *Jasmin* for voyage to China where broken up.								
1,009	1,661	*La Sierra*	24.11.1965	28,004	Bulk Carrier	St/Sc/Mv 720.0/92.4/40.1	13,800 bhp Dies H&W	Buries Markes Ltd London
Completed 12.2.1966, sister ship of *La Estancia.* In 1980 to Hong Kong owners, Ocean Trading, renamed *Bravery.* Broken up China 1992.								

Ship	Yard No	Name	Date Launched	Displacement Tons	Type	Construction and Dimensions	Horse Power/ Engines	Owners
1,010	1,662	*Orcoma*	25.1.1966	10,509	Cargo Ship	St/Sc/Mv 508.9/70.2/31.2	13,200 bhp Dies H&W	Nile Steamship Co. (Furness Withy) Liverpool
Completed 30.3.1966. In 1979 to Indonesian owners, P.T. Perusahan Pelayaran, renamed *Eka Daya Samudera.* Broken up Taiwan (Kaohsiung) 1984.								
1,011	1,663	*Donax*	5.7.1966	42,068	Oil Tanker	St/Sc/Mv 800.0/115.9/42.9	18,000 bhp Dies H&W	Shell Tankers (UK) Ltd London
Completed 16.12.1966. In 1984 to Cypriot owners, Troodos Groep, renamed *Savvas II.* Broken up India (Alang) 1992.								
N/A	1,664	*Doryssa* Oil Tanker	Cancelled					
1,012	1,665	*Nairnbank*	6.5.1966	10,541	Cargo Ship	St/Sc/Mv 513.3/67.8/31.2	7,000 bhp Dies H&W	Andrew Weir & Co. Glasgow
Completed 7.7.1966, sister ship of *Hazelbank.* In 1979 to Gulf Ltd, London, renamed *Gulf Hawk.* Broken up India (Alang) 1986.								
1,013	1,666	*Myrina*	6.9.1967	95,450	Oil Tanker	St/Sc/St 1050.0/155.3/58.0	30,000 shp Turb H&W	Deutsche Shell A.G. Hamburg
Completed 24.4.1968, first 'super-tanker' built in UK. Longer than longest slipway so when stern was completed partly launched to clear 121ft of slip to permit bows to be built. Broken up South Korea (Inchon) 1981.								
1,014	1,667	*Ulster Prince*	13.10.1966	4,478	Passenger-Cargo Ferry	St/2Sc/Mv 377.2/54.1/13.6	7,200 bhp Dies H&W	Coast Lines Ltd (Belfast SS Co.) Belfast
Completed 6.4.1967, drive-on/drive-off car ferry for Liverpool–Belfast route. First vessel on cross-Channel trade to have passenger lifts and fitted with bow thrusters for docking. In 1982 to Cypriot owners, Panmar Ferries Services, renamed *Lady M.* In 1984 to Panamanian Owners, Varsity SA, renamed *Tangpakorn* and *Long Hu* (1986), employed on Hong Kong–Kina route. In 1988 to Shun Tak Enterprises, Macau, renamed *Macmosa*, employed on Macau–Taiwan route. In 1995 to Hellenic Mediterranean Lines (under Panamanian flag), renamed *Neptunia*, employed on Bari–Cesme route. After less than a year to Panther Marine Corp. renamed *Panther* – remaining on same route. In 2000 chartered to Superferries, renamed *Vatan*, but in same year to Manar Marine Services, Panama, renamed *Manar*, moved to Dubai, operating Port Rashid-Umm Qasr route. Broken up India (Alang) 2004.								
1,015	1,668	*Fjordaas*	15.4.1967	41,079	Bulk Carrier	St/Sc/Mv 825.0/105.2/46.6	18,900 bhp Dies H&W	Agdesidens Rederi A/S Arendal, Norway
Completed 28.8. 1967. In 1979 to China Ocean Shipping Co. (PRC), renamed *Den Long Hai.* Broken up China 1991.								
1,016	1,669	*Essi Kristine*	21.11.1967	41,089	Bulk Carrier	St/Sc/Mv 825.0/105.2/46.6	18,900 bhp Dies H&W	Ruud-Pedersen Oslo, Norway
Completed 1.3.1968, sister ship of *Fjordaas.* In 1978 to China Ocean Shipping Co. (PRC), renamed *Wen Deng Hai.* No longer classified by Lloyd's last reported 1994. Broken up/Extent?								
1,017	1,670	*Skaufast*	9.8.1968	57,204	Bulk Carrier	St/Sc/Mv 855.0/137.8/46.4	18,900 bhp Dies H&W	A/S Elkland Oslo, Norway
Completed 29.10.1968. In 1978 to Greek owners, Metropolitan World Shipping, renamed *Mount Pelion.* In 1983 became *Energy Pioneer* but quickly passed to Garth Shipping co., Cardiff, renamed *Graigffion.* In 1985 to Nassau Shipping Co., renamed *Nassau Pride.* In 1988 Imperial Shipping, Bahamas, renamed *Pan Oak.* In 1991 to Turkish owners, Hilmi Sonayue Urtaklari, renamed *Anafarta S.* Broken up Pakistan (Gadani) 1992.								
1,018	1,671	*Thara*	14.5.1968	41,089	Bulk Carrier	St/Sc/Mv 825.0/105.2/46.9	18,900 bhp Dies H&W	Tonnevolds Redere A/S Grimstad, Norway
Completed 28.8.1968, sister ship of *Fjordaas.* In 1978 to China Ocean Shipping Co. (PRC), renamed *Luo Shan Hai.* No longer classified by Lloyd's last reported 1994. Broken up/ Extant?								
1,019	1,672	*Aino*	18.3.1969	57,204	Bulk Carrier	St/Sc/Mv 855.0/133.8/48.6	20,700 bhp Dies H&W	C.H. Sorensen & Sonner Arendal, Norway
Completed 16.5.1969. In 1983 to Hong Kong owners, East China Shipping, renamed *Mega Star.* In 1987 to Greek owners, Efshipping Co., renamed *Patman* and *Batman* (1989). In 1989 to Turkish owners, Somey Shipping, renamed *Anadolu 3.* In 1990 to Sonmez Denizcliik vo Ticaret, renamed *Ziya S.* In 1992 to Panamanian owners, Good Faith Shipping, renamed *Zea.* In 1997 became *Zea I*, and broken up Pakistan (Gadani).								

Ship	Yard No	Name	Date Launched	Displacement Tons	Type	Construction and Dimensions	Horse Power/ Engines	Owners
1,020	1,673	*Maplebank*	24.5.1967	10,365	Cargo Ship	St/Sc/Mv	7,000 bhp Dies H&W	Andrew Weir & Co. Glasgow
Completed 15.8.1967, sister ship of *Hazelbank*. In 1979 to Greek owners, Enaton Corp, renamed *Kavo Yossonas*. In 1985 renamed *Kowloon Countess* and broken up Pakistan (Gadani).								
1,021	1,674	*Gowanbank*	1.12.1967	10,365	Cargo Ship	St/Sc/Mv 513.3/67.8/31.2	7,000 bhp Dies H&W	Andrew Weir & Co. Glasgow
Completed 30.1.1968, sister ship of *Hazelbank*. In 1979 to Greek owners, Ogdoon Corp, renamed *Kavo Grossos*. Broken up India (Sachana) 1985.								
1,022	1,675	HMS *Charybdis*	28.2.1968	2,500	Frigate	St/2Sc/St 372.0/43.0/19.0	30,000 shp Turb H&W	Ministry of Defence
Completed 6.6.1969. A 'broad-beam' *Leander*, unlike many of sisters not rebuilt around the Exocet/Sea-Wolf weapons systems because of 1981 defence cuts. Sunk as a target, June 1993.								
1,023	1,676	*Esso Ulidia*	11.5.1970	126,538	Oil Tanker	St/Sc/St 1143.3/170.0/84.0	32,000 shp Turb H&W	Esso Petroleum Co. London
Completed 6.10.1970. The first super-tanker to be constructed in building dock. Had a short life being laid up at start of 1983 and broken up Taiwan (Kaohsiung).								
1,024	1,677	*Esso Caledonia*	29.5.1971	126,535	Oil Tanker	St/Sc/St 1143.3/170.0/84.0	32,000 shp Turb H&W	Esso Petroleum Co. London
Completed 6.9.1971, sister ship of *Esso Ulidia*. Broken up Taiwan (Kaohsiung) 1982.								
1,025	1,678	*La Pampa*	22.1.1970	17,180	Bulk Carrier	St/Sc/Mv 543.0/80.0/50.0	11,600 bhp Dies H&W	Buries Markes Ltd London
Completed 13.5.1970. In 1980 to Greek owners, Polydefkis Corp, renamed *Polydefkis*. In 1988 to Marina shipping, Bermuda, renamed *Maria Scirocco* (1988) and *Maria* (1990). In 1992 to Panamanian owners, Xin An Shipping Corp, renamed *Youth Strong*. In 1996 renamed *Yue Qiang* and broken up Bangladesh (Chittagong).								
1,026	1,679	*Bulk Eagle*	6.5.1970	17,180	Bulk Carrier	St/Sc/Mv 543.0/80.0/50.0	11,600 bhp Dies H&W	Kriship Shipping Co. London
Completed 14.9.1970, sister ship of *La Pampa*. In 1974 to Hong Kong owners, Denhart Sp and later Jardine, Matherson & Co., renamed *Eagle Arrow*. In 1985 to Panamanian owners, Libertaris Soc. De Carga, renamed *Aghia Markella*. and *Triumph* (1992). In 1993 to Shandong Shipping Co., renamed *Ever Access* and *Da Shun* (2001). Extant May 2011.								
1,027	1,680	*Sydney Bridge*	2.6.1970	35,868	Bulk Carrier	St/Sc/Mv 735.0/106.0/41.0	15,900 bhp Dies H&W	Bowring Steamship Co.
Completed 10.9.1970. In 1978 to Greek owners, Nissos Shipping Co., renamed *Amorgos*. In 1981 to Hong Kong owners, COScO, renamed *Bontrader*. Broken up India (Alang) 1997.								
N/A	1,681	Un-named Bulk Carrier	Cancelled					
N/A	1,682	Un-named Bulk Carrier	Cancelled					
N/A	1,683	Un-named Oil Tanker	Cancelled					
1,028	1,684	*Rudby*	11.12.1970	57,245	Bulk Carrier	St/Sc/Mv 855.0/133.5/66.0	23,200 bhp Dies H&W	Ropner Shipping Co. Darlington
Completed 1.3. 1971. In 1980 to Liberian owners, Rada Marine Corp, renamed *Orient Pioneer*. Foundered Indian Ocean, January 1990.								
1,029	1,685	*Olympic Banner*	7.10.1972	128,561	Oil Tanker	St/Sc/St 1132.0/171.0/68.0	32,000 shp Turb H&W	Carlow Maritime Panama
Completed 24.11.1972. In 1990 to Shell Tankers (UK), renamed *Latia*. Broken up India (Alang) 1997.								
1,030	1,686	*Olympic Brilliance*	4.8.1973	128,561	Oil Tanker	St/Sc/St 1132.0/171.0/68.0	32,000 shp Turb H&W	Lakeport Navigation Co. Panama
Completed 7.9.1973, sister ship of *Olympic Banner*. In 1990 to Shell Tankers (UK), renamed *Limnea*. Broken up Bangladesh (Chittagong) 1995.								

Ship	Yard No	Name	Date Launched	Displacement Tons	Type	Construction and Dimensions	Horse Power/ Engines	Owners
N/A	1,687	Unnamed Tanker	Cancelled					
1,031	1,688	*Iron Somersby*	8.10.1971	57,250	Bulk Carrier	St/Sc/Mv 855.0/133.5/66.0	23,200 bhp Dies H&W	Ropner Shipping Co. Darlington
Completed 7.12.1971, sister ship of *Rudby*. Immediately chartered to Broken Hill Property Co., used as ore carrier. Returned to owners in 1986, placed on Nassau registry, renamed *Somersby*. In 1987 to Karson Navigation Corp, renamed *Chia Yun*. In 1993 renamed *Chi Kuni* and broken up China (Nantong) 1993.								
1,032	1,689	*Barbro*	18.12.1971	56,915	Bulk Carrier	St/Sc/Mv 855.0/133.5/66.0	23,200 bhp Dies H&W	Rederi A/S Mascot Norway
Completed 18.2.1972, sister ship of *Rudby*. In 1981 to Korean Shipping Corp, renamed *West Junori*. In 1989 to Hanjin Transport Co., renamed *Hanjin Hedland* and *Hayarobi* (1990). Broken up Pakistan (Gadani) 1991.								
1,033	1,690	*Belinda*	26.4.1972	56,915	Bulk Carrier	St/Sc/Mv 855.0/133.5/66.0	23,200 bhp Dies H&W	Rederi A/S Mascot Norway
Completed 30.6.1972, sister ship of *Rudby*. In 1985 to Sincere Navigation Corp, renamed *Trave Ore*. In 1993 to Maritine Merchantile, renamed *Grand Arc*. In 1994 to owners in St Vincent, renamed *Grand*. Broken up 1996.								
1,034	1,691	*Mount Newman*	1.10. 1973	65,131	Bulk Carrier	St/Sc/Mv 858.0/133/72.0	23,200 bhp Dies H&W	Pacific Maritime Services Ltd Hong Kong
Completed 16.11.1973, a slightly enlarged version of *Rudby*. Ordered as *Winsford Bridge* but completed under this name after chartered on stocks by Australian National Line. Returned to owners in 1981. In 1982 to Hong Kong owners, C.Y. Tung, renamed *South Victor*. In 1987 to Queensgate Shipping Corp, renamed *Colita*. In 1990 to Pan Shipping Co., renamed *Pan Ceder*. In 1991 to Cypriot owners, Iapetos Marine, renamed *Iapetos*. Broken up India (Alang) 1996.								
1,035	1,692	*Canadian Bridge*	5.10.1974	65,135	Bulk Carrier	St/Sc/Mv 858.0/133/72.0	23,200 bhp Dies H&W	Britain Steamship Co. (Bibby Line?)
Completed 29.11.1974, sister ship of *Mount Newman*. Originally *Bedfordshire* but completed under this name after chartered on stocks. In 1977 returned reverted to original name and laid up. In 1978 to Shell, renamed *Tectus*. In 1987 to Philippine owners, Philippians Transmarine Carriers, renamed *Bocita*. In 1988 to Chinese owners, Tianjion Ocean Shipping Co., renamed *Shou an Hai*. Broken up China (Nantong) 1995.								
1,036	1,693	*World Cavalier*	23.3.1974	138,025	Oil Tanker	St/Sc/St 1133.0/171.0/86.9	36,000 shp Turb H&W	Hendale Navigation Co. Ltd London
Completed 12.6.1974. Operated under Liberian flag. Broken up South Korea (Ulsan) 1982.								
1,037	1,694	*Lotorium*	13.12.1974	138,037	Oil Tanker	St/Sc/St 1133.0/171.0/86.9	36,000 shp Turb H&W	Shell Tankers (UK) Ltd London
Completed 27.2.1975, sister ship of *World Cavalier*. In 1980 to Belgravia Tanker, renamed *Lotor*. In 1987 to Panamanian owners, Grafton Shipping, renamed *Olympic Armour II*. In 1996 to Thai owners, Thai International Tankers, renamed *Orapin Global*. Broken up Bangladesh (Chittagong) 2001.								
1,038	1,695	*Lampas*	5.7.1975	161,632	Oil Tanker	St/Sc/St 1153.0/182.0/95.0	35,496 shp Turb H&W	Airlease International (Shell Tankers) London
Completed 17.11.1975. Broken up Bangladesh (Chittagong) 1998.								
1,039	1,696	*Lepeta*	27.1.1976	161,632	Oil Tanker	St/Sc/St 1153.0/182.0/95.0	36,000 shp Turb H&W	Airlease International (Shell Tankers) London
Completed 26.7.1976, sister ship of *Lampas*. Broken up Pakistan (Gadani) 1999.								
1,040	1,697	*Leonia*	2.7.1976	161,626	Oil Tanker	St/Sc/St 1153.0/182.0/95.0	36,000 shp Turb H&W	Airlease International (Shell Tankers) London
Completed 30.12.1976, sister ship of *Lampas*. Broken up Bangladesh (Chittagong) 1998.								
1,041	1,698	*Lima*	11.12.1976	161,632	Oil Tanker	St/Sc/St 1153.0/182.0/95.0	36,000 shp Turb H&W	Airlease International (Shell Tankers) London
Completed 3.6.1977, sister ship of *Lampas*. Broken up Bangladesh (Chittagong) 1998.								

Ship	Yard No	Name	Date Launched	Displacement Tons	Type	Construction and Dimensions	Horse Power/ Engines	Owners
1,042	1,699	*Essi Camilla*	8.10.1975	63,509	Bulk Carrier	St/Sc/Mv 858.0/133/72.0	24,800 bhp Dies H&W	Ruud-Pedersen Oslo, Norway
Completed 5.1.1976, similar to Mount Newman type but with more powerful engines. In 1985 to Singapore owners, Essi Camilla Shipping Co. In 1987 to China Ocean Shipping Co. (PRC), renamed *Tao Jiang Hai.* In 1990 to Qingdao Shipping Co. (PRC). In 1999 to Shanghai Puyuang Shipping Co., renamed *Shuan Xin Feng Hai.* No longer classified by Lloyd's. Broken up/Extant?								
N/A	1,700	Un-named Bulk Carrier	Cancelled					
1,043	1,701	*Lackenby*	21.3.1977	64,640	Bulk Carrier	St/Sc/Mv 858.0/133/72.0	24,800 bhp Dies H&W	Ropner Shipping Co. Darlington
Completed 5.7.1977, sister ship of *Essi Camilla.* Originally *Otterpool* but renamed before completion. Broken up India (Alang) 1996.								
N/A	1,702	Un-named Oil Tanker	Cancelled					
N/A	1,703	Un-named Oil Tanker	Cancelled					
1,044	1,704	*Coastal Corpus Christi*	18.6.1977	172,147	Oil Tanker	St/Sc/St 1204.0/182.0/95.0	36,000 shp Turb H&W	Woodstock Shipping Co. Liberia
Completed 25.3.1980, delivery refused. In 1982 to Danesby Shipping Co., London, renamed *Carrianna Venture* and *Venturia* (1984*).* In 1988 to Feba Set Ltd, renamed *Daqing* and *Maxus Widuri* (1990). In 1997 to Singapore owners, Lingreta Marine Corp, renamed *Atlantic Blue.* Broken up India (Alang) 2002.								
1,045	1,705	*Coastal Hercules*	27.1.1978	172,147	Oil Tanker	St/Sc/St 1204.0/182.0/95.0	36,000 shp Turb H&W	Pomona Shipping Co. Panama
Completed 25.3.1980, sister ship of *Coastal Corpus Christi,* delivery refused. In 1983 to Mariana Islands SS Co., renamed *Medusa.* On 10 June 1986 hit by Iraqi air-launched missile 40nm from Kharg Island, declared a constructive total loss. Wreck broken up South Korea (Ulsan) 1987.								
N/A	1,706	Un-named Oil Tanker	Cancelled					
N/A	1,707	Un-named Oil Tanker	Cancelled					
1,046	1,708	*Appleby*	24.6.1978	64,641	Bulk Carrier	St/Sc/Mv 858.0/133/72.0	24,800 bhp Dies H&W	Ropner Shipping Co. Darlington
Completed 31.10.1978, near sister of *Lackenby* with less powerful engines. Originally for Norwegian owners under name *Golden Master* purchased and completed under this name/owner. Broken up China 1999.								
1,047	1,709	*Hornby Grange*	6.10.1978	39,626	Products Carrier	St/Sc/Mv 749.0/106.0/58.0	20,500 bhp Dies H&W	Alexander Shipping Co. (Furness Withy)
Completed 20.6.1979. In 1984 to Liberian ownership, Fest Atlantic, renamed *Santa Barbara.* In 1989 to Singapore owners, Transpetrol Navigation, renamed *Affinity.* Broken up India (Alang) 2000.								
1,048	1,710	*Elstree Grange*	27.1.1979	39,626	Products Carrier	St/Sc/Mv 749.0/106.0/58.0	20,500 bhp Dies H&W	Alexander Shipping Co. (Furness Withy)
Completed 24.10.1979. In 1984 to Liberian ownership, Fest Atlantic, renamed *Santa Lucia.* In 1989 to Singapore owners, White Tankers, renamed *Spirit.* Broken up India (Alang) 2000.								
1,049	1,711	*Isomeria*	21.3.1981	42,069	Liquid-Petroleum Gas Carrier	St/Sc/Mv 689.0/103.0/70.0	20,500 bhp Dies H&W	North Sea Marine Leasing Co. (Shell Tankers) London
Completed 30.4.1982. In 2005 to Singapore owners, MC Shipping, renamed *Galileo.* Broken up India (Alang) 2009.								
1,050	1,712	*Isocardia*	23.1.1982	39,932	Liquid-Petroleum Gas Carrier	St/Sc/Mv 689.0/103.0/70.0	20,500 bhp Dies H&W	North Sea Marine Leasing Co. (Shell Tankers) London
Completed 29.10.1982. In 1999 to Greek owners, Naftomar Shipping & Trade, renamed *Gaz Horizon.* In 2008 renamed *Horizon* and broken up India (Alang).								

<table>
<tr><th>Ship</th><th>Yard No</th><th>Name</th><th>Date Launched</th><th>Displacement Tons</th><th>Type</th><th>Construction and Dimensions</th><th>Horse Power/ Engines</th><th>Owners</th></tr>
<tr><td>1,051</td><td>1,713</td><td>Galloway Princess</td><td>24.5.1979</td><td>6,268</td><td>Passenger-Car Ferry</td><td>St/2Sc/Mv
424.0/71.0/39.0</td><td>16,000 bhp
Dies
H&W</td><td>Midland & Montagu Leasing Ltd
(British Rail/Sealink)</td></tr>
<tr><td colspan="9">Completed 22.4.1980, first and smallest of four ferries for British Rail, for Stranraer–Larne/Belfast routes. In 1990 to Stena Line when Sealink 'sold-off', renamed Stena Galloway. In 1996 following introduction of HSS ferry reduced to freight duties. In 2002 to Moroccan owners, IMTC, renamed Le Rif, employed on Algeciras–Tangier route. Extant 2011.</td></tr>
<tr><td>1,052</td><td>1,714</td><td>Ravenscraig</td><td>7.9.1979</td><td>64,651</td><td>Bulk Carrier</td><td>St/Sc/Mv
858.0/133/72.0</td><td>24,800 bhp
Dies
H&W</td><td>Orion Leasing Ltd
(British Steel)</td></tr>
<tr><td colspan="9">Completed 14.12.1979, sister ship of Lackenby. Broken up India (Alang) 1999.</td></tr>
<tr><td>1,053</td><td>1,715</td><td>St Anselm</td><td>5.12.1979</td><td>7,003</td><td>Passenger-Car Ferry</td><td>St/2Sc/Mv
425.0/71.0/39.0</td><td>20,800 bhp
Dies
H&W</td><td>Lloyds Leasing Ltd
(British Rail/Sealink)</td></tr>
<tr><td colspan="9">Completed 16.10.1980, for Dover–Calais service. In 1990 to Stena Line, renamed Stena Cambria. In 1999 to Spanish owners, UMAFISA, renamed Isla de Botafoc employed on Barcelona–Ibiza route. Laid up 2010 and sold to shipbreakers, resold and briefly renamed Winner-9, before sold to Panamanian owners, Ventouris Ferries, renamed Bari. Extant May 2011.</td></tr>
<tr><td>1,054</td><td>1,716</td><td>St Christopher</td><td>20.3.1980</td><td>6,996</td><td>Passenger-Car Ferry</td><td>St/2Sc/Mv
425.0/71.0/39.0</td><td>20,800 bhp
Dies
H&W</td><td>Barclays Mercantile Industrial Finance
(British Rail/Sealink)</td></tr>
<tr><td colspan="9">Completed 6.3.1981, sister ship of St Anselm for same service. In 1990 to Stena Line, renamed Stena Antrim and transferred to Larne–Stranraer route. In 1998 to Moroccan owners, Lignes Maritimes de Detroit, renamed Ibn Batouta, employed on Algeciras–Tangier route. Extant May 2011.</td></tr>
<tr><td>1,055</td><td>1,717</td><td>St David</td><td>25.9.1980</td><td>7,109</td><td>Passenger-Car Ferry</td><td>St/2Sc/Mv
425.0/71.0/39.0</td><td>20,800 bhp
Dies
H&W</td><td>Barclays Mercantile Industrial Finance
(British Rail/Sealimk)</td></tr>
<tr><td colspan="9">Completed 24.7.1981, sister ship of St Anselm, employed on the Stranraer–Larne/Belfast route. In 1991 to Stena Line, renamed Stena Caledonia. Remained on the North Channel routes. Still extant May 2011.</td></tr>
<tr><td>1,056</td><td>1,718</td><td>British Skill</td><td>3.7.1982</td><td>66,034</td><td>Oil Tanker</td><td>St/Sc/Mv
856.0/130/76.0</td><td>116,250 bhp
Dies
H&W</td><td>BP Thames Tanker Co.
London</td></tr>
<tr><td colspan="9">Completed 26.4.1983, designed to carry crude oil and semi-refined products Arabian Gulf–Australia. In 2002 to Singapore owners, Xin Don Shipping, renamed Ocean Skill. Broken up Bangladesh 2010.</td></tr>
<tr><td>1,057</td><td>1,719</td><td>British Success</td><td>28.3.1983</td><td>66,034</td><td>Oil Tanker</td><td>St/Sc/Mv
856.0/130/76.0</td><td>116,250 bhp
Dies
H&W</td><td>BP Thames Tanker Co.
London</td></tr>
<tr><td colspan="9">Completed 14.2.1984, sister ship of British Skill. In 2002 to Norwegian owners, International Andromeda, renamed St Andrews. In 2004 hulked and converted into off-shore storage/offloading vessel, renamed CNOOC 114.</td></tr>
<tr><td>1,058</td><td>1,720</td><td>British Steel</td><td>28.1.1984</td><td>90,831</td><td>Bulk Carrier</td><td>St/Sc/Mv
941.0/156.0/79.0</td><td>19,713 bhp
Dies
H&W</td><td>Lombard Finance
(British Steel Corporation)</td></tr>
<tr><td colspan="9">Completed 19.10.1984. In 2001 to Niagara Marine, renamed Good Luck. Extant May 2011.</td></tr>
<tr><td>1,059</td><td>1,721</td><td>English Star</td><td>23.9.1984</td><td>10,291</td><td>Cargo Ship (Refrigerated)</td><td>St/Sc/Mv
489.0/72.0/41.0</td><td>15,226 bhp
Dies
H&W</td><td>Lombard North Central
(Blue Star Line)
London</td></tr>
<tr><td colspan="9">Completed 7.1.1986. In 1987 chartered to Horn Line, Hamburg, renamed Hornsea, reverted to original name on return. Extant May 2011.</td></tr>
<tr><td>1,060</td><td>1,722</td><td>Scottish Star</td><td>23.9. 1984</td><td>10,291</td><td>Cargo Ship (Refrigerated)</td><td>St/Sc/Mv
489.0/72.0/41.0</td><td>15,226 bhp
Dies
H&W</td><td>Lombard North Central
(Blue Star Line)
London</td></tr>
<tr><td colspan="9">Completed 2.4.1985, sister ship of English Star. Extant May 2011.</td></tr>
<tr><td>1,061</td><td>1,723</td><td>Auckland Star</td><td>4.3.1985</td><td>10,291</td><td>Cargo Ship (Refrigerated)</td><td>St/Sc/Mv
489.0/72.0/41.0</td><td>15,226 bhp
Dies
H&W</td><td>Investors in Industry
(Blue Star Line)
London</td></tr>
<tr><td colspan="9">Completed 21.1.1986, sister ship of English Star. In 1987 chartered to Horn Line, Hamburg, renamed Horncliff. Reverted to original name on return. Extant May 2011.</td></tr>
<tr><td>1,062</td><td>1,724</td><td>Canterbury Star</td><td>1.7.1985</td><td>10,291</td><td>Cargo Ship (Refrigerated)</td><td>St/Sc/Mv
489.0/72.0/41.0</td><td>15,226 bhp
Dies
H&W</td><td>Investors In Industry
(Blue Star Line)
London</td></tr>
<tr><td colspan="9">Completed 4.2.1986, sister ship of English Star. Extant May 2011 but renamed Canterbury for final voyage to breakers (Alang).</td></tr>
</table>

Tanker *Skaufast* (H&W y/n 1670) 1968. (Courtesy of Lagan Legacy)

Texaco Maracaibo (H&W y/n 1656) 1964. (Courtesy of Lagan Legacy)

Thara (H&W y/n 1671) 1968. (Courtesy of Lagan Legacy)

Ship	Yard No	Name	Date Launched	Displacement Tons	Type	Construction and Dimensions	Horse Power/ Engines	Owners
1,063	1,725	*Ironbridge*	Sept.1986	90,000	Bulk Carrier	St/Sc/Mv 944.0/156.0/79.0	197,200 bhp Dies H&W	Lloyds Equipment Leasing Ltd (British Steel Corporation)
Completed June 1987. In 2001 to Greek owners, Marmara Navigation, renamed *Koutalianos.* In 2005 to Chinese owners, Hosco, renamed *Sea Ace.* Subsequently renamed *Hebei Loyalty.* Extant May 2011.								
1,064	1,726	*Seillean*	May 1988	50,928	SWOPS-Type Ship	St/2Sc/Mv 819.0/123.0/65.0	41,937 bhp Dies & Gas Turb H&W?	BP Petroleum Developments Ltd London
Completed April 1990, highly sophisticated vessel for oil production. After being employed in North Sea this vessel was sold in 1993 to Reading and Bates and moved to Brazilian waters. Currently owned by Noble Organisation of Panama, renamed *Noble Seillean.* Extant May 2011.								
1,065	1,727	*Fort Victoria*	12.6.1990	31,500	Fleet Supply Ship	St/2Sc/Mv 669.0/99.9/31.9	25,000 bhp Dies H&W	Ministry of Defence
Completed 24.6.1994. A one-stop supply ship capable of combining the functions of previous fleet tankers and stores ships. Armed for her own defence with 30mm guns and the Phalanx 20mm short-range weapon. Can operate up to five Sea King or Merlin helicopters. Extant May 2011.								
1,066	1,728	*Knock Allan*	August 1991	78,710	Oil Tanker	St/Sc/Mv 899.0/145/79.0	16,454 bhp Dies H&W	Fred Olsen Norway
Completed January 1992, registered Monrovia. In 2007 converted into oil production ship. Extant May 2011.								
1,067	1,729	*Knock Stocks*	1992	78,710	Oil Tanker	St/Sc/Mv 899.0/145/79.0	17,578 bhp Dies H&W	Fred Olsen Norway
Completed January 1993, sister ship of *Knock Allen*, registered Monrovia. In 2008 converted to oil production ship, renamed *Kalamu.* From March 2008 operating as floating production platform off Congo. Extant May 2011.								
1,068	1,730	*Knock Adoon*	1992	78,710	Oil Tanker	St/Sc/Mv 899.0/145/79.0	17,578 bhp Dies H&W	Fred Olsen Norway
Completed July 1992, sister ship of *Knock* Allen, registered Monrovia. In 1993 to Indian owners, Great Eastern Shipping Co., renamed *Jag Laadki.* In 2007 to Greek ownership, MASPAL Investments Corp, renamed *Kriti Episkopi.* Broken up Pakistan (Gadani) 2010.								
1,069	1,731	*Knock Clune*	6.3.1993	78,843	Oil Tanker	St/Sc/Mv 899.0/145/79.0	14,941 bhp Dies H&W	Fred Olsen Norway
Completed June 1993, sister ship of *Knock Allen*, registered Monrovia. In 2005 to Ardas Shipping Co., Marshell Islands, renamed *Errorless.* In 2007 to Cassidx Navigation Co., Marshall Islands, renamed *Sea Max.* In 2008 to Eldorado Shipholding (Marshall Islands), converted to ore carrier and renamed *Road Runner.* Extant May 2011.								
1,070	1,732	*Knock Dun*	1993	78,843	Oil Tanker	St/Sc/Mv 899.0/145/79.0	17,578 bhp Dies H&W	Fred Olsen Norway
Completed October 1994, a sister ship of *Knock Allen.* In 2005 to Kifisos Shipping Co., Marshall Islands, renamed *Edgeless.* Subsequently to Front Omaga Inc., renamed *Front Fighter.* Extant May 2011.								
1,071	1,733	*Erradale*	14.11.1993	82,701	Bulk Carrier	St/Sc/Mv 930.0/145.0/79.0	20,633 bhp Dies H&W	China Navigation Hong Kong
Completed April 1994. Extant May 2011.								
1,072	1,734	*Lowlands Trassey*	1995	82,830	Bulk Carrier	St/Sc/Mv 930.0/145.0/79.0	20,633 bhp Dies H&W	Enterprise Shipping & Trading Isle of Man
Completed May 1995. In 2003 to Enterprises Shipping and Transport, renamed *Iron Prince.* In 2008, renamed *Bet Prince.* Extant May 2011.								
1,073	1,735	*Knock An*	1996	134,510	Oil Tanker	St/Sc/Mv 908.0/145/79.0	20,648 bhp Dies H&W	Fred Olsen Norway
Completed October 1996. To Norwegian management, Knutsen OAS, renamed *Gerd Knutsen.* Extant May 2011.								

Ship	Yard No	Name	Date Launched	Displacement Tons	Type	Construction and Dimensions	Horse Power/ Engines	Owners
1,074	1,736	*Knock Muir*	1996	146,268	Oil Tanker	St/Sc/Mv 899.0/145/79.0	20,850 bhp Dies H&W	Fred Olsen Norway
Completed February 1996. In 2005 to Sperhios Shipping, Marshall Islands, renamed *Ellen P.* In 2008 to Front Hunter Inc., renamed *Front Hunter.* Extant May 2011.								
1,075	1737	*Schiehallion*	1997	152630	FPSO	St/barge 803.0/147.5/89.0	N/A	British Petroleum London
Completed January 1998, floating oil-production platform designed to exploit field of this name. Extant May 2011.								
N/A	1,738	N/A	Cancelled vessel?					
1,076	1,739	*Glomar C.R. Luigs*	2000	47,079	Deepwater Drillship	St/3Sc/Mv 748.5/118.0/58.0	46,000 shp Dies H&W	Global Marine International Panama
Completed March 2000. Renamed *GSF C.R. Luigs*. Extant May 2011.								
1,077	1,740	*Glomar Jack Ryan*	2000	47,079	Deepwater Drillship	St/2Sc/Mv 759.5/118.0/58.0	46,000 shp Dies H&W	Global Marine International Panama
Completed July 2000. Extant May 2011.								
1,078	1,741	*Hartland Point*	1.7.2002	22,900	Ro-Ro Ship MOD	St/2Sc/Mv 633.0/85.0/54.8	17,130 bhp Dies H&W	A. Weir & Co. Shipping London
Completed 11.12.2002. Extant May 2011.								
1,079	1,742	*Anvil Point*	2002	22,996	Ro-Ro Ship MOD	St/2Sc/Mv 633.0/85.0/54.8	17,130 bhp Dies H&W	A. Weir & Co. Shipping London
Completed March 2003. Extant May 2011.								

Workman Clark & Companies

Yard No	Name	Date Launched	Displacement Tons	Type	Construction and Dimensions	Horse Power	Owners
1	*Ethel*	20.8.1880	265	Cargo	Ir/Sc/St 150.1/21.7/10.7	60 nhp CI (2Cy) **Engines** J. Rowan & Sons Belfast	A. McMullin Belfast
Shortly after completion *c.* 1881 to A.Godin & Co., renamed *Obokh.* In 1883 to D. MacBrayne, resumed old name. Renamed *Clansman* (1910). Foundered NE of Haisborough Lighthouse, October 1924.							
2	*William Hinde*	20.10.1880	346	Cargo	Ir/Sc/St 160.7/22.7/11.7	60 nhp CI (2Cy) **Engines** J. Rowan & Sons Belfast	William Hinde Belfast
In 1890 to W.E. Davies, renamed *Charles.* In 1893 to R. Gilchrist & Co., renamed *Marquess of Bute.* Sank following collision with *Connemara* between South Stack and Skerries, March 1910.							
3	*Ethelbert*	?.1.1881	513	Cargo	Ir/Sc/St 170.0/24.6/12.8	75 nhp CI (2Cy) **Engines** Muir & Houston Glasgow	Colvils Lowden & Co. Glasgow
By 1890 owned by Fowley & Co., London. In 1908 to Italian owners, La Sicania, renamed *Motia.* Sunk submarine gunfire (*U-35*) near Ustica, Tyrrhenian Sea, June 1916. No lives lost.							
4	*Rita (?)*	? 1880	3	Yacht (Cutter)	Iron Hulled 21.0/6.7/2.8	N/A	J.A. Macnaughton Belfast
A small yacht.							
5	*Number Four*	? 1880	594	Sailing Barge	Ir & St/Sail	N/A	Dublin Port & Docks Board
Fitted with triple-expansion engine 1925. Broken up Dublin 1957.							
6							
7	*City of Cambridge*	15.8.1882	2,576	Passenger-Cargo	Ir/Sc/St 400.0/42.1/29.6	600 nhp CI (2Cy) **Engines** J.J. Thompson Glasgow	George Smith & Sons Glasgow
Sunk by submarine torpedo (*UC-17*) off Algeria, July 1917. No lives loss.							
8	*Ethelwolf*	?.7.1881	516	Cargo	Ir/Sc/St 170.0/24.6/12.8	70 nhp CI (2Cy) **Engines** Muir & Houston Glasgow	Colvils Lowden & Co. Glasgow
Wrecked on Silleiro Rocks, Vigo, December 1886. Crew of 13 rescued by German merchantman *Hanover.*							
9	*Skelligs*	22.9.1881	450	Cargo	Ir/Sc/St 160.0/26.1/12.0	70 nhp CI (2Cy) **Engines** J. Rowan & Sons Belfast	Clyde Shipping Co. Glasgow
Lost collision N of Calf of Man, May 1884.							
10	*River Forth*	5.5.1882	1,127	Cargo	Ir/Sc/St 230.0/31.7/12.2	120 nhp CI (2Cy) **Engines** Muir & Houston Glasgow	James Little & Co. Glasgow
Foundered off S of Ireland, November 1882.							

Yard No	Name	Date Launched	Displacement Tons	Type	Construction and Dimensions	Horse Power	Owners
11	*Newhaven*	19.7.1882	906	Cargo	Ir/Sc/St 201.0/31.6/13.9	95 nhp CI (2Cy) **Engines** Lees, Anderson & Co. Glasgow	R. Mackie & Co. Leith
In 1903 to Norwegian owners, H. Kuhnle, renamed *Geir.* Wrecked, Farne Island, February 1908.							
12	*Skerryvore*	12.10.1882	994	Passenger-Cargo	Ir/Sc/St 225.6/31.0/15.6	180 nhp CI (2Cy) **Engines** J. Rowan & Sons Belfast	Clyde Shipping Co. Glasgow
In 1897 to G. Bazeley & Sons, renamed *Coath.* Sunk by submarine torpedo (*U-38*) near Eastbourne, December 1916. Sixteen lives lost.							
13	*Lenore*	? 1882	102	Yacht (Schooner)	Sailing Ship 97.8/17.5/14.4	N/A	George Smith Esq. Glasgow
The private yacht of George Smith, the owner of George Smith & Sons of Glasgow.							
14	*Teelin Head*	6.2.1883	1,715	Cargo	St/Sc/St 275.4/35.3/18.1	200 nhp CI (2Cy) **Engines** J. Howden & Co. Glasgow	Ulster SS Co. Belfast
Sunk by submarine torpedo (*UC-31*) 12nm SSW of Owers LS, January 1918, cargo of potatoes. Thirteen lives lost.							
15	*River Ettrick*	?.3.1883	1,454	Cargo	Ir/Sc/St 250.0/35.2/18.0	152 nhp CI (2Cy) **Engines** J. Rowan & Sons Belfast	James Little & Co. Glasgow
In 1897 to Swedish owners, J.A. Waller, renamed *Rumina.* Captured by German submarine (*U-17*) on 22 October 1915 with cargo of wood pulp for London. Sunk following day when hit a mine off Gotland as prize crew were attempting to bring vessel to port. No lives lost.							
16	*Meraggio*	24.4.1883	1,126	Cargo	Ir/Sc/St 217.3/31.9/15.4	99 nhp CI (2Cy) **Engines** Victor Coats Belfast	Marshall Dobson & Co. Leith
By 1890 owned by MacLay & McIntyre, Leith. In 1895 to T. Jack, renamed *Inver.* Lost following collision off Coningbeg Lighthouse, February 1917.							
17	*Newington*	30.5.1883	1,125	Cargo	Ir/Sc/St 217.3/31.9/15.4	99 nhp CI (2Cy) **Engines** Victor Coats Belfast	R. Mackie & Co. Leith
In 1911 to Greek owners, A. Georgandis, renamed *Antonios.* Sunk in air attack, Suda Bay, May 1941.							
18	*Jane Clark*	30.6.1883	838	Cargo	Ir/Sc/St 208.0/29.1/14.1	96 nhp CI (2Cy) **Engines** Victor Coats Belfast	Clark & Service Glasgow
Wrecked St Mary's Island, Northumberland, December 1894. Ship had lost her bridge and compass in storm. No lives lost.							
19	*River Garry*	?.11.1883	1,339	Cargo	Ir/Sc/St 240.0/33.2/18.2	99 nhp CI (2Cy) **Engines** Muir & Houston Glasgow	James Little & Co. Glasgow
Foundered in force-12 gale off Thornton Loch, East Dunbar, loaded with coal, November 1893. All 19 crew members lost their lives.							
20	*Maria A Hinde*	19.9.1883	821	Cargo	Ir/Sc/St 208.0/29.1/14.0	96 nhp CI (2Cy) **Engines** Victor Coats Belfast	William Hinde Belfast

Yard No	Name	Date Launched	Displacement Tons	Type	Construction and Dimensions	Horse Power	Owners
In 1896 to Samuel Bros, renamed *Springbok*. In 1909 to J. Cook & Son, renamed *Glen Derry*. In 1913 to Swedish owners, J.P. Jonsson, renamed *Southgar*. Sunk following collision near Flamborough Head, April 1918.							
21	*Blackwater*	?.10.1883	538	Cargo	Ir/Sc/St 176.0/24.6/12.9	80 nhp CI (2Cy) **Engines** W. King & Co. Glasgow	J. McCormick & Co. Dublin
Lost following collision off Skerries, July 1905.							
22	*Fort George*	12.2.1884	1,756	Sailing Vessel (Four-masted Ship)	Iron Hulled 260.0/40.0/23.1	N/A	Clark & Service Glasgow
Disappeared on voyage New York–Honolulu, August 1908.							
23	*Clanrye*	5.4.1884	239	Cargo	Ir/Sc/St 138.0/20.5/10.3	55 nhp CI (2Cy) **Engines** Victor Coats Belfast	Newry Steam Packet Co. Newery
In March 1886 left Swansea for Newry with cargo of coal; never seen again. Nine lives lost.							
24	*Corra Linn*	1.4.1884	833	Cargo	Ir/Sc/St 208.0/29.2/14.1	96 nhp CI (2Cy) **Engines** W. Kemp & Co. Glasgow	J.&A. Wyllie Glasgow
Sold in 1897 to French owners, A. Deppe, 1897, renamed *Meuse*. Lost collision off Haaks, June 1906.							
25	*River Indus*	?.10.1884	3,452	Passenger-Cargo	Ir/2Sc/St 331.8/43.2/28.0	360 nhp CI (2Cy) **Engines** Muir & Houston Glasgow	James Little & Co. Glasgow
In 1896 to Japanese owners, H. Hamanaka, renamed *Nanyo Maru*. Wrecked near Quelpart Island, March 1904.							
26	*Alice M. Craig*	19.4.1884	387	Sailing Vessel (Barque)	Iron Hulled 156.5/27.7/12.8	N/A	William J. Woodside Belfast
Capsized and sank San Lorenzo, Argentina, March 1893.							
27	*Workman*	30.5.1884	387	Sailing Vessel (Barque)	Iron Hulled 156.5/27.7/12.8	N/A	Woodside & Workman Belfast
A sister ship of *Alice M Craig*. Wrecked at entrance of Rio Sao Francisco, Brazil, May 1888.							
28	*Countess of Bantry*	9.9.1884	90	Cargo	Ir/Sc/St 91.6/17.0/9.0	30 nhp CI (2Cy) **Engines** W. Kemp & Co. Glasgow	Bantry Bay SS Co. Skibbereen
Used to operate service between Bantry and Castletownbere. In 1906 another route opened between Bantry and Glengariff. The Castletownbere service ceased during the First World War and Glengariff service in 1936. Broken up 1937.							
29	*Alert*	1884		Launch			Rangoon Port Commissioners
30	*City of Bombay*	12.8.1885	4,491	Passenger-Cargo	Ir/Sc/St 404.0/48.0/29.2	630 nhp CI (2Cy) **Engines** J.&J. Thompson Glasgow	George Smith & Co. Glasgow
In 1901 taken over by J.R. Ellerman. Chartered to Allen Line 1903, 1906 and 1907. Broken up Holland (Rotterdam) 1908.							
31	*Carnmoney*	9.9.1884	1,299	Sailing Vessel (Barque)	Iron Hulled 235.5/36.2/21.0	N/A	William Porter & Sons Belfast
Boarded by German submarine (*U-49*) and sunk by explosives 150 miles W of Fastnet inbound from Buenos Aires with cargo of maize, May 1917. No lives lost.							

Yard No	Name	Date Launched	Displacement Tons	Type	Construction and Dimensions	Horse Power	Owners
32	*Watchman*	?.9.1884	466	Sailing Vessel (Barque)	Iron Hulled 171.1/28.1/13.5	N/A	W.J. Woodside & Co. Belfast
Disappeared on voyage from Rio Grande to Liverpool, November 1894.							
33	*Martha C. Craig*	8.10.1884	466	Sailing Vessel (Barque)	Iron Hulled 171.0/28.2/13.6	N/A	Woodside & Workman Belfast
Sister ship of *Watchman*. Wrecked at Mostardas, Brazil, July 1897.							
34	*Auric*	1.11.1884	423	Cargo	Ir/Sc/St 173.5/25.2/12.2	74 nhp CI (2Cy) **Engines** Victor Coats & Co. Belfast	H. Scott & Co. Belfast
Wrecked Cairnbulg near Fraserburgh, October 1897.							
35	*Fort James*	1.7.1885	1,755	Sailing Vessel (Ship)	Iron Hulled 261.2/39.9/23.0	N/A	Clark & Service Glasgow
Near sister of *Fort George*. By 1890 to J.H. Iredale & Co., Liverpool. By 1895 owned by R. Clark, Liverpool, renamed *Garsdale*. By 1898 owned by Mcvicar, Marshall & Co. Abandoned off Cape Horn after de-masted, September 1905.							
36	*Rosa*	1885	52	Sailing Vessel (Schooner)	Steel Hulled 75.9/18.1/9.7	N/A	Belfast Harbour Commissioners
37	*Star of Austria*	8.2.1886	1,708	Sailing Vessel (Ship)	Iron Hulled 264.7/38.7/23.1	N/A	J.P. Corry & Co. Belfast
The last sailing ship built for firm and their first order from WC. In 1895 disappeared rounding Cape Horn on voyage Santa Rosalia–Swansea with cargo of copper.							
38	*Polly Woodside*	7.11.1885	678	Sailing Vessel (Barque)	Iron Hulled 192.2/30.1/16.0	N/A	Woodside & Workman Belfast
In 1904 to Australian owners, A.H. Turnbull, renamed *Rona*. Hulked 1923; restored as training ship 1967. Has recently been renovated and now on permanent display.							
39	*Star of Victoria*	1887	3,239	Cargo	St/Sc/St 361.7/42.7/26.4	850 nhp CI (2Cy) **Engines** J.&J. Thompson Glasgow	J.P. Corry & Co. Belfast
Corry's first steamship began service with charter to India but subsequently fitted with refrigerated holds for New Zealand meat trade. In 1911 to Austro-Hungarian owners, Fratelli Cosulich, Trieste, renamed *Frigida*. In 1911 to Societa Importazioni Carne Congelate. In 1913 to Argentinian owners, Soc. Anonyme de Nav. Sud-Atlantica, renamed *Moinho Fluminense*. By early 1917 owned by French company, Cia des Chemins de fer Paris-Lyons, renamed *Marseille*. Broken up 1919. (Some sources say lost in collision 20.3.1917.)							
40	*Elgiva*	7.7.1886	667	Cargo	Ir/Sc/St 180.6/26.2/13.7	95 nhp CI (2Cy) **Engines** Hudson & Corbett Glasgow	Colvils, Lowden & Co. Glasgow
By 1890 owned by McGregor SS Co., Glasgow. Lost collision between Longships and Lizard Head, August 1893.							
41	*Bessfield*	7.6.1886	1,332	Sailing Vessel (Barque)	Iron Hulled 239.7/36.2/21.1	N/A	W. Porter & Sons Belfast
Broken up 1924.							
42	*Ethelbald*	14.8.1886	657	Cargo	Ir/Sc/St 180.6/26.2/13.7	95 nhp CI (2Cy) **Engines** Hudson & Corbett Glasgow	Colvils, Lowden & Co. Glasgow
By 1890 owned by McGregor SS Co., Glasgow. Wrecked near Stavanger, December 1893.							

Yard No	Name	Date Launched	Displacement Tons	Type	Construction and Dimensions	Horse Power	Owners
43	*Broughshane*	3.6.1886	325	Cargo	Ir/Sc/St 152.2/23.1/11.8	70 nhp CI (2Cy) **Engines** J.&J. Thompson Glasgow	Antrim Iron Ore Co. Belfast
In 1907 to French owners, Gaules de Mezaubran, renamed *Hirondelle.* Wrecked Sark, October 1917.							
44	*Harold*	1.2.1887	832	Cargo	Ir/Sc/St 190.3/27.1/21.4	98 nhp CI (2Cy) **Engines** Hudson & Corbett Glasgow	Colvils, Lowden & Co. Glasgow
Wrecked Grand Turk Island, March 1890.							
45	*Kathleen*	3.3.1887	336	Cargo	Ir/Sc/St 155.7/23.2/11.8	70 nhp CI (2Cy) Engines J & J Thompson Glasgow	John Milligan Belfast
Disappeared on voyage Burghead–Middlesborough, January 1914.							
46	*Corsican*	9.3.1887	338	Cargo	St/Sc/St 150.3/22.2/10.7	95 nhp CI (2Cy) **Engines** Hudson & Corbett Glasgow	J&J MacFarlane Glasgow
In 1889 to Russian owners, Steveleff of Vladivostok, renamed *Novek.* Sunk by Japanese shellfire during the siege of Port Arthur, October 1904.							
47		1888		Dock Caisson			Belfast Harbour Commissioners
48		1888		Dock Caisson			Belfast Harbour Commissioners
In 1933 WC stated these were built for the British government. However, a photograph from a 1903 advertising book shows one of them clearly marked 'Alexander Graving Dock No.2'; this completed by Harbour Commissioners in 1897, therefore they were the customers. One of these gates still exists, making it the oldest surviving WC hull.							
49	*City of Dublin*	2.1.1888	3,267	Cargo	St/Sc/St 361.7/42.7/26.4	350 nhp TE (3Cy) **Engines** J.&J. Thompson Glasgow	George Smith & Sons Glasgow
In 1900 to E. Haselhurst, London, renamed *Clavering.* Wrecked Tees, January 1907.							
50	*Clandeboye*	16.4.1887	300	Excursion Boat	St/Pd/St 225.0/24.3/8.6	230 nhp DA (2Cy) **Engines** Hudson & Corbett Glasgow	Belfast Bangor and Larne Steamboat Co. Ltd Belfast
Completed 26.5.1887, for services around Belfast Lough. In 1889 to Danish owners, Forenede Damp-Skibsselskab, renamed *Gjedser.* Hulked in 1904, broken up Germany (Kiel) 1928.							
51	*Derby Park*	1.9.1887	1,333	Sailing Vessel (Barque)	Steel Hulled 240.7/36.4/21.3	N/A	P. Iredale & Sons Liverpool
Near sister of *Bessfield.* Wrecked Penrhyn Island, Pacific, July 1888.							
52	*Macgregor*	28.1.1888	1,047	Cargo	St/Sc/St 215.4/32.1/12.5	180 nhp TE (3Cy) **Engines** Muir & Houston Glasgow	Colvils, Lowden & Co. Glasgow
Completed March 1888. Wrecked Yucatan, December 1888.							

Yard No	Name	Date Launched	Displacement Tons	Type	Construction and Dimensions	Horse Power	Owners
53							
54							
55	*Fort William*	24.7.1888	1,807	Cargo	St/Sc/St 271.2/37.1/16.0	136 nhp TE (3Cy) **Engines** W. King & Co. Glasgow	Clark & Service Glasgow
Completed August 1888. Disappeared on voyage Newcastle–Norfolk, Virginia, December 1896.							
56	*Kirklands*	23.8.1888	1,807	Cargo	St/Sc/St 271.2/37.1/16.0	190 nhp TE (3Cy) **Engines** W. King & Co. Glasgow	J. Cuthbertson & Co. Glasgow
Completed September 1888. In 1897 to Australian owners, Adelaide SS Co., renamed *Kolya.* In 1912 to Singapore owners, Warner, Barnes & Co. In 1920 to Philippines owners, Figueras SS Co., renamed *Roberto Figueras.* Broken up 1924.							
57	*Lorton*	14.4.1888	1,419	Sailing Vessel (Barque)	Steel Hulled 245.8/37.4/21.6	N/A	P. Iredale & Sons Liverpool
To Peruvian ownership without changing name. Sunk by submarine gunfire (*U-67*) off coast of Spain, February 1917. Sinking provoked powerful anti-German response in Peru which ultimately saw the country breaking off diplomatic relations and seizing nine German ships interned in Peruvian ports.							
58	*Star of England*	2.2.1889	3,511	Cargo	St/Sc/St 371.8/44.2/27.2	400 nhp TE (3Cy) **Engines** J.&J. Thompson Glasgow	J.P. Corry & Co. Belfast
Completed March 1889. One voyage to India before fitted with refrigeration equipment for New Zealand meat trade. In 1913 to Italian owners, T. Gazzolo, renamed *Purificazione.* By 1915 owned by Soc. Anon. Liva, in September sprang a leak in North Atlantic and foundered.							
59	*City of Vienna*	7.12.1889	4,672	Passenger-Cargo	St/Sc/St 412.3/46.7/29.3	700 nhp TE (3Cy) **Engines** J.&J. Thompson Glasgow	G. Smith & Sons Glasgow
Completed June 1890. Employed as transport for Boer War, 1899–1902. In 1901 taken over by J.R. Ellerman. In 1906 chartered to Allen Line for three voyages. In 1913 to Greek owners, National Greek Line, renamed *Thessalonika.* In January 1916 on voyage Greece–New York abandoned in sinking condition 350nm from Sandy Hook.							
60	*Lady Martin*	8.10.1888	1,245	Passenger-Cargo	St/Sc/St 269.6/34.2/16.4	220 nhp TE (3Cy) **Engines** Dunsmuir & Jackson Glasgow	B.&I. Steam Packet Co. Dublin
Completed November 1888, for Dublin–London route. By 1914 owned by Ottoman government, renamed *Bimbashi Riza Bey.* Appears to have been captured in 1917, operated by Cunningham Shaw, renamed *Purfleet Belle.* In 1920 to Greek owners, Embiricos Bros, renamed *Naxos.* Subsequently to A.G. Yannoulatos, renamed *Miaoulis.* Broken up 1934.							
61	*Ferry No.3*	1888	15	Steam Ferry	St/Sc/St 55.0/13.0/?	?	Belfast Harbour Commissioners
Operated between Prince's Quay and Abercorn Basin, Belfast. Cost £897. Broken up Belfast 1934.							
62	*Hippomenes*	3.4.1889	2,694	Cargo	St/Sc/St 320.4/40.2/18.3	400 nhp TE (3Cy) **Engines** Bow & M'lachaen Paisley	R.P. Houston & Co. Liverpool
Completed September 1889. In 1912 to Italian owners, G. Girogi & Co., renamed *Ippomene,* used as coal hulk at Genoa.							

Yard No	Name	Date Launched	Displacement Tons	Type	Construction and Dimensions	Horse Power	Owners
63	*Dunmore Head*	18.5.1889	2,229	Cargo	St/Sc/St 302.4/40.2/19.5	275 nhp TE (3Cy) **Engines** J.&J. Thompson Glasgow	Ulster SS Co. Ltd Belfast
Completed July 1889. Sunk by submarine torpedo (*U-62*) 135nm NW of Tory Island, outbound Manchester–Genoa with cargo of coal and ammunition, April 1917. No lives lost.							
64	*Iredale*	12.6.1889	1,573	Sailing Vessel (Barque)	Steel Hulled 256.2/38.0/22.0	N/A	P. Iredale & Porter Liverpool
Dismasted 1910 and not repaired.							
65	*Uranus*	11.7.1889	1,202	Passenger-Cargo	St/Sc/St 222.7/32.7/21.9	180 nhp TE (3Cy) **Engines** Muir & Houston Glasgow	Z.J. de Aldecoa Manila
Completed September 1889. In 1901 to Spanish owners, Cia Maritima, renamed *Z.V. de Aldecoa*. Hulked 1907.							
66	*County Down*	23.12.1889	2,210	Cargo	St/Sc/St 285.3/38.2/19.2	160 nhp TE (3Cy) **Engines** W. King & Co. Glasgow	County Steamship Co. (J.W. Woodside) Belfast
Completed April 1890. In 1899 to Swedish owners, C.B. Hofgaard, renamed *Falco*. Foundered between lista and Lindesnes on voyage Burntisland–Lulea with cargo of coal, August 1910.							
67	*City Of Dundee*	3.5.1890	3,427	Cargo	St/Sc/St 361.7/42.7/26.4	344 nhp TE (3Cy) **Engines** J. Holden & Co. Glasgow	G. Smith & Sons Glasgow
Completed August 1890. In 1901 taken over by J.R. Ellerman. Sank collision with Elders & Fyffes' *Matina* St George's Channel on route Liverpool–Algiers, October 1908.							
68	*Chichester*	22.2.1890	2,082	Cargo	St/Sc/St 285.3/38.2/19.2	200 nhp TE (3Cy) **Engines** Muir & Houston Glasgow	W.R. Rea Belfast
Completed April 1890. Wrecked in Straits of Magellan on route Iquique (Chile)–St Vincent with cargo of nitrate, August 1891.							
69	*Nuestra Senora del Carmen*	18.1.1890	389	Cargo	Ir/Sc/St 147.8/24.6/9.1	74 hp CI (2Cy) **Engines** Muir & Houston Glasgow	Goyenechea Manila
Completed February 1890. Wrecked Mariveles, July 1930.							
70	*Marlay*	20.5.1890	798	Cargo	St/Sc/St 200.2/29.2/14.0	170 nhp CI (2Cy) **Engines** V. Coates & Co. Belfast	R. Tedcastle & Co. Dublin
Completed September 1890. Foundered Dublin Bay, December 1902.							
71	*City of Perth*	23.7.1890	3,427	Cargo	St/Sc/St 361.7/42.7/26.4	354 nhp TE (3Cy) **Engines** J.&J. Thompson Glasgow	G. Smith & Sons Glasgow
Completed September 1890. In 1901 taken over by J.R. Ellerman. Sunk by submarine torpedo (*U-70*) 200 miles from Fastnet, inbound Alexandria–London, June 1917. Eight lives lost.							

Yard No	Name	Date Launched	Displacement Tons	Type	Construction and Dimensions	Horse Power	Owners
72	*Ethelwold*	14.8.1890	955	Cargo	St/Sc/St 208.1/28.1/12.7	158 nhp TE (3Cy) **Engines** D. Rowen & Co. Glasgow	Colvils, Lowden & Co. Glasgow
Completed October 1890. Broken up Briton Ferry (UK) 1912.							
73	*Celtic King*	1.11.1890	3,737	Cargo (Refrigerated)	St/Sc/St 371.8/44.2/27.2	360 nhp TE (3Cy) **Engines** J.&J. Thompson Glasgow	W. Ross & Co. London
Completed 18.1.1891. In 1898 purchased by US Navy, renamed *Celtic*. Broken up Japan (Osaka) 1929.							
74	*Helen Craig*	18.10.1890	417	Cargo	St/Sc/St 165.3/24.1/9.9	68 nhp CI (2Cy) **Engines** V. Coates & Co. Belfast	H. Craig & Co. Belfast
Completed January 1891. Broken up Ireland (Passage West) 1959.							
75	*Ramore Head*	9.2.1891	4,444	Cargo	St/Sc/St 402.1/44.7/27.8	450 nhp TE (3Cy) **Engines** J.&J. Thompson Glasgow	Ulster SS Co. Belfast
Completed April 1891. Broken up Germany (Hamburg) 1924.							
76	*Eveleen*	15.12.1890	489	Cargo	St/Sc/St 171.8/26.1/10.2	90 nhp TE (3Cy) **Engines** Muir & Houston Glasgow	John Milligen Belfast
Completed March 1891. Disappeared on voyage Aye–Belfast, May 1918. Twelve lives lost.							
77	*Ferry No.4*	1890	15	Steam Ferry	St/Sc/St 55.0/13.0/?	?	Belfast Harbour Commissioners
Cost £1,230. Withdrawn 1934, hulk used as a pontoon until broken up Belfast 1939.							
78	*Wanderer*	26.5.1891	4,085	Cargo	St/Sc/St 380.0/43.8/29.4	365 nhp TE (3Cy) **Engines** J.&J. Thompson Glasgow	T.&J. Harrison Liverpool
Completed August 1891. In 1922 to Italian owners, IN Edilizie, renamed *Enrichetta*. Broken up Italy (Genoa) 1924.							
79	*Marian Woodside*	11.2.1891	1,549	Sailing Vessel (Barque)	Steel Hulled 256.2/37.8/21.9	N/A	W.J. Woodside & Co. Belfast
Completed March 1891, near sister of *Iredale*. In 1911 to Danish owners, M. Hanson, renamed *Lindo*. Disappeared on voyage Port Natal–Albany, August 1913.							
80	*Ardanmhor*	11.6.1891	2,081	Cargo	St/Sc/St 276.3/38.3/16.0	244 nhp TE (3Cy) **Engines** J. Howden & Co. Glasgow	Clark & Service Glasgow
Completed September 1891. In 1903 to American owners, W.D. Munson, renamed *Cubana*. Broken up Briton Ferry (UK) 1914.							
81	*Archdale*	24.6.1891	1,557	Sailing Vessel (Barque)	Steel Hulled 256.2/38.0/21.9	N/A	J.H. Iredale & Co. Liverpool
Completed August 1891, near sister of *Iredale*. In 1893 to R. Russell & Co., renamed *Lord Elgin*. Wrecked, Lourenco Marques and burnt, April 1907.							
82	*Rathdown*	20.8.1891	2,145	Sailing Vessel (Ship)	Steel Hulled 279.5/41.7/24.4	N/A	R. Martin & Co. Dublin
Completed September 1891. Disappeared on voyage Yokohama–Puget Sound, October 1900.							

Yard No	Name	Date Launched	Displacement Tons	Type	Construction and Dimensions	Horse Power	Owners
83	*M.J. Hedley*	2.9.1891	442	Cargo	St/Sc/St 165.3/24.0/10.0	68 nhp CI (2Cy) **Engines** V. Coates & Co. Belfast	McCully & Co. Belfast
Completed October 1891. By 1898 owned by Hosken, Trevithick Polkinhern & Co., Penzance. Broken up Sunderland (UK) 1926.							
84	*Lough Neagh*	22.10.1891	973	Sailing Vessel (Barque)	Steel Hulled 206.0/34.1/19.0	N/A	McWilliams, Smyth & Co. Belfast
Completed November 1891. In 1895 to Italian owners F.S. Ciampa & Sons, renamed *Emilia Ciampa*. In 1910 to A.V. Canepa, renamed *Francesco C.* Sunk by U-boat (*U-34*) with explosive charge, near Sardinia, May 1917.							
85	*Dundonald*	3.10.1891	2,205	Sailing Vessel (Four-masted Barque)	Steel Hulled 284.2/42.0/24.4	N/A	T. Dixion & Sons Belfast
Completed November 1891. Wrecked Disappointment Island, Auckland Islands, March 1907.							
86	*Invermore*	31.10.1891	1,600	Sailing Vessel (Barque)	Steel Hulled 256.0/37.9/22.1	N/A	H. Hutton & Co. Belfast
Completed December 1891. Hit a wreck and sank, Cape Frio, October 1903.							
87	*Galgorm Castle*	18.11.1891	1,569	Sailing Vessel (Barque)	Steel Hulled 256.2/38.0/22.0	N/A	Northern Shipowners Co. Ltd Belfast
Completed February 1892, near sister of *Iredale*. Sunk submarine gunfire (*U-49*) 90 miles W of Fastnet, inbound Queenstown–Buenos Aires, February 1917. Eleven lives lost.							
88	*Cavo Hill*	5.3.1892	2,245	Sailing Vessel (Four-masted Barque)	Steel Hulled 284.0/41.9/24.5	N/A	Belfast Shipowners Co. Ltd Belfast
Completed April 1892, near sister of *Dundonald*. Shortly after completion to Galbraith & Moorhead, London. Wrecked Punta Espada, San Domingo, December 1894.							
89	*Howth*	23.12.1891	2,244	Sailing Vessel (Four-masted Barque)	Steel Hulled 284.4/41.9/24.5	N/A	Sir R. Martin & Co. Dublin
Completed March 1892, near sister of *Dundonald*. In 1918 to Anglo-Saxon/Shell, renamed *Horn Shell*, converted into tanker and fitted with diesel engines. Broken up Japan 1926.							
90	*Crown of Germany*	7.4.1892	2,241	Sailing Vessel (Four-masted Barque)	Steel Hulled 284.4/41.9/24.5	N/A	Crown SS Co. Ltd (J. Reid) Belfast
Completed May 1892, near sister of *Dundonald*. In 1910 to German owners, Knohr & Burchard, renamed *Fischbek*. Wrecked False Cove, Le Maire Strait, July 1910.							
91	*Southern Cross*	9.8.1892	5,050	Cargo Ship (Refrigerated)	St/Sc/St 400.4/48.1/29.6	511 nhp TE (3Cy) W&C	Wincott Cooper & Co. London
Completed September 1892. By 1898 owned by Houlder Bros & Co., London. Wrecked Vigo, Spain, December 1909.							
92							
93	*Goodrich*	11.6.1892	2,241	Sailing Vessel (Four-masted Barque)	Steel Hulled 284.2/42.1/24.5	N/A	Boyd Bros & Co. Belfast
Completed July 1892, near sister of *Dundonald*. In 1895 to Finnish owners, A.W. Soderland, renamed *Fennia*. In 1915 taken over by UK government. In 1919 to Anglo-Saxon/Shell converted into tanker and fitted with diesel engines, renamed *Fiona Shell*. Sunk by human torpedo, Gibraltar, September 1941.							
94	*Star of New Zealand*	24.1.1895	4,712	Cargo (Refrigerated)	St/Sc/St 393.5/46.8/28.0	457 nhp TE (3Cy) W&C	J.P. Corry & Co. Belfast
Completed March 1895. By 1902 on South American rather than New Zealand routes. Wrecked near Molene, inbound from Montevideo with cargo of meat, November 1915.							
95	*Senator*	17.11.1892	4,688	Cargo	St/Sc/St 400.3/45.3/29.8	430 nhp TE (3Cy) W&C	T.&J. Harrison Liverpool
Completed February 1893. In 1914 to Chilean owners, P.A. de Bruyne, renamed *Gobernador Bories*. In 1916 to American owners, Sherman SS Co., New York, renamed *Sherman*. In 1918 to US Navy, renamed *Durham*. Broken up Italy (Genoa) 1924.							

Yard No	Name	Date Launched	Displacement Tons	Type	Construction and Dimensions	Horse Power	Owners
96	*South African*	12.12.1892	438	Sailing Vessel (Barque)	Steel Hulled 171.0/27.3/13.0	N/A	Harrower & Workman Belfast
Completed February 1893. In 1900 to A. Coulon & Co., renamed *Marie Helene.* In 1903 to E.F. Troost, renamed *Alice Marie.* In 1907 to C. Dreyer, renamed *H.C. Dreyer.* Abandoned at sea on voyage Rio Grande–Mersey, January 1910.							
97	*Lauriston*	17.10.1892	2,301	Sailing Vessel (Ship)	Steel Hulled 284.6/42.0/24.4	N/A	Galbraith & Moorhead London
Completed December 1892, near sister of *Dundonald* rigged as ship. To Soviet government 1923, renamed *Tovaristsch.* Scuttled Sea of Azov, September 1943.							
98	*Ormidale*	17.8.1893	3,560	Cargo	St/Sc/St 361.0/44.5/26.5	369nhp TE (3Cy) W&C	R.&C. Allen Glasgow
Completed September 1893. In 1919 to Greek owners, S. Vlassopoulos, renamed *Istros.* Broken up Italy (Savona) 1930.							
99	*Sophie Kirk*	2.3.1893	958	Sailing Vessel (Barque)	Steel Hulled 211.3/35.3/17.2	N/A	W.J. Woodside & Co. Belfast
Completed March 1893. In 1910 to J. Wagle, renamed *Regia.* In 1913 to Italian owners, P. Schiaffino, renamed *Anirac.* Wrecked at Isabella, Brazil, February 1913.							
100	*Jeanie Woodside*	2.3.1893	962	Sailing Vessel (Barque)	Steel Hulled 211.3/35.3/17.2	N/A	W.J. Woodside & Co. Belfast
Completed April 1893 sister ship of *Sophie Kirk.* In 1910 to Norwegian owners, C. Hannevig, renamed *Martha 1.* In 1916 to C.C. Andersen, renamed *Nelly.* Disappeared on voyage Kristiansand–Savannah, January 1917.							
101	*Moya*	16.3.1893	184	Tender	St/2Sc/St 126.0/23.0/10.8	95 nhp CI (4Cy) W&C	Commissioners of Irish Lights Dublin
Out of service by 1905.							
102	*Ardandhu*	2.5.1893	2,091	Cargo	St/Sc/St 281.7/39.7/15.0	274 nhp TE (3Cy) W&C	Clark & Service Glasgow
Completed June 1893. Lost collision, Vineyard Sound, January 1900.							
103	*Xantippe*	15.5.1893	972	Sailing Vessel (Four-masted Barque)	Steel Hulled 211.3/35.3/17.3	N/A	Montgomery & Workman Belfast
Completed June 1893, near sister of *Sophie Kirk.* Disappeared during voyage to Vancouver, December 1895.							
104	*Ardanrose*	?.12.1893	2,123	Cargo	St/Sc/St 281.7/39.7/15.0	274 nhp TE (3Cy) W&C	Clark & Service Glasgow
Completed January 1894, sister ship of *Ardandhu.* In 1903 to American Owners, W.D. Munson, renamed *Paloma.* Broken up Italy (Trieste) 1924.							
105	*Ormiston*	25.10.1893	3,561	Cargo	St/Sc/St 361.0/44.4/26.2	328 nhp TE (3Cy) W&C	R.&C. Allen Glasgow
Completed November 1893, renamed *Orcadian* 1898. To Donaldson Line 1915, renamed *Polaria.* Wrecked off Alexandria, January 1918.							
106	*Poltalloch*	9.11.1893	2,254	Sailing Vessel (Four-masted Barque)	Steel Hulled 284.0/42.0/24.4	N/A	Potter Bros. London
Completed December 1893, near sister of *Dundonald.* Wrecked north of Barmouth, January 1916.							
107	*Sultan*	26.1.1894	2062	Passenger-Cargo	St/Sc/St 258.5/38.0/13.9	206 nhp TE (3Cy) W&C	Alfred Holt & Co. Liverpool
Completed April 1894, jointly operated by Holts and the Western Australian Steam Navigation Co., on Singapore–Batavia–Fremantle route. By 1898 wholly owned by Alfred Holt. In 1909 to Japanese owners, Oaki Goshi Kaisya, renamed *Kayo Maru.* Appears to have been chartered to Chinese government for a time, renamed *Wei-Hei.* Laid up 1929 and broken up Japan (Yokohama) 1930–31.							
108	*Planet Mercury*	?.5.1894	3,222	Cargo	St/Sc/St 335.0/43.7/18.4	275 nhp TE (3Cy) W&C	R.W. Leyland & Co. Liverpool
Completed June 1894. Disappeared on voyage from Portland Maine, February 1900. Thirty-five lives lost.							

Yard No	Name	Date Launched	Displacement Tons	Type	Construction and Dimensions	Horse Power	Owners
109	*Logican*	22.5.1894	4,878	Cargo	St/Sc/St 400.0/47.0/28.5	424 nhp TE (3Cy) W&C	T.&J. Harrison Liverpool
Completed August 1894. Broken up Germany (Hamburg) 1923.							
110	*Ching Wo*	4.7.1894	3,883	Passenger-Cargo	St/Sc/St 370.0/45.3/27.0	398 nhp TE (3Cy) W&C	China Mutual SS Co. London
Completed September 1894. Acquired by Holt's when C.M.S.N. taken over 1902. In 1911 to Japanese owners, Uchida Kisen K.K., renamed *Unkai Maru No.2.* In 1920 to French government, renamed *Indochina.* Broken up Italy (La Spezia) 1923.							
111	*Mount Sirion*	12.2.1895	3,280	Cargo	St/Sc/St 335.0/43.7/18.2	292 nhp TE (3Cy) W&C	Smith & Service Glasgow
Completed March 1895. In 1899 to Booth SS Co., renamed *Bernard.* In 1911 to H.&C. Grayson renamed *Redbarn.* Shortly afterwards to Greek ownership, Embiricos & Co., renamed *Lordos Byron.* Foundered near Casquets, November 1911.							
112	*Oopack*	1.9.1895	3,883	Passenger-Cargo	St/Sc/St 370.0/45.3/27.0	398 nhp TE (3Cy) W&C	China Mutual SS Co. London
Completed October 1894, sister ship of *Ching Wo.* Acquired by Holt's 1902. Sunk by submarine torpedo (*U-68*) 110 miles east of Malta, October 1918. No lives lost. The submarine was subsequently sunk by escorts, amongst captured Germans was commander Lt Cmdr Karl Doenitz, later to command U-boats in Second World War and succeed Hitler, briefly, as German head of state.							
113	*Urmston Grange*	2.10.1895	3,444	Passenger-Cargo (Refrigerated)	St/Sc/St 340.0/46.5/17.6	327 nhp TE (3Cy) W&C	Houlder Bros & Co. London
Completed November 1894. In 1906 chartered to Commercial Pacific Cable Co., converted into cable layer. In 1914 scuttled as block ship, Scapa Flow.							
114	*Mourne*	19.9.1895	3,223	Cargo	St/Sc/St 338.0/43.7/26.1	334 nhp TE (3Cy) W&C	T. Dixion & Co. Belfast
Completed October 1895. In 1899 to Booth SS Co., renamed *Basil.* Lost collision near Owers Light, November 1917.							
115	*Sarpedon*	17.10.1894	4,663	Cargo	St/Sc/St 391.5/47.2/26.1	345 nhp TE (3Cy) W&C	Alfred Holt & Co. Liverpool
Completed December 1894. In 1914 to Holt's Dutch subsidiary, N.S.M. Oceaan, no name change, reverted to British register 1915. Served as naval transport. In 1923 to German owners, Leonard R. Muller, renamed *Gotz von Berlichingen.* Broken up Germany (Hamburg) 1925.							
116	*Hector*	27.11.1894	4,660	Cargo	St/Sc/St 391.5/47.2/26.1	244 nhp TE (3Cy) W&C	Alfred Holt & Co. Liverpool
Completed February 1895, sister ship of *Sarpedon.* Enjoyed uneventful career until First World War. Initially *Fleet Messenger No.20* then became a balloon ship spotting for battleships during Dardanelles campaign. Subsequently *White Sea Ammunition Carrier No.126* and *Expeditionary Force Transport No.F01* carrying wheat from India to the Gulf, and stores and motor transport from Avonmouth to Egypt. After this *Royal Naval Collier No.2154* before ending war as *Stores Carrier No.103.* After return to owners, broken up Germany (Wilhelmshaven) 1923.							
117							
118	*Cerebus*	?.11.1894	1,754	Cargo	St/Sc/St 257.3/41.1/20.9	148 nhp TE (3Cy) W&C	Alfred Holt & Co. Liverpool
Completed December 1894, operated by East Indian Steamship Co. In 1899 to German owners, Norddeutscher Lloyd, renamed *Singora.* In 1910 to Japanese owners, Y. Hachiuma, renamed *Tamon Muru No.1.* In 1923 to Shizaki Yokichi, renamed *Kiku Maru.* Broken up Japan 1931.							
119	*Statesman*	25.5.1895	6,322	Cargo	St/Sc/St 450.0/52.5/30.6	582 nhp TE (3Cy) W&C	T.&J. Harrison Liverpool
Completed July 1895. In 1914 taken up for war service. Sunk by submarine torpedo (*UB-43*) 200 miles E of Malta, November 1916. Six lives lost.							
120	*Pak Ling*	24.7.1895	4,447	Cargo	St/Sc/St 410.0/48.1/27.4	600 nhp TE (3Cy) W&C	China Mutual SS Co. London
Completed September 1895. Acquired by Holts in 1902. Ran aground Button Island, Bonham Straits, July 1920 refloated and repaired at Shanghai. Broken up Germany (Wilhelmshaven) 1923.							

Agamemnon (WC y/n 503) 1929.

Araguaya (WC y/n 230) 1906.

Bermuda (WC y/n 490) 1927.

Dundonald (WC y/n 85) 1891.

Yard No	Name	Date Launched	Displacement Tons	Type	Construction and Dimensions	Horse Power	Owners
121	*Ardandearg*	?.7.1895	3,218	Cargo	St/Sc/St 335.0/43.6/18.2	273 nhp TE (3Cy) W&C	Clark & Service Glasgow
Completed July 1895. Sunk by submarine torpedo (*UC-54*) 86 miles from Malta, March 1918. Two lives lost.							
122	*Kintuck*	3.9.1895	4,447	Cargo	St/Sc/St 410.0/48.1/27.4	600 nhp TE (3Cy) W&C	China Mutual SS Co. London
Completed October 1895, sister ship of *Pak Ling.* Acquired by Holts 1902. Although survived U-boat attacks in December 1916 and June 1917 luck ran out in December 1917 when struck mine (*UC-17*) near Godrevy Lighthouse, Cornwall, on route London–Barry in ballast. One life lost.							
123	*Hyson*	20.11.1895	4,445	Cargo	St/Sc/St 410.0/48.1/27.4	600 nhp TE (3Cy) W&C	China Mutual SS Co. London
Completed 15.2.1896, sister ship of *Pak Ling.* In 1902 acquired by Holts when they took over China Mutual in 1902. In 1926 to Italian owners, E. Bozzo and L. Mortola, Genoa, and renamed *Maria Rosa.* Broken up Italy (La Spezia) in 1932.							
124	*Langton Grange*	29.2.1896	5,850	Cargo (Refrigerated)	St/Sc/St 420.0/54.2/29.5	455 nhp TE (3Cy) W&C	Holder Bros & Co. London
Completed May 1896. Wrecked North Bishop Rock, August 1909.							
125	*Denton Grange*	27.5.1896	5,807	Cargo (Refrigerated)	St/Sc/St 420.0/54.1/29.4	513 nhp TE (3Cy) W&C	Holder Bros & Co. London
Completed August 1896, sister ship of *Langton Grange.* Badly damaged when ran aground off Las Palmas operating as transport during Boer War. In 1901 to Macgregor, Gow & Co., London, renamed *Glenlogan.* Sunk by submarine torpedo (*U-21*) while inbound from Yokohama, Stromboli Island, 31 October 1916. No lives lost.							
126	*Centaur*	19.9.1895	1,900	Cargo	St/Sc/St 278.0/41.1/20.8	148 nhp TE (3Cy) W&C	Alfred Holt & Co. Liverpool
Completed October 1895, for Holt's East Indian Steam Ship Co. In 1899 to German owners, Norddeutscher Lloyd, renamed *Korat.* In 1911 to Japanese owners, Sensho Kogyo, renamed *Daito Maru.* Lost collision off Tsukumo, July 1917.							
127	*Charon*	20.12.1895	1,920	Cargo	St/Sc/St 278.0/41.1/20.8	148 nhp TE (3Cy) W&C	Alfred Holt & Co. Liverpool
Completed February 1896, sister ship of *Centaur* for same service. In 1899 to German owners, Norddeutscher Lloyd, renamed *Bangkok.* In 1911 to Japanese owners, Awakoko Kiodo K.K., renamed *Kiodo Maru No.13,* by 1918 owned by Uchida Kisen K.K. In 1922 to Ogina Laisyo K.K., Takoaka, renamed *Kyodo Maru No.13.* In 1933 owned by Oginuno Kaisha K.K., Fushiki, without name change. Sunk in air attack, sea of Japan, July 1945.							
128	*Patroclus*	31.3.1896	5,509	Cargo	St/Sc/St 422.0/49.4/28.6	520 nhp TE (3Cy) W&C	Alfred Holt & Co. Liverpool
Completed May 1896. In September 1907 at end of voyage from Australia ran aground off Portland Bill and badly damaged. In January 1911 sustained damage in collision with Great Eastern Railways ferry *Vienna.* In 1914 to Dutch subsidiary, N.S.M. Oceaan, requisitioned by British government 1917, returned 1919. Renamed *Palamed* 1923. In 1924 to Italian owners, Atlantide S.A. per Imprese Marittima, renamed *Australia.* Broken up Italy (Genoa) 1929.							
129	*Antenor*	11.6.1896	5,531	Cargo	St/Sc/St 422.0/49.4/28.6	521 nhp TE (3Cy) W&C	Alfred Holt & Co. Liverpool
Sister of *Prometheus,* cost £62,796. In 1914 to Dutch subsidiary, N.S.M. Oceaan, but later returned to British flag. Torpedoed February 1918 in Mediterranean; repaired. In 1925 to Italian owners, Atlantide S.A. per Imprese Marittima, renamed *Fortunato.* Broken up Italy (Genoa) 1926.							
130	*Lord Dufferin*	19.3.1896	2,270	Sailing Vessel (Four-masted Barque)	Steel Hulled 285.0/41.9/24.6	N/A	John Herron & Co. Liverpool
Near sister of *Dundonald.* Left Barry June 1896 on first transatlantic voyage for Montevideo with cargo of coal. On 7 October sailed for New York to collect cargo for Sydney, never seen again. Twenty-seven Lives lost.							
131	*Glenarm Head*	24.7.1897	3,910	Cargo	St/Sc/St 360.0/46.1/19.9	379 nhp TE (3Cy) W&C	Ulster SS Co. Belfast
Sunk by submarine torpedo (*UB-30*) near Brighton lightship, on route Southampton–Boulogne with cargo of ammunition, January 1918. Two lives lost.							

Yard No	Name	Date Launched	Displacement Tons	Type	Construction and Dimensions	Horse Power	Owners
132	*Magician*	11.9.1896	5,065	Cargo	St/Sc/St 400.0/47.0/22.4	424 nhp TE (3Cy) W&C	T.&J. Harrison Liverpool
Completed October 1896. In 1900 chartered as transport for Boer War. In 1922 to Japanese owners, Taiyo Kaiun, renamed *Magician Maru* and *Keigo Maru.* Wrecked Arena Islands, March 1923.							
133	*City of Sparta*	9.10.1896	5,179	Cargo	St/Sc/St 430.0/50.2/28.5	471 nhp TE (3Cy) W&C	G. Smith & Sons Glasgow
Completed June 1897. Taken over by Ellerman 1901. Broken up Port Glasgow (UK) 1931.							
134	*Kamakura Maru*	9.12.1896	6,123	Passenger-Cargo	St/2Sc/St 445.0/49.7/30.4	554 nhp TE (6Cy) **Engines** Berkley Curle & Co. Glasgow	Nippon Yusen K.K. Tokyo
Completed May 1897. Broken up Japan 1933.							
135							
136							
137	*Belvidere*	12.12.1896	1,516	Passenger-Fruiter	St/Sc/St 255.0/34.0/22.0	291 nhp TE (3Cy) W&C	R.&C. Allan Glasgow
Completed April 1897. Wrecked 5 miles S of Cape Maisi, Cuba, May 1898.							
138	*Beverly*	25.3.1897	1,516	Passenger-Fruiter	St/Sc/St 255.0/34.0/22.0	291 nhp TE (3Cy) W&C	R.&C. Allan Glasgow
Completed May 1897, sister ship of *Belvidere.* Chartered to Boston Fruit Co. and later United Fruit. In 1905 to Canadian owners, Atlantic and Plant SS Co., renamed *A.W. Perry.* Wrecked Halifax, June 1915.							
139	*Hidalgo*	5.12.1896	1,126	Cargo	St/Sc/St 232.3/36.2/15.2	150 nhp TE (3Cy) W&C	New York & Cuba SS Co. Vera Cruz
Completed January 1897. Lost following collision Vera Cruz, March 1912.							
140	*Pavia*	4.3.1897	2,936	Cargo	St/Sc/St 332.1/45.7/15.0	354 nhp TE (3Cy) **Engines** Berkley Curle & Co. Glasgow	Cunard SS Co. Liverpool
Completed June 1897. Broken up Barrow (UK) 1928.							
141	*Tyria*	17.4.1897	2,936	Cargo	St/Sc/St 332.1/45.7/15.0	347 nhp TE (3Cy) **Engines** Berkley Curle & Co. Glasgow	Cunard SS Co. Liverpool
Completed August 1897. In 1928 to Niger Co., renamed *Ars.* Broken up Ireland (Cork) 1930.							
142	*Cypria*	20.7.1897	2,936	Cargo	St/Sc/St 332.1/45.7/15.0	356 nhp TE (3Cy) W&C	Cunard SS Co. Liverpool
Completed January 1898. Broken up Rosyth (UK) 1937.							
143	*Royston Grange*	30.6.1897	4,018	Cargo (Refrigerated)	St/Sc/St 370.0/47.6/19.0	415 nhp TE (3Cy) W&C	Houlder Bros & Co. London
Completed December 1897. Broken up Italy (Savona) 1929.							
144	*Sado Maru*	11.8.1897	5,898	Passenger-Cargo	St/2Sc/St 445.0/49.7/30.4	554 nhp TE (6Cy) W&C	Nippon Yusen K.K. Tokyo
Completed February 1898, sister ship of *Kamakura Maru*, employed on Hong Kong–Japan–Seattle route. At first commanded by American officers but after 1912 entirely Japanese manned. Broken up Japan 1934.							

Yard No	Name	Date Launched	Displacement Tons	Type	Construction and Dimensions	Horse Power	Owners
145	*Indore*	10.3.1898	7,300	Cargo	St/Sc/St 480.0/52.3/27.0	665 nhp TE (3Cy) W&C	B. Bates & Co. Liverpool
Completed July 1898. Shortly after completion transferred to ownership of J.H. Welsford & Co., Liverpool. Broken up Italy (Genoa) 1926.							
146	*Beacon Grange*	25.1.1898	4,018	Cargo (Refrigerated)	St/Sc/St 370.0/47.6/19.0	415 nhp TE (3Cy) W&C	Houlder Bros & Co. London
Completed June 1898, sister ship of *Riyston Grange.* Wrecked Rio Gallegos, September 1921.							
147	*City of Corinth*	22.2.1898	5,443	Passenger-Cargo	St/Sc/St 430.0/50.2/28.5	471 nhp TE (3Cy) W&C	G. Smith & Sons Glasgow
Completed September 1898. Taken over by Ellerman 1901. In 1912 to French owners, Cie.De Nav Sud-Atlantique, renamed *Sequana.* During First World War taken up by French government as troopship. In May 1917 left Dakar with 665 on board, including 400 Senegalese soldiers. Torpedoed by submarine (*UC-72*) off Ile d'Yeu, 8 June 1917. As many of troops did not understand French considerable confusion and consequently losses were heavy. Two hundred and seven lives lost.							
148	*Rippingham Grange*	18.4.1898	5,790	Cargo (Refrigerated)	St/Sc/St 420.0/54.2/29.5	513 nhp TE (3Cy) W&C	Houlder Bros & Co. London
Completed 8.10.1898. In 1911 chartered to British Indian SN Co. In 1912 to New Zealand Shipping Co., renamed *Limerick.* One of ships that transported first contingent of New Zealand Expeditionary Force. Sunk by submarine torpedo (*U-86*), 140 miles from Bishops Rock, inbound from Sydney with cargo of meat, May 1917. Eight lives lost.							
149	*Workman*	4.6.1898	6,115	Cargo	St/Sc/St 450.0/52.5/30.6	585 nhp TE (3Cy) W&C	T.&J. Harrison Liverpool
Completed October 1898. Wrecked near Rio de Janeiro, December 1912.							
150	*Castilian*	19.10.1898	7,440	Passenger-Cargo	St/Sc/St 470.0/53.7/25.2	521 nhp TE (3Cy) W&C	Allen Line SS Co. Glasgow
Completed February 1899. Wrecked on Gannet Rock, Yarmouth, March 1899.							
151	*Quernmore*	?.9.1898	7,302	Cargo	St/Sc/St 480.0/52.3/27.0	521 nhp TE (3Cy) W&C	W. Johnston & Co. Liverpool
Completed November 1898. Sunk by submarine torpedo (*U-82*) 160 miles from Tory Island, July 1917. One life lost.							
152	*Brisgravia*	23.2.1899	6,575	Cargo	St/Sc/St 448.5/53.2/31.2	498 nhp TE (3Cy) W&C	Hamburg America Line Hamburg
Completed May 1899. In 1919 ceded to France as war reparation, allocated to France Line, renamed *Arkansas.* Broken up Italy (La Spezia) 1934.							
153	*Heathmore*	2.8.1898	3,147	Cargo	St/Sc/St 331.0/46.3/24.2	285 nhp TE (3Cy) **Engines** D. Rollo & Son Liverpool	W. Johnston & Co. Liverpool
Completed September 1898. In 1927 to German owners, E. Behncke, renamed *Gloria.* Broken up Germany (Lubeck) 1932.							
154	*Stentor*	31.12.1898	6,773	Cargo	St/Sc/St 442.4/52.8/30.6	521 nhp TE (3Cy) **Engines** D. Rollo & Son Liverpool	Alfred Holt & Co. Liverpool
Completed May 1899, towed to Liverpool where machinery fitted. War service as *White Sea Ammunition Carrier No.222.* In July 1922 transferred to Dutch subsidiary, N.S.M. Oceaan, not renamed. In 1926 to Philippine owners, Madrigal & Co., renamed *Don Jose.* Broken up Singapore 1932.							
155	*Yang Tsze*	16.1.1899	6,457	Cargo	St/Sc/St 450.0/53.2/30.9	620 nhp TE (3Cy) W&C	China Mutual SS Co. London
Completed March 1899. Acquired by Holts in 1902. In 1927 to Philippine owners, Madrigal & Co., renamed *Macaria (2).* Broken up Japan (Osaka) 1933.							

Yard No	Name	Date Launched	Displacement Tons	Type	Construction and Dimensions	Horse Power	Owners
156	*Ping Suey*	30.3.1899	6,457	Cargo	St/Sc/St 450.0/53.2/30.9	620 nhp TE (3Cy) W&C	China Mutual SS Co. London
Completed June 1899, sister ship of *Yang Tsze*. Acquired by Holts in 1902. In June 1916 ran aground near Cape of Good Hope, refloated and to Mitchell Cotts, sent to Hong Kong for repairs. In 1919 to Italian owners, Lloyd de Pacifico, renamed *Attualita*. Broken up Italy (Genoa) 1932.							
157	*Star of Australia*	24.6.1899	7,200	Cargo (Refrigerated)	St/Sc/St 440.0/55.1/29.7	579 nhp TE (3Cy) W&C	J.P. Corry & Co. Belfast
Completed 7.9.1899. In January 1914 to Commonwealth and Dominion Line, renamed *Port Stephens* (April 1916). In August 1918 sank *North Cambria* in collision 70 miles W of Ushant. Broken up Italy 1924.							
158	*Sicilian*	15.8.1899	6,010	Passenger- Cargo (Refrigerated)	St/Sc/St 430.0/54.2/28.2	447 nhp TE (3Cy) W&C	Allen Line SS Co. Glasgow
Completed November 1899. Renamed *Bruton* 1923. Broken up Italy (Genoa) 1925.							
159	*Lord Downshire*	2.11.1899	4,808	Cargo	St/Sc/St 406.9/48.8/29.3	463 nhp TE (3Cy) W&C	T. Dixon & Sons Belfast
Completed January 1900. In 1917 to Ulster SS Co., not renamed. Broken up Preston (UK) 1930.							
160	*Corinthian*	19.3.1900	6,240	Passenger- Cargo (Refrigerated)	St/Sc/St 430.0/54.2/28.2	447 nhp TE (3Cy) W&C	Allen Line SS Co. Glasgow
Completed May 1900, sister ship of *Sicilian*. Wrecked Bay off Fundy, December 1918.							
161	*Rathlin Head*	17.10.1899	6,753	Cargo	St/2Sc/St 469.0/53.4/32.3	520 nhp TE (6Cy) W&C	Ulster SS Co. Belfast
Completed December 1899. Broken up Rosyth (UK) 1929.							
162	*Mimiro*	30.1.1900	6,224	Cargo (Refrigerated)	St/Sc/St 440.0/55.1/29.9	570 nhp TE (3Cy) W&C	Tyser & Co. London
Completed March 1900. Transferred to Commonwealth and Dominion Line on formation, renamed *Port Hacking* (1916). In 1927 to Italian owners, A. Zanchi, renamed *Capo Nord*. Broken up Italy (Genoa) 1933.							
163							
164							
165							
166	*Irada*	19.5.1900	8,120	Passenger/ Cargo	St/2Sc/St 501.0/59.3/?	? TE (6Cy) W&C	E. Bates & Son Liverpool
Completed July 1900. Wrecked Mizen Head, December 1908.							
167	*Calderon*	17.5.1900	4,074	Cargo	St/Sc/St 378.0/47.5/24.7	534 nhp TE (3Cy) W&C?	Lamport & Holt Liverpool
Completed July 1900. In 1901 transferred to company's Belgian subsidiary. Sunk after collision with *Musketeer*, River Mersey, January 1912.							
168	*Camoens*	23.8.1900	4,074	Cargo	St/Sc/St 378.0/47.5/24.7	534 nhp TE (3Cy) W&C?	Lamport & Holt Liverpool
Completed September 1900, sister ship of *Calderon*. In 1901 transferred to company's Belgian subsidiary, reverted to British flag 1908. Scrapped Italy (Genoa) 1924.							
169	*Mechanican*	9.8.1900	9,044	Cargo	St/2Sc/St 482.0/57.3/31.5	604 nhp TE (6Cy) W&C	T.&J. Harrison Liverpool
Completed October 1900. In 1917 taken over and armed as escort. January 1918 badly damaged by submarine torpedo (*UB-35*) 8 miles from St Catherines Point, beached but total loss. Thirteen lives lost.							
170	*Indian*	24.10.1900	9,121	Passenger- Cargo	St/2Sc/St 482.9/57.2/31.8	640 nhp TE (6Cy) W&C	Leyland & Co. Liverpool
Completed December 1900. Broken up Germany (Wilhelmshaven) 1923.							

Yard No	Name	Date Launched	Displacement Tons	Type	Construction and Dimensions	Horse Power	Owners
171	*City of Athens*	7.12.1900	5,160	Cargo	St/Sc/St 430.0/50.2/28.5	471 nhp TE (3Cy) W&C	G. Smith & Sons Glasgow
Completed February 1901. Taken over by Ellerman. Sunk August 1917 by mine laid off Capetown in January by German surface raider *Wolf.* Twenty-one lives lost.							
172	*Peleus*	1.3.1901	7,441	Cargo	St/Sc/St 454.7/54.1/32.3	533 nhp TE (3Cy) W&C	Alfred Holt & Co. Liverpool
Completed May 1901. First of four similar ships. Stuck on slip when launched and it was a week later that actually took to water. In 1931 to Philippine owners, Madrigal & Co., renamed *Perseus.* Broken up Japan (Osaka) 1933.							
173	*Tydeus*	4.6.1901	7,441	Cargo	St/Sc/St 454.7/54.1/32.3	533 nhp TE (3Cy) W&C	Alfred Holt & Co. Liverpool
Completed July 1901, sister of *Peleus.* Broken up Glasgow (UK) 1931.							
174	*Paknam*	6.10.1900	2,027	Cargo	St/Sc/St 278.6/41.2/20.9	148 nhp TE (3Cy) W&C	Norddeutscher Lloyd Bremen
Completed November 1900. In 1906 to Indian owners, Bengal SN Co., renamed *Zaida.* In 1923 to Japanese owners, Yamamoto Shoji, renamed *Shunmei Maru.* Wrecked Etorofu, November 1929.							
175	*Tanglin*	21.11.1900	2,027	Cargo	St/Sc/St 278.6/41.2/20.9	148 nhp TE (3Cy) W&C	Norddeutscher Lloyd Bremen
Completed December 1900, sister ship of *Paknam.* In 1906 to Bengal SN Co., renamed *Zira.* In *c.* 1922 to Chinese owners, Shaw Hsing SS Co., renamed *Hulsing.* In 1941 taken over by Japanese government, renamed *Wako Go.* Sunk by mine off Korea, August 1945.							
176	*Carrigan Head*	9.3.1901	4,201	Cargo	St/Sc/St 370.5/46.0/28.7	438 nhp TE (3Cy) W&C	Ulster SS Co. Belfast
Completed April 1901. Broken up Rosyth (UK) 1934.							
177	*Ionian*	12.9.1901	8,265	Passenger-Cargo (Refrigerated)	St/2Sc/St 470.0/57.5/37.6	604 nhp TE (6Cy) W&C	Allen Line SS Co Glasgow
Completed November 1901, for Liverpool–Canada route. In 1909 rebuilt to accommodate 325 second-class and 800 third-class passengers. In 1914 became troopship, operating to Bombay via Suez Canal. Sunk by submarine-laid mine (*UC-51*) off Milford Haven on route Liverpool–Plymouth, October 1917. Seven lives lost.							
178	*City of Benares*	29.10.1901	6,732	Passenger-Cargo	St/Sc/St 460.5/55.3/31.0	521 nhp TE (3Cy) W&C	City Line (Ellerman) Glasgow
Completed January 1902, first 'City' for Ellerman. Accommodation for 90 passengers. Served as troopship 1914–18. Broken up Blyth (UK) 1933.							
179							
180	*City of Madrid*	7.6.1901	4,900	Cargo	St/Sc/St 406.8/48.8/29.4	552 nhp TE (3Cy) W&C	G. Smith & Sons Glasgow
Completed July 1901. In 1927 to Italian owners, G. Molfino & Co., renamed *Nitro.* Broken up Italy (Genoa) 1932.							
181	*Drayton Grange*	3.10.1901	6,592	Cargo (Refrigerated)	St/2Sc/St 450.0/55.0/ 30.6	662 nhp TE (6Cy) W&C	Holder Bros & Co. Greenock
Completed 12.12.1901. In 1912 to New Zealand Shipping Co., renamed *Tyrone.* To Union SS Co. but wrecked before handover, S of Taiaroa Head, September 1913.							
182	*Oswestry Grange*	23.1.1902	6,592	Cargo (Refrigerated)	St/2Sc/St 450.0/55.0/ 30.6	662 nhp TE (6Cy) W&C	Holder Bros & Co. Greenock
Completed March 1902, sister ship of *Drayton Grange.* In 1912 to New Zealand Shipping Co., renamed *Roscommon.* Subsequently to Union SS Co. Sunk by submarine torpedo (*U-53*) 20m NE of Tory Island outbound Manchester–Australia, August 1917. No lives lost.							
183	*Niwaru*	24.12.1901	6,450	Cargo (Refrigerated)	St/2Sc/St 450.0/55.2/30.2	583 nhp TE (6Cy) W&C	Tyser & Co. London
Completed March 1902. Transferred to Commonwealth and Dominion Line 1914, renamed *Port Lyttelton* (1916). In January 1924 ran aground Tamar Heads, Tasmania, salvaged but sold for scrap as surplus of tonnage and repair not considered viable. Broken up Italy (Genoa) 1924.							

Yard No	Name	Date Launched	Displacement Tons	Type	Construction and Dimensions	Horse Power	Owners
184	*Telemachus*	25.3.1902	7,450	Cargo	St/Sc/St 454.7/54.1/32.3	521 nhp TE (3Cy) W&C	Alfred Holt & Co. Liverpool
Completed May 1902, sister ship of *Peleus*. Between October 1915 and June 1918 *Expeditionary Force Transport No.C106* transporting stores from Canada. In 1932 to Italian owners, Ditta Luigi Pittaluga Vapori, renamed *Tasmania*. Broken up Italy 1933.							
185	*Jason*	24.5.1902	7,450	Cargo	St/Sc/St 454.7/54.1/32.3	521 nhp TE (3Cy) W&C	Alfred Holt & Co. Liverpool
Completed July 1902, sister ship of *Peleus*. War service July 1915 to March 1918. Broken up Japan (Osaka) 1931.							
186	*Lord Antrim*	13.2.1902	4,270	Cargo	St/Sc/St 375.3/47.2/28.8	499 nhp TE (3Cy) W&C	T. Dixon & Sons Belfast
Completed April 1902. In 1917 to Ulster SS Co., not renamed. Broken up Rosyth (UK) 1934.							
187	*Titian*	8.5.1902	4,170	Cargo	St/Sc/St 390.0/50.3/27.1	413 nhp TE (3Cy) W&C	Lamport & Holt Liverpool
Completed June 1902. Sunk by submarine torpedo (Austrian SMS *U-14*) off Malta, August 1917. No lives lost. Commander of submarine was Georg Ritter von Trapp.							
188	*Tintoretto*	5.7.1902	4,170	Cargo	St/Sc/St 390.0/50.3/27.1	413 nhp TE (3Cy) W&C	Lamport & Holt Liverpool
Completed August 1902, sister ship of *Titan*. Broken up Italy (Savona) 1930.							
189							
190							
191	*Keemun*	1.9.1902	7,642	Cargo	St/2Sc/St 482.0/58.2/32.8	801 nhp TE (6Cy) W&C	China Mutual SS Co. Liverpool
Completed October 1902. Acquired by Holts. During First World War regularly carried fuel oil in ballast tanks Far East–Europe. On 13 June 1918 successfully drove off attack by surfaced U-boat in Atlantic. Broken up Japan (Osaka) 1933.							
192	*Gregory Apcar*	6.10.1902	4,562	Passenger-Cargo	St/Sc/St 410.0/49.2/27.6	629 nhp TE (3Cy) W&C	Apcar & Co. Calcutta
Completed November 1902. Broken up Italy (Genoa) 1923.							
193	*Irak*	30.10.1902	8,112	Cargo	St/2Sc/St 501.0/59.3/ 32.9	831 nhp TE (6Cy) W&C	J.S. Welsford & Co. Liverpool
Completed December 1902. In 1911 to T.&J. Brocklebank, renamed *Mandasor*. In 1913 to German owners, HAPAG, renamed *Belgia*. Taken over by British government 1915, renamed *Huntstrick*. Sunk by submarine torpedo (*U-39*) 80 miles from Cape Spartel, outbound London–Salonika carrying stores and troops, June 1917. Fifteen lives lost.							
194	*Marere*	17.11.1902	6,443	Cargo (Refrigerated)	St/2Sc/St 450.0/55.2/30.2	583 nhp TE (6Cy) W&C	Tyser Line Ltd London
Completed December 1902, sister ship of *Niwaru*. Transferred to Commonwealth and Dominion Line, name not changed as sunk by submarine gunfire (*U-35*) 236 miles E of Malta on route Fremantle–Mudros with troops and supplies, January 1916. No lives lost.							
195	*Wayfarer*	19.12.1902	9,600	Cargo	St/2Sc/St 505.0/58.3/31.7	751 nhp TE (6Cy) W&C	T.&J. Harrison Liverpool
Completed February 1903. In 1923 to American owners, Dollar Line, renamed *Virginia Dollar*. In 1924 to Italian owners, Italian Metallici, renamed *Angiolina R*. In 1928 to Piemontese, renamed *Susa*. Broken up Italy (Genoa) 1932.							
196							
197	*City of Calcutta*	17.3.1903	7,380	Passenger-Cargo	St/Sc/St 471.7/56.2/31.9	546 nhp TE (3Cy) W&C	Ellerman Line Ltd Liverpool
Completed May 1903. In 1914–18 troopship. Renamed *Calcut* for voyage to breakers in Japan (Osaka) 1934.							
198	*Colonial*	30.12.1902	4,955	Cargo	St/Sc/St 400.0/48.5/19.2	470 nhp TE (3Cy) W&C	T.&J. Harrison Liverpool
Completed March 1903. In 1925 to Italian owners, Lagorara Bros, renamed *Color*. Broken up Italy (Genoa) 1929.							

Yard No	Name	Date Launched	Displacement Tons	Type	Construction and Dimensions	Horse Power	Owners
199	*Councillor*	3.4.1903	4,955	Cargo	St/Sc/St 400.0/48.5/19.2	470 nhp TE (3Cy) W&C	T.&J. Harrison Liverpool
Completed May 1903, sister ship of *Colonial.* Sunk by submarine-laid mine (*U-79*) off Galley Head, inbound San Francisco–Liverpool with cargo of barley and timber, September 1916. No lives lost.							
200	*Star of Ireland*	29.6.1903	4,331	Cargo (Refrigerated)	St/Sc/St 380.0/48.7/28.3	452 nhp TE (3Cy) W&C	J.P. Corry & Co. Belfast
Completed August 1903, for Australian meat trade. In 1915 to Nelson Steam Navigation Co., renamed *Highland Star* (1916). Laid up 1927 at Dunston-on-Tyne and broken up Inverkeithing (UK) 1930.							
201	*Pera*	10.6.1903	7,635	Cargo (Refrigerated)	St/2Sc/St 480.0/57.2/32.7	516 nhp TE (6Cy) W&C	P&O SN Co. London
Completed 23.7.1903. Sunk by submarine torpedo (*UB-48*), Mediterranean, outbound Liverpool–Calcutta, October 1917. One life lost.							
202	*Palma*	24.8.1903	7,635	Cargo (Refrigerated)	St/2Sc/St 480.0/57.2/32.7	516 nhp TE (6Cy) W&C	P&O SN Co. London
Completed 9.10.1903. Renamed *Arma* and broken up Italy (Genoa) 1924.							
203	*City of Agra*	8.9.1903	4,808	Cargo	St/Sc/St 400.0/50.2/28.9	379 nhp TE (3Cy) W&C	Ellerman Lines Liverpool
Completed October 1903, originally for R. Alexander & Co. as *Locksley Hall* but sold on stocks and completed under this name. Broken up Italy (Savona) 1932.							
204	*City of York*	17.12.1903	7,705	Passenger- Cargo	St/Sc/St 485.0/56.3/32.0	599 nhp TE (3Cy) W&C	Ellerman Line Liverpool
Completed February 1904. Renamed *City* for voyage to breakers in Japan (Osaka) 1936.							
205	*Matatua*	15.1.1904	6,500	Cargo (Refrigerated)	St/2Sc/St 448.0/56.5/30.6	800 nhp TE (6Cy) W&C	Shaw Savill & Albion Southampton
Completed February 1904. In 1928 to German owners, A. Bernstein, renamed *Ilsenstein.* Scuttled as block ship, Scapa Flow, February 1940.							
206	*Victorian*	25.8.1904	10,630	Passenger	St/3Sc/St 520.0/60.4/38.0	12,000 shp Turb W&C	J.&A. Allen Glasgow
Completed March 1905, for Canadian routes; this liner was smaller than those operating to America, with accommodation for 1,300 passengers. Originally pair of ships were to be built by WC. However, decision to change design to include turbine power and triple screws meant company felt they could not undertake two such advanced vessels at once, *Virginian* therefore built by Alexander Stephens & Sons on Clyde. *Victorian* beat sister into service by two weeks and could claim to be first turbine-driven liner on North Atlantic. In war commissioned as armed merchant cruiser and spent two and a half years with 10th Cruiser Squadron. After war served as troopship then modernised, renamed *Marloch*, returned to Canadian routes 1922. Broken up Pembroke Dock (UK) 1929.							
207	*Parana*	28.4.1904	3,900	Cargo (Refrigerated)	St/Sc/St 375.3/48.3/25.9	430 nhp TE (3Cy) W&C	Royal Mail SP Co. London
Completed June 1904. Broken Blyth (UK) 1933.							
208	*Ferry No.6*	?.?.1904	19	Steam Ferry	St/Sc/St 60.0/14.0/ ?	25 ? W&C	Belfast Harbour Commissioners
Cost of £1,420. Broken up Belfast 1934.							
209	*San Jose*	2.6.1904	3,300	Fruiter	St/Sc/St 330.0/44.6/31.6	320 nhp TE (3Cy) W&C	United Fruit Co. New Jersey
Completed 4.8.1904, fruit carrier with accommodation for 18 passengers. WC was to build nine vessels of this type for this customer (see yard numbers 210, 211, 342, 343, 344, 345, 347 and 348). Initially under British flag through wholly owned subsidiary, Tropical Fruit SS Co., Glasgow, transferred to US 1914. Sunk collision, January 1942.							
210	*Limon*	1.8.1904	3,300	Fruiter	St/Sc/St 330.0/44.6/31.6	320 nhp TE (3Cy) W&C	United Fruit Co. New Jersey
Completed 21.9.1904, sister ship of *San Jose.* Initially under British flag, Tropical Fruit SS Co., Glasgow, transferred to US 1914. Ran aground British Honduras, July 1938; refloated and broken up USA (Baltimore).							

<table>
<tr><th>Yard No</th><th>Name</th><th>Date Launched</th><th>Displacement Tons</th><th>Type</th><th>Construction and Dimensions</th><th>Horse Power</th><th>Owners</th></tr>
<tr><td>211</td><td>Esparta</td><td>12.9.1904</td><td>3,300</td><td>Fruiter</td><td>St/Sc/St
330.6/44.5/28.9</td><td>320 nhp
TE (3Cy)
W&C</td><td>United Fruit Co.
New Jersey</td></tr>
<tr><td colspan="8">Completed 27.10.1904, sister ship of San Jose. Initially on UK register, Tropical Fruit SS Co., Glasgow, transferred to US 1914. Sunk by submarine torpedo (U-123) off Jacksonville, Florida, April 1942. One life lost.</td></tr>
<tr><td>212</td><td>Star of Scotland</td><td>15.9.1904</td><td>6,230</td><td>Cargo
(Refrigerated)</td><td>St/Sc/St
440.3/55.3/ 30.3</td><td>579 nhp
TE (3Cy)
W&C</td><td>J.P. Corry & Co.
Belfast</td></tr>
<tr><td colspan="8">Completed November 1904. Transferred to Commonwealth and Dominion Line 1914, renamed Port Campbell (1916). Hit by submarine torpedo (U-53), outbound London–New York, 115 miles SW of Bishops Rock, sank two days later, April 1916. No lives lost.</td></tr>
<tr><td>213</td><td>Telamon</td><td>14.11.1904</td><td>4,510</td><td>Cargo
(Refrigerated)</td><td>St/Sc/St
383.3/47.4/28.2</td><td>350 nhp
TE (3Cy)
W&C</td><td>Alfred Holt & Co.
Liverpool</td></tr>
<tr><td colspan="8">Completed December 1904. Broken up Port Glasgow (UK) 1933.</td></tr>
<tr><td>214</td><td>Anselm</td><td>20.1.1905</td><td>5,440</td><td>Passenger-
Cargo
(Refrigerated)</td><td>St/Sc/St
400.4/50.1/19.1</td><td>819 nhp
TE (3Cy)
W&C</td><td>Booth SS Co.
Liverpool</td></tr>
<tr><td colspan="8">Completed March 1905. In 1922 to Argentinian owners, A.M. Delfino & Co., renamed Comodoro Rivadavia. In 1944 to Argentine government, renamed Rio Santa Cruz. Broken up Argentina 1961.</td></tr>
<tr><td>215</td><td>HMS Squirrel</td><td>21.12.1904</td><td>230</td><td>Coast Guard
Vessel</td><td>St/Sc/St
?</td><td>?</td><td>Admiralty</td></tr>
<tr><td colspan="8">By 1914 operating as cable vessel. Patrol duties during First World War. In early 1920s sold as private yacht, renamed Vedra.</td></tr>
<tr><td>216</td><td>City of Karachi</td><td>8.3.1905</td><td>5,547</td><td>Passenger-
Cargo</td><td>St/Sc/St
438.5/54.1/31.2</td><td>402 nhp
QE (4Cy)
W&C</td><td>Ellerman Lines
Liverpool</td></tr>
<tr><td colspan="8">Completed April 1905. Renamed Karachi for voyage to Japanese breakers (Yawata) 1934.</td></tr>
<tr><td>217</td><td>Regina</td><td>7.12.1904</td><td>1,160</td><td>Cargo</td><td>St/Sc/St
247.5/36.7/14.2</td><td>116 nhp
TE (3Cy)
W&C</td><td>R. Truffin & Co.
Havana</td></tr>
<tr><td colspan="8">Completed December 1904. Broken up 1934.</td></tr>
<tr><td>218</td><td>Delta</td><td>4.7.1905</td><td>8,053</td><td>Passenger-
Cargo</td><td>St/2Sc/St
470.2/56.5/31.6</td><td>1,251 nhp
QE (8Cy)
W&C</td><td>P&O SN Co.
London</td></tr>
<tr><td colspan="8">Completed 25.9.1905, accommodation for 163 first-class and 80 second-class passengers. Broken up Japan (Kobe) 1929.</td></tr>
<tr><td>219</td><td>Patani</td><td>6.6.1905</td><td>3,465</td><td>Cargo</td><td>St/Sc/St
370.3/49.3/30.7</td><td>379 nhp
TE (3Cy)
W&C</td><td>Elder Dempster
Liverpool</td></tr>
<tr><td colspan="8">Completed 4.8.1905. In 1930 to Italian owners, Genovese, renamed Capo Faro. Sunk by British aircraft while attempting to resupply Italian Army in North Africa, November 1941.</td></tr>
<tr><td>220</td><td>Agberi</td><td>6.7.1905</td><td>3,465</td><td>Cargo</td><td>St/Sc/St
370.3/49.3/30.7</td><td>379 nhp
TE (3Cy)
W&C</td><td>Elder Dempster
Liverpool</td></tr>
<tr><td colspan="8">Completed September 1905, sister ship of Patani. Sunk by submarine torpedo (U-87), inbound Dakar–Liverpool, 18 miles from Bardsey Island, Christmas Day 1917. No lives lost.</td></tr>
<tr><td>221</td><td>Pacuare</td><td>21.3.1905</td><td>3,891</td><td>Fruiter</td><td>St/Sc/St
367.3/46.8/29.3</td><td>577 nhp
TE (3Cy)
W&C</td><td>Elders & Fyffes
London</td></tr>
<tr><td colspan="8">Completed May 1905. Broken up Belgium (Bruges) 1936.</td></tr>
<tr><td>222</td><td>Zent</td><td>23.3.1905</td><td>3,891</td><td>Fruiter</td><td>St/Sc/St
367.3/46.8/29.3</td><td>577 nhp
TE (3Cy)
W&C</td><td>Elders & Fyffes
London</td></tr>
<tr><td colspan="8">Completed June 1905, sister ship of Pacuare. Sunk by submarine torpedo (U-66) outbound Garston–Santa Maria, off Fastnet, April 1916. Forty-nine lives lost, eleven survivors.</td></tr>
<tr><td>223</td><td>Volturnus</td><td>1904</td><td>160</td><td>Cargo</td><td></td><td></td><td>Alfred Holt & Co.
(According to list)</td></tr>
<tr><td colspan="8">This vessel appears on WC list in advertising material. However, no trace of such ship in Lloyd's or company's history. Appears to have been an error in building list.</td></tr>
</table>

<table>
<tr><th>Yard No</th><th>Name</th><th>Date Launched</th><th>Displacement Tons</th><th>Type</th><th>Construction and Dimensions</th><th>Horse Power</th><th>Owners</th></tr>
<tr><td>224</td><td>Orator</td><td>30.8.1905</td><td>3,563</td><td>Cargo</td><td>St/Sc/St
350.3/46.0/ 18.0</td><td>305 nhp
TE (3Cy)
W&C</td><td>T.&J. Harrison
Liverpool</td></tr>
<tr><td colspan="8">Completed October 1905. Sunk by submarine torpedo (U-96) 84nm WNW of Fastnet, inbound Pernambuco–Liverpool, June 1916. Five lives lost.</td></tr>
<tr><td>225</td><td>Bingera</td><td>13.9.1905</td><td>2,092</td><td>Passenger-Cargo</td><td>St/3Sc/St
300.3/40.8/17.9</td><td>498 nhp
TE (6Cy)
+Exh Turb
W&C</td><td>Austrasian United SNC
Brisbane</td></tr>
<tr><td colspan="8">Completed December 1905. Broken up Australia (Brisbane) 1924.</td></tr>
<tr><td>226</td><td>City of Glasgow</td><td>15.1.1906</td><td>6,444</td><td>Passenger-Cargo</td><td>St/Sc/St
443.0/53.6/ 30.3</td><td>481 nhp
QE (4Cy)
W&C</td><td>Ellerman Line
London</td></tr>
<tr><td colspan="8">Completed June 1906. Employed as troopship early in war but later released. Sunk by submarine torpedo (UB-118), outbound Manchester–Montréal, 21nm from Tuskar Rock, September 1918. Twelve lives lost.</td></tr>
<tr><td>227</td><td>Bellerophon</td><td>29.11.1905</td><td>8,920</td><td>Cargo</td><td>St/2Sc/St
485.3/58.4/31.0</td><td>585 nhp
TE (6Cy)
W&C</td><td>Alfred Holt & Co.
Liverpool</td></tr>
<tr><td colspan="8">Operated on Glasgow–Liverpool–Singapore–China–Japan–Vancouver–Seattle route. In 1914 became troopship and horse carrier operating between Liverpool and France. Again requisitioned for trooping duties February 1937, carried 750 troopers with their mounts and supplies from Birkenhead to Shanghai during 'China Affair'. Broken up Barrow-in-Furness (UK) 1948.</td></tr>
<tr><td>228</td><td>Veronese</td><td>14.11.1905</td><td>7,022</td><td>Cargo</td><td>St/Sc/St
465.0/59.0/ ?</td><td>3,300 ihp?
TE (3Cy)
W&C</td><td>Lamport & Holt
Liverpool</td></tr>
<tr><td colspan="8">Completed January 1906. Wrecked Leixoes, Portugal, on voyage Liverpool–Vigo–Leixour–Buenos Aires with 234 passenger and crew on board, January 1913. Twenty-seven lives lost.</td></tr>
<tr><td>229</td><td>Suva</td><td>14.12.1905</td><td>2,229</td><td>Passenger-Cargo</td><td>St/Sc/St
300.3/41.1/11.8</td><td>414 nhp
TE (3Cy)
W&C</td><td>Australasian United SN
Brisbane</td></tr>
<tr><td colspan="8">Completed March 1906, near sister of Bingera. In 1928 to Philippine owners, Madrigal & Co., renamed Sirius. The following year to Fernandez Bros, renamed Bohol. Scuttled Manila, 27 December 1941, to avoid capture by Japanese.</td></tr>
<tr><td>230</td><td>Araguaya</td><td>5.6.1906</td><td>10,537</td><td>Passenger-Cargo</td><td>St/2Sc/St
515.2/61.3/30.5</td><td>1514 nhp
QE (8Cy)
W&C</td><td>Royal Mail S.P. Co.
London</td></tr>
<tr><td colspan="8">(In company advertising material described as passenger vessel, re-rated)
Completed September 1906, one of famous 'A' class, examples of which were built by both Belfast yards. Employed as hospital ship during First World War and some time afterwards. In 1930 to Yugoslav owners, Yugoslav Lloyd, renamed Kraljica Marij. In 1940 taken over by French government, renamed Savoie, employed by Vichy government as naval transport. Sunk by American naval gunfire (USS Massachusetts), during Allied landings, Casablanca, November 1942.</td></tr>
<tr><td>231</td><td>Belgravia</td><td>10.5.1906</td><td>6,650</td><td>Cargo</td><td>St/Sc/St
448.9/53.3/31.7</td><td>402 nhp
QE (4Cy)
W&C</td><td>Hamburg America Line
Hamburg</td></tr>
<tr><td colspan="8">Completed July 1906. In 1916 to German Navy, renamed Wolf. In 1919 ceded to France, to French Line, renamed Iowa. Broken up Italy (Pola) 1934.</td></tr>
<tr><td>232</td><td>Chirripo</td><td>28.3.1906</td><td>4,041</td><td>Fruiter</td><td>St/Sc/St
374.3/47.8/29.3</td><td>666 nhp
TE (3Cy)
W&C</td><td>Elders & Fyffes
London</td></tr>
<tr><td colspan="8">Completed May 1906. Sunk by submarine-laid mine (UC-75), outbound Liverpool–Jamaica, Black Head, Belfast Lough, December 1917. No lives lost.</td></tr>
<tr><td>233</td><td>Reventazon</td><td>26.4.1906</td><td>4,041</td><td>Fruiter</td><td>St/Sc/St
374.3/47.8/29.5</td><td>666 nhp
TE (3Cy)
W&C</td><td>Elders & Fyffes
London</td></tr>
<tr><td colspan="8">Completed June 1906, sister ship of Chirripo. Sunk by submarine torpedo (UC-23) Gulf of Salinika, October 1918. Fifteen lives lost.</td></tr>
<tr><td>234</td><td>Japan</td><td>5.7.1906</td><td>6,013</td><td>Passenger-Cargo</td><td>St/Sc/St
450.2/56.4/29.6</td><td>996 nhp
TE (3Cy)
W&C</td><td>Apcar & Co.
Calcutta</td></tr>
<tr><td colspan="8">Completed 20.9.1906. Later operated by British India SN Co. Broken up Japan 1926.</td></tr>
<tr><td>235</td><td>Star of Japan</td><td>23.8.1906</td><td>6,236</td><td>Cargo
(Refrigerated)</td><td>St/Sc/St
450.0/56.4/ ?</td><td>3,000 ihp?
TE (3Cy)
W&C</td><td>J.P. Corry & Co.
Belfast</td></tr>
<tr><td colspan="8">Completed October 1906. Wrecked Pedro de Galha, west coast Africa, April 1908.</td></tr>
</table>

Yard No	Name	Date Launched	Displacement Tons	Type	Construction and Dimensions	Horse Power	Owners
236	*City of London*	20.11.1906	8,875	Passenger-Cargo	St/Sc/St 491.0/57.8/32.5	660 nhp QE (4Cy) W&C	Ellerman Lines Liverpool
	Completed February 1907, for India routes, great improvement on previous ships. Accommodation for 240 first-class and 50 second-class passengers. In 1916 commissioned as armed merchant cruiser (8x 6in) served China station. In 1919 returned to owners and UK–India routes. In 1939 troopship and later naval accommodation ship, Ceylon. Broken up Dalmuir (UK) 1946.						
237	*Howth Head*	4.10.1906	4,440	Cargo	St/Sc/St 380.4/48.4/28.8	462 nhp TE (3Cy) W&C	Ulster SS Co. Belfast
	Completed 17.11.1906. Sunk by submarine torpedo (*U-60*) 158nm NW off Fastnet, inbound New Orleans–Dublin, April 1917. Two lives lost.						
238	*Salaga*	15.12.1906	3,810	Cargo	St/Sc/St 380.5/50.3/30.9	379 nhp TE (3Cy) W&C	Elder Dempster Liverpool
	Completed 17.2.1907. Broken up Italy (Savona) 1930.						
239	*Gando*	20.12.1906	3,810	Cargo	St/Sc/St 380.5/50.3/30.9	379 nhp TE (3Cy) W&C	Elder Dempster Liverpool
	Completed 12.3.1907, sister ship of Salaga. Wrecked, beached and burnt out, Sanquin River, Liberia, January 1917.						
240	*Chyebassa*	21.2.1907	6,250	Cargo	St/Sc/St 430.2/54.3/32.0	805 nhp TE (3Cy) W&C	British India SN Co. Glasgow
	Completed 28.3.1907. Broken up Italy (Piombino) 1939.						
241	*Ceara*	16.3.1907	3,324	Passenger-Cargo (Refrigerated)	St/2Sc/St 340.0/44.8/23.5	534 nhp TE (6Cy) W&C	Lloyd Brasileiro Rio de Janeiro
	Completed July 1907. In 1927 renamed *Commandante Ripper*. Broken up Brazil (Rio de Janeiro) 1962.						
242	*Para*	30.4.1907	3,324	Passenger-Cargo (Refrigerated)	St/2Sc/St 340.0/44.8/23.5	534 nhp TE (6Cy) W&C	Lloyd Brasileiro Rio de Janeiro
	Completed July 1907, sister ship of *Ceara*. Broken up in Brazil (Rio de Janeiro) 1962.						
243							
244							
245	*San Paulo*	14.6.1907	3,583	Passenger-Cargo (Refrigerated)	St/2Sc/St 340.2/45.1/24.8	534 nhp TE (6Cy) W&C	Lloyd Brasileiro Rio de Janeiro
	Completed December 1907, near sister of *Ceara*. Foundered Rio de Janeiro Harbour, May 1921.						
246	*Rio de Janeiro*	16.8.1907	3,583	Passenger-Cargo (Refrigerated)	St/2Sc/St 340.3/45.1/24.8	534 nhp TE (6Cy) W&C	Lloyd Brasileiro Rio de Janeiro
	Completed February 1908, sister ship of *San Paulo*. In 1923 renamed *Prudente de Moraes*. In 1939 wrecked Straits of Magellan, refloated and repaired. In 1941 to Chilean Owners, R.C. Waters, renamed *California*. Foundered June 1949, Valparaiso.						
247	*Whakarua*	30.5.1907	6,600	Cargo (Refrigerated)	St/2Sc/St 450.3/55.3/30.4	650 nhp TE (6Cy) W&C	Tyser Line London
	Completed July 1907, near sister of *Niwaru*. To Commonwealth and Dominion Line 1914, renamed *Port Chalmers* (1916). Attacked by U-boat March 1917, successfully drove off attacker with gunfire. In 1926 to Italian owners, A. Zanchi, renamed *Norge*. Sunk by Allied aircraft Kerkena Island, Tunisia, December 1940, while trying to supply Italian Tenth Army.						
248	*Nerehana*	27.8.1907	6,600	Cargo (Refrigerated)	St/2Sc/St 450.3/55.3/30.4	650 nhp TE (6Cy) W&C	Tyser Line London
	Completed October 1907, sister ship of *Whakarua*. To Commonwealth and Dominion Line 1914, renamed *Port Hardy* (1916). Sunk by submarine torpedo (*U-91*), inbound Buenos Aires–Genoa, 78 miles off Cape Spartel, Tunisia, July 1918. Seven lives lost.						
249–254	Almost certainly barges produced for Lloyd Brasileiro. In *Shipbuilding at Belfast* (1933) WC claimed to have supplied 21 vessels to this customer but building list contains only nine. The remaining 12 barges produced in two batches of six (also see 257–262).						
255	*Kia Ora*	10.10.1907	6,560	Cargo (Refrigerated)	St/2Sc/St 448.3/56.5/30.5	810 nhp TE (6Cy) W&C	Shaw Savill & Albion London
	Completed November 1907. In 1935 to Italian owners, L. Pittaluga, renamed *Verbania*. Seized by British government 1940, renamed *Empire Tamar*. Scuttled at breakwater, Normandy, June 1944.						

<table>
<tr><th>Yard No</th><th>Name</th><th>Date Launched</th><th>Displacement Tons</th><th>Type</th><th>Construction and Dimensions</th><th>Horse Power</th><th>Owners</th></tr>
<tr><td>256</td><td>Verdi</td><td>23.10.1907</td><td>6,580</td><td>Passenger-Cargo (Refrigerated)</td><td>St/Sc/St 430.4/53.3/28.8</td><td>460 nhp TE (3Cy) W&C</td><td>Lamport & Holt Liverpool</td></tr>
<tr><td colspan="8">Completed December 1907. Sunk by submarine torpedo (U-53) 115nm off Eagle Island, inbound New York–Liverpool, August 1917. Six lives lost.</td></tr>
<tr><td>257–262</td><td colspan="7">As with 249–254 these numbers almost certainly refer to barges produced for Lloyd Brasileiro.</td></tr>
<tr><td>263</td><td>Bahia</td><td>15.11.1909</td><td>3,401</td><td>Passenger-Cargo (Refrigerated)</td><td>St/2Sc/St 340.2/44.8/24.8</td><td>534 nhp TE (6Cy) W&C</td><td>Lloyd Brasileiro Rio de Janeiro</td></tr>
<tr><td colspan="8">Completed March 1910, sister ship of San Paulo. In 1930 renamed Commandante Severino. Broken up 1931.</td></tr>
<tr><td>264</td><td>Minas Geraea</td><td>20.12.1909</td><td>3,401</td><td>Passenger-Cargo (Refrigerated)</td><td>St/2Sc/St 340.2/45.1/24.8</td><td>534 nhp TE (6Cy) W&C</td><td>Lloyd Brasileiro Rio de Janeiro</td></tr>
<tr><td colspan="8">Completed May 1910, sister ship of San Paulo. In 1923 renamed Affonso Penna. Sunk by submarine torpedo and gunfire (Italian Barbarigo) off Bahia, March 1943.</td></tr>
<tr><td>265</td><td>Coppename</td><td>5.12.1907</td><td>3,192</td><td>Passenger-Fruiter</td><td>St/Sc/St 339.5/42.6/15.9</td><td>486 nhp TE (3Cy) W&C</td><td>Koninklijke West-Indische Paramaribo</td></tr>
<tr><td colspan="8">Completed February 1908. In 1913 to United Fruit, transferred to US flag 1914. In 1940 to Venezuelan owners, Industria Pesca, renamed Anna Maria Gualdi. Sank internal explosion, Palermo, December 1942.</td></tr>
<tr><td>266</td><td>Marowijne</td><td>1.2.1908</td><td>3,192</td><td>Passenger-Fruiter</td><td>St/Sc/St 339.5/42.6/15.9</td><td>486 nhp TE (3Cy) W&C</td><td>Koninklijke West-Indische Paramaribo</td></tr>
<tr><td colspan="8">Completed March 1908, sister ship of Coppename. In 1912 to United Fruit, transferred to US flag 1914. Disappeared off Central America during voyage to New Orleans, August 1915. Ninety-seven lives lost.</td></tr>
<tr><td>267</td><td>Mantiqueira</td><td>6.9.1907</td><td>1,696</td><td>Cargo</td><td>St/2Sc/St 276.2/44.9/16.4</td><td>126 nhp TE (6Cy) W&C</td><td>Lloyd Brasileiro Rio de Janeiro</td></tr>
<tr><td colspan="8">Completed March 1908. Wrecked Ilha de Araras, Santa Catharina, Brazil, August 1942.</td></tr>
<tr><td>268</td><td>Bocaine</td><td>1.11.1909</td><td>1,696</td><td>Cargo</td><td>St/2Sc/St 276.2/44.9/16.4</td><td>126 nhp TE (6Cy) W&C</td><td>Lloyd Brasileiro Rio de Janeiro</td></tr>
<tr><td colspan="8">Completed December 1909, sister ship of Mantiqueira. Broken up Brazil (Rio de Janeiro) 1964.</td></tr>
<tr><td>269</td><td>Pyrineus</td><td>22.12.1909</td><td>1,696</td><td>Cargo</td><td>St/2Sc/St 276.2/44.9/16.4</td><td>126 nhp TE (6Cy) W&C</td><td>Lloyd Brasileiro Rio de Janeiro</td></tr>
<tr><td colspan="8">Completed March 1910, sister ship of Mantiqueira. Foundered 400 miles N of Rio de Janeiro, June 1956.</td></tr>
<tr><td>270</td><td>Ancona</td><td>19.12.1907</td><td>8,210</td><td>Passenger-Cargo</td><td>St/2Sc/St 482.3/58.3/26.2</td><td>1,221 nhp TE (6Cy) W&C</td><td>Soc de Navigazio a Vapore Genoa</td></tr>
<tr><td colspan="8">Completed February 1908, accommodation for 60 first-class and 2,500 third-class passengers on Italy–New York routes. Sunk by submarine torpedo, after being shelled, by German U-38 (operating under Austrian flag, Germany and Italy were not technically at war, Italy and Austria were), outbound Massina–New York, November 1915. There were 283 passengers and 163 crew on board at the time, about 200 lives lost, including nine American citizens which created major diplomatic incident.</td></tr>
<tr><td>271</td><td>Verona</td><td>31.3.1908</td><td>8,210</td><td>Passenger-Cargo</td><td>St/2Sc/St 482.3/58.3/26.2</td><td>1,221 nhp TE (6Cy) W&C</td><td>Soc de Navigazio a Vapore Genoa</td></tr>
<tr><td colspan="8">Completed May 1908, sister ship of Ancona. Employed as transport during Libyan War and employed as armed merchant cruiser at time of sinking (4x 4.7in guns). Sunk by submarine torpedo (UC-52), Straits of Messina, May 1918. Eight hundred and eighty lives lost.</td></tr>
<tr><td>272</td><td>Cartago</td><td>30.4.1908</td><td>4,940</td><td>Passenger-Fruiter</td><td>St/Sc/St 378.8/49.8/29.6</td><td>413 nhp TE (3Cy) W&C</td><td>United Fruit New Jersey</td></tr>
<tr><td colspan="8">First of new type of passenger-fruiter for United Fruit which would eventually number thirteen ships (see also yard nos: 273, 274, 280, 281, 282, 284, 285, 286, 287, 304, 305 and 306) all of around 5,000 tons with similar machinery. These ships had accommodation for 100 first-class passengers.
Completed July 1908. Initially on UK register (Tropical Fruit SS Co., Glasgow), transferred to US 1914. In 1933 chartered to States SS Co., renamed General Lee, reverted to original name on return in 1937. Converted to cargo ship. Broken up USA (Tampa) 1947.</td></tr>
</table>

Cefalu (WC y/n 514) 1930.

Chesapeake (WC y/n 494) 1927.

Drayton Grange (WC y/n 181) 1901.

Ionian (WC y/n 177) 1901.

Yard No	Name	Date Launched	Displacement Tons	Type	Construction and Dimensions	Horse Power	Owners
273	*Parismina*	20.5.1908	4,940	Passenger-Fruiter	St/Sc/St 378.8/49.8/29.6	413 nhp TE (3Cy) W&C	United Fruit New Jersey
Completed July 1908, sister ship of *Cartago*. Initially on UK register (Tropical Fruit SS Co. Glasgow), transferred to US 1914. In 1933 chartered to States SS Co., renamed *General Sherman*, reverted to original name on return 1937. Sunk by submarine torpedo (*U-624*) North Atlantic, November 1942. Twenty lives lost of 75 on board.							
274	*Heredia*	?.5.1908	4,940	Passenger-Fruiter	St/Sc/St 378.8/49.8/29.6	413 nhp TE (3Cy) W&C	United Fruit New Jersey
Completed August 1908, sister ship of *Cartago*. Initially on UK register (Tropical Fruit SS Co. Glasgow) transferred to US 1914. In 1933 chartered to States SS Co., renamed *General Pershing*. Reverted to original name on return 1937. Sunk by submarine torpedo (*U-506*) Gulf of Mexico, May 1942. Thirty-six lives lost of 62 on board.							
275	*Perseus*	25.6.1908	6,728	Cargo	St/Sc/St 443.0/52.9/32.0	534 nhp TE (3Cy) W&C	Alfred Holt & Co. Liverpool
Completed August 1908, first of nine very similar vessels. March 1915 evaded U-boat attack 40 miles W of Scilly Isles. In February 1917 sunk by mine laid by German surface raider *Wolf* off Colombo, Ceylon.							
276	*Theseus*	26.8.1908	6,728	Cargo	St/Sc/St 443.0/52.9/32.0	534 nhp TE (3Cy) W&C	Alfred Holt & Co. Liverpool
Completed October 1908, sister ship of *Perseus*. During First World War served under British, Indian, French and Canadian governments. In March 1915 attacked by submarine gunfire (*U-28*) but escaped after returning fire. Broken up Preston (UK) 1947.							
277	*Tainui*	1.9.1908	9,957	Passenger-Cargo (Refrigerated)	St/2Sc/St 477.8/61.1/31.0	1,080 nhp TE (6Cy) W&C	Shaw Savill & Albion London
Completed October 1908, for New Zealand trade. Almost lost April 1918 when abandoned after being torpedoed (*U-82*), reboarded and towed 130 miles to Falmouth where beached and salvaged. Sold for scrap 1939 but acquired by Ministry of War Transport, renamed *Empire Trader*. Hit by submarine torpedo (*U-92*) North Atlantic and scuttled, February 1943. No lives lost.							
278	*Otranto*	27.3.1909	12,124	Passenger-Cargo	St/2Sc/St 535.3/64.0/38.6	1,977 nhp QE (8Cy) W&C	Orient Steam Navigation Co. London
(In company advertising material described as passenger vessel, re-rated) Completed June 1909, for Australia routes, accommodation for 235 first-class, 185 second-class and 695 third-class passengers. At outbreak of war commissioned as armed merchant cruiser, attached to South Atlantic Squadron, fortunate to escape destruction when that force destroyed by Von Spee at Coronel. Subsequently patrol duties in Pacific and escort for Atlantic convoys. On such a voyage from New York in October 1918, with *c.* 1,100 crew and troops on board, was lost in collision with P&O's *Kashmir*. Drifted ashore off Islay, 431 lives lost, including 335 American military personnel.							
279	*Orvieto*	6.7.1909	12,124	Passenger-Cargo	St/2Sc/St 535.3/64.0/38.6	1,977 nhp QE (8Cy) W&C	Orient Steam Navigation Co. London
(In company advertising material described as passenger vessel, re-rated) Completed November 1909, sister ship of *Otranto*. Requisitioned as troopship by Australian government. Employed 1915–16 as minelayer and from May 1916 as armed merchant cruiser on convoy escort between UK and Brazil. After war returned to Australian route. Broken up Bo'ness (UK) 1931.							
280	*Abangarez*	23.1.1909	4,960	Passenger-Fruiter	St/Sc/St 378.8/50.3/29.1	413 nhp TE (3Cy) W&C	United Fruit New Jersey
Completed April 1909, sister ship of *Cartago*. Initially on UK register (Tropical Fruit SS Co., Glasgow), transferred to US 1914. In 1934 converted to cargo ship. Broken up USA (Richmond Cal) 1947.							
281	*Turrialba*	11.3.1909	4,960	Passenger-Fruiter	St/Sc/St 378.8/50.3/29.1	413 nhp TE (3Cy) W&C	United Fruit New Jersey
Completed May 1909, sister ship of *Cartago*. Initially on UK register (Tropical Fruit SS Co., Glasgow), transferred to US 1914. Broken up USA (Baltimore) 1949.							
282	*Atenas*	8.5.1909	4,960	Passenger-Fruiter	St/Sc/St 378.8/50.3/29.1	413 nhp TE (3Cy) W&C	United Fruit New Jersey
Completed July 1909, sister ship of *Cartago*. Initially under UK registry (Tropical Fruit SS Co. Glasgow), transferred to US 1914. In 1936 converted to cargo ship. Broken up USA (Baltimore) 1950.							

<table>
<tr><th>Yard No</th><th>Name</th><th>Date Launched</th><th>Displacement Tons</th><th>Type</th><th>Construction and Dimensions</th><th>Horse Power</th><th>Owners</th></tr>
<tr><td>283</td><td>Star of Canada</td><td>17.8.1909</td><td>7,280</td><td>Cargo
(Refrigerated)</td><td>St/2Sc/St
470.4/58.5/ ?</td><td>4,000 ihp?
TE (3Cy)
W&C?</td><td>J.P. Corry & Co.
Belfast</td></tr>
<tr><td colspan="8">Completed October 1909, company's first two-screwed ship. During voyage New Zealand–London was waiting offshore to load meat when gale blew up causing her to drag anchors, wrecked on Kaiti Beach, Gisborne, June 1912.</td></tr>
<tr><td>284</td><td>Almirante</td><td>22.7.1909</td><td>5,010</td><td>Passenger-
Fruiter</td><td>St/Sc/St
378.8/50.3/29.1</td><td>413 nhp
TE (3Cy)
W&C</td><td>United Fruit
New Jersey</td></tr>
<tr><td colspan="8">Completed October 1909, sister ship of Cartago. Initially on UK register (Tropical Fruit SS Co., Glasgow), transferred to US 1914. Sank in collision with USS Hisco off Atlantic City, September 1918.</td></tr>
<tr><td>285</td><td>Santa Marta</td><td>14.9.1909</td><td>5,010</td><td>Passenger-
Fruiter</td><td>St/Sc/St
378.8/50.3/29.1</td><td>413 nhp
TE (3Cy)
W&C</td><td>United Fruit
New Jersey</td></tr>
<tr><td colspan="8">Completed November 1909, sister ship of Cartago. Initially on UK register (Tropical Fruit SS Co., Glasgow), transferred to US 1914. Broken up USA (Baltimore) 1947.</td></tr>
<tr><td>286</td><td>Metapan</td><td>14.10.1909</td><td>5,010</td><td>Passenger-
Fruiter</td><td>St/Sc/St
378.8/50.3/29.1</td><td>413 nhp
TE (3Cy)
W&C</td><td>United Fruit
New Jersey</td></tr>
<tr><td colspan="8">Completed December 1909, sister ship of Cartago. Initially on UK register (Tropical Fruit SS Co., Glasgow), transferred to US 1914. In October 1914 sunk in collision, salvaged and repaired. Mined and sunk, Mediterranean, October 1943. No lives lost.</td></tr>
<tr><td>287</td><td>Zacapa</td><td>28.10.1909</td><td>5,010</td><td>Passenger-
Fruiter</td><td>St/Sc/St
378.8/50.3/29.1</td><td>413 nhp
TE (3Cy)
W&C</td><td>United Fruit
New Jersey</td></tr>
<tr><td colspan="8">Completed December 1909, sister ship of Cartago. Initially on UK register (Tropical Fruit SS Co. Glasgow), transferred to US 1914. Broken up USA (Fieldsbro, NJ) 1949.</td></tr>
<tr><td>288</td><td>Professor</td><td>30.11.1909</td><td>3,580</td><td>Cargo</td><td>St/Sc/St
350.0/46.2/14.5</td><td>310 nhp
TE (3Cy)
W&C</td><td>T.&J. Harrison
Liverpool</td></tr>
<tr><td colspan="8">Completed February 1910. In 1930 to Pentwyn SS Co., Cardiff, renamed Pentrent. Broken up Italy (Monfalcone) 1933.</td></tr>
<tr><td>289</td><td>Rangatira</td><td>16.12.1909</td><td>10,118?</td><td>Cargo
(Refrigerated)</td><td>St/2Sc/St
478.0/61.1/31.3</td><td>920 nhp
TE (6Cy)
W&C</td><td>Shaw Savill & Albion
London</td></tr>
<tr><td colspan="8">Completed February 1910. Wrecked Robin Island, South Africa, March 1916.</td></tr>
<tr><td>290</td><td>Tenet</td><td>29.1.1910</td><td>606</td><td>Cargo</td><td>St/Sc/St
187.0/29.0/ 12</td><td>1,600 ihp
TE (3Cy)
W&C?</td><td>W.A. Grainger
Belfast</td></tr>
<tr><td colspan="8">Completed February 1910. Capsized off Bishops on route Newport–Londonderry cargo of coal, October 1912.</td></tr>
<tr><td>291</td><td>Muritai</td><td>28.4.1910</td><td>7,280</td><td>Cargo
(Refrigerated)</td><td>St/2Sc/St
470.0/58.2/31.7</td><td>727 nhp
TE (6Cy)
W&C</td><td>Tyser & Co.
London</td></tr>
<tr><td colspan="8">Completed June 1910, originally sister of Niwaru changed during construction. Transferred to Commonwealth and Dominion Line 1914, renamed Port Victor (1916). In September 1917 inbound Bahia Blanca–Havre with cargo of meat, torpedoed 30 miles S of St Catharine's (UC-69) Point, managed to reach Southampton, repaired by WC and re-entered service. Broken up Barrow-in-Furness (UK) 1935.</td></tr>
<tr><td>292</td><td>St Albans</td><td>10.5.1910</td><td>4,120</td><td>Passenger-
Cargo
(Refrigerated)</td><td>St/Sc/St
367.2/47.0/24.0</td><td>588 nhp
TE (3Cy)
W&C</td><td>Eastern & Australian
SS Co.
London</td></tr>
<tr><td colspan="8">Completed July 1910. Broken up Japan (Yokohama) 1931.</td></tr>
<tr><td>293</td><td>Kansas</td><td>26.6.1910</td><td>6,074</td><td>Cargo</td><td>St/Sc/St
431.7/54.9/30.9</td><td>403 nhp
TE (3Cy)
W&C</td><td>Bucknall SS Co.
North Shields</td></tr>
<tr><td colspan="8">Completed August 1910. In 1926 to Bucknall-Ellerman Line, renamed City of Winnipeg. In 1934 renamed Winny for voyage to breakers in Japan (Yawata).</td></tr>
<tr><td>294</td><td>Aeneas</td><td>23.8.1910</td><td>10,050</td><td>Passenger-
Cargo</td><td>St/2Sc/St
493.0/60.4/28.6</td><td>641 nhp
TE (6Cy)
W&C</td><td>Alfred Holt & Co.
Liverpool</td></tr>
<tr><td colspan="8">(In company advertising material described as passenger vessel, re-rated)
Completed November 1910, for South Africa and Australia services, and this ship and her sisters allowed firm to operate a six-weekly sailing schedule. Maiden voyage (Glasgow–Liverpool–Fishguard–Las Palmas–Cape Town–Adelaide–Melbourne–Sydney) took 39 days. During war requisitioned by Australian government as troopship. In May 1918 ran aground, Rathlin Island but refloated. Returned to Australia service with accommodation for 180 first-class passengers. In 1925 following fall in demand on Australia routes, transferred to Far Eastern routes. Sunk air attack off Star Point, Devon, July 1940. Nineteen lives lost.</td></tr>
</table>

<table>
<tr><th>Yard No</th><th>Name</th><th>Date Launched</th><th>Displacement Tons</th><th>Type</th><th>Construction and Dimensions</th><th>Horse Power</th><th>Owners</th></tr>
<tr><td>295</td><td>Ascanius</td><td>29.10.1910</td><td>10,050</td><td>Passenger-Cargo</td><td>St/2Sc/St
493.0/60.4/28.6</td><td>640 nhp
TE (6Cy)
W&C</td><td>Alfred Holt & Co.
Liverpool</td></tr>
<tr><td colspan="8">(In company advertising material described as passenger vessel, re-rated)
Completed December 1910, sister ship of Aeneas. In 1914 employed as troopship for Australian Expeditionary Force and in 1917 again requisitioned. Resumed sailings to Australia 1920, refitted Palmers of Jarrow 1922. In Second World War again employed as troopship. In July 1944 torpedoed (U-621) while on route Barry–Normandy to take up duties as a depot ship. Eventually reached Liverpool where repaired by Cammell Laird. After war used to transport Jewish emigrants from Marseilles to Haifa. In 1949 to Italian owners, Cia. De Nav. Florencia, renamed San Giovannio, intended to carry Italian immigrants to Australia. Never employed and broken up Italy (La Spezia) 1952.</td></tr>
<tr><td>296</td><td>Anchises</td><td>12.1.1911</td><td>10,050</td><td>Passenger-Cargo</td><td>St/2Sc/St
493.0/60.4/28.6</td><td>640 nhp
TE (6Cy)
W&C</td><td>Alfred Holt & Co.
Liverpool</td></tr>
<tr><td colspan="8">(In company advertising material described as passenger vessel, re-rated)
Completed March 1911, sister ship of Aeneas. Requisitioned as troopship, successfully drove off attacking U-boat, September 1918. Returned to Australian service 1922. Sunk air attack off N of Ireland, February 1941. Twelve lives lost.</td></tr>
<tr><td>297</td><td>Star of India</td><td>22.9.1910</td><td>7,316</td><td>Cargo
(Refrigerated)</td><td>St/2Sc/St
470.1/58.4/31.6</td><td>756 nhp
TE (6Cy)
W&C</td><td>J.P. Corry & Co.
Belfast</td></tr>
<tr><td colspan="8">Completed October 1910. Transferred to Commonwealth and Dominion 1914, renamed Port Pirie (1916). Broken up Briton Ferry (UK) 1935.</td></tr>
<tr><td>298</td><td>Arankola</td><td>2.11.1910</td><td>4,026</td><td>Passenger/
Cargo</td><td>St/2Sc/St
390.3/50.3/22.0</td><td>1,346 nhp
QE (8Cy)
W&C</td><td>British India SN Co.
Glasgow</td></tr>
<tr><td colspan="8">Completed 20.1.1911. Broken up Japan 1937.</td></tr>
<tr><td>299</td><td>Neleus</td><td>31.1.1911</td><td>6,686</td><td>Cargo</td><td>St/Sc/St
443.0/52.7/32.0</td><td>534 nhp
TE (3Cy)
W&C</td><td>Alfred Holt & Co.
Liverpool</td></tr>
<tr><td colspan="8">Completed March 1911, sister ship of Perseus. Broken up Preston (UK) 1948.</td></tr>
<tr><td>300</td><td>Aracataca</td><td>5.1.1911</td><td>4,154</td><td>Passenger-Fruiter</td><td>St/Sc/St
376.3/48.5/ 29.1</td><td>413 nhp
TE (3Cy)
W&C</td><td>Elders & Fyffes
London</td></tr>
<tr><td colspan="8">Completed March 1911. Sunk in collision with Lamport & Holt's Moliere, Beachy Head, April 1917.</td></tr>
<tr><td>301</td><td>Vandyke</td><td>1.6.1911</td><td>10,328</td><td>Passenger-Cargo</td><td>St/2Sc/St
495.5/60.8/28.7</td><td>622 nhp
QE (8Cy)
W&C</td><td>Lamport & Holt
Liverpool</td></tr>
<tr><td colspan="8">(In company advertising material described as passenger vessel, re-rated)
Completed September 1911, for Liverpool–South America route. This ship and sisters later transferred to New York–River Plate route. Scuttled after capture by German raider Karlsruhe off Brazil, October 1914.</td></tr>
<tr><td>302</td><td>Vauban</td><td>20.1.1912</td><td>10,660</td><td>Passenger-Cargo</td><td>St/2Sc/St
495.5/60.8/28.7</td><td>622 nhp
QE (8Cy)
W&C</td><td>Lamport & Holt
Liverpool</td></tr>
<tr><td colspan="8">(In company advertising material described as passenger vessel, re-rated)
Completed April 1912. A slightly improved version of Vandyke with accommodation for 289 first-class, 130 second-class and 200 third-class passengers. In 1913 chartered to Royal Mail, renamed Alcala. Reverted to original name on return 1914. In 1930 laid up, broken up Milford Haven (UK) 1932.</td></tr>
<tr><td>303</td><td>Vestris</td><td>16.5.1912</td><td>10,494</td><td>Passenger-Cargo</td><td>St/2Sc/St
495.5/60.8/28.7</td><td>1,243 nhp
QE (8Cy)
W&C</td><td>Lamport & Holt
Liverpool</td></tr>
<tr><td colspan="8">(In company advertising material described as passenger vessel, re-rated)
Completed September 1912, sister ship of Vauban. In November 1929, south bound and two days out of New York, met heavy weather which caused cargo and coal supplies to shift resulting in the ship capsizing and sinking. Sixty-eight passengers out of 128 and 44 of crew of 197 were lost.</td></tr>
<tr><td>304</td><td>Tivives</td><td>1.8.1911</td><td>5,017</td><td>Passenger-Fruiter</td><td>St/Sc/St
378.8/50.3/29.1</td><td>412 nhp
TE (3Cy)
W&C</td><td>United Fruit
New Jersey</td></tr>
<tr><td colspan="8">Completed October 1911, sister ship of Cartago. Initially on UK register (Tropical Fruit SS Co., Glasgow), transferred to US 1914. Sunk by air-launched torpedo, Mediterranean, October 1943. Two lives lost.</td></tr>
<tr><td>305</td><td>Carrillo</td><td>17.5.1911</td><td>5,017</td><td>Passenger-Fruiter</td><td>St/Sc/St
378.8/50.3/29.1</td><td>412 nhp
TE (3Cy)
W&C</td><td>United Fruit
New Jersey</td></tr>
<tr><td colspan="8">Completed September 1911, sister ship of Cartago, originally to have been La Senora but launched under this name. Initially on UK register (Tropical Fruit SS Co., Glasgow), transferred to US 1914. Converted to cargo ship 1936. Broken up USA (Baltimore) 1948.</td></tr>
</table>

<table>
<tr><th>Yard No</th><th>Name</th><th>Date Launched</th><th>Displacement Tons</th><th>Type</th><th>Construction and Dimensions</th><th>Horse Power</th><th>Owners</th></tr>
<tr><td>306</td><td>Sixaola</td><td>24.8.1911</td><td>5,017</td><td>Passenger-
Fruiter</td><td>St/Sc/St
378.8/50.3/29.1</td><td>423 nhp
TE (3Cy)
W&C</td><td>United Fruit
New Jersey</td></tr>
<tr><td colspan="8">Completed October 1911, sister ship of Cartago. Initially on UK register (Tropical Fruit SS Co., Glasgow), transferred to US 1914. Sunk by submarine torpedo and gun fire (U-159) off Panama, June 1942. Twenty-nine lives lost out of 201 on board.</td></tr>
<tr><td>307</td><td>Egra</td><td>14.3.1911</td><td>5,108</td><td>Passenger-
Cargo</td><td>St/2Sc/St
410.0/52.8/24.7</td><td>1,062 nhp
TE (6Cy)
W&C</td><td>British India SN Co.
Glasgow</td></tr>
<tr><td colspan="8">Completed 1.6.1911, for Indian coastal trade. Broken up India (Bombay) 1950.</td></tr>
<tr><td>308</td><td>Ekma</td><td>21.10.1911</td><td>5,108</td><td>Passenger-
Cargo</td><td>St/2Sc/St
410.0/52.8/24.7</td><td>1,062 nhp
TE (6Cy)
W&C</td><td>British India SN Co.
Glasgow</td></tr>
<tr><td colspan="8">Completed 15.12.1911, sister ship of Egra. Broken up India (Bombay) 1948.</td></tr>
<tr><td>309</td><td>Waimana</td><td>12.9.1911</td><td>10,389</td><td>Cargo
(Refrigerated)</td><td>St/2Sc/St
477.6/63.1/31.3</td><td>947 nhp
TE (6Cy)
W&C</td><td>Shaw Savill & Albion
London</td></tr>
<tr><td colspan="8">Completed December 1911. In 1926 to Aberdeen Line, renamed Herminius. In 1932 reverted to owners and original name. In 1939 to Admiralty for use as basis of dummy Royal Sovereign battleship. Renamed Empire Waimana and returned to merchant service 1941. In 1946 repurchased by SSA and adopted original name. Broken up Milford Haven (UK) 1952.</td></tr>
<tr><td>310</td><td>Makarini</td><td>3.2.1912</td><td>8,491</td><td>Cargo
(Refrigerated)</td><td>St/2Sc/St
490.2/61.4/31.3</td><td>967 nhp
TE (6Cy)
W&C</td><td>Tyser & Co.
London</td></tr>
<tr><td colspan="8">Completed April 1912, could carry 1,000 emigrants in temporary accommodation in holds on outbound journeys. Initially employed by Victoria government's emigrant service. To Commonwealth and Dominion Line 1914, renamed Port Nicholson (1916). Early war service as troopship but returned to merchant service. Sunk by submarine-laid mine (UC-1) 15 miles north of Dunkirk, inbound from Australia with cargo of meat, January 1917. Two lives lost.</td></tr>
<tr><td>311</td><td>Demodocus</td><td>21.3.1912</td><td>6,700</td><td>Cargo</td><td>St/Sc/St
443.0/52.8/32.1</td><td>532 nhp
TE (3Cy)
W&C</td><td>Alfred Holt & Co.
Liverpool</td></tr>
<tr><td colspan="8">Completed May 1912, sister ship of Perseus. Taken up under Liner Requisition Scheme 1917. Torpedoed (UC-53) Mediterranean, March 1918, six lives lost, towed to Malta and repaired. In 1951 to Italian owners, Ditta Luigi Pittaluga Vapori, for £51,000, renamed Ircania. In 1956 to P. Tomei, Genoa, renamed Miriam. Broken up Italy (Trieste) 1958.</td></tr>
<tr><td>312</td><td>Laomedon</td><td>24.4.1912</td><td>6,700</td><td>Cargo</td><td>St/Sc/St
443.0/52.8/32.1</td><td>532 nhp
TE (3Cy)
W&C</td><td>Alfred Holt & Co.
Liverpool</td></tr>
<tr><td colspan="8">Completed June 1912, sister ship of Perseus. During First World War employed by governments of India, Portugal, France, Serbia and Russia, carrying frozen meat or trooping in Mediterranean. In April 1916 successfully fought off U-boat attack. Broken up Faslane (UK) 1949.</td></tr>
<tr><td>313</td><td>Hawks Bay</td><td>27.9.1912</td><td>8,491</td><td>Cargo
(Refrigerated)</td><td>St/2Sc/St
490.2/61.4/31.3</td><td>967 nhp
TE (6Cy)
W&C</td><td>Tyser & Co.
London</td></tr>
<tr><td colspan="8">Completed December 1912, sister ship of Mikarini, employed on emigrant transport after completion. To Commonwealth and Dominion Line 1914, renamed Port Napier (1916). Served as troopship in First World War. Laid up in River Blackwater 1932–36 when transferred to Cunard group fleet of Thos & Jno Brocklebank, renamed Martand. In 1938 to Italian owners, A. Zanchi, renamed Martano and Mar Blanco. In September 1943, after Italian capitulation, taken over by Germans at Ancona, used to supply army in Yugoslavia. Sunk by Allied aircraft off Zara, December 1943.</td></tr>
<tr><td>314</td><td>Pastores</td><td>17.8.1912</td><td>7,782</td><td>Passenger-
Fruiter</td><td>St/2Sc/St
470.4/55.3/30.8</td><td>620 nhp
QE (8Cy)
W&C</td><td>United Fruit
New Jersey</td></tr>
<tr><td colspan="8">Completed December 1912, first of three fruiters with accommodation for 143 first-class passengers. Initially on UK register (Caribbean SS Co., Glasgow), transferred to US 1914. Between 1917 and 1919 served as US Navy transport. In 1933–37 chartered to Colombian Line. In 1942 taken up by US Navy as transport. In 1946 to US Maritime Commission. Broken up USA (Oakland) 1947.</td></tr>
<tr><td>315</td><td>Tenadores</td><td>28.3.1912</td><td>7,782</td><td>Passenger-
Fruiter</td><td>St/2Sc/St
470.4/55.3/30.8</td><td>620 nhp
QE (8Cy)
W&C</td><td>United Fruit
New Jersey</td></tr>
<tr><td colspan="8">Completed July 1913, sister ship of Pastores. Initially on UK register (Tropical Fruit SS Co., Glasgow), transferred to US 1914. In 1917 taken up as troopship by US Navy. Wrecked on Ile d'Yeu, December 1918. No lives lost.</td></tr>
<tr><td>316</td><td>Calamares</td><td>2.9.1913</td><td>7,782</td><td>Passenger-
Fruiter</td><td>St/2Sc/St
470.4/55.3/30.8</td><td>620 nhp
QE (8Cy)
W&C</td><td>United Fruit
New Jersey</td></tr>
<tr><td colspan="8">Completed December 1913, sister ship of Pastores. Initially on UK register (Clarke & Service, Glasgow), transferred to US 1914. In 1917–19 employed as transport by US Navy. 1937 converted to cargo ship. Laid up 1938-41. 1941 taken up by US Navy as transport, 1946 US Maritime Commission. Broken up USA (Baltimore) 1947.</td></tr>
</table>

<table>
<tr><th>Yard No</th><th>Name</th><th>Date Launched</th><th>Displacement Tons</th><th>Type</th><th>Construction and Dimensions</th><th>Horse Power</th><th>Owners</th></tr>
<tr><td>317</td><td>Patia</td><td>28.1.1913</td><td>6,103</td><td>Passenger-Fruiter</td><td>St/2Sc/St
417.2/53.3/30.1</td><td>594 nhp
6,000 ihp
TE (6Cy)
W&C</td><td>Elders & Fyffes
London</td></tr>
<tr><td colspan="8">Completed May 1913, for UK–West Indies fruit/passenger service. In 1915 commissioned as armed merchant cruiser, served in 10th Cruiser Squadron until it disbanded. Sunk by submarine torpedo (UC-49) in Bristol Channel, June 1918. Sixteen lives lost.</td></tr>
<tr><td>318</td><td>Nestor</td><td>7.12.1912</td><td>14,500</td><td>Passenger-Cargo</td><td>St/2Sc/St
563.2/68.4/40.2</td><td>782 nhp
7,750 ihp
TE (6Cy)
W&C</td><td>Alfred Holt & Co.
Liverpool</td></tr>
<tr><td colspan="8">(In company advertising material described as passenger vessel, re-rated)
Completed May 1913, first of two larger ships to supplement highly successful Aeneas type on UK–Australia routes, allowing existing six-week cycle of sailings to be improved to monthly. Designed by Henry B. Wortley and costing £248,250, Nestor made maiden voyage in May 1913, arriving back in September after a round voyage of four months. From September 1915 until 1918 operated as Australian Expeditionary Force transport. Resumed previous service 1920. In 1940 passenger accommodation was reduced from 350 to 250 and later that year requisitioned, employed on Liverpool–Brisbane route initially carrying children being evacuated to Australia. Broken up Faslane (UK) 1949. During career completed 68 round voyages to Australia and steamed 2,111,607 miles.</td></tr>
<tr><td>319</td><td>Ulysses</td><td>5.7.1913</td><td>14,500</td><td>Passenger-Cargo</td><td>St/2Sc/St
563.2/68.4/40.2</td><td>782 nhp
7,750 ihp
TE (6Cy)
W&C</td><td>Alfred Holt & Co.
Liverpool</td></tr>
<tr><td colspan="8">(In company advertising material described as passenger vessel, re-rated)
Completed October 1913, sister ship to Nestor. Taken up as troopship 1915, ferrying Australian troops to Suez. By 1917 in Atlantic bringing American reinforcements to Europe. Returned to commercial service 1920. Was being refitted at Hong Kong when Japanese launched their offensive and escaped that port with hours to spare. Loaded cargo in Australia for Britain. Crossed Pacific and traversed Panama Canal during which sustained damage in collision with tanker. The captain decided to make for Newport News for repairs, despite fact that U-boats were known to be operating in area. On 11 April 1942 was torpedoed (U-160) off Florida and passengers and crew, except essential personnel, abandoned ship. Submarine fired a second torpedo which sank Ulysses immediately. No lives lost.</td></tr>
<tr><td>320</td><td>Patuca</td><td>26.4.1913</td><td>6,103</td><td>Passenger-Fruiter</td><td>St/2Sc/St
417.2/53.3/30.1</td><td>594 nhp
6,000 ihp
TE (6Cy)
W&C</td><td>Elders & Fyffes
London</td></tr>
<tr><td colspan="8">Completed October 1913, sister ship of Patia. Commissioned as armed merchant cruiser during war. Returned to owners 1919. Broken up Holland (Hendrik-Ibo-Ambacht) 1935.</td></tr>
<tr><td>321</td><td>Eumaeus</td><td>3.6.1913</td><td>6,700</td><td>Cargo</td><td>St/Sc/St
443.0/52.9/32.0</td><td>534 nhp
TE (3Cy)
W&C</td><td>Alfred Holt & Co.
Liverpool</td></tr>
<tr><td colspan="8">Completed August 1913, sister ship of Perseus. Sunk by submarine torpedo (U-55) inbound Yokohama–London, 24 miles NNW of Ile de Vierge, February 1918. No lives lost.</td></tr>
<tr><td>322</td><td>Phemius</td><td>20.9.1913</td><td>6,700</td><td>Cargo</td><td>St/Sc/St
443.0/52.8/32.1</td><td>534 nhp
TE (3Cy)
W&C</td><td>Alfred Holt & Co.
Liverpool</td></tr>
<tr><td colspan="8">Completed November 1913, sister ship of Perseus. Sunk by submarine torpedo (UC-45) outbound Liverpool–Hong Kong, 80 miles NW of Eagle Island, June 1917. No lives lost.</td></tr>
<tr><td>323</td><td>Kentucky</td><td>29.10.1912</td><td>6,590</td><td>Cargo</td><td>St/Sc/St
447.3/56.4/31.4</td><td>412 nhp
QE (4Cy)
W&C</td><td>Bucknall SS Co.
North Shields</td></tr>
<tr><td colspan="8">Completed December 1912. In 1927 to Bucknall-Ellerman Line, renamed City of Mobile. Sunk air attack, Irish Sea, September 1940. No lives lost.</td></tr>
<tr><td>324</td><td>Cardiganshire</td><td>30.9.1913</td><td>9,426</td><td>Cargo (Refrigerated)</td><td>St/2Sc/St
500.3/62.4/34.6</td><td>977 nhp
TE (6Cy)
W&C</td><td>Royal Mail SP Co.
London</td></tr>
<tr><td colspan="8">Completed November 1913, for UK–Australia/New Zealand trade, permanent accommodation for 12 first-class passengers, but removable berths could be rigged to accommodate 1,300 steerage passengers. At outbreak of war taken up as transport to move British Expeditionary Force to France. In February 1915 damaged while engaged in landing at Zeebrugge; Belgian pilot responsible was subsequently shot as German spy. Subsequently to Dardanelles campaign. In 1918 carried thousands of American troops to Europe. After war returned to civilian service. Sometimes claimed this ship was scrapped 1929 but passed to Chr. Salvesen & Co., Leith, converted to whale factory ship, renamed Salvestria. Sunk by aircraft-laid mine, July 1940, off Innkeith lighthouse. Five lives lost.</td></tr>
<tr><td>325</td><td>Carnarvonshire</td><td>18.12.1913</td><td>9,426</td><td>Cargo (Refrigerated)</td><td>St/2Sc/St
500.3/62.4/34.6</td><td>977 nhp
TE (6Cy)
W&C</td><td>Royal Mail SP Co.
London</td></tr>
<tr><td colspan="8">Completed March 1914, sister ship of Cardiganshire. Troopship in First World War. Broken up Japan (Osaka) 1936.</td></tr>
</table>

Yard No	Name	Date Launched	Displacement Tons	Type	Construction and Dimensions	Horse Power	Owners
326	*Dunaff Head*	15.1.1918	5,258	Cargo	St/Sc/St 390.4/51.8/29.8	380 nhp 3,100 ihp? TE (3Cy) W&C	Ulster SS Co. Belfast
Completed 16.3.1918. Sunk by submarine torpedo (US ex-Turkish *Batiray*) S of Iceland, outbound Glasgow–New Brunswick, March 1941. Five lives lost.							
327	*Melmore Head*	25.5.1918	5,320	Cargo	St/Sc/St 390.4/51.8/29.8	3,100 ihp? Turb W&C	Ulster SS Co. Belfast
Completed 14.9.1918, a sister ship of *Dunaff Head* fitted with turbine for comparative purposes. Sunk by submarine torpedo (*U-225*) N of Azores outbound Belfast–New Brunswick, December 1942. Fourteen lives lost out of 49 on board.							
328	*Star of Victoria*	13.11.1913	9,152	Cargo (Refrigerated)	St/2Sc/St 501.3/63.3/33.6	979 nhp TE (6Cy) +Exh Turb W&C	J.P. Corry & Co. Belfast
Completed 10.1.1914, emigrant carriers for outward journey. Transferred to Commonwealth and Dominion Line two weeks after completion, renamed *Port Melbourne* (1916). On outbreak of war taken up as troopship. In March 1917 requisitioned by Shipping Controller, redeployed as a meat carrier. In 1919 returned to owners. In 1929 refitted with Bauer-Wach exhaust turbines to reduce fuel consumption by 15–25 per cent. Laid up River Blackwater 1931, damaged by fire. Repaired on Tyne and laid up there before returning to Blackwater 1936–37. During Second World War operated on meat run without incident. Broken up Blyth (UK) 1948.							
329	*Star of England*	16.2.1914	9,152	Cargo (Refrigerated)	St/2Sc/St 501.3/63.3/33.6	979 nhp TE (6Cy) +Exh Turb W&C	J.P. Corry & Co. Belfast
Completed April 1914, sister ship of *Star of Victoria*, completed as part of Commonwealth and Dominion fleet, renamed *Port Sydney* (1916). Started war as troopship but like sister taken up by Shipping Controller. Re-engined in the same manner 1929. Broken up Preston (UK) 1948.							
330	*City of Exeter*	1.4.1914	9,373	Passenger-Cargo	St/2Sc/St 486.7/58.9/32.6	584 nhp QE (8Cy) W&C	Ellerman Lines Liverpool
Completed June 1914, for UK–India service. Just completed maiden voyage at outbreak of war, immediately requisitioned by Indian government as troopship. In 1917 damaged by mine laid by German surface raider *Wolf*, but managed to reach Bombay. After war served on India routes and later on services to South and East Africa. Broken up Dalmuir (UK) 1950.							
331	*City of Nagpur*	11.6.1914	8,331	Passenger-Cargo	St/Sc/St 465.0/52.9/34.1	492 nhp QE (8Cy) W&C	Ellerman Lines Liverpool
Completed August 1914. Wrecked Delagoa Bay, South Africa, August 1917.							
332	*City of Vienna*	17.3.1914	6,111	Cargo	St/Sc/St 420.3/55.7/30.9	424 nhp TE (3Cy) W&C	Ellerman Lines Liverpool
Completed May 1914. Wrecked Ketch Harbour, Nova Scotia, July 1918.							
333	*Ebro*	8.9.1914	8,463	Passenger-Cargo	St/2Sc/St 450.3/57.8/30.6	1,055 nhp 5,800 ihp QE (8Cy) W&C	Royal Mail SP Co. London
(In company advertising material described as passenger vessel, re-rated) Completed January 1915, for UK–West Indies service, accommodation for 250 first-class and 248 second-class passengers. Commissioned as armed merchant cruiser 1915 (8x 6in) served with 10th Cruiser Squadron until disbanded afterwards on convoy duties. After war employed Pacific Steam Navigation's service New York–Valparaiso via Panama Canal for ten years. Returned to Britain laid up River Dart 1930–35. In 1935 to Yugoslavian owners, Jugoslava Lloyd, renamed *Princesa Olga*. In 1940 to Portuguese owners, Cia Colonial de Nav., renamed *Serpa Pinto*. Employed on Lisbon–South America route and on routes to Central America. Broken up Belgium (Antwerp) 1955.							
334	*Essequibo*	6.7.1914	8,463	Passenger-Cargo	St/2Sc/St 450.3/57.8/30.6	1,055 nhp 5,800 ihp QE (8Cy) W&C	Royal Mail SP Co. London
(In company advertising material described as passenger vessel, re-rated) Completed November 1914, sister ship of *Ebro*. Very similar career, except hospital ship during First World War. When sold in 1935 became Russian *Neva* and seems to have ended career as naval auxiliary. Deleted 1963.							
335	*Pyrrhus*	25.8.1914	7,603	Cargo	St/Sc/St 455.5/56.5/32.5	572 nhp TE (3Cy) W&C	Alfred Holt & Co. Liverpool
Completed November 1914, first of a new type that succeeded *Perseus* vessels. Refurbished at end of war with extra passenger accommodation, later converted to pure cargo vessel by Elder Dempster after they acquired Holts in 1936 following the collapse of Royal Mail Group.							

Yard No	Name	Date Launched	Displacement Tons	Type	Construction and Dimensions	Horse Power	Owners
Sunk by submarine torpedo (*U-37*) NW of Cape Finisterre outbound Glasgow–Manila, February 1940. Eight lives lost out of 86 on board.							
336	*Carmarthanshire*	5.11.1914	7,823	Passenger-Cargo (Refrigerated)	St/Sc/St 470.2/58.3/32.2	735 nhp QE (4Cy) W&C	Royal Mail SP Co. London
Completed February 1915. Sometimes stated scrapped 1929. In fact, like *Cardiganshire*, sold to Chr. Salvesen & Co., Leith, converted to whale factory ship, renamed *Sourabaya*. Sunk by submarine torpedo (*U-436*) SE of Cape Farewell, inbound New York–Liverpool, October 1942. Seventy-seven lives lost out of 158 on board.							
337	*Pembrockeshire*	19.12.1914	7,823	Passenger-Cargo (Refrigerated)	St/Sc/St 470.2/58.3/32.2	735 nhp QE (4Cy) W&C	Royal Mail SP Co. London
Completed April 1915, sister ship of *Carmarthanshire*. Broken up Germany (Danzig) 1936.							
338	*Cavina*	17.1.1915	6,539	Passenger-Fruiter	St/2Sc/St 425.4/54.3/29.9	622 nhp TE (6Cy) W&C	Elders & Fyffes London
Completed March 1915. Sunk by submarine torpedo (*U-88*) 45nm WxS of Fastnet, inbound Port Limon–Avonmouth with a cargo of bananas, June 1917. No lives lost.							
339	*Coronado*	1.4.1915	6,539	Passenger-Fruiter	St/2Sc/St 425.4/54.3/29.9	622 nhp TE (6Cy) W&C	Elders & Fyffes London
Completed May 1915, sister ship of *Cavina*. Eleven days after sister sunk this vessel torpedoed off south coast of Ireland but brought into port and repaired. From autumn of 1917 to March 1919 served as naval escort. After war refitted with accommodation for 100 first-class passengers and finally entered intended service. Broken up Italy (Savona) 1935.							
340	*Ulua*	?.?.1917	7,452	Passenger-Fruiter	St/2Sc/St 425.4/54.3/29.9	622 nhp TE (6Cy) W&C	United Fruit New Jersey
Completed December 1917, reduced version of Pastores type. Accommodation for 131 first-class passengers. Initially on UK register (Clark & Service, Glasgow), transferred to US 1928. In 1942 taken up as transport by US Navy, renamed *Octans*. Returned to owners and reverted to original name 1946. Broken up USA (Baltimore) 1948.							
341	*Toloa*	22.8.1917	7,452	Passenger-Fruiter	St/2Sc/St 425.4/54.3/29.9	622 nhp TE (6Cy) W&C	United Fruit New Jersey
Completed February 1918, sister ship of *Ulua*. Initially on UK register (R. Clark, Glasgow), transferred to US 1928. In 1941 requisitioned by War Shipping Administration. Broken up USA (San Francisco) 1948.							
342	*San Mateo*	5.5.1915	3,301	Fruiter	St/Sc/St 315.2/44.2/28.8	302 nhp TE (3Cy) W&C	United Fruit New Jersey
Completed July 1915. Registered in US from completion. In 1942 taken up as transport by US Navy, renamed *Delphinus*. Returned to owners and reverted to original name 1946. Broken up USA (Mobile) 1948.							
343	*San Pablo*	15.5.1915	3,301	Fruiter	St/Sc/St 315.2/44.2/28.8	302 nhp TE (3Cy) W&C	United Fruit New Jersey
Completed October 1915, sister ship of *San Mateo*. Initially on UK register (Workman Clark & Co. Ltd, Belfast), transferred to Panamanian register in 1931 and later Honduras. Torpedoed (*U-161*) at Limon, Costa Rica, July 1942, considered beyond repair and wreck used by US Navy as target September 1943.							
344	*San Rito*	12.8.1915	3,301	Fruiter	St/Sc/St 315.2/44.2/28.8	302 nhp TE (3Cy) W&C	United Fruit New Jersey
Completed May 1916, sister ship of *San Mateo*. On UK register (Workman Clark & Co. Ltd, Belfast). Sunk by submarine torpedo (*UC-37*) 23nm SW of Khios Island on route Salonika–Port Said, February 1918. Three lives lost.							
345	*San Andres*	29.1.1918	3,301	Fruiter	St/Sc/St 315.2/44.2/28.8	302 nhp TE (3Cy) W&C	United Fruit New Jersey
Sister ship of *San Mateo*. On UK register (Clarke & Service, Glasgow). Sunk by submarine torpedo (*U-65*) 40 miles from Port Said, September 1918. No lives lost.							
346	*Tela*	21.10.1915	7,226	Passenger-Fruiter	St/Sc/St 415.3/54.7/ ?	4,900 ihp? QE (4Cy) W&C	United Fruit New Jersey
Completed February 1917. On UK register (R. Clark, Glasgow), completed as troopship. Sunk by submarine torpedo (*UB-18*) 16nm off Cape Barfleur on route Havre–Cardiff, May 1917. No lives lost.							

Yard No	Name	Date Launched	Displacement Tons	Type	Construction and Dimensions	Horse Power	Owners
347	*San Blas*	10.3.1920	3,628	Fruiter	St/Sc/St 325.0/46.3/29.2	330 nhp TE (3Cy) W&C	United Fruit New Jersey
Completed August 1920. Initially British register, transferred to Panama 1931. Sunk by submarine torpedo (*U-158*) Gulf of Mexico, June 1942. Thirty lives lost out of 44 on board.							
348	*San Bruno*	29.5.1920	3,628	Fruiter	St/Sc/St 325.0/46.3/29.2	330 nhp TE (3Cy) W&C	United Fruit New Jersey
Completed October 1920, sister ship of *San Blas*. Initially British register, transferred to Panama 1931. In 1942 taken over by War Shipping Administration. In 1949 to Italian owners, Italo-Somali, renamed *Genale*. Returned to United Fruit, renamed *Somalia*. In 1957 to Italo-Somali, renamed *Frigo America*. Broken up Brazil (Niteroi) 1973.							
349	*Mahana*	11.1.1917	11,800	Cargo (Refrigerated)	St/2Sc/St 500.9/63.5/39.6	1,119 nhp Turb **Engines** Parsons S.T. Newcastle	Shaw Savill & Albion London
Completed July 1917. Broken up Dalmuir (UK) 1953.							
350	*Mahia*	?.?.1917	7,914	Cargo (Refrigerated)	St/2Sc/St 477.6/63.1/39.7	997 nhp QE (4Cy) W&C	Shaw Savill & Albion London
Completed August 1917. Broken up Faslane (UK) 1953.							
351	*Port Darwin*	9.7.1917	8,179	Cargo (Refrigerated)	St/2Sc/St 480.4/60.3/40.8	809 nhp TE (6Cy) +Exh Turb W&C	Commonwealth & Dominion London
Completed January 1918. Broken up Barrow (UK) 1949.							
352	*Port Denison*	18.9.1917	8,179	Cargo (Refrigerated)	St/2Sc/St 480.4/60.3/40.8	809 nhp TE (6Cy) +Exh Turb W&C	Commonwealth & Dominion London
Completed May 1918, sister ship of *Port Darwin*. Sunk in air attack 6nm E of Peterhead, September 1940. Sixteen lives lost.							
353	*Fanad Head*	24.2.1917	5,200	Cargo	St/Sc/St 390.4/51.8/29.8	379 nhp TE (3Cy) W&C	Ulster SS Co. Belfast
Completed 10.6.1917. In September 1939 halted by warning shots from U30 260nm NNW of Malin Head. The crew took to boats after radioing news of attack. The aircraft carrier HMS *Ark Royal* was in area and launched Skua and Swordfish aircraft and detached destroyers to scene. The U-boat placed a prize crew on board *Fanad Head* and they were preparing to sink it with explosive charges when attacked by aircraft. The German captain refused to abandon his men and eventually recovered prize crew, after which sank *Fanad Head* with a torpedo. *U-30* then attacked by destroyers but managed to escape.							
354	*Munardan*	?.?.1917	3,813	Cargo	St/Sc/St 370.2/50.3/25.1	350 nhp TE (3Cy) W&C	Clark & Service Glasgow
Completed December 1917, shortly after completion transferred to Munson SS. In 1937 to Italian owners, Genovese, renamed *Capo Noli*. Captured in Gulf of St Lawrence by HMCS *Bras d'Or*, June 1940, taken over by Canadian government, renamed *Bic Island*. Sunk by submarine torpedo SW of Rockall, October 1942. The ship was straggling behind convoy having stopped to rescue survivors from two other ships sunk the previous day. One hundred and sixty-five lives lost (44 crew and 121 rescued), no survivors.							
355	*City of Cambridge*	26.10.1920	7,055	Cargo	St/Sc/St 454.0/58.2/34.5	647 nhp QE (4Cy) +Exh Turb W&C	Ellerman Lines Liverpool
Completed February 1921. Wrecked China Sea and burned by looters, October 1934.							
356	*Port Bowen*	17.12.1918	8,267	Cargo (Refrigerated)	St/2Sc/St 480.7/62.4/32.9	1,001 nhp Turb W&C	Commonwealth & Dominion London
Completed 20.5.1919. Wrecked Castleshore Beach, New Zealand, July 1939.							
357	*Calchas*	11.1.1921	10,304	Cargo	St/2Sc/St 490.8/62.4/39.6	8,000 ihp? Turb W&C	Alfred Holt & Co. Liverpool
Completed June 1921, for Liverpool–Far East route, cost of £532,000. Sunk by submarine torpedo (*U-107*) inbound Sydney–Liverpool (unescorted) 550nm N of Cape Verde Islands, April 1941. Twenty-four lives lost out of 113 on board.							

Yard No	Name	Date Launched	Displacement Tons	Type	Construction and Dimensions	Horse Power	Owners
358	*Port Caroline*	28.6.1919	8,267	Cargo (Refrigerated)	St/2Sc/St 480.7/62.4/32.9	1,001 nhp Turb W&C	Commonwealth & Dominion London
Completed November 1919, sister ship of *Port Bowen*. Broken up Blyth (UK) 1950.							
359	*Vandyke*	24.2.1921	13,233	Passenger-Cargo	St/2Sc/St 510.6/64.3/39.3	7,000 shp Turb W&C	Lamport & Holt Liverpool
(In company advertising material described as passenger vessel, re-rated) Completed September 1921. In 1939 commissioned as boarding vessel, later depot ship Scapa Flow. Sunk in air attack near Narvik, 10 June 1940, during Norwegian campaign. Seven lives lost.							
360	*Voltaire*	14.8.1923	13,233	Passenger-Cargo	St/2Sc/St 510.3/64.4/39.3	806 nhp 7,500 ihp QE (8Cy) W&C	Lamport & Holt Liverpool
(In company advertising material described as Passenger vessel, re-rated) Completed November 1923, sister ship of *Vandyck*. In 1939 commissioned as armed merchant cruiser (8x 6in) served Mediterranean and on convoy escort in western Atlantic. Sunk in action with German surface raider *Thor*, 700 miles W of Cape Verde Islands, April 1941, with loss of 75 lives. German vessel picked up 197 survivors.							
361	*P.15*	24.1.1916	613	Naval Patrol Vessel	St/2Sc/St 244.6/23.9/8.0	3,500 shp Turb W&C	Admiralty
Sold 1921, broken up Portsmouth.							
362	*P.16*	23.3.1916	613	Naval Patrol Vessel	St/2Sc/St 244.6/23.9/8.0	3,500 shp Turb W&C	Admiralty
Sold 1921, broken up Plymouth.							
363	*P.17*	21.10.1915	613	Naval Patrol Vessel	St/2Sc/St 244.6/23.9/8.0	3,500 shp Turb W&C	Admiralty
Sold 1921, broken up Plymouth.							
364	*San Gil*	29.7.1920	3,628	Fruiter	St/Sc/St 325.0/46.3/29.2	330 nhp TE (3Cy) W&C	United Fruit New Jersey
Completed December 1920, sister ship of *San Blas*. Initially British register, transferred to Panama 1931. Sunk by submarine torpedo (*U-103*) off coast of Virginia, February 1942. Two lives lost.							
365	*Chirripo*	11.12.1919	5,360	Passenger-Fruiter	St/Sc/St 400.0/51.3/30.0	447 nhp TE (3Cy) W&C	Elders & Fyffes London
Completed July 1920, replacement for original vessel of this name. In 1935 to German owners, Handels und Schiffahrtsgesellschaft, renamed *Westermunde*. In 1939 interned Honduras, 1941 seized by US government, operated by United Fruit until 1946 when returned to Elders & Fyffes. Broken up Preston (UK) 1952.							
366	*Pentstemon*	5.2.1916	1,250	Naval Sloop	St/Sc/St 268.0/33.6/11.0	2,000 ihp VTE (4Cy) W&C	Admiralty
Arabis-class escort. In 1920 disposed of for merchant use, Ramez Klat & Co., renamed *Lila*. In 1923 to M. Zehil, renamed *Noemi*. In 1928 to M.&J. Sitges, renamed *Sitges*. In 1931 to Chinese ownership, F.W. Tse, renamed *Hoi Lee*. In 1935 taken over by Chinese Navy and rearmed as warship, renamed *Hai Chao*, lost 1937.							
367	*Petunia*	3.4.1916	1,250	Naval Sloop	St/Sc/St 268.0/33.6/11.0	2,000 ihp VTE (4Cy) W&C	Admiralty
Sold 1922, broken up.							
368	*Appleleaf*	28.11.1916	5,900	Naval Oiler	St/2Sc/St 405.5/54.6/33.6	1,102 nhp TE (6Cy) W&C	Admiralty
Completed February 1917, originally *Texol* but completed with this name. Broken up Troon (UK) 1947.							
369	*Reventazon*	25.1.1921	5,360	Passenger-Fruiter	St/Sc/St 400.0/51.3/30.0	447 nhp TE (3Cy) W&C	Elders & Fyffes London
Sister ship of *Chirripo*. In 1935 to German owners, 'Union' Handels und Schiffahrtsellschaft, renamed *Bremerhaven*. In 1942 converted into troopship and in 1944 hospital ship.							

Kosmos II (WC y/n 522) 1931.

Llandaff Castle (WC y/n 488) 1926.

Niwaru (WC y/n 183) 1901.

Orania (WC y/n 379) 1921.

Yard No	Name	Date Launched	Displacement Tons	Type	Construction and Dimensions	Horse Power	Owners
On 29 October 1944 left Latvian port of Windau for Gotenhaven with 3,171 people on board (1,671 wounded troops, 680 civilian refugees, 511 Todt Organisation workers, 200 SS guards, 42 medical staff, 22 anti-aircraft gunners and 45 civilian crew members). On the morning of 31st attacked by Russian aircraft and hit by air-launched torpedo and two bombs which set vessel on fire, sank ten hours later. Four hundred and ten lives lost.							
370							
371							
372							
373							
374							
375	*M32*	22.5.1915	360	Coastal Monitor	St/2Sc/St 177.3/31.0/6.0	400 ihp VTE (8Cy) H&W?	Admiralty
Completed June 1915, ordered from H&W (y/n 488) built by WC on sub-contract basis. In 1920 to Dutch owners, Curacaosche SM/Shell, converted to oil tanker, renamed *Ampat*. In 1924 to French owners, F.M.T.P., renamed *Delta*. In 1946 to A. Richard, Marseille, renamed *Colette Richard*. Broken up Italy (La Spezia) 1952.							
376	*M33*	22.5.1915	360	Coastal Monitor	St/2Sc/St 177.3/31.0/6.0	400 ihp VTE (8Cy) H&W?	Admiralty
Completed June 1915, ordered from H&W (y/n 489) built by WC on sub-contract basis. In 1925 converted to minelayer, renamed *Minerva*. Subsequently employed by navy as hulk *C-23*. Now restored at Portsmouth.							
377		1916		Steam Launch			Admiralty
378		1916		Steam Launch			Admiralty
379	*Orania*	1.10.1921	9,771	Passenger-Cargo	St/2Sc/St 450.3/59.4/40.9	1,246 nhp Turb W&C	Koninklijke Lloyd Rotterdam
(In company advertising material described as passenger vessel, re-rated) Completed February 1922. Sunk collision, Leixoes Harbour, December 1934.							
380	*PC 60*	4.6.1917	613	Naval Patrol Vessel	St/2Sc/St 244.6/23.9/8.0	3,500 shp Turb W&C	Admiralty
Sold 1924, broken up.							
381	*PC 61*	19.6.1917	613	Naval Patrol Vessel	St/2Sc/St 244.6/23.9/8.0	3,500 shp Turb W&C	Admiralty
Sold 1923, broken up.							
382	*Port Auckland*	11.5.1922	8,308	Cargo (Refrigerated)	St/2Sc/St 480.8/62.4/32.9	859 nhp TE (6Cy) +Exh Turb W&C	Commonwealth & Dominion London
Completed 3.8.1922, sister ship of *Port Caroline* with different machinery. Sunk by submarine torpedo (*U-305*) North Atlantic inbound with 7,000 tons of frozen meat from Australia, March 1943. Eight lives lost out of 118 on board.							
383	*Port Campbell*	15.3.1922	8,308	Cargo (Refrigerated)	St/2Sc/St 480.8/62.4/32.9	859 nhp TE (6Cy) +Exh Turb W&C	Commonwealth & Dominion London
Completed June 1922, sister ship of *Port Auckland*. Broken up Briton Ferry (UK) 1953.							
384							
385							
386							
387							
388		1917		Stern-Wheel Hospital Ship	St/PD/St		Admiralty
A post-war publication describes these singular vessels: 'The next work to be tackled was a series of stern wheel hospital ships for the River Tigris, four of these were constructed. One was completely finished and went out under her own steam to her far-off destination, the other three being sent out to the East for re-erection. These vessels were specially equipped with every hospital convenience, and have been found very suitable for their purpose.'							
389		1917		Stern-Wheel Hospital Ship	St/PD/St		Admiralty

Yard No	Name	Date Launched	Displacement Tons	Type	Construction and Dimensions	Horse Power	Owners
390		1917		Stern-Wheel Hospital Ship	St/PD/St		Admiralty
391		1917		Stern-Wheel Hospital Ship	St/PD/St		Admiralty
392	*Diomed*	14.1.1922	10,340	Cargo	St/2Sc/St 491.0/62.4/31.1	? Turb W&C	Alfred Holt & Co. Liverpool
Completed May 1922, sister ship of *Calchas*. Transport in Second World War, notably during assault on Sicily, July 1943. Broken up Dalmuir (UK) 1952.							
393	*Torr Head*	20.3.1923	5,221	Cargo	St/Sc/St 400.1/52.3/28.4	531 nhp TE (3Cy) W&C	Ulster SS Co., Belfast
Completed May 1923. In 1933 to Chilean owners, Chilena Interoceanic, renamed *Angol*. In 1950 to Chilena Del Pacifico, renamed *Alamo*. Broken up Italy (Genoa) 1960.							
394							
395							
396							
397							
398							
399							
400	*PC 69*	11.3.1918	682	Naval Patrol Vessel	St/2Sc/St 244.6/23.9/8.0	3,500 shp Turb W&C	Admiralty
Transferred to Indian Naval Service, renamed *Pathan*. Sunk Italian submarine (*Luigi Galvani*) Indian Ocean, June 1940. Six lives lost.							
401	*PC 70*	12.4.1918	682	Naval Patrol Vessel	St/2Sc/St 244.6/23.9/8.0	3,500 shp Turb W&C	Admiralty
Sold 1926, broken up Blyth (UK).							
402	*Syringa*	29.9.1917	1,290	Naval Sloop	St/Sc/St 262.6/35.0/11.6	2,000 ihp VTE (4Cy) W&C	Admiralty
Anchusa Class escort. In 1920 to Egypt, renamed *Sollum*. Lost when ran aground at Sidi Barrani during German air attack January 1941.							
403	*Windflower*	12.4.1918	1,290	Naval Sloop	St/Sc/St 262.6/35.0/11.6	2,000 ihp VTE (4Cy) W&C	Admiralty
Sold for breaking up 1927.							
404							
405							
406							
407							
408							
409							
410							
411							
412							
413							
414	*BV 1*	1917		Barrage Vessel	St/Sc/St		Admiralty
These small auxiliary warships were designed to protect the 'Dover Barrage'. A post-war publication gives a description of these ships: 'The barrage vessels were each fitted with four powerful searchlights, and were suitable for putting up a barrage of light wherever desired. They were also fitted with guns for protection.'							
415	*BV 2*	1917		Barrage Vessel	St/Sc/St		Admiralty
416	*BV 3*	1917		Barrage Vessel	St/Sc/St		Admiralty
417	*BV 4*	1917		Barrage Vessel	St/Sc/St		Admiralty

<table>
<tr><th>Yard No</th><th>Name</th><th>Date Launched</th><th>Displacement Tons</th><th>Type</th><th>Construction and Dimensions</th><th>Horse Power</th><th>Owners</th></tr>
<tr><td>418</td><td>BV 5</td><td>1917</td><td></td><td>Barrage Vessel</td><td>St/Sc/St</td><td></td><td>Admiralty</td></tr>
<tr><td>419</td><td>BV 6</td><td>1917</td><td></td><td>Barrage Vessel</td><td>St/Sc/St</td><td></td><td>Admiralty</td></tr>
<tr><td>420</td><td>BV. 7</td><td>1917</td><td></td><td>Barrage Vessel</td><td>St/Sc/St</td><td></td><td>Admiralty</td></tr>
<tr><td>421</td><td>BV 8</td><td>1917</td><td></td><td>Barrage Vessel</td><td>St/Sc/St</td><td></td><td>Admiralty</td></tr>
<tr><td>422</td><td>BV 9</td><td>1917</td><td></td><td>Barrage Vessel</td><td>St/Sc/St</td><td></td><td>Admiralty</td></tr>
<tr><td>423</td><td>BV 10</td><td>1917</td><td></td><td>Barrage Vessel</td><td>St/Sc/St</td><td></td><td>Admiralty</td></tr>
<tr><td>424</td><td>British Lantern</td><td>11.6.1918</td><td>6,897</td><td>Oil Tanker</td><td>St/Sc/St
430.1/57.0/33.0</td><td>634 nhp
TE (3Cy)
W&C</td><td>British Tanker Co. London</td></tr>
<tr><td colspan="8">Completed August 1918. In 1936 to Royal Navy as RFA, renamed Oligarch. Badly damaged by submarine torpedo (U-453) off Libyan coast on route Gibraltar–Port Said, July 1943. The hulk, loaded with obsolete ammunition and poison gas shells, scuttled Red Sea, April 1946.</td></tr>
<tr><td>425</td><td>British Beacon</td><td>7.9.1918</td><td>6,897</td><td>Oil Tanker</td><td>St/Sc/St
430.1/57.0/33.0</td><td>634 nhp
TE (3Cy)
W&C</td><td>British Tanker Co. London</td></tr>
<tr><td colspan="8">Completed October 1918, sister ship of British Lantern. In 1936 to Royal Navy as RFA, renamed Olcades. Broken up Blyth (UK) 1953.</td></tr>
<tr><td>426</td><td>War Beetle</td><td>10.9.1918</td><td>5,177</td><td>Cargo (B Type)</td><td>St/Sc/St
400.4/52.3/28.4</td><td>517 nhp
2,500 ihp
TE (3Cy)
W&C</td><td>Shipping Controller</td></tr>
<tr><td colspan="8">Completed 14.9.1918, three and a half days after launch. In 1919 to Belgian owners, Lloyd Royal Belge, renamed Eglantier. In 1939 to Yugoslav owners, Atlantska Plovidba, renamed Sreca. By 1946 operated by Jugoslavenska Plovidba, renamed Kornat. In 1957 to Lebanese owners, P.D. Kyprianou, renamed Cheik Marcel. Broken up Japan (Osaka) 1963.</td></tr>
<tr><td>427</td><td>War Leopard</td><td>21.6.1918</td><td>5,177</td><td>Cargo (B Type)</td><td>St/Sc/St
400.4/52.3/28.4</td><td>518 nhp
2,500 ihp
TE (3Cy)
W&C</td><td>Shipping Controller</td></tr>
<tr><td colspan="8">Completed July 1918, sister ship of War Beetle. In 1919 to Italian owners, Bianchi Bros, renamed Fratelli Bianchi. In 1925 to La Polar, renamed Villa Ada. In 1927 to British owners, Turner Brightman, renamed Zeriba. In 1933 to Greek owners, Rethymnis Kulukundis, renamed Mount Cynthos. In 1939 to Japanese ownership, Yamashita Kisen, renamed Momoyama Maru. Sunk air attack off New Guinea, March 1943.</td></tr>
<tr><td>428</td><td>BD 31</td><td>1918</td><td></td><td>Boom Defence Vessel</td><td>St/Sc/St</td><td></td><td>Admiralty</td></tr>
<tr><td colspan="8">Like the earlier barrage vessels these craft were designed for the 'Dover Barrage'. However, the post-war publication makes it clear that they were a very different type: 'The boom defence vessels were intended for carrying the boom nets, and were also fitted with guns and special hauling winches for raising and lowering the nets as desired.'</td></tr>
<tr><td>429</td><td>BD 32</td><td>1918</td><td></td><td>Boom Defence Vessel</td><td>St/Sc/St</td><td></td><td>Admiralty</td></tr>
<tr><td>430</td><td>BD 33</td><td>1918</td><td></td><td>Boom Defence Vessel</td><td>St/Sc/St</td><td></td><td>Admiralty</td></tr>
<tr><td>431</td><td>BD 34</td><td>1918</td><td></td><td>Boom Defence Vessel</td><td>St/Sc/St</td><td></td><td>Admiralty</td></tr>
<tr><td>432</td><td>BD 35</td><td>1918</td><td></td><td>Boom Defence Vessel</td><td>St/Sc/St</td><td></td><td>Admiralty</td></tr>
<tr><td>433</td><td>BD 36</td><td>1918</td><td></td><td>Boom Defence Vessel</td><td>St/Sc/St</td><td></td><td>Admiralty</td></tr>
<tr><td>434–435</td><td colspan="7">These two numbers were almost certainly two further boom-defence vessels which were cancelled at the end of the war.</td></tr>
</table>

<table>
<tr><th>Yard No</th><th>Name</th><th>Date Launched</th><th>Displacement Tons</th><th>Type</th><th>Construction and Dimensions</th><th>Horse Power</th><th>Owners</th></tr>
<tr><td>436</td><td>War Argus</td><td>19.10.1918</td><td>7,910</td><td>Cargo
(Refrigerated)
(G Type)</td><td>St/2Sc/St
450.0/58.4/37.1</td><td>1,138 nhp
5,500 ihp
TE (6Cy)
W&C</td><td>Shipping Controller</td></tr>
<tr><td colspan="8">Completed 12.12.1918. In 1919 to Ocean SN Co., renamed Gallic. In 1933 to Clan Line, renamed Clan Colquhoun. In 1947 to J. Livanos & Sons, renamed Ioannis Livanos. In 1949 to Dos Oceanos Co., renamed Jenny. In 1951 to Indonesian owners, Djakarta Lloyd, renamed Imam Bondjol and Djatinegara (1952). Broken up Hong Kong 1956.</td></tr>
<tr><td>437</td><td>Nowshera</td><td>21.1.1919</td><td>7,920</td><td>Cargo
(Refrigerated)
(G Type)</td><td>St/2Sc/St
450.0/58.4/37.1</td><td>1,138 nhp
5,500 ihp
TE (6Cy)
W&C</td><td>British India SN Co.
Glasgow</td></tr>
<tr><td colspan="8">Completed 15.4.1919, sister ship of War Argus, originally War Ceres but completed under this name. Captured and sunk by German surface raider Pinguin, Indian Ocean, November 1940 inbound Australia–UK. Crew were taken prisoner.</td></tr>
<tr><td>438</td><td>Royalstar</td><td>22.11.1918</td><td>7,900</td><td>Cargo
(Refrigerated)
(G Type)</td><td>St/2Sc/St
450.0/58.4/37.1</td><td>1,138 nhp
5,500 ihp
TE (6Cy)
W&C</td><td>Blue Star Line
Liverpool</td></tr>
<tr><td colspan="8">Completed 25.1.1919, sister ship of War Argus, originally War Charon but completed under this name. Sunk by air-launched torpedo NE of Algiers on voyage Buenos Aires–Malta, April 1944. One life lost.</td></tr>
<tr><td>439</td><td>Albionstar</td><td>6.3.1919</td><td>7,900</td><td>Cargo
(Refrigerated)
(G Type)</td><td>St/2Sc/St
450.0/58.4/37.1</td><td>1,138 nhp
5,500 ihp
TE (6Cy)
W&C</td><td>Blue Star Line
Liverpool</td></tr>
<tr><td colspan="8">Completed 11.6.1919, sister ship of War Argus, originally War Hecuba but completed under this name. Broken up Briton Ferry (UK) 1948.</td></tr>
<tr><td>440</td><td>Wangaratta</td><td>30.4.1919</td><td>7,900</td><td>Cargo
(Refrigerated)
(G Type)</td><td>St/2Sc/St
450.0/58.4/37.1</td><td>1,138 nhp
5,500 ihp
TE (6Cy)
W&C</td><td>British India SN Co.
Glasgow</td></tr>
<tr><td colspan="8">Completed 9.7.1919, sister ship of War Argus, originally War Theseus but completed under this name. In 1929 to Blue Star Line, renamed Tacoma Star. In May 1941 sunk at Liverpool Docks during air raid, salvaged and repaired. Sunk by submarine torpedo (U-109) 500nm E of Hampton Roads, inbound Buenos Aries–Liverpool, February 1942. Germans reported that crew got off safely in lifeboats but radioed wrong position of sinking, as a consequence no survivors were recovered. Eighty-seven lives lost.</td></tr>
<tr><td>441</td><td>Muneric</td><td>18.4.1919</td><td>5,146</td><td>Cargo
(B Type)</td><td>St/Sc/St
400.4/52.3/28.4</td><td>517 nhp
2,500 ihp
TE (3Cy)
W&C</td><td>Clark & Service
Glasgow</td></tr>
<tr><td colspan="8">Completed 3.6.1919, sister ship of War Beetle, originally War Spider but completed under this name. In 1930 to American owners, Munson SS Co., not renamed. In 1936 to British ownership, Putney Hill SS Co. In 1939 to Bright Navigation. Sunk by submarine torpedo (U-432) S of Iceland, inbound Australia–Middlesbrough with 7,000 tons of iron ore, September 1941. Sixty-three lives lost (no survivors).</td></tr>
<tr><td>442</td><td>Ballygally Head</td><td>31.5.1919</td><td>5,180</td><td>Cargo
(B Type)</td><td>St/Sc/St
400.4/52.3/28.4</td><td>517 nhp
2,500 ihp
TE (3Cy)
W&C</td><td>Ulster SS Co.
Belfast</td></tr>
<tr><td colspan="8">Completed 26.6.1919, sister ship of War Beetle. Originally War Peewit but completed under this name. In 1924 to West Hartlepool SN Co., renamed Kepwickhall. In 1930 to French owners, Fraissinet & Co., renamed Tombouctou. Between 1940 and 1946 under control of Ministry of War transport. In 1948 to Panamanian owners, Atychides, renamed Ispahan. In 1949 to German owners, A. Wiards, renamed Monika Wiards. In 1959 to Bowring & Curry, renamed Rhoda. Broken up Japan (Osaka) 1959.</td></tr>
<tr><td>443</td><td>Gogra</td><td>9.7.1919</td><td>5,181</td><td>Cargo
(B Type)</td><td>St/Sc/St
400.4/52.3/28.4</td><td>517 nhp
2,500 ihp
TE (3Cy)
W&C</td><td>British India SN Co.
Glasgow</td></tr>
<tr><td colspan="8">Completed 20.8.1919, sister ship of War Beetle, laid down as War Tomtit launched as Gorissa and completed as Gogra. Sunk by submarine torpedo (U-124) 320nm W of Oporto, outbound Glasgow–India, April 1943. Eighty-two lives lost out of 90 on board. U-boat sunk by convoy escorts following attack, 53 lives lost.</td></tr>
<tr><td>444</td><td>Gorala</td><td>26.8.1919</td><td>5,181</td><td>Cargo
(B Type)</td><td>St/Sc/St
400.4/52.3/28.4</td><td>517 nhp
2,500 ihp
TE (3Cy)
W&C</td><td>British Indian SN Co.
Glasgow</td></tr>
<tr><td colspan="8">Completed 20.9.1919, sister ship of War Beetle, laid down as War Terrier but completed under this name. In 1924 to King Line, renamed King Edward. Sunk by submarine torpedo (U-356) NNW of Azores, outbound Hull–New York, December 1942. Twenty-three lives lost out of 48 on board. U-boat sunk by convoy escorts following attack, 46 lives lost.</td></tr>
</table>

<table>
<tr><th>Yard No</th><th>Name</th><th>Date Launched</th><th>Displacement Tons</th><th>Type</th><th>Construction and Dimensions</th><th>Horse Power</th><th>Owners</th></tr>
<tr><td>445</td><td>Kenbane Head</td><td>11.10.1919</td><td>5,180</td><td>Cargo
(B Type)</td><td>St/Sc/St
400.4/52.3/28.4</td><td>517 nhp
2,500 ihp
TE (3Cy)
W&C</td><td>Ulster SS Co.
Belfast</td></tr>
<tr><td colspan="8">Completed 19.11.1919, sister ship of War Beetle, laid down as War Whippet but completed under this name. In November 1940 formed part of convoy HX84 which was attacked by German raider Admiral Scheer off Greenland. Although the armed merchant cruiser Jarvis Bay engaged German vassal in a suicidal battle to give the convoy time to scatter Kenbane Head and four other vessels were caught and sunk. Twenty-four lives lost out of 44 on board.</td></tr>
<tr><td>446</td><td>Narenta</td><td>27.8.1919</td><td>8,266</td><td>Cargo
(Refrigerated)
(G Type)</td><td>St/Sc/St
450.2/58.3/37.1</td><td>892 nhp
5,500 shp
Turb
W&C</td><td>Royal Mail SP Co.
London</td></tr>
<tr><td colspan="8">Completed 20.2.1920, half sister of War Argus with single screw and turbine machinery, laid down as Neganti (no standard 'War' name appears to have been allocated) but completed under this name. In 1939 to Japanese owners, Nippon Suisan, renamed Kosei Maru. Sunk by submarine torpedo (USS Tunny) off Caroline Islands, April 1943.</td></tr>
<tr><td>447</td><td>Port Curtis</td><td>9.10.1919</td><td>8,287</td><td>Cargo
(Refrigerated)
(G Type)</td><td>St/Sc/St
450.2/58.3/37.1</td><td>892 nhp
5,500 shp
Turb
W&C</td><td>Commonwealth &
Dominion
London</td></tr>
<tr><td colspan="8">Completed 14.5.1920, sister ship of Narenta (no standard 'War' name appears to have been allocated). In 1936 to Counties Ship Management, London, renamed Tower Dale. In 1937 to Finnish owners, J.A. Zachariassen, renamed Kronoborg. In 1946 to the Soviet government as war prize, named Kronstadt. In 1967 to Bulgarian government, renamed Algeneb. Broken up Spain (Bilbao) 1970.</td></tr>
<tr><td>448</td><td>Nebraska</td><td>9.12.1919</td><td>8,266</td><td>Cargo
(Refrigerated)
(G Type)</td><td>St/Sc/St
450.2/58.3/37.1</td><td>892 nhp
5,500 shp
Turb
W&C</td><td>Royal Mail SP Co.
London</td></tr>
<tr><td colspan="8">Completed 4.8.1920, sister ship of Narenta (no standard 'War' name appears to have been allocated). Sunk by submarine torpedo (U-843) SW of Ascension Island outbound for Buenos Aires, April 1944. Two lives lost.</td></tr>
<tr><td>449</td><td>Canonesa</td><td>6.3.1920</td><td>8,286</td><td>Cargo
(Refrigerated)
(G Type)</td><td>St/Sc/St
450.2/58.3/37.1</td><td>892 nhp
5,500 shp
Turb
W&C</td><td>Furness-Houlder
Liverpool</td></tr>
<tr><td colspan="8">Completed 4.11.1920, sister ship of Narenta (no standard 'War' name appears to have been allocated). Sunk by submarine torpedo (U-100) 340nm W of Bloody Foreland inbound from Australia, September 1940. One life lost.</td></tr>
<tr><td>450</td><td>Nictheroy</td><td>20.5.1920</td><td>8,266</td><td>Cargo
(Refrigerated)
(G Type)</td><td>St/Sc/St
450.2/58.3/37.1</td><td>892 nhp
5,500 shp
Turb
W&C</td><td>Royal Mail SP Co.
London</td></tr>
<tr><td colspan="8">Completed 22.12.1920, sister ship of Narenta (no standard 'War' name appears to have been allocated). In 1937 to Italian owners, Achille Lauro, renamed Cuma. Sunk mine off Sicily, October 1941.</td></tr>
<tr><td>451</td><td></td><td></td><td></td><td></td><td></td><td></td><td></td></tr>
<tr><td>452</td><td></td><td></td><td></td><td></td><td></td><td></td><td></td></tr>
<tr><td>453</td><td></td><td></td><td></td><td></td><td></td><td></td><td></td></tr>
<tr><td>454</td><td>Mayari</td><td>12.3.1921</td><td>2,802</td><td>Sugar Vessel</td><td>St/Sc/St
303.0/47.2/21.7</td><td>218 nhp
TE (3Cy)
W&C</td><td>United Fruit
New Jersey</td></tr>
<tr><td colspan="8">Completed May 1921. Initially UK registered, 1928 transferred to Panama. In 1954 to Panamanian owners, Ircar, renamed Kismet. In 1955 to German owners, Hugo Stinnes, renamed Heinrich Hugo Stinnes. Broken up Germany (Altenwirdorl) 1960.</td></tr>
<tr><td>455</td><td>Macabi</td><td>14.4.1921</td><td>2,802</td><td>Sugar Vessel</td><td>St/Sc/St
303.0/47.2/21.7</td><td>218 nhp
TE (3Cy)
W&C</td><td>United Fruit
New Jersey</td></tr>
<tr><td colspan="8">Completed May 1921, sister ship of Mayari. Initially UK registered, 1928 transferred to Panama. Sunk mine Port of Spain, Trinidad, October 1942. No lives lost.</td></tr>
<tr><td>456</td><td>Manaqui</td><td>25.5.1921</td><td>2,802</td><td>Sugar Vessel</td><td>St/Sc/St
303.0/47.2/21.7</td><td>217 nhp
TE (3Cy)
W&C</td><td>United Fruit
New Jersey</td></tr>
<tr><td colspan="8">Completed June 1921, sister ship of Mayari. Initially UK registered, 1928 to Panamanian owners, Balboa SS Co. In 1937 to Furness Withy & Co. On 23 February 1942 left Belfast Lough for Kingston Jamaica and never arrived. According to some sources sunk by submarine torpedo (U-504) as approached Caribbean. However, while this U-boat was operating in area did not claim vessel as 'kill'. Recently has been suggested that was a victim of Italian submarine Morosini but this has not been confirmed. Other sources say vanished. Torpedoed/foundered? Forty-one lives lost.</td></tr>
</table>

Yard No	Name	Date Launched	Displacement Tons	Type	Construction and Dimensions	Horse Power	Owners
457	*Maravi*	6.6.1921	2,802	Sugar Vessel	St/Sc/St 303.0/47.2/21.7	217 nhp TE (3Cy) W&C	United Fruit New Jersey
Completed July 1921, sister ship of *Mayari.* Initially UK registered, 1928 transferred to Panama. In 1951 to L.R. Schmith & Co. renamed *Jane Lanng.* In 1959 to Kopsaftis Foutoulaki renamed *Aghios Symeon.* Broken up China (Shanghai) 1970.							
458							
459	*San Benito*	12.8.1921	3,724	Passenger-Fruiter	St/Sc/St 325.3/46.3/29.2	3,100 ihp? Turb-Elect **Engines** British Thompson Houston Belfast	United Fruit New Jersey
Completed 20.9.1921. Initially UK registered, transferred to Panama 1931. In 1942 requisitioned by US Navy, renamed *Taurus.* Returned to owners 1946 reverted to original name. Broken up USA (Mobile) 1953.							
460	*Dardanus*	18.4.1923	7,857	Cargo	St/Sc/St 459.5/58.4/32.6	7,000 ihp? Turb W&C	Alfred Holt & Co. Liverpool
Completed June 1923. To Glen Line 1935, renamed *Flintshire.* Reverted to original owners and name 1939. In April 1942 damaged by aircraft off Vizagapatam, Indian Ocean. Taken in tow by *Gandara*, following day both ships caught and sunk by Japanese warships in Bay of Bengal. Crew escaped in lifeboats, no lives were lost.							
461							
462	*Port Brisbane*	11.10.1923	8,315	Cargo (Refrigerated)	St/2Sc/St 480.8/62.4/32.9	859 nhp 4,500 ihp? TE (6Cy) +Exh Turb W.C	Commonwealth & Dominion London
Completed December 1923, sister ship of *Port Auckland.* Sunk by German raider *Pinguin*, Indian Ocean, November 1940. No lives lost.							
463	*Port Wellington*	8.1.1924	7,868	Cargo (Refrigerated)	St/2Sc/St 470.1/60.5/ ?	4,500 ihp? TE (6Cy) +Exh Turb W&C	Commonwealth & Dominion London
Completed February 1924, a reduced version of Port Auckland type. Scuttled following capture by German raider *Pinguin*, Indian Ocean, December 1940. No lives lost.							
464	*City of Nagpur*	30.5.1922	10,140	Passenger-Cargo	St/Sc/St 469.9/59.3/40.0	1,038 nhp QE (4Cy) W&C	Ellerman Lines Liverpool
(In company advertising material described as passenger vessel, re-rated) Completed September 1922, for India routes, accommodation for 200 first-class and 93 second-class passengers, later employed on East and West Africa routes. In April 1941, during fifth wartime voyage, outward bound and sailing independently, submarine torpedo (*U-75*) 900 miles W of Fastnet. Only one of 300 passengers and ten of 215 crew members lost, remainder rescued by destroyer after three days in lifeboats.							
465	*British Workman*	17.1.1922	6,993	Tanker	St/Sc/St 440.4/57.0/33.9	605 nhp Turb W&C	British Tanker Co. London
Completed February 1922. Sunk by submarine torpedo (*U-455*) S of Cape Pace, Newfoundland, outbound Greenock–Galveston, May 1942. Six lives lost.							
466	*British Engineer*	26.4.1922	6,993	Tanker	St/Sc/St 440.4/57.0/33.9	605 nhp Turb W&C	British Tanker Co. London
Completed June 1922, sister ship of *British Workman.* In 1952 to Panamanian owners, Vivalet Shipping & Trading, renamed *Emily.* In 1954 to Israeli owners, Traders & Shippers (Tankers), renamed *Yarkon.* Broken up Yugoslavia (Split) 1959.							
467	*Berwindmoor*	28.6.1923	6,078	Topside Tank Collier	St/Sc/St 420.3/56.4/27.8	636 nhp TE (3Cy) W&C	Berwindmoor SS Co. Oslo
Completed September 1923. In 1930 to German owners, F. Krupp, renamed *Borbeck.* By early 1945 engaged in evacuating German refugees and troops in Baltic. On 9 March disabled by Russian air attack and sunk by submarine torpedo (Russian *Sc-303*) 30 miles NE of Hela.							
468	*City of Venice*	6.2.1924	8,308	Passenger-Cargo	St/Sc/St 455.2/58.1/31.3	972 nhp QE (4Cy) W&C	Ellerman Line Liverpool
Completed April 1924, for India routes, accommodation for 133 first-class and 32 second-class passengers.							

<table>
<tr><th>Yard No</th><th>Name</th><th>Date Launched</th><th>Displacement Tons</th><th>Type</th><th>Construction and Dimensions</th><th>Horse Power</th><th>Owners</th></tr>
<tr><td colspan="8">In 1930 re-engined by WC with turbo-electric machinery. Employed as a troopship in war. In July 1943, carrying 292 men of the 1st Canadian Division and a large quantity of stores for invasion of Sicily, when sunk by submarine torpedo (U-375) off Cape Tenez, Algeria. Twenty-one lives lost out of 482 on board.</td></tr>
<tr><td>469</td><td>Arlington Court</td><td>5.4.1924</td><td>4,915</td><td>Cargo</td><td>St/Sc/St
396.6/53.1/26.5</td><td>414 nhp
TE (3Cy)
W&C</td><td>Haldin & Co.
London</td></tr>
<tr><td colspan="8">Completed May 1924. Sunk by submarine torpedo (U-43) 320 miles from Start Point, inbound from Freetown with cargo of maize, November 1939. Seven lives lost.</td></tr>
<tr><td>470</td><td>Barrington Court</td><td>14.8.1924</td><td>4,915</td><td>Cargo</td><td>St/Sc/St
396.6/53.1/26.5</td><td>414 nhp
TE (3Cy)
W&C</td><td>Haldin & Co.
London</td></tr>
<tr><td colspan="8">Completed September 1924, sister ship of Arlington Court. In 1948 to F.C. Strick & Co. (La Tunisienne Steam Nav. Co.), London, renamed Leon De Nervo. In 1951 to Puerto Rican owners, V. Tricoglu, renamed Electric. Wrecked Masirah Island, Oman, August 1960.</td></tr>
<tr><td>471</td><td>Marudu</td><td>17.5.1924</td><td>1,926</td><td>Passenger</td><td>St/Sc/Mv
263.2/41.7/18.2</td><td>355 nhp
Dies
Engines
Burmeister
& Wain
Copenhagen</td><td>Straits SS Co.
Singapore</td></tr>
<tr><td colspan="8">Completed July 1924. In 1963 to Singapore government, converted to moored training ship, renamed Singapore. Broken up Singapore 1979.</td></tr>
<tr><td>472</td><td>Atlantida</td><td>24.4.1924</td><td>4,191</td><td>Passenger-
Fruiter</td><td>St/Sc/St
350.6/50.3/29.5</td><td>669 nhp
TE (4Cy)
W&C</td><td>Standard Fruit
New Jersey</td></tr>
<tr><td colspan="8">Completed 22.5.1924. In 1942 requisitioned by US War Shipping Administration, returned to owners 1946. Broken up Belgium (Ghent) 1959.</td></tr>
<tr><td>473</td><td>Buchanness</td><td>1.10.1924</td><td>4,573</td><td>Cargo</td><td>St/Sc/St
401.6/54.3/25.3</td><td>349 nhp
TE (3Cy)
W&C</td><td>Wm Reardon – Smith &
Sons
Cardiff</td></tr>
<tr><td colspan="8">Completed November 1924. In 1931 renamed Imperial Valley. In 1948 to Memphis Shipping Co., London, renamed Memphis Town. In 1951 to Costa Rican owners, Oriental de Panama, renamed Marinella. Broken up Italy (La Spezia) 1959.</td></tr>
<tr><td>474</td><td>Skegness</td><td>13.11.1924</td><td>4,573</td><td>Cargo</td><td>St/Sc/St
401.6/54.3/25.3</td><td>349 nhp
TE (3Cy)
W&C</td><td>Wm Reardon – Smith &
Sons
Cardiff</td></tr>
<tr><td colspan="8">Completed December 1924, sister ship of Buchanness. In 1931 renamed Sacramento Valley. Sunk by submarine torpedo (U-106) W of Cape Verde Islands outbound Cardiff–Pernambuco, cargo of coal, June 1941. Three lives lost.</td></tr>
<tr><td>475</td><td>Antinous</td><td>18.11.1924</td><td>4,563</td><td>Cargo</td><td>St/Sc/St
401.6/54.3/25.3</td><td>423 nhp
TE (3Cy)
W&C</td><td>New Egypt & Levant SS
Co.
(T. Bowen-Rees Ltd)
Alexandria, Egypt</td></tr>
<tr><td colspan="8">Completed January 1925, near sister ship of Buchanness. In 1933 to Watts & Co., renamed Willesden. Sunk by German raider Thor, South Atlantic, April 1942. One life lost, but survivors spent three years in Japanese prisoner-of-war camp.</td></tr>
<tr><td>476</td><td>Errington Court</td><td>23.4.1925</td><td>4,915</td><td>Cargo</td><td>St/Sc/St
396.6/53.1/26.5</td><td>414 nhp
TE (3Cy)
W&C</td><td>Haldin & Co.
London</td></tr>
<tr><td colspan="8">Completed June 1925, sister ship of Arlington Court. In 1947 to Tarros Shipping Co., London (J. Livanos & Sons), renamed Tharros. In 1950 to Panamanian owners, Toula SA, renamed Athens. In 1954 to Monrovian owners, San Roccosa, renamed Navidad. Broken up Holland (Hendrik-Ido-Ambacht) 1965.</td></tr>
<tr><td>477</td><td>Port Dunedin</td><td>12.3.1925</td><td>7,463</td><td>Passenger-
Cargo</td><td>St/2Sc/Mv
466.9/59.8/31.3</td><td>1,112 nhp
Dies
Engines
W. Doxford
& Sons</td><td>Commonwealth &
Dominion
London</td></tr>
<tr><td colspan="8">Completed May 1925. The first motor vessel in company's fleet and first on New Zealand–UK route. Apart from collision in Thames with Blue Star's Australia Star, December 1937 an uneventful career. Broken up Italy (Genoa) 1962.</td></tr>
<tr><td>478</td><td></td><td></td><td></td><td></td><td></td><td></td><td></td></tr>
<tr><td>479</td><td></td><td></td><td></td><td></td><td></td><td></td><td></td></tr>
<tr><td>480</td><td></td><td></td><td></td><td></td><td></td><td></td><td></td></tr>
<tr><td>481</td><td>Federiko Galavic</td><td>28.1.1925</td><td>5,269</td><td>Cargo</td><td>St/Sc/St
420.6/54.7/25.0</td><td>484 nhp
TE (3Cy)
W&C</td><td>Dubrovacka Parobrodska
Yugoslavia</td></tr>
<tr><td colspan="8">Completed February 1925. In 1941 taken over by British government, renamed Radport. In 1946 returned to Yugoslavia, renamed Beograd. Broken up Yugoslavia (Split) 1970.</td></tr>
</table>

Yard No	Name	Date Launched	Displacement Tons	Type	Construction and Dimensions	Horse Power	Owners
482							
483							
484	*Jevington Court*	9.6.1925	4,544	Cargo	St/Sc/St 397.0/53.2/24.5	419 nhp TE (3Cy) W&C	Haldin & Co. London
Completed July 1925, sister ship of *Arlington Court.* Mined on passage Tyne–London with cargo of coal off Cromer, February 1940. No lives lost.							
485	*Gatun*	17.9.1925	3,362	Passenger-Fruiter	St/Sc/St 315.6/45.2/29.4	525 nhp TE (3Cy) W&C	Standard Fruit New Jersey
Completed October 1925. Broken up Italy (La Spelia) 1960.							
486	*Orestes*	14.4.1926	7,882	Cargo (Refrigerated)	St/2Sc/Mv 459.6/58.4/32.6	1,304 nhp Dies **Engines** Burmeister & Wain, Copenhagan	Alfred Holt & Co. Liverpool
Completed June 1926, for Australia–UK meat trade. In May 1942 attacked by Japanese aircraft off Madras, drove them off with anti-aircraft fire. In June attacked by three Japanese submarines 90 miles S of Sydney, fought them off using depth charges. Broken up Japan (Mihara) 1963.							
487	*Idomencus*	10.6.1926	7,882	Cargo (Refrigerated)	St/2Sc/Mv 459.6/58.4/32.6	1,307 nhp Dies **Engines** Burmeister & Wain, Copenhagen	Alfred Holt & Co. Liverpool
Completed August 1926, sister of *Orestes.* Broken up Italy (Genoa) 1962.							
488	*Llandaff Castle*	10.8.1926	10,786	Passenger-Cargo	St/2Sc/St 471.2/61.7/39.2	1,086 nhp QE (8Cy) W&C	Union-Castle Line London
(In company advertising material described as passenger vessel, re-rated) Completed January 1927, for 'round-Africa' service. In 1940 transported child evacuees to South Africa then converted to troopship. In December 1940 in convoy attacked by German raider *Admiral Hipper* but escorting cruiser drove attacker off. In early 1942 converted to infantry landing ship with accommodation for 1,150 troops, took part in the invasion of Madagascar. Sunk by submarine torpedo (*U-177*) off coast of Africa on route Dar-es-Salaam–Durban, November 1942. Three lives lost out of 313 on board.							
489	*Port Freemantle*	6.1.1927	8,072	Passenger-Cargo (Refrigerated)	St/2Sc/Mv 477.4/63.4/31.0	1,281 nhp Dies **Engines** W. Duxford & Sons	Commonwealth & Dominion London
Completed April 1927, for New Zealand–UK meat trade, 646,000cu. ft of hold space. During war employed on 'Food for Britain' trade and avoided major incident. Scrapped Japan (Osaka) 1960.							
490	*Bermuda*	28.7.1927	19,086	Passenger	St/4Sc/Mv 525.9/74.1/39.6	11,200 bhp Dies **Engines** W. Duxford & Sons	Furness-Wythy Liverpool
Completed December 1927, the largest ship WC ever built, with accommodation for 616 first-class and 75 second-class passengers on newly establish New York–Bermuda tourist route. Entered service January 1928. In June 1931 superstructure was badly damaged by fire at Hamilton, and after temporary repairs returned to builders to be reconditioned. On 20 November, while in WC's hands, there was another fire and the vessel became a constructive loss. The wreck purchased by yard who, after salvaging machinery, sold hulk for scrap. While being towed to breakers, broke adrift and went ashore on Sutherland coast, April 1933.							
491	*Tela*	24.3.1927	4,083	Passenger-Fruiter	St/Sc/St 342.0/48.0/28.2	406 nhp TE (4Cy) W&C	United Fruit New Jersey
Completed May 1927, new type smaller than pre-war *Cartago*, with accommodation for only 58 passengers. Honduras registered. Sunk by submarine torpedo (*U-504*) Caribbean on route Panama–Costa Rica, June 1942. Eleven lives lost out of 54 on board.							

Yard No	Name	Date Launched	Displacement Tons	Type	Construction and Dimensions	Horse Power	Owners
492	*Castilla*	3.3.1927	4,083	Passenger-Fruiter	St/Sc/St 341.9/48.0/28.2	406 nhp TE (4Cy) W&C	United Fruit New Jersey
Completed March 1927, sister ship of *Tela.* Honduras registered. In 1937 converted to cargo ship. Sunk by submarine torpedo (*U-107*) south of Cuba on route Mobile–Kingston, cargo of flour, June 1942. Twenty-four lives lost out of 59 on board.							
493	*Iriona*	21.4.1927	4,083	Passenger-Fruiter	St/Sc/St 341.9/48.0/28.2	406 nhp TE (4Cy) W&C	United Fruit New Jersey
Completed May 1927, sister ship of *Tela.* Honduras registered. In 1934 renamed *Civdad De Pasto.* Broken up USA (Newport) 1960.							
494	*Chesapeake*	24.11.1927	8,955	Tanker	St/Sc/Mv 476.8/63.8/35.1	997 nhp Dies W&C	Anglo-American Oil London
Completed January 1928. In 1950 to Esso Petroleum, renamed *Esso Aberdeen.* Broken up Faslane (UK) 1953.							
495							
496							
497							
498							
499							
500							
501							
502	*Divis*	16.10.1928	360	Sludge Vessel	St/2Sc/St 146.7/29.2/11.2	76 nhp TE (6Cy) W&C	Belfast Corporation
Completed November 1928. A long and, if rather insalubrious, uneventful life. Broken up Belfast 1990.							
503	*Agamemnon*	25.4.1929	7,593	Cargo (Refrigerated)	St/2Sc/Mv 459.8/59.4/29.3	1,300 nhp Dies **Engines** Burmeister & Wain, Copenhagen	Alfred Holt & Co. Liverpool
Completed September 1929, for Liverpool–Far East routes. In 1939 requisitioned converted to minelayer, renamed HMS *Agamemnon* served 1st Mine-laying Squadron. In 1943 converted at Vancouver to recreation ship for Pacific fleet for use by sailors on local leave; facilities included swimming pool, cinema theatre and brewery. Returned to commercial service 1947. Broken up Hong Kong 1963.							
504	*City of Sydney*	2.10.1929	6,986	Cargo	St/Sc/St 454.2/58.4/31.7	905 nhp TE (4Cy) +Exh Turb W&C	Ellerman Line Liverpool
Completed May 1930. In 1958 to Greek owners, Tsavliris, renamed *Nicolaos Tsavliris.* Broken up Hong Kong 1960.							
505	*Kosmos*	30.5.1929	17,800	Whale Factory Ship	St/Sc/St 554.1/77.2/49.6	988 nhp QE (4Cy) W&C	Anders Jahre Sandefjord, Norway
Completed July 1929. Captured by German raider *Thor* in Atlantic near equator on route to Curacao with full load (17,000 tons) of whale oil, September 1940. Although ship and cargo represented a valuable prize it was considered impossible to send to friendly port so scuttled.							
506	*Deebank*	23.4.1929	5,060	Cargo	St/Sc/St 421.8/56.7/26.7	565 nhp QE (4Cy) W&C	Andrew Weir & Co. Glasgow
Completed June 1929. In 1955 to Panamanian owners, Transportes Maritimos Atlantida, renamed *Deelock.* In 1967 to Japanese owners, Maeda Kisen, renamed *Zuimei Maru.* Broken up Japan (Onomichi) 1971.							
507	*Trentbank*	20.6.1929	5,060	Cargo	St/Sc/St 421.8/56.8/26.7	565 nhp QE (4Cy) W&C	Andrew Weir & Co. Glasgow
Completed November 1929, sister ship of *Deebank.* Sunk air attack off Algeria, on voyage Newport–Bougie, November 1942. Two lives lost.							
508	*Forthbank*	25.7.1929	5,060	Cargo	St/Sc/St 421.8/56.7/26.7	565 nhp QE (4Cy) W&C	Andrew Weir & Co. Glasgow
Completed December 1929, sister ship of *Deebank.* In 1953 to Italian Owners, Adriatico Tirreno Jonio Ligure, renamed *Potestas.* Broken up Hong Kong 1959.							

Pera (WC y/n 201) 1903.

Drawing of *Victorian* (WC y/n 206) 1904.

Vandyke (WC y/n 359) 1921.

Yard No	Name	Date Launched	Displacement Tons	Type	Construction and Dimensions	Horse Power	Owners
509	*Lindenbank*	5.9.1929	5,060	Cargo	St/Sc/St 421.8/56.8/26.7	565 nhp QE (4Cy) W&C	Andrew Weir & Co. Glasgow
Completed January 1930, sister ship of *Deebank*. Ran aground Arena Islands, Philippines, May 1939, refloated but sank.							
510	*Irisbank*	28.1.1930	5,627	Cargo (Refrigerated)	St/2Sc/Mv 426.7/57.4/25.7	1,246 nhp Dies W&C	Andrew Weir & Co. Glasgow
Completed May 1930. Broken up Japan (Osaka) 1961.							
511	*Lossiebank*	12.2.1930	5,627	Cargo (Refrigerated)	St/2Sc/Mv 426.7/57.4/25.7	1,246 nhp Dies W&C	Andrew Weir & Co. Glasgow
Completed June 1930, sister ship of *Irisbank*. Broken up Japan (Izumi-otsu) 1962.							
512	*Taybank*	28.4.1930	5,627	Cargo (Refrigerated)	St/2Sc/Mv 426.7/57.4/25.7	1,246 nhp Dies W&C	Andrew Weir & Co. Glasgow
Completed August 1930, sister ship of *Irisbank*. Broken up Hong Kong 1961.							
513	*Tweedbank*	14.5.1930	5,627	Cargo (Refrigerated)	St/2Sc/Mv 426.7/57.4/25.7	1,246 nhp Dies W&C	Andrew Weir & Co. Glasgow
Completed September 1930, sister ship of *Irisbank*. Broken up Hong Kong 1960.							
514	*Cefalu*	27.2.1930	5,222	Passenger- Fruiter	St/Sc/St 380.7/53.4/29.6	867 nhp QE (4Cy) W&C	Vacarro Bros & Co. (Standard Fruit) New Jersey
Completed 23.4.1930. In 1942 requisitioned by War Shipping Authority, returned 1946. Broken up Italy (La Spelia) 1960.							
515	*Musa*	29.3.1930	5,833	Passenger- Fruiter	St/Sc/St 416.4/56.3/30.9	7,850 ihp? Turb-Elect **Engines** British Thompson Houston Ltd	Balboa Shipping Co. Panama (United Fruit) New Jersey
Completed July 1930. Broken up Korea (Inchon) 1969.							
516	*Corabank*	4.9.1930	8,898	Tanker	St/Sc/Mv 477.0/63.8/35.6	997 nhp Dies W&C	Andrew Weir & Co. Glasgow
Completed August 1932. In 1937 to Japanese owners, Nippon Sekiyu KK, renamed *Rikko Maru*. Damaged submarine torpedo (USS *Sealion*), August 1944, sank Keelung Harbour, Taiwan, awaiting repairs, March 1945.							
517	*William Strachan*	9.10.1930	6,157	Tanker	St/Sc/Mv 407.5/55.2/33.6	623 nhp Dies W&C	Oppen & Sorensen Oslo, Norway
Completed January 1931. In 1951 to Italian owners, S. Tagliavia, renamed *Drepanum*. Broken up Italy (La Spezia) 1963.							
518	*Conus*	28.5.1931	8,132	Tanker	St/2Sc/Mv 452.4/62.1/33.9	714 nhp Dies **Engines** N.E. Marine Engine Co., Newcastle	Anglo-Saxon Petroleum London
Completed December 1931. Sunk by submarine torpedo (*U-97*) North Atlantic outbound Swansea–Curacao, April 1941. Fifty-nine lives lost (no survivors).							
519	*Corbis*	16.7.1931	8,132	Tanker	St/2Sc/Mv 452.4/62.1/33.9	714 nhp Dies **Engines** N.E. Marine Engine Co., Newcastle	Anglo-Saxon Petroleum London
Completed December 1932, sister ship of *Conus*. Sunk by submarine torpedo (*U-180*) off South Africa on route Bandar Abbas–Capetown with 13,100 tons of diesel fuel, April 1943. Fifty lives lost out of 60 on board.							
520	*Mavis*	11.9.1930	935	Cargo	St/Sc/St 216.2/35.1/12.1	189 nhp TE (3Cy) W&C	General Steam Navigation Co. London
Completed October 1930. Sunk in air attack, Calais Roads, May 1940. Three lives lost.							

Yard No	Name	Date Launched	Displacement Tons	Type	Construction and Dimensions	Horse Power	Owners
521	*Swift*	7.10.1930	935	Cargo	St/Sc/St 216.2/35.1/12.1	189 nhp TE (3Cy) W&C	General Steam Navigation Co. London
Completed November 1930, sister ship of *Mavis.* In 1948 to Moss Hutchison Line, Liverpool, renamed *Lormont.* In 1953 to Cypriot owners, D.T. Petropoulos, renamed *Silver Med.* In 1960 to Hong Kong owners, Wheelock Marden, renamed *Silver King* and *South Sea* (1965). In 1967 to Peseta SG Corp, renamed *Eugene.* Broken up Hong Kong 1968.							
522	*Kosmos II*	19.5.1931	16,966	Whale Factory Ship	St/2Sc/St 553.4/77.2/37.6	938 nhp QE (8Cy) W&C	Anders Jahre Sandefjor, Norway
Completed July 1931. Damaged by submarine torpedo (*U-606*) mid-Atlantic, 28 October 1942, inbound with 21,000 tons of crude oil and deck cargo of three landing craft and eight aircraft. A hundred passengers and crew were ordered to abandon ship while captain and about 50 others brought fire under control and attempted to catch up with convoy. On 29th again torpedoed (*U-624*) and sank. Thirty-three lives lost out of 150 on board.							
523							
524	*Erin*	5.4.1932	5,739	Passenger-Fruiter	St/Sc/St 415.0.0/54.7/30.4	1,084 nhp TE (4Cy) +Exh Turb W&C	Standard Fruit New Jersey
Completed May 1932. On British register (Erin SS Co., Belfast). In 1939 under control of Ministry of War Transport, renamed *Maplin* 1941. In 1947 to Elders & Fyffes, renamed *Manistee.* Broken up Newport (UK) 1960.							
525							
526							
527							
528							
529							
530	*Isipingo*	9.10.1933	7,069	Passenger-Cargo (Refrigerated)	St/2Sc/Mv 403.5/57.2/32.4	1,165 nhp Dies W&C	Andrew Weir & Co. Glasgow
Completed February 1934, for India–South Africa route and built to very high standard. This ship and her sisters had accommodation for 50 first-class passengers, described as 'spacious with the ambience of an English country house', all cabins had outside windows and private shower/toilet facilities. Unusually for British ships of era was equipped with outdoor swimming pool. There was also accommodation for 20 second-class passengers and up to 500 'natives' could be carried below decks. Broken up Hong Kong 1964.							
531	*Inchanga*	21.11.1933	7,069	Passenger-Cargo (Refrigerated)	St/2Sc/Mv 403.5/57.2/32.4	1,165 nhp Dies W&C	Andrew Weir & Co. Glasgow
Completed March 1934, sister ship of *Isipingo.* Broken up Belgium (Ghent) 1964.							
532	*Incomati*	15.2.1934	7,369	Passenger-Cargo (Refrigerated)	St/2Sc/Mv 418.5/57.2/32.4	1,165 nhp Dies **Engines** W. Duxford & Sons	Andrew Weir & Co. Glasgow
Completed April 1934, a slightly larger near-sister ship of *Isipingo.* Sunk by submarine torpedo and gunfire (*U-508*) off coast of Nigeria, July 1943. One life lost.							
533	*Durham*	27.6.1934	10,893	Cargo (Refrigerated)	St/2Sc/Mv 493.5/68.6/34.5	2,236 nhp Dies W&C	Federal Steam Navigation Co. London
Completed 21.9.1934. From June 1941 to July 1943 served as naval supply vessel. Mined August 1941 W of Pantellaria on route Malta–Gibraltar. In September further damaged at Gibraltar by limpet mine, had to be beached, refloated and brought to UK for repair. In 1965 to Panamanian owners, Astroguarda, renamed *Rion.* Broken up Taiwan (Kaohsiung) 1966.							
534	*Dorset*	28.7.1934	10,624	Cargo (Refrigerated)	St/2Sc/Mv 493.5/68.6/34.5	2,236 nhp Dies **Engines** Sulzer Bros	Federal Steam Navigation Co. London
Completed 9.11.1934, sister ship of *Durham.* One of 14 fast merchantmen forming supply convoy for Malta in Operation Pedestal. Their immediate escort and covering forces totalled 45 warships, including three aircraft carriers (*Eagle, Indomitable* and *Victorious*), two battleships (*Nelson* and *Rodney*), seven cruisers and 33 destroyers; operation is considered one of hardest-fought convoy actions of war. Subjected to constant attack, losses amongst the supply ships were heavy: ten were sunk before reaching Malta and one sank after arrival. *Dorset* was among losses, disabled and set on fire by three bomb near misses S of Sicily on 13 August 1942, subsequently scuttled. No lives lost.							

Yard No	Name	Date Launched	Displacement Tons	Type	Construction and Dimensions	Horse Power	Owners
535							
536	*Acavus*	24.11.1934	8,010	Tanker	St/Sc/Mv 465.0/59.4/33.9	502 nhp Dies **Engines** Hawthorn Lislie & Co.	Anglo Saxon/Shell Petroleum Co. London
Completed January 1935. During war converted to merchant aircraft carrier. Upper works removed and a 450ft flight deck was added (no hangar) allowing the operation of three aircraft. After war rebuilt as tanker and returned to trade. In 1952 to French owners, Soc. Maritime Shell, renamed *Iacra.* Broken up France (La Seyne) 1963.							

Windflower (WC y/n 403) 1918.

Otranto (WC y/n 278) 1909.

McIlwaine & Co.

Yard No.	Name	Date Launched	Displacement tons	Type	Construction and Dimensions	Horse Power	Owners
1–9	*Elizabeth Jane*	? 1876		Tug			Lagan Canal Co.
Sank while being towed to England.							
10	*Parkmore*	4.10.1880	261	Cargo	Ir/Sc/St 157.5/21.6/10.8	50 nhp CI (2Cy) McI & L	Antrim Iron Ore Co. Belfast
In 1914 sank following collision with *Eveleen*, Belfast Lough, outbound for Troon.							
11	*Volga*	? 1881	281	Cargo	Ir/Sc/St 155.3/21.7/10.5	50 nhp CI (2Cy) McI & L	Volana Shipping Co. Rodgers and Bright Liverpool
12	*Topic*	? 1881	268	Cargo	Ir/Sc/St 155.3/21.7/10.5	50 nhp CI (2Cy) McI & L	W.A. Grainger Belfast
13	*Albert*	? 1882	108	Harbour Ferry	Ir/Pd/St 141.0/16.0/7.9	? Co (1Cy)	Cork, Passage and Blackrock Railway Cork
Originally fitted with engines taken from the *Albert* of 1854, which was taken as part-payment for this vessel. In 1891 re-engined with compound diagonal engine by M. Paul & Co. of Dumbarton. Broken up 1927.							
14	*Monkstown*	7.3.1882	108	Harbour Ferry	Ir/Pd/St 145.3/16.0/7.9	50 nhp CO (2Cy) McI & L	Cork Passage and Blackrock Railway Cork
Sister ship of *Albert*. Broken up 1910.							
15	*Ards*	30.8.1882	133	Cargo	Ir/Sc/St 101.5/18.1/9.2	30 nhp CI (2Cy) McI & L	Dunn, Sefton & Walker Newtownards
Completed 6.10.1882. In 1884 to W. Rowland, Liverpool, renamed *Hebe*. Foundered Morecambe Bay, December 1897.							
16	*Mary E. Wadham*	2.2.1882	602	Cargo	Ir/Sc/St 192.3/27.1/15.7	96 nhp CI (2Cy) McI & L	G. Bargate Barrow
Wrecked Freshwater Bay, January 1888.							
17	*Dungonnell*	? 1883	273	Cargo	Ir/Sc/St 158.0/21.7/11.1	50 nhp CI (2Cy) McI & L	Antrim Iron Ore Co. Belfast
1889–90.							
18	*Saint Kevin*	21.6.1883	477	Cargo	Is/Sc/St 178.0/26.2/12.8	75 nhp CI (2Cy) McI & L	T. Heiton & Co. Dublin
Completed 16.8.1883. In 1911 to G. Postlethwaite, renamed *Lindale*. Wrecked Boulogne, September 1918.							
19	*Sea Fisher*	?.9.1883	274	Cargo	Ir/Sc/St 155.0/21.7/11.1	50 nhp CI (2Cy) McI & L	J. Fisher & Sons Newry
20	*Ferric*	14.12.1883	336	Cargo	Ir/Sc/St 154.0/22.6/11.5	60 nhp CI (2Cy) McI & L	H.J. Scott & Co. Belfast
Wrecked 2 miles N of Larne, January 1905.							
21	*Theme*	?.3.1884	332	Cargo	Ir/Sc/St 159.2/23.1/11.3	60 nhp CI (2Cy) McI & L	W.A. Granger Belfast
In 1889 to Volana Shipping Co. (Rodgers & Bright), renamed *Volante*. In 1913 to John Kelly, Belfast, renamed *Cultra*. In 1915 to Antrim Iron Ore Co., renamed *Glenaan*. Wrecked South Arran, January 1932.							
22	*Bay Fisher*	?.7.1884	369	Cargo	Ir/Sc/St 162.3/23.9/11.9	60 nhp CI (2Cy) McI & L	J. Fisher & Sons Newry
Sunk in collision with wreck, Crosby Channel, November 1901.							

Yard No.	Name	Date Launched	Displacement tons	Type	Construction and Dimensions	Horse Power	Owners
23	*Monarch*	4.12.1884	310	Cargo	Ir/Sc/St 155.0/22.7/11.3	60 nhp CI (2Cy) McI & L	King Belfast
Foundered off Ailsa Craig, Firth of Clyde, June 1919.							
24	*Lady Arthur Hill*	29.6.1885	271	Cross-Channel Vessel	Ir/Sc/St 150.5/23.1/10.6	56 nhp CI (2Cy) McI & L	East Downshire Shipping Co. Belfast
Still in existence 1889–90. Ultimate fate unknown.							
25	*Thesis*	?.1.1887	378	Cargo	Ir/Sc/St 167.0/25.1/11.7	60 nhp CI (2Cy) McI & L	W.A. Granger Belfast
Wrecked of Barony Point, Sound of Mull, October 1889.							
26	*Balniel*	?.7.1886	460	Cargo	Ir/Sc/St 174.0/26.1/12.6	80 nhp CI (2Cy) McI & L	Wigan Coal & Iron Co. Liverpool
In 1910 to J.B. Couper, renamed *Londoner* and *Clydevalley* (1913). This vessel brought a huge arms shipment to Larne for UVF in 1913. After being derelict in Canada for many years returned to Northern Ireland in early 1970s but attempts to preserve ship failed; broken up Lancaster (UK) 1974.							
27	*Lough Fisher*	8.10.1887	418	Cargo	St/Sc/St 168.2/25.1/11.6	61 nhp CI (2Cy) McI & L	James Fisher Newry
Completed November 1887. Sunk by submarine gunfire (*U-19*) near Helvick Head, Waterford, March 1918. Thirteen lives lost.							
28	*Titanic*	?.?.1888	1,608	Cargo	St/Sc/St 280.0/35.1/16.3	260 nhp TE (3Cy) McI & L	Smith & Service Glasgow
Completed May 1888. In 1901 to Peruvian owners, Lota & Coronel, renamed *Luis Alberto* and *Don Alberto* (1915). Hulked Valparaiso 1928.							
29	*Pioneer*	?.?.1887	79	Sailing Vessel (Schooner)	Ir/Sail 75.0/19.1/9.0	N/A	W. McDonnell Belfast
30	*Antrim*	21.7.1888	492	Cargo	St/Sc/St 174.0/26.2/12.5	98 nhp TE (3Cy) McI & L	Antrim Iron Ore Co. Belfast
Completed August 1888. Disappeared, last sighted near Scarweather lighthouse, Swansea, April 1902.							
31 (?)	*Theme*	?.?1888	332	Cargo	Ir/Sc/St 159.2/23.1/12.5	60 nhp CI (2Cy) McI & L	W.A. Grainger Belfast
By 1889 owned by Rodgers & Bright, Liverpool.							
32	*Topic*	1.1.1889	429	Cargo	Ir/Sc/St 173.0/26.2/11.8	73 nhp CI (2Cy) McI & L	W.A. Grainger Belfast
Completed January 1889. Wrecked near Tuskar Light, June 1913.							
33							
34	*Adula*	11.7.1889	772	Cargo	St&Ir/Sc/St 212.5/29.1/12.0	120 nhp TE (3Cy) McI & McC	Atlas SS Co. Liverpool
Completed September 1889. Capsized Jamaica, September 1899.							
35	*Mount Hebron*	26.10.1889	2,560	Cargo	St/Sc/St 300.0/41.5/19.3	300 nhp TE (3Cy) McI & McC	Smith & Service Glasgow
Completed November 1889. In 1899 to Belgian owners, A. Deppe, renamed *Belgique*. Foundered 6 nm NW of Casquets, November 1899.							
36	*Embiricos*	17.4.1889	1,946	Cargo	St/Sc/St 275.0/38.2/17.2	174 nhp TE (3Cy) McI & McC	A. Embiricos Andros, Greece
Completed July 1889. Wrecked off Isles of Scilly, February 1892.							
37							

Yard No.	Name	Date Launched	Displacement tons	Type	Construction and Dimensions	Horse Power	Owners
38	*Lough Fisher*	6.2.1890	289	Sailing Vessel (Schooner)	Ir/Sail 145.5/25.6/10.7	N/A	James Fisher & Sons Barrow
39	*Minnie Hind*	20.2.1890	540	Cargo	Ir&St/Sc/St 180.0/27.2/13.1	120 nhp TE (3Cy) McI & McC	W. Hinde Belfast
Completed March 1890. Almost immediately to German owners, Holm & Molzen, renamed *Wissmann*. Burned Kilindini, East Africa, August 1916.							
40	*Strait Fisher*	8.5.1890	465	Cargo	Ir&St/Sc/St 174.5/26.1/12.4	98 nhp TE (3Cy) McI & McC	James Fisher & Sons Barrow
Completed May 1890. In 1899 to W.A. Grainger, renamed *Trial*. In 1907 to H. Newhouse & Co., renamed *Eastern Counties*. Capsized and sank, Spurn Head, October 1911.							
41	*Glenarm*	19.6.1890	602	Cargo	St/Sc/St 205.5/27.6/12.6	98 nhp TE (3Cy) McI & McC	Antrim Iron Ore Co. Belfast
Completed July 1890. In 1905 to Belgian owners, Worms & Co., renamed *Cantenac*. Broken up Belgium (Ghent) 1938.							
42	*Manchester*	3.1.1891	506	Cargo	St/Sc/St 180.7/27.5/13.2	98 nhp TE (3Cy) McI & McC	Belfast & Mersey SS Co. (Lawther) Belfast
Completed January 1891. Broken up Barrow (UK) 1933.							
43	*Susannah Kelly*	18.10.1890	479	Cargo	St/Sc/St 140.7/21.6/11.2	48 nhp TE (3Cy) McI & McC	J. Kelly Belfast
Foundered on voyage Ayr–Belfast, June 1897.							
44	*Rostellan*	?.?.1891	82	Harbour Boat	St/Sc/St 95.0/16.0/?	? CI (2Cy) McI & McC	Cork, Passage and Blackrock Railway Cork
Sold in 1925 and scrapped late 1930s.							
45	*Minnie Hinde*	28.2.1891	409	Passenger-Cargo	Ir&St/Sc/St 171.0/25.1/10.4	75 nhp TE (3Cy) McI & McC	Mrs M.E. Shaw Belfast
Completed March 1891. In 1904 to Shetland Islands Co., renamed *Norseman*. In 1908 to Bolivian government, renamed *Explorador*. Foundered Manaos Harbour, March 1908.							
46	*Stream Fisher*	30.4.1891	479	Cargo	Ir&St/Sc/St 173.0/26.0/12.3	80 nhp CI (2Cy) McI & McC	James Fisher & Sons Barrow
Completed May 1891. Disappeared on voyage Antwerp–Tyne, December 1928. Twelve lives lost.							
47	*A.J. Balfour*	20.1.1892	3,467	Cargo	St/Sc/St 345.6/43.1/26.9	335 nhp TE (3Cy) McI & McC	S. Lowther Belfast
Completed June 1892. In 1896 to Ulster SS Co., renamed *Malin Head*. Wrecked Pentland Firth, October 1910.							
48	*Pioneer*	3.10.1891	539	Cargo	St/Sc/St 180.6/27.6/12.7	77 nhp TE (3Cy) McI & McC	R. Foley Cork
To J. Fisher & Sons before 1893. In 1896 owned by C.H. Ilwhner and 1897 by E.Grell, London. In 1900 to Spanish owners, M. Fernandez & Co., renamed *Compostela*. In 1912 to M. Trescastros, renamed *Castillejos*. In 1915 to T. Fierro & Sons, renamed *Valentin Fierro*. In 1916 to French owners, Gauls de Mezaubran, renamed *Duguesclin*. Shortly afterwards reverted to British ownership, T.S. Wilson and original name. Broken up 1929.							

Yard No.	Name	Date Launched	Displacement tons	Type	Construction and Dimensions	Horse Power	Owners
49	*Race Fisher*	30.4.1892	493	Cargo	St/Sc/St 173.5/26.1/12.4	76 nhp TE (3Cy) Mcl & McC	James Fisher & Sons Barrow
Completed June 1892. In January 1915 requisitioned as naval auxiliary served as munitions carrier and fleet messenger. Wrecked Stratoni Bay, Greece, January 1919.							
50	*Shannon*	31.5.1892	267	River Boat	Ir/Pd/St 160.0/21.1/8.0	83 nhp Co (2Cy) Mcl & McC	Waterford SS Co. Waterford
Spent working life on Shannon. Broken up *c.* 1918.							
51	*Glanariff*	24.9.1892	660	Cargo	St/Sc/St 201.0/29.1/13.8	136 nhp TE (3Cy) Mcl & McC	Antrim Iron Ore Co. Belfast
Completed October 1892. In 1908 to M. Manglands & Sons, renamed *Princess Ena.* In 1920 to Coast Line, renamed *Fife Coast.* In 1932 to Italian owners, G. Rizzo, renamed *Siciliano.* In 1937 to L. Mangiarotti, renamed *Mino.* In 1939 to M. Messina, renamed *Amalia Messina.* Broken up Italy 1947.							
52	*Queenstown*	?.?.1892	85	Harbour Boat	St/2Sc/St 92.0/16.0/?	? Cl (2Cy) Mcl & McC	Cork, Passage and Blackrock Railway Cork
Sold to owners in Gloucestershire in 1925. Broken up during Second World War.							
53	*Gorronammah*	6.12.1892	150	Gunboat	St/Sc/St 98.6/?/?	? TE (3Cy) Mcl & McC	Liberian government
Armed with a 6pdr QF and a 3pdr QF. Exact fate not known, out of use by early twentieth century.							
54							
55							
56	*Maria*	18.3.1893	2,642	Cargo	St/Sc/St 302.5/41.2/18.0	247 nhp TE (3Cy) Mcl & McC	A. Embiricos Andros, Greece
Completed April 1893. In 1900 to Norwegian owners, M. Jebsen, renamed *Elsa.* In 1904 to Russian Navy, renamed *Ussuri.* By 1911 in Japanese ownership, S. Tanaka, renamed *Yei Maru.* Broken up Japan 1935.							
57	*Wazzan*	16.9.1893	1,484	Passenger-Cargo	St/Sc/St 242.5/34.2/18.4	183 nhp TE (3Cy) Mcl & McC	Mersey SS Co. Liverpool
Completed November 1893. In 1902 to Spanish owners, Valenciana, renamed *Cabanal.* Broken up Italy (Genoa) 1928.							
58							
59	*Theory*	?.4.1894	541	Cargo	St/Sc/St 180.6/27.6/12.7	88 nhp TE (3Cy) Mcl & McC	W.A. Granger Belfast
Completed by WC after acquisition of yard. Lost in collision off Foreland Point, December 1919.							

APPENDIX 1

MAJOR BELFAST LOSSES IDENTIFIED AS 20%+ LOSS OF LIFE

Name	Builder (Y/N)	Fate	Number on Board	Number Lost	% Lost
Munardan	WC (354)	Torpedoed 1942	165	165	100
Wangaratta	WC (440)	Torpedoed 1942	87	87	100
HMS *Picotee*	H&W (1,069)	Torpedoed 1941	66	66	100
Muneric	WC (441)	Torpedoed 1941	63	63	100
Conus	WC (518)	Torpedoed 1941	59	59	100
Cufic	H&W (210)	Foundered 1919	45	45	100
Lady Cairns	H&W (60)	Collision 1904	22	22	100
River Garry	WC (19)	Foundered 1893	19	19	100
Ceramic	H&W (432)	Torpedoed 1942	656	655	99+
HMS *Glorious*	H&W (482–4)	Gunfire 1940	1,245	1,207	97
HMS *Algerine*	H&W (1,132)	Torpedoed 1942	122	114	93
Gogra	WC (443)	Torpedoed 1943	90	82	91
British Peer	H&W (32)	Wrecked 1896	22	18	82
Sagamore	H&W (256)	Torpedoed 1917	59	52	88
Corbis	WC (519)	Torpedoed 1943	60	50	83
Galician	H&W (348)	Torpedoed 1918	206	168	82
Zent	WC (222)	Torpedoed 1916	60	49	82
Waimarama	H&W (1,004)	Bombed 1942	107	87	81

Name	Builder (Y/N)	Fate	Number on Board	Number Lost	% Lost
Star of Bengal	H&W (86)	Wrecked 1908	146	110	75
Laurentic	H&W (394)	Mined 1917	475	354	74
San Bias	WC (347)	Torpedoed 1942	44	30	68
Titanic	*H&W (401)*	*Iceberg 1912*	*2,207*	*1,503*	*68*
Penelope	H&W (941)	Torpedoed 1944	621	415	67
HMS *Vervain*	H&W (1,101)	Torpedoed 1945	94	61	65
Heredia	WC (247)	Torpedoed 1942	62	36	58
Bohemian	H&W (71)	Wrecked 1881	57	33	58
Atlantic	H&W (75)	Wrecked 1873	957	545	57
Kenbane Head	WC (445)	Gunfire 1940	44	24	55
Carmarthanshire	WC (336)	Torpedoed 1942	158	77	49
Gorala	WC (444)	Torpedoed 1942	48	23	48
Ancona	WC (270)	Torpedoed 1915	446	*c.* 200	45
Empire Star	H&W (957)	Torpedoed 1942	103	42	41
Castilla	WC (492)	Torpedoed 1942	59	24	41
Otranto	WC (278)	Collision 1918	*c.* 1,100	431	39
Rohilla	H&W (381)	Wrecked 1914	229	84	37
Maloja	H&W (414)	Mined 1916	456	155	34
Vestris	WC (303)	Foundered 1929	325	112	34
City of Corinth	WC (147)	Torpedoed 1917	665	207	31
Voltaire	WC (360)	Gunfire 1941	272	75	28
Aragon	H&W (367)	Torpedoed 1917	2,700	610	23
Minnehaha	H&W (329)	Torpedoed 1917	153	43	28
Abosso	H&W (430)	Torpedoed 1917	300	65	22
Kosmos II	WC (522)	Torpedoed 1942	150	33	22
Warwick Castle	H&W (840)	Torpedoed 1942	462	96	21
Yorkshire	H&W (509)	Torpedoed 1939	278	58	21

APPENDIX 2

BELFAST-BUILT SHIPS THAT 'DISAPPEARED'

Name	Builder (Y/N)	Launched	Lost (age)	Type	Lives Lost	Location
Grecian	H&W (7)	1861	?/1873 12 years	Steam Cargo		Mediterranean?
Pizarro	H&W (96)	1875	3/1884 9 years	Sail		West Coast Australia
Steelfield	H&W (108)	1876	5/1889 12 years	Sail		South Atlantic
Bansei Maru 2 (Shahzada)	H&W (123)	1879	10/1918 39 years	Steam Cargo		East China Sea
Lord Downshire	H&W (148)	1882	5/1895 14 years	Sail		North Atlantic
Horn Head	H&W (165)	1884	8/1893 10 years	Steam Cargo	30	North Atlantic
Fort George	WC (22)	1884	8/1908 24 years	Sail		South Atlantic/Pacific
Clanrye	WC (23)	1884	3/1886 2 years	Steam Cargo	9	Irish Sea
Watchman	WC (32)	1884	11/1894 10 years	Sail		North Atlantic
Star of Austria	WC (37)	1886	4/1895 9 years	Sail		Cape Horn
Kathleen	WC (45)	1887	1/1914 27 years	Steam Cargo		East Coast of Britain
Palmas	H&W (212)	1888	1/1903 14 years	Steam Cargo	42	North Atlantic
Fort William	WC (55)	1888	12/1896 9 years	Steam Cargo		North Atlantic
Antrim	M&Co. (30)	1888	4/1902 14 years	Steam Cargo		St George's Channel?
Merrimac (Alexamder Elder)	H&W (223)	1890	10/1899 10 years	Steam Cargo	36	North Atlantic
Eveleen	WC (76)	1890	5/1918 27 years	Steam Cargo	12	North Channel Irish Sea
Lindo (Marian Woodside)	WC (79)	1891	8/1913 23 years	Sail		South African Coast
Rathdown	WC (82)	1891	10/1900 9 years	Sail		North Pacific

Name	Builder (Y/N)	Launched	Lost (age)	Type	Lives Lost	Location
Stream Fisher	M&Co. (46)	1891	12/1928 38 years	Steam Cargo		North Sea
Naronic	H&W (251)	1892	2/1893 6 months	Steam Cargo	74	North Atlantic
Alsternixe (Lord Templeton)	H&W (262)	1892	11/1906 15 years	Sail		Pacific
Nelly (Jeanie Woodside)	WC (100)	1893	1/1917 24 years	Sail		North Atlantic
Xantippe	WC (103)	1893	12/1895 18 months	Sail		South Atlantic/Pacific
Planet Mercury	WC (108)	1894	2/1900 6 years	Steam Cargo	35	North Atlantic
Lord Dufferin	WC (130)	1896	10/1896 7 months	Sail	27	West Coast of America
Marowijne	WC (266)	1908	8/1914 8 years	Steam Cargo	97	Caribbean
Manaqui	WC (456)	1921	3/1942 21 years	Steam Cargo	41	Atlantic/Caribbean

SELECT BIBLIOGRAPHY

In compiling these building lists I have used a wide range of electronic and published sources. This bibliography does not include everything but rather the main sources employed.

Electronic Sources

Miramar Ship Index – http://www.miramarshipindex.org.nz
The Ships List – http://www.theshipslist.com
'Red Duster' website of Merchant Navy Association – http://www.red-duster.co.uk
The uboat.net – http://www.uboat.net

Archive Sources

Harland & Wolff (H&W) Papers, Public Record Office of Northern Ireland D2850/TUR/20-2

Government Papers

UK and Irish Census
Reports of the Inspector of Factories and Workshops
Ulster Yearbooks
Report of an inquiry by the Board of Trade into working-class rents, housing and retail prices. [3864] BPP, 1908, CVII
Report of the Secretary of State for the Home Department on Accidents Occurring In Shipbuilding Yards, [7046] BPP, 1913, LX
Belfast Health Commission [Cd 7433 & 7446] BPP 1914 XXXVI

Directories and Similar

Belfast and Ulster Trades Directory
Dictionary of Business Biography
Industries of Ireland Vol.2 (The North) (Belfast 1986)
Lloyd's Register of Shipping

Articles

Armitage, A., 'Shipbuilding in Belfast: Workman Clark and Company, 1880–1935', in Fischer, L.R., *From Wheel House to Counting House; Essays in Maritime Business History in Honour of Professor Peter Neville Davies* (International Maritime Economic History Association 1992)
Bowden, F.C., 'Shipbuilders of other days: No.36 Workman Clark & Co', in *Shipbuilding and Shipping Record* (29 Dec 1949), p.785
Lynch, J.P., 'Belfast's Third Shipyard', in *Ulster Folklife*, vol.41 (1995)
Lynch, J.P., 'The Belfast Shipbuilding Industry 1919–1933', in *Ulster Folklife*, vol.43 (1997)
Lynch, J.P., 'Technology, Labour and the Growth of Belfast Shipbuilding', *Saothar*, vol.24 (1999)

Books

Bardon, J., *A History of Ulster* (Belfast, 1992)
Beckett, J.C., *Belfast: The Making of a City* (Belfast 1982)
Beckett, J.C. & Glasscock, R.E., *Belfast Origin and Growth of an Industrial City* (Belfast, 1982)
Belfast Corporation, *The Great War 1914–18* (Belfast, 1919)
Budge, I. & O'Leary, C., *Belfast: Approach to Crisis* (London, 1973)
Burnett, J., *A History of the Cost of Living* (Harmondsworth, 1969)
Cameron, S., *Belfast Shipbuilders: A Titanic Tale* (Newtownards, 2011)
Conway, *All the World's Fighting Ships 1860–1905* (London, 1979)
Conway, *All the World's Fighting Ships 1906–1921* (London, 1986)
Conway, *All the World's Fighting Ships 1922–1946* (London, 1980)
Conway, *All the World's Fighting Ships 1947–1995* (Annapolis, 1995)
Coe, W.E., *The Engineering Industry of the North of Ireland* (Newton Abbot, 1969)
Devlin, P., *Yes We Have No Bananas* (Belfast, 1981)
Dougan, D., *History of North East Shipbuilding* (London, 1968)
Dunn, L., *Famous Liners of the Past: Belfast Built* (London, 1964)
Dyos, H.J. & Aldcroft, D.H., *British Transport* (Leicester, 1971)
Dunn, L., *Famous Liners of the Past: Belfast Built* (London, 1964)
Lynch, J.P., *A Tale of Three Cities* (Basingstoke, 1998)
Lynch, J.P., *Unlikely Success Story* (Belfast, 2001)
Lynch J.P. (ed.), *Forgotten Shipbuilders of Belfast* (Belfast, 2004)
McCluskie, T., *Harland & Wolff: Designs from the Shipping Empire* (London, 1998)
McConnell, C., *The Ships of Harland & Wolff* (Carrickfergus, 2004)
Mitchell, B.R., *International Historical Statistics* (Basingstoke, 2003)
Mitchell, W.H. & Sawyer, L.A., *British Standard Ships of World War 1* (Liverpool, 1968)
Monsarret, N., *The Cruel Sea* (Schools Edition, London, 1955)
Moss, M. & Hume, J.R., *Shipbuilders to the World* (Belfast, 1986)
Pollard, S. & Robertson, P., *The British Shipbuilding Industry* (Harvard, 1979)
Pollard, S., *The Development of the British Economy 1914–1990* (London, 1992)
Pounder, C.C., *Some Notable Belfast-Built Engines* (Belfast, 1948)
Rees, H., *British Ports and Shipping* (London, 1958)
Smith, J.W. & Holden, T.S., *Where Ships are Born: Sunderland* (Sunderland, 1953)
Stevenson, J., *British Society 1914–45* (London, 1990)
Ulster Folk and Transport Museum, *Advertising Leaflet for Olympic and Titanic*, produced by White Star May 1911 (reprinted Belfast, 1987)
Wattenberg, B.J., *The Statistical History of the United States* (New York, 1976)

Interior of shed constructed at Harland & Wolff to build the 'Ton' class minesweepers in the mid-1950s. (Courtesy of Lagan Legacy)